FLORIDA

Real Estate Principles, Practices & Law

36th Edition | Linda L. Crawford

Dearborn
Real Estate Education

This publication is designed to provide accurate and authoritative information in regard to the subject matter covered. It is sold with the understanding that the publisher is not engaged in rendering legal, accounting, or other professional advice. If legal advice or other expert assistance is required, the services of a competent professional should be sought.

President: Dr. Andrew Temte
Chief Learning Officer: Dr. Tim Smaby
Vice President, Real Estate Education: Asha Alsobrooks
Development Editor: Christopher Kugler

FLORIDA REAL ESTATE PRINCIPLES, PRACTICES & LAW 36TH EDITION
©2013 Kaplan, Inc.
Published by DF Institute, Inc., d/b/a Dearborn Real Estate Education
332 Front St. S., Suite 501
La Crosse, WI 54601
www.dearborn.com

Printed in the United States of America
First revision, May 2013
ISBN: 978-1-4277-4094-6 / 1-4277-4094-1
PPN: 1610-0136

CONTENTS

INTRODUCTION

Congratulations! Your decision to pursue a career in real estate in Florida is an exciting one. You probably have many questions about real estate as a career, requirements for becoming licensed, and real estate in general. I have made every attempt to address your questions. The material is concise, yet presented in sufficient detail to facilitate your understanding. The content conforms to the Florida Division of Real Estate's prescribed Florida Real Estate Commission (FREC) Course I Syllabus for the prelicense course for sales associates.

As with any profession, the real estate profession has an abundance of terms unique to the industry. Key terms are presented at the beginning of each chapter. Learn what these terms mean and apply them in your real estate discussions. To aid your learning process, each term that is presented in a key term section is defined in the corresponding chapter. The term will appear in **boldface** type immediately preceding its definition. You should master these definitions in preparation for your licensing examination.

There are literally hundreds of real estate terms that you will use and apply in your professional career. However, only a limited number of these terms appear in the key term sections. This is because a priority system has been used to help you plan your preparation. Bolded key terms are top priority terms. Throughout the chapters you will also find italicized terms. These are important real estate terms that you should understand and be able to apply in your real estate discussions. However, it is not necessary to be able to "recite" a precise definition for italicized terms.

I have also included learning objectives for each chapter's Overview section. The objectives have been carefully selected to coordinate with the key concepts in the Course Syllabus. Think of the learning objectives as a "road map" to help guide you into your journey toward licensure. As you complete each chapter, be sure also to complete the Review Questions section that follows it so that you can see how well you have mastered the content presented in the chapter.

You will note also that in the left margins, each line of the text is numbered for easy reference. In the left margins you will find screened boxes with Florida Statute and Administrative Rule numbers below. I have cross-referenced the material in your textbook with the FREC statutes and rules. Refer to Appendix E for a table that lists each section of the FREC statutes and rules cross-referenced to the textbook chapter and section title where the legal reference is discussed. You should read the actual laws and rules in preparation for the license exam. Web links to important rules and statutes are presented throughout this textbook.

Text boxes are featured in your textbook. These boxes contain valuable information. The boxes titled To Remember contain learning crutches called acronyms to help you recall certain information. Be sure to study these. Other text boxes feature excerpts of Florida statutes and rules for easy reference. The Formula text boxes feature arithmetic formulas that you must be able to apply. You will find all of these special features very valuable as you delve into this book. I am excited for you and wish you the very best as you embark on your new career.

I would be remiss if I did not take a moment to thank the very special people who contributed to this book. Prior to developing this edition of your book, I received specific comments and suggestions that I incorporated into this edition to assure you of the very best quality textbook. Special thanks are extended to this edition's textbook reviewers: Howard Stevens, Bob Hogue School of Real Estate; Manuela B. Hendrickson, CIPS, GRI, Broker of Global Lifestyle and instructor at Bob Hogue School of Real Estate; and Valleri Crabtree, JD, CLU. Kudos to Howard, who always provides valuable input. In addition to reviewing this edition of the textbook, Howard updated the PowerPoint slides and developed the new Appendix E. Valleri was a wonderful contributor and used her legal expertise to provide suggestions used to update the federal regulations in this edition. Manuela was instrumental in making certain passages flow more smoothly. She also consulted regarding the need to update the section regarding retention of brokerage documents.

This book is coordinated with additional study tools designed to assist you with mastery of the material. Many students choose the Florida Sales Associate Prelicensing Key Point Review Audio CD, which is designed to aid aspiring real estate sales associates in successfully completing the prelicensing course, end-of-course exam, and state licensing exam. If you are concerned about the real estate math associated with this course, consider the companion book *Real Estate Math: What You Need to Know*. If you are looking for a concise overview of the entire course and practice questions to help prepare you for your licensing examination, we recommend *Florida Real Estate Exam Manual*.

I wish you the very best in your endeavor and would like to hear from you.

Linda L. Crawford
November 2012

CHAPTER 1

THE REAL ESTATE BUSINESS

OVERVIEW

The purpose of this chapter is to introduce the reader to the real estate business. The chapter discusses real estate brokerage, development, and construction.

After completing this chapter, the student should be able to:

- define *farm area*;
- distinguish among the five major sales specialties;
- define *business opportunity brokerage*;
- define *absentee owner*;
- define *USPAP*;
- distinguish among a CMA, a BPO, and an appraisal;
- define *dedication*; and
- distinguish among the three categories of residential construction.

KEY TERMS

absentee owner	comparative market analysis (CMA)	property manager
agricultural		real estate brokerage
appraisal	counselors	real estate business
broker's price opinion (BPO)	dedication	Realtor®
	deed restrictions	residential
business brokers	farm area	restrictive covenants
business opportunity brokerage	follow-up	subdivision plat map
	MLS	*USPAP*
	property management	

1

AN INTRODUCTION TO THE REAL ESTATE BUSINESS

The **real estate business** is composed of many specializations. We usually think of this as the buying and selling of properties. Actually, the real estate business is much broader than that and includes property management, subdivision and development, appraisal, financing, and counseling. Because the majority of licensed professionals are involved in sales and leasing, in this chapter we will focus on real estate brokerage.

Real estate brokers provide specialized service for others in return for compensation in the form of a commission, fee, or other valuable consideration. Today a real estate licensee is paid to handle other people's properties because the licensee is a professional who provides specialized service and expertise in at least five areas:

1. *Details of property transfer.* A competent real estate practitioner must know the economic and legal intricacies associated with transfers of title, property taxes, financing, and local zoning ordinances. Real estate practitioners must be intimately familiar with the real estate purchase and sale contract used in their locale, and they must be able to complete the form competently.

2. *Knowledge of market conditions.* No market is ever completely static. Property values are affected by changing market conditions. Changes in market conditions are due to changes in income tax laws, building moratoriums, and fluctuations in supply and demand. These price changes must be taken into consideration when preparing a comparative market analysis (CMA) for buyers and sellers. CMAs are prepared by real estate licensees to help buyers and sellers make informed decisions on pricing a property. (CMAs are discussed later in this chapter.)

3. *Knowledge of how to market real estate or businesses.* To be successful, licensees must know how to market real estate and/or businesses. The sale presentation most effective when working with a physician who is relocating to a new city may be completely different from the approach used to assist the owner of an expanding gourmet coffee bar in choosing an additional location.

   Marketing also includes expertise in locating prospects. For example, a real estate professional who specializes in finding homes for relocated physicians will develop contacts with the personnel in various local hospitals who work as liaisons with new hospital staff. While there may be exceptions, the bulk of evidence indicates that a property handled by a broker normally will be sold more quickly and with less reduction in the desired sale price than if an owner handles the sale without professional assistance.

4. *Knowledge of how to analyze buyer's needs.* Successful real estate professionals know how to analyze a buyer's needs, wants, and financial capabilities in order to help meet their goals. Good listening skills will allow the real estate professional to help the buyer focus on priorities when considering alternative properties as well as assisting with finding the right mortgage professional.

5. *Knowledge of laws that pertain to real estate.* It is critical that real estate professionals understand and apply the many laws that impact real estate. For example, regarding financing and applying for mortgage loans, laws such as the Real Estate Settlement Procedures Act (RESPA), Equal Credit Opportunity Act, and the Truth in Lending Act (TILA) are important. Knowledge and compliance with fair housing laws are also extremely important when working with the public. Real estate professionals must also understand and comply with Florida's real estate licensing laws, including regulations pertaining to brokerage relationships.

Each of these laws will be discussed in detail later in this textbook. Study the laws carefully—your career depends on it!

REAL ESTATE BROKERAGE

Real estate brokerage is the business of bringing together buyers and sellers, owners and renters, and completing real estate transactions. Real estate licensees are paid a fee or a commission for their services.

Sales and Leasing

Sales is the most prevalent and most well-known component of real estate brokerage. Owing to its annual dollar volume, real estate sales has been called the *lifeblood of the brokerage business*.

Some brokers prefer to specialize in residential property. Others specialize in commercial, industrial, or agricultural property, or only in business brokerage. Furthermore, a real estate professional might specialize exclusively in new residential construction, medical office space, or food service businesses. Regardless of the type of property handled, sale transactions are critical to the success of a real estate firm.

FIGURE 1.1   ■   Real Estate Sales Process

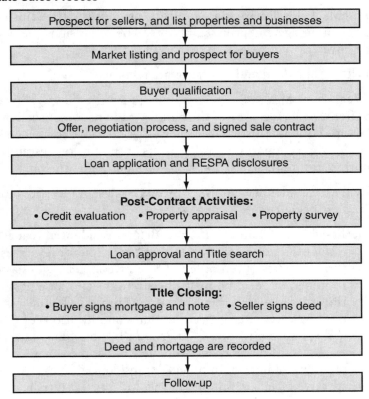

The real estate sale process is complex and involves a series of ten steps. (See also Figure 1.1, Real Estate Sales Process.)

Step One. The process begins by prospecting for sellers. The sales associate develops and presents listing presentations based on market research presented in a CMA. The presentation also includes estimating the seller's net proceeds and the listing agreement.

Step Two. Once the real estate sales associate has acquired the listing on behalf of the broker, it is time to prospect for buyers. The sales associate prepares flyers and newspaper advertisements, lists the property in the multiple listing services (MLS), and conducts open houses. During this period, the sales associate shows the property to potential buyers.

Step Three. Key to a successful sale is making sure the prospective buyer has sufficient income, a good credit history, and sufficient longevity in the workforce to be able to purchase the listed property. This process is referred to as buyer qualification.

Step Four. A qualified buyer will make an offer. The sales associate presents the offer, facilitates the negotiation process, which culminates in a signed contract for sale and purchase of the listed property.

Step Five. Most often the buyer must apply for a loan to purchase the property. The buyer receives RESPA disclosures at the time of loan application or within three business days.

Step Six. At this stage, post-contract activities include the lender's credit evaluation of the buyer and ordering an appraisal and survey of the property.

Step Seven. If the buyer has sufficient income and a good credit score, the lender will likely approve the loan application. At this stage, the lender will order a title search on the property.

Step Eight. The sales associate typically attends the title closing. At this stage, the buyer signs the mortgage and promissory note. The seller signs the deed conveying the property to the buyer.

Step Nine. The deed and mortgage are recorded.

Step Ten. The sales associate should contact the buyers and sellers within a reasonable time after the closing. One of the best ways to ensure satisfied buyers and sellers is through **follow-up**. Follow-up is what a sales associate does for buyers and sellers after the sale. The follow-up is important to all aspects of sales in real estate because it results in a good reputation, future referrals, and word-of-mouth advertising.

Real estate sales associates involved in sales and leasing often specialize in any of five major sales specialties:

1. *Residential.* Chapter 475, F.S., defines **residential** real estate as four or fewer residential units, vacant land zoned for four or fewer residential units, or agricultural property of ten or fewer acres. Residential sales associates should acquire a thorough understanding of the strengths and weaknesses of the neighborhoods in the areas in which they specialize (farm). To be successful, residential specialists need to know the best access routes and locations of schools, shopping facilities, and recreation facilities. They must be able to explain property taxes, homestead exemptions, restrictive covenants, and approximate utility costs in the area. One of the more important aspects of residential sales is knowing how to help prospective buyers obtain financing. Most real estate licensees specialize in the sale and purchase of owner-occupied residential property.

475.278(5)(a), F.S.

2. *Commercial.* To provide competent service to investors, real estate professionals who specialize in commercial sales need expertise regarding income-producing properties, investment analysis, and the various techniques for increasing after-tax cash flow. Improved residential property of more than four units, retail stores, office buildings, and shopping centers are examples of income-producing commercial properties. Contacts with financial institutions and mortgage lenders are important to facilitate commercial transactions.

3. *Industrial.* The industrial sales associate deals in three types of properties: (1) sites in industrial parks or subdivisions; (2) redeveloped industrial parcels in central areas; and (3) industrial acreage. Sales associates of industrial real estate must have technical knowledge of the needs of different industries, such as transportation requirements, including access to railroad or airport transportation; industrial construction features, such as steel versus concrete block construction; and local land-use restrictions affecting industrial properties. With the increase in technological industries, more and more industrial brokers are finding it rewarding to develop and sell beautifully landscaped and well-conceived industrial subdivisions. Almost every large city in Florida has seen the development of industrial parks.

4. *Agricultural.* **Agricultural** property is defined in Chapter 475, F.S., to mean agricultural property of more than ten acres. Professionals who specialize in the sale of farms and agricultural land must be familiar with the operation of farms and the economic problems associated with the various types of farming. One of the licensee's most important skills is the ability to communicate with farmers. Sales associates who are effective in dealing with farm operators are knowledgeable about farm operations and the federal programs affecting farm operations.

5. *Businesses.* Real estate licensees who engage in the sale, purchase, or lease of businesses are referred to as **business brokers**. This real estate activity is sometimes referred to as **business opportunity brokerage**. Business opportunity brokerage involves the sale or lease of an existing business, including the sale of tangible and intangible assets. In most states, if real property is an asset of the business, a real estate broker's license is required to sell the business. There is a *presumption* in Florida law that businesses will have some sort of real property involved, either land and physical improvements such as a building or a long-term lease. For this reason, in Florida, an active current real estate license is *required* to sell or lease business opportunities. (Business opportunity brokerage is explained in more detail in chapter 17.)

Many brokers and sales associates prefer to select one specific portion of a city and become an expert in that particular portion, known as a **farm area**. Licensees get to know almost every lot, house, and business in their farm areas. *Farming* involves maintaining data on each property, including when it was built, the sale history, typical marketing time, assessed value, the amount of property taxes, and so forth. Real estate professionals meet the people in the area and make it known that they specialize in that section of town. The farm area soon begins to produce a harvest in the form of listings and sales. Licensees create a reputation for expertise through hard work. When residents in the farm area move or decide to sell, they call on the area expert who knows what value their property will bring in the current market.

Property Management

Property management is devoted to the leasing, managing, marketing, and overall maintenance of property for others. Many investors desiring to participate in the growth of income-producing property have become absentee owners. An **absentee owner** is a property owner who does not reside on the property and who often relies on a professional property manager to manage the investment. The field of property management has experienced rapid growth and specialization, primarily because of the increase in absentee ownership.

A **property manager** is the local representative of the owner. The property manager's primary task is to produce the greatest possible net income over the longest possible time. The property manager is responsible for maintaining the property and managing the expenses. This may involve development of plans for modernization, remodeling, or alteration of existing properties, for which the cost must be clearly justified by the benefits.

As agents of absentee owners, property managers are typically responsible for rent collection, improving tenant relations, and advertising and merchandising the space. Apartment buildings, condominium developments, shopping centers, and office buildings all require efficient management. Corporations, banks, investment companies, and individuals realize that a trained property manager can usually cope with the details involved in operating income properties better than an owner, whose business expertise lies in other areas. This is particularly true for physicians, lawyers, and other professionals who recognize the tax benefits of owning income-producing real estate. Such investors normally hire qualified property managers because the investors have neither the time nor the desire to become involved in the complexities of property management.

Property managers are compensated in a number of ways. Some work for a guaranteed base amount plus a small percentage of effective gross income (total income collected).

Appraising

475.612, F.S.

Appraisal is the process of estimating the value of real property. It is an opinion given by a skilled appraiser that concludes with an estimate of the property's worth. Appraising is considered to be an art, not a science, because although the appraisal process involves mathematical calculations, and published tables and charts of the appraising trade, appraisers also use their own judgment when appraising real property.

475.25(1)(t), F.S.

Real estate brokers and sales associates may appraise real property for compensation (certain exceptions exist). However, they may *not* represent themselves as state-certified, registered trainee, or licensed appraisers unless they also hold those licenses and certifications. Florida law requires appraisers *and* real estate brokers and sales associates to abide by the *Uniform Standards of Professional Appraisal Practice (USPAP)* when conducting appraisals of real property. The **USPAP** is a set of guidelines (standards of practice) to follow when providing appraisal services. A real estate licensee who fails to abide by the *USPAP* when conducting appraisal services may be subject to disciplinary proceedings and sanctions.

475.611, F.S.
475.25, F.S.

The Florida Real Estate Appraisal Board (FREAB) regulates state-certified, licensed, and registered trainee appraisers. A state-certified or licensed appraiser must prepare an appraisal that involves a federally related transaction. (Federally related transactions are explained in detail in chapter 15.)

WEB LINK

The *USPAP* is available at www.appraisalfoundation.org. Select "USPAP (Standards)."

An appraiser carefully analyzes past sales, computes the cost to reproduce a structure, and determines the worth of future income that a property might produce. These calculations are important not only to buyers and sellers but also to mortgage lenders and insurance companies. Various levels of government also use appraisers to arrive at a value for properties condemned in order to build roads, highways, and expressways. Individual investors have learned the value of obtaining an appraisal before investing.

Appraisers charge a fee based on the time and difficulty of the work. Appraisers are not paid a commission—to reduce the possibility of a conflict of interest. If an appraiser were to be paid a percentage of the appraised value, the temptation to exaggerate the value might prove irresistible. *USPAP's* ethics rule states that it is unethical for an appraiser to accept compensation that is contingent on the value of the property. (Refer to chapter 15.)

Comparative market analysis and broker's price opinion. Sellers often ask real estate brokers and sales associates what a buyer is likely to pay for their properties. Real estate licensees may help potential sellers determine an asking price by preparing a **comparative market analysis (CMA)**. Also, sales associates and brokers prepare CMAs for buyers to help them make informed decisions when offering to purchase real property. CMAs are developed by collecting information concerning real estate activity in the area, including recent sales of similar properties, properties currently offered for sale, and recently expired listings. A CMA is a marketing tool and may *not* be referred to or be represented as an appraisal. Licensees may charge a fee or otherwise be compensated for preparing a CMA, either as a part of or in addition to the normal sale commission. However, licensees typically prepare CMAs for sellers for free as a courtesy to the sellers and to solicit new business.

A **broker's price opinion (BPO)** is a written opinion of the value of real property. Florida real estate licensees are allowed to prepare and charge for BPOs provided the BPO is *not* referred to as an appraisal. Price opinions are often requested by relocation companies and lenders involved in short sales of distressed properties. (A *short sale* produces less money than is owed the lender. The lender releases its mortgage so that the property can be sold free and clear to the new purchaser.) A licensed or certified appraiser must conduct an appraisal when the valuation assignment involves originating a federally related mortgage loan.

475.25(1)(t), F.S.

Sales associates may perform BPOs only at the direction and under the control and management of the associate's employing broker. If a sales associate or broker associate performs a BPO, the compensation must be paid to the broker and not directly to the sales associate or broker associate who prepared the BPO. The *USPAP* standards of practice do *not* apply to brokers, broker associates, and sales associates who, in the ordinary course of business, perform CMAs or broker price opinions.

Financing

If sales are the lifeblood of real estate, financing can be regarded as the lifeblood of real estate sales. Most purchases are financed. Knowledge of how to arrange financing and how to solve financing problems is essential to success in real estate. The licensee who can demonstrate how a prospective buyer can afford to buy has a tremendous advantage over the individual who only can show houses. A real estate licensee may not operate as a mortgage loan originator unless the real estate licensee also holds a Florida mortgage loan originator license. A real estate licensee may not accept a referral fee from a lender unless the real estate professional is also licensed as a mortgage loan originator. (Refer to chapter 13.)

Counseling

Real estate **counselors** provide advice to individuals and firms regarding the purchase and use of real estate investments. A counselor is typically paid a flat fee. Because few people have the education, experience in real estate, knowledge of investing, and tested judgment required to be a qualified counselor, they are few in number. Our expanding economy, the increasing complexity of problems associated with real estate, and the need for professional counseling services all indicate that counseling will grow as a real estate specialty. The services of counselors are already in demand by developers, investors, corporations, and large-scale buyers and sellers.

DEVELOPMENT AND CONSTRUCTION

Development and construction involve dividing larger parcels of land into lots, constructing roads and other off-site improvements, and then constructing buildings on the developed lots. There are three general phases of development and construction:

1. *Land acquisition and pre-development.* Developers and builders acquire raw land and then prepare the site for construction. They must carefully study zoning and land-use plans to determine what type of development is permissible. During this phase, the developer seeks approval for the proposed project from the local municipality. The developer incurs costs for engineering plans, attorney fees, surveys, and application fees.

2. *Subdividing and development. Subdividing* is the process of converting parcels of land into smaller units or lots. *Development* is the process of improving raw land so that it can be put to productive use.

    177.081, F.S.   Before work can begin, most local governments require that developers submit a subdivision plat map of a new development for review by the applicable government planning board (commission). A **subdivision plat map** is an engineer's plan for land use superimposed on a map of the land to be developed. (See Figure 10.9, Subdivision Plat Map on page 230.) The subdivision plat map indicates the proposed size and location of individual building lots, streets, and public utilities, including water and sewer lines, and other clarifying information. The developer is responsible for improving the raw land with paved streets, curbs, storm drains, and so forth. The building lots are sold to the public. Typically, the streets, curbs, and other public area improvements are dedicated to the local city or county. **Dedication** is the gift of land by an owner, in this case a developer, to a government body for a public use. A valid dedication of land from the owner to the municipality requires both an offer to dedicate (donate) the land and an acceptance by the municipality. To accomplish this, the developer typically indicates on the plat map that the streets, sidewalks, park areas, and other improvements that will not be sold to private individuals will be dedicated to the local municipality. Plat approval and recording of the plat into the public records serves as an acceptance of the dedicated streets and public areas

RESTRICTIVE COVENANTS AND DEED RESTRICTIONS

People sometimes use the terms *restrictive covenants* and *deed restrictions* interchangeably. However, deed restrictions refer to a single parcel of land, whereas restrictive covenants concern entire subdivisions.

Restrictive covenants impose limitations on the use of land in an entire subdivision. Examples of restrictive covenants that may affect a particular subdivision control such things as the minimum allowable square footage, whether the garage doors may face the street, or whether recreational vehicles and boats may be parked within view of the street.

Deed restrictions are placed by an owner who has created a restriction on future owners of the parcel of real estate. A deed restriction, for example, may prevent future landowners from selling alcoholic beverages on the site.

and obligates the local government to maintain them once they are installed. County subdivision ordinances, in effect, have combined subdividing the land into individual lots with the development phase to provide greater protection to the public.

Developers of residential subdivisions typically record in the public records restrictive covenants that affect the entire subdivision. **Restrictive covenants** affect how the land can be used and establish criteria such as minimum square footage, type of construction, architectural design, and so forth, to ensure that homes built there conform to the neighborhood. (Refer to text box, Restrictive Covenants and Deed Restrictions.) Developers use restrictive covenants to ensure that no homes will be built that might decrease the value of neighboring properties.

3. *Construction.* Licensed contractors construct buildings on the prepared site. There are three general categories of residential construction:

- *Speculative (spec) homes.* Building "on speculation" involves purchasing one or more lots and constructing a home (or homes) without a buyer in advance of construction.

- *Custom homes.* A custom builder constructs homes under contract with a buyer, often using building plans provided by architects or buyers.

- *Tract homes.* Tract homes are a type of speculative building. A new subdivision will typically feature several model homes. Buyers select a floor plan from the models and a lot on which to build in the new subdivision.

Effective marketing is critical to new construction. For large-scale developments, the use of model homes is an important part of the marketing function. While many developers employ a small sales force to show their model homes, some developers rely on help from real estate brokers to market their houses and

WHO MAY USE THE TERM *REALTOR*®?

The terms *REALTOR*® and *real estate licensee* are not synonymous. REALTORS® are members of a local Board (Association) of REALTORS®. The Florida REALTORS® and the National Association of REALTORS® are privately run professional organizations. The DBPR does not set their rules, fees, or membership requirements.

1   lots. Normally, developers pay for all advertising, and brokers agree to accept a
2   reduction in their customary sale commission to help offset this expense.

THE ROLE OF GOVERNMENT

4 The real estate business is regulated or influenced by the federal, state, and local
5 governments:

6   ■ *Local government* impacts the real estate business through property taxation and
7   regulatory activities such as occupational licensing, business tax receipts, build-
8   ing permits, building moratoriums, zoning, and building codes.

9   ■ *State government* owns and manages a large amount of property and identifies
10   coastal regions and other areas that are protected from development. State docu-
11   mentary and intangible taxes are required when ownership to real property is
12   transferred or pledged as collateral for a mortgage. (Refer to chapter 14.)

13   ■ The *federal government* impacts the real estate business through its fiscal and
14   monetary policies. Various agencies influencing the real estate field include the
15   Department of Housing and Urban Development (HUD), the Federal Housing
16   Administration (FHA), the Department of Veterans Affairs (VA), the Envi-
17   ronmental Protection Agency (EPA), and the Internal Revenue Service (IRS).
18   Subsequent chapters will cover in greater detail the role of the various units of
19   government in the real estate business.

PROFESSIONAL ORGANIZATIONS

21 Professional associations and trade organizations play an important role in the real estate
22 industry. The largest trade organization in the world is the National Association of REAL-
23 TORS® (NAR). Today, in Florida, approximately one-third of real estate licensees belong
24 to the NAR. The NAR promotes ethics and education in the real estate industry. Many of
25 the state laws designed to promote professionalism and improve ethical standards begin in
26 the NAR's REALTORS® Code of Ethics and Standards of Practice. (See chapter 4 for more
27 information concerning the Code of Ethics.)

28   The NAR's fundamental strength is the local association of REALTORS®. A **REALTOR**® is
29 a real estate professional who is a member of a local Board (or Association) of REALTORS®
30 and is affiliated with the Florida REALTORS® and the NAR. Local associations (or boards)
31 are organized across the nation. To become a member of a local association, licensees must
32 apply to and be approved by the association's membership committee. Each real estate

brokerage makes the decision regarding whether to join a local association of REALTORS®. A real estate broker is assessed local trade association dues based on the number of associates registered under the broker. Typically, the broker will require all the associates in the brokerage to also join the association, however, the trade association does not require that the associates join. If the real estate brokerage does not join an association, individual licensees within that brokerage cannot join the association.

Both the National Association of REALTORS® (NAR) and the Florida REALTORS® sponsor comprehensive educational programs for members and publish trade papers and periodicals. The NAR also sponsors affiliated organizations that offer professional designations to real estate licensees and appraisers who complete required courses in areas of special interest. These and other resources help to develop the true professional—an individual constantly seeking self-improvement.

An important service created by the NAR is the multiple listing service (MLS). The **MLS** is a database that allows real estate brokers representing sellers under a listing contract to share information about properties with real estate brokers who may represent potential buyers. The MLS compiles the listings of all member brokers making the property information available to all brokers and their associates.

Before the existence of the MLS, properties that were for sale had very little exposure outside the listing brokerage. To find properties to show a buyer that were listed by other brokerages, real estate licensees would look in the newspaper for ads placed by the listing brokerage, visit other brokers' offices to find out what properties they had available, and drive around looking for yard signs. Because the listing agreement usually specified that only the listing broker's associates could show the property, other brokerages would have to get the listing broker's permission to show the property to a buyer.

However, with the advent of the MLS and technology, it became easy to access information about all properties listed by MLS brokers. Today buyers working with licensees who are members of their local MLS will have access to information about all properties regardless of which brokerage actually has the property listed.

To participate in an MLS, brokers agree to cooperate with each other in a sharing of the commission between the listing broker and the selling broker. The terms for division of commission can vary from broker to broker. Depending on the population of an area, a broker may be a member of more than one MLS. The MLS is not a copyrighted trademark of the NAR. Anyone can create an MLS.

SUMMARY   OF   IMPORTANT   POINTS

- The five major sales specialties are (1) residential, (2) commercial, (3) industrial, (4) agricultural, and (5) businesses.
- *Farm area* refers to a selected and limited geographic area to which a sales associate devotes special attention and study.
- Business opportunity brokerage involves the sale or lease of an existing business. A real estate license is required to sell and lease business opportunities for others.
- Property management is devoted to leasing, managing, marketing, and overall maintenance of property for others. Absentee owners are property owners who

do not reside on the property and who often rely on a professional property manager to manage the investment.

- Florida law requires appraisers and real estate licensees to abide by the *Uniform Standards of Professional Appraisal Practice (USPAP)*. The *USPAP* is a set of guidelines (standards of practice) to follow when conducting appraisal services. Real estate licensees may not represent themselves as state-certified, registered, or licensed appraisers unless they also hold those licenses.

- A *comparative market analysis* (CMA) is a marketing tool that is prepared for a potential buyer or seller based on recent sales of similar properties, properties currently on the market, and recent expired listings. A CMA may not be referred to or represented as an appraisal.

- Developers must submit a subdivision plat map to the local planning board (commission). The streets, parks, and other improvements for public use are typically dedicated to the local municipality. Dedication is the gift of land by an owner to a government body for public use. The developer installs the improvements and the local municipality agrees to maintain the improvements as part of the subdivision plat approval process.

- The three categories of residential construction are (1) speculative (spec) homes, (2) custom homes, and (3) tract homes.

- A REALTOR® is a real estate professional who is a member of a local Board (or Association) of REALTORS® and is affiliated with the Florida REALTORS® and the NAR.

REVIEW QUESTIONS

1. A developer acquires a tract of land that he divides into 25 home sites. Prior to marketing the home sites, the developer must submit the subdivision plat to the
   a. Department of Housing and Urban Development.
   b. local governmental planning agency.
   c. Florida Real Estate Commission.
   d. local building code enforcement department.

2. The term *follow-up* refers to
   a. returning calls in a timely manner.
   b. completing instructions given by one's broker.
   c. following through on listing calls made to "for sale by owners."
   d. what a sales associate does for buyers and sellers after the sale.

3. Even though certain exceptions apply, an active real estate licensee is legally entitled to appraise real property for compensation concerning a nonfederally related transaction
   a. as long as she does not represent herself as a state-certified or licensed appraiser, and complies with the *USPAP*.
   b. only if the appraisal is referred to as a *comparative market analysis*.
   c. provided the compensation is based on a commission agreed on before the appraisal work is done.
   d. provided a licensed or certified appraiser signs the appraisal report.

4. The field of property management has experienced growth and specialization primarily because of
   a. the deregulation of the real estate industry.
   b. the increase in the numbers of licensees specializing in property management.
   c. the increase in the number of absentee owners.
   d. higher construction costs that have caused an increase in the number of renters.

5. Real estate licensees must comply with the *Uniform Standards of Professional Appraisal Practice (USPAP)* when conducting which value estimates?
   a. Appraisals
   b. Broker price opinions
   c. Comparative market analyses
   d. Real estate licensees are exempt from the provisions of *USPAP*

6. Appraisers are paid a fee because
   a. to accept compensation based on the appraised value is a conflict of interest.
   b. custom dictates the method of compensation.
   c. the fee would be too high if it were based on a percentage of property value.
   d. only brokers and sales associates are paid commissions for their services.

7. When a developer makes lots available for custom building in a newly developed subdivision, the overall purpose of restrictive covenants is to ensure that custom-built homes will
   a. not conflict with local zoning ordinances.
   b. not exceed the minimum square footage requirements.
   c. conform to standard building codes.
   d. not decrease the value of neighboring properties.

8. The real estate activity that is devoted to leasing, managing, marketing, and overall maintenance of property for others is referred to as
   a. commercial sales.
   b. property management.
   c. counseling.
   d. rental agents.

9. Which type of construction involves building to a buyer's specifications?
   a. Tract homes
   b. Spec homes
   c. Custom homes
   d. Model homes

10. The term *dedication* as it applies to development and construction refers to
    a. a gift of land by the owner to the local government for a public use.
    b. the builder's careful attention to construction details.
    c. recording a subdivision plat map in the public records.
    d. preparing raw land for site improvements.

11. What type of license is required to sell or lease business opportunities for another person?
    a. Business broker license
    b. Business opportunity broker license
    c. Real estate license
    d. A license is not required unless a building is being sold with the business

12. Residential real estate is defined in Chapter 475, F.S., as
    a. property zoned agricultural land of more than ten acres.
    b. five or more residential units.
    c. vacant land zoned for four or fewer residential units.
    d. all of the real estate described above.

13. The real estate profession requires
    a. skill and experience in real estate values, specialized service, and expertise.
    b. only the ability to list property.
    c. expertise in all types of real estate.
    d. that licensees also act as mortgage brokers from time to time.

14. Selecting a limited geographical area in which a real estate professional develops special expertise is referred to as
    a. farming.
    b. follow-up.
    c. subdividing.
    d. dedicating land.

15. A broker charges a prospective seller $50 for a comparative market analysis (CMA). Which statement applies?
    a. Brokers are not permitted to charge for CMAs.
    b. This is permissible, provided the broker does not represent the CMA as an appraisal.
    c. The broker must be a state-certified or licensed appraiser to do this.
    d. The CMA must be signed by a state-certified or licensed appraiser.

2

LICENSE LAW AND QUALIFICATIONS FOR LICENSURE

¹ OVERVIEW

² The purpose of this chapter is to give the reader a historical perspective of real estate
³ license law in Florida and to describe in detail the requirements for obtaining a real estate
⁴ license. The chapter discusses real estate services that require a license and exemptions
⁵ from licensure.

⁶   After completing this chapter, the student should be able to:

⁷   ■ define *sales associate*, *broker associate*, and *broker*;

⁸   ■ list the academic requirements for sales associate and broker licenses;

⁹   ■ list the application requirements for sales associate and broker licenses;

¹⁰   ■ identify services of real estate requiring licensure;

¹¹   ■ recognize exemptions from licensure; and

¹²   ■ distinguish between post-licensing education and continuing education.

¹³ KEY TERMS

broker	mutual recognition	reciprocity
broker associate	agreements	registration
caveat emptor	nolo contendere	resident
compensation	owner-developer	sales associate
license	prima facie evidence	withhold adjudication
moral turpitude	real estate services	

¹⁴ HISTORICAL PERSPECTIVE OF FLORIDA REAL ESTATE LICENSE LAW

475.001, F.S.   ¹⁵ Prior to the latter part of the 19th century, the real estate business was unorganized and
20.03, F.S.   ¹⁶ extremely competitive. The policy of **caveat emptor**, a Latin term meaning *let the buyer*
                ¹⁷ *beware*, prevailed. In 1923, the Florida Legislature passed the Real Estate License Law,
                ¹⁸ Chapter 475 of the *Florida Statutes*.

In 1925, the Florida Legislature created the Florida Real Estate Commission to administer and enforce the license law. The Legislature granted the Commission authority to keep records, conduct investigations, and the power to grant, deny, suspend, and revoke licenses. The Florida Real Estate Commission is also referred to as the *Commission* or as the *FREC*.

Today, the Division of Real Estate (DRE) provides support services to the Commission. The DRE is under the Department of Business and Professional Regulation (DBPR).

455.201, F.S.

The intent of real estate regulation is to protect the health, safety, and welfare of the public (consumer protection). The Legislature believes the profession should be regulated when:

- the unregulated practice can harm the public, the potential harm is recognizable, and the danger outweighs any anticompetitive impact that might result from regulation;
- the public is not adequately protected by other state statutes, local ordinances, or federal laws; or
- less restrictive means of regulation are not available.

STATUTES AND RULES IMPORTANT TO REAL ESTATE

Applicants must meet certain application and academic requirements and demonstrate minimal competence with regard to the real estate business. Prospective licensees must demonstrate knowledge of real estate business practices and knowledge of the Florida real estate license law and certain federal laws pertaining to real estate. To be prepared for the licensure examination and to competently perform real estate practices, the licensee must be familiar with the laws regulating the real estate business.

A brief description of the laws and rules that applicants must be familiar with are described below:

- *Florida Statute 20.* This chapter of the Florida Statutes concerns the organizational structure of Florida's government. The Florida Constitution provides for the legislative, executive, and judicial branches of government. The executive branch executes the programs and policies adopted by the Legislature. The policies are implemented by the departments of the executive branch, including the Department of Business and Professional Regulation.

- *Florida Statute Chapter 475.* This law is often referred to as the Real Estate Professional Practice Act. Chapter 475 was created by the Florida legislature to establish the legal rights and responsibilities of real estate licensees and real estate appraisers. Chapter 475 is divided into four parts. Part I pertains to real estate brokerage. Real estate licensees are responsible for knowing the provisions of this chapter. The Florida Real Estate Commission (FREC) implements, interprets, and enforces the regulatory provisions of Chapter 475.

    Part II of Chapter 475 pertains to real estate appraisers and sets forth the requirements for licensed and certified appraisers according to federal statute. The Florida Real Estate Appraisal Board (FREAB) regulates state-certified, licensed, and registered trainee appraisers. The FREAB functions very similarly to the Florida Real Estate Commission (FREC). Both quasi-judicial bodies follow the same procedures for disciplining licensees.

Part III of Chapter 475, known as the Commercial Real Estate Sales Commission Lien Act, gives a broker lien rights for earned commission. This act applies *only* to commercial property (not residential property). The lien is only against the owner's net proceeds (personal property) from the sale and does *not* attach to the commercial real property. (See also, Liens on Real Property, page 99.)

Part IV, known as the Commercial Real Estate Leasing Commission Lien Act, gives a broker lien rights for earned commission associated with a brokerage agreement to lease commercial real estate.

■ *Florida Statute 455*. This chapter of the Florida Statutes defines the general legal practice and procedure for the Department of Business and Professional Regulation (DBPR) and the licensees of all professions regulated by the DBPR, including real estate. Section 455.10 of the statute provides that an individual cannot be disqualified from practicing an occupation or profession regulated by the state of Florida solely because the person is not a U.S. citizen. Another section of this statute sets forth laws regarding Commission and Board organization, meetings, compensation, and so forth. This statute also concerns unlicensed practice of a profession, including real estate. Requirements concerning license examinations and the use of professional testing services are set forth in Chapter 455. This law also mandates what actions the DBPR may take in regulating licensees. Licensees who fail to comply with the provisions of this chapter can be disciplined by the FREC.

■ *Florida Statute 120*. This chapter of the Florida Statutes defines the procedural process by which regulatory agencies decide and implement agency action. The licensing and disciplinary process for real estate licensees is outlined in this chapter.

■ *Chapter 61J2*. Chapter 61J2 is the rules of the Florida Real Estate Commission. It is a set of administrative rules developed by the Florida Real Estate Commission, pursuant to the rulemaking process outlined in Chapter 120, Florida Statutes. Administrative rules are published in the Florida Administrative Code (FAC). The FREC promulgates these rules to expand upon the statutory provisions of Chapter 475, Florida Statutes, by addressing in greater detail, the principles of practice for the real estate profession. (Appraisal rules are in Chapter 61J1 of the FAC.)

Important federal and state laws. The Bureau of Education and Testing's *Candidate Information Booklet for Sales Associates* lists 36 Florida Statutes and one rule of the Florida Administrative Code that are tested on the state license exam. Students are also responsible for knowing the main points associated with nine Federal Regulations codified in the United States Code. The *Candidate Information Booklet* lists the applicable federal and state laws. To assist you with preparing for the state license examination, each of the required Florida Statutes and Federal Regulations is cross-referenced in this textbook. (See Appendix E.)

WEB LINK

The best way to access the Florida Statutes is using the official Online Sunshine Web site (**www.leg.state.fl.us/statutes/**).

For the most up-to-date version of the administrative rules of the Florida Real Estate Commission, go to **www.myfloridalicense.com/dbpr/re/statutes.html**. Select "Florida Administrative Code, Chapter 61J2."

Download a copy of the *Candidate Information Booklet* at **www.myfloridalicense.com/dbpr/servop/testing/booklets.html**. The booklet includes important information regarding taking the state license exam.

TWO TYPES OF REAL ESTATE LICENSES

Sales Associate	A person who performs real estate services for compensation but who does so under the direction, control, or management of a broker or an owner-developer.
Broker	A person who, for another and for compensation or other consideration (or anticipation of compensation or other consideration), performs real estate services.

Reference: Section 475.01, F.S.

GENERAL LICENSING PROVISIONS

475.01, F.S.

An individual typically begins a real estate career in Florida as a licensed **sales associate**. Applicants who have completed the required education and passed the license exam are initially licensed as voluntary inactive sales associates. Inactive sales associates can become active by finding an employer and filing the information with the Department of Business and Professional Regulation (DBPR).

Sales associates and broker associates are employed by and work under the direction and control of a broker or an owner-developer. Sales associates and broker associates are agents of their employer. An **owner-developer** is an unlicensed entity that sells, exchanges, or leases its own property. An example of an owner-developer is a real estate development company that owns land that it develops into subdivisions, and then builds and sells homes. An owner-developer's sales staff must hold active real estate licenses in order to be paid a commission or other compensation based on actual sales (that is, on a transactional basis). The sales staff is exempt from real estate licensure if paid strictly on a salaried basis.

To become a **broker** requires additional education, experience, and passing the broker license exam. While many sales associates want the prestige of a broker's license, they are not interested in opening their own real estate brokerage business. A **broker associate** is an individual who holds a broker's license but who chooses to register and work in real estate under the direction of another broker.

Application Requirements

475.175, F.S.

A person desiring to be licensed must submit an application. The application is furnished by the Department of Business and Professional Regulation (DBPR) and may be downloaded from the Internet at the DBPR's Form Center. (See Web link below.) Applicants may download, print, and mail the application, or they may apply online. Prior to accessing the online application, applicants must register one time with the DBPR using the applicant's e-mail address.

WEB LINK

You can apply for a real estate license online at the DBPR's Form Center at https://www.myfloridalicense.com/intentions2.asp?chBoard=true&boardid=25&SID=.

BACKGROUND CHECK OF CRIMINAL HISTORY

On the license application, applicants are asked if they have ever been convicted of a crime, found guilty, or entered a plea of guilty or nolo contendere (no contest) to a criminal charge, even if the applicant received a withhold of adjudication.

When the court determines that a defendant is not likely to again engage in a criminal act and that the ends of justice and the welfare of society do not require the defendant suffer the penalty imposed by law, the court may **withhold adjudication** of guilt, stay (stop) the imposition of the sentence, and place the defendant on probation. A withhold of adjudication must be disclosed on the application.

Nolo contendere is a plea of no contest entered in a criminal court of law. The defendant does not admit or deny the charges, though a fine or sentence may be imposed by the court.

1   Applicants are cautioned to complete the application carefully, particularly with
2   respect to past history concerning felonies, misdemeanors, and traffic offenses (other than
3   parking, speeding, inspection, or traffic signal violations). When responding regarding
4   past history (background questions on application), applicants who have been convicted
5   of a crime, found guilty, or entered a plea of guilty or **nolo contendere** (no contest), even
6   if court action (*adjudication*) was withheld, should attach full details of all cases with dates
7   and outcomes, including any sentence and conditions imposed. Attach to the application
8   important documentation such as copies of police records. Failure to truthfully disclose
9   this information may result in denial of a real estate license. In cases where a license has
10   already been issued, it may result in revocation of the license. An application number is
11   assigned when an application is filed online. Applicants who responded "yes" to any of the
12   background questions should mail applicable documentation with a cover letter indicat-
13   ing the application number.

14   If an applicant has a criminal history or just wants to make sure that no criminal mat-
15   ters are attached to the applicant's identity, it is best to research one's criminal history.
16   For incidences that took place in Florida, an applicant can go online to the Florida Depart-
17   ment of Law Enforcement (FDLE) Web site (see Web link on page 22) and request a copy
18   of the applicant's Florida criminal history. If a criminal matter that the applicant is aware
19   of is not listed, the applicant will need to double-check with the local court regarding the
20   status of the matter and confirm whether it was expunged. If a matter appears on the list
21   of criminal history, the applicant will know that the matter was not expunged and that
22   it must be disclosed on the license application. (*Note: Expungement of record* is a process
23   by which the record of a criminal conviction is destroyed or sealed after expiration of
24   time. Expungement is *not* automatic. Attorneys charge extra for this and applicants should
25   not assume a record has been expunged without first confirming that the matter no lon-
26   ger appears on one's criminal history.) Applicants are not required to disclose a personal
27   bankruptcy.

LICENSE APPLICATION

A Social Security number is required to apply for a real estate license. In the Full Legal Name section of the license application, applicants must enter their name as it appears on their Social Security card. Florida law requires that an applicant's Social Security number be disclosed on all professional license applications. The Social Security number is used to determine whether applicants are in compliance with child support obligations.

A real estate license application is good for two years from the date the complete application is received by the DBPR. The application expires two years after it is received by the DBPR.

Reference: Section 475.181(2) and 455.213, Florida Statutes

WEB LINK

To perform a criminal history record search go to **www.fdle.state.fl.us**. Under "Search Our Systems," select "Criminal History Records." An applicant can order an FDLE criminal history report for $24.

1 For out of state criminal history, an applicant should first contact the attorney who
2 handled the matter. The applicant should also contact the court where the matter took
3 place. If an applicant is not sure or cannot confirm the expungement of a criminal matter,
4 the applicant should disclose it. It is better to disclose only to find out that the matter did
5 not have to be disclosed than to not disclose and be charged with obtaining a license by
6 fraud! When in doubt, disclose.

7 Applicants must submit their fingerprints as part of the license application process. An
8 applicant's fingerprints are scanned and electronically submitted to the Florida Department
9 of Law Enforcement (FDLE) and to the Federal Bureau of Investigation (FBI). The purpose
10 of the fingerprinting process is to determine whether an applicant has a criminal history.
11 The DBPR has contracted with its test vendor, Pearson VUE, to provide fingerprinting
12 services for real estate applicants. Fingerprints are scanned at Pearson VUE's test sites and
13 other locations subcontracted by Pearson VUE. Once students have enrolled in the preli-
14 cense course for sales associates and have made application for a license, they are encour-
15 aged to go ahead and complete the fingerprinting process. Students do *not* have to wait until
16 the application is submitted and the course is completed before getting their fingerprints
17 scanned. In fact getting fingerprints scanned early will allow the application to be approved
18 sooner because the DBPR will not have to hold up the application approval pending the
19 results from the criminal history check.

WEB LINK

To schedule a fingerprinting appointment, contact Pearson VUE at **www.pearsonvue.com**. Select "Book Digital Fingerprinting Appointments." Applicants choose a date and time and are asked to provide demographic information (gender, eye color, and so forth). Payment is due at the time of making the appointment.

RULES PERTAINING TO NONRESIDENT LICENSEES

Any resident licensee who becomes a nonresident must notify the Commission within 60 days of the change in residency and comply with all nonresident requirements.

A Florida resident licensee who fails to notify the Commission of becoming a nonresident as prescribed in Section 475.180 may be issued a citation and fined $300.

Reference: Section 475.180, F.S., and 61J2-24.002, F.A.C.

For additional facts regarding the fingerprinting process and for instructions regarding how out-of-state applicants should submit fingerprint information, download and print the DBPR's Electronic Fingerprinting Frequently Asked Questions and Answers at **www.myflorida.com/dbpr/servop/testing/documents/finger_faq.pdf**.

1 The application fee must accompany the application. Checks and money orders are
2 accepted for applications received by mail. Online applicants may charge the fee to a
3 credit card. The notice of satisfactory completion of the prescribed course (grade report)
4 must be presented to the examination site before taking the exam.

5 A 30-day period is allowed after receipt of the application to check for errors and omis-
6 sions and to send the applicant a *notice of insufficiency* concerning any additional informa-
7 tion required. An applicant's failure to supply additional information may not be grounds
8 for denial of a license unless the applicant was notified within the 30-day period.

WEB LINK

To check the status of your application, use the DBPR Online Services at **www.myfloridalicense.com/dbpr/re/index.html**. Select "Apply For/Update Licenses" on the home page. Then select "View Application Status."

9   Any application for licensure that is not processed within the legislated time periods
10 must be considered approved. An applicant must be informed of approval or denial of the
11 application within 90 days after receipt of the last correctly submitted application. When
12 the Commission denies an application, it sends a copy of the denial to the applicant, lists
13 the reasons for the denial, and advises that the applicant has 21 days from the date of
14 receipt of the order to request a hearing in accordance with Chapter 120, F.S.

15 ## Nonresident Applicant Requirements

455.10, F.S.
475.180 (2),
F.S.

16 U.S. citizenship is *not* required of applicants. However, applicants must possess a Social
17 Security number. Furthermore, applicants do not have to be residents of Florida.

18 **Nonresident licensee requirements.** A Florida real estate licensee who moves out of
19 state and becomes a nonresident of Florida is required by law to notify the Commission
20 within 60 days of the change in residency (see text box, Rules Pertaining to Nonresident
21 Licensees). The licensee agrees to keep the licensee's mailing address current. Nonresident

MUTUAL RECOGNITION IS NOT RECIPROCITY

Reciprocity is an agreement between two states that allows a real estate licensee with a valid license in one of the states to practice real estate in both states. There is no reciprocity between Florida and any other state.

Florida instead has entered into contractual agreements with some other states known as **mutual recognition agreements.** Florida and another state enter into a contract to recognize each other's real estate license education. Mutual recognition applicants must demonstrate knowledge of Florida's real estate laws by passing a license exam that consists of 40 questions concerning Florida-specific real estate law. After demonstrating knowledge of Florida license law, the applicant is issued a Florida real estate license. Only nonresidents of Florida may use education obtained in a mutually recognized state to obtain a Florida real estate license.

1 licensees must satisfactorily complete the post-licensing and continuing education required
2 of all Florida real estate licensees. Nonresident applicants and licensees must comply with
3 all other F.S. 475 requirements and FREC rules.

61J2-26.001, F.A.C.

4 **Mutual recognition agreements.** To date, the FREC has entered into mutual recognition
5 agreements with licensing authorities in nine states: Alabama, Arkansas, Connecticut,
6 Georgia, Indiana, Mississippi, Nebraska, and Oklahoma. The intent of mutual recognition
7 agreements is to recognize the education and experience of individuals licensed in another
8 state or nation when the other jurisdiction has education and experience requirements
9 comparable to Florida's requirements. The agreements apply exclusively to *nonresidents*
10 who are licensed in other jurisdictions. A resident of Florida who is licensed in a mutual
11 recognition state *cannot* apply for a Florida real estate license under mutual recognition.

12 If a holder of a real estate license from a state with which Florida has a mutual rec-
13 ognition agreement desires a Florida real estate license, the individual submits a Florida
14 real estate license application. The applicant requests mutual recognition on the license
15 application and indicates from which state mutual recognition is being requested. An
16 applicant applying for mutual recognition must obtain a *certification of license history* from
17 the Real Estate Commission in the state where the applicant is licensed. A certification
18 of license history must contain the applicant's initial license exam information, current
19 license status, the number of active months of licensure within the preceding five years,
20 and whether any disciplinary action has been taken against the licensee. The certification
21 is submitted with the application.

22 Real estate applicants approved for licensure under mutual recognition are exempt
23 from the prelicense education course. However, the mutual recognition applicant must
24 demonstrate mastery of Florida's real estate license law by passing a written Florida-spe-
25 cific real estate law license exam. The exam consists of 40 questions worth 1 point each. A
26 grade of 30 points (75 percent) or higher is required to pass the exam. After demonstrating
27 knowledge of Florida license law, the applicant is issued a Florida real estate license. Indi-
28 viduals who receive a Florida real estate license under mutual recognition must fulfill the
29 same post-license and continuing education requirements as all other Florida real estate

MORAL TURPITUDE

Moral turpitude is conduct contrary to honesty, good morals, justice, or accepted custom. Embezzlement and crimes of larceny, including writing bad checks, are generally considered moral turpitude.

1 licensees. (Post-license education and continuing education requirements are explained
2 later in this chapter.)
3

Mutual recognition agreements also ensure that Florida licensees have an opportunity
4 for licensure in mutual recognition states. The agreements are state-specific and what is
5 required of Florida licensees varies among mutual recognition states depending on how
6 another state's license law compares to Florida's license law. A Florida real estate licensee
7 interested in obtaining a license from a mutual recognition state should contact the state's
8 Real Estate Commission for information regarding application procedures. (Refer to the
9 Web link below.)
10

WEB LINK

Florida real estate licensees interested in the requirements to obtain a Georgia real estate license under mutual recognition can find information in the "Frequently Asked Questions" section of the Georgia Real Estate Commission's Web site at **www.grec.state.ga.us/faq/faqreciprocity.html**.

61J2-26.002,
F.A.C.

Florida resident defined. For application and licensing purposes, the FREC rules define
11 a **resident** of Florida as a person who has resided in Florida continuously for a period of
12 four calendar months or more within the preceding year, regardless of whether the person
13 resided in a recreational vehicle, hotel, rental unit, or other temporary or permanent loca-
14 tion. Any person who presently resides in Florida in any of the above-described accommo-
15 dations with the intention of residing continuously in Florida for four months or longer,
16 beginning on the date the person established the current period of residence, is also con-
17 sidered a legal Florida resident. This is the test used to determine whether an applicant for
18 licensure qualifies as a nonresident under mutual recognition.
19

SALES ASSOCIATE QUALIFICATIONS FOR LICENSURE

20

475.17, F.S.
61J2-2.027,
F.A.C.

The sales associate applicant *must*

21
22
23
24
25
26
27
28

- be 18 years of age or older;
- have a high school diploma or its equivalent;
- possess a Social Security number;
- be honest, truthful, trustworthy, of good character, and have a reputation for fair dealing; and
- be competent and qualified to make real estate transactions and conduct negotiations with safety to investors and others.

1   When completing an application for licensure, the applicant must disclose

2   ■ if ever convicted or found guilty of a crime or ever entered a plea of *nolo conten-*
3   *dere* (no contest); if under investigation for civil or criminal prosecution; or if
4   any judgment or decree has been rendered wherein the charges involved **moral**
5   **turpitude** or fraudulent or dishonest dealing (refer to text box, Moral Turpitude);

6   ■ if any name or alias other than the full legal name indicated on the application
7   has ever been used, including a maiden name (*Note:* Full legal name is the name
8   as it appears on the applicant's Social Security card);

9   ■ if ever denied licensure or had a license suspended or revoked by the real estate
10   licensing agency of another state or nation;

11   ■ if ever denied registration or a license to practice any regulated profession, busi-
12   ness, or vocation, or had a registration or license suspended or revoked in this or
13   any other state or nation; and

14   ■ if ever guilty of any conduct or practice that would have been grounds for sus-
15   pension or revocation under F.S. 475 had the applicant then been licensed to
16   practice real estate in this state or elsewhere. This includes acting, or attempting
17   to act, as a real estate sales associate or broker in violation of F.S. 475 during the
18   year before the applicant filed an application, or until a valid license was issued,
19   regardless of whether compensation was an issue.

20   Applicants guilty of these offenses will be considered qualified for registration only
21 if passage of time, good behavior, or other sufficient reasons cause the Commission to
22 believe that the interests and welfare of the general public will not be endangered.

23 Moral Turpitude Case

24 A real estate licensee pled guilty to leaving the scene of an accident with injuries. The
25 courts ordered the licensee to pay monthly restitution to the victim. The victim requested
26 in writing that the FREC not impose revocation so that the licensee could continue to
27 pay restitution.

28   *Violation:* Guilty of having been convicted or found guilty of, or entered a plea of nolo
29 contendere to, regardless of adjudication, a crime in any jurisdiction which directly relates
30 to the activities of a licensed broker or sales associate, *or involves moral turpitude* (italics
31 added for emphasis) or fraudulent or dishonest dealing in violation of Section 475.25(1)
32 (f), F.S.

33   *Penalty:* The Commission imposed a six-month suspension, $2,500 fine, costs, 12
34 months probation, and ordered the licensee to attend a two-day FREC meeting.

35   Reference: DBPR Case Number 2009064637

36 Education Requirements

475.17(2), F.S.
61J2-3.008,
F.A.C.

37 Sales associate candidates must successfully complete Course I or an equivalent FREC-
38 approved prelicense course. The course is based on understanding and applying the
39 fundamentals of real estate principles and practices, real estate law, real estate license
40 law, and real estate mathematics.

61J2-3.008(8),
F.A.C.

41   Course I consists of 60 hours of instruction plus 3 hours for an end-of-course exami-
42 nation. The end-of-course examination consists of 100 questions worth 1 point each and

REGULATIONS PERTAINING TO PRELICENSE COURSES

A student may not miss more than eight hours of instruction. An instructional hour is considered to be 50 minutes. (Section 475.17, F.S.)

A student may attend makeup classes to take the end-of-course exam or a makeup exam if absences were due to student or family illness, if done within 30 days of the regularly scheduled exam time, or later with Commission approval. Makeup classes must consist of the original course material that the student missed. (61J2-3.008, F.A.C.)

The school or institution provides each student passing the end-of-course exam with a FREC-prescribed grade report of successful completion of the course. The school must submit a roster notifying the Commission of the name of each student who has satisfactorily completed the education requirements. (Section 475.175, F.S.)

The student must pass the school-administered end-of-course exam with a grade of 70 or higher. (61J2-3.008, F.A.C.)

A student failing the end-of-course exam must wait at least 30 days from the date of the original examination to retest. Within one year of the original examination, a student may retest a maximum of one time. Otherwise, a student failing the end-of-course exam must repeat the course prior to being eligible to retake the end-of-course examination. Schools must administer a different form of the end-of-course exam to a student who is retaking the exam or repeating the course. (61J2-3.008, F.A.C.)

Students may choose to complete a distance-learning course and satisfactorily complete a timed, distance learning course examination. (Section 475.17, F.S.)

The prelicense course may be taken by correspondence or other suitable means by anyone who, because of individual physical hardship, cannot attend the course where it is regularly conducted or who does not have access to distance learning courses. (Section 475.17, F.S.)

is normally organized with 45 questions on principles and practices, 45 questions on real estate law, and 10 math questions. A passing score of at least 70 is required on the end-of-course exam.

475.17(6), F.S.
61J2-3.012(2), F.A.C.

Exemptions to the prelicense course requirement. Attorneys who are active members of The Florida Bar are exempt from Course I. Additionally, individuals who have received a four-year degree in real estate from an institution of higher education are exempt from the prelicense course. (Refer to Figure 2.1, Summary of Education Exemptions, page 28.)

TIME LIMIT FOR PRELICENSE EDUCATION

If an applicant does not pass the state license exam within two years after the course completion date, the course completion expires and the applicant must again complete the prelicense education course.

The completion date is the date the student passed the prelicense end-of-course exam.

Reference: Section 475.181(2), F.S.

License Examinations

61J2-2.029, F.A.C.

When the application processing is complete and the applicant is considered to be qualified, the DBPR notifies the national testing vendor (Pearson VUE). The vendor then sends a notice informing the candidate of eligibility to take the state license examination.

Applicants schedule examination appointments directly through the testing vendor. License examinations for sales associate and broker applicants are given at test sites located throughout Florida. The license exam may also be taken in any state where the test vendor has a test center.

The examination consists of multiple-choice questions and is administered as a computerized test. The license exam is offered in English and Spanish. Students who want the Spanish version must request the Spanish language examination when making the test reservation. The passing score on the license exam is a grade of 75 percent or higher.

Students' answers are graded at the test site. Students who pass the exam are given a "pass" notification at the test site. A real estate license is mailed to students who passed the exam. New sales associates must change their license to *active* status before legally operating as a sales associate. A change from inactive to active status is accomplished by submitting form DBPR RE-10 (Request to Become Active). The form includes the sales associate's name, license number, contact information, and the employer's name, license number, and business address. The form is signed by the broker or owner-developer and the sales associate. Florida brokers may also register new licensees online at the DBPR's Web site. New licensees must not begin working until the DBPR Web site indicates that the license has been changed to *active* status under the proper broker or brokerage entity.

F I G U R E 2.1 ■ Summary of Education Exemptions

	Prelicense Course I	Prelicense Course II	Post-License	Continuing Education
4-Year Real Estate Degree*	Exempt	Exempt	Exempt	Not Exempt
Florida-Licensed Attorney**	Exempt	Not Exempt	Not Exempt	Exempt

* Exempt from FREC-approved Courses I and II but must pass license exam.

** Must be an active member of The Florida Bar. Exempt from Course I only. Must pass license exam.

Licensees can monitor the progress of their change of status request on the DBPR Web site (refer to Web link that follows).

WEB LINK

To download and print a copy of the Request to Become Active form, go to **www.myfloridalicense.com/dbpr/re/documents/DBPR_RE_11_Change_of_Status_Associates.pdf**.

To monitor the progress of a request for change of status, go to **www.myfloridalicense.com**. Select "Renew Your License" and follow the prompts.

455.217, F.S.
120.57, F.S.
120.569, F.S.
61-11.017(2)
(a), F.A.C.

Students who fail the license exam are given a failure notice at the test site. The failure notice includes a breakdown of the points scored in each major subject area. The notice also includes information about reviewing the exam, retaking the exam, and requesting a hearing to challenge the exam. Requests to review the exam must be received within 21 days after the release date on the original grade notification. Review appointments are scheduled with the test vendor. Students may only review the questions they answered incorrectly.

Applicants who fail the license exam have the right at their own expense to have an attorney review the exam with them. If during the exam review, applicants have objections to any of the exam questions and answers, they should write down their objections to the specific questions and turn in their comments to the test center employee (review monitor). Applicants may also request that the Validation Committee review the objections to specific exam questions. The request must be made in writing to the DBPR within 30 days from the date of the examination review. If the examination review results in a corrected score, the new score will apply only to the applicant who challenged the examination questions.

61J2-2.030,
F.A.C.
61-11.012,
F.A.C.

An applicant also has the right to petition for a formal hearing before the Division of Administrative Hearings. A request for a hearing before an administrative law judge must be filed within 21 days from the date of the on-site grade notice, or 21 days from the date of the letter notifying the student of the DBPR evaluation decision regarding the student's challenges. The request for a hearing is filed with the Chief, Bureau of Education and Testing, DBPR.

WEB LINK

The Department's administrative rule regarding examinations is available at **www.flrules.org/gateway/ChapterHome.asp?Chapter=61-11**.

POST-LICENSING EDUCATION

475.17, F.S.
61J2-3.020,
F.A.C.
61J2-3.008,
F.A.C.

Sales associates are required to successfully complete a prescribed post-licensing education requirement *before the first renewal* of their licenses. This requirement has the effect of placing all initial licenses in a conditional (probationary) status because failure to complete the post-licensing education requirement will cause the initial license to become null and void by operation of law. Sales associates who do not complete the 45-hour post-licensing requirement and want to continue in the real estate business are *required to requalify* for licensure by repeating the prelicense course and end-of-course exam and by again passing the state licensing exam.

Post-licensure courses are offered by accredited colleges, universities, and community colleges; area technical centers; real estate proprietary schools; and FREC-approved

TIPS REGARDING POST-LICENSE EDUCATION

Students should *not* enroll in a post-license course until first becoming licensed. If you take your post-license course before becoming licensed, the course will *not* count.

Students are encouraged to take their post-license education soon after becoming licensed. Do not wait until the last minute. Plan to complete the course *at least* 30 days *before* the expiration date on your license. Licensees who fail the post-license end-of-course exam must wait at least 30 days from the date of the original examination to retake a different form of the end-of-course examination. Therefore, it is wise to allow yourself ample time so that if you need to retake the exam you can do so prior to the expiration date on your license. If you are taking the course by distance education, your school will need time to grade your exam and electronically submit the results to the state *before* your expiration date. Furthermore, you need to allow for unexpected events such as computer problems, sickness, and emergencies.

sponsors. Post-licensure courses are offered in live classroom format and online. Students must pass the 45-hour end-of-course exam with a score of 75 percent or higher. Licensees who fail the end-of-course exam must wait at least 30 days from the date of the original examination to retake a different form of the end-of-course examination. (Alternatively, licensees who do not want to wait 30 days may choose to retake the course and, in such cases, take a different form of the end-of-course exam.) Florida-licensed attorneys who are also licensed real estate sales associates must complete the post-licensing education requirement. (Refer to Figure 2.1, Summary of Education Exemptions, page 28.)

CONTINUING EDUCATION

61J2-3.009, F.A.C.

After completing the post-licensing education requirement during the initial license period, active and inactive licensees must complete at least 14 hours of continuing education during every 2-year license period after that. Three of the 14 hours must consist of core law, which includes updates to applicable rules and statutes. While only 3 hours of core law are required in the 2-year, 14-hour renewal cycle, the legislature encourages licensees to take 3 hours of core law in each year of the renewal cycle to stay current on changes in the Florida real estate laws. A licensee who takes the 3-hour core-law course in each year of the renewal period receives 6 hours of credit toward the 14-hour continuing education requirement. The continuing education requirement may be satisfied by attending a classroom course, by completing an approved distance education course, or by attending a Commission-approved education seminar or conference.

A licensee may substitute attendance at one legal agenda session of the FREC for three classroom hours of continuing education (CE) credit. A licensee may substitute three CE credits only one time per renewal cycle. To obtain the credit, the licensee must notify the DRE at least seven days in advance of the licensee's intent to attend the FREC's legal agenda session. A licensee may not earn CE credit for attending a legal agenda session if the licensee is a party to a disciplinary action slated for that FREC legal agenda.

Active members in good standing with The Florida Bar are exempt from the continuing education requirements for real estate licensees. (Refer to Figure 2.1, Summary of Education Exemptions, page 28.)

BROKER REQUIREMENTS

Applicants who possess a Florida sales associate's license must fulfill their sales associate's post-licensing education *before* the expiration of the initial sales associate's license or before applying for a broker's license (whichever occurs first).

475.17(2)&(3), F.S. 61J2-3.008, F.A.C.

Broker applicants must successfully complete Course II or an equivalent FREC-approved course (unless qualifying as a broker under the mutual recognition provision). Course II consists of 69 hours of instruction plus 3 hours for the end-of-course examination.

475.17(2)(b), F.S.

Broker Experience Requirements

Broker applicants must fulfill an experience requirement in addition to the education requirement. A broker applicant fulfills the experience requirement by having held an active real estate license for at least 24 months during the five-year period preceding application to become a Florida real estate broker. A broker applicant can fulfill the experience requirement in one of three ways:

1. The applicant has held an active sales associate license under one or more real estate brokers for at least 24 months during the five-year period preceding application to become a Florida real estate broker. The employment can be under a Florida real estate broker or a broker licensed in another state or in any foreign jurisdiction.

2. The applicant held an active sales associate license while working as a salaried employee of a governmental agency and performing the duties authorized in Chapter 475, F.S., for at least 24 months during the five-year period preceding application to become a Florida real estate broker.

3. The applicant held an active broker license in another state or in any foreign jurisdiction for at least 24 months during the five-year period preceding application to become a Florida real estate broker.

475.17(2)(c), F.S.

The experience cannot be earned by working for an owner-developer unless the owner-developer is a licensed broker who holds a current, valid, active real estate license. A broker applicant who holds a *Florida* real estate sales associate license *must* fulfill the 45-hour post-licensing education requirement before the initial sales associate license expires in order to be eligible to obtain a Florida broker license, even if the applicant is applying real estate experience from another state. If the broker applicant does not hold a Florida real estate sales associate license, the 45-hour post-licensing education requirement does not apply.

475.17, F.S. 61J2-3.020, F.A.C. 61J2-3.008, F.A.C.

Broker Post-Licensing Education

Broker licensees are required to successfully complete post-licensing education *before the first renewal* of their licenses. If a broker does not complete the 60-hour post-licensing requirement, the broker's license becomes null and void by operation of law. However, the

PRIMA FACIE EVIDENCE

Prima facie evidence is a legal term used to refer to evidence that is good and sufficient on its face (at first view) to establish a given fact or prove a case. Unless it is refuted by evidence to the contrary, prima facie evidence will prove a case (presumptive evidence).

A real estate license indicates the licensee's name, issue date, and expiration date, and it serves as prima facie evidence that the licensee holds a current and valid license. Furthermore, official Commission documents become prima facie evidence once they are signed by the FREC chairperson or the chairperson's designee and affixed with the Commission's seal. (See also Commission General Powers and Duties, page 45.)

broker may request and receive a sales associate's license after completing 14 hours of continuing education within the 6 months following expiration of the broker's license—and provided the broker has complied with all requirements for renewal.

Any licensee who has received a four-year degree in real estate from an institution of higher education is exempt from the broker prelicense and post-license education requirements to become initially licensed (continuing education is not exempt). (Refer to Figure 2.1, Summary of Education Exemptions, page 28.)

Broker Continuing Education

Broker licensees must complete the same continuing education requirements required for sales associates. (See Continuing Education on page 30.)

REGISTRATION AND LICENSURE

475.215(2), F.S.

Registration is the process of submitting information to the DBPR that is entered into the Department's records. Information that is placed on record with the DBPR includes the name and address of each licensed broker and sales associate; the name and business address of each sales associate's employer; the sales associate's and broker's license status (active or inactive); and the person's involvement as an officer, director, or partner of a real estate business. Sales associates and broker associates licensed in Florida must be registered under their employing broker (or owner-developer, if applicable). Sales associates and broker associates may have only one registered employer at any given time. Florida licensees may also hold active licenses in other states. Individuals who do not intend to engage actively in the real estate business, such as a director of a real estate corporation, simply register this information with the DBPR so that the information can be entered into the database. However, an individual who wishes to actively engage in the real estate industry must be licensed and registered as active with the DBPR.

Licensure is obtained when an applicant passes the state license exam. Passing the license examination gives the applicant the right to request and be issued a real estate **license**. (See Figure 2.2, Real Estate License and Wallet-Sized Card.) The license

FIGURE 2.2 ■ Real Estate License and Wallet-Sized Card

1 indicates the effective date, expiration date, the name of the governor, and the DBPR
2 secretary. The licensee's full name and license status are also indicated. The two-letter
3 prefix before the license number indicates the license type. BK signifies broker; SL,
4 sales associate; BL, broker associate; BO, branch office; CQ, corporations and LLCs;
5 and PR, partnerships and LLPs. A real estate license is considered **prima facie evidence**
6 that the holder possesses a current and valid license. (Refer to the text box, Prima Facie
7 Evidence.)

REAL ESTATE SERVICES

475.01, F.S.

9 The Florida Real Estate License law identifies eight real estate-related activities referred to
10 as *real estate services* that require a Florida real estate license. **Real estate services** include
11 any real estate activity involving compensation for performing the service for another.

12 To remember the eight services of real estate, use the memory crutch (mnemonic)
13 acronym A BAR SALE, where the first letter of each service forms the memory aid.

TO REMEMBER: A BAR SALE

A Advertise real estate services

B Buy
A Appraise
R Rent or provide rental information or lists

S Sell
A Auction
L Lease
E Exchange

14 Real estate services are further defined in law to include the following activities in the
15 sale, exchange, or lease of real property, including mineral rights, business enterprises, or
16 business opportunities:

17 ■ Offer to, agree to, or attempt to perform real estate activities

- Advertise or otherwise indicate to the public that one is in the business of performing real estate services
- Direct or assist in the procurement of sellers, buyers, lessors, or lessees
- Negotiate or close a real estate transaction (*Note:* Case law has determined that the intention to close a real estate transaction is sufficient.)

Anyone who performs real estate services for another person for compensation of any type must be licensed, unless specifically exempted by law. **Compensation** is defined as anything of value or a valuable consideration, directly or indirectly paid, promised, or expected to be paid or received. Compensation includes money in the form of a salary, bonuses, commissions, and gratuities. Compensation is also things of value such as dinner, flowers, wine, gift certificates, event tickets, and so forth.

It is a violation of license law to share a commission with or to pay a fee or other compensation to an unlicensed person for the referral of real estate business clients, prospects, or customers. However, a Florida broker may pay a referral fee to a broker licensed in another state so long as the foreign broker does not violate Florida law.

INDIVIDUALS WHO ARE EXEMPT FROM A REAL ESTATE LICENSE

475.011, F.S.

Individuals may buy, sell, exchange, or lease property for themselves. Therefore, the following individuals and business entities are exempt from a real estate license in the following circumstances:

- Property owners do not need a real estate license to buy, sell, exchange, or lease their own real estate.
- Corporations, partnerships, trusts, and joint ventures may buy, sell, exchange, or lease their own property. Salaried employees of these business entities may buy, sell, exchange, or lease real property for their employer, provided the activity is incidental to their employment and they are not paid a commission or compensated on a transactional basis.

Also exempt from real estate licensure are salaried employees:

468, Part VIII, F.S.

- who work in an on-site rental office in a leasing capacity and who do not receive a commission (*Note:* There is no restriction on the duration of the rental leases for this exemption.);
- who are managers of condominiums or cooperative apartment complexes who rent individual units for periods no longer than one year and who are not paid a commission (*Note:* If the condominium or cooperative meets certain requirements, property managers must obtain community association manager licenses [CAM licenses] from the DBPR. Salaried managers of community associations are required to obtain CAM licenses.);
- of an owner-developer (real estate developer) provided they do not receive a commission;
- of a governmental agency who perform real estate services for the state or local government and who do not receive a commission (*Note:* This exemption includes persons who appraise railroad property for tax purposes.); and
- of business entities who negotiate the sale or purchase of radio, television, or cable enterprises provided the sale does not involve real property. (*Note:* If

the transaction involves the sale or lease of land, buildings, or other improvements to land, a real estate licensee must be retained for that portion of the transaction.)

Chapter 475 of the Florida Statutes exempts the following individuals from holding a real estate license:

- Persons who sell cemetery lots. (*Note:* This exemption exists because Chapter 475, F.S., excludes cemetery lots from the definition of real property.)
- Individuals who rent lots in a mobile home park or recreational travel park.
- Attorneys-at-law when acting within the scope of their professional duties in an attorney-client relationship. (*Note:* In Florida, holding a Florida Bar license does *not* entitle an attorney to compensation for performing real estate services.)
- Certified public accountants (CPAs) when performing accounting duties within the scope of their professional duties.
- A person who has been given a power of attorney (referred to as an *attorney-in-fact*) in order to sign contracts and conveyances on someone's behalf. (*Note:* A person cannot appoint another individual as an attorney-in-fact for the purpose of conducting real estate services for others.)
- Owners of time-share periods for their own use and occupancy who later offer the time-share periods for resale.
- State-certified and licensed real estate appraisers who are licensed under Chapter 475, Part II for the purpose of conducting appraisal services.
- Court-appointed individuals acting within the limitations of their duties.
- Hotel and motel clerks who rent lodging accommodations on behalf of the establishment.
- Federally regulated banks and dealers registered with the Securities and Exchange Commission (SEC) selling business enterprises to accredited investors.
- Apartment property owners or property management firms for the purpose of paying a finder's fee of no more than $50 to a tenant of the complex for a rental referral.

Practical Examples of When a Real Estate License Is (Is Not) Required

Practice Problem 1

Chris works as an office administrative assistant in the brokerage office. Chris is a salaried employee who does not have a real estate license. Last week, Chris showed a listed property to a customer because the broker was too busy to show the property to the customer. Chris walked the customer through the property pointing out its features and discussing the homeowners' association clubhouse, pool, and annual dues. Was Chris required to be licensed to show property to a customer?

Practice Problem 2

An owner-developer pays a commission to employee Sally for selling a lot in the development. Sally has an inactive real estate license. The developer is not a broker. Is this a violation?

Practice Problem 3

A court of law appoints Mathew, who is unlicensed, to sell property in an estate. Is Mathew required to be licensed in order to be compensated for selling the property?

Practice Problem 4

Broker Mariah and John have agreed to sell a parcel of land that they both own. They each own a 50 percent share of the property. John does not have a real estate license. Is John required to be licensed in order to receive 50 percent of the proceeds from the sale of the land?

Practice Problem 5

Teresa is a sales associate who is registered under the broker for Complete Real Estate Services, Inc. Teresa also works on the weekends as a leasing agent for College Town Apartments. College Town Apartments pays Teresa a salary. Is Teresa in violation of Chapter 475, F.S.?

The solutions to the Practice Problems are located on page 38.

SUMMARY OF IMPORTANT POINTS

- A *sales associate* is a person who performs real estate services for compensation or other consideration but does so under the direction, control, and management of an active broker or owner-developer.

- A *broker* is a person who, for another and for compensation or other consideration performs real estate services.

- A *broker associate* is an individual who meets the requirements of a broker but who chooses to work in real estate under the direction (employ) of another broker.

- An *owner-developer* is an unlicensed entity that sells, exchanges, or leases its own property. Sales staff must hold active real estate licenses to be paid commission. The sales staff is exempt from licensure if paid strictly on a salaried basis.

- To become a sales associate, applicants must complete (1) a 63-hour prelicense course with a score of at least 70; and (2) the application process, including the DBPR license application, fingerprints submission, background check information, affidavit of honesty (attest statement), initial license and application fee payment; and passage of the state license exam with a score of at least 75.

- Applicants must be at least 18 years of age and have earned a high school diploma or its equivalent. U.S. citizenship is not required, and applicants do not have to be Florida residents. Applicants must possess a Social Security number.

- Resident licensees who move out of the state must notify the Commission within 60 days of the change in residency.

- Sales associates must complete a 45-hour post-licensing course before the expiration of their initial license. Failure to do so will cause the sales associate license to become null and void.

- Fourteen hours of continuing education each license period is required for all real estate licensees following the initial license period.

- Individuals who have earned a four-year degree in real estate are exempt from the sales associate and broker prelicense courses as well as the post-license requirement. They are not exempt from the continuing education requirement.

- Florida-licensed attorneys who are active members of The Florida Bar are exempt from the sales associate prelicense course and from continuing education. They are not exempt from the broker prelicense education and the post-license requirement.

- Real estate services include any real estate activities involving compensation for performing the service for another. Compensation is anything of value paid or promised to be paid to an individual for performing any of the eight services of real estate.

Note to Readers

The same FREC rule may appear in several different forms: "Rule 61J2-1.011, Florida Administrative Code"; "Chapter 61J2-1.011, F.A.C."; "Commission Rule 61J2-1.011"; simply as "61J2-1.011"; etc. Similar variations apply to the same Florida law: "Chapter 475.01, Florida Statutes"; "Florida Statute 475.01"; "Section 475.01"; "s. 475.01"; "475.01, F.S."; etc.

Practical Examples of When a Real Estate License Is (Is Not) Required Solutions

(Practice Problems are located on page 36.)

Practice Problem 1 Solution

Chris performed real estate services (buying and selling activities) for others. Chris needs a real estate license. This is a violation of Chapter 475.

Practice Problem 2 Solution

The sales staff of an owner-developer is exempt from a real estate license if the staff is paid strictly on a salaried basis. In this case, a commission is paid (compensation on a transactional basis), so an active license is required. Sally would have had to be registered under her employer (the developer) with an active license status for this to be in accordance with Chapter 475.

Practice Problem 3 Solution

Court-appointed individuals acting within the limitations of their duties are exempt from real estate licensure. Mathew may sell the property in accordance with the instructions of the court. Compensation is usually paid from the assets of the estate.

Practice Problem 4 Solution

Broker Mariah and John are property owners selling a parcel of land that they both own. Property owners do not need a real estate license to sell their own property. They may split the proceeds of the sale based on their percentage share of ownership. If Mariah and John had agreed that John should receive more than his ownership share of the proceeds, this would be a violation because the additional share of the proceeds would be considered compensation. John is unlicensed and cannot be compensated for selling the property.

Practice Problem 5 Solution

A sales associate or broker associate must be registered under a broker or an owner-developer to be paid a commission. The associate can also work as a rental agent, provided the associate is paid a salary. Salaried individuals who work in a leasing capacity and who do not receive compensation on a transactional basis are exempt from a real estate license under Florida Statute 475.011. Therefore, it is not a violation of license law for Teresa to work as an agent of her broker and also receive a salary from another employer for working in a leasing capacity.

REVIEW QUESTIONS

1. A licensed sales associate may operate
   a. for any registered broker.
   b. for the broker registered as the sales associate's employer.
   c. independently if registered with the DBPR.
   d. as a broker associate.

2. A sales associate applicant is NOT required to comply with which requirement?
   a. Submit an application fee
   b. Be 18 years of age or older
   c. Be a bona fide Florida resident
   d. Possess a Social Security number

3. Which person does NOT meet the experience requirements to obtain a Florida broker's license?
   a. An applicant who has held an active California broker's license for the preceding three years
   b. An applicant who has held an active Ohio sales associate license during four of the preceding five years while employed by an Ohio broker
   c. An applicant who has held an active Florida sales associate license for the preceding two years while employed by a Florida broker
   d. An applicant who has held an active Florida sales associate license during two of the preceding five years while employed by an owner-developer

4. Which statement does NOT describe the intent of the Florida Legislature concerning regulation of professional and licensed occupations to protect the public?
   a. When the potential for harm to the public is clear
   b. When other ordinances and laws are not sufficient to protect the public
   c. Whenever deemed appropriate by the Legislature
   d. When less-constraining measures of regulation are not available or apparent

5. A sales associate applicant is NOT required to disclose which information on the license application?
   a. Convicted of a crime
   b. Proof of U.S. citizenship
   c. Maiden name, if applicable
   d. Found guilty of conduct that would have resulted in disciplinary action if the applicant had been licensed to practice real estate

6. A sales associate sells real estate for a real estate brokerage company. He also works as a sales associate for another real estate brokerage company.
   a. The sales associate is in violation of F.S. 475.
   b. The sales associate may work for both companies as long as he registers both employers with the FREC.
   c. This is legal as long as he only works part-time for each company.
   d. The sales associate must be a broker associate for this to be legal.

7. What is the Latin term for a plea of "no contest"?
   a. Prima facie
   b. Caveat emptor
   c. Writ of mandamus
   d. Nolo contendere

8. A woman helped her father sell some property he owned. The daughter is not a real estate licensee. Her father was grateful for his daughter's assistance, but the daughter declined any compensation for assisting her father. Which statement is TRUE?
   a. This was unlicensed real estate activity, and both the daughter and her father could be prosecuted.
   b. The daughter is legally allowed to sell her father's real estate and be compensated for it because she is a family member.
   c. This was a legal arrangement because the daughter did not receive compensation for performing real estate services.
   d. The daughter can be fined by the FREC for performing real estate services without a license.

9. Which event may cause the FREC to refuse to certify an individual as qualified for licensure?
   a. Dropped out of high school and later earned a GED
   b. Was convicted of fraud in an insurance scam
   c. Changed residency to a state other than the state of Florida
   d. Lost a lot of one's own money in a bad real estate investment

10. To receive a notice of satisfactory completion of Course I or Course II, a student may NOT miss more than
    a. 4 instructional hours.
    b. 6 instructional hours.
    c. 8 instructional hours.
    d. 12 instructional hours.

11. A woman received her Florida sales associate's license last year. Which requirement must she complete to become a licensed real estate broker?
    a. Successfully complete the 45-hour post-licensing course
    b. Complete 14 hours of continuing education for sales associates
    c. Document at least three closed real estate transactions
    d. Complete at least three years of experience as a sales associate before taking the broker license exam

12. A man has a North Carolina broker's license, but he is not licensed in Florida. He sells a parcel of land he owns in Florida. Assuming all else is proper, this is a legal transaction because
    a. mutual recognition agreements allow this.
    b. Florida law exempts from licensure individual owners selling their own real property.
    c. Florida has honored his nonresident broker's license.
    d. he has the knowledge and qualifications necessary to handle the transaction.

13. A sales associate applicant who has submitted a correctly completed application for the state license examination and who successfully passes the state exam may legally begin to operate as a licensee when the
    a. application and proper fees are received by the state.
    b. applicant receives a return receipt acknowledging acceptance of the application.
    c. applicant receives the canceled check as evidence of payment followed by an assigned date for the state exam.
    d. applicant is notified of having passed the state exam, has filed the appropriate form to become registered as active with the DBPR, and the DBPR Web site indicates the applicant's license status is active.

14. If the post-licensing requirement is not fulfilled before the first renewal and a sales associate licensee wishes to continue in the real estate business, the licensee
    a. must retake the state exam within one year.
    b. must requalify for licensure.
    c. is allowed a six-month grace period to meet the requirement but must hold an inactive license during that period.
    d. must retake the prelicense course within one year.

15. Services of real estate do NOT include
    a. advertising rental property lists.
    b. appraising real property.
    c. selling cemetery lots for compensation.
    d. conducting an auction of real property.

16. Which statement BEST describes who must be licensed to practice real estate in Florida?
    a. Anyone who performs any of the services of real estate
    b. Anyone who performs any of the services of real estate for another
    c. Anyone who performs any of the services of real estate for another for compensation
    d. Anyone who performs any of the services of real estate for another for compensation, unless specifically exempted by law

17. Which individual is NOT exempt from licensure under F.S. 475?
    a. Salaried employees of a governmental agency who perform real estate services for the state and do not receive commission
    b. Individual dealing in personal property only
    c. Individual serving as a personal representative and acting within the statutory limits of that designated role
    d. An employee of a real estate developer who receives a salary plus bonuses based on sales quotas

18. A salaried individual manages a condominium building and rents units for three-month to six-month periods. The manager
    a. must be licensed under F.S. 475 because leasing is one of the real estate services.
    b. must be licensed under F.S. 475 because she rents condominium units for compensation.
    c. must be licensed by the Division of Condominiums and Time Share Sales.
    d. is exempt from licensure under F.S. 475.

19. A developer purchased a tract of land and subdivided the property into individual lots. The developer hired his son, who was not licensed to sell the lots. The father agreed to pay his son a salary of $200 per week. After two weeks, the son had sold only two lots, so the father decided to add an incentive. The father promised his son that after every fifth lot was sold, he would give his son a lot free and clear. After one more week, the son had sold only one more lot. The son quit his job to go work for another developer who paid a higher weekly salary. Which statement applies to this arrangement?
   a. There is no violation of F.S. 475
   b. The son alone has violated F.S. 475
   c. Only the father has violated F.S. 475
   d. Both the father and the son have violated F.S. 475

20. FBI files reveal that six months ago a man worked as a real estate broker in Georgia, where he was charged with arson related to a large insurance claim. To avoid a long court fight without pleading guilty, the man agreed to revocation of his real estate license and entered a plea of *nolo contendere*. The FREC has just received the man's application for licensure as a sales associate disclosing the above information. The application shows that all academic requirements have been met, and a background check reveals no incriminating information other than the facts mentioned above. The FREC will probably decide that
   a. the man is not qualified for licensure.
   b. the man can be licensed based on the information on the application.
   c. because the man was never convicted of the charge in Georgia, he can be licensed in Florida.
   d. the recommendations from the references provide adequate grounds for the licensure of the man.

3

LICENSE LAW ADMINISTRATION

1 ## OVERVIEW

2 The purpose of this chapter is to discuss in detail the Florida Real Estate Commission and
3 its composition and powers. The chapter also explains license requirements, including
4 active and inactive status, license activation, and void and ineffective licenses.

5 After completing this chapter, the student should be able to:

6 ■ describe the composition and member qualifications of the Florida Real Estate
7 Commission;

8 ■ explain how members of the Commission are appointed;

9 ■ distinguish between active and inactive license status;

10 ■ explain the purpose of multiple and group licenses; and

11 ■ distinguish between void licenses and ineffective licenses.

12 ## KEY TERMS

active license	group license	quasi-judicial
address of record	ineffective	quasi-legislative
canceled	involuntary inactive	void
cease to be in force	ministerial duties	voluntary inactive
current mailing address	multiple licenses	
executive	promulgates	

13 ## FLORIDA REAL ESTATE COMMISSION

475.451, F.S.
475.04, F.S.
475.001, F.S.
455.201(1), F.S.

14 The Florida Real Estate Commission (FREC) is the regulatory body charged by the Florida
15 Legislature to protect the general public by regulating real estate brokers and broker-
16 age firms, broker associates, sales associates, and real estate schools and instructors. The
17 FREC is also charged with fostering the education of real estate licensees and permit
18 holders. This includes the regulation of proprietary real estate schools and all noncredit,

FIGURE 3.1 ■ **Composition of the Florida Real Estate Commission**

Four Active Brokers	One Active Sales Associate or Broker	Two Consumer Members
Licensed for at Least Five Years	Licensed for at Least Two Years	Never Been Licensed

1 FREC-approved courses offered by colleges, universities, community colleges, and area
2 technical centers. The objective of such regulation is to protect the public (consumer
3 protection) by ensuring that real estate licensees have at least a minimal degree of
4 competence.

Composition and Qualifications

475.02, F.S.
455.209, F.S.
20.052, F.S.
20.165, F.S.
61J2-20.040,
F.A.C.

6 The Florida Real Estate Commission (FREC) consists of seven members (See Figure 3.1, Com-
7 position of the Florida Real Estate Commission):

8 ■ Five of the members are *professional* (licensed) members of which:

9 ■ four must be Florida real estate brokers who have held active licenses during
10 the five years preceding appointment; and

11 ■ one must be either a Florida real estate broker or sales associate who has held
12 an active license during the two years preceding appointment.

13 ■ Two remaining members are *consumer* (unlicensed) members who have never
14 been real estate brokers or sales associates.

15 The governor, subject to confirmation by the state Senate, appoints Commission
16 members to four-year staggered terms. Commissioners may *not* serve more than two con-
17 secutive terms.

18 Each member of the Commission is accountable to the governor, not the DBPR, for
19 proper performance. All FREC members are exempt from civil liability while performing in
20 their official capacity. At least one of the seven members must be 60 years of age or older.

Compensation

455.207, F.S.
61J2-20.049,
F.A.C.

22 Commission members do not receive a salary. However, in lieu of salary, they are paid
23 $50 per day for each day they attend an official meeting and for each day they participate
24 in other Commission business. In addition, they receive reimbursement for expenses
25 connected with their official activities. Any travel outside the state as members of the
26 Commission requires the prior approval of the DBPR Secretary.

¹ # Meetings

455.207, F.S.

² The FREC meetings are held each month. There must be a quorum consisting of at least
³ 51 percent (or four Commission members) to conduct official business. One of the meet-
⁴ ings is designated the *annual meeting* when the Commission elects from its members a
⁵ chairperson and vice-chairperson.

⁶ ## Commission General Powers and Duties

475.25, F.S.
475.181, F.S.
475.125, F.S.
475.10, F.S.
475.05, F.S.

⁷ The powers and duties of the FREC fall into three general areas of responsibility:

⁸ 1. **Executive** powers to regulate and enforce the license law are delegated to the
⁹   Commission by the legislature.

¹⁰ 2. **Quasi-legislative** responsibilities include the power to enact and revise adminis-
¹¹   trative rules and regulations and to interpret questions regarding the practice of
¹²   real estate.

¹³ 3. **Quasi-judicial** responsibilities include the power to grant or deny license appli-
¹⁴   cations, to determine license law violations, and to administer penalties.

¹⁵ The FREC's powers and duties also include these specific responsibilities:

¹⁶ ■ *Adopt a seal.* The seal, when affixed to rules, regulations, or other official documents,
¹⁷   properly signed, becomes *prima facie evidence* that the document is authentic.

¹⁸ ■ *Foster the education of applicants and licensees.* The Commission fosters the edu-
¹⁹   cation of brokers, broker associates, sales associates, and instructors in ethical,
²⁰   legal, and business principles. It also prescribes post-licensing education require-
²¹   ments and continuing education requirements for brokers and sales associates to
²²   qualify for license renewal.

²³ ■ *Make determinations of violations.* The Commission is obligated to report any
²⁴   criminal violation of Chapter 475, when it knows of such violations, to the
²⁵   state's attorney having jurisdiction. Furthermore, the FREC must inform the
²⁶   Division of Florida Condominiums, Timeshares, and Mobile Homes when any
²⁷   disciplinary action is taken by the FREC against any of its licensees.

²⁸ ■ *Regulate professional practices.* For example, when requested and deemed appropri-
²⁹   ate, the Commission may issue an escrow disbursement order (EDO) to deter-
³⁰   mine the disposition of escrow (earnest money) deposits in the case of a dispute
³¹   when requested by the broker holding the escrowed funds. The Commission also
³²   establishes rules and regulations requiring that records be maintained by brokers
³³   and the manner in which deposits of money, funds, checks, or drafts are to be
³⁴   made in escrow, pending disbursement.

³⁵ ■ *Create and pass rules and regulations.* The Commission **promulgates** (enacts and
³⁶   publishes) rules and regulations that enforce the Florida statutory license law.

475.021(2), F.S.
455.219(1), F.S.

³⁷ ■ *Establish fees.* The Commission uses the DBPR estimates of required revenue
³⁸   to determine the amount of licensing fees needed to implement the real estate
³⁹   license law and other laws and regulations relating to the regulation of real
⁴⁰   estate practitioners.

⁴¹ ■ *Grant or deny applications for licensure.* The Commission certifies an applicant as
⁴²   qualified before a license is issued.

⁴³ ■ *Suspend or revoke licenses and impose administrative fines.* The Commission adopts,
⁴⁴   by rule, guidelines for the disciplinary actions that it imposes.

475.03, F.S.

1   With the prior approval of the attorney general, the Commission may retain inde-
2   pendent counsel to provide legal advice. However, an attorney employed to provide legal
3   advice to the Commission may not also prosecute the same case.

4   The powers of the FREC are limited to administrative matters and do not extend to
5   criminal actions. The FREC may *not* impose imprisonment as a penalty. The primary pur-
6   pose of the administrative jurisdiction granted to the Commission is to enforce duties and
7   obligations as they apply to individuals and firms actively engaged in the real estate business.
8   (See chapter 6.) The Commission makes decisions and sets policies that are carried out by
9   the Division of Real Estate (DRE).

10   The DRE provides all services required to administer the Florida Real Estate License
11   Law. However, the FREC is empowered by law to delegate by majority vote any duty
12   or duties to whichever division within DBPR the Commission feels is appropriate. The
13   FREC can also rescind, by majority vote, any delegation of duties at any time.

14   DEPARTMENT OF BUSINESS AND PROFESSIONAL
15   REGULATION (DBPR)

20.165, F.S.
455.223-
455.225, F.S.
61J2-20.048,
F.A.C.

16   The DBPR is the agency charged with licensing and regulating businesses and profes-
17   sionals in Florida. The DBPR is under the executive branch of the Governor, and it is
18   governed by Chapter 120, F.S. The agency is structured according to the requirements of
19   Chapter 20.165, F.S. The Legislature, under Chapter 455, F.S., granted authority to the
20   DBPR to investigate consumer complaints, issue subpoenas when conducting investiga-
21   tions, issue cease and desist orders to unlicensed individuals, and issue citations to indi-
22   viduals licensed by the DBPR. The chief administrator of the DBPR is the Secretary of the
23   DBPR who is appointed by the governor, subject to confirmation by the state Senate. The
24   main DBPR office is located in Tallahassee, Florida. The divisions under the Department
25   of Business and Professional Regulation that are most relevant to real estate are presented
26   below.

WEB LINK

A description of agency organization and operation of the Florida Department of Business and Professional
Regulation (DBPR) is available at www.myfloridalicense.com/dbpr/adm/AgencyOrganization.html.

27   The Division of Professions

28   The Division of Professions administers numerous professional boards. Due to the magni-
29   tude of the real estate profession, it is organized as a separate division under the DBPR.
30   The Division of Professions regulates education courses and license examinations for each
31   profession under the DBPR.

32   Division of Service Operations

33   There are two important units under the Division of Service Operations:

34   ■   The Customer Contact Center handles all incoming telephone, postal, and
35   e-mail inquiries from licensees and the general public.

1   ■ The Central Intake Unit processes all of the license applications and license fees
2   that come into the DBPR. The Central Intake Unit is also responsible for the
3   issuance of all licenses and license renewal notifications for the Department.

Division of Florida Condominiums, Timeshares, and Mobile Homes

718, F.S.
719, F.S.
720, F.S.
721, F.S

This Division provides consumer protection for Florida residents through education, complaint resolution, mediation and arbitration, and developer disclosure. It regulates condominiums, cooperatives, time-shares, and mobile home parks. The Division of Florida Condominiums, Timeshares, and Mobile Homes is also charged with providing complaint resolution for homeowner associations.

Division of Real Estate

475.021, F.S.

The Division of Real Estate performs all functions related to the regulation of general real estate in Florida. The duties of the DRE are essentially administrative and ministerial. The administrative duties include routine duties and clerical functions on behalf of the FREC. The DRE's **ministerial duties** involve record keeping.

Florida statute mandates that the DRE offices and the principal office of the Commission are located in Orlando. Additional facts concerning the DRE are presented below:

■ The Director of the DRE is appointed by the Secretary of the DBPR, subject to approval by majority vote of the FREC. The Director is a senior employee charged with the direct service assistance to the Commission.

■ The DBPR employs all DRE personnel to support FREC activities.

■ Members of the Commission, on the other hand, are appointed by the governor, subject to senate confirmation, and are *not* employees.

REAL ESTATE REGULATION

Licensing Examinations

455.217, F.S.
455.2171, F.S.
455.2175, F.S.

The Division of Professions contracts with a professional testing service for exam services. The DBPR, acting with its Division of Professions and the Division of Real Estate, must ensure that the license examinations adequately and reliably measure an applicant's ability to practice real estate.

    Florida law requires that an accurate record of each applicant's examination questions, answers, papers, grades, and grading key be stored for two years. Examinees' grades and the state examination questions are confidential. The theft of a DBPR license examination or unauthorized copying of an examination is a third degree felony.

License Fees

New applicants for licensure are assessed an initial application fee in addition to the biennial license fee. Applicants for initial licensure and for subsequent license renewal also pay an unlicensed activity fee and may be required to pay a Real Estate Recovery Fund fee,

1 if applicable. (See Real Estate Recovery Fund in chapter 6.) Applicants submit the license
2 exam and fingerprint processing fees directly to the test vendor.

455.213(12), F.S.

3 **Fee waiver for military veterans.** The initial application fee, biennial license fee, and
4 unlicensed activity fee are waived for military veterans who apply for a real estate license
5 within 24 months after honorable discharge from the Armed Forces. The fee waiver applies
6 to all licenses issued by the DBPR.

Current Mailing Address

455.275(1) and (2), F.S.
61J2-10.038, F.A.C.
61J2-24.002, F.A.C.

8 Licensees are responsible for notifying the DBPR in writing of their current mailing
9 address, e-mail address, and place of practice. **Current mailing address** is the current
10 residential address a licensee uses to receive mail through the U.S. Postal Service. A post
11 office box is an acceptable mailing address. The DBPR sends official communication to a
12 licensee at the last known mailing address or e-mail address, referred to by the DBPR as
13 the **address of record**.

14 Licensees must notify the DBPR in writing within *ten days* of a change in current
15 mailing address. Licensees may mail or fax the appropriate form to the DBPR, or licensees
16 may submit a change of address online at the DBPR Online Service Web site. Licensees
17 who fail to timely notify the DBPR of a change of address are in violation of Florida Stat-
18 ute 455 and are subject to a citation and $500 fine. Florida licensees who move out of
19 state must also comply with all nonresident requirements. (See Nonresident Application
20 Requirements in chapter 2.)

License Renewal Periods

455.203, F.S.
475.182 F.S.

22 The initial effective date of a real estate license is the date the applicant passed the license
23 exam. All real estate licenses are issued with an expiration date of either March 31 or Sep-
24 tember 30. The expiration date (March 31 or September 30) that is assigned to a particular
25 license is the date that will give the licensee as close to 24 months of licensure as possible,
26 without exceeding 24 months. License law mandates that the initial license period must
27 provide the licensee at least 18 months of licensure but not more than 24 months.

28 For example, assume the initial effective date of a sales associate license is July 25,
29 2012. What expiration date will give the licensee at least 18 months of licensure but not
30 more than a 24-month license period?

31 Hint: 24 months from the initial effective date is July 25, 2014.

32 To answer this question, ask yourself which expiration date in 2014 is *closest* to July
33 25, 2014, but *not after* July 25, 2014?

34 March comes before July so the expiration date closest to July 25, 2014, but not past
35 July 25 must be March 31, 2014. (September 30, 2014, is after July 25, 2014.) March is
36 four months prior to July so this licensee will have approximately 20 months of licensure
37 (24 months minus 4 months). Thereafter, this license will always expire every two years
38 (biennially) on March 31.

> **Practice Problem**
>
> Part 1: Assume December 29, 2012, is the date an initial license is issued. On what date will this license expire?
>
> Part 2: How many months of licensure are in the initial license period?
>
> (The solution to the Practice Problem is at the end of this chapter on page 55.)

¹ If a real estate sales associate later decides to become a broker, the broker license will ² have a new initial effective date, and that new effective date is the date the person passed ³ the broker license exam. Because the broker's license is issued with a new effective date, ⁴ it is possible that the broker license will have a different expiration date. For example, ⁵ assume the sales associate's license expired biennially on March 31. Depending on when ⁶ the sales associate passes the broker license exam, the new broker's license may have a ⁷ September 30 expiration date.

License Renewal

455.273, F.S.

⁹ Ninety days before the end of a license cycle, the DBPR sends a renewal notice to licens-¹⁰ ees. The DBPR either mails the notice to the licensee's last known address of record or it ¹¹ electronically sends the notice to the licensee's e-mail address of record. Sales associates ¹² and brokers must complete their post-license education *before the first renewal* of their ini-¹³ tial licenses. After the post-license education is satisfied and the initial license is renewed, ¹⁴ licensees must complete 14 hours of continuing education during each renewal period.

475.182, F.S.
455.02, F.S.
61J2-3.020,
F.A.C.

¹⁵ To renew a real estate license, the licensee submits a renewal application and the ¹⁶ biennial license fee. Real estate licensees must complete the applicable post-licensing ¹⁷ or continuing education requirement *before* renewing a license. When a licensee signs ¹⁸ and returns the renewal application the licensee is attesting to have completed the edu-¹⁹ cation requirement. (Refer to Post-licensing Education and Continuing Education in ²⁰ chapter 2.)

²¹ If licensees renew after the expiration date a late fee is charged. If a licensee does not ²² renew a license by the expiration date, the license reverts automatically to involuntary ²³ inactive status. (Involuntary inactive status is discussed later in this chapter.) An active ²⁴ licensee who fails to renew a license following the expiration date has 24 months in which ²⁵ to renew the license. A real estate licensee must *not* practice real estate following the ²⁶ expiration date of the license. It is also unlawful for a licensee holding a current *inactive* ²⁷ license to perform the services of real estate for compensation.

455.02, F.S.
61J2-1.015,
F.A.C.

Armed Forces exemption. A licensee in good standing who is a member of the U.S. armed ²⁹ forces is exempt from the renewal provisions during the licensee's period of active duty and ³⁰ six months after discharge from active duty. If the military duty is out of state, the exemp-³¹ tion also applies to a licensed spouse. The Armed Forces exemption applies provided the ³² licensee is not engaged in real estate brokerage activity in the private sector for profit.

³³ The DBPR may issue a temporary real estate license to the spouse of an active duty ³⁴ member of the Armed Forces who is assigned to duty in Florida. The spouse must hold ³⁵ a valid real estate license in another state or foreign jurisdiction. A temporary license ³⁶ expires six months after the date of issue and is not renewable.

INACTIVE STATUS

Voluntary Inactive   The licensure status that results when a licensee has applied to the Department to be placed on inactive status and has paid the fee prescribed by rule

Involuntary Inactive   The licensure status that results when a license is not renewed at the end of the license period prescribed by the Department

Reference: Section 475.01, F.S.

Active versus Inactive Status

475.183, F.S.
475.182, F.S.

An **active license** is required to engage in real estate brokerage services. Sales associates achieve active status by finding an employer and registering with the DBPR under the employing broker or owner-developer. Licensees who choose not to engage in the real estate business may place their licenses on inactive status. There are two types of inactive status: (1) voluntary inactive and (2) involuntary inactive.

61J2-1.014, F.A.C.

Voluntary inactive. A licensee who has qualified for a real estate license but who voluntarily chooses not to engage in the real estate business during a given period and requests such a change is placed on **voluntary inactive** status. A licensee may change an active license to a voluntary inactive license status by submitting to the DBPR the proper form. Such licensees hold a current inactive license.

Voluntary inactive licensees who subsequently wish to activate their licenses may do so at any time simply by completing the proper form requesting an active license with an active broker or owner-developer. As with an active license, a licensee may renew a current voluntary inactive license indefinitely. Voluntary inactive licensees who satisfactorily complete the prescribed continuing education courses every two years must pay the appropriate fees to qualify for renewal of a voluntary inactive license. A license that is not renewed at the end of the license period reverts automatically to involuntary inactive status, except in the case of initial licenses when post-licensing education requirements have not been completed satisfactorily.

475.01(g), F.S.
61J2-3.010, F.A.C.

Involuntary inactive. If a licensee fails to renew an active or voluntary inactive license before the expiration date (other than the first renewal), the license reverts automatically to **involuntary inactive** status. The licensee must complete continuing education and renew the license to either active or voluntary inactive status within the next two years. A license is placed in involuntary inactive status for no more than two years. After two years the license automatically expires (becomes null and void) by operation of law without further FREC or DBPR action.

455.273, F.S.

Ninety days before expiration of an involuntary inactive license, the DBPR notifies licensees of this upcoming deadline. Once a license becomes void, the individual must reapply for licensure, retake the 63-hour prelicense course, and again pass the license exam.

475.183, F.S.
455.271(6), F.S.
61J2-3.010,
F.A.C.
61J2-1.014,
F.A.C.

Involuntary inactive licensees may activate their licenses during the two-year period following expiration of a valid current license only after satisfactorily completing FREC-prescribed courses of instruction. When a licensee has been involuntary inactive for:

- 12 months or less, licensees may satisfy the education requirement by completing 14 hours of FREC-approved continuing education; or

- more than 12 months but less than 24 months, licensees are required to complete 28 hours of a Commission-prescribed education course.

There is another situation that causes a license to be placed in involuntary inactive status. If a sales associate's broker is disciplined and as a result the broker's license is suspended or revoked, the sales associate's license will be automatically placed in involuntary inactive status. This is because a sales associate can only perform real estate services for compensation under the direction of the sales associate's employer. A sales associate's license is returned to active status as soon as a new employer is chosen and the information is filed with the DBPR.

Other License Classifications

475.183(2), F.S.
61J2-24.005,
F.A.C.

Void. When a license is **void** it no longer exists. A license becomes void when the following situations occur:

- When a license has been involuntary inactive for more than two years, the license becomes null and void without any further action by the DBPR or FREC.

- A license that has been revoked following a disciplinary proceeding becomes void. Revocation of a license is a *permanent* penalty (the licensee is put out of the real estate business forever). However, there are two exceptions to permanent revocation. A licensee whose license has been revoked for the following two reasons may reapply for a sales associate's license after five years have passed:

  1. A licensee filed for renewal but did not comply with the continuing or post-licensing education requirements prior to the expiration date

  2. An individual filed an application for a license that contained false or fraudulent information (for example, an applicant failed to disclose a prior criminal conviction)

- A person who no longer wants to engage in the real estate business can voluntarily cancel being licensed. When a license is **canceled** it is void. Cancellation of a license is effective on the date it is approved by the Commission. Cancellation does not involve disciplinary action.

Ineffective. When a license is **ineffective**, the license exists but the licensee cannot use it. A license becomes ineffective when the following situations occur:

  1. *Inactive.* Real estate licensees may *not* perform real estate services with an inactive license.

     - A licensee who has met all of the requirements for licensure but chooses not to work in the real estate industry may request a change in license status to voluntary inactive.

     - If a licensee fails to renew a license prior to the expiration date (other than the first renewal), the license is automatically placed in involuntary inactive status.

475.31, F.S.

- When a broker's license is suspended or revoked, no disciplinary action is taken against the sales associates and broker associates registered under that broker. However, the licensees registered under the disciplined broker cannot continue working because their employer's license is either void (revoked) or ineffective (suspended). The DBPR places the licenses of any sales associates and broker associates registered under the penalized broker on involuntary inactive status. The sales associates and broker associates are free to seek another employer and register as active under the new employer. Otherwise, the licensee should request a change of status to voluntary inactive status.

2. *Suspended.* If the result of a disciplinary proceeding is to suspend a license, the licensee is prevented from working for a period of time. The license is ineffective during the period of suspension.

Cease to be in force. When certain events occur, a license will **cease to be in force** (the licensee cannot conduct business) until the DBPR is properly notified. For example, if a sales associate leaves one brokerage firm and wants to work for another brokerage firm, the DBPR must be informed of the associate's new employer. Until the sales associate is registered under the new employer, the sales associate cannot work. The license ceases to be in force (also known as *ceases to be in effect*) until the sales associate has registered with the new broker. Otherwise, the sales associate would be *acting as a broker* (performing real estate services without being registered under an employing broker).

475.23, F.S.

The Commission must be notified within ten days when either of the following actions occurs:

- *A broker or registered school changes business address.* When a broker or real estate school changes business address, the new location must be registered and a fee paid. When a broker opens a new brokerage office, no new brokerage business may be conducted (the license ceases to be in effect) until the FREC is notified of the new business location and it is properly registered.

- *A sales associate or real estate instructor changes employer.* A sales associate must be registered under an employing broker. Therefore, a sales associate (or an instructor) who changes employer may not work under the new employer until the FREC has been informed and the associate (or instructor) is registered under the new employer.

If a licensee fails to give proper notification of a change in business address or a change in employer within ten days, it may result in a FREC administrative discipline proceeding.

When a broker or a real estate school changes business address, the brokerage firm or school permit holder must file with the Commission a notice of the change of address, along with the names of any sales associates or instructors who are no longer employed by the brokerage or school. Sales associates who are no longer employed with the broker of record will be placed on *involuntary inactive status.* The notification to the Commission fulfills the change of address notification requirements for sales associates who remain employed by the brokerage and instructors who remain employed by the school. When a broker changes the business address, the licenses of the sales associates remain in force. The same is true for instructors working for a real estate school that changes its business address.

Multiple Licenses

475.215, F.S.

Multiple licenses are issued to a broker who qualifies as the broker for more than one business entity. For each business that a person is a broker, a separate broker license must be obtained. A broker who holds more than one Florida broker license is said to hold **multiple licenses**. Because sales associates and broker associates may have only one registered employer at a time, sales associates and broker associates may *not* hold multiple licenses. For example, Jane Doe is the broker for both Extra-Fine Real Estate Services and Midnight Realty, two separate brokerage entities. Jane needs multiple broker licenses to qualify both brokerage entities.

Group License

61J2-6.006, F.A.C.

A **group license** is sometimes issued to sales associates or broker associates who are registered under an owner-developer. An owner-developer may own properties in the names of various entities. If the entities are all connected so that ownership and control is with the same individual(s), sales associates and broker associates employed by the owner-developer may be issued a group license.

The owner-developer sends an affidavit to the DBPR with a list of all the legal company names used by the owner-developer. This allows the associate to sell for all of the affiliated entities owned by the owner-developer. Owner-developers are not required to hold real estate licenses if they only sell their own properties. The owner-developer is registered with the DBPR under a pseudo number (not a license) that is entered into the DBPR records. To activate a sales associate license under an owner-developer, the sales associate and the developer complete the appropriate section of form DBPR RE 10. The sales associate's name and license number are entered on the form. The owner-developer's name, business location address, and pseudo number are entered on the form. In actual practice, the sales associate (or broker associate) is issued a real estate license and no distinction regarding group license is made on the associate's license. For example, Joseph Jones is an owner-developer. He owns and controls two development companies, Happy Estates and Excellent Homes. If associate Alice is employed by Mr. Jones to sell properties for both development companies, she has a group license. Alice has one sales associate license and one employer (Mr. Jones).

Registration of Proprietary Real Estate Schools

475.451, F.S.
475.04, F.S.
61J2-17.009, F.A.C.
61J2-3.008, F.A.C.

Each person, school, or institution in Florida that offers courses or training programs designed to aid applicants in becoming licensed real estate sales associates or brokers must be registered and receive a permit. This requirement does not apply to accredited colleges, universities, community colleges, or area technical centers when transferable college credit courses are involved (their noncredit courses are not exempt). However, all courses conducted by institutions exempt from obtaining a permit must meet the equivalency standards established by the FREC. This means that the Commission is not required to recognize students from exempt institutions as qualified to take a state licensing examination until and unless those courses have been approved by the FREC as equivalent to the Course I and Course II standards.

475.4511, F.S.

Proprietary schools of real estate are prohibited from advertising or making representations that are known to be false, inaccurate, misleading, or exaggerated. The content of advertisements must conform to specified guidelines. A proprietary real estate school may not promise or guarantee employment or placement of a student or prospective student on the basis of training to be provided unless the school actually offers the student a bona fide employment contract.

A school permit may be suspended for:

61J2-17.013, F.A.C.

- guaranteeing that students will pass a state examination;
- offering a refund to students who fail;
- representing that a state agency endorses the school;
- obtaining a list of questions that appear on any state examination;
- representing that the school or an instructor has obtained questions from such an examination; or
- furnishing anyone, student or otherwise, questions purported to be from a state examination.

61J2-17.015, F.A.C.

Furthermore, real estate schools and their instructors may not recruit for employment opportunities for any real estate brokerage firm during classroom instructional time. Each school permit holder must post in every classroom and administrative area, and read at the beginning of each course, the following statement: *"Recruiting for employment opportunities for any real estate brokerage firm must be accomplished outside the prescribed classroom instructional time. Noncompliance should be reported to the Commission."*

REAL ESTATE EDUCATION AND RESEARCH FOUNDATION

475.045, F.S.
215.37, F.S.
61J2-25, F.A.C.

The 1985 Florida Legislature established the Florida Real Estate Commission Education and Research Foundation. The Foundation is administered by the Florida Real Estate Commission. The Foundation funds worthy real estate education projects and real estate research. The Foundation is required to give priority to "projects with the greatest potential for direct or indirect benefit to the public." The law lists a number of other purposes, objectives, and duties, all centered around the Foundation's overall purpose, which is "to create and promote educational projects to expand the knowledge of the public and real estate licensees in matters pertaining to Florida real estate." To carry out its duties, the Foundation may solicit advice and information from real estate licensees, universities, colleges, real estate schools, and the general public.

Foundation activities and projects are funded from income derived from the real estate portion of the Professional Regulation Trust Fund. The director of the DRE is responsible for submitting to the Commission, in advance of each fiscal year, a budget for expenditure of funds to conduct proposed activities. The Commission then reviews and approves the proposed budget. A report of the Foundation's activities and accomplishments must be published annually.

Practice Problem Solution

(This Practice Problem is located on page 49.)

Part 1: 24 months from the initial effective date is December 29, 2014. September 2014 is closer to December than is March 2014. Therefore, the expiration date is September 30, 2014.

Part 2: September is 3 months before December. Therefore, the initial license period is for approximately 21 months (24 months minus 3 months).

SUMMARY OF IMPORTANT POINTS

- The Commission consists of seven members: five professional members and two consumer members. Four of the professional members must have held active broker licenses during the five years preceding appointment. The fifth professional member must have been licensed as an active broker or sales associate for the two years preceding appointment.

- The Commission's powers are primarily quasi-judicial and quasi-legislative. The FREC exercises its quasi-legislative powers when it adopts rules. It exercises its quasi-judicial powers when it hears complaints, disciplines licensees, and grants or denies Recovery Fund claims.

- Licensees must notify the DBPR within ten days of a change in mailing address.

- Sales associates and brokers must complete post-license education before the first renewal of the initial license. Failure to complete the post-license education prior to the expiration of the initial license will result in a null and void license.

- There are two types of inactive status: voluntary and involuntary. A licensee who has qualified for a real estate license but who voluntarily chooses not to engage in the real estate business may request voluntary inactive status. Involuntary inactive status occurs when a licensee fails to renew an active or voluntary inactive license before the expiration date.

- A void license no longer exists. When an individual performs real estate services with a void license, that activity is considered unlicensed activity. A license becomes void when an involuntary inactive status has continued more than two years. When the FREC revokes a real estate license, the license becomes void. A license that is voluntarily surrendered by the licensee is canceled by the FREC without the involvement of disciplinary action. Once canceled, the license is void.

- An ineffective license exists, but the licensee cannot use it. A licensee who has an ineffective license may not perform real estate services. A license is ineffective during the time that it is in voluntary inactive status. An involuntary inactive license is also ineffective; however, after two years in involuntary inactive status, the license will become void. When a real estate license is suspended, it is ineffective during the period of suspension. If a broker's license is suspended or revoked, the licenses of the sales associates and broker associates registered under

that broker are placed in involuntary inactive status. Once new employment is
secured, the license status is changed to active.

■ A licensee in good standing who is a member of the U.S. armed forces is exempt
from license renewal provisions during active duty and for six months after
discharge from active duty. The armed forces exemption is valid, assuming
the service member is not actively engaging in real estate practices during the
exemption period. This is another example of an ineffective license.

■ "Multiple licenses" refers to those cases in which a broker holds more than one
broker's license.

■ A group license is issued to a sales associate or a broker associate employed by
an owner-developer (real estate developer) who owns properties in the name of
various entities. A group license entitles the licensee to work for the separate
sales projects owned by the owner-developer.

REVIEW QUESTIONS

1. The statements below are true with respect to the members of the Florida Real Estate Commission EXCEPT that they
   a. are a mix of real estate practitioners and consumer members.
   b. are accountable to the governor for proper performance.
   c. are DBPR employees.
   d. depend on the DRE for their administrative assistance.

2. Members of the FREC are appointed by the
   a. governor and confirmed by the Secretary of State.
   b. governor and confirmed by the DBPR Secretary.
   c. DBPR Secretary and confirmed by the governor.
   d. governor and confirmed by the state Senate.

3. The Commission's purpose is to regulate
   a. real estate brokers, broker associates, and sales associates.
   b. real estate schools and instructors.
   c. real estate brokerage firms.
   d. all of the above.

4. Real estate licensees on active duty with the U.S. Army are required to renew their licenses
   a. every two years.
   b. on discharge.
   c. within one year after discharge.
   d. within six months after discharge.

5. The term of office for each Commission member is
   a. two years.
   b. four years.
   c. five years.
   d. seven years.

6. The members of the Commission receive
   a. no compensation for their services.
   b. only a per-diem fee when on official business.
   c. $50 per day when on official business, plus expenses.
   d. an annual salary equal to a state legislator's annual salary.

7. A licensee's status as registered with the DBPR is broker associate. Which statement is FALSE regarding this licensee?
   a. The licensee holds an active license.
   b. The licensee is broker-qualified.
   c. The licensee has an employer.
   d. The licensee may hold more than one Florida broker associate license.

8. The Commission is NOT empowered to
   a. make determinations of violations.
   b. impose administrative fines.
   c. levy fines and imprisonment as penalties for certain crimes.
   d. adopt an official seal that, when used on a document, certificate, proceeding, or act of the Commission, is prima facie evidence of its authenticity in all matters of law in this state.

9. Specific responsibilities of the FREC do NOT include
   a. determining the amount of licensing fees needed to operate the Commission.
   b. reporting criminal violations to the state's attorney.
   c. informing the Division of Florida Condominiums, Timeshares, and Mobile Homes of disciplinary action against any of its licensees.
   d. providing the services necessary for the preparation and administration of licensing examinations.

10. Which power is NOT granted to the DBPR under Florida Statute 455?
    a. Issue citations
    b. Investigate consumer complaints
    c. Appoint FREC members
    d. Issue subpoenas

11. A sales associate recently moved from Dunedin, Florida, to High Springs, Florida.
    a. The sales associate must notify the DBPR of her change in current mailing address within 60 days of the change.
    b. The sales associate must notify the DBPR of her change in current mailing address within 10 days of the change.
    c. If the sales associate does not change brokers, she is not required to notify the DBPR of her change in mailing address.
    d. The sales associate's license is automatically canceled until she notifies the DBPR of her change in current mailing address.

12. A sales associate is employed by a broker. The broker's license is suspended. This action causes the sales associate's license to be
    a. placed in involuntary inactive status.
    b. suspended.
    c. revoked.
    d. unaffected.

13. When an active broker changes a business address and the broker notifies the FREC within the required ten days, the licenses of the sales associates
    a. remain in force.
    b. cease to be in force.
    c. are null and void.
    d. are temporarily ineffective.

14. If an active licensee fails to renew her third two-year license before the expiration date on the license, the license will
    a. revert automatically to involuntary inactive status at the end of the license period.
    b. be suspended automatically.
    c. be canceled, and the licensee will have to retake both the course and the licensing exams.
    d. be canceled, and the licensee will have to retake the licensing exam only.

15. An involuntary inactive license will automatically become void without further action by the FREC or the DBPR after
    a. two years.
    b. four years.
    c. five years.
    d. ten years.

16. Who may NOT reactivate a license to active status?
    a. A voluntary inactive sales associate
    b. A licensed corporate director of a real estate company
    c. An involuntary inactive broker
    d. A sales associate who did not complete post-licensing education prior to the expiration of the initial license

17. An owner-developer owns several properties with different names, but all are business entities closely connected and controlled by the owner-developer. A sales associate working for that owner-developer may legally obtain
    a. a group license.
    b. multiple licenses.
    c. either a group license or multiple licenses, but not both.
    d. neither a group license nor multiple licenses.

18. A broker moves his real estate office to a new, trendy location. He is so busy coordinating the move that he forgets to notify the DBPR. The broker's license
    a. will cease to be in force.
    b. is null and void.
    c. is automatically suspended.
    d. is canceled.

19. An initial real estate license is issued on September 10, 2012. When will it expire?
    a. March 31, 2013
    b. March 31, 2014
    c. September 10, 2014
    d. September 30, 2014

20. A broker decides to relocate her real estate brokerage office. She notifies the DBPR of the change in business address. She also informs the DBPR of the names of two sales associates who are no longer associated with her brokerage. The sales associates' licenses will be
    a. suspended until they find new employment.
    b. canceled.
    c. null and void.
    d. placed on involuntary inactive status.

CHAPTER 4

BROKERAGE RELATIONSHIPS AND ETHICS

OVERVIEW

This chapter begins with a general explanation of the law of agency and then details the various types of brokerage relationships practiced in Florida. The chapter also explains the licensee's duties and obligations to principals and customers. The terms *misrepresentation* and *fraud* are defined, and fraudulent activities are discussed. The chapter concludes with a section about professional ethics.

After completing this chapter, the student should be able to:

- distinguish between the terms *general agent* and *special agent*;
- describe which legal provisions apply only to residential real estate transactions;
- describe the duties of a transaction broker;
- describe the duties and disclosure requirements that single agents have to their principals;
- define a *dual agent*;
- describe the purpose and requirements of the no brokerage relationship notice;
- list the no brokerage relationship duties;
- describe the process of transition from a single agent to a transaction broker;
- identify actions that will terminate an agency; and
- recognize activities that would constitute fraud.

KEY TERMS

agent	fraud	residential sale
at arm's length	general agent	single agent
customer	misrepresentation	special agent
designated sales associates	no brokerage relationship	subagents
dual agent	principal	transaction broker
fiduciary	puffing	universal agent

LAW OF AGENCY

When a person delegates authority to someone to act on his or her behalf, an agency relationship has been created. Agency relationships fall within the body of law called *law of agency*.

There are two types of law that society looks to for guidance regarding agency relationships: common law and statutory law.

775.01, F.S.

Common law (sometimes referred to as unwritten law) is law based on usage, general acceptance, and custom. It is judge-made law manifested in decrees and judgments of the courts (case law) as opposed to statutory law. Common law originated in England and was later incorporated into the U.S. legal system. Under the English common law, servants owed absolute loyalty to their masters. This absolute loyalty is one of the fundamental principles of the agency relationship. Agency law derives from common law.

Statutory law includes the written statutes and rules enacted by legislatures and other governing bodies. In addition to the statutory laws of agency, real estate license law and the Florida Real Estate Commission (FREC) rules directly affect and regulate the brokerage relationships among real estate licensees, buyers and sellers, and the public.

Agency Relationships in General Business Dealings

In general, a person who delegates authority to another is referred to as the *principal*. A person who accepts the authority (and responsibilities, duties, and obligations associated with that authority) is referred to as the *agent*. An **agent** is the person entrusted with another's business. An agent is authorized to represent and act for the principal.

The agency relationship creates a *fiduciary relationship* with the principal. A *fiduciary* acts in a position of trust and confidence for another. The fiduciary owes complete allegiance to the principal. A fiduciary relationship contrasts with the common public relationship that exists in normal trading transactions where people with adverse interests deal **at arm's length** with one another. People dealing at arm's length conduct negotiations on their own behalf without trusting the other's fairness or integrity and without being subject to the other's control or influence. In such cases, the legal doctrine of *caveat emptor* (let the buyer beware) applies. Agency relationships exist in many business transactions such as between an attorney (agent) and client (principal). An agency relationship may exist in certain real estate transactions. (This will be explained in detail in the next section of the chapter.)

There are three types of agents characterized by the extent of authority delegated to an agent in general business dealings: (1) universal agent, (2) general agent, and (3) special agent.

A **universal agent** is authorized by the principal to perform all acts that the principal can personally perform and that may be lawfully delegated to another. An attorney who manages the trust agreement of a mentally disabled adult is a universal agent for that client (the principal). Duties of the attorney-agent would include, for example, overseeing the principal's financial affairs, medical care, employment opportunities, and living arrangements.

A **general agent** is authorized by the principal to perform acts associated with the continued operations of a particular job or a certain business of the principal. A property manager, for example, acts as a general agent if authorized to show and rent apartments, collect rents, supervise maintenance and upkeep of the property, handle tenant relations, and perform bookkeeping duties. A sales associate is a general agent of the employing broker.

A **special agent** is authorized by the principal to handle only a specific business transaction or to perform only a specific act. If you hire a certified public accountant (CPA) to prepare your tax return and, if necessary, to answer any inquiries from the IRS concerning the tax return, the CPA is acting as a special agent for you (the principal). A real estate licensee may act as a special agent with buyers or sellers. This occurs when the buyer or seller and the brokerage firm enter into a single agent relationship. The broker agrees to represent the buyer or seller with regard to a single business transaction. Not all real estate brokers act as agents of buyers and sellers. (See Single Agent Relationship on page 66.)

BROKERAGE RELATIONSHIPS IN FLORIDA

475.255, F.S.
475.01, F.S.

Historically, there has been confusion among buyers and sellers regarding what role real estate licensees have in real estate negotiations. Sellers assumed that real estate licensees represented their interests because sellers traditionally paid the commission. However, the payment of commission or the promise of compensation alone is *not* what determines whether a brokerage relationship exists. A brokerage relationship can be accidently (inadvertently) created by a licensee's actions and words. For example, referring to a prospective purchaser as "my buyer" or "my client" may imply that the licensee is representing the buyer when in actuality the brokerage is representing the seller. Because of this confusion, the Florida legislature passed the Brokerage Relationship Disclosure Act. The Brokerage Relationship Disclosure Act is intended to inform and educate the public regarding the types of authority (brokerage relationships) that can be granted to a broker and the duties brokers have in each type of brokerage relationship.

Brokerage Relationship Options

Licensees have three basic options in all real estate transactions concerning the role the real estate brokerage firm will assume for buyers and sellers:

1. The brokerage firm may work as a transaction broker for the buyer and/or the seller.
2. The brokerage firm may work as a *single agent* of either the buyer or the seller (but *not* for both buyer and seller in the same transaction).
3. The parties may agree that the brokerage firm will not represent the buyer or the seller at all. This situation is referred to as *no brokerage relationship*. The brokerage firm simply facilitates the transaction.

In Florida, a real estate licensee may enter into a brokerage relationship either as a transaction broker or as a single agent with prospective buyers and sellers. Alternatively, the customer may desire not to be represented in any capacity by the brokerage firm. For example, property owners who have found buyers for their own homes (for-sale-by-owners, also referred to as FSBOs) may want a knowledgeable real estate firm to handle the paperwork regarding the transaction. However, a FSBO seller may not need or desire the broker to represent or negotiate on the seller's behalf. In such cases, FSBOs may elect no brokerage relationship with the brokerage firm.

475.01, F.S.
475.272, F.S.

It is illegal in Florida for a real estate licensee to operate as a dual agent. The term **dual agent** means a broker who represents as a fiduciary both the prospective buyer and the prospective seller in a real estate transaction. When a broker represents a buyer or a seller as a **fiduciary**, the broker is in a relationship of trust and confidence between the broker as agent and the seller as principal or the buyer as principal. A fiduciary relationship is created when a real estate broker accepts employment as a single agent of the seller or the buyer. In an agency relationship, the broker owes fiduciary duties to the principal. Florida real estate license law prohibits a broker from creating a fiduciary relationship with both the buyer and the seller.

Residential Transactions

475.278, F.S.

Chapter 475 mandates certain duties and obligations in each type of brokerage relationship. These duties and obligations apply to *all* real estate transactions. However, written disclosures are required only when dealing in residential real estate transactions.

A **residential sale** is defined as the sale of improved residential property of four or fewer units, the sale of unimproved residential property intended for use as four or fewer units, or the sale of agricultural property of ten or fewer acres. Furthermore, the disclosure requirements do *not* apply to:

- nonresidential transactions;
- the rental or leasing of real property, unless an option to purchase all or a portion of the property improved with four or fewer residential units is given;
- auctions;
- appraisals; and
- dispositions of any interest in business enterprises or business opportunities, except for property with four or fewer residential units.

(*Note:* Licensees are no longer required to give customers a written disclosure when a transaction broker relationship is chosen.)

Transaction Broker Relationship

475.278, F.S.
475.01, F.S.

Under Florida law, it is *presumed* that all licensees are operating as transaction brokers unless a single agent or no brokerage relationship is established, in writing, with the customer. A **transaction broker** is a broker who provides limited representation to a buyer, a seller, or both in a real estate transaction, but who does *not* represent either party in a fiduciary capacity or as a single agent. In this relationship, the seller (or the buyer) is considered to be a customer of the real estate broker and *not* a principal. In a transaction broker relationship the buyer or seller (customer) is not responsible for the acts of a licensee.

Chapter 475 defines **customer** to mean a member of the public who is or may be a buyer or a seller of real property and may or may not be represented by a real estate licensee in an authorized brokerage relationship. Therefore, the seller (or the buyer) who chooses limited representation is a customer under the transaction broker relationship. A licensee may enter into a transaction broker relationship with both parties (buyer and seller) in a real estate transaction. The seven duties of the transaction broker in this limited form of representation are as follows:

1. *Deal honestly and fairly.* Licensees owe a duty of good faith and honesty to customers. A broker's customers are entitled to rely on any material statement related to a real estate transaction that is made by a licensee.

2. *Account for all funds.* The broker must account for all funds entrusted to him or her with regard to a real estate transaction. Such holdings are considered trust funds or escrow funds. Money and valuables entrusted to a broker must be kept separate from the broker's funds. The broker is not entitled to any trust or escrow funds until the transaction is concluded at a title closing. Brokers are required to keep complete records of all transactions and funds as well as to make available to the Department of Business and Professional Regulation (DBPR) such books, accounts, and records as will enable the DBPR to determine whether the broker is in compliance with Chapter 475.

3. *Use skill, care, and diligence in the transaction.* The broker, for example, must keep informed of current zoning and other developments that may affect the value of the property and must use diligence in facilitating the transaction.

4. *Disclose all known facts that materially affect the value of residential real property and are not readily observable to the buyer.* Licensees have a duty to disclose to buyers all known facts that materially affect the value of residential property. For example, a licensee is obligated to inform the buyer if there are cracks in the tile floor under the wall-to-wall carpeting caused from the foundation settling.

    Questions sometimes arise regarding whether certain information concerning the seller or previous occupants of a property must be disclosed to prospective buyers. Federal fair housing law and the Florida statutes specifically mandate that the fact that an occupant of real property is infected or has been infected with human immunodeficiency virus (HIV) or diagnosed with acquired immune deficiency syndrome is *not* a material fact in a real estate transaction. This is personal medical information and must not be disclosed without prior authorization. Furthermore, Florida statute mandates the fact that a property was, or was at any time suspected to have been, the site of a homicide, suicide, or death is *not* a material fact in a real estate transaction. A cause of action will not arise against a property owner or a real estate licensee for failure to disclose any of the information or events listed above.

5. *Present all offers and counteroffers in a timely manner.* Unless a party has previously directed the licensee otherwise in writing, the licensee must present all oral and written offers and counteroffers in a timely manner even if a valid contract exists.

6. *Exercise limited confidentiality, unless waived in writing by a party.* This limited confidentiality will prevent disclosure that the seller will accept a price less than the asking or listed price; that the buyer will pay a price greater than the price submitted in a written offer; of the motivation of any party for selling or buying property; that a seller or buyer will agree to financing terms other than those offered; or of any other information requested by a party to remain confidential.

7. *Perform any additional duties that are mutually agreed to with a party.* A real estate licensee must be careful not to accept duties beyond the scope of limited representation. To do so might create an unintended fiduciary relationship with a customer. For example, a transaction broker may not promise complete allegiance

475.5015, F.S.

689.25, F.S.
760.50, F.S.

1   to a customer because to do so could be interpreted by a court of law to have cre-
2   ated a fiduciary relationship.

3   In a transaction broker relationship, the parties to a real estate transaction are giving
4   up their rights to the undivided loyalty of a licensee. This aspect of *limited representation*
5   allows a licensee to facilitate a real estate transaction by assisting both the buyer and the
6   seller. However, a licensee will not work to represent one party to the detriment of the
7   other party when acting as a transaction broker to both parties. Real estate licensees are
8   no longer required to give customers a written transaction broker notice. However, licens-
9   ees must still fulfill the duties of a transaction broker when that form of representation is
10   selected. The seven duties listed above apply to all real estate transactions (residential and
11   otherwise) when the parties have agreed to a transaction broker relationship. (See Figure
12   4.1, Brokerage Relationship Duties.)

13 ## Single Agent Relationship

475.278, F.S.
475.01, F.S.

14   A seller (or a buyer) may want to be represented by a real estate broker. In this case, the
15   real estate broker is a single agent who represents the seller as a fiduciary in selling the
16   home or the buyer in finding a home. The Florida real estate license law defines a **single
17   agent** as a broker who represents, as a fiduciary, either the buyer or the seller, but *not both*,
18   in the same transaction. In a single agent relationship, the seller (or the buyer) is the prin-
19   cipal and the real estate broker is the agent. The term **principal** is used to mean the party
20   with whom a real estate licensee has entered into a single agent relationship.

21   **Subagents** are persons authorized to assist and represent the agent. A subagent has
22   the same duties as the agent. A broker's sales associates are general agents of the broker
23   and subagents of the broker's principals. For example, in a single agent relationship, the
24   broker is an agent of the principal. The broker's sales associates and broker associates are
25   subagents of the broker's principals. Sales associates and broker associates owe the same
26   fiduciary obligations to the broker's principals as does their broker. (*Note:* This is true
27   regardless of whether the associates, for tax purposes, are employees or independent con-
28   tractors of the broker.)

F I G U R E 4.1 ■ Brokerage Relationship Duties

Duty	No Brokerage	Transaction	Single Agent
Deal honestly and fairly	✔	✔	✔
Disclose all known facts that affect value of residential property	✔	✔	✔
Account for all funds	✔	✔	✔
Use skill, care, and diligence		✔	✔
Present all offers and counteroffers		✔	✔
Exercise limited confidentiality		✔	
Perform additional duties that are mutually agreed to		✔	
Confidentiality			✔
Obedience			✔
Loyalty			✔
Disclosure (full)			✔

The nine duties a real estate licensee owes to a buyer or seller who engage the real estate brokerage as a single agent are as follows:

1. *Deal honestly and fairly.* (See page 65 for explanation.)

2. *Loyalty.* The agent as fiduciary in a real estate transaction must avoid any situation that might breach the duty of undivided loyalty to the principal. The overriding rule is that a broker may not adopt an attitude that is adverse to the interests of the principal or act for himself or herself or some other person whose interests are contrary to those of the principal. Loyalty (faithfulness) requires the broker to always place the principal's interests above those of other persons with whom the broker deals. Courts have ruled (case law) that for brokers to be loyal to their principals, they cannot exercise duties in such a manner as to profit themselves or anyone else at the expense of the principal. The duty of loyalty includes, for example:

   ■ obtaining the most favorable price and terms for the principal;

   ■ acting on behalf of the principal;

   ■ not acting for parties with adverse interest in the same transaction;

   ■ never concealing the identity of the purchaser to induce the principal to sell;

   ■ disclosing to the principal if the agent becomes personally interested in the principal's property; and

   ■ never advancing the agent's or another person's interest at the expense of the principal.

3. *Confidentiality.* Much of the information a broker gains while employed by the principal is confidential. An agent may not reveal to a third party, without the principal's permission, personal or private information that might lessen the principal's bargaining position. For example, a licensee may not tell a buyer that a seller is forced to sell owing to poor health or loss of a job without the principal's permission. Brokers may not divulge confidential information learned during the course of the single agency even after the transaction is concluded and the agent-principal relationship is ended. A broker is never free to use confidential information to the disadvantage of or reveal any harmful or unfavorable information about a former principal.

4. *Obedience.* An agent is obligated to act in good faith according to the principal's lawful instructions. The broker-agent is at all times obligated to act in conformity with the principal's instructions as long as those instructions are legal and relevant to the contractual relationship. If a broker feels that carrying out the principal's legal directions will harm the principal, then the broker must promptly inform the principal of all known facts along with the broker's opinion. However, if the principal will not change the instructions, the broker must either carry them out or withdraw from the relationship.

   Brokers may not violate the law. For example, if a principal instructs a listing broker not to show the property or sell to a member of a particular minority or ethnic group, the broker may not obey the principal's instructions because doing so would violate the law. In such an instance, the broker must inform the principal that to restrict certain groups of people from seeing or purchasing a listed property is a violation of the fair housing laws.

5. *Full disclosure.* It is a broker-agent's duty to keep the principal fully informed at all times of all the facts or information that might affect the transaction or the

value of the property. An agent is obligated to disclose facts regarding a property's true worth. Agents may be held responsible for material facts they should have known and communicated to their principal but did not. Also, broker-agents must inform their seller principals, for example, of the buyer's financial condition, the status of the earnest money deposit, or if a personal relationship exists between the agent and the buyer. All material facts must be revealed to the principal even if the disclosure of such facts might cause the transaction to fail.

Full, fair, and prompt disclosure also includes notifying the principal if the broker is personally interested in buying the listed property. In such an event, the broker must clearly terminate the agent-principal relationship and inform the principal of all facts regarding the property that the broker has learned while in an agent's capacity. Otherwise, the broker could buy from the principal and subsequently sell at a higher price and keep the profit ("overage," "secret profit," or "secret commission"). To do so could be construed as fraud, misrepresentation, concealment, and/or dishonest dealing and could expose the broker to liability to both seller and buyer for the full amount of the secret profit. It might further give rise to disciplinary proceedings against the licensee.

6. *Account for all funds.* (See page 65 for explanation.)

7. *Skill, care, and diligence in the transaction.* A broker's obligations extend beyond merely selling a listing or locating a suitable property for a buyer. A real estate broker holds himself or herself out to the public as specially qualified by reason of experience, ability, and knowledge. If a broker's principal is a buyer, then the broker should attempt to obtain the property at the lowest price possible. If the broker's principal is a seller, then the broker should try to get the seller the most favorable price. This includes researching a property thoroughly to advise the seller of a reasonable listing price. Brokers should discuss with their principals any anticipated tax consequences and advise them to seek expert tax advice when appropriate. The duty of using skill, care, and diligence does not end with the signing of a contract. It continues via numerous services by the agent until the transaction is closed. If an agent does not perform with the required degree of skill, care, and diligence, the agent becomes liable to the principal for the damages the principal may have sustained and may be disciplined by the FREC.

8. *Present all offers and counteroffers in a timely manner.* (See page 65 for explanation.)

9. *Disclose all known facts that materially affect the value of residential real property and are not readily observable to the buyer.* (See page 65 for explanation.)

The nine duties listed above apply to *all* real estate transactions (residential and otherwise) when the parties have agreed to a single agent relationship. (See Figure 4.1, Brokerage Relationship Duties, page 66 and Figure 4.2, Single Agent Disclosure Form, page 69.)

BROKERAGE RELATIONSHIP LIMITATIONS

- If the brokerage firm has a transaction broker relationship with the seller, the brokerage firm can also work with the buyer, in the same transaction, as a transaction broker or in no brokerage relationship. The brokerage firm *cannot* represent the buyer as a single agent if the firm has a transaction broker relationship with the seller.

- If the brokerage firm is representing the seller as a single agent, the brokerage firm can work with the buyer, in the same transaction, in no brokerage relationship. The brokerage firm *cannot* represent the buyer as a single agent or work with the buyer as a transaction broker if the firm is also representing the seller as a single agent.

The brokerage relationship limitations described above apply, even if the buyer and seller are working with different sales associates in the same brokerage firm.

FIGURE 4.2 ■ Single Agent Disclosure Form

SINGLE AGENT NOTICE

FLORIDA LAW REQUIRES THAT REAL ESTATE LICENSEES OPERATING AS SINGLE AGENTS DISCLOSE TO BUYERS AND SELLERS THEIR DUTIES.

As a single agent, (insert name of Real Estate Entity and its Associates) owe to you the following duties:

1. Dealing honestly and fairly;
2. Loyalty;
3. Confidentiality;
4. Obedience;
5. Full disclosure;
6. Accounting for all funds;
7. Skill, care, and diligence in the transaction;
8. Presenting all offers and counteroffers in a timely manner, unless a party has previously directed the licensee otherwise in writing; and
9. Disclosing all known facts that materially affect the value of residential real property and are not readily observable.

Seller or (buyer) _____   _____
Signature   Date

_____   _____
Signature   Date

> ## TO REMEMBER: FOUR UNIQUE DUTIES OF A SINGLE AGENT
>
> A single agent owes nine duties to the principal. Four of the duties apply only to single agent relationships.
>
> C   Confidentiality
> O   Obedience
> L   Loyalty
> D   Disclosure (full)

No Brokerage Relationship

475.278(4), F.S.

The seller (or the buyer) can choose not to be represented by a real estate broker. In such a situation, the broker would simply facilitate the sale (or the purchase) of real property without entering into either a single agent relationship or transaction broker relationship. A broker working in a **no brokerage relationship** capacity with a seller can enter into a listing agreement with that seller and be paid a commission. Similarly, a brokerage firm working in a no brokerage relationship capacity can work with a buyer. Florida law does not require that prospective buyers and sellers be represented. A real estate licensee working in a no brokerage relationship capacity with a buyer or a seller has the following three duties:

1. Deal honestly and fairly.
2. Disclose all known facts that materially affect the value of residential real property that are not readily observable to the buyer.
3. Account for all funds entrusted to the licensee.

(See Figure 4.3, No Brokerage Relationship Disclosure Form, page 71.)

Disclosure Requirements

475.278, F.S.

The duties of the chosen relationship must be fully described and disclosed in writing to a buyer or the seller, either as a separate and distinct disclosure document or included as part of another document, such as a listing agreement or buyer broker agreement. If the disclosure document is incorporated into a listing or buyer broker agreement, a signature line must be inserted immediately following the disclosure information. It is not sufficient to only have a signature line at the bottom of the listing or buyer broker agreement. The single agent disclosure must be made before, or at the time of, entering into a listing agreement or an agreement for representation, or before the showing of property, whichever occurs first. The no brokerage relationship notice must be disclosed in writing before the showing of property.

When incorporated into other documents, the required disclosure notice must be of the same size as, or larger type than, other provisions of the document and must be conspicuous in its placement to advise customers (or principals in a single agent relationship) of the brokerage duties. The first sentence must be printed in uppercase and bold type. The list of duties must be presented on the disclosure in the same order as listed in the statute. The disclosure notice may include information concerning the real estate brokerage such as the company name and logo, address, phone number, e-mail address, and so forth.

F I G U R E 4.3 ■   **No Brokerage Relationship Disclosure Form**

NO BROKERAGE RELATIONSHIP NOTICE

FLORIDA LAW REQUIRES THAT REAL ESTATE LICENSEES WHO HAVE NO BROKERAGE RELATIONSHIP WITH A POTENTIAL SELLER OR BUYER DISCLOSE THEIR DUTIES TO SELLERS AND BUYERS.

As a real estate licensee who has no brokerage relationship with you, (insert name of Real Estate Entity and its Associates) owe to you the following duties:

1. Dealing honestly and fairly;
2. Disclosing all known facts that materially affect the value of residential real property which are not readily observable to the buyer; and
3. Accounting for all funds entrusted to the licensee.

Seller or (buyer) _____

Signature _____   Date _____

_____   _____

Signature   Date

Although the disclosure notice provides for the customer's (principal's) signature, the signature is not mandatory (except for the transition to transaction broker notice and the designated sales associate disclosure discussed later in this chapter). If a customer or principal desires to proceed with the relationship but refuses to sign or initial the disclosure document, the licensee should include a copy of the disclosure in the file with a note indicating the date the disclosure was presented and that the buyer or the seller refused to sign the document. Under Florida law, it is presumed that all licensees are operating as transaction brokers unless another brokerage relationship is established. Therefore, there is no requirement to give a written transaction broker disclosure notice to the buyer and/or the seller.

Exceptions to Disclosure Requirements

475.278(5)(b), F.S.

Certain interactions a licensee has with buyers and sellers do not constitute a brokerage relationship. These situations are described in the real estate license law. When a licensee has an encounter with a buyer or seller under these specific situations, the licensee is *not* required to give a prospective buyer or a prospective seller a disclosure notice. The six situations that do not create a brokerage relationship are as follows:

1. When the licensee knows that a single agent or a transaction broker represents a prospective seller or a prospective buyer
2. At a bona fide "open house" or model home showing that does not involve eliciting confidential information; the execution of a contractual offer or an agreement for representation; or negotiations concerning price, terms, or conditions of potential sale
3. During unanticipated casual encounters between a licensee and a prospective seller or a prospective buyer that do not involve eliciting confidential information; the execution of a contractual offer or an agreement for representation; or negotiations concerning price, terms, or conditions of a potential sale

4. When responding to general factual questions from a prospective seller or a prospective buyer concerning properties that have been advertised for sale

5. Situations in which a licensee's communications with a prospective buyer or a prospective seller are limited to providing either written or oral communication that is general, factual information about the qualifications, background, and services of the licensee or the licensee's brokerage firm

6. When an owner is selling new residential units built by the owner and the circumstances or setting should reasonably inform the potential buyer that the owner's employee or single agent is acting on behalf of the owner, whether because of the location of the sales office or because of office signage or placards or identification badges worn by the owner's employee or single agent

If during any of the situations described above, a member of the public begins to provide confidential information or begins to negotiate concerning price, terms, and so forth, the licensee would at that point present the person with the appropriate disclosure notice depending on the circumstances and desire of the parties.

Transition to Another Relationship

475.278, F.S.

A licensee may change from one brokerage relationship to another as long as the buyer or the seller, or both, give consent before the change occurs. For example, a single agent relationship may be changed to a transaction broker relationship at any time during the relationship between the agent and principal, provided the agent first obtains the principal's written consent to the change in relationship. To gain the principal's written consent to a change in relationship, the buyer or seller (or both) *must* either sign or initial the consent to transition to transaction broker notice set forth in Chapter 475. Note that this disclosure notice requires the buyer's or seller's signature (or initials) before the licensee may change from one brokerage relationship to another. If the principal refuses to sign or initial the consent to transition notice, the broker must continue to act as a single agent.

Assume that a brokerage firm represents seller Rebecca as a single agent. Buyer Mike enters the brokerage firm with the purpose of finding a home to purchase. Buyer Mike is not working with any other real estate company. Buyer Mike indicates that he wants the real estate firm to represent him in the real estate negotiations and to work solely in his best interest. Therefore, Buyer Mike has indicated to the licensee that he desires single agency representation. The licensee must give Buyer Mike the single agent notice before entering into a buyer agency agreement or before showing Mike any property.

Because Buyer Mike has entered into a single agent relationship with the brokerage firm, the sales associate may not show Seller Rebecca's home to the buyer. This is because a broker may not be a single agent of the buyer *and* a single agent of the seller in the same transaction. This is true even if Rebecca and Mike use different sales associates with the same company because the single agent agreement is with the brokerage firm. If a real estate broker represents both parties in a transaction in a fiduciary capacity, an illegal **dual agent** relationship is created. Because the seller and the buyer have each entered into single agent relationships with the brokerage firm, they must both give written consent to transition (change) to transaction broker relationships in order for Buyer Mike to be shown Seller Rebecca's home. This is the purpose of allowing a licensee to transition from one agency status to another.

The consent to transition to transaction broker notice includes wording regarding the principal's permission to allow the single agent to transition to a transaction broker. The notice also includes a list of the duties that a transaction broker owes to the customer. The consent to transition to transaction broker notice can either be a separate document or be included as part of another document, for example, in the listing agreement. Refer to page 70 for information concerning the required format of the disclosure notice. (See Figure 4.4, Consent to Transition to Transaction Broker.)

A licensee may also transition from a transaction broker relationship to a single agent relationship. Furthermore, a licensee may transition from any one of the brokerage relationships to another relationship. However, there is no specific disclosure language provided in the Florida license law for these situations. The licensee will have to accomplish the transition in a manner sufficient to withstand civil challenge under the common law.

FIGURE 4.4 ■ Consent to Transition to Transaction Broker

FLORIDA LAW ALLOWS REAL ESTATE LICENSEES WHO REPRESENT A BUYER OR SELLER AS A SINGLE AGENT TO CHANGE FROM A SINGLE AGENT RELATIONSHIP TO A TRANSACTION BROKERAGE RELATIONSHIP IN ORDER FOR THE LICENSEE TO ASSIST BOTH PARTIES IN A REAL ESTATE TRANSACTION BY PROVIDING A LIMITED FORM OF REPRESENTATION TO BOTH THE BUYER AND THE SELLER. THIS CHANGE IN RELATIONSHIP CANNOT OCCUR WITHOUT YOUR PRIOR WRITTEN CONSENT.

As a transaction broker, _____ (insert name of Real Estate Firm and its Associates) provides to you a limited form of representation that includes the following duties:

1. Dealing honestly and fairly;
2. Accounting for all funds;
3. Using skill, care, and diligence in the transaction;
4. Disclosing all known facts that materially affect the value of residential real property and are not readily observable to the buyer;
5. Presenting all offers and counteroffers in a timely manner, unless a party has previously directed the licensee otherwise in writing;
6. Limited confidentiality, unless waived by a party. This limited confidentiality will prevent disclosure that the seller will accept a price less than the asking or listed price, that the buyer will pay a price greater than the price submitted in a written offer, of the motivation of any party for selling or buying property, that a seller or buyer will agree to financing terms other than those offered, or of any other information requested by a party to remain confidential; and
7. Any additional duties that are entered into by this or by separate written agreement.

Limited representation means that a buyer or seller is not responsible for the acts of the licensee. Additionally, parties are giving up their rights to the undivided loyalty of the licensee. This aspect of limited representation allows a licensee to facilitate a real estate transaction by assisting both the buyer and the seller, but a licensee will not work to represent one party to the detriment of the other party when acting as a transaction broker to both parties.

_____ I agree that my agent may assume the role and duties of a transaction broker.

[must be initialed or signed]

Designated Sales Associates

475.2755, F.S.

In a nonresidential real estate transaction where the buyer and seller each have assets of $1 million or more, the broker at the request of the buyer and seller may designate two sales associates to act as single agents for the buyer and seller in the same transaction. The two sales associates in such an arrangement are referred to as **designated sales associates**. Note that in a residential transaction this would be an illegal dual agency.

In this arrangement, the broker serves as an advisor to each designated sales associate—*not* to the buyer or the seller. The broker serves as a neutral party helping to facilitate the process without giving guidance or representation to the parties in the transaction. The designated sales associates have the duties of a single agent and must give the buyer and the seller a special disclosure notice. The buyer and seller *must* sign the disclosure notice stating that their assets meet the threshold and requesting that the broker use the designated sales associate form of representation. A transition notice is not required. (See Figure 4.5, Designated Sales Associate.)

Record Keeping

475.5015, F.S.

Florida law requires brokers to retain agreements that engage the services of a broker. Brokers must retain brokerage relationship disclosure documents and buyer broker agreements for five years for all residential transactions that result in a written contract to purchase and sell real property and all nonresidential transactions that use designated sales associates. This requirement includes files of properties that may have failed to close. If a transaction fails to close, the licensee should retain the brokerage relationship disclosure documents with the purchase and sale contract, escrow documentation, and other documents associated with the property, and place them in the "dead" (failed to close) file. The Commission may discipline a licensee for failure to abide by any provision in Section 475.278, F.S., including the duties owed to customers and principals, disclosure requirements, and record-keeping requirements set forth in law.

Terminating a Brokerage Relationship

Generally speaking, a transaction broker relationship or a single agent relationship is terminated when the objectives have been accomplished according to the terms of the contract that created the brokerage relationship and notice is given to the other party. A principal is justified in revoking a single agent relationship with the broker if the broker-agent breaches any of the fiduciary duties.

A brokerage relationship between a principal (or a customer) and a broker may be terminated for any one of the following reasons:

- Fulfillment of the brokerage relationship's purpose (for example, finding a ready, willing, and able buyer).
- Mutual agreement to terminate the brokerage relationship.
- Expiration of the terms of the agreement. (If no term is specified, the courts have ruled that a brokerage relationship may be terminated after a "reasonable" time.)
- Broker renounces the single agent relationship by giving notice to the principal or the broker renounces the transaction broker relationship by giving notice to the customer.

F I G U R E 4.5 ■   Designated Sales Associate

I have assets of one million dollars or more. I request that (*Insert Name of Broker*) use the designated sales associate form of representation.

_____

Signature of Buyer or Seller (circle one)

SINGLE AGENT NOTICE

FLORIDA LAW REQUIRES THAT REAL ESTATE LICENSEES OPERATING AS SINGLE AGENTS DISCLOSE TO BUYERS AND SELLERS THEIR DUTIES. As a single agent, (Insert name of Real Estate Entity) and its Associates owe to you the following duties:

1. Dealing honestly and fairly;
2. Loyalty;
3. Confidentiality;
4. Obedience;
5. Full disclosure;
6. Accounting for all funds;
7. Skill, care, and diligence in the transaction;
8. Presenting all offers and counteroffers in a timely manner, unless a party has previously directed the licensee otherwise in writing; and
9. Disclosing all known facts that materially affect the value of residential real property and are not readily observable.

_____   _____
Seller or (buyer)   Signature Date

FLORIDA LAW PROHIBITS A DESIGNATED SALES ASSOCIATE FROM DISCLOSING, EXCEPT TO THE BROKER OR PERSONS SPECIFIED BY THE BROKER, INFORMATION MADE CONFIDENTIAL BY REQUEST OR AT THE INSTRUCTION OF THE CUSTOMER THE DESIGNATED SALES ASSOCIATE IS REPRESENTING. HOWEVER, FLORIDA LAW ALLOWS A DESIGNATED SALES ASSOCIATE TO DISCLOSE INFORMATION ALLOWED TO BE DISCLOSED OR REQUIRED TO BE DISCLOSED BY LAW AND ALSO ALLOWS A DESIGNATED SALES ASSOCIATE TO DISCLOSE TO HIS OR HER BROKER, OR PERSONS SPECIFIED BY THE BROKER, CONFIDENTIAL INFORMATION OF A CUSTOMER FOR THE PURPOSE OF SEEKING ADVICE OR ASSISTANCE FOR THE BENEFIT OF THE CUSTOMER IN REGARD TO A TRANSACTION. FLORIDA LAW REQUIRES THAT THE BROKER MUST HOLD THIS INFORMATION CONFIDENTIAL AND MAY NOT USE SUCH INFORMATION TO THE DETRIMENT OF THE OTHER PARTY.

- Principal revokes a single agent relationship or the customer revokes a transaction broker relationship, by giving notice. (In this case, the principal or the customer may be liable for damages, such as advertising expenses, incurred by revoking the brokerage relationship prior to the termination date of the listing contract or exclusive buyer contract.)
- Death of a seller's broker or the seller before the broker finds a ready, willing, and able buyer.
- Death of the buyer's broker or the buyer before the broker finds a suitable property for the buyer.
- Destruction of the property or condemnation by eminent domain.
- Bankruptcy of the principal or the customer.

Practical Examples of Duty to Disclose

Michael was transferred to Seattle, so he wanted to sell his Florida residence. Harbor Realty entered into a single agent relationship with Michael. Harbor Realty later transitioned to a transaction broker relationship with Michael. Sales associate Merissa was working with Michael on behalf of Harbor Realty. Michael told Merissa that the air conditioner compressor would run for about an hour and then overheat and stop running. Merissa knew that Michael was anxious to sell, so she did not mention the air conditioning compressor to the buyer.

Practice Problem 1

Does the fact that Michael had a transaction broker relationship with Harbor Realty excuse nondisclosure of the air conditioning compressor's condition?

Practice Problem 2

Can the sales associate be disciplined for failing to inform the buyer that the compressor would overheat?

Practice Problem 3

Can Merissa's broker be held accountable for not disclosing the air conditioning compressor's condition to the buyer?

The solutions to the Practice Problems are located on page 78.

MISREPRESENTATION AND FRAUD

The law allows real estate agents to enthusiastically describe the value of real estate and/or the potential of the property. Licensees may not, however, exaggerate, conceal, or misrepresent by making statements they know to be untrue. **Puffing** is the term used to describe a licensee's boasting of a property's benefits. For example, the statement "The apartment has a fantastic view" is puffing because the prospect is clearly able to assess the view, and the statement is the licensee's opinion. However, if the licensee had instead said, "The apartment has a fantastic view of the lake," when in fact the lake is not visible from the apartment, the statement is untrue and would be illegal misrepresentation.

Misrepresentation is the misstatement of fact or the omission or concealment of a factual matter. Misrepresentation can lead to fraud. The elements of a cause of action for **fraud** are: (1) the licensee made a misstatement or failed to disclose a material fact, (2) the licensee either knew or should have known that the statement was not accurate or that the undisclosed information should have been disclosed, (3) the party to whom the statement was made relied on the misstatement, and (4) the party to whom the statement was made was damaged as a result.

The law prohibits deceptive practices. For example, it is fraudulent and dishonest dealing by trick, scheme, or device for a licensee to:

- knowingly sell or offer for sale any property covered by a mortgage that also covers other property sold, unless the particular property sold or offered for sale may be released from the mortgage any time before foreclosure sale on payment of an amount less than that remaining due from the purchaser after the sale;

- induce any person to buy property by promising that the licensee or the owner will resell or repurchase the property at any future time, unless there is proof that the guaranteed repurchase agreement has been approved by an agency of the State of Florida or there is evidence that the repurchase has been accomplished as promised;

- offer lotteries and schemes of sale involving the sale of chances or similar devices whereby it is represented that the purchaser is to receive property in an order to be determined by chance, whereby the price will depend on chance or the amount of sales made, or whereby the buyer may or may not receive any property; and

- invite the public to solve puzzles on the pretense of a drawing to receive property free, at a nominal price, or at cost.

Any representation made by a broker may later become the basis for charges of fraud, breach of contract, or breach of trust. In general, a purchaser has only a limited right to rely on the statements of a broker. However, if a broker invites trust and then betrays that trust, the broker is guilty of breach of trust. This legal concept brings to light an important ethical principle relating to those engaged in the sale of real estate: Whenever the trust or confidence of a buyer or seller is invited, by actions or words, that trust or confidence, once given, must not be betrayed.

PROFESSIONAL ETHICS

Defining *ethics* is like trying to pick up mercury with one's fingers. Even philosophers disagree on exactly how to define ethics. While there are no hard-and-fast standards that constitute ethical behavior, everyone knows what ethical conduct is.

A licensee can easily determine if a course of action is ethical by asking, "Would I want someone else to act in the same manner toward me?" Failure to apply the Golden Rule results in a double standard: how you treat others and how you expect others to treat you.

Ethics is not in conflict with enterprise or profit. Time and time again, ethical performance has proved to be good business. The most important factor influencing real estate agents to operate ethically is their personal code of behavior. The most important factor influencing real estate agents to operate unethically is the behavior of their employers and, then, other real estate agents.

Ethics should not have to be regulated or dictated by government. In fact, all the laws in the world will not prevent unethical conduct. It is a matter of personal integrity when individuals—and real estate agents as a group—take care to be honest in all dealings with others. Just a few unethical brokers or sales associates will reflect on the entire industry. Licensees have a moral duty to behave ethically and to take action against the practices of any licensees who act unethically. Real estate agents have a duty to support efforts to raise the qualifications of new brokers and sales associates, not to limit competition but to improve professional standards within the industry.

Some acts may be legal but unethical. For example, a broker regularly may include in all employment contracts with sales associates a clause stating that all rights to listing commissions cease ten days after a sales associates leaves the firm for any reason. Suppose a marginal employee brings in a listing for a $400,000 commercial building, the first listing that sales associate has had in 12 months. The broker accepts the listing, then two days later lets the sales associate go. The broker may not have broken any laws, but the broker's actions are unethical.

Professionalism and a Code of Ethics

As you no doubt have concluded, the real estate business is becoming increasingly complex, with rapid changes and constant pressures. A real estate brokerage firm is only as good as its reputation, and a good reputation can result only from a history of ethical business practices. Because just one dishonest or unethical person in a firm may destroy years of honest effort by others, ethical service is the only focal point around which a lasting reputation and career can be built. Licensees must strive for individual ethical conduct and strive to maintain a high standard of ethical professionalism within the industry.

Most professional and trade organizations have requirements designed to raise the professional and ethical standards of their members. The National Association of REALTORS® (NAR) adopted its Code of Ethics in 1913. The Code emphasizes fair dealings in three major areas: (1) with clients, (2) with other real estate brokers, and (3) with the general public. Through the years, the NAR's "Code of Ethics and Standards of Practice" has been updated and has proved helpful to everyone in the real estate business because it contains practical applications of business ethics and statements of good practices that everyone in the business should know and carefully follow. Today, to maintain membership in the NAR, REALTOR® members must complete three hours of ethics training every four years.

Practical Examples of Duty to Disclose

(Practice Problems are located on page 76.)

Practice Problem 1 Solution

No, transaction broker relationship duties include the duty to disclose all known facts that affect value of residential property. The fact that a transaction broker relationship existed did not relieve Harbor Realty from the duty to disclose the air conditioning compressor's condition.

Practice Problem 2 Solution

Yes, Merissa can be charged with Section 475.278, F.S.; failure to disclose facts that materially affect the value of property.

Practice Problem 3 Solution

Yes, the brokerage relationship is between Harbor Realty and the buyer. The broker for Harbor Realty, in addition to the sales associate, can be disciplined for not disclosing the air conditioning compressor's condition.

SUMMARY OF IMPORTANT POINTS

- A person who delegates authority to another is the *principal*. A person who accepts the authority is the *agent*. An agent is authorized to represent and act for the principal. The agency relationship creates a *fiduciary* relationship with the principal. A fiduciary acts in a position of trust and confidence with the principal.

- A real estate licensee may act as a special agent with buyers or sellers. This occurs when the buyer or seller, but not both, and the brokerage firm enter into a single agent relationship. In this relationship, the buyer or seller is the principal and the broker is the agent.

- In all real estate transactions, there are three options concerning the role the real estate brokerage firm will assume: (1) transaction broker for the buyer and/or the seller, (2) single agent of either the buyer or the seller, and (3) no brokerage relationship.

- Licensees may not operate as dual agents. A dual agent is a broker who represents both the buyer and the seller as a fiduciary.

- The duties and obligations in each type of brokerage relationship apply to all real estate transactions.

- A written disclosure is required for residential transactions when a single agent relationship or a no brokerage relationship is chosen. The single agency disclosure must be made before, or at the time of, entering into a listing agreement or an agreement for representation, or before the showing of property, whichever occurs first. The no brokerage relationship disclosure must be made before the showing of property.

- A *residential sale* is defined as the sale of improved residential property of four or fewer units, the sale of unimproved residential property intended for use as four or fewer units, or the sale of agricultural property of ten or fewer acres.

- Under Florida Law, it is presumed that all licensees are operating as transaction brokers unless another brokerage relationship is chosen. A transaction broker provides limited representation to a buyer, a seller, or both, but does not represent either in a fiduciary capacity or as a single agent.

- License law mandates that a real estate broker working in a no brokerage relationship capacity has three duties: (1) deal honest and fairly, (2) disclose all known facts that materially affect the value of residential real property that are not readily observable to the buyer, and (3) account for all funds entrusted to the licensee.

- License law mandates that a real estate broker working as a transaction broker has the duties required in a no brokerage relationship plus four additional duties: (1) use skill, care, and diligence; (2) present all offers and counteroffers; (3) exercise limited confidentiality; and (4) perform additional duties that are mutually agreed to.

- F.S. 475 mandates that a real estate broker working as a single agent has the duties required in a no brokerage relationship plus the first two additional duties required in a transaction broker relationship. Four duties apply exclusively to a broker working as a single agent: (1) confidentiality, (2) obedience, (3) loyalty, and (4) full disclosure.

- A real estate broker may change from a single agent relationship to a transaction broker relationship only with the express written permission of the principal. The principal must sign or initial the Consent to Transition to Transaction Broker disclosure before the change can occur.

- Brokers must retain brokerage relationship disclosure documents and buyer broker agreements for five years for all residential transactions that result in a written contract to purchase and sell real property and all nonresidential transactions that use designated sales associates.

- In a nonresidential transaction and where the buyer and the seller each have assets of $1 million or more, the broker, at the request of the buyer and the seller, may designate two sales associates to be *designated sales associates*. In such situations, one sales associate acts as a single agent for the buyer and the other sales associate acts as a single agent for the seller. The broker is not considered a dual agent but rather a neutral party advising the designated sales associates to help facilitate the process. The buyer and seller must sign the Designated Sales Associate disclosure listing the duties of a single agent and affirming that the buyer and seller each have assets of at least $1 million.

R E V I E W   Q U E S T I O N S

1. Which disclosure notice must be given before a single agent can change to a transaction broker?
   a. No brokerage relationship
   b. Single agent
   c. Consent to transition to transaction broker
   d. Transaction broker

2. A man is so cautious that he refuses to sign all disclosure documents. Your office policy is to include a note in his file indicating the time, date, place, and circumstance under which you made the disclosure that the man refused to sign. You may NOT work with the man under which circumstance?
   a. List the man's home as a single agent
   b. Provide limited representation to the man in locating a new home
   c. Provide real estate services to the man in a no brokerage relationship
   d. Change from a single agent to a transaction broker to show the man's home to an in-house buyer-principal

3. The brokerage relationship disclosure requirements in Chapter 475, F.S., apply to the
   a. sale of a 20-unit apartment complex.
   b. sale of a condominium unit.
   c. residential lease agreement in a duplex.
   d. sale of a book store business and real property.

4. Which statement BEST describes the duty of loyalty in a single agent relationship?
   a. The broker must act in the best interest of the principal.
   b. The broker must disclose all latent defects to prospective buyers.
   c. The broker is held to a standard of care that requires knowledge concerning the land and physical characteristics of the property.
   d. The broker must be able to account for all funds received on behalf of the principal.

5. A real estate broker who works in a limited capacity for both the buyer and the seller in the same transaction is
   a. a dual agent.
   b. a transaction broker.
   c. bound to fiduciary duties to both the buyer and the seller.
   d. a single agent of both the buyer and the seller.

6. A licensee of ABC Realty must give the no brokerage relationship notice to
   a. a buyer who has a single agent relationship with XYZ Realty.
   b. every prospective buyer and prospective seller in all cases.
   c. a for-sale-by-owner (FSBO) seller before showing the FSBO home to a buyer customer of ABC Realty.
   d. every prospective buyer who walks through an open house listed by ABC Realty.

7. A broker has listed a seller's property. The seller has disclosed to the broker that the ceramic tile is loose in the dining room because the cement did not adhere to the tile. The loose tile is not readily visible because it is covered with an area rug to protect the seller's toddler. The broker has satisfied his legal obligation if he tells the buyer
   a. that the floor appears to be in good condition.
   b. that ceramic tiles in the dining room are loose.
   c. that the buyer can order an inspection at his own expense if he is concerned about the floor.
   d. nothing unless he is asked specifically about the tile floor's condition.

8. A transaction broker has all of the duties listed below EXCEPT
   a. limited confidentiality.
   b. to use skill, care, and diligence.
   c. to disclose all known facts that materially affect the value of residential real property and are not readily observable to the buyer.
   d. obedience.

9. A brokerage relationship is terminated under which circumstance?
   a. The broker agent renounces the brokerage relationship.
   b. The purchase and sale contract is signed.
   c. At the will of either party without notice.
   d. An offer is accepted.

10. A seller lists her home for $116,900. The seller tells the sales associate that she needs to get at least $112,000 for the home. Following Sunday's open house, the sales associate receives two offers on the home. The first offer for $116,900 is contingent on the seller's financing a portion of the down payment. The second offer is for $112,000, with the buyer to secure her own financing. The sales associate should
    a. seek his broker's advice regarding which offer to present.
    b. present the full-price offer to the seller.
    c. present the second offer to the seller.
    d. present both offers, explaining the details of each to the seller.

11. In the common public relationship that exists in a typical real estate transaction, buyers and sellers are said to be dealing
    a. in a fiduciary capacity.
    b. at arm's length with each other.
    c. in an agency status with each other.
    d. under the doctrine of ethical confidentiality.

12. If a principal gives the broker instructions that will result in loss or harm to the principal, the broker
    a. is justified in not carrying out such instructions.
    b. should carry out such instructions without question.
    c. should carry out only that portion of the instructions that will not cause loss or harm to the principal.
    d. should inform the principal of possible harm inherent in the instructions, and then either do as instructed or withdraw from the relationship.

13. A broker's obligations to consumers with whom the brokerage firm has no brokerage relationship include the duty of
    a. full disclosure.
    b. accounting for all funds.
    c. loyalty.
    d. limited confidentiality.

14. Designated sales associates are best described as
    a. single agents for the buyer and the seller in nonresidential transactions where the buyer and the seller meet certain asset thresholds.
    b. the sales associates designated to represent the buyer and the seller in a transaction broker relationship.
    c. undisclosed dual agents.
    d. the sales associates in charge of the required brokerage disclosure forms for the brokerage office.

15. Which relationship is a general agency relationship?
    a. Brokerage company employed under a listing contract
    b. Relationship between the employing broker and a broker associate
    c. Sales associate working with a prospective buyer
    d. Relationship between a sales associate and the seller who has listed property with the brokerage

16. A real estate licensee makes a nonfactual statement about a property and the buyer accuses the licensee of fraud. The buyer is NOT required to prove that the
    a. misstatement was made by the licensee.
    b. misstatement made by the licensee was material to the transaction.
    c. buyer was damaged by the misstatement.
    d. information misstated could be proved to be false with due diligence.

17. A transaction broker involved in a residential sale discovered before the closing that a large recycling facility will be built approximately three-quarters of a mile from the home site. The transaction broker should
    a. disclose the information to both the buyer and the seller.
    b. inform only the buyer of this fact.
    c. inform only the seller of this fact.
    d. ignore the information to protect the transaction.

18. A real estate sales associate must disclose to a prospective buyer that
    a. a former occupant of the property committed suicide in the home.
    b. the seller has been diagnosed with HIV.
    c. the family room addition does not comply with local building codes.
    d. families of other racial groups live in the immediate area.

5

REAL ESTATE BROKERAGE OPERATIONS

OVERVIEW

This chapter concerns the day-to-day operations of a real estate office. Statutory requirements detail principal office and branch office regulations as well as rules governing signs, advertising, record keeping, and conduct. This chapter discusses the broker's role as an expert and the proper handling of escrow funds, fees for rental information or rental lists, and compensation. The chapter also describes the various forms of business entities that may be encountered and that are permitted to engage in real estate brokerage activities in Florida.

After completing this chapter, the student should be able to:

■ identify the requirements for a broker's office(s);

■ explain what determines whether a temporary shelter must be registered as a branch office;

■ list the requirements related to sign regulation;

■ list the requirements related to the regulation of advertising by real estate licensees;

■ explain the term *immediately* as it applies to earnest money deposits;

■ describe the four settlement procedures available to a broker who has received conflicting demands or who has a good-faith doubt as to who is entitled to disputed funds;

■ explain the rule regarding the advertisement of rental property information or lists or negotiation of rentals;

■ describe the obligations placed on a sales associate who changes employers; and

■ contrast the features of the various types of business organizations.

KEY TERMS

arbitration	escrow disbursement order	litigation
blind advertisement	(EDO)	mediation
commingle	general partnership	ostensible partnership
conflicting demands	good faith	point of contact
conversion	immediately	information
corporation	interpleader	policy manual
declaratory judgment	kickback	sole proprietorship
deposit	limited liability company	telephone solicitation
earnest money	limited liability partnership	trust funds
escrow account	limited partnership	

BROKERAGE OFFICES

475.42; F.S.
475.22, F.S.
61J2-10.022,
F.A.C.

All active Florida real estate brokers are required to have an office and to register the office with the Department of Business and Professional Regulation (DBPR). A broker's office must consist of at least one enclosed room in a building of stationary construction that will provide privacy to conduct negotiations and closings of real estate transactions. The broker's books, records, and real estate transaction files are to be kept in the office. Florida law does not require the broker to have a telephone, desk, business checking account, or an escrow account. If local zoning permits, the broker's office may be in the broker's residence, provided the required sign is displayed properly. A broker may have an office or offices in another state, provided the broker agrees in writing to cooperate with any investigation initiated under Chapter 475, F.S.

Sales associates are *not* permitted to open offices of their own. They must be registered from and work out of an office maintained and registered in the name of their employer.

Branch Offices

475.24, F.S.
61J2-10.023,
F.A.C.

If a broker desires to conduct business from additional locations, the broker must register each additional location as a branch office and pay the appropriate registration fees.

The Florida Real Estate Commission (FREC) may insist that a broker open and register a branch office whenever the FREC decides that the business conducted at a place other than the principal office is of such a nature that the public interest requires registration of a branch office. Further, any office will be considered a branch office if the advertising of a broker, who has a principal office elsewhere, is such that it leads the public to believe that the office of concern is owned or operated by the broker in question.

A *temporary shelter* in a subdivision being sold by a broker is not a branch office if the shelter is intended only for the protection of customers and sales associates. But if sales associates are assigned there, necessary sales supplies are on hand, and sale transactions are concluded there, then the temporary structure must be registered as a branch office. In short, the permanence, use, and character of activities customarily conducted at the office or shelter determine whether it must be registered.

61J2-10.023,
F.A.C.

Registrations issued to branch offices are *not* transferable. To illustrate, suppose a broker decides to close one branch office and open a new branch office at a different location. Even though these actions may take place at the same time, the registration of the closed

Example of a Sole Proprietor with a Trade Name Sign

office may not be transferred to another office. The new location must be registered and the
fee paid. A broker may reopen a branch office in the same location during the same license
period by requesting a reissue of the branch office license without paying an additional fee.

Office Signs

475.22, F.S.

Active real estate brokers must display an official sign on either the exterior or interior
of the entrance to their principal office and all branch offices. The sign(s) must be easily observed and read by anyone entering the office. The sign must contain the following
information:

- Trade name (if one is used)
- Broker's name
- The words, "Licensed Real Estate Broker" or "Lic. Real Estate Broker"

Refer to the example of an office sign. The registered trade name is Little Mo Realty,
the broker's name is Murl H. Crawford, and the required wording "Licensed Real Estate
Broker" appears on the sign.

The names of the sales associates and broker associates are *not* required on the entrance
sign. However, if the associates' names appear on the sign, the names must be below the
name of the broker(s) and the appropriate title, sales associate or broker associate, must
appear next to each associate's name.

A line or observable space must separate the names of the real estate brokers from
the names of the sales associates or broker associates (Refer to the previous example of an
office sign.)

Example of a Brokerage Corporation Sign

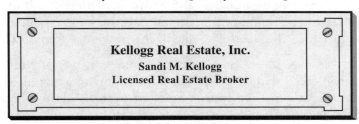

FALSE ADVERTISING

A person may not disseminate or cause to be disseminated by any means any false or misleading information for the purpose of offering for sale, or for the purpose of causing or inducing any other person to purchase, lease, or rent, real estate located in the state or for the purpose of causing or inducing any other person to acquire an interest in the title to real estate located in the state.

Reference: 475.42(1)(o), F.S.

If the brokerage entity is a partnership, corporation, limited liability company (LLC), or limited liability partnership, the sign must contain the following information:

- Name of the firm or corporation (or trade name, if one is used)
- Name of at least one active broker
- The words, "Licensed Real Estate Broker" or "Lic. Real Estate Broker"

ADVERTISING

475.01(1), F.S.

Anyone who advertises or represents that they are providing real estate services is acting as a real estate broker. Therefore, advertising is considered under Florida law to be a broker activity. All advertising must be in the name of the brokerage and under the supervision of the broker. Sales associates may not advertise real estate services in their own names. The broker is accountable for all advertising, regardless of who actually prepares the advertisement. Publication of false or misleading information by means of radio, television, or written matter for the purpose of inducing someone to buy, lease, rent, or acquire an interest in title to real property is illegal. If a sales associate prepares a misleading ad, both the broker and the sales associate can be disciplined. Advertising includes letterhead stationery and flyers, business cards, yard signs and billboards, newspaper and magazine ads, Internet, radio and television, promotional materials, and so forth.

61J2-10.025, F.A.C.

All advertising must be worded so that reasonable people will know that they are dealing with a real estate licensee. A licensee may not advertise real estate services in such a way as to mislead the public that the offer is being made by a private individual rather than a real estate licensee. Advertisements must clearly reveal the licensed name of the brokerage firm. Advertisements that fail to disclose the license name of the brokerage firm are **blind advertisements**. For example, an advertisement that provides only a post office box number, telephone number, and/or street address is a blind ad and is prohibited. If sales associates create promotional materials, such as refrigerator magnets and notepads, they must include the licensed name of the brokerage firm on them.

Licensees may insert their personal names in ads provided they include their last name as registered with the DBPR. Advertisements created by sales associates must be supervised directly by their broker. Sales associates and their brokers should review advertisements for accuracy and also make certain the ad is canceled when, due to sale or listing

ADVERTISING KEY CONCEPTS

- All advertisements must include the name of the brokerage firm.

- If a licensee inserts a personal name in the ad, the licensee's last name as registered with the DBPR must also be included.

- Licensees may use their nickname in advertisements provided they also include their legal name as registered with the DBPR.

- The brokerage firm's address and phone number are not required to be included in the advertisement (*Note:* Exception regarding Internet advertisement, as discussed below).

1 expiration, the property is no longer on the market. Licensees may indicate their nickname
2 on business cards and in advertisements but only if their legal name as registered with the
3 DBPR is also indicated (for example, Robert "Bob" Smith). Sales associates may indicate
4 their after-hours phone number and/or address on their business cards provided the card
5 also includes the name of the brokerage firm. FREC does not require that the brokerage
6 firm's phone number or address be included in ads.

61J2-10.025, F.A.C.

7 FREC rules mandate that real estate advertisements must not be fraudulent, false,
8 deceptive, or misleading. Licensees must take care when constructing real estate adver-
9 tisements to make certain they are not misleading. Take a look at the example of an adver-
10 tisement below. Is this ad misleading?

11 **EXAMPLE:** Spacious 4BR, 3BA home in Crystal Pines Subdivision. New roof
12 July 2012. Home is on wooded lot. Call Alfonzo "Fonzie" Lombardi, Excellent
13 Realty, 333-222-4444.

14 Is the phone number in the above example Alfonzo's direct number or that of the bro-
15 kerage firm? If the phone number of the licensee appears directly below the company name
16 (or directly next to it), it gives the appearance that it is the brokerage phone number. To
17 prevent someone from considering this ad to be misleading, the licensee, after identifying
18 the brokerage, should make clear that the phone number is the licensee's personal number
19 and not the brokerage firm's main business number. It is recommended that when using
20 only the licensee's phone number in the ad the word *direct*, *cell*, or something similar be
21 inserted adjacent to the phone number. Doing so informs the public that the number is
22 not the brokerage phone number, but that of the licensee. Therefore, a better constructed
23 advertisement follows:

24 **EXAMPLE:** Spacious 4BR, 3BA home in Crystal Pines Subdivision. New roof
25 July 2012. Home is on wooded lot. Excellent Realty. Call Alfonzo "Fonzie" Lom-
26 bardi, (mobile) 333-222-4444.

27 **Internet sites.** When advertising on an Internet site, the name of the brokerage firm
28 must appear adjacent to or immediately above or below the point of contact information.
29 **Point of contact information** refers to any means by which to contact the brokerage firm
30 or individual licensee, including mailing address(es), physical street address(es), e-mail
31 address(es), telephone number(s), or facsimile (fax) telephone number(s).

F I G U R E 5.1 ■ **Telephone Solicitation**

Florida Law	Federal Law
No solicitation calls registry	National Do Not Call Registry
Calls restricted to 8:00 AM to 9:00 PM	Calls restricted to 8:00 AM to 9:00 PM
$10,000 fine for violation	$11,000 fine for violation
FSBO exception	No FSBO exception—must check registry (federal law supersedes state law)

475.25(1)(c),
F.S.
61J2-10.025,
F.A.C.

1   The rules regarding advertising real property do not prevent real estate licensees from
2   selling their own property. Real estate licensees who own property and are selling the
3   property "by owner" may place their own classified advertisements. Licensees may include
4   their personal contact information in the ads, such as the home phone number and street
5   address of the property. It is not necessary for a licensee to indicate in the advertisement
6   that the seller is a real estate licensee. However, because a licensee has superior knowl-
7   edge and expertise in real estate, to reduce liability the "by owner" licensee-seller should
8   disclose prior to entering into serious negotiations that the seller is a real estate licensee.
9   Disclosure of this fact should also be documented in the sale contract. Such disclosure is
10 mandated in the National Association of REALTORS® Standards of Practice. The NAR
11 requires that member REALTORS® who advertise unlisted real property for sale or lease in
12 which they have an ownership interest disclose their status as owners (or landlords) and as
13 REALTORS®. Licensees considering selling property that they own "by owner" should first
14 consult with their broker and review the office policy manual. Some brokers expect the
15 licensee to list the property through the brokerage office.

Telephone Solicitation

501.6, F.S.

17 *Telemarketing* is the use of the telephone as a marketing tool to solicit services directly to
18 the public. Telemarketing is regulated by state and federal law. The Telephone Consumer
19 Protection Act of 1991 (TCPA) is a federal law concerning telephone solicitations. A
20 **telephone solicitation** is defined as the initiation of a telephone call for the purpose of
21 encouraging the purchase of, or investment in, property, goods, or services. The TCPA
22 established a National Do Not Call Registry for consumers who wish to avoid telemarket-
23 ing calls. Consumers at no charge may request to be on the list. Telemarketers must first
24 search the national registry before making telemarketing calls. Calls are restricted to the
25 hours of 8:00 AM to 9:00 PM.

26 The federal law covers both interstate (between states) and intrastate (within state)
27 telemarketing calls. The law exempts (1) political solicitations; (2) telephone surveys
28 (callers purporting to take a survey, but who also offer to sell goods or services, must com-
29 ply with the do-not-call registry); and (3) charitable solicitations. Violators of the federal
30 law may be fined up to $11,000 for each illegal call.

31 Florida's telemarketing law is administered through the Department of Agriculture
32 and Consumer Services. Florida maintains a no sales solicitation calls registry for consum-
33 ers at an initial charge of $10 ($5 each year thereafter). Florida has made its registry part

of the National Do Not Call Registry. Violators of Florida's Telemarketing Act may be fined $10,000 per call.

A major difference between the state and federal telemarketing laws is that the Florida law exempts real estate licensees who solicit listings in response to a "For Sale" yard sign. (See Figure 5.1, Telephone Solicitation.) However, the federal law does not exempt calls to for-sale-by-owners (FSBOs). The Federal Communications Commission (FCC) recently ruled that under the federal law, real estate sales associates may *not* call for-sale-by-owners (FSBOs) and homeowners with expired listings to solicit for listings if the owners' names are listed on the National Do Not Call Registry, even if the homeowner's telephone number appears on a yard sign or in a newspaper ad. The federal law provides the following exceptions:

- A sales associate representing a potential buyer may call the FSBO seller, but only if they have an actual buyer interested in the property and to negotiate a sale.

- A sales associate may contact individuals with whom the associate has had an established business relationship, even if those customers' numbers are on the national registry. For example, the company that previously listed a property may contact the former customer to solicit new business for up to 18 months after the business transaction has been concluded.

- Sales associates may contact a customer for three months after a business inquiry or application (such as a customer who registered at an open house or a FSBO seller who requested information from a sales associate).

If a sales associate calls a FSBO or an expired listing under the exceptions listed above and the homeowner requests not to be called, the sales associate must comply. Telemarketers must state their names, the business name, and the business telephone number. Telemarketers may not block their phone numbers. Businesses that use telemarketing must develop and adhere to written procedures regarding the firms' calling policies. Businesses must advise and train their personnel and independent contractors engaged in telephone solicitation regarding do-not-call list maintenance and procedures. Real estate companies that wish to use telemarketing in their business strategy must obtain the list of phone numbers in the registry. Licensees must search the national registry at least quarterly and delete from their call lists the phone numbers of consumers who have registered.

Sales associates beware—even though the state law exempts real estate licensees for the purpose of soliciting for listings, the federal law does not. Don't end up in a federal court—know the law *before* telemarketing for business!

Fax solicitations. FCC rules mandate that it is unlawful to send unsolicited advertisements to a residential or business fax machine without the recipient's prior express invitation or permission. The four requirements a sender must meet before sending an unsolicited advertising fax to a consumer are summarized below:

1. Sender must have an established business relationship with the recipient or written consent from the recipient prior to sending unsolicited advertising faxes.

2. Sender must have received the recipient's fax number voluntarily from the recipient in the context of the established business relationship.

3. Sender must clearly state on the first page of the advertisement that the recipient has the right to opt-out of receiving future unsolicited advertising faxes.

4. Sender must honor opt-outs received from recipients within 30 days of receipt.

KEY CONCEPTS REGARDING ESCROW ACCOUNTS

- Broker may open an escrow account in a Florida bank, savings association, or credit union.

- Broker must be a signatory on the escrow account.

- Broker must review, sign, and date the monthly reconciliation statements.

- Broker must review the company's escrow accounting procedures.

- If the broker chooses not to open an escrow account, the funds may be held by a title company or in an attorney's trust account.

- Brokers must maintain records of real estate transactions for five years regardless of whether escrow funds were pledged (or two years after litigation if beyond the five-year period).

WEB LINK

The FCC has published a guide regarding unwanted fax solicitations at **www.fcc.gov/guides/fax-advertising**.

To learn more about the National Do Not Call Registry, visit the FCC Web site at **www.fcc.gov/encyclopedia/do-not-call-list**.

To find out more regarding the Florida Do Not Call Program, visit **www.800helpfla.com/nosales.html**.

Download and print an informative FAQ regarding Florida's telemarketing law at **www.800helpfla.com/telemkt.html**.

1 ## ESCROW OR TRUST ACCOUNTS

475.25(1)(k), F.S.
61J2-14.008, F.A.C.

2 Typically, when a buyer makes an offer on real property, the buyer includes with the offer
3 a deposit to show good faith that the buyer is serious about purchasing the property. A
4 **deposit** is a sum of money, or its equivalent, delivered to a real estate licensee as **earnest**
5 **money** or a payment, or partial payment in connection with a real estate transaction. Such
6 deposits are also referred to as *good-faith deposits* or *binder deposits*.

7 An **escrow account** is an account for the deposit of money a disinterested third party
8 (for example, the broker) holds in trust for others; hence the term **trust funds**. Trust funds
9 include cash, checks, money orders, and items that can be converted into cash such as
10 deeds and personal property. In addition to earnest money deposits brokers hold in trust
11 for others money associated with leasing property such as rent deposits and security depos-
12 its. Brokers are not required to keep earnest money deposits separate from rental deposits.
13 However, tracking trust funds is easier when separate escrow accounts are established for
14 funds associated with sales and funds associated with rentals.

61J2-14.009, F.A.C.

15 **Immediately defined.** Florida real estate license law mandates the time frame for deposit-
16 ing escrow funds. Sales associates who receive a binder deposit from a customer or princi-
17 pal must deliver it to their broker-employer no later than the *end of the next business day*.
18 When a sales associate or an employee (such as a receptionist) of the brokerage company
19 accepts funds on behalf of the brokerage company, the broker is accountable for those

funds. Therefore it is extremely important that brokers train their personnel regarding the importance of turning over all earnest money in a timely manner.

61J2-14.008, F.A.C.

Brokers must place trust funds into an escrow account **immediately**, which means no later than the *end of the third business day* after their sales associate (or an employee of their brokerage company) has received it. The three-business-day time period coincides with the day that the sales associate must turn over the deposit to the broker.

Assume a sales associate receives a deposit from a prospective buyer on a Tuesday (no legal holidays are involved).

■ The sales associate has until the end of the next business day (Wednesday) to deliver the deposit to the broker.

■ The broker has until the end of the third business day (Friday) to deposit the funds. The three-business-day time period for the broker to deposit the funds begins on the day the sales associate is required to deliver the funds to the broker. (In this example, the first day of the three-business-day period is Wednesday.)

Now assume that the sales associate receives a deposit from a prospective buyer in the brokerage office on Tuesday (no legal holidays are involved) and the sales associate turns the check over to the broker that same day (Tuesday). When must the broker deposit the funds into the escrow account?

The day of receipt of the escrow deposit was Tuesday. The broker must deposit the funds by the end of business on the third business day after the brokerage received the funds. The three business days are Wednesday, Thursday, and Friday. Therefore, the broker has until the end of the third business day (Friday) to deposit the funds. So the fact that the sales associate delivered the escrow check to the broker on Tuesday rather than waiting until Wednesday made no difference regarding when the broker was required to deposit the funds. When computing the day for the broker to deposit the funds, the day the buyer (or lessee if this is a rent deposit) gives the funds to the brokerage is not counted in the broker's days. The first day of the three-business-day time period always begins on the business day after the check is given to the brokerage. Keep in mind that a broker does not have to wait until the third business day to deposit the funds. The broker can make the deposit earlier. The broker can also receive the deposit directly without the involvement of a sales associate. The same rule applies in this case: The broker has until the end of the third business day to make the deposit.

If an escrow check is made out to the sales associate personally, the best course of action is to ask the prospective buyer to write a new check payable to the broker's escrow account. However, if this is not practical, the sales associate should immediately endorse the check and include the words, "For Deposit Only to the (name of the escrow account)" and turn it over to the broker.

673.1131, F.S. 14.008(1), F.A.C.

Postdated checks and insufficient funds. Occasionally a licensee may be given a post-dated check (considered a promissory note) as an earnest money deposit. Extreme caution should be taken in handling such deposits. The seller's approval *must* be obtained before accepting the postdated check. Once accepted, the broker should secure the instrument in a proper place, such as an office safe, until the date on the check becomes current, and then immediately deposit the check into the broker's escrow account. A broker will not be held responsible for the nonpayment of an escrow check, *provided* the broker timely deposits the check into the escrow account and the broker's own culpable negligence did not cause the check not to be honored.

KEY REPORTING DEADLINES REGARDING ESCROW ACCOUNTS

- Sales associates must deliver escrow deposits to their broker by the end of the *next business day*.

- Brokers must deposit escrow funds by the end of the *third business day*.

- Brokers must notify the FREC in writing of conflicting demands or of a good-faith doubt within *15 business days*.

- Brokers must institute one of the settlement procedures within *30 business days* of receiving conflicting demands or of having a good-faith doubt.

- If a broker requests an EDO and the escrow dispute is either settled or goes to court before the EDO is issued, the broker must notify the FREC within *10 business days*.

61J2-24.002(gg), F.A.C.
61J2-14.014, F.A.C.
61J2-14.008, F.A.C.

Acceptable depositories. Brokers may maintain either an interest-bearing or noninterest-bearing escrow account in a Florida commercial bank, credit union, or savings association. Some brokers do not want the responsibility and liability of maintaining an escrow account. Instead they may choose to have a Florida-based title company that has trust powers to maintain the escrow funds, or alternatively, if designated in the sale contract, a Florida attorney may escrow the funds.

61J2-14.008(2)(b), F.A.C.

Title company and attorney escrow accounts. When a deposit is placed with a title company or with an attorney, the following procedure must be used:

- The real estate licensee who prepared or presented the sale contract must indicate on the purchase and sale agreement the title company's name (or attorney's name, if applicable), address, and telephone number.

- No later than ten business days after each deposit is due under the terms of the sale contract, the licensee's broker must request a written verification of receipt of the deposit. The broker's request to the title company (or to the attorney) must be in writing. If the deposit is held by a title company or by an attorney nominated in writing by the seller or the seller's agent, the verification is waived.

- No later than ten business days after the date the broker made the written request for verification of the deposit, the broker must provide the seller's broker with a copy of the written verification. If the title company (or attorney) failed to provide the broker with a written verification, this information must be given to the seller's broker no later than ten business days after the request for verification of the deposit. If the seller is not represented by a broker, the licensee's broker must notify the seller directly.

Sometimes, the purchase and sale contract will require the buyer to make more than one earnest money deposit. For example, the contract may state that the buyer is to make a $5,000 earnest money deposit at the time the contract is accepted by the seller and then a second deposit of $15,000 30 days after the date the contract is signed by the seller. When the contract requires more than one earnest deposit, the procedure described above must be employed for every deposit specified in the purchase and sale agreement.

Real estate license law governs only broker's escrow accounts. A broker may be subject to administrative discipline for failing to follow the procedure described above. However, because real estate license law governs only broker escrow accounts, the FREC has no jurisdiction over the title company or the attorney that was used as an escrow agent. The broker is required under Chapter 475, F.S., to deliver the funds to the escrow agent within the same time frame required for depositing the funds into the broker's escrow account. Therefore, the broker must deliver the funds to the escrow agent no later than the end of the third business day after the deposit was received by the brokerage.

Interest-bearing escrow accounts. If the broker's escrow account is an interest-bearing account, the broker must get written permission from all parties before placing the funds in this type of account. The written authorization must specify who is entitled to the interest earned. The broker may receive the interest earned, but only if it is specifically agreed to by all parties. A broker can be disciplined by the FREC for failure to secure the written permission of all interested parties prior to placing trust (escrow) funds in an interest-bearing escrow account.

Record keeping. Brokers must keep business records, books, and accounts in compliance with Florida law and Commission rules and make them available for audit or spot checks by the DBPR at any reasonable time. Records must be preserved for at least *five years* from the date of receipt of money, funds, deposits, or checks entrusted to the broker. Furthermore, records must be retained for at least five years from the date of any executed agreement, including buyer brokerage agreements, listing agreements, offers to purchase, rental property management agreements, rental or lease agreements, or any other written or verbal agreement that engages the services of the broker. If a broker's records have been the subject of litigation or have served as evidence for litigation, the relevant records must be preserved for two years beyond the conclusion of the civil action or the conclusion of an appellate proceeding, but in no case, for less than five years.

475.5017, F.S.
475.5015, F.S.
61J2-14.012,
F.A.C.

Money to maintain escrow account. A broker is allowed to place in the sales escrow account an amount up to $1,000 of personal or brokerage funds. Brokers may keep up to $5,000 of their own monies in a property management escrow account. It is advisable that brokers keep sales escrow funds separate from property management escrow funds. However, Florida law does not require separate sales escrow accounts and property management escrow accounts. If a broker maintains sales escrow funds and property management escrow funds in a single escrow account, the amount of personal funds or brokerage funds in the account cannot exceed $5,000.

61J2-14.010
(2), F.A.C.

A broker who maintains an escrow account must be a signatory on the account. The escrow account must be properly reconciled each month, and the broker must review, sign, and date the monthly reconciliation. Many brokers rely on a bookkeeper or an accountant to handle the day-to-day deposits and disbursements. However, Florida law holds the broker accountable for reviewing the brokerage firm's escrow accounting procedures to ensure compliance with Florida license law.

Misappropriation of escrow funds. Brokers may not intermingle or commingle (mix) escrow deposits with other types of funds. To **commingle** funds is the illegal practice of mixing a buyer's, seller's, tenant's, or landlord's funds with the broker's own money or of mixing escrow money with the broker's personal funds or brokerage funds. All trust funds deposited in an escrow account must be kept in that account until the transaction is closed or other fulfillment of an escrow condition occurs or until otherwise legally disposed of. Misappropriation of another's property will expose the broker to charges of conversion. **Conversion** is the unauthorized control or use of another person's personal property.

Notice and Settlement Procedures

475.25(1)(d)1, F.S.
61J2-10.032(1)(a), F.A.C.

Conflicting demands. **Conflicting demands** occur when the buyer and seller make demands regarding the disbursing of escrowed property that are inconsistent and cannot be resolved. If a broker who maintains an escrow account receives conflicting demands on escrowed property, the broker must notify the FREC, in writing, within 15 business days of receiving the conflicting demands unless specifically exempted.

455.2235, F.S.

Further, the broker must institute one of the four settlement (or escape) procedures within 30 business days from the time the broker received the conflicting demands. For example, if a broker waits 10 business days to report the conflicting demands, the broker has just 20 business days remaining to implement one of the settlement procedures.

The four settlement procedures are as follows:

1. *Mediation.* If all parties give written consent, the dispute may be mediated. **Mediation** is an informal, nonadversarial process intended to reach a negotiated settlement. If the *nonbinding* mediation process is not successfully completed within 90 days following the party's last demand for the disputed funds, the licensee must employ one of the other three settlement procedures.

2. *Arbitration.* **Arbitration** is a process whereby, with the prior written consent of all parties to the dispute, the matter is submitted to a disinterested third party. Each side presents its case to a third party, who makes a *binding* judgment in favor of one side or the other. The parties must agree in advance to abide by the arbitrator's final decision.

3. *Litigation.* If the disputing parties cannot agree, a disputing party may file a lawsuit so that the matter can be resolved in a court of law. Such a legal process is referred to as **litigation**. The litigation can involve either of two court procedures:

   I. *Interpleader.* If the broker does not have a financial claim to the disputed escrow funds, the broker can deposit the funds with the court registry. The broker is then excused from the case, and the disputing parties argue their case in court. This court procedure is known as **interpleader**.

475.25(1)(d), F.S.
61J2-10.032(2), F.A.C.

   II. *Declaratory judgment.* Brokers who believe they are entitled to a portion of disputed funds can file a court action known as a **declaratory judgment**. In this court procedure, the judge declares each party's rights to the disputed escrow funds.

TO REMEMBER: FOUR SETTLEMENT PROCEDURES

M Mediation (nonbinding)
A Arbitration (binding)
L Litigation
E Escrow disbursement order

4. *Escrow disbursement order (EDO).* The broker may request that the Commission issue an **escrow disbursement order (EDO)**, a determination of who is entitled to the disputed funds. The FREC will not issue an EDO if the funds are held in an attorney's escrow account or are being held by a title company. An EDO

procedure is only available if the funds are held in a brokerage escrow account. If the broker is informed in writing that the Commission will not issue an EDO, the broker must use one of the other settlement procedures. In such an instance, the broker must notify the Commission which settlement procedure will be used. FREC rules require a broker to notify the Commission within ten business days if the dispute is settled between the parties or if the matter goes to court before the EDO is issued.

If the real estate licensee promptly employs one of the four settlement procedures and abides by the resulting order or judgment, a complaint may not be filed against the licensee for failure to account for or deliver escrowed property (the broker has immunity from disciplinary action).

There are three exceptions to the notice and settlement procedures for sales escrow accounts:

1. Brokers who are entrusted with an earnest money deposit concerning a residential sale contract used by HUD in the sale of HUD-owned property are exempted from the notice and settlement procedures in Chapter 475, F.S. In such cases, the broker is required to follow HUD's Agreement to Abide, Broker Participation Requirements.

2. If a buyer of a residential condominium unit timely delivers to a licensee written notice of the buyer's intent to cancel the contract as authorized by the Condominium Act, the licensee may return the escrowed property to the purchaser without notifying the Commission or initiating any of the settlement procedures. (See also chapter 8, page 183.)

3. If a buyer of real property in good faith fails to satisfy the terms specified in the financing clause of a contract for sale and purchase, the licensee may return the escrowed funds to the purchaser without notifying the Commission or initiating any of the settlement procedures. (Although *not* required by law, licensees are cautioned that they may be exposing themselves to civil liability if they release escrowed funds without first getting the parties to agree as to who is entitled to the funds. The Florida REALTORS® have developed preprinted forms that can be used to obtain the written permission of all parties to release escrowed funds.)

Good-faith doubt. If a broker has a *good-faith doubt* as to which party should receive the escrowed property, the broker must notify the FREC, in writing, within *15 business days* after having such doubt and institute one of the settlement procedures (described earlier) within *30 business days* after having such doubt. The term good faith is used to describe a party's honest intent to transact business, free from any intent to defraud the other party, and generally speaking, each party's faithfulness to the duties or obligations set forth by contract. Therefore, if the broker doubts the parties' good faith, the law requires that the broker abide by the notice requirement and initiate one of the settlement procedures in a timely manner. Individuals must look to case law for interpretations of what specific circumstances constitute a good-faith doubt. Situations that may constitute good-faith doubt by the broker include the following:

■ The transaction closing date has passed, and the broker has not received identical instructions from both the buyer and seller regarding how to disburse escrowed funds.

NOTICE

PURSUANT TO FLORIDA LAW: If the rental information provided under this contract is not current or accurate in any material aspect, you may demand within 30 days of this contract date a return of your full fee paid. If you do not obtain a rental you are entitled to receive a return of 75 percent of the fee paid, if you make demand within 30 days of this contract date.

Reference: 61J2-10.030, F.A.C.

- The transaction closing date has not passed, but one or more parties have expressed the intention not to close and the broker has not received identical instructions from the buyer and seller regarding how to disburse escrowed funds.

- One party to a failed transaction does not respond to a broker's inquiry about escrow disbursement. In this situation, the broker may send a certified notice letter, return receipt requested, to that nonresponding party stating that a demand has been made on the escrowed funds and that failure to respond by a designated date will be regarded as authority for the broker to release the funds to the demanding party. (*Note:* Although *not* required by law, to limit the broker's potential liability, it is advisable before releasing the trust funds to secure the postal return receipt as proof the notice was delivered.)

Title company or attorney as escrow agent. If a title company or an attorney is the escrow agent, the broker has no obligation to report an escrow dispute to the FREC or to institute a settlement procedure. Generally, a title company or the attorney will not disburse funds without authorization from the parties to the transaction. Usually, if the parties cannot come to an agreement regarding the funds the matter is submitted to a court of law for resolution.

Monies Paid in Advance for Performing Real Estate Services

721.20(6), F.S.

Sometimes a broker will receive commission or partial compensation before completing the real estate service. When this occurs the broker is entrusted with funds that must be placed into the broker's escrow or trust until the services are completed. Once the service is completed the broker has earned the compensation and may at that time transfer the funds into the broker's operating account. However, the Time-Share Act prohibits a real estate licensee from collecting an advance fee for the listing of a time-share unit.

RENTAL INFORMATION AND LISTS

475.453, F.S.
61J2-10.030, F.A.C.

Some real estate brokerage firms offer prospective tenants a list of properties available for rent. However, very few brokerage firms sell this information. Rental companies or anyone who advertises rental property information or lists in any manner is acting as a broker or a broker's representative and is subject to the laws regulating licensed occupations.

Accordingly, any broker or sales associate who furnishes rental information to a prospective tenant for a fee must provide the prospective tenant with a contract or receipt that contains a provision for repayment under specified conditions. It must state that a prospective tenant who does not obtain a rental is entitled to be repaid 75 percent of the fee paid if requested within 30 days of the contract/receipt date.

If the information provided to the prospective tenant is not current or is inaccurate in any material respect, the broker must repay 100 percent of the fee to the prospective tenant on demand. Any demand from the prospective tenant for the return of any part or all of the fee must be made within 30 days from the date the broker or sales associate contracted to provide services. Such demands may be made orally or in writing. The contract or receipt agreement must follow FREC guidelines, and the licensee must send a copy to the DBPR within 30 days of the first use.

Advertising rental property information or lists that are not current or are materially inaccurate is illegal. Any person who violates the requirements outlined above is guilty of a misdemeanor of the first degree, is subject to a fine of up to $1,000 and/or imprisonment of up to one year, and is subject to license suspension or revocation.

BROKER'S COMMISSION

Antitrust Laws

542, F.S.

The real estate industry is subject to state and federal antitrust laws. At the federal level, the Sherman (1890), Clayton (1914), and Federal Trade Commission (1914) acts and subsequent amendments deal with preserving competition and ensuring against restraint of trade. It is illegal for real estate brokers to conspire to fix commissions or fees for the services they perform. Local real estate boards and multiple listing services may not fix commission rates or splits between cooperating brokers.

61J2-10.028, F.A.C.

The amount of commission to be paid is negotiable, and it is arrived at by agreement between the broker and buyer or seller. If no specific agreement exists, a judicially determined commission will apply. Neither the FREC nor Florida law establishes or regulates the amount of commission paid. The sharing of brokerage compensation by a licensee with a party to the real estate transaction, with full disclosure to all interested parties, is allowed under Chapter 475, F.S.

Liens on Real Property

475.42(1)(j), F.S.
61J2-24.001(3) (ee), F.A.C.

Residential property. A broker may place a lien on real property for nonpayment of commission *only* if the broker is expressly authorized to do so in a contractual agreement. Otherwise, when a buyer or seller refuses to pay a broker's commission after the commission has been earned, the broker would be required to take legal action to collect the monies due by filing a suit against the party for the amount due. The broker would have to obtain a civil judgment against the party who owed the commission. The FREC is authorized to suspend or revoke a real estate license for the unauthorized recording of a *lis pendens* or a lien or other instrument that affects the title of real property or that encumbers real property.

475, Part IV, F.S.

Commercial Real Estate Sales Commission Lien Act. Chapter 475, Part III, known as the Commercial Real Estate Sales Commission Lien Act, gives a broker lien rights for earned commission. This act applies *only* to commercial property as defined in Chapter 475. The lien is only against the owner's net proceeds (personal property) from the sale and does *not* apply to the commercial real property.

To establish a broker's lien rights, the broker must disclose to the owner (seller) at or before the time the owner executes the brokerage agreement for the listing (and subsequent sale) of commercial property, that Chapter 475, Part III, creates lien rights for commission earned by the broker. Commission includes any fee or other compensation that the owner agrees to pay the broker for licensed real estate services specified in the brokerage agreement. The disclosure must state that the Commercial Lien Act provides that when a broker has earned a commission under a brokerage agreement, the broker may claim a lien against the owner's net sales proceeds for the broker's unpaid commission. The lien against the owner's net proceeds takes priority as of the date of recording a commission notice claiming the commission owed. Priority of the lien does *not* relate back to the date of the brokerage agreement.

Commercial Real Estate Leasing Commission Lien Act. Chapter 475, Part IV, known as the Commercial Real Estate Leasing Commission Lien Act, gives a broker lien rights for earned commission associated with a brokerage agreement to lease commercial real estate. If the landlord is the person obligated to pay the leasing commission, the broker's lien attaches to the landlord's interest in the commercial real estate. If the tenant is the person obligated to pay the leasing commission, the broker's lien attaches to the tenant's leasehold estate.

Sales Associate's Commission

All monies earned by sales associates as a result of any real estate service must be paid to the sales associates by their employer and not directly by the buyer or seller. Sales associates are compensated by splitting commissions paid to their broker-employer. What split is retained by a broker and what split is received by a sales associate is usually agreed upon when they reach an independent contractor agreement. The closing agent for a real estate transaction can legally prepare a check payable to a real estate sales associate for the sales associate's share of the commission. The check may be given to the associate at the closing provided the broker has given the closing agent written authorization and instructions regarding the specific amount of commission the associate is to be paid for the particular transaction. (A blanket authorization cannot be given to a closing agent.)

Under Florida law a sales associate may not operate as a broker, nor operate independently. Therefore, all commissions and all listings are legally the property of the broker. Sales associates are prohibited from initiating any suit or action for compensation in connection with a real estate transaction against any person *except* the person registered as their employer. Sales associates who accept listings, deposits, or commissions from any source *must* accept them in the name of their broker and with the express consent of that broker.

Kickbacks

475.25(2)(h), F.S. 61J2-10.028, F.A.C.

A **kickback** (or *rebate*) is an unearned fee paid to a licensee associated with a real estate transaction for non-real-estate services (payment for something other than one of the eight services of real estate). Below is a list of important facts regarding kickbacks and rebates:

- Prior to the payment and receipt of the kickback, the buyer and seller must be fully informed of all facts regarding the kickback. For example, assume a broker refers buyers to Nifty Blinds and receives $25 for each buyer who purchases window treatments from Nifty. The broker, prior to the payment and receipt of the

$25, must fully advise all parties in the transaction of the arrangement that the broker has with Nifty Blinds.

- The kickback must not violate the Real Estate Settlement Procedures Act (RESPA). RESPA prohibits the payment of a kickback or unearned fee associated with a settlement (closing) service, including title searches, title insurance, attorney services, surveys, credit reports, and appraisals. A person paid a fee regarding settlement services must have actually rendered (performed) the service. (See also page 156.)

- The person receiving the kickback must be properly licensed if a license is required to perform the service. (In Florida, a real estate licensee must also be licensed as a mortgage loan originator to be legally paid a fee for referring prospective borrowers to a mortgage lender.)

- Real estate licensees are prohibited from sharing a commission with an unlicensed person for real estate services. However, Florida law does allow the sharing of part of the commission to the buyer or seller in a real estate transaction, provided the rebate is disclosed to all interested parties. Sharing a portion of the commission with a party to the transaction is an example of a legal (permissible) kickback or rebate. The commission is property of the broker; therefore, the sales associate should refer to the office policy manual or discuss the matter with the broker before presenting this incentive to the buyer or seller.

- Florida law prohibits a real estate licensee from paying an *unlicensed* person money for the referral of real estate business. However, Florida license law does provide that a property management firm or the owner of an apartment complex may pay a finder's fee (or referral fee) of no more than $50 to an unlicensed person who is a tenant of the apartment complex for the referral of a prospect who becomes a tenant of the apartment complex.

CHANGE OF EMPLOYER

475.23, F.S.

Sales associates who change employers are required to take certain actions before they may legally work for the new employer. A sales associate's license ceases to be in force when a sales associate changes employer. The DBPR must be notified within ten days after the change by filing a *Change of Broker/Employer* (DBPR RE-10) form, disclosing the name and address of the new employer. Sales associates may not perform real estate services until they are properly registered with their new employer. The request of change of registration also serves to notify the DBPR of the termination of employment with the former employer.

475.25(1)(b), F.S.

After leaving a former employer, a sales associate who diverts a buyer or seller of the former employer from completion of a transaction may sustain liability for breach of fiduciary to the former employer and possibly to the party that hired the former employer. Recall that sales associates and broker associates are agents of their employing broker (principal) and as such a fiduciary duty exists. To divert buyers or sellers or use confidential information is both unethical and illegal in Florida. Additionally, a sales associate may have agreed contractually to a noncompete agreement.

Because of the fiduciary relationship between sales associate and employer, the obligations of the sales associate do not end with termination of employment. The sales associate is prohibited from disclosing confidential information learned as a result of employment. A licensee is further prohibited from doing anything that might discredit the former employer or damage the goodwill of the employer's business.

FIGURE 5.2 ■ **Business Entities**

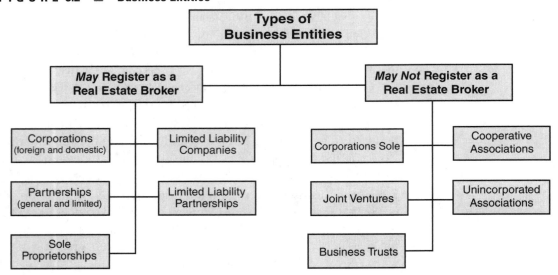

1 A sales associate who duplicates records, listings, or confidential information from the
2 office of a former employer without consent is guilty of breach of trust, even though the
3 sales associate may have placed those items in the employer's records.

4 If a sales associate takes the original records from an employer's office, as opposed to
5 duplicating them, then the sales associate is guilty of larceny (theft) and is exposed to
6 administrative penalties by the FREC, civil action in court, and criminal penalties.

7 **Office policy manual.** Every real estate brokerage firm should have a policy and procedures
8 manual for its sales associates and employees. A **policy manual** is a collection of office
9 rules and regulations created to inform sales associates and employees of the standards and
10 procedures in that particular office. Brokers are *not* required to have a policy manual. A
11 policy manual helps to eliminate the necessity for new personnel to be constantly asking
12 questions regarding floor time, listing and sales quotas, vacation schedules, advertising,
13 commissions, and so forth.

MEMBERSHIP IN ORGANIZATIONS

61J2-
24.002(2)(aa),
F.A.C.
61J2-10.027,
F.A.C.

15 Real estate licensees may not represent themselves as members of a professional trade
16 organization or use, for example, the term REALTOR®, unless entitled to do so by means of
17 membership, payment of dues, and so forth. Licensees may be fined $300 for representing
18 themselves as REALTORS® when they are not current members of the NAR. Sales associ-
19 ates, brokers, and state-certified appraisers can be issued a $300 citation for representing
20 themselves as such when their license status is inactive.

TYPES OF BUSINESS ENTITIES THAT MAY REGISTER

475.161, F.S.
475.15, F.S.
475.01(1)(a),
F.S.

22 A broker may choose from a variety of business entities. (See Figure 5.2, Business Enti-
23 ties.) Sole proprietorships, partnerships (both general and limited), limited liability part-
24 nerships, corporations, and limited liability companies may be registered as real estate

brokers and/or brokerage entities. Chapter 475.01, F.S., defines the term *broker* to include any person who is a general partner, officer, or a director of a partnership or corporation that acts as a real estate broker.

All real estate brokerage entities must register with the DBPR. Registration includes the names of every licensed and unlicensed general partner of a real estate brokerage general partnership or limited partnership and every officer and director of a real estate brokerage corporation. Every member of a member-managed real estate brokerage limited liability company must also register. A person licensed as a sales associate or broker associate may *not* register as a general partner, a member of a member-managed real estate limited liability company, a manager of a manager-managed real estate limited liability company, an officer, or director of a brokerage corporation.

Sole Proprietorships

A **sole proprietorship** is a business owned by one person. It is easy to organize and flexible to operate. A sole proprietor who holds a current and valid broker's license may run a real estate brokerage business. Brokers may use their own name or a fictitious name as a trade name once it has been registered with the DBPR. (See Trade Names on page 106.)

Sole proprietors are personally liable not only for their own actions but also for the actions of any employees acting within the scope of their employment. A sole proprietorship may be dissolved by ceasing business activities and notifying the Commission, or by expiration of the license, court order, or death of the owner.

Partnerships

620, F.S.
475.15, F.S.

A **general partnership** is an association of two or more persons for the purpose of jointly conducting a business. Each general partner is responsible for all the debts incurred in the conducting of that business; each has the power to bind the other or others in transactions; and each is entitled to receive a share of the profits in an amount agreed on by the parties. A general partnership is created by a contract that may be written, oral, or implied from the conduct of the parties.

Real estate brokerage general partnerships. Brokers may choose to form a general partnership. Requirements regarding real estate brokerage partnerships include the following:

- The partnership must register with the DBPR under the partnership name.
- At least one partner must be licensed as an active broker.
- Partners who will deal with the public and perform services of real estate must be licensed as active brokers.
- Sales associates and broker associates may *not* be general partners in a real estate brokerage partnership.

61J2-5.018, F.A.C.
61J2-5.019, F.A.C.
61J2-4.009, F.A.C.

Any change in the composition of a partnership must be reported to the DBPR. If the partnership has only one active broker (broker of record) and that broker dies, resigns, or is removed from office, the broker of record must be replaced within 14 calendar days. No new brokerage business may be conducted by the partnership or by a licensee registered with the partnership until a new active broker is identified and registered under the partnership. Failure to timely appoint another active broker will result in the automatic cancellation of the partnership registration, and the licenses of all people associated with the partnership will become involuntary inactive. It is the responsibility of every active broker in the real estate brokerage partnership to see that the partnership and all of its partners and sales associates have current and appropriate registration and licenses.

Limited partnerships. A **limited partnership** is created by a written instrument filed with the Florida Department of State. There must be one or more general partners and one or more limited partners to qualify under the law. The limited partners must make an invest- ment of cash or of property, but not of services.

620, F.S.
475.15, F.S.

The liability of the general partner(s) is nearly the same as in a general partnership. Limited partners are *not* liable to creditors of the partnership unless the limited partners' names appear in the partnership name (with certain exceptions) or the limited partners take part in the control of the business. Limited partners are liable only for any unpaid part of their pledged contribution, any assets of the partnership in their hands, and any distribution made to them while the partnership is insolvent.

Real estate brokerage limited partnerships. Requirements regarding real estate brokerage limited partnerships include the following:

- The limited partnership must register with the DBPR under the limited partner- ship name.
- General partners who will deal with the public and perform services of real estate must be licensed as active brokers.
- At least one general partner must be licensed as an active broker.
- All other general partners must register (names and addresses are disclosed) with the DBPR for identification purposes.
- Sales associates and broker associates may *not* be general partners in a real estate brokerage limited partnership; however, they may be limited partners (regarded in the same light as stockholders in a corporation).
- Limited partners are not required to register with the DBPR.

Ostensible partnership. An **ostensible partnership** (or quasi partnership) is not inten- tionally created. Rather, the conduct of two or more persons creates the "appearance" that a partnership exists. It is considered to be fraudulent and deceitful if the public is deceived into believing that a partnership exists. In such as situation, the courts may consider a partnership to exist. Under the law the parties can be held liable for each others debts and torts (wrongful acts). Real estate licensees who operate as ostensible partners may be subject to license suspension.

Brokers sometimes do business in the same office building. This is permissible provided each brokerage displays its own office sign and uses separate telephone numbers. Each bro- kerage must have and register its own business name (name of broker or trade name) and indicate the brokerage name on separate letterhead, business cards, and so forth.

Limited Liability Partnerships

The partners in a **limited liability partnership** enjoy protection from personal liability in much the same way as limited partners in a limited partnership. Limited liability partners are not liable for obligations or liabilities of the partnership arising from contract, errors or omissions, negligence, malpractice, or wrongful acts committed by another partner or by an employee, agent, or representative of the partnership. A limited liability partner is liable for any errors, omissions, negligence, malpractice, or wrongful acts committed by that partner, or any person under the partner's direct supervision and control in any activity in which the wrongful act occurred, or for any debts for which the partner agreed in writing to be liable. The partners in a limited liability partnership are not subject to the limitations imposed on limited partners in a traditional limited partnership. Registered limited liability partnerships must file with the Florida Department of State. The name of a registered limited liability partnership must include the words "Registered Limited Liability Partnership" or the abbreviation "L.L.P." or the designation "LLP" as the last words or letters of its name.

Corporations

607, F.S.
475.15, F.S.
61J2-
24.002(2)(x–y),
F.A.C.
61J2-5.012-
.20, F.A.C.

A **corporation** is an artificial person or legal entity created by law and consists of one or more persons. A corporation is formed by filing articles of incorporation with the Florida Department of State. Both foreign and domestic corporations may register as brokerage entities. A *foreign corporation* is a corporation organized under the laws of another state but that does business in Florida. *Domestic corporations* are incorporated in the state of Florida and do business in Florida. The owners of the corporation are the stockholders. The stockholders elect the board of directors to manage the corporation. The officers, president, vice president, secretary, and treasurer, carry out the directives of the board.

In Florida, a corporation may be formed as a real estate brokerage firm after providing proof of legal corporate existence. Requirements regarding real estate brokerage corporations include the following:

- The corporation must register with the DBPR under the corporation name; this is accomplished by completing the brokerage corporation application. (If the brokerage is going to operate under a trade name, that information is also entered on the application.)
- At least one of the officers or directors must be licensed as an active broker (the *principal broker* or *qualifying broker*).
- Active Florida brokers, inactive Florida brokers, and unlicensed people may serve as officers and directors of a real estate brokerage; however, officers and directors who will deal with the public and perform services of real estate must be licensed as active brokers.
- All officers and directors who are not licensed must be registered with the DBPR for identification purposes; this is accomplished by submitting each individual's name, residence address, office held, and percentage of ownership when completing the management information section of the brokerage corporation application.
- Inactive brokers and unlicensed individuals may perform managerial functions for the brokerage corporation that do not involve real estate functions, such as administrative matters, bookkeeping, and accounting duties.
- Sales associates and broker associates may not be an officer or director in a real estate brokerage corporation; a sales associate or broker associate may be issued a citation and fined for serving as an officer or director of a brokerage corporation.
- Sales associates and broker associates may be shareholders of a real estate brokerage corporation.

61J2-5.018,
F.A.C.

If the only active broker of a brokerage corporation dies, resigns, or is removed from office, the vacancy must be filled within 14 calendar days. New brokerage business may

TRADE NAMES

No person shall operate as a broker under a trade name without causing the trade name to be noted in the records of the Commission and placed on his license, or so operate as a member of a partnership or as a corporation or as an officer or manager thereof, unless such partnership or corporation is the holder of a valid current registration.

Reference: Section 475.42, F.S.

not be performed by the corporation or by a licensee registered with the corporation until a new active broker is designated and registered. Failure to meet the 14-day deadline will result in the automatic cancellation of the brokerage firm's registration, and the licenses of all its officers, directors, and sales associates will become involuntary inactive. If, on the other hand, the corporation has more than one active broker and one of the brokers dies or resigns, the corporate registration and the licenses of the officers, directors, and sales associates are not affected by the vacancy. It is the responsibility of every active corporate officer and director to see that the corporation and all officers, directors, and sales associates have current and appropriate registration and licenses.

617, F.S.
61J2-5.012-
.020, F.A.C.

Nonprofit corporations. A *nonprofit corporation* is organized in substantially the same manner as a corporation for profit. Chapter 475, F.S., does not make a distinction between profit and nonprofit corporations. However, any broker who is considering forming a nonprofit corporation for real estate brokerage activity should consult a tax advisor before proceeding.

Limited Liability Companies

608, F.S.

A **limited liability company** (LLC) is a form of business organization that offers the best features of a corporation and a partnership. It provides the owners protection from personal liability for business debts in the same way a corporation does, but the IRS treats an LLC as a partnership for tax purposes. Income is taxed only once, as in a partnership. An LLC has great flexibility in how it passes income and deductions to its members. Limited liability companies are formed under Chapter 608, F.S.

BUSINESS ARRANGEMENTS AND ENTITIES THAT MAY NOT REGISTER AS BROKERS

A *corporation sole* is an ecclesiastical or church organization and should not be confused with a corporation for profit. It is normally headed by a bishop or other clerical official who has been empowered by a church to hold title to church property. However, the title descends to successors in office and not to heirs. A broker should exercise caution in dealing with a corporation sole. Before dealing with a corporation sole, a broker should obtain

1 a written opinion from a lawyer who has experience in such titles. A corporation sole can-
2 not be registered as a real estate broker.

3   A *joint venture* (or joint adventure) is a temporary form of business arrangement often
4 encountered in the real estate business. The joint venture structure is normally used when
5 two or more parties combine their efforts to complete a single business transaction or a
6 fixed number of business transactions. No written agreements are required for the forma-
7 tion of a joint venture. The rights, duties, and obligations of joint venturers are similar
8 to those of partners in a partnership, except that they are restricted to the transaction for
9 which the joint venture was formed.

609, F.S.
475.011(2), F.S.

10   Real estate brokers often combine their efforts in real estate transactions to create a
11 joint venture. A joint venture, when composed of separate real estate brokers, can broker
12 real property. In such a case, the joint venture would not be required to register with the
13 DBPR because each of the individuals is registered and licensed. If two parties form a joint
14 venture to provide real estate services for compensation, both parties must be licensed real
15 estate brokers.

16   A *business trust* is a form of business entity that may be formed to engage in transactions
17 involving its own real property. A business trust is formed by any number of persons who
18 make an investment at a stipulated amount per unit. The monies collected in this manner
19 are then used to buy, develop, and/or sell real estate. Title to real property acquired by a
20 business trust is taken in the name of a trustee or group of trustees. A business trust cannot
21 be registered with the DBPR as a real estate broker. However, any employee who buys or
22 sells real property for a trust and is compensated on a transaction basis must be licensed.

619, F.S.

23   A *cooperative association* is permitted to conduct commercial business and to convey,
24 sell, or buy its own property, but it cannot be registered as a real estate broker. (See also
25 chapter 8.)

26   *Unincorporated associations* are generally recognized as groups of people associated for
27 some noncommercial common purpose. They are not regarded as partners and are not
28 incorporated. An example would be a group of property owners in a subdivision who orga-
29 nize for such purposes as beautification, planning, maintenance, or even the performance
30 of services such as garbage removal. Such associations can incur liabilities, and members
31 are liable for debts to creditors in the same manner as partners. For example, each member
32 is liable for all the debts, but as to each other, the members are liable only for their indi-
33 vidual proportionate share. Unincorporated associations sometimes buy or sell their own
34 real property through a trustee or board of trustees. Unincorporated associations may not
35 be registered as real estate brokers.

36 # TRADE NAMES

865.09, F.S.
475.42(1)(k),
F.S.
61J2-10.034,
F.A.C.
61J2-9.007,
F.A.C.

37 A *trade name* is a business name other than the legal name of the person doing business.
38 The letters *T/A* are used to indicate "trading as." *Fictitious name* refers to the name regis-
39 tered with the Department of State. The letters *D/B/A* refer to "doing business as." Sole
40 proprietors and business entities may choose to operate under these designations.

41   An individual broker or brokerage entity may use a trade name and applicable desig-
42 nation after that name is registered with the DBPR. Chapter 475 (license law) does *not*
43 require a sole proprietor or brokerage entity to register a trade name with the Department of
44 State. However, if another business entity has previously registered that name with the
45 Department of State, the brokerage may not use the name. If a brokerage corporation

or partnership conducts business under a fictitious name, the business must comply with the Florida Fictitious Name Act and register the fictitious name with the Department of State.

621.12, F.S.
608.406, F.S.
475.161, F.S.

Broker associates and sales associates must have their licenses issued in their legal names. They may not be licensed or registered under a trade name. However, a broker associate or a sales associate is allowed to form a professional corporation, limited liability company, or professional limited liability company. In this case, the DBPR issues the license in the licensee's actual (legal) name and includes the entity designation on the face of the license. For example, Florida law requires that a professional corporation include the words "professional association" or the abbreviation "PA" in the name. Therefore, the sales associate license could state, for example, Jane Doe, PA. Florida law further mandates that a professional limited liability company include the words "professional limited company" or the abbreviation "PL" in the name. A sales associate license could state, for example, John Doe, PL. Florida law requires that a limited liability company include "limited liability company" or "limited company" or the abbreviation "LLC" or "LC" in the name. In such a case, a license could state, for example, Jane Doe, LLC.

A real estate sales associate or broker associate may form a professional corporation, limited liability company, or professional limited liability company for income tax purposes only, and this is *not* to be confused with a brokerage business entity. Sales associates and broker associates must work under a broker or an owner-developer.

SUMMARY OF IMPORTANT POINTS

- To have active status, a real estate broker is required to open an office and register it with the DBPR.
- The brokerage office sign must contain (1) the trade name (if applicable), (2) the broker's name, and (3) the words "Licensed (or Lic.) Real Estate Broker." If desired, the names of the sales associates and broker associates may be added below the broker's name(s), provided the appropriate title (sales associate or broker associate) appears after their name. A line or space must separate the brokers' names from the associates' names.
- Blind advertising fails to disclose the license name of the brokerage firm and provides only a post office box number, telephone number, and/or street address.
- *Point of contact information* refers to the information provided on the Internet for contacting a brokerage firm or individual licensee, including mailing addresses, physical street addresses, e-mail addresses, telephone numbers, and FAX telephone numbers. The brokerage firm name must be above, below, or adjacent to point of contact information.
- Licensees who include their personal name in advertisements must use their last name as registered with the DBPR.
- A *telephone solicitation* is a telephone call placed for the purpose of encouraging the purchase of, or investment in, property goods, or services. Telemarketers (including real estate licensees) must search the National Do Not Call Registry before making telemarketing calls. Violators of the federal Telephone Consumer Protection Act may be fined up to $11,000 per call. The penalty for violating Florida's Telemarketing Act is $10,000 per call.

- An *escrow account* is an account for the deposit of money held by a third party in trust for another for safekeeping. Brokers may open escrow accounts in a Florida bank, savings association, or credit union. The broker must be a signatory on the escrow account. If the broker chooses not to open an escrow account, the funds may be held by a title company or in an attorney's trust account.

- Sales associates must deliver binder deposits to their broker-employer no later than the end of the next business day. Brokers must deposit the funds into their escrow account no later than the end of the third business day after the brokerage received the funds.

- If the broker's escrow account is an interest-bearing account, the broker must get written permission from all parties before placing the funds into the account. The written authorization must specify who is entitled to the interest earned. The broker may receive the interest.

- Brokers must maintain records of real estate transactions for five years, regardless of whether escrow funds were pledged (or two years after litigation, if beyond the five-year period).

- *Commingle* is the illegal practice of mixing a buyer's, seller's, tenant's, or landlord's funds with the broker's own money or mixing escrow money with the broker's personal funds or brokerage funds. Brokers are allowed to place up to $1,000 of personal or brokerage funds in a sales escrow account or up to $5,000 of personal or brokerage funds in a property management escrow account.

- Brokers must notify the FREC in writing of conflicting demands or of a good-faith doubt within 15 business days. Brokers must institute one of the settlement procedures within 30 business days of receiving conflicting demands or of having a good-faith doubt. The four settlement procedures are (1) mediation, (2) arbitration, (3) litigation, and (4) escrow disbursement order.

- Some real estate brokerage entities offer prospective tenants a list of properties available for rent. Very few brokerage firms sell the information; however, if the brokerage charges a fee for the rental information, the tenant must receive a receipt that outlines two refund provisions: (1) if the rental information is in error, 100 percent refund; and (2) if the prospective tenant is unable to find a suitable rental, a 75 percent refund. The request for refund must be made verbally or in writing within 30 days following the day of purchase.

- Failing to provide accurate and current rental information for a fee is a first-degree misdemeanor. The penalty for a first-degree misdemeanor is a fine of not more than $1,000 and/or up to one year in jail.

- A *kickback* occurs when a broker receives money from someone other than the buyer or the seller, such as for referring a buyer or seller to a particular vendor for services. Buyer and seller must be fully informed prior to the payment.

- Florida law prohibits a real estate licensee from paying money to an unlicensed person for the referral of real estate business.

- Florida law allows the sharing of part of the commission to the buyer or seller in a real estate transaction, provided the rebate is disclosed to all interested parties.

- Types of business entities that may register as a brokerage entity include the following: sole proprietorship, general partnership, limited partnership, limited liability partnership, corporation, and limited liability company.

- An *ostensible partnership* (or quasi-partnership) is created when the actions of two or more persons create the appearance that a partnership exists. Licensees who operate as ostensible partners may be subject to license suspension.
- Sales associates and broker associates may not be members of the board of directors or officers of a real estate brokerage corporation.
- Sales associates and broker associates are not allowed to register as general partners of a real estate brokerage general or limited partnership.

R E V I E W   Q U E S T I O N S

1. John Anderson is a licensed real estate sales associate. Under which name may he register and be licensed?
    a. Complete Real Estate Sales Services
    b. John Anderson Brokerage
    c. John Anderson, LLC
    d. John Anderson and Partners

2. A sales associate receives a binder deposit from a prospective buyer on Thursday morning. Later that same day, the associate gives the binder deposit to his broker. By the end of business on what day of the week must the broker deposit the funds into her escrow account?
    a. Friday
    b. Monday
    c. Tuesday
    d. Wednesday

3. Real estate brokerage trust funds may NOT be deposited into a
    a. title company in Florida that has trust powers.
    b. credit union in Florida.
    c. commercial bank in Florida.
    d. life insurance company in Florida.

4. In connection with escrow accounts, the Florida Real Estate Commission has rules and regulations that
    a. permit the depositing of personal funds into an escrow account as long as adequate records are kept.
    b. prohibit the depositing of more than $1,000 of personal funds into a sales escrow account.
    c. require deposits to be placed in an escrow account by the sales associate.
    d. require escrow disbursement orders to be prepared when making all deposits.

5. Real estate sales associates who receive checks payable to them as deposits on the purchase of real property must
    a. endorse the checks, deposit them in their employers' accounts, and maintain good records.
    b. endorse the checks and immediately turn them over to their employers.
    c. deposit the checks immediately in their own accounts and notify their employers of the transactions.
    d. deposit the checks immediately and give their employers the equivalent amounts in the form of checks or cash.

6. Which statement is FALSE regarding escrow accounts?
   a. The escrow account may be either interest-bearing or noninterest-bearing.
   b. A broker may choose to have an attorney or a Florida title company maintain the escrow account.
   c. It is illegal for the broker to keep any earned interest even if the buyer and the seller give written permission.
   d. A broker must get written authorization from the buyer and the seller prior to placing escrow funds in an interest-bearing escrow account.

7. A dispute arises between the buyer and seller as to which one is entitled to escrowed property. The broker should first
   a. mediate the matter.
   b. arbitrate the matter with the consent of both parties.
   c. notify the FREC in writing, unless exempted from the notice requirements.
   d. submit the matter to a court of law for adjudication.

8. An individual who paid for rental information but did not obtain a rental is entitled to repayment of
   a. the fee.
   b. the fee if requested within 10 days of the contract/receipt date.
   c. 75 percent of the fee if requested within 10 days of the contract/receipt date.
   d. 75 percent of the fee if requested within 30 days of the contract/receipt date.

9. A woman purchased a rental list one week ago from a real estate broker. She inspected an apartment described in the list. The apartment manager told her that cats were not allowed. She had specifically looked at the apartment because the rental list indicated that pets were allowed. Immediately, the woman orally demanded and should legally receive from the broker
   a. nothing, because the demand is not in writing.
   b. 75 percent of the fee paid.
   c. 100 percent of the fee paid.
   d. nothing, because the broker may not be held accountable for the actions of the property manager.

10. If the license issued to the only active broker of a real estate corporation becomes void for any reason, another active broker must be appointed within 14 calendar days. Failure to appoint another active broker will result in what action against the corporation's registration?
    a. Automatic cancellation
    b. Denial
    c. Automatic suspension
    d. Revocation

11. A broker decides to incorporate his new real estate business in order to reduce his personal liability. The broker must do each requirement EXCEPT
    a. register the brokerage entity with the DBPR.
    b. file the articles of incorporation with the Florida Department of State.
    c. register all officers and directors of the company with the DBPR.
    d. file the articles of incorporation with the Secretary of the DBPR.

12. Which statement is TRUE regarding a lien filed by a broker under the Commercial Real Estate Sales Commission Lien Act?
    a. The lien applies to commission only and does not include other fees the owner agrees to pay in the brokerage agreement.
    b. The lien is filed against the real property covered in the brokerage agreement.
    c. The lien takes priority as of the date of the brokerage agreement.
    d. The broker must disclose to the owner at the time of signing, or before the owner signs the brokerage agreement, that Chapter 475, Part III, creates lien rights for commission earned by the broker.

13. To form a general partnership, two or more persons must
    a. agree to share equally in the profits and losses.
    b. agree to engage in business together and share in the profits and losses.
    c. be personally qualified and licensed as real estate brokers.
    d. invest equal amounts of money in the business and each be entitled to a share of the profits.

14. One difference between a general partnership and a limited partnership is that
    a. only a general partnership may be registered as a real estate broker.
    b. limited partners must make a cash or property investment.
    c. while both have general partners, there must be two or more general partners in a limited partnership.
    d. limited partners must be licensed as either active or inactive sales associates.

15. Which business entity may be registered as a real estate broker?
    a. Corporation sole
    b. Cooperative association
    c. Limited partnership
    d. Business trust

16. A broker has conflicting demands from a buyer and a seller regarding an escrow deposit. The broker may employ all of the escape procedures listed below EXCEPT
    a. request an escrow disbursement order.
    b. provided all of the parties consent, submit the matter to arbitration.
    c. request an informal hearing before the FREC to resolve the matter.
    d. through an interpleader, submit the matter to a court proceeding for determination of the rightful claimant.

17. A broker is getting prepared to open Sunnyside Realty as a sole proprietorship and is placing an order to have an entrance sign made. Which wording does NOT need to be included on the sign?
    a. Sunnyside Realty
    b. The broker's legal name
    c. Licensed real estate broker
    d. 1000 Sunset Blvd.

18. A licensed real estate broker and an attorney who specializes in contract law form a joint venture for the purpose of locating and selling to investors raw land that is suitable for commercial development. Which statement is true regarding this arrangement?
    a. The attorney is exempt from the requirement to hold a broker's license because she is an attorney.
    b. They have formed an illegal ostensible partnership.
    c. Because they are performing real estate services for compensation, they both must be licensed real estate brokers.
    d. A joint venture is not required to register with the DBPR; therefore, there is no need for both parties to hold real estate licenses.

19. A broker receives conflicting demands concerning a roof inspection report. Both the buyer and seller claim the earnest money deposit. The broker must
    a. provide written notification to the FREC within 10 business days.
    b. follow the written instructions of the broker's buyer or seller.
    c. institute one of the statutory settlement procedures within 30 business days after the last demand.
    d. request an escrow disbursement order from the DBPR.

20. The sales commission rates applicable to the various types of property sold in Florida are determined by
    a. FREC rules and regulations.
    b. agreement between each broker and buyer or seller.
    c. the local board of REALTORS®.
    d. agreement between each seller and buyer.

21. When a sales associate decides to leave the employ of her broker to work for another broker, she
    a. may take copies of all listings she personally obtained while employed by her former broker.
    b. must notify the DBPR within ten days of her change in broker-employer.
    c. may telephone sellers of her former employer to encourage them to cancel their listing agreements with the former employer and then list with her new broker.
    d. must apply for a new real estate license under the name of her new broker.

22. A broker decides to organize his brokerage as a limited partnership. What must he accomplish?
    a. File the limited partnership agreement with the Florida Department of State
    b. Register the limited partnership with the DBPR
    c. Register all general partners with the DBPR
    d. All of the above

23. In Florida, listings obtained and any commissions paid by the buyer or seller are
    a. legally the sales associate's property.
    b. jointly owned by the sales associate and the sales associate's employer.
    c. legally classified as the property of the employing property owner.
    d. legally the property of the sales associate's employer.

24. Which statement is FALSE concerning the payment of an unearned fee or kickback?
    a. A real estate licensee may be paid a fee for referring buyers to a title company, provided the buyer is informed in advance of the facts concerning the fee.
    b. A real estate licensee may share part of the commission with the buyer or seller in a real estate transaction.
    c. A real estate licensee must also be licensed as a mortgage broker to be legally paid a fee for referring buyers to a mortgage lender.
    d. The payment of a kickback must not violate RESPA.

25. Two brokers from different brokerages agree to work with one another to market a prestigious marina in Naples, Florida. One broker is particularly knowledgeable regarding marinas and the other is an expert on the Naples real estate market, so they decide to combine their expertise on this particular listing. This business arrangement is referred to as
    a. an ostensible partnership.
    b. a general partnership.
    c. a joint venture.
    d. a limited partnership.

CHAPTER

6

COMPLAINTS, VIOLATIONS, AND PENALTIES

OVERVIEW

This chapter details the step-by-step procedures for investigations and hearings via the complaint process. The chapter describes many types of violations of the laws and rules governing real estate activities and the possible consequences that may result. Finally, the Real Estate Recovery Fund is explained regarding its function when damages are suffered in a real estate transaction owing to a wrongful act of a Florida licensee.

After completing this chapter, the student should be able to:

■ explain the procedures involved in the reporting of violations, the investigation of complaints, and the conduct of hearings;

■ describe the elements of a valid complaint;

■ describe the composition of the probable-cause panel;

■ describe events that would cause a license to be denied;

■ recognize actions that would cause a license to be subject to suspension or revocation;

■ identify individuals who would be eligible to seek reimbursement from the Real Estate Recovery Fund; and

■ describe the monetary limits imposed by law on the Real Estate Recovery Fund.

KEY TERMS

administrative complaint	final order	probable cause
citation	formal complaint	recommended order
complaint	formal hearing	stipulation
complainant	informal hearing	subpoena
Division of Administrative Hearings (DOAH)	legally sufficient	summary suspension
	notice of noncompliance	

PROCEDURES FOR INVESTIGATIONS AND HEARINGS

In Florida, the legal bases for investigations and hearings are:

- Chapter 120, F.S. (Administrative Procedure Act);
- Chapter 455, F.S. (Regulation of Professions and Occupations);
- Chapter 475, F.S. (Florida Real Estate License Law);
- Chapter 28, Sections 101 through 110 (Division of Administrative Hearings [DOAH] Rules), Florida Administrative Code (F.A.C.); and
- Chapter 61J2 (Florida Real Estate Commission), Florida Administrative Code (F.A.C.).

475.021, F.S.

The Division of Real Estate (DRE) is assigned the responsibility for investigative functions related to real estate. This includes DRE investigations to verify information provided by applicants as well as investigations of complaints against licensees. Based on its findings, the DRE prosecutes licensees before the Florida Real Estate Commission.

455.225, F.S.
455.203(7), F.S.
120.62, F.S.

The DRE investigates applications for licensure to determine whether all requirements and qualifications have been met. The investigative process also includes determining whether licensed brokers and sales associates are guilty of violating the laws of Florida or some other state or federal law. An investigator may require a report (such as escrow records), make an inspection of the broker's office, or make other investigative demands only as authorized by statute. Any person who is asked to respond to a request or demand for an oral statement by a state agency is entitled to a copy of the transcript in the same manner as any other public record request under Chapter 119, F.S., provided the agency had the proceeding transcribed. (*Note:* State agencies are required to tape-record official proceedings; however, they are not required to transcribe official proceedings.)

COMPLAINT PROCESS—SEVEN STEPS

Seven steps are involved in the process of dealing with complaints of alleged violations:

1. A complaint is filed
2. Investigation of the complaint
3. Probable cause determination
4. Formal complaint is issued if probable cause is found
5. Informal hearing or formal hearing is conducted
6. Final order is issued
7. Judicial review (appeal) of the final order

Step 1: Filing the Complaint

475.25, F.S.
455.225, F.S.

The complaint process begins when a **complaint** (an alleged violation of a law or rule) is filed with the Department of Business and Professional Regulation (DBPR). Any complaint that is filed in writing and is legally sufficient will be investigated. A complaint is **legally sufficient** if it contains facts indicating that a *violation* of any of the following has occurred:

- Florida statute
- Any existing, legally enacted DBPR rule
- Any existing, legally enacted FREC rule

Anyone may file a complaint against a licensee, an applicant, or an unlicensed person for actions believed to be in violation of Chapter 475, F.S. The alleged violation(s) need not pertain to real estate transactions and need not have taken place in Florida. A Uniform Complaint Form is available from the DBPR.

The DBPR may investigate an anonymous complaint or one made by a confidential informant if the complaint is in writing and is legally sufficient; if the alleged violation of law or rules is substantial; and if the Department has reason to believe, after preliminary inquiry, that the alleged violations in the complaint are true.

WEB LINK

You can download the Uniform Complaint Form at the DRE's Form Center. The address is **www .myfloridalicense.com/dbpr/re/forms.html**. Scroll down to the middle of the page under Complaint Forms. Select "RE-2200 Uniform Complaint Form for Real Estate."

Consumers may also file a complaint online. Go to **www.myfloridalicense.com/dbpr/** and select "File a Complaint."

Step 2: Investigation

The Department may initiate an investigation on its own if it has reasonable cause to believe that a licensee has violated a Florida statute, Department rule, or FREC rule. Furthermore, the Department may conduct an investigation without notification to anyone subject to the investigation if the act under investigation is a criminal offense.

455.225, F.S.

If the original **complainant** (person who files the complaint) withdraws the complaint or otherwise indicates a desire not to cause it to be investigated or prosecuted to completion, the Department may continue with the investigation and the Commission may take the appropriate final action on the complaint. When an investigation of a subject is undertaken, the DBPR will forward a copy of the complaint to the subject or to the subject's attorney. The subject of the investigation may submit a written response to the complaint. The response must be considered by the probable-cause panel. A complaint and all information obtained during any resulting investigation must be treated as confidential until ten days after probable cause has been found to exist or the subject of the investigation waives the privilege of confidentiality, whichever occurs first.

The DBPR is empowered to administer oaths; take depositions; and examine respondents, witnesses, and complainants. It can also issue subpoenas to obtain records, documents, or information that is material to the investigation. A Department investigator interviews the subject of the allegation(s), and, if applicable, an audit is performed of any escrow account(s). Once the investigative process is completed, and provided the complaint is legally sufficient, the Department prepares a written investigative report that then is submitted to the probable-cause panel.

The report consists of the investigative findings and contains recommendations regarding the existence of **probable cause** (reasonable grounds for prosecution) and a recommended course of action.

120.60, F.S.
455.225(8),
F.S.

Summary suspension. In rare situations, during the investigative process, the DBPR or the DRE may uncover something so serious that it cannot allow the licensee to continue to endanger the public welfare. For example, the investigator may discover that a broker has stolen thousands of dollars from the escrow account. In such extreme circumstances, the DBPR or the FREC may decide that the licensee cannot be allowed to continue to practice real estate during the normal disciplinary process. Such situations require emergency action. The DBPR Secretary (or a legally appointed designee) has the authority to issue a **summary suspension** (also referred to as an *emergency suspension order* or *final summary order*).

When it has been demonstrated that a summary suspension is necessary, due process does not require a hearing prior to the emergency suspension, provided a formal proceeding for suspension or revocation is promptly instituted.

Step 3: Probable Cause

455.225(4), F.S.
61J2-20.009, F.A.C.

Chapter 455, F.S., mandates that the determination as to whether probable cause exists is made by majority vote of a board's probable cause panel, or by the DBPR, if the profession does not have a board. The FREC *probable-cause panel* is composed of two current members or one current and one former member of the FREC. The panel must include at least one professional member. If a former professional board member serves on the panel, the former Commissioner must currently hold an active real estate license. A consumer member, if available, may serve on the probable-cause panel.

455.207(4), F.S.

Probable-cause proceedings are not open to the public, and the remaining FREC members are prohibited from attending. The segregation of the Commission members allows the probable-cause panel to serve in a "grand jury" type of arrangement. Because the remaining commissioners do not participate in the probable-cause proceedings, they are able to maintain objectivity in the matter if it comes before the Commission in an informal hearing.

The probable-cause panel's sole responsibility is to determine whether probable cause exists. The probable-cause panel reviews the facts of the case and the staff attorney's recommendations. After a complete review of the record, the probable-cause panel makes a determination as to whether probable cause exists. If the complaint information presented to the probable-cause panel is not adequate in content, the panel may request, and the DBPR must provide, any available or necessary additional information. A request for additional information must be made within the time frame set forth in the statute.

The probable-cause panel must make a decision within 30 days after receipt of the final investigative report, unless an extension is granted by the Secretary of the Department. If the panel fails to act within the statutory time limit (plus legal extensions), the Department may make a determination in the case. If probable cause is found, the DBPR (or the FREC) must give timely written notice to a licensee's broker or employer when a formal complaint has been filed against a sales associate or a broker associate.

If the panel finds that probable cause does not exist, the DBPR is allowed ten days to override that decision and to file charges. Furthermore, if the Department finds that the panel was unwise in deciding that probable cause existed, it may choose not to prosecute a complaint. In such cases, the Department refers the matter to the FREC. The Commission may retain independent legal counsel, employ investigators, and continue the investigation if it deems necessary.

If the panel finds that probable cause does not exist, it may simply dismiss the case, or it may dismiss the case with a *letter of guidance* to the subject. (See Summary of Types of Administrative Penalties, page 126.) Once the probable-cause proceeding has been concluded, the complainant and the subject of the investigation are sent written notification of the outcome.

Step 4: Formal Complaint

455.225, F.S.

If probable cause is found to exist, the probable-cause panel will direct the Department to file a formal complaint against the subject of the investigation (respondent). A **formal complaint**, also referred to as an **administrative complaint**, is an outline of allegations of facts and charges against the licensee. When an administrative complaint is mailed to a licensee, the licensee also receives an Election of Rights. The licensee is instructed to select one of three options in the Election of Rights and return the completed Election of Rights form to the DBPR on or before the 21st day after receipt of the administrative complaint. The licensee may choose to:

1. not dispute the allegations of fact and request an informal hearing;

2. dispute the allegations of fact and request a formal hearing; or

3. not dispute the allegations of fact and waive the right to be heard.

Sometimes a licensee-respondent and the licensee's attorney (if the licensee has legal counsel) will meet with a DRE attorney prior to a hearing to discuss a possible settlement and enter into a stipulation. A **stipulation** is an agreement as to the facts of the case and the penalty reached between the attorneys for the DRE and the licensee or licensee's attorney. To be effective, any agreed upon stipulation must be approved by the FREC. The licensee and the licensee's legal counsel, where there is one, are encouraged to appear before the FREC to defend the stipulation. The FREC will approve or deny the stipulation during a Commission meeting. If the FREC denies the stipulation, it usually provides guidance to the DRE attorney concerning additional penalties it believes appropriate in order for it to support a revised stipulation.

Step 5: Case Is Presented in Either an Informal Hearing or a Formal Hearing

455.225(5), F.S.
120.57(2), F.S.
120.569, F.S.
61J2-2.032,
F.A.C.

If the licensee-respondent's case was not resolved with a stipulation, the respondent's case will either be heard by the FREC in an informal hearing or the case may be heard before an administrative law judge in a formal hearing. The licensee-respondent must admit to the alleged facts to be entitled to an informal hearing. If the licensee-respondent disputes the alleged facts that are made in the complaint, the licensee-respondent's case must be heard by an administrative law judge in a formal hearing. The licensee-respondent must be given at least 14 days' notice of a hearing. The notice of the hearing informs the licensee-respondent of the time, place, and nature of the hearing. The notice also includes a statement regarding the legal authority and jurisdiction under which the hearing is being held.

120.575(3), F.S.
455.2273(5),
F.S.
120.52, F.S.

An informal hearing is an expedited way of resolving the disciplinary case provided the licensee does not dispute the alleged facts stated in the complaint. During an **informal hearing**, normally held at a regular Commission meeting, the licensee-respondent is given an opportunity to explain the details of the case with supporting evidence and/or witnesses. Any commissioners who served on the probable-cause panel for the particular complaint may not participate in this informal hearing. If any party raises an issue of disputed fact during an informal hearing, the hearing is terminated and a formal hearing will be scheduled before an administrative law judge. The FREC will determine based on the admitted facts

455.225, F.S.
120.60(5), F.S.
120.57(1), F.S.

whether the licensee is guilty of the charges alleged in the complaint. If the licensee is found guilty of the charges, the FREC will determine which penalties are appropriate based on the details of the case, taking into consideration any *mitigating* circumstances (reasons to reduce the impact of the violation), and it will issue a final order. (Refer also to Step 6 below.)

If the licensee-respondent requests a **formal hearing** or if the licensee-respondent disputes the allegations, the DBPR requests that the case be prosecuted under Chapter 120, F.S. Hearings under Chapter 120 are conducted by full-time Florida administrative law judges who are employed by the **Division of Administrative Hearings (DOAH)**. The DOAH may legally employ only those persons who have been members of The Florida Bar in good standing for the preceding five years. Administrative law judges are not subject to control, supervision, or direction by any party, commission, or department of state government. Once an administrative law judge is assigned, the DBPR may take no further action except as a litigating party.

The administrative law judge has the power to swear witnesses, to take their testimony under oath, and to issue subpoenas. A **subpoena** is a command to appear at a certain time and place to give testimony or to produce records. Failure to comply with a subpoena could result in a finding of contempt of court.

455.2273(5), F.S.
120.57(3), F.S.
120.52, F.S.

The administrative law judge prepares and submits to the DBPR and to all other parties a **recommended order** that includes the administrative law judge's findings and conclusions and the recommended penalty, if any, in accordance with the Commission's range of penalties as set forth in rule. Any party of record in the case may submit (within the statutory time limit) written exceptions to the administrative law judge's recommended order.

WEB LINK

To learn more about the formal hearing process, visit the Florida Division of Administrative Hearings Web site at **www.doah.state.fl.us/ALJ/**. Click on "Statutes and Rules."

Step 6: Final Order

475.31, F.S.
455.225, F.S.
120.57, F.S.
61J2-24.001, F.A.C.

The FREC (with the members who served on the probable-cause panel excused) issues the **final order** in each disciplinary case. The final order is FREC's final decision as to innocence or guilt and the determination of the appropriate penalty. The FREC issues a final order at the conclusion of an informal hearing. If the matter was heard by an administrative law judge in a formal hearing, the FREC must review and consider the administrative law judge's findings and recommended order before issuing its final order.

The respondent may appear in person or be represented by an attorney or both. Independent legal counsel represents the Commission in disciplinary proceedings. The Commission members who did not serve on the probable-cause panel consider the administrative law judge's report and recommended order, plus any filed exceptions to the report and the accused party's final arguments, if any. After all final arguments are heard, the Commission members make a determination and issue the final order, concluding the quasi-judicial process.

The final order must be in writing. It must include the facts established during the proceeding and state each conclusion of law separately. A copy of the final order is mailed to each party in the case. The notice must inform the recipient of the appeal process. The final order becomes effective 30 days after it has been entered. A licensee has the right to practice real estate during the complaint process and up until the final order becomes effective.

Step 7: Judicial Review (Appeal)

475.37, F.S.
120.68, F.S.

The licensee-respondent may challenge the final order within 30 days by filing an appeal. The petition of judicial review (notice of appeal) must be filed with the DBPR and with the appropriate district court. The licensee may request a *stay of enforcement*. A stay of enforcement, if granted, stops the enforcement of a suspension or revocation in the final order pending the outcome of the appeal process. To obtain a stay of the final order, the district court of appeals must issue a *writ of supersedeas*. A writ of supersedeas is an order issued by a court containing a command to stay (stop), in this case, the DBPR from suspending or revoking a real estate license pending the outcome of the appeal process.

If the reviewing court finds that a material error in procedure by the FREC has affected the fairness of the hearing or the correctness of the action taken, the case will be sent back to the FREC for corrective action. Unless the court finds legitimate grounds to set aside, modify, remand for further FREC proceeding, order additional action by the FREC, or order some auxiliary relief under Florida Statute 120.68, the court is required to affirm (support) the action taken by the Commission.

The DBPR is authorized to seek judicial review of any final order issued by the Commission. If a FREC final order is affirmed, reversed, or set aside, a mandate (copy) is filed with the Commission attesting to that event. The respondent's rights and privileges as a licensee will be restored as of the date of filing, if the final order is reversed. Thereafter, the matters examined and the charges alleged cannot be reexamined in any other proceedings concerning the licensure of that person or party. When the inquiry or proceeding is in reference to an application to become licensed, the application must be approved and processed. If a court reverses or sets aside a final order, the court may award attorney's fees and costs to the aggrieved prevailing party.

Stipulation Case

Florida DBPR vs. R. G. Hansen, Respondent

What follows is information concerning an actual case (DBPR 2009006963). This case was resolved in a stipulation. The information has been summarized for education purposes.

Stipulation:

Petitioner, Florida DBPR, Division of Real Estate (DBPR), and Respondent, R. G. Hansen, hereby stipulate and agree that the Florida Real Estate Commission issue a Final Order adopting and incorporating the provision of this Stipulation as final agency action in this case.

Stipulated Facts and Conclusions of Law:

1. Respondent at all times held a valid active sales associate license.
2. Respondent admits that the DBPR served the Respondent with an Administrative Complaint charging Respondent with violation of provisions of Chapter 455 and 475, Florida Statutes.
3. Respondent neither admits nor denies the factual allegations in all counts of the Administrative Complaint.
4. Respondent was found guilty of having failed to advertise property or services in a manner in which reasonable persons would know they are dealing with a real

estate licensee. Respondent failed to include the licensed name of the brokerage firm in an advertisement, and having placed or caused to be placed an advertisement that is fraudulent, false, deceptive, or misleading in form or content, in violation of Rule 61J2-10.025, Florida Administrative Code, and Section 475.25(1)(c), Florida Statute.

Stipulated Disposition:

1. Respondent shall pay a fine of $500 and $650 in costs.

2. Respondent shall attend one two-day FREC general meeting. Respondent is placed under probation for a period of two years. Respondent must pass the 28-hour reactivation course. The education herein is in addition to any requirement for respondent to maintain his real estate license.

3. Noncompliance with the terms of this Stipulation shall result in the suspension of Respondent's license without notice to Respondent or further hearing, until Respondent submits satisfactory proof of compliance to the DBPR. The suspension period shall not exceed ten years.

4. A summary of the action of Final Order shall be published in the FREC *News and Report.*

5. The parties understand that this Stipulation is subject to the approval of the DBPR and of the FREC.

6. Respondent executes this Stipulation to avoid further administrative action with respect to these causes.

7. The FREC has not taken prior disciplinary action against Respondent.

VIOLATIONS AND PENALTIES

475.455, F.S.
475.42, F.S.
475.25, F.S.
61J2-24.002, F.A.C.

For the purposes of the following discussion, the term *license* also includes the terms *registration, certification,* and *permit.* The grounds and penalties for these actions are numerous and are listed in the following sections.

Grounds for Denial

Denial of an applicant's request for licensure keeps the applicant from becoming licensed to practice real estate in Florida. Several reasons for denial exist. Some denials result from errors made in the application process, or from failing the state licensing examination. When such instances occur, the applicant may correct or file a new application, or submit an application to retake the exam.

Examples of grounds for license denial are:

■ neglecting to answer completely all questions on the application;

■ neglecting to forward the proper fees with the application request;

■ neglecting to correct errors or omissions on applications returned; and

■ failing to complete successfully the required written examination.

475.181, F.S.
475.17, F.S.

Other grounds for denial are more serious and result in an applicant being denied licensure. Examples of cause for license denial are that the applicant:

■ lacked minimum qualifications;

REVOCATION OR CANCELLATION WITHOUT PREJUDICE

A license may be revoked or canceled if it was issued through the mistake or inadvertence of the Commission. Such revocation or cancellation shall not prejudice any subsequent application for licensure filed by the person against whom such action was taken.

Reference: Section 475.25(2), F.S.

1   ■ did not possess the character required by the provisions of Florida Statutes 455
2   and 475;
3   ■ did not possess the general competence to deal with the public, or complaints
4   against the applicant were received by the FREC or the DBPR;
5   ■ was guilty of acts that would have resulted in revocation or suspension of a
6   license had the applicant already been licensed;
7   ■ acted in violation of any provision of F.S. 475.42 or was at the time subject to
8   discipline under F.S. 475.25; and
9   ■ received assistance or cheated while taking a state exam.

10   If the FREC denies an applicant on two occasions, the applicant may appeal to the
11   Division of Administrative Hearings (DOAH). The DOAH makes a recommendation to
12   the FREC, which may adopt or reject the DOAH recommendation. A judicial court may
13   only vacate the order of the FREC if it denied the applicant due process or breached a
14   mandate of law. A court of law cannot force the FREC to issue a license because Florida
15   statutes reserved the power to grant or deny a real estate license to the FREC.

Grounds for Suspension

475.42, F.S.
475.25, F.S.

17   Suspension of an individual's license is a temporary penalty. The maximum period for
18   which the FREC may suspend a license is ten years. Florida statutes refer to many acts that
19   are illegal, any one of which may result in license suspension. Each illegal act constitutes
20   grounds for suspension or revocation of licensure, depending on the seriousness attached
21   to the offense by the Commission. A second suspension for the same or a different viola-
22   tion may result in revocation of the license, registration, certification, or permit.

Grounds for Revocation

475.31, F.S.
475.25, F.S.
455.227, F.S.
61J2-24.005,
F.A.C.

24   The most severe type of administrative penalty that the FREC is authorized to impose is
25   revocation of a license. Revocation of a license is permanent. When the FREC revokes
26   a license, that licensee is put out of the real estate business. Exceptions to "permanent"
27   occur when a licensee has filed for renewal but has not complied with the continuing or
28   post-licensing education requirements prior to the expiration date or when an individual
29   filed an application for licensure that contained false or fraudulent information. In such
30   cases, the applicant may not reapply for a sales associate's license for five years unless the

SUMMARY OF TYPES OF ADMINISTRATIVE PENALTIES

- *Denial* of license application (or refusal to renew a license).

- *Letter of reprimand* is a letter that is placed in the licensee's file describing a minor incidence of misconduct that resulted in no disciplinary action (also called a *letter of guidance*).

- *Notice of noncompliance* is a warning for a minor violation (an initial offense only) that allows a licensee 15 days to correct the minor infraction without consequence (nonresponse could result in disciplinary action).

- *Citation* concerns violations that are of no substantial threat to the public involving a fine that currently ranges from $100 to $500.

- *Probation* allows the licensee to continue to practice real estate under the guidance of the FREC for a period of time while completing conditions specified by the FREC such as to complete education courses, attend FREC meetings, and satisfy all of the terms of the penalty.

- *Fine* may be up to $5,000 for each violation of Chapter 455 and Chapter 475.

- *Suspension* of a license (for up to 10 years).

- *Revocation* of a license is permanent (with continuing education and license application exceptions).

Commission specifies a lesser period of time in the final order based on mitigating factors presented by the licensee. At their discretion the FREC is empowered to revoke a licensee's license for any of the causes that constitute grounds for suspension or denial. Suspension or revocation plus a $5,000 fine is the minimum penalty for obtaining a license by fraud, misrepresentation, or concealment.

When a real estate broker's license is suspended or revoked, all licenses issued to sales associates who work for the penalized broker are placed in involuntary inactive status. If the revoked or suspended broker is a partnership or corporation, affected sales associates, partners, officers, and directors may request registration with a new employer or in the same partnership or corporation if it reorganizes to requalify under Florida statutes and FREC rules.

TYPES OF PENALTIES

475.42, F.S.

There are three types of penalties that may be imposed for violations of the real estate license law: administrative, civil, and criminal.

LICENSURE REISSUE

The Department shall reissue the license of a licensee against whom disciplinary action was taken upon

certification by the Commission that the licensee has complied with all of the terms and conditions of the

final order imposing discipline.

Reference: Section 475.25(3), F.S.

1   ## Administrative Penalties

475.25, F.S.
455.227, F.S.
61J2-24.001,
F.A.C.

2   The Commission may impose an administrative penalty for violations of the law or rules
3   and regulations. Possible administrative penalties imposed by the FREC include denial
4   of an application for a license; refusal to recertify a license for renewal; revocation of a
5   license; suspension of a license for not more than ten years; a fine not to exceed $5,000 for
6   each separate violation of Chapters 455 and 475, F.S.; and probation, reprimand, or other
7   penalty (for example, publication of the disciplinary action taken against a licensee and
8   the requirement to complete additional education).

9   The FREC may, in addition to other disciplinary penalties, place a licensee on *proba-*
10 *tion.* The Commission is empowered to set the time period and conditions of probation.
11 Probationary conditions may include, for example, requiring the licensee to attend a pre-
12 license or post-license course or other educational offering, to submit to and successfully
13 complete the state-administered examination, or to be subject to periodic inspections by
14 a DBPR investigator.

455.225(3), F.S.
120.695, F.S.
61J2-24.003,
F.A.C.

15 The DBPR/DRE may issue a **notice of noncompliance** as a first response to a minor
16 violation by a licensee. The notice must identify the specific statute(s) and rule(s) vio-
17 lated, provide information on how to comply, and state the time to comply. The FREC sets
18 the guidelines for which violations warrant a notice of noncompliance. The Commission
19 has established by rule minor violations that do not endanger the public health, safety,
20 and welfare and that do not demonstrate a serious inability to practice the profession. Rule
21 24.003, F.A.C., lists the various violations for which a notice of noncompliance may be
22 issued for a first-time offense, including, for example, a sales associate serving as an officer
23 of a brokerage corporation. A notice of noncompliance may also be issued if a broker fails
24 to register a trade name, does not have the proper office entrance sign, or neglects to sign
25 the escrow account reconciliation in instances where the account balances. If a licensee
26 fails to take action to correct the minor violation within 15 days after being notified, the
27 licensee may be issued a citation. However, if the violation is not listed in the citation
28 rule, the licensee may be subjected to other disciplinary penalties.

455.228, F.S.
455.224, F.S.
61J2-24.002,
F.A.C.

29 DBPR investigator-auditors have the authority to immediately issue citations in the
30 field for minor violations discovered during an investigation or audit. **Citations** involve
31 fines that currently range from $100 to $500 per offense and may include other assess-
32 ments (for example, require educational course attendance). Several of the more common
33 offenses cited include failure to timely notify the DBPR of a licensee's current mailing
34 address or of a change in the current mailing address, failure to secure the written permis-
35 sion of all interested parties prior to placing trust funds into an interest bearing escrow

account, and advertising in a manner in which a reasonable person would not know that one is dealing with a licensee or brokerage. A licensee receiving a citation has 30 days to accept or reject the alleged violation(s), as specified in the citation. If the licensee does not dispute the matter, the citation penalty will become effective (a final order) and the case will be closed. If the licensee disputes the alleged violation(s), the licensee must file a written objection. The licensee will be allowed to state his or her case and, based on the merits, will have the case dismissed or carried forward to a formal hearing. If the licensee fails to pay the fine in a timely manner, the FREC will file an administrative complaint.

The FREC is limited to issuing administrative penalties on real estate licensees. The Commission can *not* issue a penalty of incarceration (jail sentence). The FREC does *not* have the authority to order restitution to an injured party. If the acts of a licensee harm a consumer, the injured party may seek damages in a court of law.

Civil Penalties

Civil penalties may be enforced by the courts if a person has performed any real estate services without a license. The courts may rule that no sale commission is due.

Criminal Penalties

775.081-3, F.S.
455.2277, F.S.

A violation of Florida Statute 475 or any lawful order, rule, or regulation is legally a misdemeanor of the second degree (except as noted below). It may be punishable by a fine of not more than $500 and/or by imprisonment for not more than 60 days. A corporation may only be fined, because a corporation cannot be imprisoned. All imprisonment penalties or fines, except administrative fines, must be obtained in a court of law because the Commission lacks the authority to assess such penalties.

475.453(3)(a), F.S.

First-degree criminal penalties. There is one violation of real estate license law that is a first-degree misdemeanor: failing to provide accurate and current rental information for a fee.

The penalty for a first-degree misdemeanor is a fine of not more than $1,000 and/or up to one year in jail.

455.227(2), F.S.

Other penalty actions. The assessing of one of the three types of penalties (administrative, civil, or criminal) does not prevent or affect the prosecution of any other proceeding. The same facts that are the basis for the prosecution of violations of the real estate license law may prove to be an offense committed under other state statutes. Both violations may be charged, but the punishment (fine and/or sentence) cannot be greater than the highest prescribed in either statute. However, the Commission may, in addition to any other disciplinary action imposed, assess costs related to the investigation and prosecution of a case, excluding attorney's fees.

475.42(1)(a), F.S.
455.228, F.S.

Unlicensed practice of real estate. The Secretary of the DBPR assigns a probable cause panel and a hearing officer to hear cases of unlicensed activity. The DBPR can issue fines of up to $5,000 per count to a person it finds guilty of unlicensed activity.

The DBPR may issue a cease and desist order to an unlicensed person who has violated F.S. 475, F.S. 455, or any other statute relating to the practice of real estate. The DBPR may also file a proceeding in the name of the state requesting the circuit court to issue an injunction or a *writ of mandamus* ordering the unlicensed activity to stop. If the person found guilty of unlicensed activity refuses to pay a fine issued by the DBPR,

1 it may seek enforcement of the penalty through a civil court. The DBPR must refer
2 any criminal matters to the State Attorney's Office. The state attorney may institute
3 criminal prosecution against an unlicensed person. It is a felony of the third degree for
4 a person to perform real estate services for compensation without a real estate license.
5 The criminal penalty for a third-degree felony is a fine of not more than $5,000 and/or
6 up to five years in jail.

WEB LINK

The DBPR maintains a Web page dedicated to unlicensed activity. Go to the DBPR Web site at www.myfloridalicense.com/dbpr/reg/UnlicensedActivity.html. Consumers may call 866-532-1440 toll free to report unlicensed activity.

FREC DISCIPLINARY GUIDELINES

455.2273, F.S.
61J2-24.003, F.A.C.
61J2-24.002, F.A.C.
61J2-24.001, F.A.C.

8 The Commission uses guidelines that apply to each specific ground for disciplinary action
9 that it may impose. The purpose of these disciplinary guidelines is to give notice to licensees
10 of the range of penalties that normally will be imposed for each count (offense) during a
11 formal or informal hearing. A finding of *mitigating* (less severe) circumstances or *aggravating*
12 (more severe) circumstances allows the Commission to impose a penalty other than those
13 provided. The extent of a penalty, ranging from least to most severe, is reprimand to suspen-
14 sion and revocation or denial. Combinations of these and other penalties are permitted.
15 Grounds and penalties are listed in Figure 6.1, Disciplinary Guidelines (see page 136) in
16 numerical order by statute.

REAL ESTATE RECOVERY FUND

475.482, F.S.
215.37, F.S.

18 The Florida Real Estate Recovery Fund's purpose is to reimburse an individual or business
19 entity judged by a Florida court to have suffered monetary (compensatory) damages as a
20 result of an act committed by a broker or sales associate who:

- was at the time the alleged act was committed, the holder of a current, valid, active real estate license issued under Chapter 475;
- was not the seller, buyer, landlord, or tenant in the transaction (except as noted below) nor an officer or director of a corporation, a member of a partnership, a member of a limited liability company, or a partner of a limited liability partner-ship which was the seller, buyer, landlord, or tenant in the transaction; and
- was acting solely in the capacity of a real estate licensee in the transaction.

28 A claim for recovery will not be considered unless a civil suit resulted in a final judg-
29 ment against an *individual licensee* as defendant (not merely against a real estate brokerage
30 entity). A claimant must cause a *writ of execution* to be issued on the judgment, and the
31 results (an asset search) must show that insufficient funds or property are available to sat-
32 isfy the judgment. The claimant must also execute an affidavit showing that the final judg-
33 ment is not on appeal or, if it was the subject of an appeal, that the appellate proceedings
34 have concluded and show the outcome of the appeal. The filing of a bankruptcy petition
35 by a licensee does not relieve a claimant from the obligation to obtain a final judgment
36 against the licensee in order to recover from the fund. The FREC may waive the require-
37 ment for a final judgment if a bankruptcy court obstructs obtaining such a judgment.

KEY CONCEPTS OF RECOVERY FUND

- Reimburses consumers who are financially injured by a licensee

- Licensee must hold active license at time of alleged act and acted in capacity of a real estate licensee in the transaction

- Spouse of the offending licensee (judgment debtor) is not eligible for reimbursement

- A civil suit was filed, a final judgment issued against licensee, and an attempt was made to collect on the judgment

- Claim must be made within two years of the alleged act or within two years of the discovery of the alleged act

- Maximum payment from one judgment (single transaction) is $50,000

- Maximum payment based on multiple judgments (more than one transaction) against a licensee is $150,000

- At time of payment from fund due to misconduct, license is automatically suspended until money plus interest is repaid to the fund

- Punitive damages and interest cannot be reimbursed from the fund

- A broker who complies with an escrow disbursement order and is later sued may be reimbursed from the fund without penalty

Time limit to file a claim. A claim must be made within two years of either the alleged violation or discovery of the alleged violation. However, in no case may a claim for recovery be made more than four years after the date of the alleged violation.

475.484, F.S.

Monetary limits of claims. Payments for claims arising out of the same transaction are limited, in total, to $50,000 or the unsatisfied portion of a judgment claim, whichever is less, regardless of the number of claimants or parcels of real estate involved in the transaction. Payments for claims based on judgments against one broker or sales associate may not exceed, in total, $150,000.

475.482(3), F.S.

A total of $1 million is the authorized limit for the fund at any one time. Funds are accumulated by charging each active and inactive licensee a recovery fund fee when a new license is issued or an existing license is renewed. In addition, fines imposed by the FREC and collected by the DBPR are transferred into the fund under Section 475.482(4), F.S. The collection of these special fees stops when the limit is reached, and it begins again when the amount drops below $500,000. At that time, a fee of $3.50 per year for brokers and $1.50 per year for sales associates is added to the license fee for both new and renewed licenses. The Chief Financial Officer makes all payments from the fund following receipt of a voucher signed by the DBPR Secretary.

475.484(7), F.S.

Mandatory suspension. Suspension of a licensee's license is mandatory on payment of any amount from the Real Estate Recovery Fund in settlement of a claim to satisfy a judgment against any licensee as described in 475.482(1), F.S. The license is automatically suspended on the date of payment from the recovery fund and will not be restored until the licensee has repaid the amount paid from the fund in full (plus interest).

Claim resulting from an EDO. If a broker who complied with an escrow disbursement order is later required by a court of law to pay damages as a result of legal actions taken by the buyer or seller in the transaction, the FREC is authorized to order reimbursement to the broker for the amount of the judgment against the broker up to $50,000. No disciplinary action will be taken against a broker who had previously requested an EDO and followed its instructions. The broker's license will not be suspended, and no repayment to the fund is required.

To be eligible for reimbursement, the broker must notify the FREC of the court case and the broker-defendant must diligently defend in court the disputed actions concerning the transaction. Furthermore, Florida Statute provides for the Commission to pay the broker-defendant's reasonable attorney's fees and court costs and, if the plaintiff prevails in court, the plaintiff's (person who filed the lawsuit) reasonable attorney's fees and court costs. In cases other than those regarding compliance with an EDO, court costs and attorney's fees may not be awarded. In all cases, punitive damages, treble (triple) damages, and interest may not be recovered from the fund.

Licensee as buyer or seller. A real estate licensee who was the buyer or seller (lessor or lessee) in a real estate transaction may also make a claim against the fund *provided* the licensee did *not* act in the capacity of a real estate agent. In other words, if a licensed person is the buyer or seller of real property and suffers monetary damages as a result of an act committed by another licensed broker or sales associate who did act in the capacity of an agent, the fact that the victim is licensed will not prevent the victim from seeking reimbursement from the fund.

475.483, F.S.

Individuals who cannot make a claim. The following individuals cannot make a claim for recovery from the fund:

- The spouse of the offending licensee (judgment debtor).
- A licensee who acted as a single agent or transaction broker in a real estate transaction that is the subject of the claim.
- An individual whose claim is against a licensee who owned the property under contract, and the licensee was dealing for licensee's own account. (The licensee was not acting as a broker or sales associate.)
- A person who files a claim against a licensee who did not hold a valid and current license at the time of the transaction.
- Individual who obtains a judgment against a real estate brokerage entity only rather than against a licensed individual.

Real Estate Recovery Fund Case

P. Warner, Claimant vs. D. Hughes, Licensee

What follows is information concerning an actual Recovery Fund Claim (RFC 2010018090). The information has been summarized for education purposes.

Findings of Fact:

1. Claimant is a nonlicensee and is unrelated to the licensee.
2. Licensee held a valid real estate license at the time of the transaction.

3. Hughes acted solely as a broker in accepting earnest money deposits totaling $44,800 related to claimant's purchase of three parcels of Florida real property.

4. None of the transactions closed and the licensee failed to account for or return the deposits upon claimant's demand, and converted said sums to licensee's own use.

5. Claimant notified the FREC of his intention to make a claim against the licensee and the Recovery Fund, within two years of the date the claimant became aware of the licensee's misappropriation of escrow funds.

6. A final judgment against the individual licensee arising from the violation of his duties as a real estate licensee was entered in circuit court and the time for appeal of the judgment has passed.

7. Claimant has attempted to execute on the judgment but after reasonable inquiry has been unable to locate assets of the licensee.

8. The claim does not exceed the $50,000 cap imposed by Florida statute and total claims paid based on judgments against licensee do not exceed, in total, $150,000.

Order:

1. The FREC ordered payment from the Recovery Fund in the amount of $44,800 be made to the claimant.

2. The license of the licensee shall be automatically suspended upon the date of payment from the Recovery Fund and may not be reinstated until the licensee has repaid in full, plus interest, the amount paid from the Recovery Fund.

3. Within 30 days of the filing date of this order, the licensee may institute a review proceeding by filing the Notice of Appeal with the appropriate district court of appeals.

LEGAL TERMS TO KNOW

As a final focus on license law and to assist you in learning important but often difficult-to-understand real estate terms in the legal realm, the following definitions and examples are provided to supplement those in the text, cases, and glossary:

- *Breach (as in breach of duty or breach of contract).* The breaking of a promise or obligation, either by an act of commission or omission; default; nonperformance.

- *Commingle (intermingle).* To mix the money or other personal property of a buyer or seller with a broker's own money or property; to combine escrow money with personal or business funds.

- *Concealment.* The withholding of information or a material fact. *Example:* In a fiduciary relationship, the broker has a duty to speak, unless the principal knows the information or fact.

- *Conversion.* Brokers may not use earnest money funds for their personal use. A licensee's personal use or misuse of client (or customer) monies.

- *Culpable negligence.* Guilty of failing to use the care a reasonable person would exercise. *Example:* Broker does not give ordinary, careful attention to the brokerage and does not exercise reasonable control over the brokerage's agents.

- *Failure to account for and deliver.* The act of failing to pay money to a person entitled to receive it. *Example:* Broker's failure to pay an earnest money deposit at the title closing in accordance with the contract for sale and purchase.

- *Fraud.* Intentional deceit for the purpose of inducing another to rely on information to part with some valuable thing belonging to him or her or to surrender a legal right. *Example:* Seller or broker not disclosing known defects or remaining "silent" under such circumstances when the buyer could not have verified for himself or herself.

- *Material fact.* A piece of information that is relevant to a person making a decision and that affects the value of the real property. *Example:* Information about the condition of a property, such as known defects or code violations.

- *Misrepresentation.* An untrue statement of fact. An incorrect or false misrepresentation of the facts. *Example:* Failing to indicate in a newspaper that a listed property is advertised by a real estate licensee.

- *Moral turpitude.* Conduct contrary to honesty, good morals, justice, or accepted custom. Case law has further defined moral turpitude to mean a depravity against society. *Example:* Embezzlement and crimes of larceny, including writing bad checks, are generally considered moral turpitude.

Practical Examples of Legal Terms

Practice Problem 1

Broker Joe is the property manager for a duplex that rents for $1,000 per unit. Last month, he collected the rent from each tenant at the beginning of the month. Because Joe was having trouble making his mortgage payments, he used the $2,000 to pay his lender. Two weeks later, Joe received a commission check from a sale and then paid the owner of the duplex the $2,000 of rent. Which legal term applies to Broker Joe's misuse of the rent money?

Practice Problem 2

Late Friday evening, Morris gave Susan, a sales associate with XYZ Brokerage, $1,000 in cash as a binder deposit with an offer. Susan was uncomfortable holding that much cash, so she used the bank night depository to place the money in her checking account. Susan then wrote a check to the escrow account for $1,000. Which legal term describes Susan's actions?

Practice Problem 3

On July 14, Broker Bill received an earnest money check for $5,000 payable to John Stetson, Attorney Trust Account. Bill placed the check in his desk drawer until he was able to get it to the attorney's office. When he received a copy of the closing statement before closing, the buyer noted that the earnest money was not mentioned. The attorney had no record of an earnest money deposit. Which legal term best describes this situation?

The solutions to the Practice Problems are located on page 135.

SUMMARY OF IMPORTANT POINTS

- Seven steps comprise the complaint process:

  1. A complaint (an alleged violation of a law or rule) is filed with the DBPR.

  2. If the complaint is legally sufficient, the DBPR conducts an investigation and notifies the licensee-respondent. The complaint and the information obtained during the investigation are kept confidential until ten days after probable cause has been found to exist. The DBPR's investigative report is forwarded to the probable-cause panel. In rare situations deemed to be too serious to allow the licensee to continue to practice real estate while the complaint process proceeds, the DBPR Secretary may issue a summary (emergency) suspension.

  3. The probable-cause panel consists of two FREC members. The probable-cause panel makes a determination as to whether probable cause exists.

  4. If probable cause is found, the DBPR issues a formal (administrative) complaint. An Election of Rights is mailed with the complaint to the licensee. The licensee has 21 days to (1) not dispute the allegations of fact and request an informal hearing, (2) dispute the allegations of fact and request a formal hearing, or (3) not dispute the allegations of fact and waive the right to be heard. The licensee-respondent may enter into a stipulation (an agreement as to the facts of the case and the penalty reached between the attorneys for the DRE and the licensee).

  5. If there are no disputed facts, the Commission (probable-cause panel members are excused) decides the case and imposes the penalty in an informal hearing held during a regular FREC meeting. If the licensee-respondent requested a formal hearing or if the respondent disputes the allegations, the case is heard by a Florida administrative law judge in a formal hearing. The administrative law judge prepares a recommended order.

  6. The FREC imposes the final order (members of the probable-cause panel do not participate). The final order becomes effective 30 days after it has been entered.

  7. The licensee-respondent may appeal the final order.

- The FREC may impose an administrative penalty for violations of law or rules and regulations. A citation is issued for violations that are of no substantial threat to the public. Such citations carry fines ranging from $100 to $500. The DBPR may issue a notice of noncompliance as a first response to a minor violation. More serious offenses are punishable by fines of up to $5,000 for each violation of Chapters 455 and 475 and/or a suspension of up to 10 years. In extreme cases, the FREC may revoke a license.

- Failing to provide accurate and current rental information for a fee is a misdemeanor of the first degree, punishable in a court of law by a fine of up to $1,000 and/or by imprisonment of up to one year.

- All other violations of license law are misdemeanors of the second degree, punishable by a fine of up to $500 and/or by imprisonment of up to 60 days.

- Unlicensed practice of real estate for compensation is a felony of the third degree. The penalty is a fine of up to $5,000 and/or up to five years in jail.

1   ■   The real estate recovery fund is a separate account used to reimburse people
2   who have suffered monetary damages as a result of license law violations by
3   a licensee. Claims are limited to $50,000 per transaction and no more than
4       $150,000 against one licensee involving multiple transactions. The license is
5   automatically suspended upon payment from the fund until the fund is reim-
6   bursed (EDO exception).

Practical Examples of Legal Terms Solutions

(Practice Problems are located on page 133.)

Practice Problem 1 Solution

Broker Joe is guilty of conversion. He used the landlord's money to make his
mortgage payment. If the checks were made payable to Joe, he should have
deposited them in his escrow account.

Practice Problem 2 Solution

Sue has commingled trust funds. Sue is required to deliver the $1,000 to her bro-
ker. By depositing the funds in her checking account, Sue has commingled the
buyer's money with her own money.

Practice Problem 3 Solution

Because Broker Bill did not deposit the check with the attorney's trust account,
Bill can be charged with failing to account for or deliver escrowed property.
According to administrative rule, Bill could receive an administrative fine not to
exceed $5,000 and up to a five-year suspension.

FIGURE 6.1 ■ **Disciplinary Guidelines: 61J2-24.001, F.A.C. (Effective date, July 2010)**

	PENALTY RANGE	
Violation	**First Violation**	**Second and Subsequent Violations**
(a) Section 475.22, F.S. Broker fails to maintain office or sign at entrance of office	(a) Reprimand to $500 administrative fine	(a) 90-day suspension and $1,000 administrative fine
(b) Section 475.24, F.S. Failure to register a branch office	(b) Reprimand to $500 administrative fine	(b) 90-day suspension and $1,000 administrative fine
(c) Section 475.25(1)(b), F.S. Fraud, misrepresentation, and dishonest dealing	(c) $1,000 to $2,500 administrative fine and 30-day suspension to revocation	(c) $2,500 to $5,000 administrative fine and 6-month suspension to revocation
Concealment, false promises, false pretenses by trick, scheme or device	$1,000 to $2,500 administrative fine and 30-day suspension to revocation	$2,500 to $5,000 administrative fine and 6-month suspension to revocation
Culpable negligence or breach of trust	$1,000 to $2,500 administrative fine and 30-day suspension to revocation	$2,500 to $5,000 administrative fine and 6-month suspension to revocation
Violating a duty imposed by law or by the terms of a listing agreement; aided, assisted or conspired with another; or formed an intent, design or scheme to engage in such misconduct and committed an overt act in furtherance of such intent, design or scheme	$1,000 to $2,500 administrative fine and 30-day suspension to revocation	$2,500 to $5,000 administrative fine and 6-month suspension to revocation
(d) Section 475.25(1)(c), F.S. False, deceptive or misleading advertising	(d) $250 to $1,000 administrative fine and 30- to 90-day suspension	(d) $1,000 to $5,000 administrative fine and 90-day suspension to revocation
(e) Section 475.25(1)(d), F.S. Failed to account or deliver to any person as required by agreement or law, escrowed property	(e) $250 to $1,000 administrative fine and suspension to revocation	(e) $1,000 to $5,000 administrative fine and suspension to revocation
(f) Section 475.25(1)(e), F.S. Violated any rule or order or provision under Chapters 475 and 455, F.S.	(f) $250 to $1,000 administrative fine and suspension to revocation	(f) $1,000 to $5,000 administrative fine and suspension to revocation
(g) Section 475.25(1)(f), F.S. Convicted or found guilty of a crime related to real estate or involving moral turpitude or fraudulent or dishonest dealing	(g) $250 to $1,000 administrative fine and 30-day suspension to revocation	(g) $1,000 to $5,000 administrative fine and suspension to revocation
(h) Section 475.25(1)(g), F.S. Has license disciplined or acted against or an application denied by another jurisdiction	(h) $250 to $1,000 administrative fine and 30-day suspension to revocation	(h) $1,000 to $5,000 administrative fine and suspension to revocation
(i) Section 475.25(1)(h), F.S. Has shared a commission with or paid a fee to a person not properly licensed under Chapter 475, F.S.	(i) $250 to $1,000 administrative fine and 30-day suspension to revocation	(i) $1,000 to $5,000 administrative fine and suspension to revocation

FIGURE 6.1 ■ **Disciplinary Guidelines: 61J2-24.001, F.A.C. (Effective date, July 2010) (Continued)**

PENALTY RANGE

Violation	First Violation	Second and Subsequent Violations
(j) Section 475.25(1)(i), F.S. Impairment by drunkenness, or use of drugs or temporary mental derangement	(j) Suspension for the period of incapacity	(j) Suspension for the period of incapacity
(k) Section 475.25(1)(j), F.S. Rendered an opinion that the title to property sold is good or merchantable when not based on opinion of a licensed attorney or has failed to advise prospective buyer to consult an attorney on the merchantability of title or to obtain title insurance	(k) $250 to $1,000 administrative fine and 30-day suspension to revocation	(k) $1,000 to $5,000 administrative fine and suspension to revocation
(l) Section 475.25(l)(k), F.S. Has failed, if a broker, to deposit any money in an escrow account immediately upon receipt until disbursement is properly authorized. Has failed, if a sales associate, to place any money to be escrowed with his registered employer	(l) $250 to $1,000 administrative fine and 30-day suspension to revocation	(l) $1,000 to $5,000 administrative fine and suspension to revocation
(m) Section 475.25(1)(l), F.S. Has made or filed a report or record which the licensee knows to be false or willfully failed to file a report or record or willfully impeded such filing as required by State or Federal Law	(m) $250 to $1,000 administrative fine and 30-day suspension to revocation	(m) $1,000 to $5,000 administrative fine and suspension to revocation
(n) Section 475.25(1)(m), F.S. Obtained a license by fraud, misrepresentation or concealment	(n) $250 to $1,000 administrative fine and 30-day suspension to revocation	(n) $1,000 to $5,000 administrative fine and suspension to revocation
(o) Section 475.25(1)(n), F.S. Confined in jail, prison or mental institution; or through mental disease can no longer practice with skill and safety	(o) $250 to $1,000 administrative fine and suspension to revocation	(o) $1,000 to $5,000 administrative fine and suspension to revocation
(p) Section 475.25(1)(o), F.S. Guilty for the second time of misconduct in the practice of real estate that demonstrates incompetent, dishonest or negligent dealings with investors	(p) $1,000 to $5,000 administrative fine and a 1 year suspension to revocation	
(q) Section 475.25(1)(p), F.S. Failed to give Commission 30-day written notice after a guilty or nolo contendere plea or convicted of any felony	(q) $500 to $1,000 administrative fine and suspension to revocation	(q) $1,000 to $5,000 administrative fine and suspension to revocation

FIGURE 6.1 ■ Disciplinary Guidelines: 61J2-24.001, F.A.C. (Effective date, July 2010) (Continued)

PENALTY RANGE

Violation	First Violation	Second and Subsequent Violations
(r) Section 475.25(1)(r), F.S. Failed to follow the requirements of a written listing agreement	(r) $250 to $1,000 administrative fine and suspension to revocation	(r) $1,000 to $5,000 administrative fine and suspension to revocation
(s) Section 475.25(1)(s), F.S. Has had a registration suspended, revoked or otherwise acted against in any jurisdiction	(s) $250 to $1,000 administrative fine and 60-day suspension to revocation	(s) $1,000 to $5,000 administrative fine and suspension to revocation
(t) Section 475.25(1)(t), F.S. Violated the Uniform Standards of Professional Appraisal Practice as defined in Section 475.611, F.S.	(t) $250 to $1,000 administrative fine and 30-day suspension to revocation	(t) $1,000 to $5,000 administrative fine and suspension to revocation
(u) Section 475.25(1)(u), F.S. Has failed, if a broker, to direct, control, or manage a broker associate or sales associate employed by such broker	(u) $250 to $1,000 administrative fine and suspension to revocation	(u) $1,000 to $5,000 administrative fine and suspension to revocation
(v) Section 475.25(1)(v), F.S. Has failed, if a broker, to review the brokerage's trust accounting procedures in order to ensure compliance with this chapter	(v) $250 to $2,500 administrative fine and suspension to revocation	(v) $1,000 to $5,000 administrative fine and suspension to revocation
(w) Section 475.42(1)(a), F.S. Practice without a valid and current license	(w) $250 to $2,500 administrative fine and suspension to revocation	(w) $1,000 to $5,000 administrative fine and suspension to revocation
(x) Section 475.42(1)(b), F.S. Practicing beyond scope as a sales associate	(x) $250 to $1,000 administrative fine and suspension to revocation	(x) $1,000 to $5,000 administrative fine and suspension to revocation
(y) Section 475.42(1)(c), F.S. Broker employs a sales associate who is not the holder of a valid and current license	(y) $250 to $1,000 administrative fine and suspension to revocation	(y) $1,000 to $5,000 administrative fine and suspension to revocation
(z) Section 475.42(1)(d), F.S. A sales associate shall not collect any money in connection with any real estate brokerage transaction except in the name of the employer	(z) $250 to $1,000 administrative fine and suspension to revocation	(z) $1,000 to $5,000 administrative fine and suspension to revocation
(aa) Section 475.42(1)(g), F.S. Makes false affidavit or affirmation or false testimony before the Commission	(aa) $250 to $1,000 administrative fine and suspension to revocation	(aa) $1,000 to $5,000 administrative fine and suspension to revocation
(bb) Section 475.42(1)(h), F.S. Fails to comply with subpoena	(bb) $250 to $1,000 administrative fine and suspension	(bb) $1,000 to $5,000 administrative fine and suspension to revocation
(cc) Section 475.42(1)(i), F.S. Obstructs or hinders the enforcement of Chapter 475, F.S.	(cc) $250 to $1,000 administrative fine and suspension to revocation	(cc) $1,000 to $5,000 administrative fine and suspension to revocation

F I G U R E 6.1 ■ **Disciplinary Guidelines: 61J2-24.001, F.A.C. (Effective date, July 2010) (Continued)**

PENALTY RANGE

Violation	First Violation	Second and Subsequent Violations
(dd) Section 475.42(1)(j), F.S. No broker or sales associate shall place upon the public records any false, void or unauthorized information that affects the title or encumbers any real property	(dd) $250 to $2,500 administrative fine and suspension to revocation	(dd) $1,000 to $5,000 administrative fine and suspension to revocation
(ee) Section 475.42(1)(k), F.S. Failed to register trade name with the Commission	(ee) $250 to $1,000 administrative fine	(ee) $1,000 to $5,000 administrative fine and suspension to revocation
(ff) Section 475.42(1)(l), F.S. No person shall knowingly conceal information relating to violations of Chapter 475, F.S.	(ff) $250 to $1,000 administrative fine and suspension	(ff) $1,000 to $5,000 administrative fine and suspension to revocation
(gg) Section 475.42(1)(m), F.S. Fails to have a current license as a broker or sales associate while listing or selling one or more timeshare periods per year	(gg) $250 to $1,000 administrative fine and suspension	(gg) $1,000 to $5,000 administrative fine and suspension to revocation
(hh) Section 475.42(1)(n), F.S. Licensee fails to disclose all material aspects of the resale of timeshare period or timeshare plan and the rights and obligations of both buyer or seller	(hh) $250 to $1,000 administrative fine and suspension	(hh) $1,000 to $5,000 administrative fine and suspension to revocation
(ii) Section 475.42(1)(o), F.S. Publication of false or misleading information; promotion of sales, leases and rentals	(ii) $250 to $1,000 administrative fine and suspension to revocation	(ii) $1,000 to $5,000 administrative fine and suspension to revocation
(jj) Section 475.451, F.S. School teaching real estate practice fails to obtain a permit from the department and does not abide by regulations of Chapter 475, F.S., and rules adopted by the Commission	(jj) $250 to $1,000 administrative fine and suspension	(jj) $1,000 to $5,000 administrative fine and suspension to revocation
(kk) Section 475.453, F.S. Broker or sales associate participates in any rental information transaction that fails to follow the guidelines adopted by the Commission and Chapter 475, F.S.	(kk) $250 to $1,000 administrative fine and suspension	(kk) $1,000 to $5,000 administrative fine and 90-day suspension to revocation

FIGURE 6.1 ■ **Disciplinary Guidelines: 61J2-24.001, F.A.C. (Effective date, July 2010) (Continued)**

	PENALTY RANGE	
Violation	**First Violation**	**Second and Subsequent Violations**
(ll) Section 475.5015, F.S. Failure to keep and make available to the department such books, accounts, and records as will enable the department to determine whether the broker is in compliance with the provisions of this chapter	(ll) $250 to $1,000 administrative fine and suspension to revocation	(ll) $1,000 to $5,000 administrative fine and 90-day suspension to revocation
(mm) Section 455.227(1)(s), F.S. Failing to comply with the educational course requirements for domestic violence	(mm) $250 to $1,000 administrative fine and suspension to revocation	(mm) $1,000 to $5,000 administrative fine and suspension to revocation
(nn) Section 455.227(1)(t), F.S. Failing to report in writing to the Commission within 30 days after the licensee is convicted or found guilty of, or entered a plea of nolo contendere or guilty to, regardless of adjudication, a crime in any jurisdiction.	(nn) $250 to $1,000 administrative fine and suspension to revocation	(nn) $1,000 to $5,000 administrative fine and suspension to revocation
(oo) Section 455.227(1)(u), F.S. Termination from a treatment program for impaired practitioners as described in Section 456.076 for failure to comply, without good cause, with the terms of the monitoring or treatment contract entered into by the licensee or failing to successfully complete a drug or alcohol treatment program	(oo) $250 to $1,000 administrative fine and suspension to revocation	(oo) $1,000 to $5,000 administrative fine and suspension to revocation

R E V I E W   Q U E S T I O N S

1. The probable-cause panel includes
   a. a total of two members.
   b. at least one professional member.
   c. at least one current member.
   d. all of the above.

2. A person is eligible to seek recovery from the Real Estate Recovery Fund if
   a. that person received a final judgment against a licensee in a legal action and the case was based on a real estate brokerage transaction (assuming no specific exceptions apply).
   b. that person is a licensed broker who acted as the agent in the transaction that is the subject of the claim.
   c. that person's claim is based on a real estate transaction in which the broker did not hold a valid, current, and active license at the time of the transaction.
   d. any of the above events has occurred.

3. The decision as to whether probable cause exists is made by a majority vote of the
   a. Commission.
   b. Commission or the Department, as appropriate.
   c. administrative law judges.
   d. probable-cause panel (or the Department if there is no panel).

4. Which action would cause a license to be revoked without prejudice?
   a. A licensee accepted an earnest money deposit on a property that he knew was encumbered by an undisclosed lien.
   b. The broker obtained his license by means of fraud, misrepresentation, or concealment.
   c. A sales associate received her license as a result of an administrative error by the Division of Real Estate.
   d. For the referral of real estate business a licensee shared a commission with a person (not party to the transaction) who did not have a real estate license.

5. Which offense is a misdemeanor of the first degree?
   a. Failing to provide current and accurate rental information for a fee.
   b. Publishing false or misleading information to induce a buyer to purchase real property.
   c. Failing to timely deposit earnest money into the escrow account.
   d. Failing to timely notify the FREC of conflicting demands.

6. Who prepares and submits a recommended order of findings and conclusions in a complaint case?
   a. Court of law
   b. Administrative law judge
   c. Probable-cause panel
   d. The DBPR

7. Any final order issued by the DBPR Secretary or a legally appointed designee that results from circumstances that pose an immediate danger to the public's health, safety, or welfare is called a
   a. petition for review.
   b. stay of enforcement.
   c. summary or emergency suspension.
   d. license revocation.

8. A buyer gives the broker a $47,500 earnest money deposit. The broker defrauds the buyer of the $47,500. The buyer sues the broker and is awarded a judgment in the amount of $62,500 for the original $47,500 deposit plus $15,000 for punitive damages. Because the buyer was unable to collect the judgment from the broker, the buyer requests relief from the Florida Real Estate Recovery Fund. How much can the buyer receive from the Recovery Fund?
   a. $15,000
   b. $47,500
   c. $50,000
   d. $62,500

9. The DBPR is authorized to investigate a written complaint filed against a licensee
   a. if the alleged complaint is legally sufficient.
   b. only if the claimant has been harmed by the actions of the licensee.
   c. only if the alleged violation was committed in the State of Florida.
   d. only if all of the above conditions have been met.

10. Neglecting to correct omissions or errors on a license application returned by the DBPR to the applicant for correction is considered grounds for
    a. suspension of an applicant's rights.
    b. denial of the application.
    c. revocation of the application.
    d. administrative revocation.

11. If a broker's license is suspended, the licenses of all sales associates working for that broker are
    a. placed in involuntary inactive status.
    b. denied.
    c. suspended.
    d. revoked.

12. One of the grounds for the suspension or revocation of a licensee's license is the unauthorized use or retention of money or property, otherwise known as
    a. concealment.
    b. conversion.
    c. culpable negligence.
    d. commingling.

13. A licensee received a citation for $500 for operating as a sales associate without a registered employer. The sales associate feels the citation was issued in error. How should the sales associate proceed?
    a. File a written objection within 30 days
    b. File a written objection within 15 days
    c. Request a hearing before the FREC within 30 days
    d. Request a civil court hearing within 15 days

14. When payment from the Real Estate Recovery Fund is made to satisfy a claim against a licensee and the claim was not the result of the broker complying with an escrow disbursement order, the Commission's action against the licensee must be
    a. citation.
    b. probation.
    c. automatic suspension.
    d. emergency suspension.

15. Which type(s) of penalties may be imposed for violations of the real estate license law?
    a. Civil penalties only
    b. Administrative penalties only
    c. Civil and administrative penalties only
    d. Criminal, civil, and administrative penalties

16. The Florida Real Estate Commission may NOT impose which disciplinary penalty?
    a. Imprisonment
    b. Probation
    c. Administrative fine
    d. Denial of a license application

17. One penalty that the Commission may NOT legally levy is to
    a. deny the issuance of a license.
    b. deny the payment of compensation.
    c. suspend a license.
    d. revoke a license.

18. The collective amount to be paid from the Real Estate Recovery Fund as a result of any one real estate transaction may NOT exceed
    a. $25,000.
    b. $50,000.
    c. $75,000.
    d. $150,000.

CHAPTER

7

FEDERAL AND STATE HOUSING LAWS

1 ## OVERVIEW

2 For many families the purchase of a home is the largest single investment they will make
3 during their lifetime. The federal government and all state governments have enacted laws
4 to ensure that the public interest in real estate is adequately protected. This chapter high-
5 lights some of the laws most important to Florida real estate practitioners. Licensees should
6 study these laws to make certain they comply with the laws to better serve the public.

7 After completing this chapter, the student should be able to:

8 ■ describe the features of the Civil Rights Acts of 1866, 1964, and 1968;

9 ■ recognize examples of steering, redlining, and blockbusting;

10 ■ describe the features of the Truth in Lending Act, the Equal Credit Opportunity
11 Act, and the Real Estate Settlement Procedures Act; and

12 ■ describe the provisions of the Florida Residential Landlord and Tenant Act.

13 ## KEY TERMS

annual percentage rate (APR)	handicap status	triggering terms
blockbusting	property report	Truth in Lending Act (TILA)
Civil Rights Act of 1866	public accommodations	
Fair Housing Act	redlining	
familial status	servicing disclosure statement	
good faith estimate	special information booklet	
	steering	

FEDERAL FAIR HOUSING LAW

Civil Rights Act of 1866

The **Civil Rights Act of 1866** prohibits any type of discrimination based on *race* in *any* real estate transaction (sale or rental) *without exception*. This law is still in force today. A suit can be filed in a federal court under the 1866 Civil Rights Act. The court may award actual (monetary) damages and punitive damages for racial discrimination.

The Civil Rights Act of 1866 states that:

> *All citizens of the United States shall have the same right, in every State and Territory, as is enjoyed by white citizens thereof to inherit, purchase, lease, sell, hold, and convey real and personal property.*

WEB LINK

To view the Civil Rights Act of 1866, visit http://teachingamericanhistory.org/library/index .asp?document=480.

Jones v. Mayer. Joseph Lee Jones filed a complaint in 1965 in District court alleging that Alfred H. Mayer Company had refused to sell him a home because he was black. The famous legal case known as *Jones v. Alfred H. Mayer Company* reached the Supreme Court in 1968. The court upheld the Civil Rights Act of 1866. The Civil Rights Act of 1866 prohibits *all racial discrimination without exception*. The Supreme Court declared that the 1866 Act still applies today, and that it prohibits all racial discrimination (public and private) in the sale of all real property (residential and commercial). Remember, when race is involved, *no exemptions apply*. This court decision allows a person who has experienced discrimination on the basis of race to sue the individuals who committed the alleged discrimination despite certain exemptions in the Civil Rights Act of 1968 (discussed below) when the discrimination is based on race.

WEB LINK

Title VIII of the Civil Rights Act of 1968 (Fair Housing Act) is published in the United States Code and is available at www.law.cornell.edu/uscode/text/42/chapter-45.

Civil Rights Act of 1964 (Titles II and III)

The Civil Rights Act of 1964 was landmark legislation that ended racial segregation in schools, the workplace, and public accommodations. Title II of the 1964 Civil Rights Act prohibits discrimination on the basis of race, color, religion, and national origin in places of public accommodation engaged in interstate commerce, including hotels, motels, restaurants, gas stations, and places of entertainment. Title III prohibits state and municipal governments from denying access to public facilities on the grounds of race, color, religion, or national origin.

Civil Rights Act of 1968: The Fair Housing Act

The **Fair Housing Act** (Act) is contained in Title VIII of the Civil Rights Act of 1968. The Act prohibits discrimination on the basis of race, color, religion, sex, and national origin when selling or renting residential property. This law covers residential dwellings and apartments, as well as vacant land acquired for the purpose of constructing residential dwellings.

In 1988, Congress passed the Fair Housing Amendment Act that expanded federal civil rights protections. Families with children younger than 18 and pregnant women were now a protected class, which the Act refers to as **familial status**. The second protected class included in the 1988 amendment was handicap status. **Handicap status** includes individuals with mental or physical impairments that limit major life activities. As a result of the 1988 amendment, there are seven protected classes:

- Race
- Color
- Religion
- Sex
- Handicap status
- Familial status
- National origin

To help recall the seven protected classes, think of how to spell "fresh corn" but without the vowels (FRSH CRN). No protection is given under the Fair Housing Act to individuals based on age, occupation, marital status, or sexual orientation. However, fair housing laws passed by state and local governments may expand the classes afforded fair housing protection in its jurisdiction.

The Fair Housing Act covers two categories of housing:

1. Single-family houses

   - Residential property that is *not* privately owned (for example, dwellings owned or operated by the federal government)
   - Privately owned residential property if a real estate licensee is employed to sell or rent the property
   - Residential property owned by a person who owns four or more residential units in total
   - Residential property when the owner, during the immediate past two-year period, sells two or more houses in which the owner was not a resident

2. Multifamily housing

   - Multifamily dwellings of five or more units
   - Multifamily dwellings of four or fewer units if the owner does not reside in any of the units

Housing for older persons. Certain housing for older persons is exempt from the familial status protection under the Fair Housing Act provided:

1. all units are occupied by persons 62 years of age or older; or
2. at least 80 percent of the units are occupied by one or more persons 55 years of age or older, and housing policies are published and followed that demonstrate an intent to be housing for persons 55 and older.

Real estate transactions exempted under the act. Although most property is covered by the Fair Housing Act, there are exemptions.

It is important to note that these exemptions apply only if two conditions are met: (1) A real estate licensee was not involved, and (2) there was no discriminatory advertising. The exemptions are as follows:

- Seller owns three or fewer single-family dwellings and sells or rents the property
- Seller was not living in the single-family house and was not the most recent resident when the property was sold or rented (Only one sale is exempt within a 24-month period.)
- Rentals in multifamily dwellings with four or fewer family units as long as the owner lives in one of the units

Remember, even though the situations described above are exempt from the Fair Housing Act, if racial discrimination occurs, the individual can be sued under the Civil Rights Act of 1866.

Special exemptions under the act. Housing operated by religious organizations and private clubs is exempt from the Fair Housing Act provided the housing is *not* operated for commercial purposes:

1. Religious organizations may restrict dwelling units they own or operate to members of their religion if the organization does not otherwise discriminate in accepting its membership.
2. Private clubs may restrict rental or occupancy of its units to its members.

Activities prohibited. Discrimination against any of the protected classes in the sale or rental of housing, financing of housing, or the provision of brokerage services is illegal. It is a violation of the Fair Housing Act to do any of the following activities:

- Channel homeseekers to or away from particular neighborhoods because they are members of a protected class (commonly known as **steering**)
- Use the entry, or rumor of the entry, of a protected class into a neighborhood to persuade owners to sell (commonly known as **blockbusting**)
- Deny loans or insurance coverage by a lender or insurer that present different terms or conditions for homes in certain neighborhoods (commonly known as **redlining**)
- Refuse to rent to, sell to, negotiate with, or deal with a member of a protected class
- Quote different terms, conditions, or privileges for buying or renting
- Advertise that housing is available only to people of a certain race, color, religion, sex, national origin, handicap status, or familial status
- Deny membership in or use of any real estate service, broker's organization, or multiple listing service
- Make false statements concerning the availability of housing for inspection, rent, or sale

Fair housing poster. The Fair Housing Act requires the use of an equal opportunity poster. The poster features the equal housing logo and a statement pledging adherence to the Fair Housing Act. The poster (Figure 7.1) is available without charge from the Department of Housing and Urban Development (HUD). The poster must be displayed at real estate offices and other businesses involved in the housing industry. In the event a discrimination complaint is made against a broker, HUD considers failure to prominently display the equal housing opportunity poster in the broker's place of business as evidence of discrimination. HUD considers any charge of discrimination to be true unless disproved by

FIGURE 7.1 ■ **Equal Housing Opportunity Poster**

U.S. Department of Housing and Urban Development

We Do Business in Accordance With the Federal Fair Housing Law

(The Fair Housing Amendments Act of 1988)

It is Illegal to Discriminate Against Any Person Because of Race, Color, Religion, Sex, Handicap, Familial Status, or National Origin

- In the sale or rental of housing or residential lots
- In the advertising the sale or rental of housing
- In the financing of housing

- In the provision of real estate brokerage services
- In the appraisal of housing
- Blockbusting is also illegal

Anyone who feels he or she has been discriminated against may file a complaint of housing discrimination:
   1-800-669-9777 (Toll Free)
   1-800-927-9275 (TDD)

U.S. Department of Housing and Urban Development
Assistant Secretary for Fair Housing and Equal Opportunity
Washington, D.C. 20410

Previous editions are obsolete

form HUD-928.1 (2/2003)

1   evidence to the contrary. The burden of proof is placed on the broker to prove no discrimi-
2   nation has occurred in such cases.

3   **Regulation.** Complaints of housing discrimination under the Fair Housing Act are filed
4   with HUD. If a discriminatory housing practice has occurred, HUD issues the parties to the
5   complaint a *Charge of Discrimination*. A hearing is then scheduled before a HUD admin-
6   istrative law judge. Either party may elect instead to have the matter heard in Federal
7   court. An injunction (court order to stop the discriminatory practice), actual (monetary)
8   damages, and punitive damages may be awarded for discriminatory practices. Furthermore,
9   the Florida Real Estate Commission may initiate an administrative proceeding against a
10   licensee found guilty of a discriminatory act.

Fair Housing Case

U.S. Department of HUD, on behalf of Steve Times and Betty Brinson, Complainant vs. Annette Banai, Janos Banai, Sylvia Arias, and Manhattan Group Real Estate, Inc., Respondents

What follows is information concerning federal case (HUDALJ 04-93-2060-8). The information has been summarized for education purposes.

In the aftermath of Hurricane Andrew, Steve Times and Betty Brinson (Complainants) sought to rent a place to live until repairs could be made to their home.

Janos and Annette Banai (Respondents) resided in New York. They owned a home in Hollywood, Florida, that they rented out on previous occasions using the services of a rental agent. Sylvia Arias was a licensed sales associate for Manhattan Group Real Estate, Inc. The Respondents listed their residence with the brokerage. The Respondents indicated that they wanted to rent the residence to hurricane disaster victims.

The Complainants responded to a newspaper advertisement placed by Arias and her brokerage firm on behalf of the owners. Arias showed the Complainants the house, and the Complainants indicated they wanted to rent the home. Before finalizing the rental, Arias called the Respondent to discuss the agreement. Arias told the Respondents that she had found "a very nice couple to rent the house." Ms. Banai (the Respondent) asked "what kind of people" they were. The conversation included, in part:

    Respondent: "Are they Hispanic?"

    Arias: "No."

    Respondent: "Are they black?"

    Arias: "Yes."

    Respondent: "No, I cannot rent the house to black people because I live in part of the house and because of what the neighbors will say about something like that."

    Arias: "We are not supposed to discriminate in that way."

    Respondent: "Look for someone else."

Arias contacted the Complainants and told them, in part:

    Arias: "I am very, very sorry to tell you that you are not going to be able to rent the house. I contacted the owners, and the owners said they did not want persons of color in their house."

    Complainants: "What does that mean, because we're black?"

    Arias: "Yes."

Arias showed the Complainants other rentals. Arias also reported the incident to her broker. The broker asked why Arias had identified the couple's race to the owners. Arias answered that the Respondents had asked her. The broker told Arias that she should have refused to respond to the question and that she should have stated that the race of the applicants is irrelevant to the transaction.

The broker sent a letter to the Respondents indicating that Manhattan Group could not be a party to any type of discriminatory practices, that the owners should rent to the couple. Further, if the owners refused to rent to the couple, Manhattan Group was withdrawing from the listing contract with the owners.

Findings:

- A preponderance of evidence directly and unambiguously establishes that Ms. Banai refused to rent to Complainants solely because they were black.

- By answering the owner's inquiry concerning race, the sales associate violated Fair Housing law. Arias "facilitated and participated in Ms. Banai's refusal to rent to Complainants and thereby made a dwelling unavailable because of race [and] color."

- Because Ms. Arias was a sales associate for Manhattan Group Real Estate, Inc., at the time Arias violated the act, the brokerage is vicariously liable for Ms. Arias' actions.

Order:

- Respondents Annette and Janos Banai, Sylvia Arias, and Manhattan Group Real Estate, Inc. are permanently enjoined from discriminating with respect to housing because of race or color.

- The Banais were found guilty of discrimination and ordered to pay a $10,000 civil penalty to the Secretary of HUD and compensatory damages of $35,000 each to Times and Brinson for emotional distress, inconvenience, and lost housing opportunity.

- Arias was fined $100 and required to attend fair housing training.

Appeal:

- Annette and Janos Banai appealed to the United States Court of Appeals, Eleventh Circuit (NO. 95-4377). The appeals court affirmed the $70,000 in compensatory damages to Steve Times and Betty Brinson.

WEB LINK

To learn more about the Fair Housing Act, download the booklet *Equal Opportunity for All* at www.hud.gov/offices/adm/hudclips/forms/files/1686.pdf.

Americans with Disabilities Act of 1990

The Americans with Disabilities Act (ADA) of 1990 is a federal statute designed to remove barriers that prevent qualified individuals with disabilities from enjoying the same opportunities that are available to persons without disabilities. The act prohibits discrimination in places of **public accommodations** and in commercial facilities. Public accommodations are facilities open to the public, including sales and rental establishments, hotels, and shopping centers. ADA requirements also apply to private entities that own, lease, or operate commercial facilities, including real estate brokerage offices, even if the broker's office is located in a private residence. Buyers who purchase older homes with plans to turn the structures into offices may face costly unanticipated expenses to modify or upgrade the facility to ADA standards.

ADA governs employment practices regarding discrimination in hiring and reasonable accommodations in the workplace. ADA also mandates accessibility standards in public accommodations through design specifications such as width of doorways, height of light switches, grab bars in bathrooms, and so forth. If the broker's office is in a private residence, the accessibility standards apply to that portion of the home that is used exclusively as an office and to the portions of the house that are available to customers, including bathrooms. The accessibility standards do not apply to any portion of the home that is used exclusively as a personal residence.

WEB LINK

To learn about the ADA, visit **www.ada.gov**.

FEDERAL LAWS REGARDING LAND AND THE ENVIRONMENT

Interstate Land Sales Full Disclosure Act

The Interstate Land Sales Full Disclosure Act is a federal law that regulates the sale or lease of land. The law is intended to prevent fraudulent marketing schemes through the mail or other means of interstate commerce that may occur when land is being sold without being seen by out-of-state buyers.

The Interstate Land Sales Full Disclosure Act is administered by the secretary of the Department of Housing and Urban Development (HUD) through its Office of Interstate Land Sales Registration. The law requires developers to register their developments with HUD and to disclose to prospective buyers important facts regarding the real estate. The law has two components:

1. *Antifraud provision.* Developers of 25 or more lots must provide each purchaser with a disclosure document referred to as a **property report**. The property report contains relevant information about the real estate and must be delivered to each purchaser before the signing of the contract. Purchasers who received the property report prior to signing the contract may cancel the contract within seven days. Purchasers who did not receive the property report before signing the contract may cancel the contract any time within two years from the date of signing. The sale and purchase contract must clearly state the purchaser's right(s) to cancel.

2. *Registration requirement.* Land developers must register subdivisions of 100 or more lots by filing a statement of record with HUD.

WEB LINK

To learn more about the provisions of the Interstate Land Sales Full Disclosure Act, visit **www.hud.gov/offices/hsg/ramh/ils/buyinglots.pdf**.

Coastal Zone Management Act

The Coastal Zone Management Act (CZMA) is administered by the Environmental Protection Agency (EPA). CZMA encourages states (and Native American tribes) to care for wetlands, floodplains, estuaries, beaches, dunes, barrier islands, and coral reefs (as well as the fish and wildlife using those habitats) found within its jurisdictions. States and Native American tribes affected include areas bordering the Atlantic, Pacific, and Arctic Oceans, Gulf of Mexico, Long Island Sound, and Great Lakes. While most laws typically impose mandatory duties and responsibilities, compliance with this law is voluntary. To encourage participation, the CZMA makes federal financial assistance available to any coastal state or territory that is willing to assume the responsibility to develop and implement a comprehensive coastal management program.

1   In 1990, Congress reauthorized the CZMA. In this reauthorization, Congress identi-
2   fied nonpoint source (NPS) pollution as a major factor in pollution of coastal waters.
3   NPS pollution is caused by rainfall or snowmelt moving over and through the ground.
4   As the runoff moves, it picks up and carries away natural and human-made pollutants.
5   These pollutants are eventually deposited into lakes, rivers, wetlands, coastal waters, and
6   ground waters. Nonpoint source pollution includes excess fertilizer, herbicides, oil, grease,
7   and toxic chemicals found on or in the soil. Congress recognized that effective solutions
8   to nonpoint source pollution could be implemented at the state and local levels. There-
9   fore, in the Coastal Zone Act Reauthorization Amendments of 1990 (CZARA), Congress
10 called upon states with federally approved coastal zone management programs to develop
11 and implement coastal nonpoint pollution control programs.

WEB LINK

To learn about coastal zone management, visit the EPA's Web site at http://epa.gov/agriculture/lzma
.html#Summary of Coastal Zone Management Act and Amendments.

12   FEDERAL LAWS REGARDING MORTGAGE LENDING

13   Truth in Lending Act and Regulation Z

14 The **Truth in Lending Act (TILA)** is Title 1 of the Consumer Credit Protection Act. Most
15 of the requirements imposed by TILA are contained in Federal Regulation Z; therefore,
16 the terms Truth in Lending Act and Regulation Z are often used interchangeably. The law
17 became effective in 1969 and has been amended as recently as 2009. In 2010, the Dodd-
18 Frank Wall Street Reform and Consumer Protection Act created the Consumer Financial
19 Protection Bureau, consolidating most federal consumer financial protection authority
20 under a single bureau. The Consumer Financial Protection Bureau supervises banks and
21 credit unions and also enforces federal consumer financial laws, including the Truth in
22 Lending Act. The bureau was established in 2012 as part of the Dodd-Frank Act.

23 **Purpose of TILA and Regulation Z.** TILA is intended to inform borrowers of the true cost
24 of obtaining a loan. The law ensures that credit terms are disclosed in a meaningful and
25 uniform way so consumers can compare credit terms more readily and knowledgeably.
26 Before its enactment, consumers were faced with various credit terms and rates. It was
27 difficult to compare loans because they were seldom presented in the same format. Under
28 TILA, all creditors must use the same credit terminology and expressions of rates.

29 In addition to providing a consistent system for disclosures, TILA includes substan-
30 tive protections. It gives consumers the right to cancel certain credit transactions, regu-
31 lates certain credit card practices, and provides a means for fair and timely resolution
32 of credit billing disputes. TILA and Regulation Z do not, however, mandate how much
33 interest banks may charge or whether they must grant loans to consumers. The law does
34 *not* attempt to regulate interest rates.

35 TILA applies to consumer loans only; it does not apply to business, commercial, or
36 agricultural credit, or to credit extended to governmental agencies.

37 **Mortgage loans covered under TILA.** Regulation Z generally applies when a loan is secured
38 by a residence (residential real estate loans intended for the purchase or construction of a

1   consumer dwelling are considered to be consumer loans under TILA). Specifically, TILA
2   applies to

3   ■   loans to purchase or construct any consumer dwelling (prior to 2009 applied to a
4   principal residence only),

5   ■   refinanced home loans, and

6   ■   home equity loans (including home equity lines of credit).

7   **Required disclosures.** Regulation Z requires four important disclosures regarding the cost
8   of credit (see Figure 7.2, Truth in Lending Disclosure Statement Example):

9   ■   *Annual percentage rate.* The finance charge must be stated as an **annual percent-**
10   **age rate (APR).** The APR includes the interest rate and other loan costs and
11   represents the true annual cost of credit. The APR is expressed as an effective
12   yearly interest rate. The disclosure of the APR is central to the uniform credit
13   cost disclosure. It is common to see an ad that states "mortgage interest rates at 6
14   percent" followed by a parenthetical statement such as "(annual percentage rate
15   6.25 percent)" or "(APR 6.25%)." APR is a function of the amount financed, the
16   finance charge, and the payment scheduled. The APR is rounded to the nearest
17   ⅛ percent.

18   ■   *Finance charge.* Finance charge is the total dollar amount the loan will cost over
19   its entire life. Charges that must be disclosed include interest charges, discount
20   points or buydown fees, loan finder's fees, servicing fees, notary fees, and required
21   life insurance. Not included in finance charges are title insurance, legal fees,
22   appraisal fees, survey fees, notary fees, credit reports, and deed preparation.

23   ■   *Amount financed.* This is expressed as the total amount of credit provided by the
24   lender.

25   ■   *Total payments.* The total amount the borrower will have paid after making all of
26   the scheduled payments.

27 **Timing of disclosure.** All required disclosures must be made in writing and either given
28 to the borrower at the time of loan application or sent within three business days of appli-
29 cation, and effective 2009, at least seven business days before consummation (a timing
30 waiver is available for a bona fide emergency). The lender may not charge an application
31 fee until after the disclosures have been provided (the applicant may be charged a credit
32 report fee). Lenders must deliver to the borrower a copy of the appraisal report three busi-
33 ness days before closing the loan.

34 **Triggering terms.** TILA makes "bait and switch" advertising a federal offense. For exam-
35 ple, if a subdivision developer advertises homes for sale with a down payment of $1,000,
36 the seller must accept $1,000 as the complete down payment or be in violation of the
37 law.

FIGURE 7.2 ■ Truth in Lending Disclosure Statement Example

Annual Percentage Rate (APR)	Finance Charge	Amount Financed	Total of Payments
The cost of credit as a yearly rate	The dollar amount the credit will cost	The amount of credit provided by the lender	The amount borrower will have paid after all payments as scheduled
4.375%	$27,939.86	$76,439.00	$104,378.86

TILA is also concerned that consumers may be misled by being given truthful, but inadequate, information in advertising. While it does not require creditors to advertise credit terms, it does provide that if they advertise certain credit terms, called **triggering terms**, they must include additional disclosures. Trigger terms include the

- amount or percentage of any down payment,
- number of payments,
- period (term) of repayment,
- amount of any payment, and
- amount of any finance charge.

Advertisements containing any of the triggering terms must also disclose the following:

- Amount or percentage of down payment
- Terms of repayment
- Annual percentage rate, using that term, and if the rate may be increased in the future, that fact must also be disclosed

The Truth in Lending Act allows general phrases such as "owner will finance" and "favorable financing terms available." Such expressions are too general to trigger additional disclosure requirements.

Three-day right of rescission. The borrower has the right to rescind (cancel) the loan contract up to midnight of the *third business day* following the signing of the loan documents. The right of rescission can be waived by the borrower for financial reasons. The right of rescission applies to most consumer loans but does *not* apply to loans to purchase or construct a home. If refinancing with a new lender, the right of rescission applies. If refinancing with the same lender, only additional money added to the original loan (if any) may be rescinded. The three business day right of rescission applies to

- home equity lines of credit;
- second mortgages; and
- refinance loans.

Equal Credit Opportunity Act (ECOA)

The Equal Credit Opportunity Act (ECOA) is enforced by the Federal Trade Commission. The ECOA is a federal law that requires financial institutions and firms engaged in extending credit to make credit available with fairness and without discrimination on the basis of race, color, religion, national origin, sex, marital status, age, or receipt of income from public assistance programs. (See Figure 7.3, Summary of Protected Classes.)

Real Estate Settlement Procedures Act (RESPA)

RESPA is a consumer protection law, administered by the Consumer Financial Protection Bureau, intended to ensure that buyers are informed regarding the amount and type of charges they will pay at closing. RESPA also attempts to eliminate kickbacks and referral fees that increase closing costs. RESPA applies to federally related residential loans. RESPA covers loans secured with a mortgage on a one-family to four-family residential property.

FIGURE 7.3 ■ Summary of Protected Classes

Law	Race	Color	Religion	Sex	Handicap Status	Familial Status	National Origin	Marital Status	Age	Public Assistance Income
Civil Rights Act 1866	✔	✔								
Fair Housing Act (as amended)	✔	✔	✔	✔	✔	✔	✔			
Equal Credit Opportunity Act (Lending)	✔	✔	✔	✔			✔	✔	✔	✔

These include most purchase loans, assumptions, refinances, property improvement loans, and equity lines of credit. Transactions *exempt* from RESPA include

- loans to finance the purchase of 25 acres or more;
- loans for home improvement or to refinance or any other type of loan if its purpose is not to purchase or transfer title;
- loans to finance the purchase of a vacant lot if none of the loan proceeds will be used to place a residential structure or mobile home on the lot;
- sale or transfer of property involving only an assumption of an existing loan (if the lender does not have to approve the assumption) or sale subject to an existing loan;
- construction loans, except those intended for conversion into permanent loans;
- permanent loans to finance construction of a one-family to four-family structure when the lot is owned by the borrower; and
- loans to finance the purchase of property when the primary purpose is resale of the property.

RESPA disclosures at time of loan application or within three business days. When borrowers apply for a mortgage loan, they must be given the following disclosures:

- **Special Information Booklet**, published by the Department of Housing and Urban Development (HUD), contains consumer information regarding closing services (required for purchase transactions only) the borrower may be charged for at closing, describes the home buying process, and explains both the Good Faith Estimate and the HUD-1 Settlement Statement
- **Good Faith Estimate (GFE)** of closing (settlement) costs, listing the charges the buyer is likely to pay at closing. The standardized GFE facilitates shopping among settlement service providers. If the lender allows the borrower to shop for third-party settlement services, the lender must provide the borrower a list of acceptable service providers.
- **Servicing Disclosure Statement**, which discloses to the borrower whether the lender intends to service the loan or transfer it to another lender or servicing company

If the borrower did not receive the disclosures at the time of loan application, the lender must mail them within three business days of receiving the loan application.

WEB LINK

You can download a copy of the Buying Your Home: Settlement Costs and Helpful Information booklet at http://portal.hud.gov/hudportal/HUD?src=/program_offices/housing/ramh/res/sfhrestc. Select either the Microsoft Word or PDF version for download.

Affiliated business relationships. Sometimes, several businesses that offer settlement (closing) services are owned or controlled by a common corporate parent. These businesses are known as *affiliates*. When a lender, real estate broker, or other closing participant refers a borrower to an affiliate for a settlement service (for example, when a real estate broker refers a buyer to a mortgage broker affiliate), RESPA requires the referring party to give the borrower an Affiliated Business Arrangement (AFBA) Disclosure. This form explains to borrowers that they are not required, with certain exceptions, to use the affiliate and are free to shop for other providers. The AFBA must include an estimate of the affiliated business provider's charges. Except in cases where a lender refers a borrower to an attorney, credit reporting agency, or real estate appraiser to represent the lender's interest in the transaction, the referring party may not require the consumer to use the affiliated business.

Purchase of title insurance. RESPA prohibits a seller from requiring the home buyer to use a particular title insurance company as a condition of sale. Generally, the lender will require title insurance. The borrower can shop for and choose a company. However, if the seller is paying for the owner's title insurance policy, the law does not prohibit the seller from choosing the title company.

HUD-1 settlement statement. The closing agent must provide borrowers with the HUD-1 Settlement Statement at closing. The HUD-1 statement shows all of the charges imposed on the borrower and the seller and any credits due the borrower and the seller. It itemizes the actual closing costs of the loan transaction. The HUD-1 was revised in 2010 to help consumers determine if their actual closing costs were within established tolerance requirements. The HUD-1 includes a chart that compares the charges quoted in the GFE with the actual charges applied at closing. Some of the charges may not increase; others may not increase more than 10 percent. If requested by the borrower, the closing agent must provide a copy of the HUD-1 statement one business day before the actual settlement. The HUD statement must include all information the closing agent has at that time.

Escrow for taxes and insurance. RESPA limits the amount lenders can require borrowers to place in escrow for property taxes and hazard insurance. The lender must perform an annual escrow account analysis. An excess of $50 or more must be returned to the borrower.

Kickbacks, fee-splitting, and unearned fees. It is illegal under RESPA for anyone to pay or receive a fee, kickback, or anything of value because they agree to refer settlement service business to a particular person or organization. For example, a mortgage lender may not pay a real estate broker a fee for referring a buyer to the lender. In Florida, sales associates must hold mortgage broker's licenses to legally be paid a fee for referring prospective borrowers to affiliated mortgage lenders. It is also illegal for anyone to accept a fee or part of a fee for services if that person has not actually performed settlement services for the fee. For example, a lender may not add to a third party's fee, such as an appraisal fee, and keep the difference. RESPA does not prevent title companies, mortgage brokers, appraisers, attorneys, closing agents, and others, who actually perform a service in connection with the mortgage loan or the closing, from being paid for the reasonable value of their work.

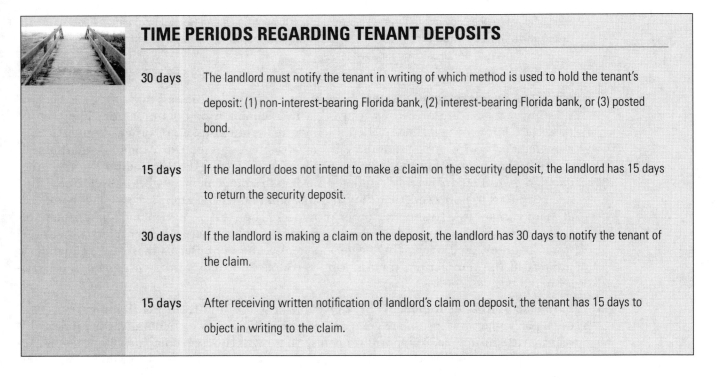

TIME PERIODS REGARDING TENANT DEPOSITS

30 days   The landlord must notify the tenant in writing of which method is used to hold the tenant's deposit: (1) non-interest-bearing Florida bank, (2) interest-bearing Florida bank, or (3) posted bond.

15 days   If the landlord does not intend to make a claim on the security deposit, the landlord has 15 days to return the security deposit.

30 days   If the landlord is making a claim on the deposit, the landlord has 30 days to notify the tenant of the claim.

15 days   After receiving written notification of landlord's claim on deposit, the tenant has 15 days to object in writing to the claim.

It is a crime for someone to pay or receive an illegal referral fee. The penalty can be a fine, imprisonment, or both. The borrower may also be entitled to recover three times the cost of settlement service charges that were illegally referred or charged with no actual service provided by bringing a private lawsuit (also referred to as *triple* or *treble damages*).

WEB LINK

To learn more about RESPA, visit the RESPA home page at http://portal.hud.gov/hudportal/HUD?src=/ program_offices/housing/rmra/res/respa_hm.

STATE LAW REGARDING MORTGAGE LENDING

Florida Fair Lending Act

This law prohibits certain practices related to high-cost home loans. A *high-cost home loan* means a loan for a consumer credit transaction that is secured by the consumer's principal dwelling and features high points and or fees. What constitutes "high" is defined in the federal law. The Florida Fair Lending Act was created to prevent abusive practices regarding such loans. Abusive practices include, for example, making consumer loans based on equity in the home rather than based on the borrower's ability to pay the loan payments; and loans that finance the points and fees so that the lender receives immediate income, thereby encouraging lenders to repeatedly refinance the same property. Two of the most significant features of the Florida Fair Lending Act are:

1. Prepayment penalty. A lender may include a prepayment penalty for up to the first 36 months from the creation of the loan, but only if the borrower has also

been offered a choice of another product without a prepayment penalty, and the borrower has been given a written disclosure of the terms of the prepayment fee.

494.0078, F.S.
494.00791(9), F.S.

2. No refinancing. No lender or its affiliate may refinance a loan to the same borrower within the first 18 months when doing so does not reasonably benefit the borrower.

STATE HOUSING AND GROWTH MANAGEMENT LAWS

Florida Fair Housing Act

760.21, F.S.

The objective of Florida's Fair Housing Act is to provide for fair housing throughout the state. The Florida act is similar in scope to the federal Fair Housing Act. However, whenever the federal Fair Housing Act is in conflict with or broader in scope than the Florida act, the federal act prevails.

Growth Management Act

163.3180, F.S.

Florida's Growth Management Act of 1985 requires that cities and counties prepare a comprehensive plan of land use. (See also chapter 20.) The act also contains a concurrency provision that requires that the infrastructure be in place before new development can begin.

STATE LAWS REQUIRING REAL ESTATE DISCLOSURES

Deceptive and Unfair Trade Practices Act (Florida's "Little FTC Act")

501, Part II, F.S.

The Deceptive and Unfair Trade Practices Act (Florida's "Little FTC Act") declares that unfair methods of competition, unconscionable acts or practices, and unfair or deceptive acts or practices in the conduct of any trade or commerce are unlawful. When Chapter 501 and Chapter 475 are in conflict, real estate licensees selling real property in Florida must abide by the Florida real estate law.

RESPA and HUD require that licensees disclose in writing to buyers before the buyer signs the purchase agreement that, on closing the sale, additional costs may be required of the buyer. Brokerage firms in Florida provide prospective purchasers of real property with a list of closing items that may be costs to the buyer. However, firms do not have to list brokerage commissions, advance hazard insurance costs, or escrow items such as taxes and insurance.

FLORIDA RESIDENTIAL LANDLORD AND TENANT ACT

The intent of the Residential Landlord and Tenant Act is to place Florida landlords of residential properties and their tenants on a more equitable basis in their legal relationship. The law applies only to the rental of dwelling units (residential tenancies). It does not apply to commercial leases; medical facilities; transient accommodations (motels and hotels); or cooperative apartments, condominiums, or mobile home parks when used as transient accommodations.

Under present Florida law, an 18-year-old is entitled to enter into a rental agreement.

83.49, F.S.

Deposits and advance rents. A security deposit is typically paid to guarantee that the property will be left in good condition. Rent in advance is also often paid (typically the last month's rent). When money is given to a landlord as a security deposit or advance rent, the landlord is obligated to account for such deposits in one of three ways:

1. Hold the money in a separate noninterest-bearing Florida bank account and not commingle, hypothecate, that is, pledge as security for a debt, or use any such funds until due to the tenant.

2. Hold the money in a separate interest-bearing Florida bank account and pay the tenant at least 75 percent of any annualized average interest rate or 5 percent per year simple interest, and not commingle, hypothecate, or use any such funds until due to the tenant.

3. Post a surety bond with the clerk of the circuit court in the county in which the rental property is located in the total amount of the security deposits and advance rents or $50,000, whichever is less, and pay the tenant 5 percent per year simple interest. If the landlord chooses this method, the landlord is not obligated to place the funds (deposits) into a special account.

The landlord must inform tenants in writing, within 30 days from the receipt of advance rent or security deposit, of the manner in which the tenant's funds are being held. Typically, this written notification is accomplished by indicating in the lease how the deposit and advance rent money is held. In the notice to the tenant, the landlord also must show the bank name and address, the amount deposited, the rate of interest (if any), and the date interest payments will be made to the tenant. The landlord is required to pay or credit the interest at least once each year. If the landlord is acting in the role of a licensed real estate agent, or if the landlord has hired a broker to act as agent, the real estate licensee must abide by the escrow requirements specified in Chapter 475. (See also chapter 5.)

83.51, F.S.

Landlord's obligation to maintain premises. A landlord's obligations to tenants include the following:

- Maintain the rented dwelling unit in a condition that meets all building, housing, and health codes in the community. (If no codes have been established for the area, the law requires that the premises be maintained in "good repair and capable of resisting normal forces and loads.")
- Provide exterminating service for insect and rodent control.
- Provide garbage receptacles and pickup.
- Provide working equipment for heat plus running hot water.

The landlord is allowed to charge tenants for services, provided the charges are included in the rental agreement. If the dwelling unit is a single-family home or a duplex, the landlord is required to install working smoke detectors prior to the beginning of the lease period.

Landlords may not be held responsible for conditions caused or created by negligent or wrongful acts of tenants or their guests. A landlord is not required to maintain a mobile home when a tenant is renting the landlord's lot.

83.52, F.S.

Tenant's obligations. A tenant's obligations include the following:

- Comply with applicable building, housing, and health codes.
- Keep occupied premises, including the dwelling's plumbing fixtures, clean and sanitary.
- Use reasonable care in the operation of all plumbing, electrical, heating, and air-conditioning equipment.
- Conduct self and make sure guests behave so as not to disturb the peace of other tenants.

83.53, F.S.

Landlord's access to premises. A tenant may not unreasonably withhold consent for a landlord to enter rented premises from time to time to:

- inspect the premises;
- make necessary or agreed-on repairs, decorations, alterations, or improvements;
- supply agreed-on services; and
- exhibit or show the premises.

In case of emergency or when necessary to protect or preserve the premises, a landlord is entitled to enter a dwelling unit at any time. However, the law prohibits a landlord from abusing this right of access to harass a tenant. If the rent is current and the tenant notifies the landlord of an intended absence, the landlord may not enter the premises during the period of absence, except with the tenant's consent or in an emergency. Except in emergencies, landlords are obligated to enter rented premises at times reasonable and convenient for the tenant. The statute mandates that at least 12 hours is reasonable notice.

83.49(3), F.S.

Vacating premises. When a tenant vacates a rental unit at the end of a lease agreement, the landlord must abide by certain time restrictions as follows:

- The landlord has *15 days* to return the security deposit and any accrued interest, if applicable, provided the landlord does *not* intend to make a claim on the security deposit.
- The landlord has *30 days* to notify the tenant if the landlord intends to impose a claim on the deposit.

The notification must be in writing and be sent by certified mail to the tenant's last-known mailing address. The notice must include the reason for the claim. Failure to give the required notice to the tenant within the 30-day period forfeits the right to claim part of the deposit. The deposit must then be returned to the tenant with any accrued interest.

If a tenant is properly notified of the landlord's claim on the security deposit, the tenant is allowed 15 days after receipt of the landlord's notice to file an objection. The date established by delivery of the landlord's notice begins the tenant's 15-day period. If a dispute must be settled in court, the law states that the prevailing party in the litigation is entitled to receive reimbursement for court costs plus reasonable attorney's fees from the other party.

The Florida Landlord and Tenant Act relieves brokers of the duty to notify the FREC of disputes regarding security deposits and advance rent. Section 83.49, F.S., provides that brokers holding security deposits and advance rent may *disburse* the funds from the rental escrow account without complying with the Commission's escrow dispute and notification procedures, provided the broker has fully complied with the Florida Landlord and Tenant Act. (See chapter 5.)

SUMMARY OF EVICTION PROCESS

The landlord serves the tenant a written notice allowing three days (excluding weekends and legal holidays) for the tenant to pay the rent or to vacate the premises.

If the tenant does not pay the rent or moves, the landlord may begin legal action to evict by filing a *complaint for eviction* in county court.

If the court agrees with the landlord, the tenant is notified in writing. The tenant has five days (excluding weekends and legal holidays) to respond in writing to the court.

If the tenant does not respond or if a judgment is entered against the tenant, the clerk of the county court issues a *writ of possession* to the sheriff.

The sheriff notifies the tenant that eviction will take place after a 24-hour notice has been posted.

83.56 (1), F.S.

Termination of rental agreements by the tenant. If a landlord fails to maintain rented premises or fails to comply with the terms and conditions of the rental agreement, a tenant may terminate the agreement by following this procedure:

1. The tenant first must give written notice to the landlord citing the noncompliance and stating the intent to cancel the agreement if the noncompliance is not corrected.
2. Thereafter, the landlord has seven days to correct the noncompliance and resolve the problem.
3. If the noncompliance is not corrected within seven days after delivery of the tenant's complaint to the landlord, the tenant is entitled to terminate the agreement.

In those cases in which a tenant does not desire to terminate the rental agreement but does want to correct a landlord's noncompliance, the law provides alternative courses of procedure:

- If the dwelling unit is habitable despite the landlord's failure to comply, the tenant may remain in occupancy of the premises, and the law states that the rent may be reduced by a court in proportion to the loss in rental value caused by the failure to comply.

- If the dwelling unit is rendered untenable (uninhabitable) owing to the landlord's failure, the tenant may not be liable for the rent during the period the premises remain untenable, if the court agrees with the tenant's assertions. This is a departure from the requirements of a nonresidential lease under which the landlord has no obligation to repair damaged premises unless the obligation is specifically contained in the lease agreement.

83.56 (2), F. S.
83.56(3), F.S.

Termination of rental agreements by the landlord. If a tenant fails to comply with a lease or rental agreement, the landlord may terminate the agreement by following the three-step procedure previously mentioned. The same period of seven days is allowed for compliance

NOTE REGARDING TEST ANXIETY

If you are concerned or even panicky about taking the end-of-chapter practice quizzes and the practice exam, as well as the state licensing examination, obtain in advance a personal copy of the author's *Florida Real Estate Exam Manual for Sales Associates and Brokers*. It contains, among other valuable sections, a section entitled "Successful Exam-Taking Strategies" and two sample exams, both designed and proven to improve your test-taking ability and scores.

by the tenant. However, if the tenant's noncompliance is *failure* to pay rent when due, the following procedure is required for a landlord to terminate the agreement:

1. The landlord must give the tenant written notice demanding either payment of rent within three business days or possession of the premises. The written notice can be mailed, personally delivered, or if the tenant is absent from the place of residence, attached to the door of the dwelling. It is always advisable to be accompanied by another person to witness delivery of the notice. The three-day time limit begins from the time the notice is posted by mail or delivered at the residence, not including weekends or holidays.

2. The tenant has three business days to either pay the rent or surrender the premises. If the tenant continues the default in payment of rent after the allotted days have lapsed, the landlord must resort to formal eviction to have the tenant removed.

3. If the tenant vacates the rented premises, the landlord then is required to give the tenant written notice by certified mail of any claim on the tenant's security deposit or advance rent held by the landlord, as described previously.

Eviction requirements. From time to time, a landlord has to evict tenants from rented dwelling units. In any eviction process the landlord must adhere to the following procedure:

1. The tenant must be notified in writing that the landlord is demanding possession of the premises. The notice may be mailed to or served on the tenant or posted on the door of the tenant's residence. The landlord keeps a copy of the notice and indicates the date mailed or delivered.

83.59, F.S.

2. If the tenant does not surrender the premises to the landlord within three business days after notification for nonpayment of rent (seven days for all other breaches of the rental agreement), the landlord must file a *complaint for eviction* in the court of the county where the dwelling is located. This complaint identifies the premises and cites the reasons that justify recovery of the property. The sheriff's department usually delivers the complaint to the tenant.

83.60, F.S.

3. The tenant is allowed five business days to file a reply defending himself or herself against the complaint. If the tenant decides to defend continued possession, the courts must decide the case.

4. If the tenant merely continues to occupy the premises without answering the landlord's complaint, the landlord must obtain a final judgment from the court.

A landlord is entitled to have the motion for final judgment advanced on the court's calendar if the court approves the request.

5. After entry of judgment in favor of the landlord, the clerk of the court issues a writ to the sheriff to put the landlord in possession after a 24-hour notice has been posted on the premises.

6. At the time the sheriff executes (signs) the writ of possession or at any time thereafter, the landlord or the landlord's agent may remove any personal property found on the premises. Subsequent to executing the writ of possession, the landlord may request that the sheriff stand by to keep the peace while the landlord changes the locks and removes the personal property from the premises.

When a tenant refuses to vacate and defends for continued possession, it sometimes takes one to two months to complete the entire eviction procedure. In the meantime, any unpaid rent creates a lien in favor of the landlord. That lien applies to all property of the tenant except beds, bedclothes, and wearing apparel, either on or off the rented premises. This general lien dates from the date a judgment is issued by a court in favor of the landlord. Any right or duty stated in Florida's Landlord Tenant Law is enforceable by civil action. This means that all legal remedies sought by either tenant or landlord under this statute are pursued through the civil courts.

83.62, F.S.

WEB LINK

You can learn more about Florida's Residential Landlord Tenant Act. The Florida Statutes are available at **www.leg.state.fl.us/welcome/index.cfm**. Under the Senate seal, select "Florida Statutes," then "Title VI, Civil Practice and Procedure," and then "Chapter 83."

The Division of Consumer Services has published a consumer brochure concerning Florida's Landlord/Tenant Law. You can download the brochure at **www.800helpfla.com/landlord_text.html**.

SUMMARY OF IMPORTANT POINTS

- The Civil Rights Act of 1866 prohibits racial discrimination in all real estate transactions without exception.

- The *Jones v. Mayer* case upheld the Civil Rights Act of 1866.

- The Civil Rights Act of 1968 (known as the Fair Housing Act) protects people from discrimination because of their race, color, religion, sex, handicap status, familial status, or national origin in the sale or rental of housing or residential lots. The Fair Housing Act does not protect individuals based on age, occupation, marital status, or sexual orientation.

- There are several exemptions from the Fair Housing Act that apply to individuals selling or renting their own property. However, if racial discrimination occurs, the individual is in violation of the Civil Rights Act of 1866. If a real estate licensee is involved in the transaction, the Fair Housing Act applies.

- Prohibited activities under the Fair Housing Act include refusing to rent to, sell to, negotiate with, or deal with a member of a protected class; quoting different terms or conditions for buying or renting; advertising that housing is available only to people of a certain race, color, religion, sex, national origin, handicap status, or familial status; denying membership in or use of any real estate brokerage services, brokers' organization, or MLS; and making false statements concerning the availability of housing for inspection, rent, or sale.

- The Fair Housing Act also prohibits blockbusting (inducing homeowners to sell their property by making misrepresentations regarding the entry of minority persons in order to cause a turnover of properties in the neighborhood); steering (channeling home seekers to or away from particular neighborhoods because they are members of a protected class); and redlining (denying loans or insurance coverage or offering loans or insurance coverage with different terms or conditions for homes in certain neighborhoods).

- The Americans with Disabilities Act (ADA) prohibits discrimination in places of public accommodation and commercial facilities such as hotels and real estate offices.

- The Interstate Land Sales Full Disclosure Act allows a purchaser who received the required property report prior to signing the contract to cancel the contract within seven days.

- The Truth in Lending Act is implemented by Federal Reserve Regulation Z and requires lenders to disclose the annual percentage rate (APR) and all costs associated with credit. The law gives borrowers three business days to cancel most consumer loan contracts except loans to purchase or construct a home.

- The Equal Credit Opportunity Act (ECOA) ensures that financial institutions make credit available without discrimination on the basis of race, color, religion, national origin, sex, marital status, age, or receipt of income from public assistance programs.

- The Real Estate Settlement Procedures Act (RESPA) requires disclosures at time of mortgage loan application or within three business days: Special Information Booklet, Good Faith Estimate, and Servicing Disclosure Statement.

- The Florida Residential Landlord Tenant Act requires landlords (1) to maintain security deposits and advance rent in a separate non-interest-bearing escrow account, (2) to maintain security deposits and advance rent in a separate interest-bearing account and pay the tenant five percent interest or 75 percent of interest earned, or (3) to post a surety bond for the lesser of the amount of the funds or $50,000 and pay the tenant five percent interest. If a real estate broker holds the funds on behalf of the landlord, the broker must abide by real estate license law concerning escrow funds.

REVIEW QUESTIONS

1. The federal statute that prohibits a private homeowner from discriminating strictly on the basis of race if selling, renting, or leasing is the
   a. 1968 Fair Housing Act.
   b. 1866 Civil Rights Act.
   c. 1934 National Housing Act.
   d. 1968 Interstate Land Sales Full Disclosure Act.

2. The law that requires that lenders disclose the annual percentage rate (APR) of interest is the
   a. Real Estate Settlement Procedures Act (RESPA).
   b. Federal Housing Act (FHA).
   c. Florida Deceptive and Unfair Trade Practices Act ("Little FTC Act").
   d. Regulation Z (Truth in Lending Act).

3. The federal 1968 Fair Housing Act prohibits discrimination based on
   a. race, color, religion, sex, national origin, familial status, or handicap status.
   b. race or age.
   c. religion, age, race, familial status, or handicap status.
   d. race, color, religion, age, or national origin.

4. The Truth in Lending Act
   a. does not affect real estate financing credit.
   b. attempts to regulate maximum interest rates charged consumers.
   c. requires disclosure of finance charges as well as annual percentage rates of interest.
   d. accomplishes all of the above.

5. The Real Estate Settlement Procedures Act (RESPA) was enacted to
   a. establish a maximum cost for all closing items.
   b. ensure that sellers are informed regarding the amount and types of expenses expected at closing.
   c. ensure that buyers are informed regarding the amount and types of expenses to be expected at closing.
   d. establish a minimum cost for all closing items.

6. If requested by the borrower, and to the extent that information is available to the closing agent, the borrower must be provided with which item at least one business day before closing?
   a. HUD-1 Settlement Statement
   b. Borrower's Special Information Booklet
   c. Guaranteed amount of settlement costs
   d. Notice of title-closing-agent selection

7. As part of the preparation for a closing, a listing broker referred a property owner to an appraiser. The appraiser completed the appraisal and charged the owner $250, which was entered on the RESPA settlement statement. The appraiser gave the listing broker $50 for the referral, which the broker accepted. According to RESPA
   a. the listing broker also must be licensed as an appraiser.
   b. the appraiser has not violated the law as long as the appraiser is state certified.
   c. both the broker and the appraiser have violated the law.
   d. the arrangement is entirely legal.

8. Which transaction is exempt from RESPA requirements?
   a. The sale of a house where the only financing is assumption of an existing loan
   b. A construction loan that will become a permanent loan only after the building is completed
   c. A loan to purchase a new house in a new subdivision
   d. An adjustable-rate mortgage loan to purchase a five-year-old residence

9. The intent of the Florida Landlord and Tenant Act is to
   a. give the tenant a legal advantage in a relationship with the landlord.
   b. make the landlord-tenant relationship more equitable.
   c. provide landlords the legal assistance needed to create an advantageous relationship.
   d. regulate residential and commercial rental property.

10. When security deposits or advance rents are required by a landlord in Florida, such funds
    a. must always be kept in a separate account.
    b. may be deposited in the landlord's account if a sufficient surety bond has been posted.
    c. must always be placed in an interest-bearing account.
    d. must bear interest at the rate of 7 percent.

11. The sales associates in a real estate office have been instructed to send all of their Spanish-speaking prospects to a new subdivision "beautifully designed with a Spanish flavor." This is an example of
    a. steering.
    b. subordination.
    c. alienation.
    d. blockbusting.

12. A landlord who rents a duplex to two tenants is obligated to provide
    a. working equipment for air-conditioning.
    b. an operable washer and dryer.
    c. a designated parking space.
    d. working smoke detectors.

13. Which disclosure requirement is required to be given to tenants in multifamily buildings of five or more units?
    a. No brokerage relationship notice
    b. Notice of where deposit is held within 30 days
    c. 15-day cancellation privilege
    d. Transaction broker notice

14. If a tenant vacates rented premises promptly when a lease or tenancy expires, the landlord must
    a. inform the tenant within 45 days if the landlord claims part of the security deposit.
    b. return the tenant's security deposit within 30 days or explain any exception.
    c. inform the tenant within 25 days if part of the tenant's deposit will be claimed.
    d. inform the tenant within 30 days if part of the tenant's deposit will be claimed.

15. The Fair Housing Act does NOT apply to which category listed below?
    a. A property owner of a single-family home who owns two residential properties and is selling the single-family property "for sale by owner"
    b. Residential property owned by the county government
    c. Single-family home listed by a real estate sales associate
    d. Twenty-unit multifamily apartment building

16. If a tenant's rent is current and the tenant notifies the landlord of an intended absence, the landlord
    a. may not enter the tenant's rented premises without the tenant's consent except in an emergency.
    b. may enter only if accompanied by a second party.
    c. may enter without any restriction.
    d. may not enter the tenant's rented premises without first obtaining a sheriff's affidavit.

17. How long does a landlord have to correct a noncompliance after receiving written notice from a tenant?
    a. 7 days
    b. 10 days
    c. 2 weeks
    d. 30 days

18. A landlord must follow designated procedures in evicting a tenant. The first step in a legal eviction is to
    a. personally deliver a written notice demanding possession.
    b. notify the tenant by mail of the landlord's demand for possession.
    c. attach a notice to the door of the premises that possession of the premises is demanded.
    d. do any of the above.

19. The law that requires that lenders furnish borrowers with a good-faith estimate of closing costs is the
    a. Truth in Lending Act.
    b. Real Estate Settlement Procedures Act.
    c. Consumer Credit Protection Act.
    d. Fair Housing and Lending Act.

20. Which phrase may legally be included in an advertisement to sell real estate?
    a. "Cute cottage home, perfect for first-time buyer"
    b. "Beautiful neighborhood rich in ethnic heritage"
    c. "Spanish-speaking community"
    d. "Quiet neighborhood, no young children please"

8 PROPERTY RIGHTS: ESTATES, TENANCIES, AND MULTIPLE OWNERSHIP INTERESTS

OVERVIEW

This chapter begins with a description of the physical components of real property. It goes on to discuss various types of estates and the rights that are included in each type of estate. It describes multiple ownership interests as well as special ownership interests, including the constitutional homestead. The chapter concludes with a thorough presentation of cooperatives, condominiums, and time-shares.

After completing this chapter, the student should be able to:

- define *land*, *real estate*, and *real property*;
- list and explain the physical components of real property;
- explain the four tests courts use to determine if an item is a fixture;
- distinguish between real and personal property;
- describe the bundle of rights associated with real property ownership;
- list the principal types of estates (tenancies) and describe their characteristics;
- describe the features associated with the Florida homestead law;
- distinguish among cooperatives, condominiums, and time-shares; and
- describe the five main documents associated with condominiums.

DEFINITION OF REAL PROPERTY

Real property or real estate means any interest or estate in land and any interest in business enterprises

or business opportunities, including any assignment leasehold, subleasehold, or mineral right; however,

the term does not include any cemetery lot or right of burial in any cemetery, nor does the term include the

renting of a mobile home lot or recreational vehicle lot in a mobile home park or travel park.

Reference: Section 475.01, F.S.

KEY TERMS

common elements	homestead	remainderman
concurrent ownership	joint tenancy	right of survivorship
condominium	land	riparian rights
condominium documents	leasehold estate	separate property
cooperative	life estates	tenancy at sufferance
declaration of	littoral rights	tenancy at will
condominium	marital assets	tenancy by the entireties
elective share	nonfreehold estate	tenants in common
estate for years	personal property	time-share
estate in severalty	proprietary lease	trade fixture
fee simple estate	prospectus	undivided interest
fixtures	real estate	
freehold estate	real property	

THE NATURE OF PROPERTY

In medieval times kings and lords owned the land, and the common people worked the land under the *feudal* system of ownership. In the United States today the *allodial* system, which grew out of the English feudal system, allocates full property ownership rights to private individuals.

Land refers not only to the *surface* of the earth but also to everything attached to it by nature, such as trees and lakes. Land also includes products of nature beneath the surface, such as oil and limestone. Technically, land extends downward to the center of the earth and upward into the air to infinity.

Real estate refers to the land and all *improvements* permanently attached to the land. Improvements are artificial (human-made) things attached to land, such as homes, factories, fences, streets, sewers, and other additions.

Real property includes all real estate plus the legal *bundle of rights* inherent in the ownership of real estate. (The bundle of rights is explained in detail under General Property Rights later in this chapter.) The terms *real property* and *real estate* are often used interchangeably. (See the definition of real property in the text box above.) However,

F I G U R E 8.1 ■ Physical Components of Land

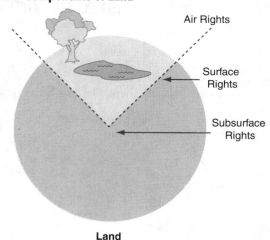

Land
Earth's surface—including trees and
water, land and minerals—to the center
of the earth, and the airspace above.

some references reserve the term *real property* to include the concept of a bundle of rights associated with ownership. Real property, therefore, includes not only the real estate (land plus improvements) but also the legal interests, rights, and privileges associated with the ownership of real estate.

Physical Components of Land

An owner's rights to use the physical components of surface, subsurface, and air are referred to as *surface rights, subsurface rights,* and *air rights.* (See Figure 8.1, Physical Components of Land.)

Surface rights. Surface rights include land and water rights. Two types of water rights are:

1. **Riparian rights** are associated with land abutting the banks of a river, stream, or other watercourse.
2. **Littoral rights** are associated with land abutting tidal bodies of water such as an ocean, sea, or lake.

Subsurface rights. These consist of an owner's rights to underground minerals, petroleum, natural gas, and so forth, often referred to as *mineral rights.*

Air rights. Air rights involve that space above a tract, extending up to a height established by law (e.g., building rights, easements, aerial navigation).

Most real property transactions include all three physical components in the exchange of ownership rights. However, it is entirely possible for the seller to retain one or even two of the components if the buyer and seller agree. For example, the Met Life Building in New York City was built by purchasing the air rights over Grand Central Station. The surface and subsurface components of that parcel continue to perform the same function as before construction of the Met Life Building. Another example of the separation

DEFINITIONS ASSOCIATED WITH WATER RIGHTS

Accretion	The process of land buildup from water-borne rock, sand, and soil
Alluvion	New deposits of land as a result of accretion; alluvion deposits commonly occurring at the mouth of large rivers (The landowner is entitled to all new soil deposits.)
Erosion	Gradual loss of land due to natural forces (A landowner may lose land through the natural process of erosion.)
Reliction	Gradual receding of water, uncovering additional land (The new land usually belongs to the landowner of the area that was previously covered by water.)

1 of components of real estate occurred near Jay, Florida. Before the oil supply there was
2 exhausted, owners often sold or leased the subsurface component, including oil rights,
3 while retaining the surface and air rights.

Personal Property

5 The two basic types of property are real property and personal property. (See Figure 8.2,
6 Real Versus Personal Property.) Property that is not real property is **personal property** (also
7 known as *chattel*). A savings account, a car, and jewelry are all personal property. Just as the
8 term *realty* is used to denote real property, the term *personalty* is used to indicate personal
9 property. It is important to distinguish between real property and personal property in a
10 real estate transaction. All personal property included in the sale should be identified in
11 the contract for sale, or the seller is entitled to remove the property.

FIGURE 8.2 ■ Real Versus Personal Property

Real Estate or Real Property
Land and anything permanently
attached to it

Personal Property
Movable items not attached to
real property; items severed
from real property

Fixture
Item of personal property converted
to real property by attaching it to the
real property with the intention that it
become permanently a part thereof

Trade Fixture
Item of personal property attached to
real property that is owned by a tenant
and is used in a business; legally
removable by tenant

1   Real property can become personal property by the *act of severance*. For example, tim-
2   ber is real property, but when cut it becomes personal property by the act of severance.
3   Vice versa, personal property can become real property by *attachment*.

4   ## Fixtures

5   **Fixtures** are objects that were personal property but have been permanently attached to or made
6   part of real estate and thus are now real property. A bathtub, for example, was personal property
7   in its container in a warehouse, but once permanently attached in a home, it became real
8   property. Some items, such as drapes, ceiling fans, and chandeliers, are more difficult to
9   classify. In those cases where contracting parties have not had the foresight to include
10 such items in a real estate sale contract, the courts generally use the following set of *tests*
11 to decide if an item is a fixture:

12 **Intent of the parties.** As in most points of law, intent of the party placing an article on or
13 in real property is of primary importance. Statements made by an owner to witnesses may
14 indicate the intent to make an item a fixture. For example, including a washer and dryer in
15 a sale contract as part of the real property would remove any doubt about the owner's inten-
16 tion. In disputes between buyer and seller, the terms and conditions of the sale contract usu-
17 ally are strictly enforced unless there is some indication that the buyer was misled.

T O   R E M E M B E R :   T E S T   F O R   F I X T U R E S

I	Intent of the parties
R	Relationship between parties
M	Method of annexation
A	Adaptation of the article

---

18 **Relationship between the parties.** In this test the courts seek to determine the exact nature
19 of the relationship between the parties. Is it buyer and seller or landlord and tenant? Ordi-
20 narily, residential tenants are required to leave any item they have attached to the landlord's
21 real property. However, if a building is leased as a retail store and display racks are attached
22 to the walls and counters are attached to the floor, the courts generally rule that such items
23 are trade fixtures and may be removed. A **trade fixture** is an article that is attached by a com-
24 mercial tenant as a necessary part of the tenant's trade or business and is personal property.

25 **Method of annexation.** The manner in which an article is attached to real property gener-
26 ally indicates whether it is a fixture or personal property. Normally, if removing the item
27 would result in damage to real property, the article is classified as a fixture. A set of built-in
28 storage cabinets in the utility room would normally be considered a fixture if removing it
29 would damage the wall.

30 **Adaptation of the article.** This test seeks to determine if an article was designed for, or
31 necessary to, the normal use of a specific property. If the item is adapted or custom-built
32 to fit the property, it will likely be considered a fixture even though it is moveable. For
33 example, hurricane shutters are considered to be fixtures because they are custom-made to
34 fit specific windows in a structure even though they are not on the windows at all times.
35 The shutters are placed on the windows when a storm is approaching and removed when
36 the danger has passed. Another example of a fixture would be draperies that have been
37 custom-made using the same decorative pattern as the wallpaper.

1 These tests should not be necessary if all personal property to be sold with the real
2 estate is listed in the sale contract. This eliminates misunderstanding and possible litiga-
3 tion. Frequently, a potential buyer will ask an owner who is anxious to sell, "Do the washer
4 and dryer go with the house, or are you taking them with you?" To which the owner might
5 reply, "Oh, yes!" (yes, what?), or the owner might even make a forthright statement like
6 "They go with the house." In either case the buyer would be well advised to list the washer
7 and dryer in the sale contract to remove any doubt.

GENERAL PROPERTY RIGHTS

9 The practical result of the allodial system has been government recognition and protec-
10 tion of private rights of ownership. Real property ownership rights (or bundle of rights)
11 include the:

12 ■ *right of disposition*. This right permits the owner to sell, mortgage, dedicate, give
13   away, or otherwise dispose of all or any portion of the property.

14 ■ *right of use (control)*. This right entitles the owner to uninterrupted use and
15   control of the owner's land in any manner consistent with local laws. In earlier
16   times, this right was almost absolute. As the density of population increased, it
17   became necessary to enact legislation to ensure that one owner's use of land did
18   not and would not interfere with his neighbors' use of land.

19 ■ *right of possession*. This right allows an owner to occupy the premises in privacy
20   with maximum legal control over entry and use of that property. An owner
21   acquires the right of possession of a property on the day that owner becomes
22   legally entitled to the rents or income from such property, even though the
23   owner may not have set foot on the land itself.

24 ■ *right of exclusion (quiet enjoyment)*. This right is formal recognition that "a man's
25   home is his castle." An owner has the right to control entry onto the owner's
26   land without interference and to collect damages for certain forms of trespass.
27   Other parties must have permission to enter the land of an owner with this right.
28   This right has also been modified by judicial decisions and legislation.

TO REMEMBER: BUNDLE OF RIGHTS
D   Disposition (sell or give away)
U   Use (control)
P   Possession (occupy)
E   Exclusion (quiet enjoyment)

ESTATES AND TENANCIES

30 Estate refers to the degree, quantity, nature, and extent of the bundle of rights in real prop-
31 erty. The terms *estate* and *tenancy* are to be used interchangeably. Estates are divided into
32 two broad classifications: freehold (unknown duration) and nonfreehold (known dura-
33 tion). (See Figure 8.3, Estates in Real Property.)

F I G U R E   8.3 ■   Estates in Real Property

Freehold Estates are estates of ownership.
- Fee Simple (Absolute) is the most comprehensive estate and it is inheritable.
- Life Estate is measured by a natural life span ("for the life of").
  - Estate in Reversion occurs when property returns to the grantor.
  - Remainder Estate occurs when property goes to a third party.
  - Vested Remainderman refers to someone whose legal name is specified.
  - Contingent Remainderman refers to someone whose legal name is not specified (such as, first-born child).

Nonfreehold Estates (Leasehold) are estates of possession.
- Estate for Years is a written lease agreement with a specific starting and ending date.
- Tenancy at Will is either an oral agreement or one that has no specific ending date.
- Tenancy at Sufferance occurs when the lease period has ended and the tenant is a holdover.

Freehold Estates

A **freehold estate** is an ownership interest for an indefinite period. That interest can be inherited (fee simple estate) or can be measured by the lifetime of an individual (life estate).

Fee simple estate. The most comprehensive collection of real property freehold rights is the fee simple estate. A **fee simple estate** means absolute and complete ownership, subject only to governmental restrictions (for example, taxation and police powers). Sometimes called *fee* and sometimes *fee simple absolute*, all these terms identify an ownership interest with complete power to use, to dispose of, and to allow the property to descend to heirs. It is the highest type of real property interest recognized by law.

Life estate. Life estates, which exist today, are another type of freehold estate. The owner has considerably fewer rights than the owner of a fee simple estate. The life estate owner owns the property for only the period of the lifetime of an individual (the owner or other designated person). During the time an owner enjoys a life estate, the owner must maintain the property and not permit *waste* (anything that reduces the value of property) to occur. The life estate owner also must pay the taxes and property insurance and keep current any mortgage(s) or lien(s) to preserve the property.

When the life estate ends, the property reverts (returns) to the original grantor (previous owner) or goes to a third party, called a **remainderman**. If the life estate reverts to the original grantor, an *estate in reversion* (reversion estate) is created. For example, John Smith transfers his property to his mother, Mary Smith, for her lifetime. The property is to return to John (the grantor) upon Mary's death. Mary has a life estate, and John has an estate in reversion.

If the life estate is to go to a remainderman, the remainderman owns a *remainder estate* while the life estate exists. The instrument (typically a deed) that establishes the life estate also designates the remainderman. The remainderman acquires either a fee simple estate in severalty or concurrent ownership if more than one remainderman is designated. For example, Sue Jones's deed states that she owns the property for her lifetime and that upon her death, the property will transfer to her sons, Matt and Adam (the remaindermen). Sue has a life estate, and Matt and Adam have a remainder estate.

Nonfreehold or Leasehold Estates

Nonfreehold estates have a known duration and do *not* involve an ownership interest. *Nonfreehold* or *less-than-freehold* estates grant the right to use and possess (but not own) real property. Nonfreehold estates are also referred to as leasehold estates.

A **leasehold estate** (tenancy) is an interest in real property that a tenant possesses. Leasehold estates are measured in calendar time. Under a lease, the tenant possesses a leasehold estate and the landlord (property owner) possesses a *reversion estate*. At the end of the leasehold estate, possession and use of the property reverts to the property owner. There are three types of leasehold estates: estate for years, tenancy at will, and tenancy at sufferance. (See Figure 8.3, Estates in Real Property.)

Estate for years. An **estate for years** (or tenancy for years) is a tenancy with a specific starting and ending date. It exists for a designated period, which may be any length of time from less than a year to a period of many years (such as a 99-year lease). An estate for years is a leasehold estate that is created by a written lease agreement. An estate for years establishes an interest in real property for the tenant (right to use, possession, and exclusion) but does not convey actual title (or ownership) or the right of disposition. (Refer also to General Property Rights on page 174.)

Tenancy at will. A **tenancy at will** is a lease agreement that has a beginning date but no fixed termination date, such as a week-to-week or a month-to-month agreement. For example, assume Harry does not intend to use his lake cabin for a while, so Harry allows his friend Bill to live in the cabin for $100 per week. A tenancy at will has been created because Bill has been given permission to use the cabin and a rental rate has been agreed upon, but no ending date was established.

83.57, F.S.

Florida statute refers to this as a *tenancy without specific term*. Tenancies at will may be written or oral agreements. Notice for termination of tenancies at will is set in statute and is based on the time interval between rent payments:

- Week to week—7 days' notice
- Month to month—15 days' notice

Other actions that will terminate a tenancy at will include sale of the property or the death of the owner or renter.

Tenancy at sufferance. A **tenancy at sufferance** occurs when a tenant stays in possession of the property beyond the ending date of a legal tenancy without the consent of the landlord. The tenant has no estate or title but only "naked" possession and is not entitled to notice to terminate. The payment and acceptance of rent alone shall not be construed to be a renewal of the lease. However, if the tenant's *holding over* is continued with the written consent of the lessor, then the tenancy becomes a tenancy at will under Florida law.

83.04, F.S.

Sole Ownership and Concurrent Ownership

Sole ownership and concurrent ownership are ways in which people hold freehold estates. When title to property is held by one person, it is called an **estate in severalty** or sole ownership. (To help you remember, think of "severed" ownership.) Ownership by two or more persons at the same time is **concurrent ownership**. There are three types of estates (tenancies) with concurrent owners: tenancy in common, joint tenancy, and tenancy by the entireties. (Refer to Figure 8.4, Sole Ownership Versus Concurrent Ownership.)

F I G U R E 8.4 ■ Sole Ownership Versus Concurrent Ownership

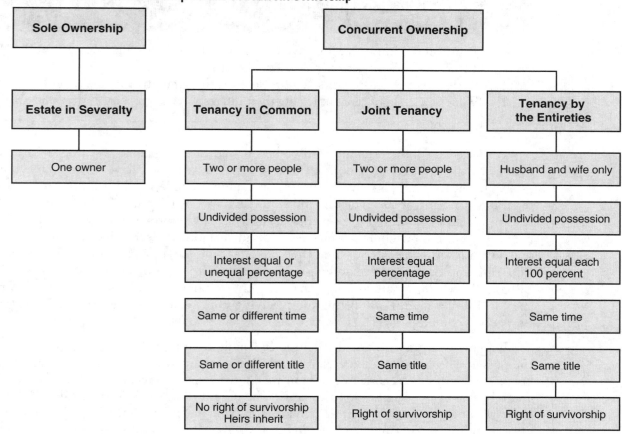

1 **Tenancy in common.** When two or more persons wish to share the ownership of a single
2 property, they may choose to do so as **tenants in common.** It is the most frequently used form
3 of co-ownership, except for husband-and-wife ownership. Tenants in common may acquire
4 title at different times or at the same time. As tenants in common, each owns an "undivided
5 interest" in the property. An **undivided interest** is interest in the entire property, rather than
6 ownership of a particular part of the property. For example, Sally and Kathy own a house as
7 tenants in common. Sally holds two-thirds interest in the entire property, and Kathy owns
8 one-third interest in the entire property. When Sally and Kathy die, their interest in the
9 property will descend to their heirs. On Sally's death, for example, her two-thirds interest in
10 the property will descend to her legal heirs (or as instructed in her will).

11 **Joint tenancy.** A major difference between a joint tenancy and a tenancy in common is
12 that **joint tenancy** is characterized by the right of survivorship. **Right of survivorship**
13 means that the share of a co-owner who has died goes to the surviving co-owner(s) and
14 not to the deceased tenant's heirs. Joint tenants have an undivided interest in real prop-
15 erty. A joint tenancy can exist only when the four "unities" of *possession, interest, title,* and
16 *time* are present.

TO REMEMBER: FOUR UNITIES OF A JOINT TENANCY		
P	Possession	Joint tenants have the same rights of undivided possession
I	Interest	Joint tenants have equal ownership interest
T	Title	Joint tenants acquire title on the same instrument (deed)
T	Time	Joint tenants acquire their interests in the property at the same time

689.21, F.S.

Today a true joint tenancy cannot be created unless specific wording in the deed conveying the property provides for survivorship. Under present law a deed conveying an estate in joint tenancy to ensure survivorship must include wording similar to "as joint tenants with right of survivorship and not as tenants in common." This continues that feature of joint tenancy that prevents disposition of the property by will or descent to heirs. As joint tenants die, their shares are divided among the surviving tenants until only one owner is left. The sole survivor then has a fee simple estate in severalty. For example, Bob, Bill, and Betty own ten acres as joint tenants with right of survivorship. If Bob dies, Bill and Betty will remain as joint tenants, with each having a 50 percent share of ownership. If Bill dies later, Betty is the sole surviving joint tenant. At the time of Bill's death, Betty owns the property in severalty.

A joint tenant who wants to sell his or her share of a property may do so. However, the person who buys that share cannot be a joint tenant with the other original owners, but instead will be a tenant in common without the right to receive any property on the death of one of the original joint tenants. The tenant in common's share can be disposed of by will, descent, or other arrangement. For example, John, Jim, Jill, and Jane own an office building as joint tenants with right of survivorship. Jim sells his ownership interest (25 percent) to Sally. Sally is a tenant in common while John, Jill, and Jane remain joint tenants. If John should die, his interest will be divided between Jill and Jane. If Sally should die, her interest will go to her heirs or according to her will.

Tenancy by the entireties. A **tenancy by the entireties** is basically a joint tenancy between husband and wife. The four unities of a joint tenancy with right of survivorship must exist, and the two co-owners must be married to each other at the time they take title. This estate has its origin in the common-law attitude that a husband and wife are one ownership entity. The deed or other instrument of conveyance does not have to state expressly that a tenancy by the entireties exists. If the parties are truly husband and wife, the estate is implied. While not mandatory, the deed should reflect a tenancy by the entireties to serve notice to others that such an estate exists, such as John P. Smith and Sally R. Smith, a married couple.

When one spouse dies, that individual's ownership interest automatically transfers to the surviving spouse by *right of survivorship*. Neither spouse may will any portion of the spousal interest in an estate by the entireties. This unique form of co-ownership can be divided by annulment or by divorce. In the event of death, the survivor emerges as the severalty (sole) owner of the property. In the event of annulment or divorce, the tenancy by the entireties is ended, and a tenancy in common results.

SPECIAL OWNERSHIP INTERESTS

Homestead

222, F.S.

Homeowners (including single persons) in Florida may homestead their permanent (principal) residence. Declaring one's residence as a **homestead** entitles the owners to certain protections and benefits including the following:

- *Protection of the homestead.* The homesteaded property is protected from forced sale for debts owing to personal loans, credit card debt, and so forth. However, the protection does not prevent foreclosure for nonpayment of property taxes, special assessments, mortgages, vendors' liens, or construction liens secured with the homesteaded property.

- *Tax exemption.* The Florida Constitution allows a tax exemption from assessed property value. The current homestead tax exemption is up to $50,000 for qualifying homesteads and is deducted from the assessed value when calculating taxable value. (See also chapter 18.)

- *Size of homestead.* The size of homesteaded property is restricted to 160 acres outside a municipality (city) or up to ½ acre if the property is located within the city.

- *Protection of the family.* According to Florida Statute, if a married person dies and the family homestead was titled in that deceased person's name only (in severalty), by operation of law (even if a will states otherwise), the surviving spouse receives a life estate and the children (lineal descendants) receive a remainder estate. If there are no children, the surviving spouse receives a fee simple estate in the homestead. The purpose of the homestead law, therefore, is to protect the family and prevent it from being displaced from the homestead.

Other Protections for the Surviving Spouse

732.2065, F.S.

Elective share. Florida law provides protection for a surviving spouse who has been excluded from the deceased spouse's will. In such cases the surviving spouse may elect to file within 120 days (4 months) a claim of **elective share**. Elective share consists of 30 percent of the net estate (real and personal property) of the deceased spouse. In addition to the elective share, the surviving spouse will also receive:

- Homestead property. The surviving spouse is entitled to homestead-exempt property regardless of whether the survivor files for elective share.

- Property owned by the couple as tenants by the entirety. All property titled in both spouses names as tenants by the entireties automatically transfers to the surviving spouse.

Distribution of Assets Resulting from Divorce

In Florida, when a husband and wife divorce, the court generally sets apart to each spouse the spouse's nonmarital assets. Nonmarital assets are **separate property** and include any property the husband or wife owned separately prior to the marriage and property acquired during the marriage by inheritance or gift.

61.075, F.S.

1 Florida law provides for the divorcing couple's **marital assets** to be divided *equitably*.
2 Marital assets include any property acquired during the marriage individually by either
3 spouse or jointly by them. The Florida court begins with the premise that the distribution
4 of marital assets should be equal. The court then takes into account all relevant factors
5 such as the economic circumstances of the parties, the duration of the marriage, any inter-
6 ruption of personal careers or educational opportunities of either party, the contribution
7 of one spouse, and the personal career or educational opportunity of the other spouse, and
8 so forth.

COOPERATIVES, CONDOMINIUMS, AND TIME-SHARING

Background

11 In Florida the Cooperative Act (719, F.S.), the Condominium Act (718, F.S.), and the
12 Florida Vacation Plan and Timesharing Act (721, F.S.) establish rights and obligations of
13 the developer, the association, and unit owners and buyers. These statutes all require that
14 before the sale of developer residential shared housing, purchasers be provided with cer-
15 tain disclosure statements. These statements include, for example, property description,
16 form of title-interest, description of common areas and amenities, existence of judgments
17 or liens, management arrangements, escrow provisions for deposits, restrictions on the
18 sale or transfer of units, apportionment of common expenses, construction completion
19 date, estimated operating budget, estimated closing costs, and copies of key documents.

20 The Division of Florida Condominiums, Timeshares, and Mobile Homes of the Depart-
21 ment of Business and Professional Regulation is the state agency charged with ensuring
22 compliance with the laws regulating all three of these multiple-ownership forms. Because
23 Florida is perhaps the most active of the states in producing and promoting multiple-
24 ownership dwelling units, a complete description of cooperatives, condominiums, and
25 time-sharing is appropriate here.

Cooperatives

719, F.S.

27 A **cooperative**, cooperative association, or co-op is normally organized as a corporation.
28 The corporation holds title to the land and improvements. Authority and control of the
29 corporation may be vested in an elected board of directors or trustees. Some apartments may
30 be more expensive than others, depending on size and location. The owners purchase shares
31 of stock in the corporation. The important result of the stock purchase is that ownership of
32 the stock entitles the purchaser to a **proprietary lease** and the right to occupy the unit for
33 the life of the corporation.

34 Section 719.117, F.S., stipulates that ad valorem (according to valuation) taxes and
35 special assessments by taxing authorities be assessed against each cooperative parcel sepa-
36 rately. The taxes and special assessments levied constitute a lien on only the individual
37 unit and not on any other portion of the cooperative property. Owners-shareholders may
38 deduct their real estate taxes and mortgage interest from taxable income. Each individual
39 shareholder must pay the corporation a monthly assessment based on a proportional share
40 of the amount necessary for the payment of common expenses such as operating and main-
41 tenance expenses. If an owner-shareholder fails to pay the monthly assessment fees, the
42 corporation may place a lien on the individual unit and eventually foreclose on the unit.

DEFINITION OF A COOPERATIVE

Cooperative means that form of ownership of real property wherein legal title is vested in a corporation or other entity and the beneficial use is evidenced by an ownership interest in the association and a lease or other evidence of title or possession granted by the association as the owner of all the cooperative property.

Reference: Section 719.103, F.S.

1 The corporation, or its governing board, may stipulate that shareholders sell their stock to
2 either a board-approved buyer or back to the corporation itself. Some cooperatives require
3 that owners-shareholders sell their stock at the original purchase price, thereby depriving
4 the unit stockholders of any profit. Most cooperatives prohibit the sale of stock shares to
5 anyone until the buyer is approved by the corporation or association.

719.503, F.S.

6 **Disclosures and cancellation period.** The developer is required to include a disclosure in
7 the sale contract stating that the buyer of a residential cooperative unit may cancel the
8 contract within *15 calendar days* of signing the contract and receipt by the buyer of all
9 items required by F.S. 719. The contract for resale of a residential cooperative unit must
10 include a clause stating that the buyer acknowledges receipt of the articles of incorpora-
11 tion of the association, the bylaws and rules of the association, and the question and
12 answer sheet at least *three business days* prior to signing the contract. If the buyer has not
13 received these required documents prior to signing the contract, the contract for resale
14 must include a clause stating that the buyer may cancel the contract within *three busi-
15 ness* days of receipt of these required documents. The buyer's right to cancel the contract
16 terminates at closing. A contract for sale of a residential cooperative unit that does not
17 include either disclosure is voidable by the buyer.

18 ## Condominiums

718, F.S.

19 A **condominium** is a form of real property consisting of condominium units and com-
20 mon elements. An individual owns a unit exclusively and owns an undivided fractional
21 (proportionate) share of the common elements. **Common elements** are legally attached
22 to each unit and are transferred with the unit when it is sold. The structural parts of the
23 building and usually the land are common elements. The roof, walls (other than interior
24 unit walls), hallways, elevators, and recreation facilities are examples of common ele-
25 ments. (Refer to Figure 8.5, Condominium Ownership.) A deed to a unit conveys the
26 unit to the purchaser together with its proportionate ownership interest in the common
27 elements. Each unit owner's share of ownership in the common elements is in the same
28 proportion so that the unit owner will share in the cost of operating the condominium. For
29 example, all things being equal, the owner of a 1,000-square-foot condo will usually pay a
30 larger share of the operating costs than will the owner of an 800-square-foot condo.

FIGURE 8.5 ■ Condominium Ownership

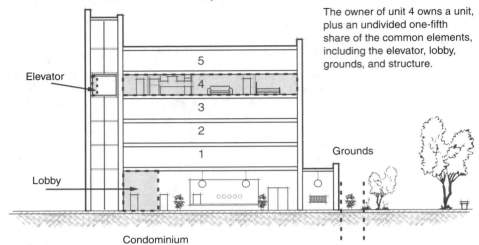

The owner of unit 4 owns a unit, plus an undivided one-fifth share of the common elements, including the elevator, lobby, grounds, and structure.

Condominium documents are a set of written instruments describing the condominium and the association. The individual legal documents that are included in the condominium documents are explained below.

- *Declaration of condominium.* A condominium is created by recording the **declaration of condominium** in the county records of the county where the property is located. The declaration contains legal descriptions of the property, including the units. It also describes each unit owner's undivided share in the common elements, membership and voting rights in the association, and covenants and restrictions on the use of the units and common elements.

- *Articles of incorporation of the association.* The operation of a condominium is carried out through its association, usually a not-for-profit corporation. The articles of incorporation create the corporate entity responsible for operating the condominium.

- *Bylaws of the association.* This document describes the operational requirements of the association. It provides for the administration of the association including procedures for calling meetings, determining voting requirements, and so forth. Each purchaser, by accepting title to a unit, automatically becomes an association member and is bound by the association rules and regulations.

- *Frequently Asked Questions (FAQ) and Answers.* The FAQ informs prospective purchases about restrictions on the leasing of a unit, information concerning assessments, and whether and in what amount the unit owners or the association are obligated to pay rent or land use fees for recreational facilities.

- *Estimated Operating Budget.* The *estimated operating budget* provides detailed estimates of various common expenses that are to be shared by the unit owners. An annual operating budget must be prepared reflecting all anticipated costs for management, maintenance, fire and extended coverage insurance, liability insurance, garbage collection, property taxes on common elements, utilities for common areas, and reserves for capital expenditures and deferred maintenance. Once adopted, the budget forms the basis for the monthly assessment fees each unit owner must pay.

718.503, F.S.
718.504, F.S.
61J2-23.001,
F.A.C.
61J2-23.002,
F.A.C.

Disclosures and cancellation period. The developer is required to file the condominium documents with the Division of Florida Condominiums, Timeshares, and Mobile Homes, prior to offering units for sale. Developers of 20 or more new residential units must also prepare a **prospectus** and file it. A copy of the prospectus must be given to prospective purchasers. The prospectus summarizes some of the major points detailed in the condominium documents. The developer must include a disclosure in the sale contract stating that the buyer of a new residential unit may cancel the contract within *15 calendar days* of signing the contract and of receipt by the buyer of the condominium documents (the prospectus and the documents detailed above). The Commission requires licensees who advertise, list for sale, or sell time-share units to provide additional disclosures in the listing contract, advertisements, and contracts for sale and purchase.

If purchasing from a private party (resale), the buyer is entitled to a copy of the declaration of condominium, the articles of incorporation of the association, the bylaws, the rules of the association, the FAQ, and a copy of the most recent year-end financial information, at the seller's expense. Buyers must also receive a copy of the governance form. This form is provided by the Division of Florida Condominiums, Timeshares, and Mobile Homes. The governance form summarizes the role of the board of directors and the rights of the unit owners. (See Figure 8.6, Condominium Disclosures.)

The contract for resale of a residential condominium unit must include a clause that states that the buyer acknowledges receipt of the condominium documents and that the prospective buyer may cancel the contract within *three business days* after the date of execution of the contract *and* receipt by the buyer of the condominium documents. (*Note:* The cancellation period does not begin to run until the condominium documents have been delivered. A buyer should verify that all documents have been received *before* signing receipt for delivery of the documents.)

If a prospective buyer chooses to timely cancel the contract, a real estate licensee may return the escrowed binder deposit to the prospective purchaser without first securing the seller's permission, provided the licensee was notified in writing that the buyer is

FIGURE 8.6 ■ Condominium Disclosures

	Developer (20+ Units New Residential)	Resale
Prospectus	✔	
Estimated operating budget	✔	
Most recent year-end financial report		✔
Rules of the association		✔
Governance form		✔
Declaration	✔	✔
Articles of incorporation	✔	✔
Bylaws	✔	✔
FAQ	✔	✔

canceling the contract during the statutory time period for cancellation. Even if the seller objects, the Real Estate License Law states that the licensee may return the deposit to the purchaser without having to notify the Commission of conflicting demands. (See also Disposition of Escrow Deposits, chapter 5.)

Condominium advantages. Condominium ownership has the following advantages:

- Property taxes are assessed and collected on each unit, just as if it were a detached single-family unit; property taxes and mortgage interest paid on an owner's unit plus their proportionate share of property taxes and mortgage interest paid on the common elements are deductible from taxable income.

- Default in payment of taxes or mortgage by an owner of one unit may result in foreclosure of only that unit; it does not affect the other unit owners.

- Building costs on a room-for-room, square-foot by square-foot basis typically are lower in a condominium than in a single-family structure.

- Common elements include features such as a recreation center, swimming pool, tennis courts, and so forth.

- Increased security, property appreciation, and pride of ownership are not available to apartment renters.

Condominium disadvantages. Condominium ownership has the following disadvantages:

- Unit owners must abide by restrictions on the use of their unit and common elements.

- Unit owners are personally involved in the operation of the condominium association.

- Nonpayment of the monthly maintenance fee (association dues) may create a lien against the owner's unit.

- A reserve fund is established for future expenses such as a new roof; however, if the fund is not adequate, the owners are charged a special assessment. Special assessments are levied when the association determines that there is either not enough money in the budget for a certain expenditure, or the expenditure was not anticipated and therefore was not included in the annual budget.

- Unit owners usually are not able to enlarge their units.

- Right-of-first refusal provisions reserved by many associations allow the association to purchase a unit at the fair market value before it is offered for sale to the public, slowing down the sale of the owner's unit.

WEB LINK

You can learn more about Florida's Condominium Act. The Florida statutes are available at **www.leg.state.fl.us/ welcome/index.cfm**. Directly under the Senate seal, select "Florida Statutes," then "Title XL Real and Personal Property," and then "Chapter 718."

The Division of Florida Condominiums, Timeshares, and Mobile Homes publishes a helpful brochure, "A Guide to Purchasing a Condominium." It is available at **www.myflorida.com/dbpr/lsc/documents/ purchasing_guide.pdf**.

Time-Sharing

721, F.S.

A few owners can afford to pay full price for a second home strictly for vacation use in attractive surroundings. On the other hand, thousands of buyers can afford a second home in their favorite vacation area if they pay only a small, fractional part of the full price. As a result, time-sharing, a spin-off of the recreational condominium concept, was born.

The property is first organized as a condominium. Each unit is divided into time segments of ownership, usually 52 weeks. A deed or some evidence of ownership is prepared for each ownership segment. **Time-share** ownership involves an undivided interest in a living unit according to the number of weeks purchased. For example, if one week is purchased, the buyer owns a 1/52 interest in the unit. Size, location, amenities, and time of year all affect the purchase price of the time-share unit.

475.011, F.S.
721.20, F.S.
61J2-23.001,
F.A.C
61J2-23.002,
F.A.C.

Time-Share Act. Potential buyers of time-share units in Florida are protected by the Condominium Act and by the Florida Vacation Plan and Timesharing Act, Chapter 721, F.S. Chapter 721 applies to all time-share plans consisting of more than seven time-share periods over a span of at least three years and in which the facilities or accommodations are located within the State of Florida. The Vacation Plan and Timesharing Act requires a developer disclosure that purchasers may cancel the contract within *ten calendar days* of contract signing or receipt of the public offering statement, whichever is later. Under the provisions of this act, sales personnel selling time-share plans of any type must be licensed as a real estate broker, broker associate, or sales associate except as provided in s. 475.011. Owner-developers who develop and sell time-share units may hire unlicensed salespersons. The salespersons must be salaried employees who are not paid a commission and who do not receive compensation on a transactional basis (for example, bonuses based on sales quotas). It is unlawful for a real estate licensee to collect an advance fee for the listing of a time-share unit. Licensees who list or sell time-share units must be familiar with the disclosures required under Florida Statute 721.

Time-share ownership. In actual practice, the form of time-share ownership is normally divided into two types: interval ownership and right-to-use.

1. *Interval ownership.* Interval ownership is fee simple ownership and contains the same rights as any other property conveyed by deed. The deed must be recordable in the public records. The owner has the right to sell, rent, will, or give away the property. In Florida and most other states, the original declaration of condominium must disclose the type of ownership estate that the deeds to the condominium units will convey.

2. *Right-to-use.* Rights granted with the right-to-use forms of time-sharing are temporary in nature. A leasehold interest is long-term, usually 20 years to 40 years. After a specified period, which could be from 1 year to 99 years, such rights revert back to the developer-seller. Right-to-use time-sharing is a much greater gamble than is interval ownership, in part because of a court ruling that under some bankruptcy conditions, those rights already bought and paid for are unenforceable.

S U M M A R Y   O F   I M P O R T A N T   P O I N T S

- *Land* refers to the surface of the earth and everything attached to it by nature.
- *Real estate* refers to the land and improvements.
- *Real property* includes all real estate plus the bundle of rights.
- Physical components of land are surface rights, subsurface rights, and air rights.
- Any tangible asset that is not real property is personal property (or chattel).
- Four tests regarding fixtures are (1) intent of the parties, (2) relationship between the parties, (3) method of annexation, and (4) adaptation of the article.
- The bundle of rights consists of the following: right of disposition, right of use (control), right of possession, and the right of exclusion (quiet enjoyment).

- A *freehold estate* is an ownership interest for an indefinite period. Fee simple is the most comprehensive freehold estate, and it is inheritable. A life estate is also a freehold estate, but it is measured by an individual's natural life span.

- A *leasehold estate*, or nonfreehold estate, is a tenant interest in real property measured in calendar time. The three types of leasehold estates are estate for years, tenancy at will, and tenancy at sufferance.

- An *estate for years* is a tenancy with a specific starting and ending date.

- A *tenancy at will* is a lease agreement that has a beginning date but no fixed termination date.

- A *tenancy at sufferance* occurs when a tenant retains possession of the property beyond the ending date of a legal tenancy without the consent of the landlord (tenant holds over).

- Sole ownership and concurrent ownership are ways that people hold freehold estates. An estate in severalty is created when title to property is in one person's name (sole owner). Ownership by two or more persons at the same time is concurrent ownership.

- The three types of concurrent ownership are (1) tenancy in common, (2) joint tenancy, and (3) tenancy by the entireties.

- Tenants in common have an undivided interest in the entire property. This interest can be left in a will or pass to heirs if there is no will.

- The four unities of a joint tenancy are (1) possession, (2) interest, (3) title, and (4) time. Joint tenancies are characterized by right of survivorship (when one co-owner dies, the deceased's share goes to the surviving co-owner).

- To create a tenancy by the entireties, the co-owners must be married to each other at the time they take title. Share automatically transfers to the surviving spouse by right of survivorship.

- Floridians may file for homestead of their permanent residence. Doing so allows a tax exemption from assessed value of up to $50,000.

- Purchasers of a unit in a cooperative buy shares of stock in a corporation. A proprietary lease entitles the purchaser to the right to occupy the unit.

- A *condominium* is real property consisting of condo units and common elements. A condominium is created by recording the declaration of condominium. The articles of incorporation create the corporate entity responsible for operating the condominium.

- Developers of 20 or more residential condo units must give purchasers a copy of the prospectus.

- There is a 3-business-day cooling off period to cancel a condominium contract for sale from a property owner. There is a 15-calendar-day notice to cancel a condominium contract for sale from a developer.

R E V I E W   Q U E S T I O N S

1. The most comprehensive interest in real property that an individual may possess is a(n)
   a. estate for years.
   b. life estate.
   c. remainder estate.
   d. fee simple estate.

2. Physical components of real property do NOT include
   a. surface.
   b. air space.
   c. equitable rights.
   d. subsurface.

3. Fixtures are items that
   a. are fixed, or attached, to real property.
   b. were once personal property but are now real property.
   c. have been incorporated as a part of real property.
   d. are all of the above.

4. A husband and wife decide to get a divorce. In addition to their Florida homesteaded property, they own a vacant lot in the same subdivision acquired in both of their names during the marriage. How will the lot be distributed?
   a. The lot is considered to be separate property and will be distributed equally between the husband and wife.
   b. Because the real estate is community property, each spouse is entitled to a one-half interest in the lot.
   c. The interest in the lot will revert to a life estate and will be distributed to the lineal descendants.
   d. The lot is a marital asset and will be distributed equitably.

5. The bundle of rights associated with real property does NOT include
   a. use.
   b. possession.
   c. disposition.
   d. utility.

6. A man and a woman were recently wed. The woman owns a residential lot that was purchased before the marriage. The lot is considered to be
   a. separate property.
   b. a marital asset.
   c. a tenancy in common.
   d. an estate by the entireties.

7. At the expiration of the lease period and before renegotiation of the lease, a tenant continued to occupy the apartment. The tenant's position is called
   a. a tenancy at will.
   b. a tenancy at sufferance.
   c. a freehold estate.
   d. an estate in reversion.

8. A woman received a new microwave for Christmas. The microwave was installed above her range by screwing the unit to the kitchen cabinets and venting it through the attic. The microwave would be considered
   a. a fixture.
   b. a chattel.
   c. separate property.
   d. personal property.

9. The homestead tax exemption is deducted from the
   a. market value of a property.
   b. assessed value of a property.
   c. sale price of a property.
   d. total cost, including all improvements.

10. A husband and wife own a home with title in both names. The husband owns two small farms in his name only, acquired before the marriage. They have one minor child and one adult son. The husband dies. Which is MOST correct?
    a. The widow owns a life estate in all property.
    b. The property is split equally among the widow and the children.
    c. The widow owns all of the home and may claim 30 percent of the two farms.
    d. The widow owns 30 percent of all of the real estate.

11. The real estate protected by homestead rights is limited to
    a. 640 acres outside a city or town and one acre in town.
    b. 160 acres outside a city or town and one-half acre in town.
    c. 40 acres outside a city or town and one-half acre in town.
    d. 160 acres outside a city or town or one-half acre in town.

12. A constitutional homestead is owned by a man, who is head of a family consisting of himself, his wife, and their three children. The man dies unexpectedly. After his death, the widow
    a. owns the homestead.
    b. owns a life estate in the homestead, and the children are vested remaindermen.
    c. may claim elective share rights of 30 percent of the homestead, and the children divide the remainder.
    d. may claim all of the above.

13. Which estate features right of survivorship?
    a. Leasehold estate
    b. Estate by the entireties
    c. Tenancy at will
    d. Tenancy in common

14. Chapter 475, F.S., defines real property as any interest or estate in
    a. land, improvements, leaseholds, subleaseholds, mineral rights, cemetery lots, or any assignment thereof.
    b. land, improvements, business enterprises and business opportunities, leaseholds, subleaseholds, mineral rights, mobile homes, or any assignment thereof.
    c. land, business enterprises and business opportunities, leaseholds, subleaseholds, mineral rights, cemetery lots, mobile home lots, or any assignment thereof.
    d. land, business enterprises and business opportunities, including any assignment, leasehold, subleasehold, or mineral rights.

15. In Florida, cooperatives and time-shares are regulated by the
    a. Division of Real Estate.
    b. Division of Florida Condominiums, Timeshares, and Mobile Homes.
    c. Department of Housing and Urban Development.
    d. Florida Real Estate Commission.

16. A condominium unit buyer has how long to cancel the purchase contract following the signing of an agreement with a developer?
    a. 3 days
    b. 10 days
    c. 15 days
    d. 20 days

17. Developers of condominium projects with 20 or more units must give buyers
    a. a copy of the prospectus.
    b. the names and business addresses of real estate sales associates assigned.
    c. the names of all current unit owners.
    d. the names of unit owners, unit numbers, and amounts due from unit owners delinquent in monthly assessment fees.

18. Which characteristic applies to condominium ownership?
    a. The corporation holds title to land and improvements.
    b. The purchaser receives shares of stock in the corporation.
    c. A proprietary lease entitles the purchaser to occupy a unit.
    d. The purchaser receives a deed to a particular unit.

19. All these apply to the constitutional homestead exemption EXCEPT
    a. protection from forced sale for nonpayment of certain debts.
    b. deduction of up to $50,000 from the assessed value of the homesteaded property, if claimed.
    c. claimants must hold title to the property and use the home as their principal residence.
    d. it automatically creates a tenancy by the entireties if the person filing for homestead is married.

20. A woman paid cash for a 60-acre lemon grove in Citrus County. The estate is for an indefinite period of time. The woman does NOT own which type of estate in the property?
    a. Fee simple estate
    b. Freehold estate
    c. Leasehold estate
    d. Estate in severalty

9

TITLES, DEEDS, AND OWNERSHIP RESTRICTIONS

OVERVIEW

This chapter concerns the legal instruments and methods used to transfer title to real property. The chapter also discusses the following concepts regarding title to real property: voluntary and involuntary alienation, title insurance, the two types of notice to title, the essential elements of a valid instrument of conveyance, certain covenants found in deeds, and governmental and private restrictions on ownership.

After completing this chapter, the student should be able to:

- differentiate between voluntary and involuntary alienation;

- explain the various methods of acquiring title to real property;

- describe the conditions necessary to acquire real property by adverse possession;

- list and describe the various types of governmental and private restrictions on ownership of real property;

- distinguish between actual notice and constructive notice;

- distinguish between an abstract of title and a chain of title;

- explain the different types of title insurance;

- describe the essential elements of a deed; and

- list and describe the four types of statutory deeds.

KEY TERMS

abstract of title	encroachment	opinion of title
acknowledgment	equitable title	owner's policy
actual notice	escheat	percentage lease
adverse possession	further assurance	police power
alienation	general lien	quiet enjoyment
assignment	general warranty deed	quitclaim deed
chain of title	grantee	seisin
condemnation	granting clause	specific liens
construction lien	grantor	sublease
constructive notice	gross lease	testate
deed	ground lease	title
easement	habendum clause	title insurance
easement appurtenant	intestate	title search
easement by necessity	lender's policy	variable lease
easement by prescription	lien	warranty forever
easement in gross	lis pendens	
eminent domain	net lease	

TITLE TO REAL PROPERTY

In 1821, Florida was purchased from King Ferdinand of Spain. This action placed all of the acquired land, except for the few Spanish private land grants, in the public domain. Title to most of the land in Florida can be traced back to *patents* signed by various presidents transferring land to private ownership. Once in the hands of private owners, title has been and continues to be customarily conveyed by a legal instrument, normally a deed.

Many authorities refer to a voluntary transfer of title from one private party to another private party as a *private grant*, whether by deed, will, or other legal instrument. A transfer of title from any level of government to a private party is called a *public grant*, whether by patent, deed, or other conveyance.

A person who holds vested ownership rights in property is said to have **title**. The right referred to may be a limited or a full bundle of rights, depending on the type of estate conveyed with the title. Therefore, title to real property is a legal concept signifying ownership of the collection of rights called an *estate*. The new owner receives the estate as specified in a deed or other legal instrument of conveyance. Sometimes a person contracts to receive legal title in the future. **Equitable title** is a beneficial interest in real estate that implies that an individual will receive legal title at a future date. (See also Title Theory on page 260.)

ACQUIRING LEGAL TITLE

Alienation is the act of transferring ownership, title, or an interest in real property from one person to another. The alienation may be voluntary (with the owner's control and consent) or involuntary (without control and consent of the owner).

F I G U R E 9.1 ■ Involuntary Alienation

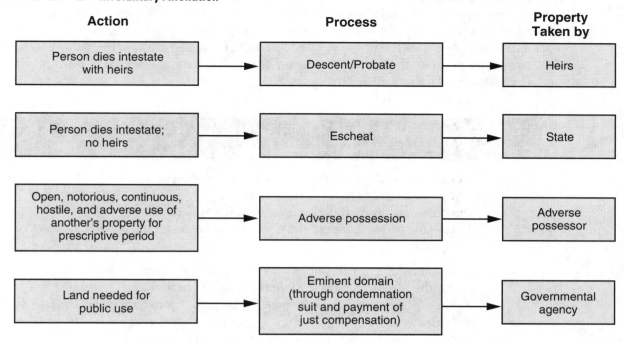

Voluntary Alienation

Deed. The normal real estate transaction involves the sale of property under a contract and is usually consummated by delivery of a deed. A *deed* is defined as a written instrument used to convey an interest in real property. Thus, a deed conveys *legal title*.

732.501, F.S.

Will. A will is a legal instrument used to convey title to real and personal property after the person's death. To die **testate** indicates the *decedent* (deceased person) prepared a will before death. Conveyance of property according to a *last will and testament* is voluntary alienation because the person who left a will—the *testator* (male) or *testatrix* (female)—intended to gift property to a particular individual. A gift of real property is a *devise* and the recipient of the gift is the *devisee*. A gift of personal property is a *bequest* and the recipient is the *beneficiary*.

Involuntary Alienation

732.01, F.S.

Descent. When a person dies without leaving a will (**intestate**), all the property the deceased owned at the time of death passes (descends) to the legal descendants. The legal descendants are known as *heirs*. Priorities as to their entitlement to share in the estate are fixed by Florida probate law. (See Figure 9.1, Involuntary Alienation.)

732.107, F.S.

Escheat to the state. **Escheat** provides for a government, normally a state government, to take the property of an owner who dies intestate and without any known heirs entitled to receive the property. The power of escheat is a practical solution to ensure that property is always owned by someone. In many states, this power extends to personal property as well as to real property.

95.18(1), F.S.

Adverse possession. **Adverse possession** arises when the true owner of record fails to maintain possession and the property is seized by another. If the true owner "sleeps on his rights" and does not use the legal means available to remove a hostile trespasser, the owner will lose the right to the property after a period of time. In Florida, the person attempting to acquire property by adverse possession must comply with all of the conditions listed in the following To Remember box.

TO REMEMBER: CONDITIONS FOR ALIENATION BY ADVERSE POSSESSION

H   Hostile possession of the property (without owner's permission), to the exclusion of the true owner or any who may contest it

O   Open possession with no attempt to conceal occupancy

T   Taxes paid on the property by the adverse possessor during all the years of possession

C   Claim of title, even an imperfect one, exists (sometimes called color of title), thus creating a reasonable basis for the action

A   Adverse possession must continue for seven or more consecutive years without the consent of the owner

N   Notorious and flagrant public possession of the property

Always seek competent legal advice before acquiring real property if the title is based on adverse possession.

Eminent domain. **Eminent domain** gives government the right to take land from an owner through a legal process referred to as **condemnation**, as long as the taking is for a public purpose. The government must pay a fair price for any land taken under eminent domain. The government may exercise this power (or delegate it to railroad and utility companies) regardless of whether the owner wants to part with the property. Therefore, it is a form of involuntary alienation.

Types of Notice

In early English history, conveyances of freehold interests in real property did not depend on written instruments. (See also Freehold Estates, chapter 8.) Instead, the parties conducted their business on the land, and the townspeople assembled around them to witness the event. The seller orally announced to the townspeople that he was transferring the land to the buyer. He symbolically "did the deed" by handing the buyer a twig or a clump of earth to give the world *actual notice* of the transfer of ownership rights. Today, there are two types of notice that have equal legal priority:

1. **Actual notice** is direct knowledge acquired in the course of a transaction. When the townspeople witnessed the transfer of earth or twig from one party to another, they had actual notice of the transfer of ownership rights. Assume that a seller discloses orally to the buyer that there is a construction lien on his home for an unpaid pool repair job. The seller has given the buyer actual notice that there is a lien on the property.

2. **Constructive notice** (or *legal notice*) is accomplished by recording the information in the public records. When the pool company records a construction lien on the property for the unpaid repair job, it gives the world constructive notice of the lien.

695.03, F.S.

Recording a properly executed and "acknowledged" instrument of conveyance puts the world on notice regarding an owner's interests in real property. All instruments affecting ownership of real property *may* be recorded in the public records of the county in which the property is located. (Florida law does not require documents to be recorded.) When properly recorded, these instruments are considered notice to the world, with precisely the same effect and authority as if the owner had given actual notice. All people dealing with the real property are bound by all recorded documents. Recordation of a conveyance protects both the holder of the title and the public from fraud because the true ownership of real property is open to verification by the public. To be recorded a deed must first be acknowledged by the grantor and the acknowledgment must be witnessed and certified by a notary public. **Acknowledgment** is the formal declaration before a notary public by the grantor that the signing is a free act. Other requirements for recording include the signatures of two witnesses. In Florida, the notary public taking the acknowledgment may be one of the witnesses. (See Figure 9.2, Short Form of Acknowledgment.)

Condition of Title

A **chain of title** is the complete successive record of a property's ownership. Beginning with the earliest owner, title may pass to many individuals. Each owner is "linked" to the next so that a "chain" is formed. A chain of title can be traced through linking conveyances from the present owner back to the earliest recorded owner.

712.02, F.S.

A **title search** is an examination of all of the public records to determine whether any defects exist in the chain of title. Recorded instruments such as deeds, divorce decrees, wills, and mortgages are included. In actual practice, the search does not go all the way back in history to the original land grant. State statute determines how far back into history the search must go. Florida's Marketable Record Titles Act limits the search to 30 years. Thus the original source of title, known as the *root of title*, goes back 30 years. The law extinguishes certain interests in real property and cures certain defects arising before the root of title. Therefore, it is necessary to search only from the current owner to the root.

F I G U R E 9.2 ■ Short Form of Acknowledgment (695.25, F.S.)

STATE OF: **Florida**

COUNTY OF: **Pinellas**

The foregoing instrument was acknowledged before me this **15th** day of **July**, 20**12**, by **Martha Sammis** who is personally known to me or has produced **a driver's license (or other type of proof)** as identification.

(NOTARY SEAL)

Notary's Signature
Notary Public

My Commission Expires: **January 1, 2015**

LIS PENDENS

A *lis pendens* (Latin for *action pending*) is a notice recorded in the public records (constructive notice) of a pending legal action that involves real estate. The notice of pending legal action states the names of the parties, the object of the action, and a legal description of the property.

A lender initiating a lawsuit to foreclose on a mortgage will file a lis pendens in the county where the property is located. The lis pendens informs the public that a legal action is pending against the property. If the owner attempts to sell the property and a title search is conducted by the prospective buyer, the buyer will learn of the pending litigation.

A title search establishes current ownership and claims that affect the title. If there is a gap in the chain, it may be necessary to establish ownership by a court action known as a *suit to quiet title*. All possible claimants to the property are allowed to present evidence during a court proceeding. A judgment is filed after all of the evidence is considered. Often, the procedure requires obtaining quitclaim deeds to establish ownership. (See also Quitclaim deed on page 200.)

An **abstract of title** is a summary report of what the title search found in the public record. The person who prepares this report is called an *abstractor*. The abstractor searches the public records and then prepares a condensed history of the various events and proceedings that affected the title throughout the last 30 years. All recorded liens and encumbrances are included, along with their current status. However, the abstract of title does *not* reveal such items as encroachments or forgeries, or any interests or conveyances that have not been recorded.

Some buyers will accept an **opinion of title** executed by an attorney who has studied the abstract of title. The opinion will list any defects or clouds on the title, such as liens, easements, or other encumbrances, and it will include the attorney's opinion of whether the seller has a *marketable title* (merchantable title). Most attorneys do *not* guarantee the opinion of title. It is an opinion only, backed by legal training and experience. If the opinion should prove to be in error, negligence must usually be proved for the attorney's client to receive reimbursement.

The limited protection afforded buyers of real property by an opinion of title led to the need for title insurance. **Title insurance** is a contract that protects the policyholder from losses arising from defects in the title. Florida law does not require title insurance; however, it is a unique type of insurance because it protects a policyholder against loss from an occurrence that has happened in the past, such as a forged deed somewhere in the chain of title. Other insurable title defects include, for example, flaws due to incorrect marital status (failure to reveal a marriage where the spouse has a title interest), and incapacity of a grantor due to mental incompetence. (See also Elements of a Deed on page 198.) The title insurance company will defend a lawsuit based on an insurable defect, and it will pay claims up to the face amount of the policy if the title proves to be defective. Policies do not cover exceptions (exclusions) listed in the policy, such as an unrecorded easement or a lien arising after the policy was issued.

475.25(2)(j),
F.S.
61J2-24.001,
F.A.C.

1 Brokers must handle statements regarding title to property with extreme caution. Real
2 estate licensees are not qualified to render an opinion of title. Licensees must advise the
3 buyer to either contact an attorney or a title insurance company to determine the condi-
4 tion of the seller's title. Florida law requires that when questions of title arise, licensees
5 first must obtain a current opinion from an attorney before quoting an opinion that title to
6 a property is good or marketable. Real estate licensees are further required to advise pro-
7 spective buyers to have their attorneys examine the abstract or to obtain a title insurance
8 policy. In the event a licensee knows that the title to a property is not marketable or that
9 liens exist, the licensee is required to inform prospective buyers of all such conditions.

10 There are two types of title insurance: (See Figure 9.3, Title Insurance Comparison.)

11 1. **Owner's policy** is issued for the total purchase price of the property. It helps to
12 protect the new owner (or the owner's heirs) against unexpected risks such as
13 forged deed signatures and damages for any defect in the title (unless listed as an
14 exception in the policy). A one-time premium is paid when the policy is issued.
15 The policy is *not* transferable to another owner.

16 2. **Lender's policy** is issued for the unpaid mortgage amount. The lender policy
17 (or *mortgagee policy*) protects the lender against title defects. Unlike the owner's
18 title insurance, the lender's title insurance is transferable. If the mortgage lender
19 sells the mortgage to another investor, the title insurance is *assignable* to the new
20 mortgagee. The lender policy will protect the new owner of the mortgage up
21 to the unpaid balance of the mortgage loan. Most lenders require lender's title
22 insurance as a condition of issuing a mortgage loan.

WEB LINK

Florida uses a standardized insurance policy known as the American Land Title Association (ALTA) form. The form is available to ALTA members at **www.alta.org**. Other helpful information is available at **www .homeclosing101.org/test.cfm**.

23 DEEDS

24 A **deed** is a written instrument that conveys title to real property. It is an instrument of
25 conveyance whereby title to real property is transferred from one party to another. The
26 two parties to a deed are the **grantor** (owner giving title) and the **grantee** (new owner
27 receiving title). The deed must be signed by a *competent* (of sound mind and legal age)
28 grantor and witnessed by two people to be valid. The grantee need not be competent nor
29 sign the deed.

FIGURE 9.3 ■ Title Insurance Comparison

Owner Policy	Lender (Mortgagee) Policy
Issued for purchase price	Issued for loan amount
Claim will pay up to the purchase price	Claim will pay up to current loan balance
Benefits owner and owner's heirs	Benefits mortgage lender
Not transferable	Transferable (assignable)
Seller typically pays this closing expense	Buyer typically pays this closing expense
One-time premium	One-time premium

Elements of a Deed

The formats of deeds may differ because the wording is immaterial, as long as the intent to convey title is clearly expressed. Certain elements must be present in a deed to spell out clearly the necessary intent and the property to which it applies.

TO REMEMBER: ELEMENTS OF A DEED	
C	Consideration (valuable or good)
E	Execution (signed by a competent grantor and two witnesses)
D	Description of property
D	Delivery and acceptance (voluntary)
I	Interest or estate being conveyed (habendum clause)
N	Names of a grantee and grantor
G	Granting and other appropriate clauses

Clauses in a Deed

Historically, deeds contained several formal covenants or clauses. (Refer to Figure 9.4, Example of a General Warranty Deed.)

- The *premises* section of a deed names the parties to the deed and the date of the deed. The date should be the date of execution by the grantor. (See ①, Figure 9.4.) The premises contains the **granting clause** with the necessary words used to convey the property: *grants, bargains, and sells* or similar words. (See ②, Figure 9.4.) Usually, the premises section also states that some consideration was given, but the entire amount of consideration need not be shown. Blank lines are provided to insert the County and State information and space is provided for the legal description.

- The **habendum clause**, so named because in medieval times it began with the Latin phrase *habendum et tenendum* ("to have and to hold"), limited the estate or tenancy being conveyed. Today, the habendum clause starts with the words "to have and to hold." Then, usually, the word "forever" follows if the estate is fee simple or the words "for the life of the grantee" if it is a life estate. Any other restrictions or limitations on the property's use, such as reservation by the seller to retain mineral rights to the land, are usually entered before or after the habendum clause. (See ③, Figure 9.4.)

- The covenant of **seisin** (also *seizin*) is a promise that the grantor owns the property and has the right to convey title. (See ④, Figure 9.4.)

- The covenant *against encumbrances* states that the property is free from liens or other encumbrances except as noted in the deed. This clause gives the grantee notice of all encumbrances (liens, restrictions, and so forth) associated with the property. (See ⑤, Figure 9.4.)

These covenants cannot, and do not, guarantee a marketable title. The clauses are only as good as the grantor. If the grantor is insolvent or unreliable, the covenants are of little or no value.

F I G U R E 9.4 ▪ Example of a General Warranty Deed

SPACE ABOVE THIS LINE FOR PROCESSING DATA ⸺⸺⸺⸺⸺⸺⸺⸺⸺⸺ SPACE ABOVE THIS LINE FOR RECORDING DATA ⸺⸺⸺⸺

This Warranty Deed,① *Made the _____ day of _____ , _____ , by*

_____ ,

hereinafter called the Grantor, to _____ ,

whose post office address is _____ ,

hereinafter called the Grantee.

(Wherever used herein the terms "Grantor" and "Grantee" include all the parties to this instrument and the heirs, legal representatives,
and assigns of individuals, and the successors and assigns of corporations, wherever the context so admits or requires.)

Witnesseth, *That the Grantor, for and in consideration of the sum of $ _____ and other valuable considerations, receipt whereof is hereby acknowledged, hereby grants, bargains, sells, aliens, remises, releases, conveys and confirms unto the Grantee all that certain land, situate in _____ County, State of _____ , viz:②*

Together, *with all the tenements, hereditaments and appurtenances thereto belonging or in anywise appertaining.* **To Have and to Hold,** *the same in fee simple forever.* ③

And *the Grantor hereby covenants with said grantee that the grantor is lawfully seized of* ④ *said land in fee simple; that the grantor has good right and lawful authority to sell and convey said land, and hereby warrants the title to said land and will defend the same against the lawful claims of all persons whomsoever; and that said land is free of all encumbrances, except taxes accruing subsequent to December 31, 20____* ⑤
In Witness Whereof, *the said Grantor has signed and sealed these presents the day and year first above written.*

Signed, sealed and delivered in the presence of:

Witness Signature (as to first Grantor)	Grantor Signature **L.S.**
Printed Name	Printed Name
Witness Signature (as to first Grantor)	Post Office Address
Printed Name	
Witness Signature (as to Co-Grantor, if any)	Co-Grantor Signature, (if any) **L.S.**
Printed Name	Printed Name
Witness Signature (as to Co-Grantor, if any)	Post Office Address
Printed Name	

STATE OF _____)

COUNTY OF _____)

I hereby Certify that on this day, before me, an officer duly authorized to administer oaths and take acknowledgments, personally appeared

_____ known to me to be the person_____ described in and who executed the foregoing instrument, who acknowledged before me that _____ executed the same, and an oath was not taken. (Check one:) ❑ Said person(s) is/are personally known to me. ❑ Said person(s) provided the following type of identification: _____

NOTARY RUBBER STAMP SEAL

Witness my hand and official seal in the County and State last aforesaid

this _____ day of _____ , A.D. _____

Notary Signature _____

Printed Name _____

©form Design, Seminole Paper & Printing Co., Inc., 1994

This form included with permission of Seminole Paper & Printing Co., Inc., 60 W. 3rd Street, Miami, Florida 33101.

Statutory Deeds

There are four types of statutory deeds: (1) quitclaim deed, (2) bargain and sale deed, (3) special warranty deed, and (4) general warranty deed. These deeds are called *statutory deeds* because the law provides for a short form of deed in which the covenants or warranties mentioned are implied to exist just as if they were written out in complete and detailed form. These four deeds are described below, starting with the one that has the fewest covenants and warranties (quitclaim deed) and ending with the one that has the most covenants and warranties (general warranty deed).

Quitclaim deed. The **quitclaim deed** is a deed by which the grantor quitclaims unto the grantee all of the *grantor's* rights, title, and interest to the property, if any. The grantor makes no warranties about the quality or extent of the title being conveyed. This form of deed is useful for clearing existing or potential *clouds* on the title. A cloud might be some unreleased lien or encumbrance that may superficially impair or cast doubt on the title's validity, such as a recorded mortgage that has been paid in full, but with no satisfaction of mortgage recorded. To clear the title of these possible trouble spots, the grantor releases any claim or interest in the property. Instead of the usual wording *grants, bargains, and sells*, the quitclaim deed uses the words *remise, release,* and *quitclaim*. The quitclaim deed does not contain a covenant of seisin. This allows the grantor to sign a deed transferring any and all interests, without claiming ownership of any right of title whatsoever. The grantor does not warrant to defend the title interest conveyed or to transfer a valid interest. When a quitclaim deed cannot be acquired, a *suit to quiet title* usually produces a clear title.

Bargain and sale deed. Normally, a bargain and sale deed consists of the granting clause, habendum clause, and covenant of seisin. However, in the *bargain and sale deed,* the grantor does not covenant or warrant to defend the title against any future claims or attacks on the title. The bargain and sale deed is sufficient to convey all the title the grantor has, but it does little to protect the grantee from clouds or claims on the title. A bargain and sale deed might be appropriate when an out-of-state property owner desires to sell several parcels of land through a Florida real estate auctioneer. Serious buyers who attend the auction know that they must do their due diligence in advance of attending the auction if they intend to bid on any of the parcels. The buyers know that the seller will not be purchasing title insurance. In such situations the seller typically delivers to the buyer a bargain and sale deed. Also, officers of the court often convey the real property under their control by means of a bargain and sale deed.

Special warranty deed. Another type of deed is the *special warranty deed*, a deed in which the grantor does not warrant the title (assume any responsibility for the title) in any way or manner except against acts by the grantor or the grantor's representative. In other words, the grantor guarantees that nothing has been done to encumber or cloud the title during the grantor's ownership. This is the type of deed that most large corporations use when selling property. Special warranty deeds are also used by lenders who have foreclosed on and have taken title to property. The grantor (lender) only assumes title responsibility for the period that the property was owned by the lender thus avoiding title liability for the period prior to foreclosure.

General warranty deed. The **general warranty deed** (or sometimes the *full covenant and warranty deed*) contains all the covenants and warranties available to give the grantee every possible future guarantee to title protection. In addition to the covenant of seisin and the covenant against encumbrances, the general warranty deed contains three unique covenants:

1. **Quiet enjoyment** guarantees peaceful possession undisturbed by claims of title.

689, F.S.

2. **Further assurance** guarantees the grantor will sign and deliver any legal instrument that might be required to make the title good in the future.

3. **Warranty forever** guarantees the grantor will forever warrant and defend the grantee's title against all lawful claims. (See Figure 9.4, Example of a General Warranty Deed.)

Special Purpose Deeds

Legal problems may be encountered when property is being conveyed from one owner to another. Several types of deeds have evolved to provide solutions for these and other situations in which an owner cannot or refuses to sign a deed.

When an owner cannot sign a deed. Under certain circumstances, a property owner may be unable to sign a deed. Three types of deeds used in such cases are:

733.301, F.S.
475.011(1), F.S.

1. *Personal representative's deed.* A *personal representative* is an individual either appointed by will or by order of a court to settle the estate of a deceased person. The testator typically identifies a trusted person to serve as personal representative who will be charged with carrying out the provisions of the will under the direction of the court in which the will was probated. If an owner should die without leaving a will, the probate court having jurisdiction will appoint a personal representative to settle the decedent's affairs. A personal representative's deed is used to formalize and record the transfer of title. It should show the full consideration paid for the property and contain a covenant of no encumbrances.

2. *Guardian's deed.* A *guardian* acts on behalf of a minor (or other ward) and is also a fiduciary. Normally, the permission of a court is required for a guardian to sell or convey property belonging to the minor. When authorized by the courts, a guardian's deed legally conveys the minor's property.

3. *Committee's deed.* One of the essentials of a valid deed is a competent grantor. When an owner is declared legally incompetent or is committed to an institution, a committee is often appointed by the court to administer the affairs of the incompetent. The committee functions under the direction of the court if conveying or disposing of the incompetent's estate. All members of a committee must sign the deed. A committee also must adhere to fiduciary disclosure requirements.

When an owner does not sign a deed. All foreclosures on real property in Florida must follow prescribed legal procedures that eventually lead to a public auction of the property. The *final judgment* given to the lender that authorizes sale of the property usually requires that the sale be under the direction of the clerk of the circuit court. A *certificate of title*, prepared by the plaintiff's (lender's) attorney and given as a result of judicial foreclosure, will show ownership and any outstanding liens and encumbrances. No covenants are given, and the buyer assumes all risks for title defects. Extreme caution should be taken when purchasing property at a foreclosure sale.

Legal Requirements

If a sale contract does not specify the type of deed to be given by the seller, Florida law requires that the property be conveyed by a general warranty deed. A *deed* is an instrument

1 used to convey (transfer) an estate or interest in real property (it is a conveyance
2 instrument). Transfer of title to property is not effective until the conveyance instrument
3 (usually a deed) is delivered to and accepted by the grantee.

4   In Florida, all deeds to real property are subject to a state documentary stamp tax. (See
5 page 317 for state documentary stamp tax calculations.)

6 OWNERSHIP LIMITATIONS AND RESTRICTIONS

7 The two general categories of restrictions are *public* (government) and *private*. Both have
8 several subcategories of restrictions and limitations. (Refer to Figure 9.5, Ownership
9 Restrictions.)

10 Public or Government Restrictions on Ownership

11 The three most important subcategories of public or governmental limitations on owner-
12 ship of real property are (1) police power, (2) eminent domain, and (3) right of taxation.

TO REMEMBER: GOVERNMENT RESTRICTIONS
P Police power
E Eminent domain
T Taxation

13 **Police power.** The U.S. and state constitutions provide for the government to apply any
14 restrictions deemed necessary in the interest of the general health, welfare, or safety of its
15 citizens. Under police power, the use of real property may be regulated. From these powers
16 come the many ordinances and regulations governing zoning, building codes, health

F I G U R E   9.5 ■ **Ownership Restrictions**

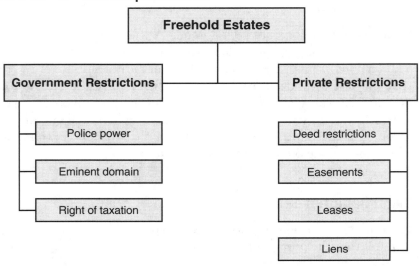

1 standards, city planning, and rent controls. State governments have delegated the exercise
2 of police powers to county, city, and local governments. **Police power** represents the
3 broadest power of the government to limit or regulate the rights of property owners. The
4 owner's use and occupancy of the property can be restricted without any compensation
5 to the owner whatsoever. Zoning, for example, can prevent an owner from using property
6 in the most profitable manner, and the owner can't recover from the government lost
7 revenue caused by the zoning.

8 **Eminent domain.** Eminent domain is referred to as a *taking for just compensation*. The con-
9 stitutions of the U.S. government and state governments grant the power (right) to take
10 private property for a public use. Amendment 5 to the U.S. Constitution prohibits taking
11 private property for a public purpose without just compensation. In Florida, an owner who
12 believes a fair price was not offered for the property taken may go to court and ask a jury,
13 in a condemnation proceeding, to settle the question of what constitutes a fair price.

14 **Right of property taxation.** This power was specifically limited to the various states by the
15 U.S. Constitution. Citizens pay for the benefits and protection provided by the various
16 levels of government. Property is usually the primary basis for local taxation. Local taxing
17 authorities can foreclose on real property for nonpayment of taxes.

Private Restrictions on Ownership

19 Private limitations on ownership of real property usually include deed restrictions, ease-
20 ments, leases, and liens.

TO REMEMBER: PRIVATE RESTRICTIONS

D	Deed restrictions
E	Easements
L	Leases
L	Liens

21 **Deed restrictions.** Probably the most common and the broadest restrictions to private
22 property ownership are deed restrictions and restrictive covenants. Deed restrictions are a
23 part of the deed and affect a particular property. Restrictive covenants are recorded along
24 with the subdivision plat and usually affect an entire subdivision. The limitations may
25 be either perpetual (continue indefinitely) or for a specified period of time. While the
26 restrictions are in effect, they restrict the use of the property for the first owner and all
27 subsequent owners. Any restriction that does not discriminate against race, color, religion,
28 sex, national origin, families with children, handicap, or public policy may be included in
29 a deed (or in the restrictive covenants).

30 **Easements.** An **easement** is a right to use a portion of an owner's land for a specific pur-
31 pose. Easements do not convey ownership (possession). Most commonly, an easement
32 entails the right of a person (or the public) to use the land of another in a certain manner,
33 such as utility easements, railroad right-of-ways, and ingress-egress easements. Easements
34 can be terminated by agreement, abandonment, or by court order. Some easements are
35 created by a written agreement between the parties that establishes the easement right.
36 Two such examples are *easement appurtenant* and *easement in gross*. (See Figure 9.6, Ease-
37 ment Appurtenant and Easement in Gross.)

FIGURE 9.6 ■ Easement Appurtenant and Easement in Gross

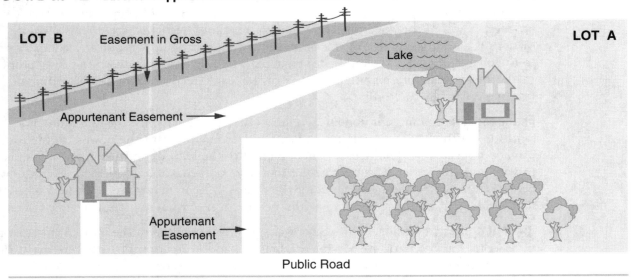

The owner of Lot B has an appurtenant easement across Lot A to gain access to the lake. The utility company has an easement in gross across both parcels of land for its power lines. Note that Lot A also has an appurtenant easement across Lot B for its driveway.

1 ■ An **easement appurtenant** benefits an adjacent parcel of land. An easement
2 appurtenant allows an owner the use of a neighbor's property, such as the right to
3 cross parcel A to reach parcel B.

4 ■ An **easement in gross** benefits an individual or a business entity and is not
5 related to a specific adjacent parcel. For example, utility easements are easements
6 in gross. The easement allows the utility company to access the land, trim trees,
7 and so forth to maintain utility equipment.

8 Certain types of easements must be created through a court of law. Two such examples
9 are *easement by necessity* and *easement by prescription*.

10 ■ With an **easement by necessity**, if a landowner subdivides land, conveying part
11 of it in a way that causes a parcel to be landlocked, the court may authorize
12 creation of an easement by necessity to allow property owners to enter and exit
13 their landlocked property.

14 ■ An **easement by prescription** is created by longtime usage. Such easements are
15 created and must be recognized after 20 years of open, continuous, uninterrupted
16 use. (Note the similarity to adverse possession; however, the adverse user in an
17 easement by prescription acquires only an easement and not title.)

18 ■ Unlike an easement, an **encroachment** is the unauthorized use of another's prop-
19 erty. For example, a fence or garage located beyond a legitimate boundary with-
20 out the owner's consent is an infringement or intrusion on property. When an
21 encroachment has continued for more than seven years, it may create an *implied
22 easement*. If encroachments are not known and a contract for sale is created
23 before a survey reveals that one exists, the title might be unmarketable and the
24 contract might be voidable.

1 **Leases.** While a lease constitutes an interest in real property, it does not convey owner-
2 ship. A *lease* is an agreement between the landlord (lessor) and a renter (lessee) that grants
3 the lessee the right of possession and use of the property for a specified time in return for
4 compensation. Florida law requires that a lease for more than one year be in writing and
5 be signed to be enforceable. Any oral contract or agreement between the lessor and lessee
6 is legally a *tenancy at will*. In fact, all oral leases and all written leases that do not fix a defi-
7 nite date for termination are tenancies at will. Leases for one year or less are enforceable,
8 even when not in writing, if the terms can be verified and a termination date was agreed
9 on. The five requirements of a valid lease are as follows: (1) names and signatures (if the
10 lease is for more than one year) of the lessor and lessee, (2) legal capacity of the lessor and
11 lessee to enter into a contract, (3) consideration, (4) the term of the tenancy, and (5) the
12 property identification. A lease for real property for an indefinite term or for longer than
13 one year must be in writing and signed by the lessor, lessee, and two witnesses.

14 Leases should be prepared by an attorney experienced in their preparation. Two wit-
15 nesses must sign the lease as verification of its proper execution if it is for more than one
16 year. Florida Supreme Court-approved formats for residential leases of one year or less may
17 be completed by nonattorneys. Fill-in-the-blank lease forms approved by the court should
18 be used by licensees. Leases of longer duration should be completed only by attorneys.
19 Attorneys are authorized to draft leases on someone else's behalf. A property owner *may*
20 *not* delegate the authority to draft a lease to a nonattorney.

21 The major characteristics of five common types of leases are described below. (See also
22 Figure 9.7, Types of Lease Agreements.)

1. In a **gross lease**, the tenant (lessee) pays a fixed (base) rent and the landlord
   (lessor) pays all expenses associated with the property, including taxes, utilities,
   insurance, and repairs. However, it is not uncommon for the tenant to pay unit-
   related utility costs. Most residential and office building leases are gross leases
   (also known as *straight leases* or *flat leases*).

2. In a **net lease**, the tenant (lessee) pays fixed rent plus property costs such as
   maintenance and operating expenses (taxes, insurance, and utilities). Net leases
   are typically used on commercial property. The terms, *net, net-net,* and *triple-net*
   are often used in commercial real estate. The number of "nets" indicates that
   the tenant is assuming more and more of the expenses. In a triple-net lease, the
   tenant pays all operating and other expenses in addition to the fixed rent. These

FIGURE 9.7 ■ Types of Lease Agreements

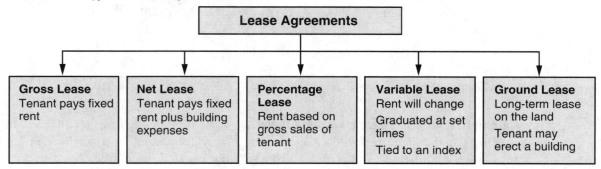

expenses include taxes, insurance, assessments, maintenance, utilities, and other charges associated with the property.

3. In a **percentage lease**, the tenant pays rent based on gross sales received by doing business on the leased property. Percentage leases are common with large retail stores, especially in shopping centers. A percentage lease can be either net or gross.

4. In a **variable lease**, the tenant pays specified rent increases at set future dates. A variable lease is usually tied to an index, such as the consumer price index (CPI).

5. In a **ground lease**, the tenant leases the land only and erects a building on the land. Ground leases (or *land leases*) are long-term leases that will run for terms up to 99 years. Ground leases are characterized by separate ownership of the land and building(s).

The five types of leases described above are not mutually exclusive. A triple-net lease, for example, can have its base rent increases tied to an index (a variable lease) and also require the tenant to pay a percentage of gross sales.

Calculating the rent owed for a percentage lease. Typically percentage leases involve a base or minimum monthly rent plus a percentage of the gross sales in excess of an amount specified in the lease.

For example, assume that a lease calls for monthly minimum rent of $1,000 plus 3 percent of annual gross sales in excess of $325,000. What is the annual rent for the year if the annual gross sales were $450,700?

1. Step One. Begin by determining how much of the gross sales are subject to the 3 percent charge.

    $450,700 total gross sales − $325,000 = $125,700 subject to 3 percent

2. Step Two. Multiply the amount subject to the 3 percent charge.

    $125,700 × .03 = $3,771 additional annual rent

3. Step Three. Add the additional annual rent to the base rent to determine total annual rent due.

    $1,000 × 12 months = $12,000 annual base rent
    $12,000 annual base rent + $3,771 additional rent = $15,771 total rent

---

Practice Problem 1

A lease calls for a minimum rent of $2,800 per month plus 4 percent of annual gross sales in excess of $500,000. What is the annual rent if the annual gross sales were $725,500?

(The solution to the Practice Problem is at the end of this chapter on page 211.)

Calculating rent owed for a variable lease. A variable lease features rent that changes at set times as specified in the lease agreement. A variable lease (or sometimes index lease) provides for adjustments of rent according to changes in a price index.

For example, assume that a building rents for $12 per square foot with an index of 1.5. The index increases to 1.8. What is the adjusted rental rate?

1. Step One. Begin by calculating how much the rent prices increased.

$$1.8 \text{ rate} - 1.5 \text{ rate} = .3 \text{ difference in index}$$
$$.3 \text{ difference} \div 1.5 \text{ original rate} = .20 \text{ or } 20 \text{ percent increase}$$

2. Step Two. Add the percent increase to the base index of 1.0, then multiply the rent per square foot times this figure.

$$.20 \text{ increase} + 1.0 \text{ base index} = 1.20$$
$$\$12 \text{ per square foot} \times 1.20 = \$14.40 \text{ adjusted rental rate}$$

Alternative solution:

1. Step One remains the same.

2. Step Two. Multiply the percent increase by the beginning rent per square foot. Then add this amount to the beginning rent per square foot.

$$.20 \text{ increase} \times \$12 \text{ per square foot} = \$2.40 \text{ rental increase}$$
$$\$2.40 + \$12 = \$14.40 \text{ adjusted rental rate}$$

Practice Problem 2

A tenant's lease requires a payment of $2,000 per month. The lease provides for an adjustment based on an index of 1.2. The index increases to 1.6. What is the new rent payment?

(The solution to the Practice Problem is at the end of this chapter on page 211.)

(*Note*: If, as a student, you would like additional practice with math calculations, consider purchasing *Real Estate Math: What You Need to Know*, by the author of your textbook. *Real Estate Math* contains more than 350 practice math problems with step-by-step solutions.)

Assignment and sublease. A lease may be assigned to another party or a tenant (lessee) may choose to sublet the leased property.

- **Assignment** of a lease occurs when a lessee (tenant) assigns to another person all of the leased property for the remainder of the lease.

- **Sublease** is used to give another person only part of an existing lease. This can occur in one of two ways:

  1. A lessee (tenant) assigns only a portion of the leased property. For example, a college student who rents a 3-bedroom home might sublet one of the bedrooms to another student.
  2. A lessee (tenant) assigns all of the property for a period that is less than the remaining term of the lease (such as for the summer only). Subleasing is also called *subrogation* and *subordination* of space. The original tenant remains obligated for the lease terms.

Sale or transfer of title of rental property. When a leased property is sold, the lease is binding on the new owner. The Florida Residential Landlord and Tenant Act provides that when a residential rental property is sold or the title of the rental property is otherwise transferred from one owner to another, the tenants' security deposits and advance rents must be transferred to the new owner. If the property owner changes the designated rental agent, all security deposits or advance rents being held by the former rental agent must be transferred to the new agent with an accounting showing the amounts to be credited on each tenant's behalf.

726.102(8), F.S.

Liens. A lien is a right or legal interest given to a creditor or a unit of government to have a debt satisfied out of some specific property belonging to a debtor. Liens can entitle the holder (lienor) to have property sold, regardless of the desires of the owner (lienee). Liens are usually recorded with the clerk of the circuit court in the county where the property is located. As a debtor, the property owner has no choice but to pay the lienor or have the property disposed of by the courts in order to satisfy the lien. A lien is an encumbrance on the title to real property. However, not all encumbrances on property are liens. Encumbrances can also be easements, covenants, deed restrictions, encroachments, and governmental regulations.

General and Specific Liens

Liens are broadly classified as voluntary or involuntary. (See Figure 9.8, Liens.) *Voluntary liens* are ones the owner places against the property to secure payment of a long-term debt, such as a mortgage lien. *Involuntary liens* are created by law to protect interests of persons who have valid monetary claims against the owner of real property. Liens are further divided into two major classifications: general liens and specific liens.

General lien. A general lien is not restricted to one property but may affect all properties of a debtor. A general lien attaches to all of the lienee's (debtor's) real property located in the county where the lien is recorded. General liens include judgment liens, income tax liens, and estate tax liens.

- *Judgment lien.* A judgment lien is an involuntary lien attaching to real property when a judgment is obtained against the owner. A judgment lien is a general lien on all property of the debtor (unless specifically exempt by law) in the county where the judgment was recorded into the public records. In Florida, a judgment lien remains a lien on real property until it has been paid or expires by passage of time.

- *Income tax (IRS) lien.* Florida does not have a state income tax. However, failure to pay federal income taxes can result in a lien on property of the delinquent taxpayer. A federal tax lien, once filed, becomes a lien on all property owned by the taxpayer at the time of filing as well as on all future property acquired by the taxpayer until the lien is satisfied.

- *Estate tax lien.* Federal estate tax liens are imposed against a decedent's taxable assets automatically upon death. They do not require recording or filing. The tax rate is progressive as the worth of the estate increases. While Florida has no inheritance tax, it does have an estate tax designed to collect up to the maximum allowable federal estate tax credit for state death taxes paid. If Florida did not receive this tax, the federal government would.

Specific lien. Liens classified as specific do not affect all of the debtor's property but apply only to certain specified property. **Specific liens** include the following:

- *Property tax and special assessment lien.* Municipal governments have been delegated the authority to levy real property taxes and special tax assessments. Unlike other debts and liens, property taxes and special assessments become liens as soon as the assessment is complete.

  The courts have ruled that special assessments may be levied only against properties that are benefited by an increase in value. Special assessment liens are ahead of private liens in priority and second only to real property tax liens. (Property taxes and special assessments are discussed in greater detail in chapter 18.)

- *Mortgage lien.* When a lender makes a loan using real estate as security, the property owner signs a mortgage document that creates a lien against the property. Mortgage liens are voluntary liens because they are made with the owner's consent. The date the mortgage is filed and recorded with the clerk of the circuit court establishes the priority of the lien against other claims on the property. If the borrower (mortgagor) defaults, the lender (mortgagee) can proceed to force sale of the property to satisfy the debt.

- *Vendor's lien.* If a buyer of property (vendee) is unable to make the full down payment required, a seller (vendor) frequently will allow a *purchase-money mortgage* to make up the amount of money the buyer is unable to produce. Actually, any portion of the sale price remaining unpaid to the vendor creates a vendor's lien. This is an equitable lien of the grantor (seller) on the land conveyed in the amount of the unpaid purchase price. A vendor's lien is enforceable only against the party obtaining title from the vendor. It does not apply against later purchasers unless a written mortgage has been executed and placed in the public records. A valid vendor's lien is enforceable by foreclosure. Priority is established by the recording date of the purchase-money mortgage.

- *Construction lien.* This lien is based on the principle of law called *unjust enrichment*. Unjust enrichment means that property owners may not use the labor or material of another party to add value to their property without reimbursement to that party. A **construction lien** (or *mechanic's*, *materialman's*, or *laborer's lien*) is a statutory right of material suppliers or laborers to place a lien on property that has been improved by their supplies and/or labor. This lien must be filed with the clerk of the circuit court not later than 90 days after the last supplies are delivered or the last labor is performed in order to assume priority over any mortgage liens created after the first material/work appeared on the property affected. This, in effect, allows a construction lien filed after work is completed to become retroactive to the first delivery of material or first day of work. If a mortgage is placed on the property during the period when construction is in progress, a lien filed after construction is completed will precede the mortgage in priority. Once filed, a construction lien is effective for one year. The party who places the lien on the property must initiate court action to collect the debt during the lien's one-year life or forfeit the privilege. This lien may be discharged or canceled by expiration of time, payment of the debt, or court action through a suit.

Lien Priority

When there are two or more liens on a property, the *priority* of the liens determines the order in which the liens will be satisfied (paid off) if the property must be sold. The priority of most liens is the date and time that the lien was recorded in the public records. Lien priority is important because the lienor (creditor) receives no compensation until all liens senior to the lienor's lien have been fully satisfied.

Real estate (property) tax liens and special assessment liens take priority over all other liens. They are automatically *superior* to any other lien (see Figure 9.8, Liens). IRS liens are *not* superior liens. The priority of IRS liens and other liens is based on the recording date. However, construction (mechanics') liens are an exception to the priority rule regarding the recording date. A construction lien's priority in a foreclosure sale is retroactive to the date the work was first performed or materials were first delivered to the property.

The priority of liens may be changed by a written agreement known as a *subordination agreement*. Under a subordination agreement, the holder of a prior lien (lien with an earlier recording date) agrees to allow a junior lien holder's interest to move ahead of the prior lien.

F I G U R E 9.8 ■ Liens

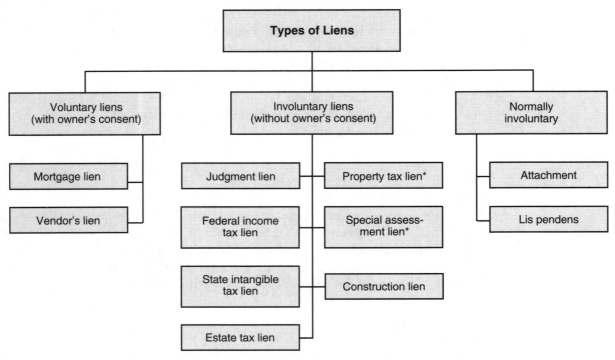

*Superior lien (ahead of other liens)

Practice Problem 1 Solution

(Practice Problem 1 is located on page 206.)

$725,500 total gross sales − $500,000 = $225,500 subject to 4 percent

$225,500 × .04 = $9,020 additional annual rent

$2,800 × 12 months = $33,600 annual base rent

$33,600 annual base rent + $9,020 additional rent = $42,620

Practice Problem 2 Solution

(Practice Problem 2 is located on page 207.)

1.6 rate − 1.2 rate = .4 difference in index

.4 difference ÷ 1.2 original index = .3333 or 33 percent increase (rounded)

.33 increase + 1.0 base index = 1.33

$2,000 × 1.33 = $2,660 new rent payment

SUMMARY OF IMPORTANT POINTS

- *Alienation* is the act of transferring ownership, title, or an interest in real property from one person to another. Alienation may be voluntary (with the owner's control and consent) or involuntary (without control and consent).

- Voluntary alienation is accomplished using a deed or a will. Involuntary alienation occurs (1) when a person dies intestate (without leaving a will) and the property descends to decedent's heirs, (2) when property transfers to the state through escheat because the owner died intestate and had no known heirs, (3) by adverse possession when the true owner fails to maintain possession and the property is seized by another, and (4) by eminent domain through a condemnation proceeding.

- *Actual notice* is direct knowledge acquired during a transaction; whereas, constructive notice is recording the information in the public record.

- A *chain of title* is the complete successive record of a property's ownership. An abstract of title is a summary report of what exists in the public record.

- The two types of title insurance are (1) owner policy, which is not transferrable and protects for the purchase price of the property; and (2) lender (mortgagee) policy, which is transferable and protects for the balance of the mortgage loan.

- The two parties to a deed are the grantor (owner giving title) and the grantee (new owner receiving title). The deed must be signed by a competent grantor and witnessed by two people. The grantee does not sign the deed.

- The premises section of a deed names the parties to the deed and the date of the deed. The premises section contains the granting clause with the words used to convey the property. The habendum clause indicates the type of estate being conveyed. The seisin clause is a promise that the grantor has the legal right to convey title.

- The four types of statutory deeds are (1) quitclaim, (2) bargain and sale, (3) special warranty, and (4) general warranty. A general warranty deed provides the most comprehensive guarantee and contains three unique covenants: (1) quiet enjoyment, (2) further assurance, and (3) warranty forever.

- Public (government) restrictions on ownership include police power, eminent domain, and taxation. Private restrictions include deed restrictions, easements, leases, and liens.

- The five common types of leases are (1) gross lease, (2) net lease, (3) percentage lease, (4) variable lease, and (5) ground lease.

- Assignment occurs when a tenant assigns to another all of the leased property for the remainder of the lease. A sublease occurs when a tenant assigns only a portion of the leased property or the tenant assigns all of the property for a portion of the remaining term of the lease.

- A general lien may affect all properties of a debtor. General liens include the following: judgment, income tax (IRS), and estate tax liens. A specific lien affects only a particular property. Specific liens include property tax and special assessment, mortgage, vendor, and construction liens.

- Lien priority of most liens is the date and time a lien was recorded in the public records. However, property tax liens and special assessment liens take priority over all other liens (including IRS liens), regardless of date.

Note to Readers

A real estate broker or sales associate is allowed by Florida statutes to draw listing and sale contracts, but not deeds, unless conveying property in which the licensee owns an interest. In addition, only residential lease forms previously discussed may legally be completed by licensees. The drawing of any other lease, deed, or giving an opinion of title may be construed as the unlicensed practice of law.

R E V I E W   Q U E S T I O N S

1. Which type of easement gives an electric company the authority to install and maintain electric power lines?
   a. In gross
   b. Prescription
   c. Appurtenant
   d. Implied

2. Rent is $1,800 per month plus 3 percent of gross sales. The total rent for last month was $2,400. The gross sales for the same month were
   a. $20,000.
   b. $24,000.
   c. $30,000.
   d. $60,000.

3. Courts at various levels have ruled that
   a. constructive notice is superior to actual notice.
   b. actual notice is superior to constructive notice.
   c. neither constructive notice nor actual notice is required.
   d. constructive notice and actual notice have equal legal priority.

4. A 92-year-old man is being forced from his home because of a governmental taking. The home has been in his family for four generations. What recourse, if any, does he have?
   a. He can file an injunction to stop the taking.
   b. He can pay the delinquent property taxes to prevent the foreclosure.
   c. He may request a condemnation proceeding to protest the amount of compensation being offered by the governmental body.
   d. He may do all of the above.

5. For a deed to be valid, a competent
   a. grantor, grantee, and two witnesses must sign the instrument.
   b. grantor and two witnesses must sign the instrument.
   c. grantee and two witnesses must sign the instrument.
   d. grantee only must sign the instrument.

6. The type or form of deed most commonly used to clear clouds on the title of real property is the
   a. general warranty deed.
   b. special warranty deed.
   c. bargain and sale deed.
   d. quitclaim deed.

7. If the sale contract does not specify the type of deed to be delivered, the seller is required to provide a
   a. general warranty deed.
   b. special warranty deed.
   c. bargain and sale deed.
   d. quitclaim deed.

8. The process of taking property under the power of eminent domain is called
   a. escheat.
   b. foreclosure.
   c. condemnation.
   d. voluntary alienation.

9. The type of deed in which the grantor does not warrant the title in any manner
   EXCEPT against the grantor's acts or the acts of the grantor's representatives is
   called a
   a. general warranty deed.
   b. special warranty deed.
   c. bargain and sale deed.
   d. quitclaim deed.

10. The covenant against encumbrances in a deed is designed to guarantee that the
    a. grantor has not encumbered the property in any manner except as noted on the deed.
    b. grantee is responsible for any unpaid encumbrances.
    c. grantee has not encumbered the property.
    d. grantor will not encumber the property.

11. The purpose of recording a deed is to
    a. comply with real estate license law.
    b. effect the transfer of ownership.
    c. give actual notice of ownership.
    d. give constructive notice of ownership.

12. In answering questions pertaining to quality of title, real estate licensees are
    a. required to give opinions because of their role as experts.
    b. required to advise prospective buyers to have a lawyer render an opinion or
       obtain title insurance.
    c. allowed to give their opinions because of their role as experts.
    d. allowed to give their opinions only when specifically asked by the buyer.

13. The seisin clause in a deed specifies
    a. the type of estate being conveyed.
    b. the improvements being transferred with the land.
    c. the rights reserved by the grantor.
    d. that the grantor actually owns the property and has the right to sell it.

14. The deed that contains the covenant guaranteeing that the grantor will forever be
    responsible for warranting title and will defend the title and possession is a
    a. general warranty deed.
    b. special warranty deed.
    c. public patent deed.
    d. bargain and sale deed.

15. The provision in a deed that names the parties and contains the granting clause is the
    a. premises.
    b. encumbrance clause.
    c. habendum clause.
    d. seisin clause.

16. An owner placed a condition in the deed that stipulated that a commercial building could NOT be erected on the property until at least the year 2020. This is an example of
    a. police power.
    b. a deed restriction.
    c. subdivision restrictive covenants.
    d. governmental restriction on ownership.

17. An example of an encumbrance on title to real property does NOT include
    a. an easement.
    b. a deed restriction.
    c. a lien.
    d. a premises clause in the deed.

18. When a lis pendens is filed properly with the county clerk, it becomes a type of
    a. attachment on the subject property.
    b. vendor's lien.
    c. constructive notice.
    d. easement by prescription.

19. Which lien is first in priority?
    a. A property tax lien effective on January 1, 2011
    b. A special assessment lien certified on December 31, 2010
    c. A first mortgage lien filed on July 15, 2011
    d. A construction lien filed on November 30, 2010

20. A business has a five-year variable lease for a suite in an office park. The first year of the lease calls for rent of $21.50 a square foot based on a beginning index of 189. The index increases to 195 at the beginning of the second year. What is the new rental rate?
    a. $22.18
    b. $22.58
    c. $22.89
    d. $23.05

21. A married couple signed a contract to purchase a home in a residential subdivision. When the couple had the lot surveyed before closing, they discovered that the contractor had built the neighbor's garage three inches inside the west boundary of their lot. The garage in its present location is an example of
    a. a deed restriction.
    b. an easement by prescription.
    c. an implied easement.
    d. an encroachment.

22. When a pathway to a property has been used continuously and without interruption for more than 20 years, it creates an
    a. implied easement.
    b. encroachment.
    c. alienation by adverse possession.
    d. easement by prescription.

23. Soon after a man's death a deed was discovered in his desk. The deed is for the man's home and it deeded the property to a charitable organization. The man is survived by his son Andrew, who discovered the deed. The man died intestate. Based on this information, the house belongs to the
    a. state because the man died intestate.
    b. charitable organization because the deed conveyed ownership to it.
    c. legal heir because the deed was never delivered and accepted.
    d. legal heir because the deed was not signed by the grantee.

24. The owner's title insurance policy is
    a. issued for an amount no greater than the purchase price of the property and is transferable.
    b. issued for an amount no greater than the purchase price of the property and is not transferable.
    c. a separate policy for the amount of the unpaid balance of the mortgage and is transferable.
    d. a separate policy for the amount of the unpaid balance of the mortgage and is not transferable.

25. A retail business rents a space in a mall. The lease calls for a base rent of $1,500 a month plus 5 percent of the annual gross sales that exceed $360,000. If the annual gross sales are $472,000, what is the total annual rent for the business?
    a. $7,100
    b. $23,600
    c. $36,000
    d. $41,600

10

LEGAL DESCRIPTIONS

1 ## OVERVIEW

2 This chapter introduces the various methods used to locate and describe the boundaries of
3 real property. Basic to the real estate business is a working knowledge of legal land descrip-
4 tions. Unless property can be located accurately, the best of contracts and the combined
5 efforts of the most knowledgeable brokers in the world will be defeated. Purchasers (and
6 title companies and lenders, if applicable) want to be certain of the exact location, size,
7 and shape of the property to be conveyed. In addition, once a property has been located
8 accurately, that particular parcel must then be described to prepare deeds, mortgages, and
9 other instruments affecting transfer of ownership.

10 After completing this chapter, the student should be able to:

11 ■ explain the necessity for legal land descriptions;

12 ■ list and explain the various methods of describing real property;

13 ■ calculate the number of acres in a parcel described by the government survey system;

14 ■ identify the location of a township by township and range number; and

15 ■ number the sections of a township.

16 ## KEY TERMS

base line	metes-and-bounds description	range
government survey system (GSS)	monument	sections
	patent	survey
legal description	point of beginning (POB)	township
lot and block	principal meridians	

17 ## PURPOSES OF LEGAL DESCRIPTIONS

18 The primary purpose of a **legal description** is to describe a particular piece of property in a way
19 that uniquely identifies that parcel from any other parcel. A legal description is so specific that
20 given only the legal description, a surveyor can locate and identify a given parcel.

Before land could be conveyed it had to be surveyed to establish the parcel's boundaries and to create the legal description. A **survey** is a drawing of a parcel of land showing its boundary lines and includes the legal description of the property. (See Figure 10.1, Boundary Survey.) Surveys have been around since the beginning of land ownership.

There are five additional purposes of surveying property and developing legal descriptions for each parcel:

1. Obtain current and accurate boundary information required to write a legal description.
2. Establish the exact quantity of area within a described tract, whether it is described in square miles, acres, or square feet.
3. Reestablish boundaries that may have become lost or obliterated.
4. Obtain data required to divide a large tract into smaller units for development and sale.
5. Identify and describe encroachments, if any.

THE EVOLUTION OF LEGAL DESCRIPTIONS

The first private land ownership began when the government conveyed land to private individuals. A **patent** (the original deed) is a certificate issued by the federal or a state government that transfers land to a private individual. In colonial times, if settlers wanted to purchase land they would apply for a patent to the land, pay the purchase price, and hire a surveyor to mark the boundaries and create the legal description of the land. In those days the metes-and-bounds method of legal description was used throughout the 13 colonies. The settlers would take the survey and patent to the county courthouse and record their purchases.

Following the Revolutionary War, the new federal government became the owner of all the land previously claimed by England. The government wanted an efficient way to survey all of the newly acquired land. The government chose a massive undertaking known as the Government Survey System which was based on a large grid of parallel lines.

TYPES OF LEGAL DESCRIPTIONS

There are three types of legal descriptions used today: (1) metes-and-bounds, (2) government survey system, and (3) lot and block descriptions.

Description by Metes-and-Bounds

The **metes-and-bounds description** is the oldest type of survey method. Today, surveyors use computer software and laser equipment to create the most accurate surveys possible. The metes-and-bounds method is used for both regular and irregular shaped parcels. Metes refers to *distance* and bounds refers to *direction*.

A metes-and-bounds description begins at an exact starting point, called a **point of beginning (POB)**. The POB must be accurate; otherwise the entire description is in error. A reader who understands the metes-and-bounds method can draw the boundaries of the parcel from the description. Starting at the POB, the first boundary is determined from the legal description that indicates the direction and the distance to the first corner of the

F I G U R E 10.1 ■ Boundary Survey

BOUNDARY SURVEY
–IN–
SECTION 10, TOWNSHIP 9 SOUTH, RANGE 19 EAST
ALACHUA COUNTY, FLORIDA

LEGEND:

F.M. = FIELD MEASUREMENT
( ) = PLAT MEASUREMENT
O = FOUND REBAR & CAP SIZE & NO. SHOWN ON PLAN
● = FOUND NAIL & DISK LS#4788 P.C.P.
Ⓓ = DRAINAGE MANHOLE
P.C.P. = PERMANENT CONTROL POINT
P.T. = POINT OF TANGENCY
P.C. = POINT OF CURVATURE
P.S.I. = POINT OF STREET INTERSECTION
Ⓔ = ELECTRIC TRANSFORMER
Ⓒ = CABLE TELEVISION PEDESTAL
⊠ = WATER METER
C/S = CONCRETE SLAB
T.B.M. = TEMPORARY BENCH MARK
⊠ = GAS METER
⊠ = ELECTRIC METER
A/C = AIR CONDITIONER
R/W = RIGHT OF WAY
PLS = PROFESSIONAL LICENSED SURVEYOR
LB = LICENSED BUSINESS
R.P. = RADIUS POINT

LEGAL DESCRIPTION:

LOT 26, BLUES CREEK UNIT – 4, A PORTION OF A PLANNED
UNIT DEVELOPMENT AS RECORDED IN PLAT BOOK "S". PAGE 3,
OF THE PUBLIC RECORDS OF ALACHUA COUNTY, FLORIDA.

SURVEYOR'S NOTES:

1. THIS SURVEY WAS BASED FROM FOUND MONUMENTATION
WHICH, IN THIS SURVEYOR'S OPINION BEST REPRESENTS
THE ORIGINAL SURVEY FOR THIS TRACT OF LAND.

2. BEARINGS AS SHOWN HEREON HAVE BEEN BASED FROM A BEARING
OF N15° 40' 45"E, AS SHOWN FOR THE CENTER LINE OF N. W. 53RD. WAY
ON THE RECORD PLAT OF BLUES CREEK UNIT – 4.

3. THE MEASUREMENTS FOR THIS SURVEY WERE MADE IN ACCORDANCE
WITH THE UNITED STATES STANDARD.

4. THIS SURVEYOR HAS REVIEWED THE MAPS ISSUED BY THE FEDERAL
EMERGENCY MANAGEMENT AGENCY FOR THE NATIONAL FLOOD INSURANCE
PROGRAM; AND IT HAS BEEN DETERMINED FROM THESE MAPS THAT THIS
PARCEL LIES IN ZONE C – AREAS OF MINIMAL FLOODING. COMMUNITY
PANEL NO. 120001 0275 A DATED SEPTEMBER 28, 1984.

F I G U R E 10.2 ■ Compass Directions

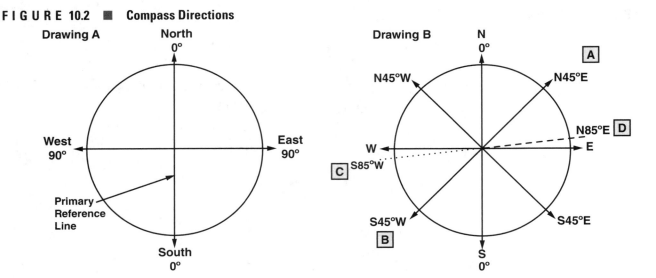

1 parcel, followed by another direction and distance to a second corner, and so on, eventu-
2 ally returning to the POB so that the parcel is enclosed within its boundaries. The surveyor
3 identifies each corner of the parcel with a visible marker called a **monument**. Surveyors in
4 colonial times often used objects found on the site as monuments, such as "the large oak
5 tree." Today monuments are made of concrete, iron, or brass, and they are carefully placed
6 by the U.S. Army Corps of Engineers or trained private land surveyors.

7   The direction of a boundary line is expressed using compass directions. Distances are
8 measured in feet, usually to the nearest one-hundredth of a foot. Plotting a metes-and-
9 bounds description is not as difficult as it might appear. The POB and *all* turning points
10 (corners of the parcel) should be regarded as being the exact center of a circle.

11   A compass has four primary directions: north, south, east, and west. If we draw a
12 straight line connecting north and south, and a second line connecting east and west, the
13 circle is divided into four quarters or *quadrants*. (See Drawing A in Figure 10.2, Compass
14 Directions.) The line running north and south is the *primary reference line*. Metes-and-
15 bounds descriptions will always begin with either north or south followed by a certain
16 number of degrees, up to a maximum of 90 degrees. The direction that follows the number
17 of degrees indicates whether the direction is east or west of due north or south.

18   Let's begin by plotting *North 45 degrees East*. Using Drawing B in Figure 10.2, place
19 your pencil in a vertical (north-south) position over the circle. The first word in the
20 description "North" indicates that we will begin with north as our primary direction so
21 our pencil lead should face upward (north). The second direction is "East" so rotate your
22 pencil in an easterly direction (to the right on the drawing). How far is 45 degrees? It is
23 half way between zero degrees (due north) and 90 degrees (due east). (Refer to Line A on
24 Drawing B in Figure 10.2.)

25   The reason why the number of degrees cannot exceed 90 is that one would pass the
26 point midway between north and south and begin to move toward the other primary ref-
27 erence direction. For example, let's plot *South 85 degrees West*. Begin with your pencil in
28 a vertical (north-south) direction with the pencil lead facing south (downward). Move
29 85 degrees to the west (to the left on the drawing). Because 85 degrees approaches 90,
30 we can draw a line very close to due west. (See line C on Drawing B in Figure 10.2.)

What would happen if you were to plot *North 95 degrees West?* (I know—I just told you descriptions don't exceed 90 degrees, but let's see why.) Again place your pencil in a vertical position, this time with the pencil lead facing upward (north). If you rotate the pencil 95 degrees to the west, notice that you pass due west (90°) and end up five degrees into the lower half of the circle. Therefore, the description should have begun with the primary reference direction of south. Let's rewrite the description properly as *South 85 degrees West.* Place your pencil in the vertical position with the pencil lead facing south. Rotate your pencil to the west 85 degrees which is just five degrees shy of 90 degrees. We have confirmed that the line is correctly labeled as *South 85 degrees West.* (Refer to Line C on Drawing B in Figure 10.2.)

Notice that the opposite of S45°W (Line B in Figure 10.2) is N45°E (Line A in Figure 10.2). The number of degrees does not change, only the compass directions. What is the opposite of S85°W? It is N85°E. (Refer to Line D in Figure 10.2.)

Practice Problem 1

What is the opposite of N45°W? To help you answer this question, refer to Figure 10.2, Drawing B. (The solution is at the end of this chapter on page 231.)

Practice Problem 2

Now, without referring Figure 10.2, what is the opposite of S15°E? Hint: the number of degrees do not change, only the compass directions. (Check your answer at the end of this chapter on page 232.)

To be more accurate, directions are actually given in degrees, minutes, and seconds. Minutes and seconds are more precise measurements smaller than one degree. Each degree is divided into 60 minutes. Therefore, half way between one degree and two degrees is one degree, 30 minutes. Each minute is then divided into 60 seconds. The symbols for degrees (°), minutes ('), and seconds (") are used so that, for example, 15 degrees 25 minutes 20 seconds would be written 15°25'20".

Description by Government Survey

Following the Revolutionary War, when the federal government decided to open an area for settlement, it first commissioned a survey for that entire area. The intent of the **government survey system (GSS)** (also known as the *U.S. System of Rectangular Surveys,* and the *Public Domain Survey*) was to create a large grid with every square of the grid uniquely identified. Over time, the government commissioned the GSS in 30 states (other than the original 13 colonies and a few other states). The GSS is based on intersecting lines. Once understood, the GSS is simple and accurate and describes property in concise symbols and words, resulting in a kind of land description shorthand.

Principal meridian and base line. A beginning reference was established in the center of the territory to be surveyed. The beginning reference is the intersection of a north/south line called a **principal meridian** and an east/west line called a **base line**. In all, 36 principal meridians and base lines were established and named in the United States. (See Figure 10.3, Government Survey System.)

The Tallahassee Principal Meridian and Base Line are the reference lines that govern surveys in Florida. The Tallahassee Principal Meridian was established in the early 1800s,

FIGURE 10.3 ■ **Government Survey System**

FIGURE 10.3 ■ **Government Survey System**

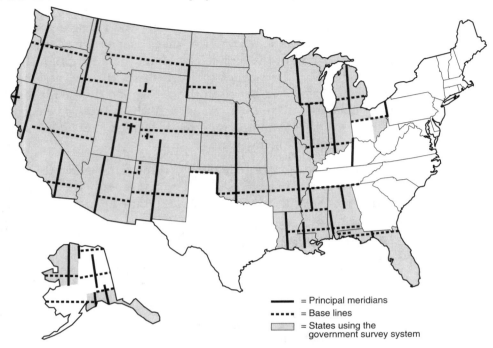

1   and it intersects with the base line in the city of Tallahassee, Florida. (See Figure 10.4,
2   Map of Florida Showing Principal Meridian and Base Line.)

3   **Range.** To create the grid system, surveyors established vertical (north/south) *range lines*
4   parallel to the principal meridian (PM) every six miles. This resulted in a series of lines six
5   miles apart on either side of the PM. Each resulting six-mile-wide vertical (north/south)
6   strip of land on either side of the PM is called a **range**. (See Figure 10.5, Map of Florida
7   Showing Selecting Range and Township Lines.)

8   Each range is numbered beginning at the PM. The first vertical (north/south) strip of
9   land to the east of the PM is numbered Range 1 East or more concisely, R1E. (Refer to the

FIGURE 10.4 ■ **Map of Florida Showing Principal Meridian and Base Line**

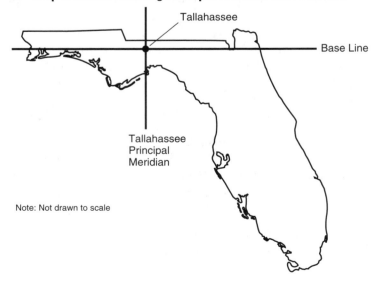

F I G U R E 10.5 ■ **Map of Florida Showing Selected Range and Township Lines**

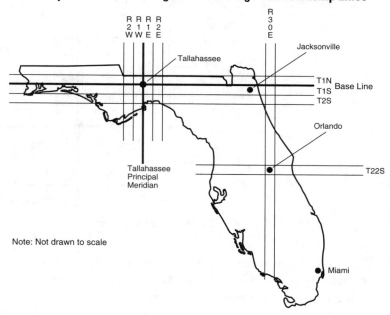

shaded column labeled R1E in Figure 10.6, T2S, R3E.) The range numbers increase by one moving farther from the PM. For example, the next range east of the PM is R2E, then R3E, and so on. The numbering also begins with 1 to the west of the PM. The first range west of the PM is R1W, then R2W, and so on.

Township. The surveyors also established horizontal (east/west) *township lines* parallel to the base line (BL) every six miles. This resulted in a series of lines six miles apart on either side of the BL. Each resulting six-mile-wide horizontal (east/west) strip of land on either side of the BL is called a township tier or simply township. (To help remember that township tiers are horizontal strips, think of tiers of a wedding cake.) (See Figure 10.5, Map of Florida Showing Selected Range and Township Lines.)

Each township tier is numbered beginning at the BL. The first horizontal (east/west) strip of land above (north of) the base line is numbered Township 1 North, or more concisely, T1N. The township line numbers increase by one moving farther from the BL. For example, the next township tier north of the BL is T2N, then T3N, and so on. The numbering also begins with one below (south of) the base line. The first township tier south of the BL is T1S (the shaded row in Figure 10.6, T2S, R3E), then T2S, and so on.

T O   R E M E M B E R

The directions of township lines and range lines may be easily remembered by thinking of the words this way:

F I G U R E 10.6 ■ **T2S, R3E**

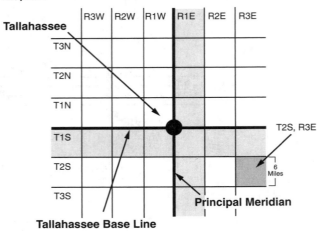

1   The resulting grid pattern formed by the crossing (or intersection) of range lines and
2   township lines produced a series of squares six miles square known as **townships**. A town-
3   ship contains 36 square miles.

4   Note that the term *township* has two meanings: In addition to an (east/west) strip of
5   land north or south of a base line, the term also refers to the square formed by the intersec-
6   tion of two range lines and two township lines. Each 36-square-mile township (six miles
7   on each side) is identified by the strip of townships (the township tier) and the range in
8   which it is located. For example, T2S, R3E is located in the second tier of townships south
9   of the base line and the third range east of the principal meridian. (Refer to the shaded
10   township in Figure 10.6, T2S, R3E.)

Practice Problem 3

Locate and shade in the townships numbered T2N, R2E and T3S, R1W on the
drawing below. (The solutions are at the end of this chapter on page 232.)

	R3W	R2W	R1W	R1E	R2E	R3E
T3N						
T2N						
T1N						
T1S						
T2S						
T3S						

Sections. Each township is further divided into 36 **sections**. Each section is one square mile or 640 acres. Sections are numbered in an S-pattern, beginning in the northeast (upper right) corner of the township with section number 1. The sections are numbered from one in the northeast corner and then consecutively to the west through section 6. The section numbers then wrap around in an S-pattern. The second horizontal row begins directly under section 6 and progresses west to east (left to right) from 7 to 12. Section 13 is directly under section 12, and one moves west (to the left) with section 18 last in that row. This method of numbering is repeated until section number 36 is reached in the southeast, or lower right, corner of every township. The numbering pattern of sections repeats itself inside each township.

At first, this may seem odd to number sections this way, however, in the 1800s surveyors measured the one mile distances with metal chains and walked the sections on foot. Imagine surveyors departing the original 13 states and walking toward the west. This is why section 1 is located in the northeast corner of the township. Because of the primitive methods and tools they used at the time, surveyors found it more efficient and less tiring to measure the sections using this particular numbering sequence. (To help remember the number system, think of the pattern people usually walk when doing their weekly grocery shopping at the supermarket as they go down one aisle and up another.) (See Figure 10.7, Sections in a Township.)

In writing a legal description of a section, it is customary to show the section number first, then the township tier number and direction, and last the range number and direction. For example, *Section 36, Township 1 South, Range 1 West of the Tallahassee Principal Meridian and Base Line* identifies Section 36 within the township that is located immediately southwest of the intersection of the principal meridian and base line. It is abbreviated to *Sec 36, T1S, R1W.* (Refer to the shaded Section 36 in Figure 10.7.)

The survey of Lot 26 presented in Figure 10.1 is also identified as in Section 10, Township 9 South, Range 19 East of Alachua County, Florida.

F I G U R E 10.7 ■   Sections in a Township

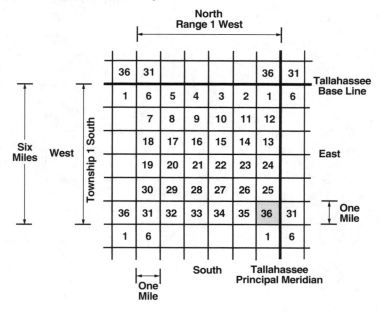

MEASURES AND TERMS ASSOCIATED WITH THE GOVERNMENT SURVEY SYSTEM

Check	A square 24 miles on each side created by intersecting guide meridians and correction lines; used to adjust the grid pattern of squares because of the curvature of the earth. A check contains 16 townships.
Township	A square 6 miles on each side (6 miles square) containing 36 square miles (36 sections); also an (east-west) strip of land north and south of a baseline (tier).
Section	A square 1 mile on each side (1 mile square) containing 1 square mile (640 acres).
Quarter section	160 acres, measuring 2,640 feet by 2,640 feet. Historically, it was the area of land originally granted to a homesteader. Today, the 160 acres is still used to establish the limits of homesteaded property outside the boundaries of municipality. (See also page 179.)
Government lot	Fractional pieces of land less than a full quarter section located along the banks of lakes and streams. Government lots were identified by a specific lot number, which became the legal description for that parcel.

Practice Problem 4

Number the sections in the township below. (The solutions are at the end of this chapter on page 232.)

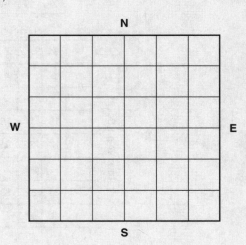

How to Use the Government Survey System

Locating sections. Suppose you want to locate a section of land in Florida, and this is the legal description given to you: "All of Section 36, Township 1 South, Range 1 West, Tallahassee Principal Meridian and Base Line." The numbers assigned to the township tier and range tell you immediately that you are dealing with property very near Tallahassee because the range (1 West) is the first six-mile segment immediately west of the principal meridian. The tier of townships (1 South) must be the first six-mile strip immediately south of the horizontal base line. Considering how sections are numbered, Section 36 cannot be anywhere except in the lower right corner of the township numbered T1S, R1W. Therefore, the section you seek begins five miles south of the intersection of the Tallahassee Principal Meridian and Base Line and immediately west of the Tallahassee Principal Meridian.

Subdividing sections. Each section is theoretically a square with all sides measuring one mile and contains 640 acres within its boundaries. It is important to remember the exact number of acres in a section because the 640 figure is used for many purposes. One reason is that the section is the basic reference when writing a legal description of land. It is also the reference when calculating acreage in subdivided tracts. Each section can easily be divided into halves, or into quarters, and so on, down into smaller divisions until the particular property one wants to locate or describe has been pinpointed.

Suppose you are interested in only a quarter section, 160 acres, of Section 36. First, divide the entire section into fourths by drawing a straight vertical line through the center of the section and a straight horizontal line through the center of the section. The two lines are perpendicular to each other and cross in the exact center of the section. The quarter section now situated in the upper right corner of the section is called the *Northeast Quarter*, the one in the lower right corner is the *Southeast Quarter*, and so on around the section. (See Figure 10.8, Section 36.) Directions are always given in terms of the direction from the center of the section where the two dividing lines intersect.

Quarter sections contain 160 acres. Suppose you are interested in a tract smaller than 160 acres. You can divide any quarter just as you did the section. Furthermore, you can keep on dividing the results until you find the tract in which you are interested.

Assume you need to find a 2½-acre tract located somewhere near the center of Section 36. The legal description given you is "SW¼ of the NE¼ of the SE¼ of the NW¼ of Section 36." Beginning with the section, divide it into quarters to start locating the property. In locating property from a legal description, it is necessary to start with the last part of the description and read from right to left. So, because you have located Section 36, move to the last fraction in the description (NW¼) and separate that quarter section from the whole. Move to the next fraction (SE¼), divide the previously located quarter section (NW¼) into four parts, and focus your attention on the resulting southeast quarter. Move to the next fraction (NE¼), divide the SE¼ of the NW¼ into four parts, and locate the northeast quarter of that division. You still have one more fraction (SW¼) remaining, so divide the last located parcel (NE¼) into fourths once more. When you find the southwest quarter of that division, you have located the tract described.

Calculating size. To find the number of acres in a tract, two approaches are possible:

1. Take 640 (the number of acres in one section) and divide by the bottom number (the denominator) of each fraction in the legal description.

FIGURE 10.8 ■ Section 36

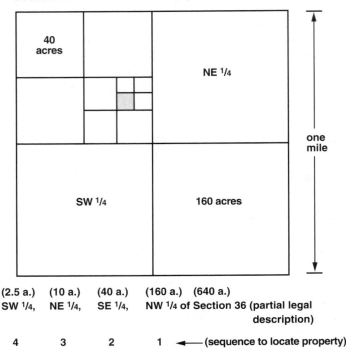

(2.5 a.)   (10 a.)   (40 a.)   (160 a.)   (640 a.)
SW ¼,   NE ¼,   SE ¼,   NW ¼ of Section 36 (partial legal
description)

4   3   2   1 ◄── (sequence to locate property)

EXAMPLE: The SW¼, NE¼, SE¼, NW¼ of a certain section contains how many acres?

$$640 \div 4 = 160; 160 \div 4 = 40; 40 \div 4 = 10; 10 \div 4 = 2.5;$$
$$\text{or } 640 \div 4 \div 4 \div 4 \div 4 = 2.5 \text{ acres}$$

2. Multiply the denominators of each fraction together and then divide 640 by the result.

EXAMPLE: The SW¼, NE¼, SE¼, NW¼ of a certain section contains how many acres?

$$4 \times 4 \times 4 \times 4 = 256$$
$$640 \div 256 = 2.5 \text{ acres}$$

The previous exercise to determine the size of a given tract demonstrates, among other things, that generally, the longer a legal description, the smaller the number of acres contained in the parcel described. With practice, one becomes familiar with the fact that a description containing four one-fourths will always result in a 2½-acre tract. A description with only three one-fourths will result in a 10-acre parcel. If fractions other than fourths are used, the method for calculating acreage is the same.

***And* in a legal description.** What will you do if you are required to find the total acreage of a tract with a legal description that contains the word *and* within the description? For example:

SE¼ of the NW¼ *and* NE¼ of the SW¼

You should multiply the denominators as previously mentioned. First, however, multiply only the denominators that immediately precede the *and*. Next, multiply the

ADDITIONAL SURVEY MEASURES AND TERMINOLOGY

Acre	43,560 square feet (approximately 208.71 ft. × 208.71 feet)
Bench mark	A permanent reference mark (PRM) affixed to an iron post or brass marker that is embedded in the sidewalk or street, used to establish elevations and altitudes above sea level on surveyed parcels.
Mile	5,280 feet in length

denominators that follow the *and*. Then, find the acreage for each. Finally, add the two answers to find the total acreage in the legal description.

> **Practice Problem 5**
>
> How many acres are there in the previous example? (The solution is at the end of this chapter on page 232.)
>
> **Practice Problem 6**
>
> How many acres are there in the legal description N½ of the NE¼ of the SW¼ and the SE¼ of the NW¼? (The solution is at the end of this chapter on page 232.)

Description by Lot and Block Numbers

Probably the most common type of legal description used for single-family dwellings located in developed subdivisions is the **lot and block** method of land description. The lot and block method can be used only where *plat maps* have been recorded in the public records (also called *plat method, description by recorded plat,* or *description by recorded map*). The platted subdivision is divided into large areas called *blocks*, and each block is subdivided into smaller areas called *lots*. The lots are usually numbered for convenience in identifying them. If the lots are numbered, the blocks may be assigned letters to eliminate confusing block numbers with lot numbers. For example, the shaded lot in Figure 10.9, Subdivision Plat Map, is Lot 5, Block B of Glendale Estates Subdivision.

A plat map is an engineer's plan for land use superimposed on a map of the land in question. The plat map shows the lot divisions and street locations, and it may provide for dedication of streets, parks, and school sites to the county or community. It shows actual dimensions for lots, streets, and other planned improvements. The plat map must show the location of the fixed monuments established and placed in the ground and the survey data needed to locate each lot, block, and street with reference to the permanent monuments. The entire tract is probably referenced to the government survey system. The subdivision is given a name. The plat map is recorded in the county courthouse under the subdivision name by book and page number. This makes the plat map a part of the public records, and it makes any further legal description of the lots a simple matter.

F I G U R E 10.9 ■ Subdivision Plat Map

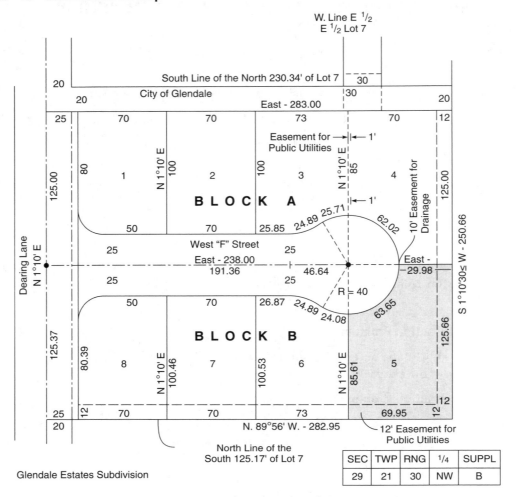

Glendale Estates Subdivision

SEC	TWP	RNG	1/4	SUPPL
29	21	30	NW	B

1   The various methods of legal description are *not* mutually exclusive. A lot and block
2   description in a plat, for example, located in Florida is created within section(s) of land in
3   the government survey system. The location of Lot 26 (see Figure 10.1, Boundary Survey,
4   on page 219) is described using the government survey system as in Section 10, Town-
5   ship 9 South, Range 19 East of Alachua County, Florida. A developer hired a surveyor to
6   stake out parcels using the metes-and-bounds method. The Boundary Survey (Figure 10.1)
7   indicates the surveyor's metes-and-bounds description of Lot 26. And the lot and block
8   description of Lot 26 (see Figure 10.1) is worded, "Lot 26, Blues Creek Unit— 4, a portion
9   of a planned unit development as recorded in Plat Book 'S', page 3, of the public records
10 of Alachua County, Florida."

11 **Tax maps.** Every parcel of land within a tax district is assessed for tax purposes. To accom-
12 plish this task, each parcel is assigned a Parcel ID (PID) number (or *assessor's parcel num-*
13 *ber*) by the county property appraiser's office. The PID numbers are used to prepare *tax*
14 *maps*. They are scaled drawings based on recorded plat maps of all the parcels within a tax
15 district showing the exact location of the property, dimensions, and the amount of the
16 assessed value of each parcel. The information is used each year to prepare the tax roll.
17 PID numbers are sometimes used to identify a particular parcel.

Practice Problem 7

A property costs $21,780 per acre. What is the cost per square foot of the property? (The solution is at the end of this chapter on page 232.)

Practice Problem 8

A rectangular property measures 880 yards by ¾ of a mile. How many acres are contained in the parcel? (The solution is at the end of this chapter on page 232.)

S U M M A R Y   O F   I M P O R T A N T   P O I N T S

- The following three types of legal descriptions are used today: (1) metes-and-bounds, (2) government survey system, and (3) lot-and-block description.

- Metes-and-bounds is the most accurate method to describe both regular- and irregular-shaped parcels. The method is based on distances (metes) and directions (bounds). Metes-and-bounds descriptions begin and end with a starting point called a point of beginning (POB).

- Corners of parcels of land are identified using markers called monuments.

- The Government Survey System was commissioned by the federal government to survey land, except in the original 13 states and a few other states. This method of legal description relies on intersecting north-south and east-west lines that form a grid system.

- In Florida, the Tallahassee Principal Meridian and Base Line intersect in Tallahassee. The Principal Meridian runs north-south and the Base Line runs east-west. A series of lines parallel to the Principal Meridian were established every six miles forming six-mile-wide strips that run north and south and are called ranges. Parallel lines established every six miles on either side of the base line form east-west strips of land called tiers or townships.

- Township also describes a square that is six miles on each side (six miles square) and contains 36 square miles (36 sections).

- A section is a square that is one mile on each side (one mile square) and contains one square mile or 640 acres. Sections are numbered within a township, beginning at the top right corner and numbered right to left (sections one through six), then the next row of sections is numbered left to right (sections seven through 12), and so on.

- To calculate the acres in a government survey legal description, multiply the denominators of each fraction together and then divide 640 by the result. If the word *and* appears in the description, calculate the acres on each side of the word *and* separately and then add the two acreages together.

- Lot-and-block descriptions are used where plat maps of single-family subdivisions have been recorded in the public records. The platted subdivision is divided into blocks, and each parcel within the block is a lot.

Practice Problem 1 Solution

(Practice 1 is located on page 221.) The number of degrees do not change, only the compass directions. The opposite of North is South. The opposite of West is East. Therefore, the opposite of N45°W is S45°E.

Practice Problem 2 Solution

(Practice 2 is located on page 221.) The number of degrees do not change, only the compass directions. The opposite of South is North. The opposite of East is West. Therefore, the opposite of S15°E is N15°W.

Practice 3 Solution

	R3W	R2W	R1W	R1E	R2E	R3E
T3N						
T2N						
T1N						
T1S						
T2S						
T3S						

(Practice 3 is located on page 224.)

Practice 4 Solution

N

6	5	4	3	2	1
7	8	9	10	11	12
18	17	16	15	14	13
19	20	21	22	23	24
30	29	28	27	26	25
31	32	33	34	35	36

W   E

S

(Practice 4 is located on page 226.)

Practice Problem 5 Solution

(Practice 5 is located on page 229.) The word and is in the middle of the description; therefore, the acreage must be calculated separately for the description before the "and" and after the "and."

$$640 \div 4 \div 4 = 40 \text{ acres}$$
$$640 \div 4 \div 4 = 40 \text{ acres}$$
$$40 + 40 = 80 \text{ acres}$$

Practice Problem 6 Solution

(Practice 6 is located on page 229.)

$$640 \div 2 \div 4 \div 4 = 20 \text{ acres}$$
$$640 \div 4 \div 4 = 40 \text{ acres}$$
$$20 + 40 = 60 \text{ acres}$$

Practice Problem 7 Solution

(Practice 7 is located on page 231.) An acre contains 43,560 square feet.

Cost divided by square feet in an acre = Cost per square foot
$$\$21,780 \div 43,560 = \$0.50 \text{ per square foot}$$

Practice Problem 8 Solution

(Practice 8 is located on page 231.) There are 3 feet per yard. 880 yards is equivalent to $880 \times 3 = 2,640$ feet in length. A mile is 5,280 feet in length. Therefore, ¾ of a mile is equivalent to $5,280 \times .75 = 3,960$ feet in length.

$2,640 \times 3,960 = 10,454,400$ square feet. $10,454,400 \div 43,560 = 240$ acres

R E V I E W   Q U E S T I O N S

1. The NW¼ of the NE¼ of the SW¼, Section 20, Township 4 South, Range 2 East, describes a tract of
   a. .125 acre.
   b. .5 acre.
   c. 10 acres.
   d. 64 acres.

2. Calculate the number of acres contained in the following legal description: NE¼ of the SE¼ and the SE¼ of the NE¼ and the N½ of the NE¼.
   a. 30 acres
   b. 80 acres
   c. 120 acres
   d. 160 acres

3. In the metes-and-bounds method of description
   a. *metes* refers to direction, and *bounds* refers to distance.
   b. *metes* refers to distance, and *bounds* refers to direction.
   c. *metes* refers to distance, and *bounds* refers to measurement.
   d. *metes* refers to metric, and *bounds* refers to boundaries.

4. The government survey system is especially adapted to describing
   a. lots in platted subdivisions.
   b. odd-shaped tracts of land carved out of former land grants.
   c. land in concise symbols and words.
   d. parcels with human-made or natural physical features.

5. What is the designation of a township located three township tiers south of the base line and five ranges east of the principal meridian?
   a. R3S, T5E
   b. T3S, R5E
   c. R7E, T2S
   d. T3N, R5E

6. A check is a square with each side measuring
   a. 1 mile.
   b. 6 miles.
   c. 24 miles.
   d. 36 miles.

7. The tract of land located inside a square formed by intersecting range lines and township lines is called
   a. an acre.
   b. a check.
   c. a section.
   d. a township.

8. The vertical strip of land six miles wide beginning at the principal meridian and extending six miles east along the length of the principal meridian is called
   a. Range 1 East.
   b. Township 1 East.
   c. Tier 1 East.
   d. Section 6.

9. If you have located a township designated as T1N, R1E, the township due north of that township is
   a. T1N, R2E.
   b. T1S, R1E.
   c. T2N, R1E.
   d. T2N, R2E.

10. Which statement is FALSE concerning townships?
    a. A township contains 36 sections.
    b. A township contains 36 square miles.
    c. A township is 6 miles square.
    d. A township contains 36 acres.

11. In writing the legal description of a section, which is the standard sequence?
    a. Range number, township number, section number
    b. Section number, township number, range number
    c. Township number, range number, section number
    d. Section number, range number, township number

12. The north boundary of Section 36, Township 1 South, Range 1 West is located
    a. 6 miles south of the principal meridian.
    b. 35 miles west of the base line.
    c. 25 miles west of the principal meridian.
    d. 5 miles south of the base line.

13. A legal description that reads, in part, "the North one-half of the Northeast one-quarter of the Northwest one-quarter Section 12, Township 42 South, Range 12 East" describes a tract of
    a. 20 acres.
    b. 10 acres.
    c. 5 acres.
    d. 2½ acres.

14. A man owned the NW¼ of a section. He sold the W½ of that NW¼. How many acres does the man still own?
    a. 40 acres.
    b. 80 acres.
    c. 160 acres.
    d. 640 acres.

15. Plat maps used in the lot and block method of legal description show
    a. the grid system of government squares.
    b. dimensions of streets and improvements.
    c. the numerical street address for each lot.
    d. distance and direction from the point of beginning.

11

REAL ESTATE CONTRACTS

1 ## OVERVIEW

2 Nearly every business transaction is based on a contract. Key to every contract is the
3 *promise*. In a real estate contract, the seller promises to convey title to the real estate, and
4 the buyer promises to pay the purchase price. Contract promises are *enforceable* by law,
5 provided the contract meets certain requirements. A contract defines the parties' legal
6 relationship and spells out their rights and duties.

7 After completing this chapter, the student should be able to:

8 ■ list and describe the essentials of a real estate contract;

9 ■ describe the differences between formal contracts and parol contracts;

10 ■ distinguish among bilateral, unilateral, implied, express, executory, and executed
11 contracts;

12 ■ describe the various ways in which an offer is terminated;

13 ■ describe the various methods of terminating a contract;

14 ■ explain the remedies for breach of a contract;

15 ■ describe the effect of the statute of frauds and the statute of limitations;

16 ■ describe the elements of an option; and

17 ■ differentiate among the various types of listings.

KEY TERMS

assignment	liquidated damages	statute of limitations
bilateral contract	meeting of the minds	unenforceable contract
buyer brokerage agreement	mutual assent	unilateral contract
competent	net listing	valid
contract	novation	valuable consideration
enforceable contract	open listing	vendee
exclusive-agency listing	option contract	vendor
exclusive-right-of-sale	parol contract	void
listing	procuring cause	voidable
good consideration	statute of frauds	

PREPARATION OF CONTRACTS

To draft the wording of legal documents or legal instruments for others is considered practicing law. Because very few real estate licensees are attorneys, real estate brokers and sales associates may *not* prepare deeds, mortgages, promissory notes, or most other legal documents. Licensees who prepare such instruments could lose their licenses, regardless of whether they receive compensation. Real estate licensees may *not* draw lease agreements. However, licensees may fill in the blanks on Florida Supreme Court preapproved lease instruments for lease periods that do not exceed one year. Real estate licensees are allowed to assist buyers and sellers with the drawing of four types of contracts:

1. *Listing agreement.* A listing agreement is a broker's employment contract with a seller. Typically, it is the sales associate who obtains the listing on behalf of the broker.

2. *Buyer brokerage agreement.* A buyer brokerage agreement is an employment contract with a buyer.

3. *Sale and purchase contract.* A sale and purchase contract is a contract between a buyer and seller. If the licensee acts as agent or facilitator for one or both of the contracting parties, the licensee may prepare the sale and purchase contract.

4. *Option contract.* An option contract is an agreement to keep open for a specified period of time an offer to sell or lease real property. In order to reduce liability it is strongly advised that licensees recommend to the buyer or the seller to have a real estate attorney draw option contracts. (See Options Contracts, page 248.)

Real estate brokerage offices typically use standardized listing agreements, buyer brokerage agreements, sale and purchase contracts, and option contracts. The Florida REAL-TORS® and other professional groups have developed standardized contracts for use by their members. This is desirable because the use of standardized contracts improves efficiency and greatly reduces liability. Each of these contracts is explained in this chapter.

UNENFORCEABLE CONTRACTS

An *unenforceable contract* is a contract that cannot be proved or will not be recognized by a court. A contract may contain all of the essentials of a contract, yet still not be enforceable. A contract may be unenforceable because it is not in writing, as required by the statute of frauds, because the statute of limitations has passed, or because the property is destroyed.

ESSENTIALS OF A CONTRACT

A **contract** is an agreement between two or more parties to do or not to do certain things, supported by a sufficient consideration. A **valid** contract is one that complies with the provisions of contract law and contains four essential elements:

1. Competent parties
2. Offer and acceptance (mutual assent)
3. Legal purpose
4. Consideration

Contracts may be in writing or oral. However, contracts that involve a transfer of real property must be in writing to be legally enforceable. The parties to an oral real estate contract may have a valid contract (one that contains all of the essential elements), but the contract will not be enforceable in a court of law if it is not in writing. (There are two exceptions to this requirement. See Statute of Frauds, page 238, and Transfer of Real Property, page 239.)

Competent Parties

Not all persons have the ability or capacity to make a valid contract. A person who is insane, intoxicated, or legally a minor may have only limited contractual capacity. A minor's contract (a contract by an individual under the legal age to contract), for example, is **voidable**. The minor may choose to void the contract. However, an adult is bound to honor the contract if the minor chooses to go through with the transaction.

The parties to a contract are **competent** if they have the *legal capacity to contract*, meaning they have no mental defects or insanity and are both of legal age to contract. A sane person contracting with an insane person or an adult contracting with a minor produces a voidable contract.

Offer and Acceptance

Mutual assent refers to the making and acceptance of an offer. The parties must come to a **meeting of the minds**, meaning they must reach an agreement on all terms in the contract. One party (the *offeror*) makes an offer, and the other party (the *offeree*) accepts that offer. A complete and mutual understanding must exist to produce a meeting of the minds.

The contract is formed at the instant that acceptance of the offer is communicated to the offeror. Therefore, a contract is formed on the acceptance of an offer and communication of the acceptance.

Legal Purpose

The provisions spelled out in a contract must not be prohibited by law. For example, a sale and purchase contract (or sale contract) that provides for payment of commission to an unlicensed person is a contract with an illegal purpose. The contract would not be enforceable in a court of law.

Consideration

Consideration is whatever is given in exchange for something else. People often think of consideration as the money exchanged by the parties. Legally, however, consideration is the *obligation* that each party makes to the other to make the contract enforceable. Each party to the contract must obligate himself or herself by placing some consideration in the agreement. A promise undertaken by one party must be supported by a promise undertaken by the other party. Mutual promises to do or not to do some specific act are sufficient consideration, even though the benefit or sacrifice may not be equal. A common misconception is that the good-faith deposit (earnest money) in a real estate sale contract is the consideration. The good-faith deposit is made by a buyer to assure the seller that the buyer is serious about the transaction and the buyer intends to purchase the property. In real estate sale contracts, the seller normally promises to sell and convey, and the purchaser promises to pay for the property. There are two types of consideration:

1. **Valuable consideration** is the money or a promise of something that can be measured in terms of money.
2. **Good consideration** is a promise that cannot be measured in terms of money, such as love and affection.

Either type of consideration is sufficient to enforce a contract. The law generally does not concern itself with the relative fairness of consideration. What is exchanged need not have the same measurable value. The law will accept that the parties thought the consideration to be fair because they freely agreed to the exchange.

STATUTE OF FRAUDS

725.01, F.S.

The **statute of frauds** requires that contracts *conveying an interest* in real property, and contracts that are not to be performed within one year of the date created, must be in writing and signed to be enforceable. An **enforceable contract** is a legally binding contract that the courts will recognize. Contracts covered by Florida's statute of frauds include the following:

- Purchase and sale contracts
- Option contracts
- Deeds and mortgage instruments
- Lease agreements for a term longer than one year
- Listing agreements for a term longer than one year

VOID AND VOIDABLE CONTRACTS

Void   A **void** contract does not meet all of the required elements of a valid contract and, therefore, has no legal effect.

Voidable   A **voidable** contract is a contract, but because of the manner or method in which it was brought about, one of the parties is permitted to avoid any contractual duties. A minor's contract is voidable because the minor can choose to void the contract.

The fact that a real estate sale contract is oral does *not* make the contract illegal. However, verbal agreements are difficult to prove and therefore will not be enforced by a court of law if there is a dispute between parties. However, it is possible that an oral real estate contract is a valid contract. For example, if a buyer and seller verbally agree to a purchase and sale of real estate, and the buyer pays part of the purchase price and takes possession of the property or has made improvements to the property, the courts will recognize the contract.

STATUTE OF LIMITATIONS

The **statute of limitations** designates the period of time during which the terms of a contract may be enforced. It protects people from being compelled to perform or otherwise be sued after a period of time has expired. The times vary, depending on whether it is an oral contract or a written contract:

- Written contracts—five years
- Oral contracts—four years
- Partly written and partly oral—five years for the written portion and four years for the oral portion

TRANSFER OF REAL PROPERTY

In addition to the four essential elements required in any contract, to be enforceable in court, real estate sale and purchase contracts must be in writing and signed by all parties who are bound by the agreement. Real estate contracts are *not* required to be witnessed or notarized.

> **TO REMEMBER: ELEMENTS OF A VALID AND ENFORCEABLE REAL ESTATE SALE CONTRACT**
>
> C   Competent parties
> O   Offer and acceptance (meeting of the minds)
> L   Legal purpose
> I   In writing and signed (statute of frauds)
> C   Consideration (valuable or good)

A contract does not have to be in any particular format to be valid, as long as it contains all of the essential elements. The contract should have an unambiguous property identification. Because a contract is an agreement designed to spell out clearly the meeting of the minds between parties on a particular subject, it creates certain enforceable rights. It also provides remedies for the affected parties if the contract is breached.

CONTRACT CATEGORIES

Contracts can be classified by their method of formation, their content, or their legal effect. The first classification is *formal* and *informal* contracts.

Formal and Informal Contracts

Formal contract. Historically, a formal contract was in written form and under seal. The seal has evolved from the old wax impression on a document to the word *seal* or the letters *L.S.* (*locus sigilli*, Latin for "the place of the seal") that appear after the signatures of parties signing the contract. The term *formal contract* also refers to a contract that depends on a particular form. For example, a negotiable instrument such as a promissory note is referred to as a formal contract. Today, the seal is *not* required to make contracts valid.

Parol (informal) contract. An oral agreement is a **parol contract**. Some oral real estate contracts are recognized by law as enforceable. (See Statute of Frauds, page 238.)

Other Contract Classifications

The very name of the contract classification often indicates the way in which the contract was arranged, the requirements for its performance, or even the type of parties bound by the contract. Contracts can be either *bilateral* or *unilateral*.

Bilateral and unilateral contracts. A **bilateral contract** obligates both parties to perform in accordance with the terms of the contract. A sale contract is an example of a bilateral contract because *both* the seller and the buyer are obligated to perform.

A **unilateral contract** obligates only one party to an agreement. There is no obligation on the part of the other party involved. An example of a unilateral contract is the ordinary *option*.

If the person asking for an option (the *optionee*) gives a consideration to the person granting the option (the *optionor*), the optionor is obligated not to sell to anyone other than the optionee during the life of the option. The optionee, however, is not obligated to buy. An optionee may choose to exercise the option. The optionor then is bound to honor the option on notification of the optionee's intent to exercise it. The option (unilateral contract) becomes a bilateral contract when the optionee has promised to exercise the option specified in the contract.

Express or implied contracts. Contracts may be classified as either *express* or *implied*.

An *express contract* exists when all the terms and conditions have been spelled out and a meeting of the minds is reached in words of agreement and mutual understanding. An express contract may be either written or parol; that is, it may be in writing or oral or be a combination of the two. The primary requirements in an express contract are mutual understanding and agreement.

An *implied contract* is one in which some or all of the obligations or conditions of a contract are not stated expressly (in words) but may be reasonably implied by the acts of the parties or by the nature of the transaction. Every day, we enter into implied contracts. For example, if a person walks into a restaurant and orders dinner, an implied contract has been created. It is implied that the customer will pay for the service after enjoying the meal without actually discussing the actual payment or agreeing to pay for the meal until after the service has been rendered. In real estate dealings if a *for sale by owner* (FSBO) seller knowingly accepts the services of a real estate licensee and the licensee is the procuring cause of the sale, a real estate commission may be due. Obviously, implied contracts are not a professional way of transacting real estate business.

The various categories of contracts are *not* mutually exclusive. For example, a particular contract may be described as *parol, bilateral,* and *express.*

Executory or executed contracts. Contracts also may be referred to as *executory* or *executed* contracts.

Assume a contract has been formed between parties but something remains to be done by one or both parties to fulfill the conditions of the contract. It is an *executory contract* because it is not yet a fully performed contract. A real estate sale contract, between the time of signing the contract and the time of closing the transaction, is an executory contract.

When all parties to a contract have completely performed all the obligations and promises contained in the contract, it is an *executed contract.* For instance, a real estate sale contract becomes an executed contract after the title closing and all the promises of both buyer and seller have been fulfilled.

CONTRACT NEGOTIATION

In the normal sequence of forming a contract, one party begins by making an *offer.* Assume that Rebecca is selling a parcel of land that she owns. Ken makes an *offer* to purchase the lot from Rebecca for $34,000. Ken is the *offeror* (the person making the offer) and Rebecca is the *offeree* (the person who receives the offer).

Frequently, the offeree will make a *counteroffer* by altering the terms of the original offer. For example, if Rebecca decides to make a counteroffer of $35,500 and asks Ken to pay all of the closing costs, Rebecca has replaced Ken's original offer with a counteroffer. When a counteroffer is made, it kills the original offer and substitutes a new offer in its place.

When a counteroffer is made, the role of both parties also changes. Because Rebecca's counteroffer is based on new terms and conditions, she has "changed hats" and is now the offeror. Likewise, Ken is receiving the new terms and conditions, so he has become the offeree. It is not uncommon for a series of offers and counteroffers to take place before a meeting of the minds is accomplished. Once a meeting of the minds is reached, that is, when one party accepts the offer of the other party and communicates such acceptance, a contract has been formed. Both parties then are obligated to perform according to the contract.

An offer is terminated when any of the following happens:

- *Counteroffer.* A counteroffer indicates a willingness to contract, but on terms or conditions different from those contained in the original offer. It is *not* an acceptance because it indicates an unwillingness to agree to the terms of the original offer. The original offer is dead forever and cannot be later accepted.

475.5018, F.S.

- *Acceptance.* Communication of the acceptance of an offer creates a contract. An acceptance must comply strictly with the terms of the offer. Letters and telegraphic communication can be part of a valid sale contract. If Rebecca had accepted Ken's offer of $34,000 for her property instead of making a counteroffer, the offer would have become a contract on that acceptance and its communication.

- *Rejection.* To effectively terminate an offer, a rejection must be communicated by the offeree to the offeror. If Rebecca had chosen to reject Ken's offer, the offer would have terminated when Rebecca communicated the rejection to Ken.

- *Withdrawal by offeror.* An offeror may withdraw (or *revoke*) the offer at any time until notice of the offeree's acceptance is received by the offeror or the offeror's designated agent. Suppose, for example, that Rebecca decides to withdraw her counteroffer of $35,500. She may do so as long as this is communicated to Ken before he accepts her counteroffer.

- *Lapse of time.* Ordinarily, when an offer is made, a time limit for acceptance of the offer is specified. The offer terminates after expiration of that time. If no time limit for acceptance is specified, the offeree is considered to have a *reasonable length of time.* This time period is based on such considerations as the method of communication used, the location of the parties involved, and the terminology and nature of the offer.

- *Death or insanity.* The death or insanity of either the offeror or the offeree terminates the offer. An offer is not assignable (transferable); it may be accepted only by the person to whom it is made.

- *Destruction of the property.* Destruction of the subject matter terminates the offer.

TO REMEMBER: WAYS AN OFFER IS TERMINATED	
W	Withdrawal by offeror
I	Insanity
L	Lapse of time
D	Death
C	Counteroffer
A	Acceptance
R	Rejection
D	Destruction of the property

REMEDIES FOR BREACH OF CONTRACT

Specific performance	Court orders the other party to perform according to the terms of the contract.
Liquidated damages	Amount of damages (usually the earnest money deposit) stipulated in the contract. If the buyer breaches the contract, typically the seller claims the earnest money deposit as liquidated damages.
Rescission	Cancellation of the contract and restoration of the parties to their original positions
Compensatory damages	Involves a lawsuit to recover the actual amount of the monetary loss to either party (also known as *unliquidated* damages)

TERMINATION OF CONTRACTS

A contract is terminated when any of the following happens:

- *Performance.* When both parties have fully performed the terms and conditions of a contract, the purpose of the contract has been accomplished and the contract is terminated. The emphasis is on full performance of each and every contract term or condition. This is, of course, the desired outcome of any contract. However, sometimes contracts are terminated for other reasons.

- *Mutual rescission.* An agreement between the contracting parties to terminate their respective duties under the contract is referred to as *mutual rescission*. Both parties must mutually agree to discontinue the contract.

- *Impossibility of performance.* Performance may be impossible and beyond the control of the parties. For example, destruction of the physical improvements is a good excuse for impossibility of performance. The death of the buyer or the seller will usually be considered a reason for impossibility of performance, unless the real estate contract provides otherwise.

- *Lapse of time.* Certain circumstances, such as lapse of time, will cause a contract to be terminated by operation of law. For example, a contract may be terminated as a result of the expiration of the statute of limitations. The words "*time is of the essence*" in a contract mean that dates and time limits in the contract must be met.

- *Bankruptcy.* The bankruptcy of one of the parties will not in itself discharge the contract. If the bankrupted party is the seller, however, control of the asset will come under the control of the courts. A court-appointed trustee will be charged with liquidating the asset.

- *Breach.* A contract is breached when one of the parties fails to perform and the law does not recognize the reason for failure to perform as valid. The aggrieved party may sue over a breach of contract.

Remedies for Breach

The Florida Real Estate Commission ordinarily has no authority or jurisdiction over breach of contract actions. There are four legal remedies for breach of a contract:

1. *Specific performance*. If awards of money damages do not afford sufficient relief, the wronged party may sue for specific performance to have the courts force the other party to perform as the contract specifically states. This action is termed a *relief in equity* because such judgments are awarded in a court of equity.

2. *Liquidated damages*. Frequently the parties will stipulate an amount of money in the contract (usually the earnest money deposit) to be paid in the case of default by the buyer. This amount is referred to as **liquidated damages** to the seller.

3. *Rescission*. To rescind is to cancel or annul the contract. The court orders the parties placed back to their original positions as if the contract had never existed. This relieves both parties from their respective obligations under the contract. An injured buyer is entitled to the return of any earnest money, and the seller is obligated to return any earnest money or payment received.

4. *Compensatory damages*. Another remedy for breach of contract is a suit for damages. Usually the party bringing suit seeks an amount of money equal to the extent of loss suffered (*compensatory damages*). A wronged party may find that a certain property was misrepresented but decide to accept the property and, in addition, sue for damages. On the other hand, the buyer may decide to refuse the property and still sue for damages.

Assignment and Novation

Assignment refers to a transfer of rights and duties under a contract. Except where the terms and conditions of the contract provide otherwise, or where specifically prohibited by law, a contract is assignable (transferable). A person who assigns or transfers legal rights in a contract to another party or person is called the *assignor*. The person to whom legal rights in a contract are transferred or assigned is called the *assignee*.

An assignor does not escape the obligation to perform the terms and conditions of the contract or to see that they are performed by the person to whom it was assigned, unless given a release from the other party to the original contract. If an assignor either accidentally or intentionally assigns the same thing(s) to two or more assignees, the first assignee to notify the other party to the contract prevails over all other assignees.

The parties to a contract may agree to substitute another person's obligation to perform. **Novation** is the substitution of a new party for the original one. The effect is to discharge the original party from the obligation.

CONTRACTS IMPORTANT TO REAL ESTATE

475.25(1)(r), F.S.

Four types of contracts are important to real estate brokers and sales associates because they are parties to negotiation of these contracts: (1) listing contracts, (2) buyer brokerage agreements, (3) option contracts, and (4) sale and purchase contracts.

One: Listing Contracts

In Florida, a listing contract may be written, oral, or implied. Written listing contracts must include the following:

- A definite expiration date
- Identification of the property
- Price and terms
- Fee or commission
- Signature(s) of the owner(s)

475.25(1)(r), F.S. 61J2-24.002(2)(k), F.A.C.

Florida law requires that a copy of the contract must be given to the owner(s) within 24 hours of execution. Furthermore, Chapter 475, F.S. forbids including an automatic renewal clause in a listing. Any extension of the listing agreement must be negotiated.

Even though Florida law recognizes oral listing contracts, all listings should be in writing because the listing contract is a broker's employment contract. If litigation should result from some misunderstanding, default, or breach, it is easier to find a remedy by showing the written terms and conditions rather than trying to prove the terms or conditions of an oral listing. However, listing contracts are not covered by the statute of frauds (*unless* they are for more than one year). Therefore, oral listing contracts are enforceable with the proper amount of evidence and testimony.

Power to bind the seller or buyer. A broker does not have the authority or power to sign a contract for the buyer or the seller or to bind the buyer or the seller to a contract unless the power to do so is specifically granted.

Power of attorney is a written legal document designating some other person as an *attorney-in-fact*. The attorney-in-fact then may bargain and sign for the person who granted the power of attorney, provided that power is specific. A real estate licensee occasionally may come in contact with either a general power of attorney or a special power of attorney. The *general power of attorney* authorizes the attorney-in-fact to act generally for the principal in all matters. The *special power of attorney* limits the attorney-in-fact to one specified area of activity or one special act, such as signing a contract for sale or purchasing a designated property. When power of attorney is granted for acts related to title to real property, the instrument must be witnessed, acknowledged, and recorded in the public records.

Usually with listing agreements, you can assume that the seller has not given power of attorney to the broker. The signatures of both parties (seller and agent) on the listing contract may create some special situations.

Conditions created by listing contract. Exclusive-right-of-sale listings and exclusive-agency listings are usually bilateral contracts because both parties are obligated to perform. Open listing agreements are usually unilateral contracts because the only promise made is that the seller promises to pay a commission if the broker causes a transaction to be consummated.

The licensee is to find a purchaser or effect a sale. If required to *find a purchaser*, the licensee must (1) produce a buyer who is ready, willing, and able to buy at the terms specified by the seller or (2) take to the seller a buyer's offer that subsequently becomes a contract. A licensee who has performed either of the above actions is entitled to a commission, even if the buyer and seller finally negotiate a sale on different terms.

COMPARISON OF LISTINGS

Type of Listing	Agent	Commission
Open	One or more brokers	Only to broker who sells property
Exclusive-agency	One broker	To listing broker if not sold by owner
Exclusive-right-of-sale	One broker	To listing broker no matter who sells

1 If required to *effect a sale*, the licensee must not only find a buyer ready, willing, and
2 able to buy on the terms specified or other terms accepted by the seller, but the licensee
3 must also ensure that the transaction actually closes.

Types of Listings

5 Listings commonly used in the real estate business are *open listings*, *exclusive-agency listings*,
6 and *exclusive-right-of-sale listings*. Any of these listings, under certain conditions, also may
7 be *net listings*.

8 **Open listing.** A seller gives an **open listing** to any number of brokers who can work simul-
9 taneously to sell the owner's property. The seller reserves the right to sell the property and
10 to list it with other brokers. The first broker to secure a buyer who is ready, willing, and
11 able to purchase at the terms of the listing is the *procuring cause* and earns the commis-
12 sion. If the owner sells the property, no broker is entitled to a commission. In the event
13 of a sale, the seller is not obligated to notify any of the brokers that the property has been
14 sold. Open listings benefit only the seller. Therefore, few brokers accept them. (See also
15 Broker's Compensation, page 247.)

16 **Exclusive-agency listing.** A seller gives an **exclusive-agency listing** to one broker who
17 handles the transaction. The seller reserves the right to sell the property without paying a
18 commission, unless the buyer was introduced to the property by the broker or others acting
19 under the broker. If the broker or another person acting under the broker's authority sells the
20 property before the seller is able to do so, the broker is entitled to a commission.

21 **Exclusive-right-of-sale listing.** The **exclusive-right-of-sale** (or *exclusive-right-to-sell*) **list-**
22 **ing** is the most advantageous listing from the broker's viewpoint. The seller gives the
23 listing to a selected broker, who then becomes the exclusive real estate agent of the owner
24 for the sale of the property during the time the listing contract is in effect. The broker
25 therefore is assured of a commission regardless of who sells the property. Even if the owner
26 sells the property during the contract period, the broker is entitled to a commission.

27 **Net listing.** An open, exclusive-right-of-sale, or exclusive-agency listing can also be a net
28 listing. A **net listing** is created when a seller agrees to sell a property for a stated accept-
29 able minimum amount, referred to as the *seller's net*. The broker retains the proceeds in
30 excess of the seller's net as commission. The seller's net plus the broker's commission
31 and closing costs equal the total sale price. Net listings are legal in Florida, however, the
32 broker may not misrepresent the value of the property to gain a financial advantage. The

broker and seller jointly arrive at a listing price. The broker then retains, as commission, all proceeds of the sale after the costs of sale are paid and the seller receives the agreed-on net amount.

Multiple listing. A *multiple listing* refers to a service provided by brokers and not to a specific type of listing. It is created by a clause included in exclusive-right-of-sale and exclusive-agency listing agreements that allows the broker to convey listing information to a multiple listing service (MLS). An MLS serves as a clearinghouse for listings obtained by REALTOR® member brokers and then shared with other MLS member brokers through a published list of properties for sale. Any members of MLSs, regardless of the brokerage company they work for, can show their buyers the listings of other MLS members and receive compensation (part of the commission) if the buyer purchases the property.

Broker's Compensation

Generally, the broker's compensation is specified in the listing or buyer brokerage agreement. (Buyer brokerage agreements are discussed later in this chapter.) The compensation can be in the form of a commission or a brokerage fee. The compensation is computed as a percentage of the total sale price, a flat fee, or an hourly rate. The amount of a broker's commission is negotiable.

The broker earns the commission. The broker then splits the commission with a cooperating broker (if applicable). The employing broker splits the commission with the sales associate involved with the sale. Sales associates must receive compensation from their employing brokers and not directly from the seller, buyer, or other brokers. Some brokers have adopted a 100 percent commission plan. Sales associates in these offices pay the broker a monthly service fee for the use of the office space, telephones, and clerical support. In return, associates receive 100 percent of the commissions from the sales transactions they negotiate for the broker.

To be paid a commission, the broker must:

■ hold a current, active real estate license at the time the listing is entered into and the real estate services are conducted;

■ be employed by the seller and/or the buyer through a listing agreement or buyer broker agreement; and

■ be the procuring cause. (*Note:* Payment could also result from a referral.)

To be a **procuring cause**, the broker must have started the chain of events that resulted in a sale. The facts dictate who is the procuring cause. The person whose efforts cause the parties to enter into a contract is generally considered to be the procuring cause. The broker who has a current listing agreement with the seller is not necessarily the procuring cause. That broker may be entitled to a fee when another broker sells the property, but procuring cause goes to the broker that brings the buyer.

Procuring cause disputes between licensees are usually settled through an arbitration hearing. Disputes between a broker and a buyer or seller may be litigated in court.

Two: Buyer Brokerage Agreements

A **buyer brokerage agreement** is an employment contract with the buyer. The broker is employed as the buyer's transaction broker, single agent, or as a nonrepresentative of the buyer. Buyer broker agreements typically include the following:

- The parties to and term of the agreement (beginning and ending dates)
- General characteristics of the property being sought by the buyer, including type of property, price range, and location
- Broker's obligations
- Buyer's obligations
- Retainer and compensation (either as a dollar amount or a percentage of purchase price)
- Protection period
- Early termination of the agreement and dispute resolution (buyer and broker agree to mediate first)
- Authorized brokerage relationship

WEB LINK

The National Association of REALTORS® Real Estate Buyer's Agent Council maintains a Web site at www.rebac.net.

To learn more about buyer brokers, visit the National Association of Exclusive Buyer Agents Web site at www.naeba.org.

Three: Option Contracts

An **option contract** is an agreement to keep open for a specified period of time an offer to sell or lease real property. The property owner (*optionor*) grants a prospective buyer (*optionee*) the exclusive right to buy the property within a specified period for a specified price and terms. Option contracts must be in writing and signed because they fall under the statute of frauds. The optionee can easily turn option contracts into sale contracts by notifying the optionor in writing that the option is being exercised.

Unilateral contract. One major difference exists between an option and a sale contract. In an option contract, the owner (optionor) is bound to perform the terms of the option if required to do so by the optionee. The optionee, however, may elect to walk away from the transaction because the option contract grants the optionee a right, *not* an obligation to buy the property. This makes the option a *unilateral* contract. In the normal bilateral sale contract, if either party does not perform all of the terms, the other party may sue for breach of contract.

Consideration. The optionee pays a fee (valuable consideration) for the right to purchase the property for a specified price within a specified period of time. The option contract may provide that the money paid to purchase the option be applied as a part of the purchase price in the event the option is exercised. If the optionee does not exercise the option, the fee (consideration) is usually retained by the optionor.

Information required. Options must contain all of the terms and provisions required for a valid contract. The option must clearly specify the length of time the option is effective, the names of the contracting parties, the price of the property, a complete legal description, and the terms of the fee paid.

Options assignable. Unless prohibited in the terms of the agreement, an option contract is assignable (transferable).

Licensee requirements. Real estate licensees may *draw* option contracts. There is no case law indicating otherwise, and the legal counsel for the DBPR has indicated that licensees may draw options. However, because there isn't any case law that specifically addresses licensees and option contracts (only sale contracts), some attorneys disagree with this position. Licensees are encouraged to either fill in the blanks on standardized option contract forms or recommend to the buyer or to the seller to have option contracts drawn by real estate attorneys. After all, you don't want to make your mark in real estate by being the subject of precedent-setting case law!

475.43, F.S. Licensees who are really interested in obtaining an option on a property as a true optionee must first divest themselves of their role as licensees. The licensee must give a valuable consideration (substantial and not nominal) for the option contract. They must inform the property owners that they are not functioning as real estate brokers or sales associates but are personally interested in acquiring an option on the property.

Four: Sale and Purchase Contracts

The parties to a sale and purchase contract (sale contract) are the **vendor** (or seller) and the **vendee** (or buyer). Unlike the option contract, a real estate sale contract (also a *purchase agreement* or *contract for sale and purchase*) is a *bilateral* contract because it contains promises to perform by both parties.

Information contained in sale contracts. Sale contracts must be in writing and signed and contain all of the terms and provisions required for a valid contract. Although the Florida statute of frauds requires that sale contracts be in writing, courts have required that oral sale contracts be honored in some instances. (See Statute of Frauds, page 238.)

Also, letters and telegraphic communications can be part of a valid sale contract. Information spelled out in the contract includes the following:

- Names of the vendor and vendee (or their legal representatives)
- Legal description (preferred) or street address of the property
- Consideration
- Purchase price
- Financing or cash terms
- Type of deed the seller will deliver (general warranty deed unless agreed otherwise)
- Title evidence required and type of estate (fee simple estate unless agreed otherwise)
- Terms of expenses and any prorations to paid
- Personal property to be left with the real property
- Date, time, and place of closing
- When possession of the property will occur

The consideration in a sale contract is the promises that the buyer and seller make to one another. However, it is also a good idea to include a provision for an earnest money (binder) deposit and when it is to be paid. Earnest money is *not* required to make the contract valid. However, it shows the buyer's intent to go through with the transaction. The contract usually states that the seller may retain the earnest money deposit as liquidated damages if the buyer breaches the contract.

Unless otherwise stated in the contract, the seller must convey a clear and merchantable title. Licensees may be guilty of fraud and subject to disciplinary action if they are aware of any title problem and do not inform the buyer before a contract is entered into or any part of the purchase price is paid. Most sale contracts require that the seller provide the buyer with an up-to-date abstract or a title insurance policy. If no such requirement is included in the sale contract, then the seller need not deliver either.

When the property is co-owned by a married couple, or if it is the homestead and ownership is in only one spouse's name (*in severalty*), both spouses must sign the real estate sale contract. If the seller's spouse signs the sale contract, that spouse indicates a willingness to convey ownership rights and to relinquish homestead interest when the time comes to sign the deed that transfers title. If the buyer's spouse signs the sale contract, that spouse also becomes bound to purchase the property. Then, in the event of failure to perform, either party can be sued. If only one spouse signs a contract to purchase, only that spouse is accountable.

Disclosures

Florida has enacted mandatory disclosure laws. These laws help consumers make informed decisions regarding real estate transactions. Most real estate contracts refer to the disclosures in the real estate contract or the disclosures may be a separate form.

Material defects disclosure. Sellers of residential real property must disclose material defects concerning the property. The use of an "as is" provision in a contract for the sale of real property does not circumvent the duty to disclose all known material defects.

Johnson v. Davis, a well-known legal case in Florida, set legal precedence concerning material defects. Mr. and Mrs. Davis entered into a contract to purchase a home from Mr. and Mrs. Johnson. Before the closing, Mrs. Davis inquired regarding peeling plaster around the corner of a window frame and stains on the ceilings. The sellers indicated that a minor problem with the window had been corrected a long time ago and that the stains on the ceiling resulted from wallpaper glue and ceiling beams being removed. Prior to closing the buyers entered the then vacant home following a downpour to find water "gushing" in from around the window frame and the ceiling of the family room. The Davises ordered a roof inspection and were informed that the roof was defective and it would need to be replaced. The Davises sued to rescind the contract and to get a refund of their deposit. The Florida Supreme Court found in favor of the Davises and stated that:

> *"We hold that where the seller of a home knows of facts materially affecting the value of the property which are not readily observable and are not known to the buyer, the seller is under a duty to disclose them to the buyer."*

The case is considered important because prior to the *Johnson v. Davis* decision, the courts had favored the seller under the philosophy of *caveat emptor* (buyer beware). This Supreme Court decision makes sellers accountable to truthfully disclose the condition of the property. A later case (*Rayner v. Wise Realty Co. of Tallahassee*) extended the duty to disclose material defects to real estate licensees. Although *Johnson v. Davis* concerned residential property, licensees are cautioned to always use sound ethical standards when dealing in all types of real property.

RADON GAS DISCLOSURE

Notification shall be provided on at least one document, form, or application executed at the time to, or prior to, contract for sale and purchase of any building or execution of a rental agreement for any building. Such notification shall contain the following language:

RADON GAS: "Radon is a naturally occurring radioactive gas that, when it has accumulated in a building in sufficient quantities, may present health risks to persons who are exposed to it over time. Levels of radon that exceed federal and state guidelines have been found in buildings in Florida. Additional information regarding radon and radon testing may be obtained from your county health department."

Reference: Section 404.056(5), F.S.

404.056, F.S.

Radon gas disclosure. A radon disclosure statement on real estate sale and lease contracts is required on at least one document before or at the time of executing a sale contract or a rental agreement. At present, the disclosure consists only of what radon is; it does not require testing to disclose radon gas levels before a sale or lease.

WEB LINK

Visit the EPA's Consumer's Guide to Radon Reduction at **www.epa.gov/radon/pubs/consguid.html**. The EPA has developed a video concerning radon in real estate. The video "Breathing Easy: What Home Buyers and Sellers Should Know About Radon" is intended for consumers and real estate professionals. View it online at **www.epa.gov/radon/video/breathing_easy.wmv**.

Lead-based paint. When purchasing or renting pre-1978 housing, the Residential Lead-based Paint Hazard Reduction Act requires that:

- sellers and landlords must disclose to prospective buyers and tenants the presence of known lead-based paint in residential property built prior to 1978;

- sale contracts must include a disclosure about lead-based paint;

- an EPA pamphlet regarding the danger of lead-based paint must be given to buyers and tenants prior to the sale or lease of residential property built before 1978; and

- sellers must allow homebuyers a ten-day period during which to conduct an inspection for the presence of lead-based paint. (Sellers are *not* required to pay the cost of the inspection.)

Renovations and demolitions of properties built before 1978 can create lead dust and chips that would be harmful to children and adults. Because of this hazard and to prevent possible lead contamination, the Environmental Protection Agency (EPA) issued a rule that became effective in April, 2010. The rule requires contractors who disturb paint in these properties to be certified and follow specific work practices. To become certified, a renovator must successfully complete an eight-hour training course offered by an accredited training provider.

1   When a real estate licensee lists pre-1978 property for sale, it becomes the responsibil-
2 ity of the licensee to make certain sellers comply with the law. The Federal law does not
3 require the testing or removal of lead-based paint. The focus of the law is disclosure of
4 lead-based paint dangers and its presence.

WEB LINK

Visit the EPA's Office of Pollution Prevention and Toxics Web site at **www.epa.gov/oppt/lead/**. The EPA
pamphlet *Protect Your Family From Lead in Your Home* is available at **www.epa.gov/lead/pubs/leadpdfe.pdf**.

553.996, F.S.

5 **Energy efficiency brochure.** The Florida Building Energy-Efficiency Rating Act requires
6 that buyers, before signing the sale contract, receive an information brochure notifying
7 the purchaser of the option for an energy-efficiency rating on the building. The brochure
8 contains a notice to residential purchasers that the energy-efficiency rating may qualify
9 the purchaser for an energy-efficient mortgage from a lending institution. The act also
10 created a uniform, statewide energy-efficiency rating system for rating new and existing
11 residential, commercial, and public buildings.

WEB LINK

For helpful information concerning energy, visit the Florida Solar Energy Center at **www.fsec.ucf.edu/en/**.

720.401, F.S.

12 **Homeowners' association disclosure.** Florida law requires sellers of property subject to a
13 mandatory homeowners' association to provide buyers with a disclosure summary regarding
14 the association, the existence of restrictive covenants, and any assessments that the asso-
15 ciation imposes. (Refer to Figure 11.1, Homeowners' Association Disclosure Summary.)
16 The disclosure summary must be supplied by the developer or by the current owner.

FIGURE 11.1 ■ Homeowners' Association Disclosure Summary

1 . As a purchaser of property in this community, you will be obligated to be a member of a homeowners' association.

2 . There have been or will be recorded restrictive covenants governing the use and occupancy of properties in this community.

3 . You will be obligated to pay assessments to the association. Assessments may be subject to periodic change. If applicable, the current amount is $_____ per _____. You will also be obligated to pay any special assessments imposed by the association. Such special assessments may be subject to change. If applicable, the current amount is $_____ per _____.

4 . You may be obligated to pay special assessments to the respective municipality, county, or special district. All assessments are subject to periodic change.

5 . Your failure to pay special assessments or assessments levied by a mandatory homeowners' association could result in a lien on your property.

6 . There may be an obligation to pay rent or land-use fees for recreational or other commonly used facilities as an obligation of membership in the homeowners' association. If applicable, the current amount is $_____ per _____.

7 . The developer may have the right to amend the restrictive covenants without the approval of the association membership or the approval of the parcel owners.

8 . The statements contained in this disclosure form are only summary in nature, and, as a prospective purchaser, you should refer to the covenants and the association governing documents before purchasing property.

9 . These documents are either matters of public record and can be obtained from the record office in the county where the property is located, or if not recorded, can be obtained from the developer.

Purchaser's signature   _____

Date   _____

PROPERTY TAX DISCLOSURE SUMMARY

Buyer should not rely on the seller's current property taxes as the amount of property taxes that the buyer may be obligated to pay in the year subsequent to purchase. A change of ownership or property improvements triggers reassessments of the property that could result in higher property taxes. If you have questions concerning valuation, contact the county property appraiser's office for information.

In addition to providing the Homeowners' Association Disclosure Summary, the contract for sale and purchase must state that:

- the buyer should not sign (execute) the contract without first receiving and reading the homeowners' disclosure summary;

- if the disclosure summary is not provided to the buyer before executing the contract for sale and purchase, the contract is voidable;

- to void the contract, the buyer must give the seller or the seller's agent written notice of the buyer's intention to cancel the contract within three calendar days after receipt of the disclosure summary or prior to closing, whichever occurs first; and

- the right to void the contract cannot be waived by the buyer. (The right terminates at closing.)

689.261, F.S.

Property tax disclosure. Prospective buyers of residential property must be presented a disclosure summary concerning ad valorem taxes before or at the time of execution of the contract for sale. The purpose of the disclosure summary is to caution prospective buyers that they cannot rely on the amount of the seller's property taxes as an indication of the taxes purchasers will be required to pay in the year following purchase of the property.

The disclosure may be either attached to the contact for sale, or the wording may be inserted into the contract. If the disclosure is not inserted into the contract, the contract must refer to and incorporate by reference the disclosure summary. The reference to the disclosure must include, in prominent language, a statement that the potential purchaser should not execute the contract without first reading the required disclosure summary. The wording of the disclosure summary is presented in the text box.

WEB LINK

You can download the property tax disclosure summary contained in the Florida statute. The Florida statutes are available on the Internet at **www.leg.state.fl.us/welcome/index.cfm**. Directly under the Senate seal, select "Florida Statutes," then "Title XL Real and Personal Property," and then "Chapter 689." The summary is in section 689.261, F.S.

125.69, F.S.

Building code violation disclosure. A seller who has been cited for a building code violation and is the subject of a pending enforcement proceeding must disclose in writing to the buyer the following information prior to title closing:

- The existence and nature of the violation and proceedings

- A copy of the pleadings, notice, and other applicable documents received by the seller
- Notice that the buyer will be responsible for compliance with the applicable code and with the orders issued in the county court proceeding

The statute does not address the liability of the seller regarding the costs associated with the code violation. Liability costs should be addressed and negotiated in the contract for sale and purchase. The seller must forward to the code enforcement agency the name and address of the new owner and a copy of the disclosures given to the buyer within five days after the title transfer. A seller who violates this provision creates a rebuttable (i.e., disputable with evidence) presumption of fraud and may become the subject of a civil case.

SUMMARY OF IMPORTANT POINTS

- Real estate licensees are allowed to assist buyers and sellers with the preparation of four types of contracts: (1) listing contracts, (2) buyer brokerage agreements, (3) option contracts, and (4) sale and purchase contracts.
- The statute of frauds requires that contracts that convey an interest in real property be in writing and signed to be enforceable. The statute of frauds applies to purchase-and-sale contracts, option contracts, and lease agreements and listing agreements of more than one year.
- The statute of limitations designates that written contracts are enforceable for five years. Oral (parol) contracts are enforceable for four years.
- A *valid contract* is one that complies with the provisions of contract law and contains four essential elements: (1) contractual capacity of the parties, (2) offer and acceptance, (3) legality, and (4) consideration.
- Real estate contracts must contain the four essential elements, be in writing, and be signed by all parties who are bound to the agreement. Real estate contracts are not required to be witnessed or notarized.
- *Valuable consideration* is the money or a promise of something that can be measured in terms of money. *Good consideration* is a promise that cannot be measured in terms of money.
- A bilateral contract obligates both parties to perform in accordance with the terms of the contract. A unilateral contract obligates only one party to an agreement.
- The *offeror* is the person who makes an offer. The *offeree* is the person who receives the offer.
- A contract is terminated when any of the following occurs: performance, mutual rescission, impossibility of performance, lapse of time, bankruptcy, and breach.
- The four legal remedies for breach of a contract are (1) specific performance, (2) liquidated damages, (3) rescission, and (4) compensatory damages.
- *Assignment* refers to a transfer (from assignor to a new assignee) of rights and duties under a contract.
- *Novation* is the substitution of a new party for the original one.
- Written listing contracts must include the following information: a definite expiration date, identification of the property, price and terms, fee or commission,

and signature of the owner. A copy of the contract must be given to the owner within 24 hours of execution. Listing contracts may not feature an automatic renewal clause.

■ *Power of attorney* is a written legal document designating some other person as an attorney-in-fact. An attorney-in-fact is authorized to perform certain acts for another as authorized in the power of attorney.

■ An *open listing* is given to one or more brokers. The seller reserves the right to sell the property and to list with other brokers. Only the broker who sells the property is entitled to commission.

■ An *exclusive-agency listing* is given to one broker. The seller reserves the right to sell the property. The listing broker is entitled to commission unless the property is sold by the owner.

■ An *exclusive-right-of-sale listing* is given to one broker who is assured of a commission regardless of who sells the property.

■ A *net listing* is created when a seller agrees to sell a property for a stated acceptable minimum amount. The broker retains, as commission, all proceeds of the sale after the costs of the sale are paid and the seller receives the agreed-on net amount.

■ A *buyer brokerage agreement* is an employment contract between a broker and a buyer.

■ An *option contract* is a unilateral contract to keep open for a specified period of time an offer to sell or lease real property. The property owner (optionor) grants a prospective buyer (optionee) the exclusive right to buy the property within a specified period for a specified price and terms.

■ The parties to a sale and purchase contract are the vendor (seller) and the vendee (buyer). Real estate sale contracts are bilateral contracts.

■ Sellers must disclose material defects to a potential buyer even if selling the property "as is."

■ A radon gas disclosure is required prior to or at the time of executing real estate sale and lease contracts. The disclosure explains what radon gas is and the possible health hazards associated with radon gas; however, it does not require a radon gas inspection.

■ A lead-based paint disclosure must be given to buyers and renters of residential units built prior to 1978. Sellers must disclose the presence of any known lead-based paint, and buyers and renters must be given an EPA pamphlet.

■ Prior to signing the sale contract, purchasers must receive an informational brochure about energy efficiency that informs them of the right to have an energy-efficiency rating performed on the structure.

■ Florida law requires sellers of property subject to a mandatory homeowners' association to provide buyers with a disclosure summary regarding the association, the existence of restrictive covenants, and any assessments that the association imposes.

■ Purchasers must be given a property tax disclosure concerning ad valorem taxes before or at the time of executing the sale contract. The disclosure cautions buyers not to rely on the amount of the seller's property taxes as an indication of future property taxes the purchaser will pay.

■ The seller must disclose to the buyer any pending building code violations.

R E V I E W   Q U E S T I O N S

1. Which group of legal instruments may legally be prepared by a licensed real estate broker?
   a. Listing contracts, buyer brokerage agreements, commercial leases, and deeds
   b. Leases, option contracts, promissory notes, and buyer brokerage agreements
   c. Listing agreements, buyer brokerage agreements, sale contracts, and option contracts
   d. Mortgages, promissory notes, commercial leases, and option contracts

2. Failure to comply with the statute of frauds
   a. may not constitute an illegal act but would always invalidate a sale contract.
   b. would have to do with whether a contract is in writing.
   c. concerns adherence to prescribed time frames of enforcement.
   d. is prima facie evidence that there is intent to commit fraud.

3. Which contract does NOT come under the jurisdiction of the statute of frauds?
   a. Lease agreements for one year or less
   b. Option contract
   c. Sale contract
   d. Listing agreement for more than one year

4. A valid real estate sale contract is one that
   a. contains all of the essential elements and is in writing.
   b. has been acknowledged.
   c. requires witnessing.
   d. transfers title to real property.

5. An adult contracting with a minor is an example of failure to meet which essential of a real estate contract?
   a. Legality of the object
   b. Offer and acceptance
   c. Meeting of the minds
   d. Competent parties

6. Canceling a daughter's property indebtedness in a contract due to love and affection is an example of
   a. good consideration.
   b. valuable consideration.
   c. insufficient consideration.
   d. inadequate consideration.

7. A contract that is NOT in writing is referred to as
   a. a formal contract.
   b. a parol contract.
   c. a unilateral contract.
   d. an executory contract.

8. When a contract has been formed but an undertaking remains to be performed by one or both parties, it is an example of
   a. an implied contract.
   b. an express contract.
   c. an executory contract.
   d. a unilateral contract.

9. Which statement is FALSE regarding counteroffers?
   a. The original offer is terminated by the counteroffer.
   b. The original offeree becomes the offeror.
   c. A contract is created when the new offeree accepts the counteroffer and communicates the acceptance to the new offeror.
   d. The offeror and offeree remain the same even though the terms are modified.

10. An offer is NOT terminated by
    a. a counteroffer.
    b. an acceptance.
    c. a rejection.
    d. an extension.

11. A contract may be terminated for which reasons?
    a. Mutual rescission
    b. Performance
    c. Breach
    d. All of the above

12. A woman gave an exclusive-right-of-sale listing to a broker to find a buyer for her residential lot. While the woman was vacationing with her family, a buyer signed an offer to purchase the woman's lot at the full price and terms of the listing agreement.
    a. Because this is an exclusive-right-of-sale listing, the broker is authorized to accept the offer on the woman's behalf.
    b. The broker may accept the offer on the woman's behalf, as long as she gets the woman's signature on the contract immediately upon the woman's return.
    c. The exclusive-right-of-sale listing does not give the broker the authority to accept the offer on the woman's behalf.
    d. The broker may accept the offer because it is a full-price offer.

13. A man and a woman enter into a written agreement. The man will mow the woman's lawn every week during the mowing season and every third week during the winter. In the middle of the summer, the man has back surgery. He hands over his lawn maintenance contracts to a friend, who assumes the responsibility for all of the man's customers for the remainder of the contract period. Which term describes this situation?
    a. Breach
    b. Assignment
    c. Specific performance
    d. Mutual rescission

14. Which applies to exclusive-right-of-sale listings?
    a. The broker is due a commission regardless of who finds the buyer.
    b. The listing may be submitted to the MLS by the listing broker.
    c. The seller must consent to the terms of the listing agreement.
    d. All of the above apply.

15. Which disclosure regarding radon is required when purchasing or leasing real property in Florida?
    a. A disclosure statement in the contract indicating that the house has been tested for radon and that the test indicated a safe level of radon.
    b. An estimate of the cost for a required radon test.
    c. A disclosure statement in the contract indicating that the seller is required to have the property tested for radon at the seller's expense if requested by the buyer.
    d. A disclosure statement in the contract explaining radon gas.

16. A 15-year-old teenager entered into a contract with a man, who is of legal age to contract.
    a. The teenager is obligated to honor the terms of the contract.
    b. The man may divest himself of his obligations under the contract because the contract is invalid.
    c. The teenager may choose to divest himself of his obligations under the contract.
    d. This contract is a void contract.

17. Normally, a sale contract involving real property contains a provision that in case of breach by the buyer, the earnest money deposit will be regarded as
    a. compensatory damages to the seller.
    b. liquidated damages to the seller.
    c. compensatory damages to the broker.
    d. liquidated damages to be divided between seller and buyer.

18. The most advantageous type of listing from the broker's point of view is
    a. an open listing.
    b. an exclusive-agency listing.
    c. an exclusive-right-of-sale listing.
    d. a net listing.

19. Which statement is FALSE concerning Florida's building code violation disclosure?
    a. The seller is responsible for the costs associated with the code violation.
    b. The seller must inform the code enforcement agency regarding the name and address of the buyer within five days of the title closing.
    c. Copies of the pleadings and other documents concerning the code violation must be given to the buyer.
    d. The disclosure requires a statement that the buyer is responsible for compliance with the building code.

20. A couple have decided to make a written offer to purchase a quaint little home built in the 1950s. Which task is NOT required prior to signing the sale contract?
    a. The couple must be given a copy of the EPA pamphlet concerning lead-based paint hazards in the home.
    b. The seller must disclose any known presence of lead-based paint.
    c. The couple must have the home inspected for lead-based paint.
    d. The real estate sale contract must include a disclosure concerning lead-based paint.

C H A P T E R

12

REAL ESTATE FINANCE

OVERVIEW

Because most real property transactions involve some type of financing, real estate licensees must understand this aspect of the business. Fluctuating interest rates, deregulation of
financial institutions, and varying rates of inflation have in the past created shock waves
among institutional lenders and mortgage specialists. As a result, new practices and variations of former lending procedures evolved. Licensees must keep current in the real estate
finance area.

After completing this chapter, the student should be able to:

- distinguish between title theory and lien theory doctrines;

- distinguish between the mortgage instrument and the note;

- explain the provisions of the various mortgage clauses;

- differentiate among FHA, VA, and conventional mortgages;

- describe the features of amortized, adjustable, package, and purchase-money
  mortgages;

- explain the purpose of an estoppel certificate;

- calculate the loan-to-value (LTV) ratio, given the purchase price and down payment amounts; and

- calculate the down payment, given the purchase price and LTV ratio.

KEY TERMS

acceleration clause	entitlement	nonconventional loan
adjustable-rate mortgage (ARM)	equity of redemption	note
amortized mortgage	estoppel certificate	package mortgage
assignment of mortgage	home equity loans	partial release clause
assumption	hypothecation	prepayment clause
balloon payment	index	prepayment penalty
biweekly mortgage	loan-to-value (LTV) ratio	purchase-money mortgage (PMM)
blanket mortgages	margin	receivership clause
contract for deed	mortgage	satisfaction of mortgage
conventional loan	mortgagee	statutory redemption period
deed in lieu of foreclosure	mortgage insurance premium (MIP)	subordination clause
defeasance clause	mortgagor	wraparound mortgage
due-on-sale clause	negative amortization	

LEGAL THEORIES OF MORTGAGES

Lien Theory

697.02, F.S.

In most states today, including Florida, the *borrower* retains title to the property. The lender is protected with a lien on the real property to secure the payment of the mortgage debt. If the borrower defaults on the mortgage debt, the lender will foreclose to recover the money owed.

Title Theory

In some states, title to the mortgaged property is conveyed to the *lender* through a mortgage deed, or to a trustee through a deed of trust. If the borrower defaults, the lender may take possession of the property. The borrower retains equitable title to the property. Once the debt is paid in full, the lender conveys legal title to the borrower.

LOAN INSTRUMENTS

Two instruments are involved in a mortgage loan: (1) the *promissory note*, which is the actual promise to repay, and (2) the *mortgage*, which creates the lien interest.

Promissory Note

673.1041, F.S.

A promissory note (or *mortgage note*, or sometimes a *bond*) must accompany all mortgages in Florida. The **note** is the legal instrument that represents the evidence of a debt. A note is a promise to repay that makes the borrower personally liable for the obligation. It represents the borrower's promise to pay the lender according to the agreed-upon terms of the loan.

The note is usually a separate legal instrument and must be signed by the borrower. The note states the amount of indebtedness, interest rate, repayment method, and term or

FIGURE 12.1 ■ **Mortgage Financing**

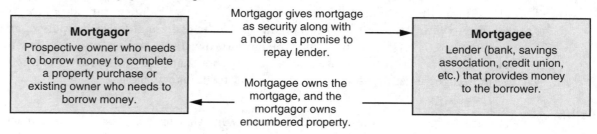

1 time period to repay. The mortgage note lists the penalties that will be assessed if the bor-
2 rower doesn't make the monthly mortgage payments. It also warns the borrower that the
3 lender can *call* the loan (demand repayment of the entire loan before the end of the term)
4 if the borrower violates the terms of the mortgage. The note is usually *not* recorded.

WEB LINK

Download the Fannie Mae/Freddie Mac Uniform Florida fixed rate note for single family property at www.efanniemae.com/sf/formsdocs/documents/notes/doc/3210w.doc.

5 Mortgage

6 A **mortgage** is an instrument that pledges the property as security (collateral) for a debt. It
7 is the legal document that represents the lien on the real estate that secures the debt. For
8 the lender, the property becomes security, legally sufficient to ensure recovery of the loan.
9 **Hypothecation** refers to the pledging of property as security for payment of a loan without
10 surrendering possession of the property. Mortgages identify the property being used to
11 secure a loan and contain the borrower's promises to fulfill certain other obligations to
12 the lender. A mortgage instrument must be in writing to be enforceable. The mortgage
13 is recorded to establish constructive notice of the lien and to establish priority ahead of
14 subsequent liens.

15 **Parties to a mortgage.** There are two parties to a mortgage: (1) the **mortgagor**, or bor-
16 rower (debtor), and (2) the **mortgagee**, or lender (creditor). The mortgagor owns the
17 property, and the mortgagee owns the mortgage. A mortgage is regarded as an investment
18 or *chattel* (personal property) by the mortgagee and, like other such investments, may be
19 sold to another investor if desired. (See Figure 12.1, Mortgage Financing.)

20 Assignment of Mortgage

701.01, F.S.

21 When a homebuyer borrows money to purchase a home, the borrower (mortgagor) signs a
22 promissory note and mortgage instrument. The mortgage and promissory note are property
23 of the mortgagee (lender). The mortgagee may choose to sell the negotiable instruments
24 rather than continue to receive the monthly payments from the mortgagor.

25 When ownership of a mortgage is transferred from one company or individual to
26 another, it is called an *assignment*. This process is accomplished by executing an **assign-**
27 **ment of mortgage**. The assignment of mortgage is a legal instrument that states that the
28 mortgagee assigns (transfers) the mortgage and promissory note to the purchaser. The
29 assignment of mortgage is signed by the assignor (mortgagee) and delivered to the assignee
30 (investor). The assignee becomes the new owner of the debt and security instrument.

The individual or company purchasing the mortgage will receive an **estoppel certificate** (estoppel letter) verifying the amount of the unpaid balance, the rate of interest, and the date to which interest has been paid prior to the assignment. The purpose of an estoppel certificate is to stop a claim that the amount owed is different from the actual unpaid balance, or that the interest rate is an amount other than the contracted rate. If requested, the mortgagee must provide an estoppel letter to the mortgagor.

WEB LINK

Download the Fannie Mae Assignment of Mortgage at www.efanniemae.com/sf/formsdocs/documents/specialpurpose/pdf/3742.pdf. Note that this instrument indicates that the purchaser (assignee) is Fannie Mae.

Satisfaction of Mortgage

701.04(1), F.S.

Chapter 701, F.S., requires that lenders provide the mortgagor payoff information. The mortgagee must provide an estoppel certificate stating the unpaid principal balance, interest due, and the per diem rate. On that joyous occasion when the mortgagor pays the debt in full, the mortgagee executes a **satisfaction of mortgage** (or a *release of mortgage*). Florida statute requires that the mortgagee cancel the mortgage and send the recorded satisfaction to the mortgagor within 60 days. This document returns to the mortgagor all interest in the real property that had been conveyed to the mortgagee. Recording the satisfaction of mortgage in the public records shows that the mortgage lien has been removed.

Foreclosure

In Florida, foreclosure requires a judicial process. Foreclosure is enforcement of the mortgage lien. Typically, foreclosure is caused by the mortgagor's failure to pay the mortgage payments. However, the mortgagor's failure (default) to perform any requirements stipulated in the mortgage may also cause foreclosure (for example, the mortgagor's failure to pay the property taxes).

If default on the mortgage occurs, the mortgagee has two remedies:

1. *Initiate a suit on the promissory note.* The mortgagee may choose to sue on the note, obtain a judgment, then execute the judgment against any real or personal property of the mortgagor. This judgment may be levied against any of the mortgagor's property except property that is specifically exempted (such as homestead property, unless it is the property on which the default is based).

2. *Initiate a foreclosure proceeding.* The mortgagee may foreclose on the property that is subject to the mortgage lien. The foreclosure process begins with the mortgagee accelerating the due date of all remaining payments and then filing a lawsuit to foreclose. On receiving final judgment, the sale is advertised (public notice of the sale), and the property is sold at public auction to the highest bidder. Once the sale has taken place, the Clerk of the Court files a Certificate of Sale with the court. The court then reviews the sale to ensure a fair price has been paid. If the court is in agreement, the sale is confirmed; if not, another sale is ordered.

On confirmation of the sale, the clerk files a Certificate of Title and title passes to the purchaser. The clerk then disburses the sale proceeds in accordance with the final decree. Any excess proceeds are paid to the mortgagor. If, however, the proceeds are not sufficient to satisfy the outstanding debt, the mortgagee may request that the court issue a *deficiency judgment* against the person(s) who signed the note. When granted, a deficiency decree can extend to include all real and personal property belonging to the maker of the note, except a homestead. The doctrine of *caveat emptor* applies in foreclosure sales; that is, the purchaser is presumed to know that the purchase is subject to any prior liens of record or interests for which there is constructive notice. The mortgagee may undertake foreclosure procedures and a suit based on the note as two separate actions. However, they are usually undertaken simultaneously.

Sometimes the parties will agree to settle the matter without going to court. This can be accomplished with a **deed in lieu of foreclosure**. The process is sometimes referred to as a *friendly foreclosure* because it is a *nonjudicial* procedure (it does not involve a law suit). The defaulting borrower gives title (the deed) to the lender to avoid judicial foreclosure. The lender takes title to the property subject to existing liens.

Equity of Redemption

Equity of redemption allows the mortgagor to prevent foreclosure from occurring by paying the mortgagee the principal and interest due plus any expenses the mortgagee has incurred in attempting to collect the debt and initiating foreclosure proceedings. In Florida, the right of equity of redemption (or *equitable right of redemption*) ends once the property has been sold at a foreclosure sale. Some states (not Florida) provide mortgagors with a **statutory redemption period** that allows the mortgagor to redeem a foreclosed property for a specified period of time after the foreclosure sale.

MORTGAGE CLAUSES

Borrower's Covenants and Agreements

A mortgage is a contract between mortgagor and mortgagee and, therefore, must contain the essential elements of a contract to be valid. (Refer to chapter 11.) Mortgage lenders in Florida commonly use the Fannie Mae-Freddie Mac Single Family Uniform Mortgage Instrument. This standard mortgage instrument contains certain uniform covenants (warranties). An explanation of the most important clauses in the uniform mortgage instrument follows.

WEB LINK

It may be helpful to download a copy of the Fannie Mae/Freddie Mac Uniform Mortgage Instrument. Refer to the mortgage when reviewing the covenants and agreements to a mortgage described below. To download a copy of the mortgage instrument, go to www.freddiemac.com/uniform/doc/3010-FloridaMortgage.doc.

Promise to repay. The borrower (mortgagor) promises to pay principal and interest according to the terms of the note. The mortgagor also agrees to pay escrowed items, prepayment charges, and late fees, if applicable.

Taxes; liens. The borrower agrees to pay all taxes, assessments, and fines that could create a lien with superior priority over the mortgage (security) instrument. This clause also stipulates that the mortgagor will pay community association dues, if applicable.

Property insurance. The mortgagor promises to keep the property insured against loss by fire and hazards included in an *extended coverage* policy. The lender may require the mortgagor to pay a one-time charge for flood zone determination and, if applicable, flood insurance coverage. If the borrower fails to maintain hazard insurance, the lender may obtain insurance coverage, at the lender's option, and charge the borrower for the expense.

Most lenders require that the mortgagor pay in advance monthly installments for property taxes and insurance. The monthly escrow payment is $1/12$ of the anticipated taxes and insurance premium for the year. These payments are held in an *escrow* account for the mortgagor. The borrower makes payments before the taxes and insurance are due. When the taxes and insurance premiums are due, the lender pays the expenses out of the escrowed funds. The insurance must cover at least the unpaid balance of the mortgage. If a loss occurs, the insurance pays the mortgagee up to the unpaid balance of the mortgage.

Occupancy. The borrowers agree to use the property as their principal residence for at least one year, unless the lender otherwise agrees in writing.

Maintenance and covenant of good repair. The mortgagor promises to keep the property in good condition, maintain the property, and prevent waste. The lender is authorized to make reasonable inspections of the property.

Due-on-sale clause. If all or any part of the property or any interest in the property is sold or transferred without the lender's prior written consent, the lender may require immediate payment in full. The **due-on-sale clause** allows the mortgagee to call due the outstanding loan balance plus accrued interest. In effect, this clause prevents another party from assuming the mortgage and requires that the mortgage debt be paid in full when the property is sold.

Acceleration clause. The **acceleration clause** authorizes the mortgagee to accelerate or advance the due date of the entire unpaid balance if the mortgagor fails to fulfill any promises stated in the mortgage instrument. The acceleration clause gives the lender the power to declare the entire unpaid mortgage loan due and payable and to foreclose on the property if the mortgagor does not remedy the default. The foreclosure process cannot begin unless the entire debt is delinquent. Without the acceleration clause, the mortgagee could sue a delinquent mortgagor for only the monthly payments that are in arrears. The borrower is given 30 days from the date of the *notice of acceleration* to pay all sums secured by the mortgage instrument. If the borrower fails to pay the debt within the specified time period, the borrower is considered to be in default. The Fannie Mae-Freddie Mac Uniform Single Family Mortgage Instrument includes in the acceleration clause the remedies for curing defaults.

Right to reinstate. This clause is based on the equity of redemption. It deals with the mortgagor's right to reinstate the original repayment terms in the note *after* the mortgagee has initiated the acceleration clause. It gives the mortgagor the right to have foreclosure proceedings stopped before the foreclosure sale, provided that the mortgagor pays all sums that would be due if no acceleration had occurred plus all expenses incurred by the mortgagee in enforcing the mortgage.

Defeasance clause. The **defeasance clause** is so named because it "defeats" the prior action when the borrower-mortgagor has made the final payment on the loan. Recall that in title theory states, the mortgaged property is conveyed to the lender through a mortgage deed. Therefore, in title theory states, the defeasance clause defeats the conveyance of legal title and returns the legal title to the borrower-mortgagor. In lien theory states, the lender is protected with a lien on the property that pledges the property as collateral

IMPORTANT MORTGAGE CLAUSES

Acceleration	Upon default, accelerates the entire debt due and payable
Defeasance	In title theory states, requires the lender to convey legal title to the borrower once the debt is repaid; in lien theory states, requires the lender to release the mortgage lien when the debt is repaid
Due-on-sale	Upon sale (alienation), loan is due and payable
Escalator	Tied to an event or a contingency, it allows the lender to increase the interest rate
Exculpatory	Lender agrees not to hold borrower personally liable for the debt
Open-end	May borrow additional funds secured by the same mortgage
Prepayment	Conditions to repay debt in advance of due date
Prepayment penalty	Allows extra charge if any amount of the loan is paid off early
Receivership	Appointment of a receiver for income-producing property
Subordination	Lender agrees to step down in priority of lien

until the debt is paid in full. Once the debt is repaid, the defeasance clause defeats the mortgage lien and the property is no longer pledged as collateral. Constructive notice that the mortgage is defeated is accomplished when the lender-mortgagee executes and records a satisfaction of mortgage. (See Legal Theories of Mortgages, page 260, and Satisfaction of Mortgage, page 262.)

Other Mortgage Provisions

Prepayment clause. A **prepayment clause** allows the borrower to pay off part or all of the debt, without penalty or other fees, prior to maturity. In Florida, a borrower has the right to prepay a mortgage loan unless the mortgage instrument states otherwise. A prepayment clause is normally included in FHA and VA mortgages on real property. A prepayment clause typically stipulates conditions and terms under which the mortgage loan may be prepaid.

Prepayment penalty clause. The lender may choose to charge a **prepayment penalty** for early payment, if provided for in the mortgage instrument.

Special Mortgage Provisions

Escalator clause. This clause permits the lender to increase the interest rate. The action is usually tied to an event or a contingency, such as the transition of a property from owner-occupied to investment property during the initial year of the mortgage.

Exculpatory clause. This clause requires that the lender waive the right to a deficiency judgment against the borrower. It relieves the borrower of personal liability to repay the loan.

Open-end clause. This allows the borrower to increase the loan amount as long as the total debt does not exceed the original amount of the loan. It's also called a *mortgage for future advances* and amounts to an expandable loan. The lender often reserves the right to adjust the interest rate to current market rates.

Land Development Loans

Developers commonly purchase land for development by securing seller financing. The developer usually requests that the seller agree to a **subordination clause**. This clause provides that the lender (usually the seller) voluntarily will permit a subsequent mortgage to take priority over the lender's otherwise superior mortgage (the act of yielding priority). This arrangement allows the developer to secure a construction loan from a traditional lending institution.

Blanket mortgages cover a number of parcels, usually building lots. The developer uses proceeds from the sale of individual lots to pay off the blanket mortgage. A **partial release clause** commonly used in blanket mortgages provides for the release of individual parcels from the blanket mortgage upon payment of a specified amount. The partial release clause stipulates the conditions under which the mortgagee (lender) will grant a release of lots, free and clear of the mortgage.

Income Property

Mortgage loans on income-producing property typically include a receivership clause. If the borrower of income-producing property does not make timely payments on the mortgage loan, the lender wants the income from the property to be used to make the mortgage payments. A **receivership clause** allows a receiver to be appointed to collect income from the property and use the income to make mortgage payments in the event of default.

TYPES OF MORTGAGE LOANS

Mortgage loans can be grouped into two general categories: (1) conventional loans and (2) nonconventional loans. A **conventional loan** is one that is not insured or guaranteed by a government agency. The lender assumes the full risk of default in a conventional loan. Nonconventional loans include FHA-insured and VA-guaranteed loans. **Nonconventional loans** typically require a smaller down payment compared with conventional loans because with nonconventional loans, the government provides some risk protection to the lender.

Federal Housing Administration (FHA Government-Insured Loan)

The National Housing Act of 1934 created the FHA to stimulate the housing market following the Depression. A major focus of FHA is to stimulate homeownership. The FHA is a government agency within the Department of Housing and Urban Development (HUD). The agency functions as an insurance company, insuring mortgage loans made by approved lenders. FHA does *not* make loans to borrowers. The FHA does not process loans or build houses.

FHA does *not* regulate interest rates. Lenders set their own interest rates for FHA-insured loans to reflect money market conditions. Lenders may charge FHA borrowers *points*, a charge by the lender designed to increase the lender's yield (see chapter 13).

The FHA insures mortgages for various types of properties. The most popular programs are listed below.

- Title I FHA loans include home improvement loans and land development loans.

- Title II, Section 203(b) is the most popular home mortgage program of the National Housing Act. Section 203(b) fixed-rate mortgage loans require a small down payment for the purchase or construction of one-family to four-family residences. (The Section 203(b) loan program is explained in detail in this chapter.)

- Section 234 provides financing for condominium units.

- Section 245 is a graduated-payment loan program.

- Section 251 is an adjustable-rate loan program.

Section 203(b) Loan Program

Mortgage insurance premium. The FHA insures mortgage loans to protect lenders in the event that borrowers default. The FHA is the largest government insurer of mortgages in the world. The cost of the mortgage insurance is passed on to the borrower.

Borrowers pay an *up-front mortgage insurance premium* (UFMIP). The percentage of the UFMIP is based on the type (new or refinance) and term (15-year or 30-year) of the mortgage. On a new 30-year mortgage, the UFMIP is 1.75 percent of the loan amount. For example, on a $250,000 FHA loan, the UFMIP would cost the borrower $4,375. The UFMIP is paid at closing and can be financed into the mortgage amount. Loans to finance condominium units do not require UFMIP.

In addition to the UFMIP, the borrower is also charged an annual **mortgage insurance premium (MIP)**. Currently, the MIP is 1.25 percent of the base loan amount on a 30-year residential loan with the required minimum down payment. The annual MIP is divided by 12 and paid monthly as part of the monthly mortgage payment. For example, on a $250,000 FHA loan, the MIP would cost the borrower $3,125 a year. One-twelfth of the MIP ($260.42) would be added to the monthly mortgage payment to cover the MIP. The MIP must be included in the proposed monthly expense when calculating the buyer's qualifying ratios. The MIP is automatically canceled after five years or when the loan-to-value ratio reaches 78 percent, whichever is longer. However, because an UFMIP is not charged on FHA condominium loans, the monthly MIP is paid for the life of the FHA condo loan. UFMIP and MIP go into an FHA fund for repaying lenders if borrowers default.

FHA down payments. A major benefit of FHA-insured loans is that the down payment is much smaller than required for conventional mortgage loans. Borrowers are required to make a down payment (minimum cash investment) of at least 3.5 percent of the sale price or the appraised value, whichever is less. Closing costs may not be used to meet the minimum 3.5 percent down payment requirement. Borrowers must have a good credit history (minimum credit score of 580) to qualify for maximum financing. FHA loans are especially attractive to homebuyers with steady incomes who have limited savings because the down payment for an FHA mortgage can be a gift, a loan from a family member, or from a governmental agency. Gift donors are restricted primarily to a relative of the borrower but can also be certain organizations such as a labor union or charitable organization. The down payment may not come from funds provided by the lender, the seller or builder, or any other person or entity that financially benefits from the transaction.

FHA 203(b) loan limits. To make sure that FHA loan programs serve low- and moderate-income households, FHA sets limits on the amount that can be borrowed based on area home values. For example, for the year 2012, the maximum FHA loan for a single-family residence in Gainesville, Florida, and Tallahassee, Florida, is $271,050. However, in Orlando the maximum FHA loan is $353,750 and $423,750 for an FHA loan to purchase a single-family residence in Fort Lauderdale and Miami. Lenders make FHA-insured loans in even $50 increments.

WEB LINK

A schedule of FHA mortgage limits by area is available at **https://entp.hud.gov/idapp/html/hicostlook.cfm**.

FHA example. A single-family residence in Tallahassee, Florida, sells for $218,000. The FHA appraiser estimates the value of the property to be $220,000. What is the borrower's minimum cash investment (down payment)?

The down payment is calculated on the lesser of the sale price or appraised value:

$218,000 × .035 = $7,630 minimum down payment

What is the maximum mortgage amount?

The reciprocal of 3.5 percent is 96.5 percent (100% − 3.5% = 96.5%)
$218,000 × .965 = $210,370 mortgage loan
(rounded down to even $50 increment = $210,350;
the $20 difference is then added to the down payment)

What is the cost of the UFMIP?

$210,350 loan × .0175 = $3,681.13 UFMIP

What is the cost of the monthly MIP?

$210,350 loan × .0125 = $2,629.38
$2,629.38 ÷ 12 months = $219.11 monthly

(*Note:* This example assumes the borrower has a good credit history and the example does not take into account borrower's closing costs.)

Additional FHA-insured loan features. Other major features of FHA-insured loans are listed here:

- Fully assumable. FHA requires complete qualification of the buyer assuming the loan. All assumed loans (and new FHA loans) are for owner-occupied use only (no investor loans). The lender must release the original mortgagor from liability

VA LOAN ELIGIBILITY

- *90 days of active duty* during any one of five wartime periods (WW II, Korea, Vietnam, Persian Gulf, and Iraq)
- *181 days of active duty* during the time periods between the five war periods (peacetime)
- *24 months of active duty* on or after September 8, 1980 (except during the Persian Gulf War)
- *6 years of service* in the Reserves or National Guard

if the assuming mortgagor is found creditworthy and executes an agreement to assume and pay the mortgage debt.

- No prepayment penalty. The loan may be paid off early without penalty.
- Minimum property standards. HUD promotes improved housing standards. HUD requires an inspection of the property to assure that it meets HUD's minimum property standards. However, FHA does not warrant the condition of the property. FHA encourages buyers to have a home inspection conducted.

Veterans Affairs Mortgage (VA or GI Loan)

In 1944, the Servicemen's Readjustment Act (GI Bill of Rights) was passed to aid returning World War II veterans. This act and subsequent acts gave the Department of Veterans Affairs (VA) the authority to *partially guarantee* mortgage loans made to veterans by private lenders. The partial guarantee covers the top portion of the loan.

Eligibility requirements. Only veterans, surviving spouses of veterans, and active military personnel may apply for a VA loan. Local lenders issue VA loans. However, the VA does have the power to make direct loans to veterans in areas where VA loans are not available. Specific eligibility requirements based on minimum days of active duty are presented in the text box, VA Loan Eligibility.

VA loans may be used to purchase, refinance, or construct a home, including farm residences, condominiums, and manufactured homes. VA loans for alterations, repairs, and improvements to an existing home are also available. Up to four units of multifamily property may be financed by a VA loan provided the veteran resides in one of the units.

VA loan guarantee. The VA establishes loan guarantee limits referred to as the VA loan guarantee or the maximum entitlement. The 2011 maximum entitlement (guarantee) is $104,250. A veteran's **entitlement** is the maximum amount the government guarantees the lender will be paid in the event the borrower defaults.

A veteran begins by applying to the VA for a certificate of eligibility. The *certificate of eligibility* states the amount of entitlement available to the veteran borrower. The VA loan guarantee program uses a scale that establishes each veteran's entitlement based on the loan amount. (Refer to text box, VA Home Loan Guarantee Entitlement.) A veteran who has used the entitlement in the past may only now be eligible for a portion of the

VA HOME LOAN GUARANTEE ENTITLEMENT

Loan Amount	Guaranteed Amount
0 to $45,000	50 percent of the loan amount
$45,001 to $144,000	Minimum guaranty is $22,500, with a maximum guaranty of up to 40 percent of the loan up to $36,000
More than $144,000	Up to $104,250 or 25 percent of the loan amount

1　entitlement. The unused portion is available to the veteran borrower up to the maximum
2　guarantee. When a VA loan is paid off, the veteran's maximum entitlement is reinstated.

3　**Loan amount.** The VA does *not* set loan limits. The amount that a veteran may bor-
4　row is dependent on the value of the real estate. The loan may not exceed the amount
5　stated in the Certificate of Reasonable Value (CRV). The CRV is based on the property
6　value estimated by a VA approved appraiser. The other limiting factor is the veteran's
7　income and ability to make the monthly mortgage payments. The veteran borrower's total
8　monthly obligations may not exceed 41 percent of total monthly gross income. (See also
9　Figure 12.3, Qualifying Ratios, page 279.)

10　Because the maximum VA guarantee is $104,250 or 25 percent of the loan amount,
11　most lenders observe a maximum loan amount of $417,000 ($104,250 ÷ .25 = $417,000),
12　or alternatively, four times the veteran's guarantee. If a veteran has sufficient income to
13　qualify for a higher loan amount, the $104,250 maximum guarantee still would apply, and
14　the veteran would make a down payment of 25 percent of the amount over $417,000.

15　**VA funding fee.** The VA requires a *funding fee* or *user's fee* to help the government defray
16　the cost of foreclosures. Currently the funding fee is 2.15 percent of the loan amount with
17　no down payment for first-time users. Funding fee expenses may be added to the maximum
18　loan amount and financed over the life of the loan. If a veteran has a service-connected
19　disability, the funding fee is waived.

20　**Closing costs.** The lender may charge reasonable closing costs. However, these costs may
21　*not* be included in the VA loan. Closing costs vary among lenders. The veteran borrower
22　or the seller may pay the following closing costs or the closing costs may be shared:

23　■ VA appraisal
24　■ Credit report
25　■ Loan origination fee (usually 1 percent of the loan)
26　■ Discount points
27　■ Title search and title insurance
28　■ Recording fees
29　■ State transfer fees
30　■ Survey

Assumability of VA loans. Because they do not have due-on-sale clauses, VA loans are assumable (even by nonveterans). VA loans made prior to March 1, 1988, are assumable without a credit check of the new mortgagor. However, both seller and buyer will be liable in case of default, unless the buyer qualifies and completes all substitution documents. For VA loans made on or after March 1, 1988, the buyer must qualify. The buyer must pay an assumption or transfer fee to the lender plus an assumption fee to the VA. The seller is then released from liability for the VA loan.

Other loan features. Additional features of the VA loan are listed below:

- The interest rate varies based on market conditions and is negotiated between the borrower and the lender.
- Down payments are *not* required on VA loans (except as noted above and for the purchase of manufactured homes).
- Borrowers pay 1/12 of estimated annual property taxes and hazard insurance with each month's principal and interest mortgage payment (PITI).
- The maximum loan term is 30 years.
- Veterans may prepay all or a portion of the mortgage loan ahead of schedule without penalty (no prepayment penalty).
- The VA loan *guarantee* differs from the FHA program that *insures* loans.
- VA loans do *not* require mortgage insurance premiums (MIP).

WEB LINK

Visit the U.S. Department of Veterans Affairs Loan Guaranty Service at **www.benefits.va.gov/homeloans/** for additional information.

Conventional Mortgage Loans

Private lenders make conventional loans. Conventional loans usually have a lower loan-to-value (LTV) ratio than either FHA or VA loans. In other words, conventional loans require a larger down payment (equity) as compared with FHA and VA. Lenders typically require a 20 percent down payment for conventional loans. Loans for more than 80 percent (20 percent down) LTV require borrowers to buy private mortgage insurance (PMI). PMI insures that portion of the mortgage loan that exceeds the 80 percent of value. Conventional loans are available for 90 percent or 95 percent LTV if the borrower buys PMI insurance. (See also page 280.)

Interest rates for conventional mortgages reflect market conditions and are negotiated between the lender and the borrower. Fixed-rate conventional mortgages typically contain a due-on-sale clause, meaning that they are not assumable.

Subcategories of Mortgages

Before 1930, buyers commonly used so-called *term mortgages* to purchase real property. With a term mortgage (or *straight-term mortgage*), buyers paid interest only until the full term of the mortgage expired. They then paid all the principal or refinanced the loan. It is a *nonamortizing loan*. Term mortgages are used today but generally for short-term financing, such as construction loans.

Amortized mortgage. Today, the most popular loan payment plan is the fully amortized, level-payment plan mortgage. *Webster's* defines the word *amortize* as meaning to extinguish

FIGURE 12.2   ■   **Allocation of Payments to Interest and Principal**

Payments on a $100,000 loan at 8 percent for 30 years. Monthly payment is $734.

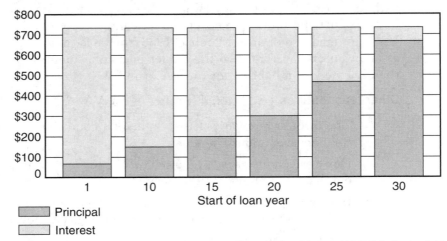

Used with permission from *Mastering Real Estate Principles, Fifth Edition Update,* by Gerald R. Cortesi. ©2010 Kaplan, Inc. Published by DF Institute, Inc., d/b/a Dearborn™ Real Estate Education.

or deaden. An **amortized mortgage** is gradually and systematically killed or extinguished by equal regular periodic payments.

When the various components of a mortgage loan are known (the amount borrowed, the rate of interest, and the term or number of years), the level or constant monthly payment can be calculated by using a financial calculator (or compound interest tables). Each monthly payment includes both interest and principal. Although the borrower pays the same amount each month, on a fixed-rate mortgage, the portion used to pay interest decreases each month, while the portion used to repay principal increases each month. On a 30-year fixed-rate mortgage, the payments during the first few years are used almost entirely to pay interest; payments during the last few years are almost entirely principal repayment. (See Figure 12.2, Allocation of Payments to Interest and Principal.)

Biweekly mortgage. A **biweekly mortgage** loan is amortized the same way as other loans with monthly payments, except the borrower makes a payment every two weeks. The amount paid is equal to one-half the normal monthly payment. Because there are 52 weeks in the year, the borrower makes 26 biweekly payments. Therefore, the borrower makes the equivalent of an extra month's payment each year (26 half-size payments equal 13 full-month payments instead of 12). This saves the borrower considerable interest and the loan is paid off sooner.

Partially amortized mortgage. With a *partially amortized mortgage* the buyer makes regular payments smaller than are required to completely pay off the loan by its date of termination. In other words, the payments do not fully amortize the loan. A single large final payment, including accrued interest and all unpaid principal, then becomes due on the loan maturity date (referred to as a **balloon payment**). In Florida, a partially amortized mortgage must be clearly identified as such on the face of the mortgage, with the amount of the final balloon payment disclosed.

Package mortgage. A **package mortgage** loan includes both real and personal property as security for the debt. A buyer uses a package mortgage, for example, when purchasing a

FOUR WAYS TO PURCHASE MORTGAGED PROPERTY

1.   Cash

2.   Subject to the mortgage

3.   Assumption of an existing mortgage

4.   Novation

restaurant complete with cooking equipment and other personal property that serve as a part of the collateral for the debt.

Purchase-money mortgage. A **purchase-money mortgage (PMM)** is a mortgage given as part of the buyer's consideration for the purchase of real property. The PMM is delivered when the deed is transferred as a simultaneous part of the transaction. It is usually a mortgage taken back by a seller from a buyer in lieu of purchase money. A purchase-money mortgage is used to fill a gap between the buyer's down payment and a new first mortgage or an assumed mortgage. Title passes to the buyer, and the seller retains a vendor's lien right as security for the debt.

METHODS OF PURCHASING MORTGAGED PROPERTY

A buyer may purchase mortgaged property in at least four ways:

1. *Cash*. The mortgage may be paid in full from the sale proceeds, a satisfaction of mortgage recorded, and the property delivered free and clear of the mortgage lien at the time of closing.

2. *Subject to the mortgage*. If the existing mortgage does not contain a due-on-sale clause, the mortgaged property may be purchased *subject to* the mortgage. Here both the existing mortgage and the existing note remain the obligation of the seller. The buyer is responsible for regular payments on the mortgage to retain possession. If the buyer fails to make payments or defaults, the mortgagee can proceed to foreclose. If the foreclosure sale does not satisfy the mortgage debt, a deficiency judgment can be sought against the *original* mortgagor, the seller, who has remained responsible for the mortgage although the property was sold. A *subject to* buyer does not become personally responsible for paying the seller's debt.

3. *Assumption of an existing mortgage*. An **assumption** of the mortgage obligates the buyer to assume liability for the debt. Both buyer and seller are equally liable in the event of default.

4. *Novation*. Until the mortgage loan is paid off, the seller is liable for the note that was signed at the time the original mortgage loan was created. The seller can be released from the liability of the note when a buyer assumes the mortgage by securing a release from the lender. Novation is the substitution of a new debtor (the buyer) and release of a former debtor (the seller) for an existing debt by mutual agreement and with approval of the lender.

Contract for Deed

A **contract for deed** (also called a *land contract*, or an *installment sale* contract) is a financing devise that is used when a buyer does not have sufficient cash to make a down payment acceptable to the seller. The buyer makes a small down payment and takes possession of the property. The seller finances the rest of the purchase price and the buyer makes installment payments on the loan. Legal title remains with the seller until the loan is repaid. The buyer has *equitable* title, which qualifies the buyer for a homestead tax exemption.

Only an attorney should prepare a contract for deed. In case of buyer default, regular foreclosure proceedings are required, just as though it were a seller-held mortgage.

Wraparound Mortgage

A **wraparound mortgage** envelops an existing mortgage and is subordinate (junior) to it. The existing mortgage stays on the property, and the new mortgage "wraps" around it. A wraparound mortgage is commonly taken by a seller who continues to be responsible for payments on a first mortgage. The seller takes a mortgage from the buyer for an amount that includes the existing mortgage balance. Wraparounds are not limited to seller financing. If the seller does not want to finance the sale, a third-party lender could take a wraparound mortgage.

Certain conditions must be present to make a wraparound mortgage economically feasible. First, a property must have an existing mortgage that does *not* have a due-on-sale clause. Second, the interest rate on the existing mortgage should be less than that on the wraparound mortgage. And third, the owner must have sufficient equity in the property to make the wraparound economically worthwhile.

Assume that the buyer is unwilling to enter into a contract for deed but is willing to enter into a wraparound mortgage for $60,000 purchase price and $4,000 down. The seller would take back from the buyer a wraparound mortgage at perhaps 10 percent interest and would receive 10 percent interest on the combined sums of the old $40,500 mortgage and the new $15,500 mortgage. The buyer would have a $56,000 mortgage at 10 percent and make payments to the seller on that basis. If the underlying mortgage is at 8 percent, the seller would receive 2 percent interest on the $40,500 mortgage and 10 percent on the $15,500 loaned in the wraparound. ($810 + $1,550 = $2,360) That's a net return of 15 percent on the $15,500. ($2,360 ÷ $15,500 = .1523) The seller keeps the old mortgage in the seller's name and makes payments just as if the property had not been sold.

OTHER TYPES OF FINANCING

Record-setting high interest rates in the early 1980s caused mortgage lenders to seek new and "creative" financing techniques that were more affordable to potential homebuyers. At the present time, lenders have more or less settled down to two choices: (1) fixed-rate mortgages (discussed previously) and (2) adjustable-rate mortgages. Several lesser-used financing techniques will also be covered here briefly.

Adjustable-Rate Mortgage

An **adjustable-rate mortgage (ARM)** is a loan characterized by a fluctuating interest rate over the term of the loan. The ARM is originated at the initial interest rate. The rate can then increase or decrease, based on an objective economic indicator called an index. As the index changes, the interest rate on the loan changes at preset intervals. The primary components of adjustable-rate mortgages are:

Index. Lenders legally are allowed to link the interest rate of an ARM with any recognized **index** (for example, U.S. treasury securities). The index moves up and down with fluctuations in the nation's economy. The index must not be controlled by the lender, and it must be verifiable by the borrower.

Margin. The **margin** (or *spread*) is the percentage added to the index. The margin represents the lender's cost of doing business plus profit. The margin percentage remains constant over the life of the loan.

Calculated interest rate. The calculated interest rate is arrived at by adding the index to the lender's margin:

$$\text{Index} + \text{Margin} = \text{Calculated interest rate}$$

Assume the borrower has an ARM tied to the one-year T-bill rate with a margin of 2.25. If the T-bill rate is 4 percent, the calculated interest rate is:

$$4 \text{ percent index} + 2.25 \text{ percent margin} = 6.25 \text{ percent calculated interest rate}$$

Adjustment period. The interest rate on an ARM adjusts periodically based on the adjustment period established in the mortgage loan documents. For example, the interest rate may adjust annually or for a longer term such as three years or seven years.

Rate caps. ARMs typically include rate caps to limit how much the interest rate may change. A *periodic rate cap* limits the amount the rate may increase at any one time. For example, the interest rate may be capped to not increase more than two percent during an adjustment period. ARMs typically also cap the total amount the interest rate may increase over the life of the loan. For example, the loan might have a *life-time cap* or ceiling of six percent over the life of the loan.

Payment cap. A payment cap limits the amount the monthly payments can increase during any year. If interest rates rise sharply but the payments do not because of a payment cap, the unpaid interest is added to the loan balance. **Negative amortization** occurs when the mortgage payments are not large enough to cover the interest expense. The result is the unpaid principal balance of the mortgage loan increases.

Teaser rate. Sometimes a lender will offer borrowers an initial below-market interest rate or *teaser*. The low rate is usually offered for the first year of the loan, with a sharp annual rate increase at the next rate adjustment period to bring the loan in line with the agreed upon index.

Shared-Appreciation Mortgage

The *shared-appreciation mortgage* (SAM) is also called an *equity-participation loan*. The lender gives the borrower a lower interest rate in exchange for a share of the future increase in the property's value. The mortgagor and mortgagee agree to the percentage split and the term of the loan. At maturity (or when the property is sold before maturity) the property is appraised to determine the amount due the lender.

Reverse Mortgage

Homeowners age 62 and older who have paid off their mortgage or have only a small mortgage balance remaining are eligible to participate in HUD's reverse mortgage program. The program allows homeowners to borrow against the equity in their homes. Homeowners can receive payments in a lump sum, on a monthly basis (for a fixed term or for as long as they live in the home), or on an occasional basis as a line of credit. The size of reverse mortgage loans is determined by the borrower's age, the interest rate, and the home's value.

Unlike ordinary home equity loans, a HUD reverse mortgage does not require repayment as long as the borrower lives in the home. Lenders recover the principal and interest when the home is sold. The remaining value of the home goes to the homeowner or to the homeowner's survivors. If the sale proceeds are insufficient to pay the amount owed, HUD will pay the lender the amount of the shortfall. The Federal Housing Administration, which is part of HUD, collects an insurance premium from the borrower to provide this coverage.

WEB LINK

The American Association of Retired Persons (AARP) has comprehensive information concerning reverse mortgages at **www.aarp.org/money/credit-loans-debt/**.

Growing-Equity Mortgage

The *growing-equity mortgage* (GEM) rapidly increases the equity in a property by increasing the monthly payments by a certain percentage each year and applying these increases to the principal. Lenders like the shorter maturity date. Borrowers see their equity grow more quickly and see savings in interest as a result of their quicker payoff.

Home Equity Loans

Homeowners use **home equity loans** to finance consumer purchases; consolidate existing credit card debt; and pay for college tuition, medical expenses, or home improvements. Because the interest on most home equity loans is tax deductible, they are more popular than other types of consumer credit.

Home equity loans are secured by the borrower's residence. The original mortgage remains in place. The home equity is usually a second mortgage (junior to the original mortgage). The dollar amount of a home equity loan is based on the amount of equity. The borrower may take a lump-sum amount or access a *line of credit*. The interest rate usually is adjustable and is based on the lender's prime rate. The LTV ratio of both mortgages combined is typically limited to 80 percent of the property's value.

Buydowns

A *buydown* occurs when a party (such as the seller or developer) pays an upfront fee to the lender. In exchange for the fee, the mortgagor's loan interest rate is reduced, generally for the first one year to three years. A builder, for example, might buy down the interest rate for the first three years from 7 percent to 5 percent so that a buyer-borrower can qualify for a larger loan. A builder would rather make an additional cash payment to the lender than reduce the price on a home in a new development.

QUALIFYING THE BUYER

The constantly changing real estate financing market requires that licensees keep up with the various mortgage types and formats available in their local areas. Before attempting to qualify a buyer, licensees should make sure that required written brokerage relationship disclosures have been made. Brokerage relationship disclosure is important because licensees need to obtain confidential information to help determine appropriate loan amounts, financing plans, and affordable income-expense ratios. Qualifying a buyer involves two separate but important processes:

1. Determining the potential buyer's real property needs (housing objectives)
2. Determining the potential buyer's economic capability to satisfy those needs (financial abilities)

Discussions of the following subjects and procedures are designed to assist licensees in reaching decisions in these two areas.

Determining Potential Buyers' Real Property Needs

Licensees must listen carefully to potential buyers to separate wishes from actual needs. Then licensees must help buyers set goals and priorities regarding housing features, neighborhoods, and prices. Licensees should encourage buyers to focus on needs first and then to add wants as economic conditions permit.

A licensee should spend the time necessary to learn a potential buyer's family size, hobbies, ages of family members, distances family members are willing to drive to and from work, plus anything else that might contribute to understanding the potential buyer's needs. If breadwinners regularly bring work home from the office, they may need a quiet, controllable home workspace. Only after housing objectives have been discussed is a licensee prepared to examine financial ability.

Determining Potential Buyers' Economic Capabilities

For some licensees, gauging economic capability is the more difficult part of the qualifying process. It need not be. Recognize that this is a sensitive area, one that is regarded as private information and no one else's business. However, if licensees are up to date on the financial options currently available to buyers, they find it easier to begin this portion of the qualifying process by reviewing the options available to buyers. Talking about loan options, demonstrates professionalism, introduces buyers to consideration of a down payment and monthly payments, and helps to develop confidence in the licensee.

One proven technique for economic qualification is the *explain-and-request technique*. After a brief summary of available financial options, a licensee explains the need to ask the prospective buyer some general questions and then requests permission to ask the questions. Work with reasonably general questions: "Have you a fairly good idea of how much you plan to invest as a down payment?" "Have you thought about the approximate amount you would feel comfortable with as a monthly mortgage payment?" Amounts the buyer provides may or may not be realistic. But the buyer responses will confirm such information or bring to the surface any misconceptions about the market value of real estate and how much home the buyer can afford.

Why Qualify Potential Buyers?

The reasons for qualifying potential buyers fall into four areas:

1. Saves time
2. Increases confidence in sales associate
3. Fits buyers to properties
4. Retains buyers

Begin to qualify buyers with questions related to general information (name, address, and so forth), then gradually work into items of a more specific, personal nature (income, expenses, etc.).

Qualifying for Mortgage Loans

Mortgage lenders use income ratios to qualify potential borrowers. For a lender to be able to sell mortgages in the secondary market (described in the next chapter), the mortgages must meet designated expense/income ratio requirements. FHA, VA, and conventional lenders all use gross monthly income to calculate qualifying ratios for borrowers. Lenders also want to know what percentage of total monthly income is already obligated to pay other debt.

Housing expense ratio. The *housing expense ratio* (HER) is calculated by taking monthly housing expenses for principal, interest, property taxes, and hazard insurance (PITI) and dividing by the applicant's monthly gross income.

$$\text{Monthly housing expenses (PITI)} \div \text{Monthly gross income} = \text{HER}$$

Total obligations ratio. The *total obligations ratio* (TOR) is a measure of a borrower's total installment obligations divided by monthly gross income. The TOR includes monthly expenses found on the borrower's credit report, such as credit card payments, auto payments, student loan payments, and child support payments, in addition to the PITI.

$$\text{Total monthly obligations} \div \text{Monthly gross income} = \text{TOR}$$

FHA-insured mortgage loans. The expenses used in the HER for FHA-insured loans include the monthly mortgage principal and interest payments, property taxes, hazard insurance, *and* FHA mortgage insurance (PITI). FHA requirements currently allow up to 31 percent for the HER and up to 43 percent for the TOR. (See Figure 12.3, Qualifying Ratios.)

VA-guaranteed mortgage loans. To qualify loan applicants, the VA uses a TOR (currently 41 percent) and a Table of Residual Incomes calculated for different regions in the United States. (See Figure 12.3.)

FIGURE 12.3 ■ Qualifying Ratios

	Housing Expense Ratio (HER)	Total Obligations Ratio (TOR)
FHA	31%	43%
VA		41%
Conventional		36%

Conventional mortgage loans. Conventional mortgage lenders typically use Fannie Mae or Freddie Mac benchmark ratios. Fannie Mae emphasizes the total debt (or total obligations) to income ratio (TOR). Fannie Mae's TOR is 36 percent. (See Figure 12.3.)

EXAMPLE 1:   A potential buyer's monthly housing expenses total $1,470 and monthly gross income is $5,880. What is the buyer's housing expense ratio?

$1,470 monthly housing expense ÷ $5,880 monthly gross income = .25 or 25%

EXAMPLE 2:   The buyer's total monthly obligations are $2,058 and the buyer's monthly gross income is $5,880. What is the buyer's total obligations ratio?

$2,058 total monthly obligations ÷ $5,880 monthly gross income = .35 or 35%

Practice Problem 1

An FHA borrower has monthly housing expenses of $1,512 and monthly total debt obligations of $1,944. The borrower's gross monthly income is $5,400. What is this borrower's housing expense ratio (HER) and the total obligations ratio (TOR)?

(The solution to the Practice Problem is at the end of this chapter on page 282.)

Mortgage Loan Underwriting

Property purchased with any type of mortgage first must be qualified by the lender. After the property has been appraised, surveyed, and the title searched, the loan underwriter will make a decision about the property. The purchaser also must be qualified. Lenders generally use five major qualifying guidelines in borrower qualification and risk analysis:

1. The quantity and quality of the borrower's income (Does the borrower have the ability to repay the debt?)
2. Other assets of value (What is the proposed mortgagor's net worth, and what is the ratio of total liabilities to total assets?)
3. Past credit history (Is the borrower willing to repay the debt?)
4. Loan-to-value ratio (How much equity is the borrower investing?)
5. The borrower's credit score (In today's marketplace, an applicant's credit score is an important component of all loan decisions. The strength of the credit score determines the interest rate offered to the applicant and also dictates the amount

of supporting documentation required for the loan application.) (See also Credit Scores later in the chapter.)

Loan underwriting (borrower qualification and property qualification) should not be confused with *buyer qualification*, which has to do with what the buyer wants and can afford. The loan underwriting process begins with the FNMA/FHLMC Uniform Residential Loan Application for all one-family to four-family homes.

Quantity and quality of income (ability to pay debt). Prospective borrowers must provide information to lenders about their present employment, financial history, and present obligations. In addition, federal regulations require lenders to obtain documented proof, such as tax returns and financial statements. Lenders use this information to make a decision about loan approval or rejection. The lender is interested in the borrower's debt-paying ability and the risk involved. The quantity of the borrower's income is the *amount* earned. However, amount alone is not sufficient because the *probable duration* of income is also important when the debt obligation may extend up to 30 years. So the *quality* of the income is also evaluated—the length of time of the applicant's present employment and probable continuation of that employment. Lenders also evaluate demands on a prospective borrower's income, that is, income taxes, installment credit amounts, proposed mortgage payments, and property taxes.

Other assets of value (sufficient security for debt). The second area of concern in analyzing a loan application is the total value of the mortgaged property plus other assets belonging to the applicant. Other real estate, savings accounts, stocks, bonds, and equity in personal property are examples of assets that could act as sources of funds for mortgage payments if the applicant's income is interrupted.

Credit history (willingness to repay debt). The third area of concern is the applicant's willingness to repay debts, based on credit history, obtainable from a local credit bureau. The existing national network of credit bureaus permits a comparatively rapid check of buyers, even of new residents from other states.

Loan-to-value ratio. The **loan-to-value (LTV) ratio** is the relationship between the amount borrowed and the appraised value (or purchase price) of a property. Lenders use this ratio as the measure of financial risk associated with lending and borrowing money. The higher the LTV ratio, the lower the lender's safety cushion, should the borrower default. Although the LTV typically falls between 60 percent and 90 percent, it can fall outside this range.

Loan-to-Value Ratio Formula:

Loan amount ÷ Price (or value) = Loan-to-Value (LTV) ratio

EXAMPLE: A home was purchased with a down payment of $36,000 and a loan of $200,000 at 6.5 percent for 30 years. Monthly payments are $1,264.14. What is the LTV ratio?

$$\$200,000 \text{ loan} \div \$236,000 \text{ purchase price}$$
$$= .84745 \text{ or } 85\% \text{ LTV ratio}$$

HOW TO OBTAIN YOUR CREDIT REPORT

The Fair and Accurate Credit Transaction Act (FACT Act) makes it possible for consumers to monitor their credit reports at no cost. The government allows consumers to request a free copy of their credit report every 12 months from each of the three credit bureaus—Equifax, Experian, and TransUnion. Consumers can request all three reports at once or spread out their requests over the 12-month period.

To request your report, go to the centralized source, a combined effort by the three national bureaus, at **www.annualcreditreport.com**. This is the only site that participates with the government program, so don't be fooled by "free credit report" gimmicks from other sites. You can download and print your credit report online or request your credit report by mail. You can also order by telephone at 877-322-8228.

Practice Problem 2

What is the loan-to-value (LTV) ratio for a home purchased for $315,000 with a loan of $283,500?

(The solution to the Practice Problem is at the end of this chapter on page 282.)

1   **Credit scores.** A credit score is a number that assists lenders with predicting whether a
2   borrower is likely to make timely credit payments. Lenders use credit scores to measure
3   potential risk of making a loan. Higher credit scores mean that an applicant is more likely
4   to be approved and pay a lower interest rate on new credit.

5   FICO® scores are the most widely used credit scores. Credit scores are based on infor-
6   mation found in a consumer's credit report. Scores reflect a consumer's payment history,
7   amount owed, how much available credit is being used, length of credit history, and
8   whether the consumer has recently applied for or opened new credit accounts. FICO
9   scores range from 300 to 850. FICO scores above 700 are a sign of good financial health.
10 FICO scores below 600 indicate high risk to lenders and could result in denial of a credit
11 application. Lenders buy FICO scores from three national credit reporting agencies.
12 (See text box, How to Obtain Your Credit Report.)

WEB LINK

To learn more about credit scores, go to **www.myfico.com/CreditEducation/CreditScores.aspx**.

Practice Problem 1 Solution

(Practice Problem 1 is located on page 279.)

$1,512 ÷ $5,400 = .28 or 28% housing expense ratio (HER)

$1,944 ÷ $5,400 = .36 or 36% total obligations ratio (TOR)

Practice Problem 2 Solution

(Practice Problem 2 is located on page 281.)

$283,500 ÷ $315,000 = .9 or 90% loan-to-value (LTV) ratio

SUMMARY OF IMPORTANT POINTS

- The two legal theories of mortgages are (1) title theory (title conveys to the lender/mortgagee through a mortgage deed) and (2) lien theory (title remains with borrower/mortgagor and lender has a lien against property). Florida is a lien theory state.

- The two instruments created with a mortgage loan are (1) promissory note, the promise to repay and represents evidence of a debt; and (2) mortgage, which creates the lien interest and pledges the property as security for the debt.

- Assignment of mortgage transfers ownership of a mortgage from one company or individual to another.

- Once the borrower has repaid the mortgage loan in full, the mortgagee executes and records in the public record a satisfaction (release) of mortgage to remove the mortgage lien. Florida statute requires that the mortgagee send the recorded satisfaction to the mortgagor within 60 days.

- When a mortgage default occurs, the lender can initiate a suit on the promissory note or initiate a foreclosure proceeding.

- Equity of redemption allows the mortgagor to prevent foreclosure by paying the mortgagee the principal and interest due plus any expenses the mortgagee has incurred in attempting to collect the debt.

- The due-on-sale clause allows the mortgagee to call due the outstanding loan balance plus accrued interest. The clause prevents another party from assuming the mortgage.

- The acceleration clause authorizes the mortgagee to accelerate the due date of the entire unpaid loan balance if the mortgagor fails to fulfill any promises stated in the mortgage instrument.

- The defeasance clause, in title theory states, requires the lender to convey legal title to the borrower once the debt is repaid; in lien theory states, this clause requires the lender to release the mortgage lien when the debt is repaid.

- Federal Housing Administration (FHA) is a government agency that insures mortgage loans made by approved lenders. FHA does not make loans nor does it regulate interest rates. Borrowers pay an up-front mortgage insurance premium (UFMIP) and an annual mortgage insurance premium (MIP). The annual premium is paid monthly as part of the monthly mortgage payment. Borrowers are required to make a down payment of at least 3.5 percent. Section 203(b) FHA program insures fixed-rate loans on one- to four-family residences.

- The Department of Veterans Affairs (VA) partially guarantees mortgage loans. Private lenders provide VA loans to veterans, surviving spouses of veterans, and active military personnel. The VA also has the power to make direct loans to veterans. A veteran's entitlement is the maximum amount the government guarantees the lender will be paid in the event the borrower defaults. A veteran's certificate of eligibility states the amount of entitlement available to the veteran borrower. Down payments are not required on VA loans. The VA charges a funding (user) fee to help the government defray the cost of foreclosures. VA loans do not have due-on-sale clauses; therefore, they are assumable (even by nonveterans).

- Conventional loans are written by private lenders and are not guaranteed or insured by the federal government. Conventional loans typically require a larger down payment, compared with FHA and VA loans, and therefore have a lower LTV ratio. Borrowers must pay for private mortgage insurance (PMI) for the portion of the loan above 80 percent LTV. Fixed-rate conventional mortgage loans have a due-on-sale clause, so they are not assumable.

- A *fully amortized mortgage* is one with regular payments each month of principal and interest. The monthly payment remains the same each month; however, the amount applied to principal increases each month, and the amount applied to interest decreases each month.

- With a *partially amortized mortgage*, the buyer makes regular payments smaller than what is required to completely pay off the loan by the date of termination. A single large final payment, called a balloon payment, of accrued interest and remaining unpaid principal is made at loan maturity.

- An *adjustable-rate mortgage* (ARM) is a financing technique in which the lender can raise or lower the interest rate according to a recognized and verifiable index. The margin is the percentage added to the index to cover the lender's costs plus profit. The index plus the margin equals the calculated interest rate.

R E V I E W   Q U E S T I O N S

1. In a fully amortized, level-payment plan mortgage, the portion of the monthly payment that goes to reducing the principal
   a. remains constant throughout the loan term.
   b. gradually increases with each payment throughout the duration of the loan term.
   c. gradually decreases with each payment throughout the duration of the loan term.
   d. fluctuates based on the prevailing interest rates.

2. A term mortgage differs from a level-payment, fully amortized mortgage because of the
   a. index chosen.
   b. number of points that may be charged.
   c. method of repayment.
   d. criteria used to qualify the borrower.

3. In a mortgage transaction in Florida, the legal evidence of the personal debt is the
   a. property (collateral).
   b. note.
   c. mortgage instrument.
   d. borrower's credit history.

4. A financing vehicle in which the vendor holds title to the property until the buyer has met the stated obligations is a
   a. balloon mortgage.
   b. purchase-money mortgage.
   c. contract for deed.
   d. term mortgage.

5. In title theory states, the mortgage clause that provides that the conveyance of title to the lender is defeated when all of the terms of the agreement have been fulfilled is the
   a. penalty clause.
   b. release clause.
   c. defeasance clause.
   d. insurance clause.

6. If a foreclosed property fails to bring sufficient proceeds at the foreclosure sale to pay the debt, the lender
   a. must absorb the loss as a bad investment.
   b. may seek recovery of the loss from the Real Estate Recovery Fund.
   c. may obtain an interpleader judgment for the amount of deficit.
   d. may obtain a deficiency judgment for the amount of deficit.

7. A home was purchased with a down payment of $50,000 and a loan of $200,000 at 6 percent interest for 20 years. Monthly payments are $1,432.86. What is the loan-to-value ratio?
   a. 25 percent
   b. 70 percent
   c. 75 percent
   d. 80 percent

8. Which is considered an advantage of home equity loans?
   a. The interest rate is typically lower than the prevailing home mortgage rate.
   b. Home equity loans do not create a lien against the borrower's residence.
   c. The interest on most home equity loans is tax deductible.
   d. All of the above are considered home equity loan advantages.

9. The current maximum FHA loan available for a single-family dwelling is
   a. dependent on the location.
   b. $108,000.
   c. $203,000.
   d. $417,000.

10. A couple purchased their first home in January. The interest rate was based on the property being owner-occupied. In May of the same year, the couple decided to live on their sailboat and make a two-year trip around the world. They rented their home to a friend. The lender soon notified the couple in writing of the mortgagee's intent to increase the interest rate on their loan to the investor rate of interest. The lender was proceeding under which of the following clauses?
    a. Acceleration clause
    b. Escalator clause
    c. Defeasance clause
    d. Release clause

11. The maximum amount of a VA loan is
    a. $417,000.
    b. $104,250.
    c. $89,912.
    d. not a legislated limit for qualified borrowers.

12. A man wants to buy a small restaurant and is considering financing the restaurant equipment in addition to the real estate. If the man pledges the personal property in addition to the real estate as collateral for the mortgage, the man's mortgage is
    a. an equipment mortgage.
    b. a package mortgage.
    c. an all-inclusive mortgage.
    d. a chattel mortgage.

13. A borrower who is in default on a mortgage is allowed to prevent the lender from foreclosing on the property by paying the mortgagee the delinquent principal and interest, plus any expenses the mortgagee has incurred in attempting to collect the payments. This right is referred to as
    a. novation.
    b. a satisfaction of mortgage.
    c. the equity of redemption.
    d. an acceleration clause.

14. A lender declares all the unpaid balance due and payable as a result of default. The lender is exercising the
    a. acceleration clause.
    b. due-on-sale clause.
    c. defeasance clause.
    d. escalator clause.

15. The person who borrows money to help pay for the purchase of real property is called at various times the
    a. lender.
    b. mortgagee.
    c. lienor.
    d. mortgagor.

16. The mortgage provision that relieves the mortgagor from any personal liability for the debt so that the mortgagee can look only to the mortgaged property for reimbursement in the event of default is the
    a. novation.
    b. estoppel certificate.
    c. exculpatory clause.
    d. subordination clause.

17. A mortgage
    a. creates a lien.
    b. is a contract.
    c. must be in writing.
    d. has all the above characteristics.

18. When a vendee buys "subject to the mortgage," the
    a. vendee becomes responsible for the note.
    b. original obligation is substituted with a new note by novation.
    c. vendor is relieved of the obligation for the promissory note.
    d. vendor remains responsible for the note.

19. Blanket mortgages
    a. are illegal.
    b. typically include a partial release clause.
    c. include equipment and other personal property.
    d. have all the above traits.

20. A couple has just made the final mortgage payment on their home. What document must the mortgagee file on their behalf?
    a. Lis pendens
    b. Novation
    c. Satisfaction of mortgage
    d. Estoppel certificate

21. A new mortgage accepted by the seller as part of the purchase price is
    a. a wraparound mortgage.
    b. a shared-appreciation mortgage.
    c. an assumption of the mortgage.
    d. a purchase-money mortgage.

22. If a mortgagee does NOT want the mortgage to be paid ahead of schedule, the mortgage will normally contain
    a. a prepayment penalty clause.
    b. a redemption clause.
    c. a defeasance clause.
    d. an acceleration clause.

23. A mortgagor defaulted on a mortgage encumbering an apartment complex. Once the foreclosure proceedings were filed, the lender appealed to the courts to appoint
    a. a receiver.
    b. an on-site manager.
    c. an attorney to handle the case.
    d. an arbitrator.

24. Which statement is TRUE regarding the mortgagor's minimum cash investment on an FHA loan?
    a. Closing costs paid by the buyer may be applied toward satisfying the cash requirement.
    b. Seller-paid closing costs may be included when calculating the cash investment amount.
    c. A loan from the seller may be used to satisfy the cash requirement.
    d. A gift from a relative may be used to satisfy the cash requirement.

25. An FHA loan is a
    a. government-insured loan.
    b. government-guaranteed loan.
    c. private loan that is insured with mortgage insurance.
    d. loan in which the mortgagor is protected against financial loss in the event of default.

26. Which applies to FHA 203(b) loans?
    a. The loan program applies to loans for one-family to four-family residences.
    b. The maximum insurable loan limit varies from area to area.
    c. Borrowers are required to pay a one-time upfront mortgage insurance premium.
    d. Each of the above applies to 203(b) loans.

27. A potential FHA borrower's monthly housing expense is $504, the total monthly gross income is $1,800, and the total monthly obligations are $648. What is the monthly housing expense ratio for the borrower?
    a. 28 percent
    b. 36 percent
    c. 38 percent
    d. 43 percent

28. The loan-to-value ratio is 80 percent. A buyer wants to acquire a property with a purchase price of $116,000. Calculate the required down payment.
    a. $20,000
    b. $23,200
    c. $32,800
    d. $92,800

29. The primary purpose of an estoppel certificate is to
    a. prevent foreclosure.
    b. relieve the mortgagor of personal liability for the debt.
    c. verify the loan balance.
    d. prevent transfer of title to the mortgagee.

30. Which expense is NOT charged to FHA borrowers?
    a. Annual mortgage insurance premium
    b. Up-front mortgage insurance premium
    c. Funding fee
    d. All of the above expenses are charged to FHA borrowers.

13

THE MORTGAGE MARKET

¹ ## OVERVIEW

² This chapter discusses the money supply; primary and secondary markets; the Financial
³ Institutions Reform, Recovery, and Enforcement Act of 1989 (FIRREA); and potential
⁴ borrowers. The very strong thread that connects all of these individuals, institutions, and
⁵ agencies is money, in the form of mortgage loans.

⁶ After completing this chapter, the student should be able to:

⁷ ■ describe the factors that influence the supply and demand for mortgage funds;

⁸ ■ distinguish between the primary and secondary markets;

⁹ ■ understand the mortgage practices of commercial banks, savings associations,
¹⁰ mutual savings banks, and life insurance companies;

¹¹ ■ distinguish between a mortgage loan originator and mortgage lender;

¹² ■ describe the three methods the Fed uses to control the supply of money in
¹³ circulation;

¹⁴ ■ describe the function of Fannie Mae, Ginnie Mae, and Freddie Mac; and

¹⁵ ■ calculate the cost of discount points and the approximate yield resulting from
¹⁶ discounts.

¹⁷ ## KEY TERMS

conforming loans	monetary policy	open market operations
demand deposits	mortgage lender	primary market
discount points	mortgage loan originator	reserve requirements
discount rate	mortgage broker company	SAFE Act
disintermediation	Office of Thrift Supervision	secondary mortgage market
intermediation	(OTS)	

THE MORTGAGE MARKET AND MONEY SUPPLY

Like other markets, the mortgage market is tied irrevocably to the *law of supply and demand.* An economic fact of life is the inverse relationship between available mortgage money and mortgage interest rates. When the amount of available mortgage money goes down, mortgage interest rates go up, and vice versa. The supply of mortgage money available at any given time depends (1) on the continuous and orderly flow of money into various types of financial institutions and (2) on the amount borrowed by the federal government.

All lenders in the mortgage market are tied together by long-term credit lending with real property as security. Also, despite their different locations and operating policies, all lenders are mutually dependent on the overall supply of money existing in the nation. For this reason, price movements of money in different areas are related. When a corporation in San Francisco borrows $50 million from a mutual savings bank in Boston, the money available in the mortgage market is depleted by that amount. The result could be higher interest rates for loans made in Orlando, for example.

Thus, each geographical area is a component of the entire mortgage market. The entire mortgage market is, in turn, only one component of the vast financial system called the *overall capital market.* As interrelated parts, each is responsive to changes affecting the whole system. In fact, it is the total demand for money interacting with the total available supply of money that determines the interest rate, or cost, of mortgages.

At any given time, a number of businesses or institutions are renting mortgage money to other businesses or individuals. The rent paid for the use of money is called *interest.* When money is plentiful and available from many sources, the supply of money exceeds the demand, creating an *easy money market* situation. The interest charged for money loaned during an easy money market is less than in a *tight money market.* A tight money market exists when demand for funds exceeds the available supply, resulting in an increase in the interest charged for money.

The *demand* for mortgage money is increased or decreased by the following six major influences:

1. Changes in the number and size of households
2. Shifts in geographic preference for households
3. Existing inventory of structures
4. Changes in employment rates and income
5. Changes in costs of real property services, taxes, and maintenance
6. Changes in construction costs

Influences on the *supply side* of the mortgage money market also are varied. Because they are considered long-term loans, mortgages do not compete directly with the short-term demand for funds. Mortgages must compete directly with other long-term claims for money. The long-term claims are corporate stocks and bonds and long-term bonds issued by the various federal, state, and local governments. As a consequence, the mortgage, stock, and bond markets are all in competition for the overall supply of funds in what is called the *nation's capital market.*

Another important influence on the mortgage market is the refinancing of the national debt. The U.S. government owes the owners of short-term and long-term securities trillions of dollars. At the present time, this debt is refinanced periodically by the sale of new securities on the open market. When the U.S. Treasury sells enough securities to pay interest on $500 billion, for example, it drains a large amount of money from the capital market. This drainage results in less funds available for the mortgage market and higher interest rates.

FEDERAL REGULATORY BODIES

Federal Reserve System

The Federal Reserve (commonly called *the Fed*) is the central bank of the United States. It was founded by Congress to provide the nation with a safer and more stable monetary system. The Federal Reserve System (FRS) consists of a 7-member Board of Governors and 12 Reserve Banks located in major cities across the nation. The members of the Board of Governors are appointed by the President and confirmed by the U.S. Senate.

Today, the Federal Reserve's duties include (1) conducting the nation's monetary policy, (2) supervising and regulating banking institutions and protecting the credit rights of consumers, and (3) maintaining the stability of the financial system. **Monetary policy** refers to the actions undertaken by the Fed to influence the availability and cost of money and credit to promote national economic goals. The Federal Reserve is charged with the responsibility for setting monetary policy.

The Federal Reserve also has regulatory and supervisory responsibilities over banks that are members of the FRS. Additionally, the Board is responsible for the development and administration of regulations that implement major federal laws governing consumer credit, such as the Truth in Lending Act and the Equal Credit Opportunity Act.

The Fed uses three economic tools (or methods) of monetary policy, listed below in the order most often used (See Figure 13.1, Federal Reserve System Economic Tools to Influence Money Supply):

1. *Open-market operations*. The Fed's principal and most effective tool for implementing monetary policy is open-market operations. **Open-market operations** involve the purchase and sale of U.S. Treasury and federal agency securities. The purchase or sale of these securities results in an increase or decrease of money in circulation. For example, when the Fed decides to *sell* securities through open-market bulk trading, the FRS holds the funds received from the sale. This reduces the supply of money in circulation, which, in turn, causes a drop in loanable funds and causes interest rates to rise. Higher interest rates cause some business and individuals to postpone borrowing. As borrowing drops off, the economy slows down and inflation (if any) is reduced. When an increase in economic activity seems needed, the Fed *buys* securities, thereby releasing money back into normal circulation and increasing loanable funds.

2. *Discount rate*. The second most commonly used method of controlling the supply of money is changing the discount rate. The **discount rate** is the interest rate charged member banks for borrowing money from the Fed. (Do not confuse *discount rate* with *discount points* discussed later in this chapter.) If the discount rate is increased, member banks have to pay a higher interest rate for money borrowed from their district bank. The higher interest rate is passed on in the form of higher interest to consumers. This reduces the number of loans made because consumers become reluctant to borrow. Because increasing or decreasing the discount rate has the greatest impact on the cost of short-term credit, the discount rate is

F I G U R E 13.1 ■ Federal Reserve System Economic Tools to Influence Money Supply

Open-market operations	Purchase and sale of U.S. Treasury securities
	Fed purchases securities: Money supply increases and interest rates decrease.
	Fed sells securities: Money supply decreases and interest rates increase.
Discount rate	Interest rate charged to member banks to borrow money from the Fed
	Discount rate increased: Fewer loans are made and money supply decreases.
	Discount rate decreased: More loans are made and money supply increases.
Reserve requirement	Amount of funds that an institution must hold in reserve against deposit liabilities as determined by the Fed
	Reserve requirement increased: Money supply decreases and interest rates increase.
	Reserve requirement decreased: Money supply increases and interest rates decrease.

considered to be the least effective economic tool for influencing the interest rates of long-term real estate loans.

3. *Reserve requirements.* The third method the Fed uses to influence the supply of money is the change in reserve requirements. The **reserve requirements** are the amount of funds that an institution must hold in reserve against deposit liabilities. Institutions must hold reserves in the form of vault cash or deposits with Federal Reserve Banks. Changing the reserve requirement is regarded as perhaps the most abrupt or drastic way to influence the supply of money. Because most member banks have large amounts of time deposits and demand deposits, a very small increase in percentage of reserve requirements has an immediate impact on the amount of funds taken out of circulation.

WEB LINK

To learn more about the Federal Reserve System, visit **www.federalreserve.gov**.

Federal Home Loan Bank System

The Federal Home Loan Bank System (FHLBS) was created to provide the same regulatory and administrative services for the nation's savings associations that the FRS provides for commercial banks. Patterned after the Fed, the FHLBS includes 12 district Federal Home Loan Banks (FHLBs). They constitute a permanent pool of reserve credit for savings association member institutions and ensure a source of mortgage funds when local funds are insufficient. The Financial Institutions Reform, Recovery, and Enforcement Act of 1989 (FIRREA) created the **Office of Thrift Supervision (OTS)** to charter and regulate member federal savings associations. FIRREA also created the Federal Housing Finance Board (FHFB) to supervise mortgage lending by the 12 regional FHLBs.

All federally chartered savings associations are required to be members of their district FHLB. While membership is optional for state-chartered savings associations, mutual savings banks, and insurance companies, many of these—that meet federal standards and can qualify—elect to join because only member institutions are allowed to borrow from their district FHLB for up to one year without collateral. Longer-term loans, such as real estate loans, must be secured by collateral.

Federal Deposit Insurance Corporation

The Federal Deposit Insurance Corporation (FDIC) insures deposits in banks and savings associations. The FDIC is an independent agency of the federal government. It is funded by premiums that banks and savings associations pay for deposit insurance coverage and from earnings on investments in U.S. Treasury securities.

Deposit accounts are insured to $250,000 per depositor in each bank or thrift that the FDIC and the National Credit Union Administration (NCUA) insures. Savings, checking, IRAs, and certain types of retirement accounts are currently insured to $250,000; however, the coverage limit will return to $100,000, except for IRAs and certain retirement accounts, effective January 1, 2014. (*Note:* The Helping Families Save Their Homes Act of 2009 extended the increased deposit insurance limit through December 31, 2013.) The Federal Deposit Insurance Reform Act of 2005 merged the Bank Insurance Fund (which formerly insured federally chartered banks) and the Savings Association Insurance Fund (which formerly insured federally chartered savings associations) into a new Deposit Insurance Fund (DIF) that insures both banks and savings associations.

PRIMARY MORTGAGE MARKET

The primary mortgage market is made up of primary lenders that *originate* new mortgage loans for borrowers. A **primary market** is the market where securities or goods are actually created. For example, if a commercial bank lends a homebuyer the money to buy a house via the use of a mortgage loan, that would be a primary market activity. The dominant primary lenders are commercial banks (CBs), savings associations (SAs), mutual savings banks, selected credit unions, and mortgage companies. Together, these lenders originate more than 95 percent of all residential mortgage loans.

SAFE Mortgage Licensing Act

In response to the recent mortgage loan crisis, Congress passed the Secure and Fair Enforcement of Mortgage Licensing Act (SAFE Act). The **SAFE Act** is intended to improve the accountability and tracking of residential mortgage loan originators (MLOs), enhance consumer protection, reduce fraud, and provide consumers with easily accessible information regarding an MLO's professional background. The SAFE Act sets a minimum standard for licensing and registering mortgage loan originators. (MLOs were previously licensed as mortgage brokers.)

The SAFE Act requires employees of banks, savings associations, credit unions, and farm credit institutions, that are regulated by a Federal banking agency and who engage in residential mortgage loan origination, to register with the Nationwide Mortgage Licensing System (NMLS). Mortgage loan originators must submit fingerprints for a criminal background check. MLOs who are not employed by agency-regulated institutions are licensed by the states. Employees of bank holding companies and their nonbank subsidiaries who act as MLOs are subject to state licensure and associated state regulation, in addition to registration with the NMLS.

The SAFE Act requires state-licensed MLOs to complete pre-licensure education courses, pass a written qualification exam, and take annual continuing education courses. The SAFE Act also requires all MLOs to submit fingerprints to the NMLS for submission to the FBI for a criminal background check. State-licensed MLOs must also provide authorization for the NMLS to obtain an independent credit report.

494.001, F.S.

Mortgage loan originator (MLO). A **mortgage loan originator** (MLO) is a person who solicits or offers to solicit mortgage loans, accepts or offers to accept mortgage loan applications, negotiates the terms or conditions of new or existing mortgage loans on behalf of a borrower or lender, processes mortgage loan applications, or negotiates the sale of existing mortgage loans to noninstitutional investors for compensation. The SAFE Mortgage Licensing Act requires MLO's who are not employed by a federal agency-regulated institution to obtain a Florida loan originator license. If a loan application is approved, the loan originator earns a negotiated *loan origination fee*.

Mortgage broker. A **mortgage broker** is a person who conducts loan originator activities through one or more licensed loan originators employed by the mortgage broker or as an independent contractor to the mortgage broker. Mortgage brokers do *not* make loans. Instead, mortgage brokers *arrange* loans for prospective borrowers with various mortgage lenders. Mortgage brokers do not service loans.

Mortgage lender. A **mortgage lender** is a person or business entity that makes mortgage loans or services mortgage loans for others or, for compensation, sells or offers to sell mortgage loans to noninstitutional investors. Mortgage lenders are not depository institutions. Mortgage lenders originate loans and then package the loans together and sell the entire package. Mortgage lenders primarily make VA and FHA loans and then sell the loans in the secondary mortgage market. Mortgage loan originators who are employed by a mortgage broker or mortgage lender must be registered with the NMLS. MLOs employed by a mortgage broker or a mortgage lender must also be state-licensed if the mortgage broker or mortgage lender is not a federal agency-regulated institution.

Mortgage lenders secure short-term funds from other lenders (for example, commercial banks) that enable them to originate mortgage loans until they are sold on the secondary market or to large financial institutions. This process is referred to as *warehousing* because the mortgage lenders use the loans as security for the short-term financing and the loans are "stored" for a short period of time until they are sold as a package. Mortgage lenders often serve as *loan correspondents* (local representatives) for life insurance companies (LICs), enabling LICs to use their insurance policy funds and pension funds to invest in mortgage instruments. Mortgage lenders typically earn loan origination fees plus servicing fees. Today, mortgage lenders are the largest originators of residential real estate loans.

Intermediation and Disintermediation

Intermediation is a process practiced by financial thrift institutions that serve as financial *intermediaries (middlemen)* between depositors and borrowers. Intermediation occurs when thrift institutions accept depositors' savings. Thrift institutions are financial institutions that hold savings deposits. Savers deposit funds into commercial banks, savings associations, and mutual savings banks, which then lend the funds to homebuyers and other borrowers. Intermediation results in the availability of mortgage money.

Disintermediation occurs when funds are withdrawn from intermediary financial institutions, such as banks and savings associations, and are invested in instruments yielding a higher return. Disintermediation is the process of bypassing the intermediary financial institutions (or middlemen).

Commercial Banks

Commercial banks are the primary reservoirs of commercial credit in this country and the largest group of financial institutions in both assets and numbers. The amount invested in real property mortgages by CBs has been increasing over the past few years. CBs hold **demand deposits** (checking accounts), as do federally chartered SAs and credit unions.

CBs are chartered by either a state or the federal government (referred to as *national banks*). National banks are supervised by the Comptroller of the Currency and are members of the FRS. The chartering agency prescribes the rules and regulations that govern the business operations of a bank. If chartered by the federal government, a CB must display the word *National* or the initials *NA* (National Association) somewhere in their name. State-chartered CBs are regulated by state agencies, and membership in the FRS is optional; however, as a practical matter, almost all state banks are members of the FRS.

Commercial banks make conventional, FHA, and VA mortgage loans, and they have long been recognized as specialists in construction loans for both residential and commercial projects. Most banks also have concentrated on equity loans (lines of credit); that is, loans to homeowners based on the amount of equity in their homes.

Savings Associations

Savings associations (SAs), formerly called *savings and loan associations* (S&Ls), are also referred to as *thrifts* and as *savings banks*. S&Ls, prior to deregulation, were the major source of residential real estate loans. Today, most SAs invest the bulk of their assets in residential mortgages and home equity loans. They adhere to strict underwriting guidelines established by the secondary mortgage market. (See Secondary Mortgage Market, page 296.)

SAs are chartered by either the state or the federal government. If a savings association is federally chartered, either *Federal* or *FA* (Federal Association) must appear in the name of the association. SAs' experience with residential mortgages makes them expert in underwriting and making mortgage loans on single-family houses. Practically all SAs prefer to make conventional mortgage loans, although they may make both FHA and VA loans.

Mutual Savings Banks

Mutual savings banks (MSBs) are state chartered and are similar to SAs. They are mutually owned (no stockholders). While CBs are located in all 50 states, most of the approximately 470 MSBs are concentrated in the Northeast. MSBs are active investors in FHA and VA loans all over the nation. By using mortgage bankers and other representation in fast-growing capital-deficit areas, MSBs are able to extend their lending activities into such areas whenever they choose to do so.

Mortgage Companies

Since the 1980s, the volume of loan originations has shifted from savings associations to mortgage companies. **Mortgage companies** originate loans with either their own funds or borrowed capital. They package the loans and sell them to institutional investors and secondary market participants.

Mortgage companies, also known as *mortgage lenders*, are not financial intermediaries because they do not accept savings deposits. The principal activity of mortgage companies is to originate and service loans on residential and income properties. Mortgage companies charge interest and earn fees on the loans that they originate. From these fees, mortgage companies pay interest on any interim funds borrowed, cover operating expenses, and earn a profit. Today, mortgage companies account for more than half of all single-family loan originations.

Life Insurance Companies

Life insurance companies (LICs) are regulated by the laws of the states in which they operate. LICs are *not* thrift institutions, nor are they organized for the primary purpose of financing real property. As insurance companies, they generate enormous amounts of funds that represent huge amounts of the public's savings, mostly in the form of policy-holders' reserves. LICs, through mortgage lenders or other loan correspondents, invest in loans secured by large-scale commercial and industrial real estate. LICs also contribute to the availability of residential mortgage funds by buying residential mortgages in bulk as a part of the secondary mortgage market. LICs have invested billions of dollars in mortgage loans.

Rural Housing Service

The Rural Housing Service (formerly called the Farmer's Home Administration) is an agency of the U.S. Department of Agriculture. It offers direct loans and other services to farmers, rural residents, and rural communities, enabling them to purchase and operate farms, homes, and businesses. Loan programs fall into three categories:

1. Originate new loans
2. Insure loans (in much the same way as FHA)
3. Guarantee loans (in much the same way as VA)

Actions and interactions of the primary and secondary mortgage markets are illustrated in Figure 13.2, Primary and Secondary Mortgage Markets.

SECONDARY MORTGAGE MARKET

Portfolio lenders hold mortgage loans in their portfolios and service the loans. However, most lenders sell the loans in the secondary mortgage market. The **secondary mortgage market** is an investor market that buys and sells existing mortgages. The existence of a

FIGURE 13.2 ■ Primary and Secondary Mortgage Markets

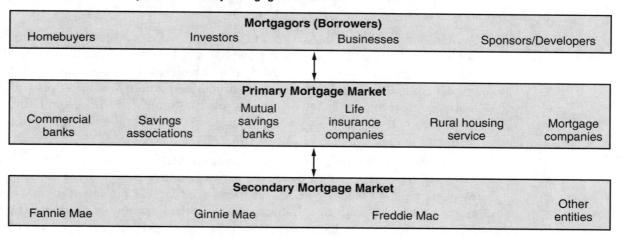

1 secondary mortgage market makes the primary mortgage market more efficient because
2 mortgage originators are able to sell their loans more quickly and obtain funds to originate
3 additional loans. The secondary market is the principal source of mortgage capital in the
4 United States.

5 Lenders sell some of the loans on the secondary market to private mortgage investors.
6 Private investors include banks, life insurance companies, and pension funds. However,
7 most of the loans are sold to government-owned enterprises. Fannie Mae, Freddie Mac,
8 and Ginnie Mae are the three major enterprises that purchase mortgages on the secondary
9 market.

10 Mortgage originators package loans they make with other loans and either sell the
11 package as a whole or keep the package and sell securities that are backed by the loans
12 in the package. Ginnie Mae provides liquidity to the mortgage market by guaranteeing
13 mortgage-backed securities. Approximately two-thirds of all residential mortgage loans
14 originated in the United States are now sold in the secondary mortgage market and used
15 as collateral for the issuance of mortgage-backed securities.

16 **Fannie Mae.** Fannie Mae (Federal National Mortgage Association or FNMA) was estab-
17 lished by Congress in 1938. Fannie Mae's initial goal was to stimulate the housing industry
18 following the Great Depression. Fannie Mae also created the first secondary market for
19 mortgage loans.

20 In 2008 Fannie Mae became a government-owned enterprise. Until that time, it was
21 organized as a completely privately owned corporation that issued its own stock.

22 Fannie Mae keeps low-cost capital flowing to mortgage lenders across the nation. Fan-
23 nie Mae does *not* lend money directly to homebuyers. Instead it works with lenders to
24 make sure they don't run out of mortgage funds. Fannie Mae provides large builders and
25 real estate companies *master commitments* in amounts of $25 million and more for funds
26 for up to 12 months in advance. In this way, Fannie Mae assures the mortgage lenders of
27 available funds.

Fannie Mae operates exclusively in the secondary mortgage market by providing two important functions:

1. Fannie Mae purchases FHA, VA, and conventional mortgages from lenders and holds the mortgages in its portfolio. For loans to be sold to Fannie Mae, they must be written in accordance with Fannie Mae's requirements (guidelines). For example, the mortgages must be Fannie Mae-Freddie Mac approved uniform mortgage instruments. Fannie Mae also sets limitations on the size and kind of loans they will buy. Loans that meet Fannie Mae guidelines are referred to as **conforming loans**.

2. Fannie Mae issues mortgage-backed securities (MBSs) in exchange for pools of mortgages from lenders. MBSs are securities guaranteed by pools of mortgages. By pledging large blocks of mortgage loans as collateral, Fannie Mae can issue mortgage-backed securities that are sold to a broad market of investors. The MBSs provide the lenders with a more liquid asset to hold or sell. Fannie Mae MBSs are highly liquid investments and are traded through securities dealers and brokers.

Freddie Mac. Freddie Mac (Federal Home Loan Mortgage Corporation, or FHLMC) was created by Congress in 1970. Freddie Mac is also now a government-owned enterprise. Freddie Mac is subject to regulatory oversight by both the Secretary of HUD and the Secretary of the Treasury Department. Freddie Mac provides a secondary market for loans originated by SAs. Most of the loans Freddie Mac handles are conventional loans. Savings associations can sell qualified mortgages to Freddie Mac for cash, then use the cash to make new mortgage loans.

Ginnie Mae. Ginnie Mae (Government National Mortgage Association or GNMA) has always been a government-owned and financed corporation. Ginnie Mae is part of the Department of Housing and Urban Development (HUD).

Ginnie Mae's mission statement is "To expand affordable housing in America by linking global capital markets to the nation's markets." Ginnie Mae accomplishes its mission by guaranteeing securities that are backed by pools of mortgages. The mortgages in the MBSs are mostly FHA and VA mortgages (and some mortgages originated through the Rural Housing Service). Ginnie Mae's guaranty allows mortgage lenders to obtain a better price for their mortgage loans in the secondary market.

Ginnie Mae serves as a *guarantor* of mortgage-backed securities (MBSs). Ginnie Mae MBSs are often referred to as Ginnie Mae pass-through securities. A *pass-through security* refers to the payments of the underlying mortgages (principal and interest) that are passed through to the investor. MBSs are created by pooling a group of similar (same interest rate and maturity date) mortgages. The mortgage pool is then used as collateral for the issuance of the MBS. Ginnie Mae does not issue, sell, or buy mortgage-backed securities, or purchase mortgage loans. Ginnie Mae-approved private institutions issue the MBSs. In exchange for a fee, Ginnie Mae guarantees the timely payment of principal and interest to the investors. Ginnie Mae mortgage-backed securities are the only MBSs to carry the *full faith and credit guarantee* of the U.S. government.

WEB LINK

To learn more about the secondary mortgage market, visit these Web sites:

Fannie Mae: **www.fanniemae.com**

Ginnie Mae: **www.ginniemae.gov**

Freddie Mac: **www.freddiemac.com**

LENDER CHARGES

Mortgage Discounting

Years ago, a system of discounting was created to make FHA and VA mortgage loans competitive with conventional mortgage loans. Lenders are allowed to charge **discount points** for FHA and VA loans. This extra, upfront fee increased the real yield, or annual percentage rate (APR), to the lender. With the discount points added on, the interest rate earned on FHA and VA loans then approximated the yield from conventional loans made at higher interest rates. Subsequently, FHA and VA mortgage interest rates have been allowed to float freely in the mortgage market, thereby following prevailing market rates in the same way as conventional mortgage rates. Today, lenders charge points as an interest rate adjustment factor. In other words, an up-front charge is imposed to increase the actual yield from a mortgage without showing an increase in the interest rate on the mortgage.

Discount points are based on the loan amount, not on the selling price. When calculating the actual borrower's cost in dollars added by the discount points, each point is equal to 1 percent of the loan amount (1 point equals 1 percent).

> **EXAMPLE:** On a $40,000 loan for which the lender is charging 6 points, find the dollar cost of the points. Take 6 percent of $40,000.

$$\$40,000 \times .06 = \$2,400$$

When the lender receives the $2,400, only $37,600 is needed from the lender's funds to make up the total $40,000 that is loaned to the borrower. However, the lender will receive interest based on the entire $40,000 during the full term of the loan. The real yield to a lender includes not only this interest but also the $2,400 paid as a mortgage discount.

Practice Problem 1

A borrower is getting a loan for $225,000 at 5 percent interest, and the lender is charging 2 points. What will the borrower pay for the points?

(The solution to the Practice Problem is at the end of this chapter on page 301.)

Lenders use computers or prepared tables to determine the number of discount points that must be paid. However, as a general rule of thumb, each discount point paid to the lender will increase the lender's yield (return) by approximately ⅛ of 1 percent (.00125). In using the rule of thumb, for each discount point charged by a lender, add ⅛ percent to the stated (contract) mortgage interest rate to estimate the lender's yield (and cost to the borrower) from the loan.

> **EXAMPLE:** A buyer wants to obtain a mortgage of $180,000, and a lender agrees to make the loan at 5½ percent interest plus 6 points up front. What will the approximate yield be to the lender?
>
> To the quoted interest rate of 5½ percent, add ⅛ of 1 percent for each point, or ⁶⁄₈, which reduces to ¾:

$$\tfrac{1}{8} \times 6 = \tfrac{6}{8} = \tfrac{3}{4}$$

Add the ¾ to the mortgage interest rate of 5½ percent, and the lender's real yield is approximately 6¼ percent on the money actually loaned:

$$¾\% + 5½\% = 6¼\% \text{ approximate yield}$$

Frequently, a lender will state that mortgages are "going at" 96 or 94, for example. This is a different way of quoting discount points. It means that the lender is willing to lend only 96 percent or 94 percent of the face value of a mortgage loan. If the seller, the buyer, or a third party is willing to come up with the remaining 4 percent or 6 percent, then the lender will make the loan. It means exactly the same thing as quoting 4 points or 6 points. Regardless of the method used, the real interest rate earned for the lender will be increased approximately ⅛ of 1 percent for each point charged up front.

Discounting interacts with the previously discussed FRS control of the money supply. Suppose the national economy is booming and inflation threatens to get out of hand. The Fed decides to decrease the amount of money in circulation as an inflation control effort. Securities are sold to absorb part of the money in circulation, and the discount rate at which banks are permitted to borrow is raised. The money supply drops and interest rates rise. Mortgage rates go to 6½ percent, but some lenders raise their interest rates to only 5½ percent. To offset the apparent 1 percent loss in yield, most lenders would make their mortgage loans at 5½ percent plus an 8-point discount. This means the lender actually would be lending only 92 percent of the amount needed; the additional 8 percent of the loan would come from the person(s) attempting to obtain the loan.

Practice Problem 2

A borrower is getting a loan for $225,000 at 5 percent interest, and the lender is charging 2 points. What is the approximate return to the lender?

(The solution to the Practice Problem is at the end of this chapter on page 301.)

Other Sources of Income to Lenders

In addition to discount points charged for making a loan, lenders frequently levy other charges. Normally, a lender charges the borrower a *loan origination fee*. Amounts vary, but the fee is typically 1 percent or 2 percent of the loan amount. The lender usually charges the borrower all expenses encountered in obtaining credit reports, preparing loan documents, and processing a mortgage loan application.

Another source of income to lenders takes the form of *commitment fees*. The developer of a subdivision, a shopping center, or an apartment complex often needs to obtain a written commitment from a financial institution certifying that permanent financing will be provided when the project is completed. The point here is that the financial institution is willing to become the permanent lender in the future, but first the developer must find a lender of construction money. With the written commitment of the future permanent lender, called a *takeout commitment*, it is much easier to find a construction money lender. When the project is built, the permanent lender advances the amount committed, and the developer repays the construction lender. Most lenders that issue a takeout commitment charge a nonrefundable fee for making the commitment. The borrower, in this case the developer, is required to pay the fee at the time the commitment is made.

Some lenders "service" (handle the loan payment collecting and record keeping) the mortgages they originate and then sell them to large financial institutions or other secondary market institutions. This is an additional source of income for such lenders. Today, *servicing fees* typically range from ⅜ to ¾ of 1 percent of the unpaid balance of loans serviced. Fannie Mae and Freddie Mac have traditionally paid a ⅜ of 1 percent (.375) servicing fee, and Ginnie Mae has normally paid .44 percent to lenders that continue to service mortgages sold to those agencies. If a lender averages a ⅜ of 1 percent service fee for several blocks of mortgages totaling $100 million, it earns a gross income of $375,000 per year from that source alone. As might be expected, lenders are generally eager to retain servicing of any loans sold to institutional investors.

Practice Problem 1 Solution

(Practice Problem 1 is located on page 299.)

$225,000 × .02 (2 percent) = $4,500 cost of points

Practice Problem 2 Solution

(Practice Problem 2 is located on page 300.)

⅜ + 5% = 5⅜% reduced to 5¼% return to the lender.

SUMMARY OF IMPORTANT POINTS

- The Federal Reserve has three economic tools to influence money supply: (1) the purchase and sale of U.S. Treasury securities known as open-market operations, (2) increasing or decreasing the discount rate charged to member banks that borrow money from the Fed, and (3) increasing or decreasing the amount of funds that institutions must hold in reserve against deposit liabilities known as the reserve requirement.

- The Federal Deposit Insurance Corporation (FDIC) insures deposits in banks and savings associations. Deposit accounts are insured to $250,000 per depositor in each bank or thrift that the FDIC insures.

- A *primary market* is the market where securities or goods are created. The primary mortgage market consists of lenders that originate new mortgage loans for borrowers.

- Mortgage loan originators (MLOs) do not make loans. They are middlemen (intermediaries) between borrowers and lenders. MLOs take loan information from a prospective borrower and "shop" for a lender offering the best rates and terms. Once a successful match is made and the loan is approved, the MLO earns a fee.

- A mortgage lender (mortgage company) originates loans and packages them to investors. Mortgage lenders may use their own money or money borrowed from other lenders. Mortgage lenders also service loans.

- *Intermediation* is the process of consumers depositing funds into savings accounts at financial institutions. Lenders serve as intermediaries using borrowers' savings to provide funds to others for investment and borrowing.

- *Disintermediation* occurs when savers withdraw funds from intermediary financial institutions, bypassing them to invest elsewhere, thereby reducing the amount of funds available to the financial institutions.

- A *secondary mortgage market* is an investor market that buys and sells existing mortgages. Secondary market participants include Fannie Mae, Freddie Mac, and Ginnie Mae. Fannie Mae deals in conventional, FHA, and VA loans. Conforming loans are loans that meet Fannie Mae guidelines. Fannie Mae provides a secondary market for loans originated by commercial banks. Freddie Mac is primarily a secondary market for conventional loans. It provides a secondary market for loans originated by savings associations. Ginnie Mae is a government agency under HUD. Ginnie Mae approved mortgage-backed securities (MBSs) are the only ones that carry the full faith and credit guarantee of the federal government. The mortgages in these MBSs are mainly FHA and VA mortgages.

- *Discount points* are an upfront charge paid at closing to increase the lender's yield. One discount point is equal to one percent of the loan amount. Each discount point increases the yield by about ⅛ of one percent.

R E V I E W   Q U E S T I O N S

1. A couple purchased their home for $125,000. They financed the purchase with an 80 percent conventional loan. The mortgagee charged 2½ points. Calculate the actual cost in dollars of the points.
   - a. $1,600
   - b. $2,000
   - c. $2,500
   - d. $3,125

2. Which individual must be state-licensed as a mortgage loan originator?
   - a. Employee who processes loans for First National Bank of Orlando
   - b. Employee of Bank of Florida who works as a bank teller
   - c. Employee who works as a loan originator for a mortgage brokerage company that is not federally regulated
   - d. Employee who works as a loan originator for First USA Credit Union

3. When the Fed increases the reserve requirement
   - a. the supply of money increases.
   - b. the supply of money decreases.
   - c. inflation usually immediately follows.
   - d. mortgage interest rates decline immediately.

4. A commercial bank sold a group of 2,000 mortgages directly to Fannie Mae. This is an example of
   - a. primary market activity.
   - b. secondary market activity.
   - c. loan correspondence.
   - d. intermediation.

5. Fannie Mae currently buys and sells
   - a. FHA mortgages.
   - b. VA mortgages.
   - c. conventional mortgages.
   - d. all three types of mortgages.

6. Which statement does NOT apply to Fannie Mae?
   - a. Loans that meet Fannie Mae guidelines are called conforming loans.
   - b. Fannie Mae provides master commitments for large real estate projects.
   - c. Fannie Mae created the first secondary market for mortgage loans.
   - d. Fannie Mae deals directly with homebuyers.

7. Which entity originates loans and typically services the loans but is NOT a financial intermediary?
   - a. Mortgage company
   - b. Mortgage loan originator
   - c. Life insurance company
   - d. Fannie Mae

8. When the Fed purchases securities, what happens?
   a. The supply of money in circulation is reduced.
   b. Interest rates begin to rise.
   c. Loanable funds are released into circulation.
   d. Pressure is applied to increase the discount rate.

9. How does the Federal Reserve compete with other financial institutions for consumer funds?
   a. Sells mortgages on the secondary market
   b. Increases the federal deficit
   c. Regulates thrift institutions
   d. Sells treasury bonds

10. The market where mortgage loans are created, supplying funds to finance real estate purchases directly to borrowers, is referred to as the
    a. primary market.
    b. secondary market.
    c. capital market.
    d. real estate market.

11. The primary purpose of Fannie Mae is to
    a. reduce and stabilize mortgage interest rates.
    b. purchase real estate loans to replenish the supply of mortgage money.
    c. make loans to low-income families.
    d. do all of the above.

12. The demand for residential real estate mortgage money is influenced by
    a. household formations.
    b. shifts in geographic preference for housing.
    c. household income.
    d. any of the above.

13. The Office of Thrift Supervision regulates
    a. savings associations.
    b. commercial banks.
    c. credit unions.
    d. the Rural Housing Service.

14. The discount rate is
    a. 1 percent of the loan amount.
    b. a rate adjustment factor used to increase the lender's yield on a loan.
    c. the interest rate charged member banks for borrowing funds from the Federal Reserve Bank.
    d. approximately ⅛ of 1 percent for each point charged.

15. The primary purpose of Freddie Mac is to
    a. purchase conventional loans from savings associations.
    b. regulate savings associations.
    c. insure mortgage loans.
    d. regulate conventional mortgage loan interest rates.

16. When investors bypass thrift institutions for direct investment elsewhere, the process is called
    a. loan correspondence.
    b. intermediation.
    c. disintermediation.
    d. capital-deficit area support.

17. Sources of income to lenders include all of the following EXCEPT
    a. the discount rate.
    b. origination fees.
    c. servicing fees.
    d. commitment fees.

18. The rule of thumb used to convert discount points to an annual percentage rate is that each discount point increases the yield by approximately
    a. ⅛ of 1 percent.
    b. ¼ of 1 percent.
    c. ½ of 1 percent.
    d. 1 percent.

19. A lender charged 7 percent plus 3 points. What is the approximate yield on this loan?
    a. 7¼ percent
    b. 7⅜ percent
    c. 7½ percent
    d. 7¾ percent

20. The most commonly used method of controlling the national money supply is for the Fed to
    a. engage in open-market activities.
    b. change the discount rate.
    c. change the reserve requirement.
    d. issue new currency.

14

COMPUTATIONS AND TITLE CLOSING

1 ## OVERVIEW

2 Real estate brokers and sales associates must understand closing statements and should be
3 capable of computing the various simple arithmetic problems to be solved in arriving at
4 the figures entered on the closing statements provided to the contracting parties. Many
5 adults have had little or no occasion to work with fractions, decimals, percentages, and
6 the like for years. The first section of this chapter assumes little or no prior knowledge
7 about these subjects and their application.

8 After completing this chapter, the student should be able to:

9 ■ compute a sale commission;

10 ■ calculate the percent of profit or loss, given the original cost of the investment,
11 the sale price, and the dollar amount of profit or loss;

12 ■ amortize a level-payment plan mortgage when given the principal amount, the
13 interest rate, and the monthly payment amount;

14 ■ prorate the buyer's and seller's expenses using either the 30-day-month method
15 or the 365-day method;

16 ■ calculate the dollar amount of transfer taxes on deeds, mortgages, and notes; and

17 ■ allocate taxes and fees to the proper parties and compute individual costs.

18 ## KEY TERMS

arrears	level-payment plan	profit
credit	pre-closing inspection	prorate
debit	principal	

COMPUTATIONS

Fractions, Decimals, and Percentages

When a whole unit or number is divided into equal parts, each of the parts is a fraction (and a percent) of the whole unit. For example, if a city block is divided into two equal parts, each of the parts is ½ (or 50 percent) of a city block.

Parts of a fraction. When dealing with fractions, the number *below* the line is called the *denominator*. The denominator always indicates the total equal parts in a whole unit. In the example of the city block above, each part was ½. The lower number indicates the total number of equal parts (two) in the entire city block. If the fraction ¼ had been used, the denominator would have indicated that the city block was divided into four equal parts.

The number in a fraction that appears *above* the line dividing the numbers is called the *numerator*. The numerator indicates how many of the equal parts of the whole unit are being counted. For example, in the fraction ¾, the top number indicates three equal parts are being counted, and the bottom number shows a total of four equal parts, so you are talking about all but one equal part of something (all but ¼).

Changing fractions to decimals. The line separating the numerator from the denominator means division (the top number is divided by the bottom number). If you are dividing a fraction using a calculator, enter the numerator first, then the division key, followed by the denominator. For example, in the fraction ½: press 1, followed by the division key, then press 2. Press the equal sign key (=) and the answer displayed is 0.5. You have now converted (changed) a fraction (½) into a decimal number (.5).

Changing decimals to percentages. To change a decimal to a percent, move the decimal point two places to the right and add the percent sign (%). (This is the same as multiplying the decimal number by 100.) If only one decimal number is involved, add a zero to the right of the number.

> **E X A M P L E S :** .5 = .50 = 50%
>
> 1.5 = 1.50 = 150%

Changing percentages to decimals. To change any percentage to an equivalent decimal, simply place a decimal point two places to the left of the number and drop the percent sign. (This is the same as dividing the percentage figure by 100.)

> **E X A M P L E S :** 34% = .34
> 150% = 1.50

If only one number is involved, add a zero to the left to permit moving the decimal point two places to the left.

> **E X A M P L E :** You want to calculate in dollars the 7½ percent commission on a house sale price.

Convert the fractional part of the decimal number:

> ½% = 1 ÷ 2 = .5

Next, convert the entire commission percentage to a decimal number.

> 7½% = 7.5% = .075

Thus, the decimal number .075 is used to calculate the sale commission.

F I G U R E 14.1 ■ Decimal Place Values

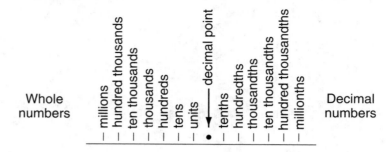

1 Assume the sale price is $130,000. Calculate the commission.

2 $$\$130,000 \times .075 = \$9,750$$

3 **Decimal place values.** A great deal of the basic arithmetic required to compute routine real
4 estate problems involves decimal numbers. This review of decimals will be more meaning-
5 ful if you refresh your memory on the decimal system of place values and the importance
6 of the decimal point in separating whole numbers from fractional parts of whole numbers.
7 The chart of decimal place values shown as Figure 14.1 should be memorized if you do not
8 already know the place values. Notice that the *whole numbers* are to the *left* of the decimal
9 point. The *decimal fractions* of a whole number are to the *right* of the decimal point.

10 **Working with decimals.** To divide a whole number by a decimal, for example, 41,500
11 divided by 1.85: first, enter 41500 into your calculator, press the division key, then enter
12 1.85. When you press the equal sign key, the answer will appear in the display, as demon-
13 strated in the calculator method on the following page.

Sale Commissions

15 If the broker has been hired to list and sell the property for the seller, the seller is normally
16 responsible for paying the commission. If a buyer brokerage agreement exists, the buyer
17 may be responsible for the commission. The commission is agreed to in the listing con-
18 tract and/or the buyer brokerage agreement.

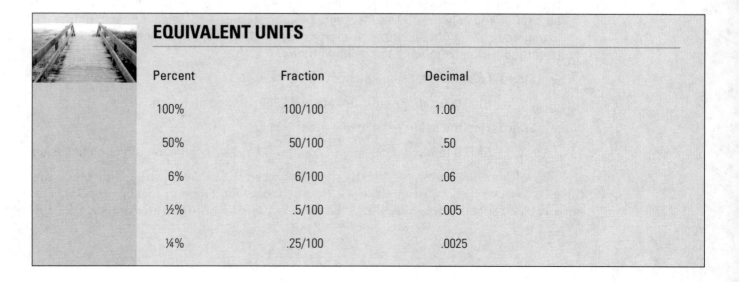

EQUIVALENT UNITS

Percent	Fraction	Decimal
100%	100/100	1.00
50%	50/100	.50
6%	6/100	.06
½%	.5/100	.005
¼%	.25/100	.0025

Calculator Method:

$41{,}500 \div 1.85 =$

Press	Display
4 then 1 then 5 then 0 then 0	41500
÷ (the division key)	41500
1 then . then 8 then 5	1.85
= (equals sign)	22432.432

Let's begin with an example of a commission calculation. In this example the property is listed and sold by the same sales associate.

EXAMPLE: Suppose a broker's listing agreement specifies that 6½ percent commission is to be paid on the sale price. A sales associate for the firm lists and sells the property and is to receive 55 percent of the 6½ percent sale commission. How much will the sales associate earn after selling the property for $62,000?

Step 1: Find the total sale commission.

$62,000 sale price × .065 rate = $4,030 total commission

Step 2: Find the sales associate's commission.

$4,030 total commission × .55 split = $2,216.50 sales associate's commission

More frequently, a property is listed with one brokerage company and sold by another brokerage through the MLS system. Members of the MLS (who are also members of their local REALTOR® association) make an offer of cooperation ("co-broke" or "co-op") when they place their listings in the MLS. When another brokerage sells the listing, it will receive the portion of the total commission that was specified by the listing brokerage.

EXAMPLE: A broker's listing agreement specifies a 7 percent commission is to be paid on the sale price. The MLS agreement specifies a 50-50 split between the listing and selling offices. If the property sells for $100,000, how much commission is earned by the listing and the selling offices?

Step 1: Find the total sale commission.

$100,000 sale price × .07 rate = $7,000 total commission

Step 2: Find the selling and listing office's split.

$7,000 total commission × .50 split = $3,500 selling/listing office commission

The selling commission is typically shared between the broker of the selling office and the sales associate who works for the selling office that found a buyer for the property. The same is true for the listing office and the sales associate who listed the property for the brokerage company. The percentage that sales associates earn is negotiated between each sales associate and the employing broker taking into consideration the sales associate's experience and production.

> **E X A M P L E :** Let's assume that the sales associate receives 60 percent of the total selling office commission. How much commission did the sales associate earn on the previous example? How much did the broker receive for the same transaction?
>
> **Step 1:** Calculate the sales associate's split of the selling office commission.
>
> > $3,500 selling office commission × .60 split = $2,100 sales associate's commission
>
> **Step 2:** Calculate the broker's split of the selling office commission.
>
> > $3,500 selling office commission × .40 split = $1,400 broker's commission

Today 100 percent commission arrangements are popular. A sales associate in a 100 percent commission office receives the entire commission due the respective brokerage office. Instead of splitting the commission with the broker, the sales associate pays a specified share of office expenses plus a fixed monthly fee.

A broker who lists a property with higher-than-normal value may agree to a graduated sale commission. This provides an incentive for the broker to get the seller the very best price possible.

> **E X A M P L E :** The broker has a listing with a seller, and the parties agree to a graduated commission structure. The commission is 5 percent on the first $200,000 of sale price, 6½ percent on the next $100,000 of sale price, and 8 percent on the amount over $300,000. What is the total commission if the property sells for $325,000?
>
> **Step 1:** Calculate the first increment of commission.
>
> > $200,000 × .05 rate = $10,000 first increment commission
>
> **Step 2:** Calculate the second increment of commission.
>
> > $100,000 × .065 rate = $6,500 second increment commission
>
> **Step 3:** Calculate the third increment of commission.
>
> > $25,000 remaining portion of sale price × .08 rate = $2,000 third increment commission
>
> **Step 4:** Add the commission increments to determine the total commission.
>
> > $10,000 + $6,500 + $2,000 = $18,500 total commission

Percentage Applied to Selling Price, Cost, and Profit

Profit is how much you make over and above your cost. It may be expressed as an amount or as a percent of your cost.

> **Profit Formula:**
>
> Amount made on sale ÷ Total cost = Percent profit
>
> **Loss Formula:**
>
> Amount lost on sale ÷ Total cost = Percent loss

EXAMPLE: A lot cost $8,000 and sold for $10,000, yielding a $2,000 profit. What is the percentage of profit?

$$\$2,000 \div \$8,000 = .25 \text{ or } 25\% \text{ profit}$$

EXAMPLE: A lot cost $10,000 and sold for $8,000, resulting in a $2,000 loss. What is the percentage of loss?

$$\$2,000 \div \$10,000 = .20 \text{ or } 20\% \text{ loss}$$

EXAMPLE: A lot sold for $6,000, making a 25 percent profit. What was the cost of the lot?

$$100\% \text{ cost} + 25\% \text{ profit} = \$6,000$$
$$125\% = \$6,000 \text{ selling price}$$
$$\$6,000 \text{ selling price} \div 1.25 = \$4,800 \text{ cost}$$

EXAMPLE: A lot sold for $10,000, representing a 20 percent loss. What was the cost of the lot?

$$100\% - 20\% = \$10,000$$
$$80\% = \$10,000$$
$$\$10,000 \text{ selling price} \div .80 = \$12,500 \text{ cost}$$

Mortgage Amortization

Mortgages used to purchase residential property usually call for regular, equal payments that include both interest payments and payments on the unpaid balance of the debt (**principal**). This type of mortgage is called the **level-payment plan** or, more commonly, a fixed-rate *amortized mortgage*, because the regular, periodic payments remain the same. However, the amount of the payment that goes for interest gradually decreases, and the amount assigned to amortizing the debt (principal) gradually increases.

To calculate how much money is to be regarded as interest and how much is to be paid on the principal, three facts are needed:

1. The outstanding amount of the debt (principal)
2. The rate of interest
3. The amount of the payment per period (usually monthly)

Interest rates for mortgages are expressed as annual interest rates. Thus, a $60,000 mortgage at 10 percent simply means that the interest rate is 10 percent per year. To find the monthly interest actually paid, first determine what 10 percent of $60,000 will amount to for the entire year. Dividing this amount by 12 (the number of months) gives the amount of interest for one month. When the principal amount changes, the calculation

AMORTIZING A MORTGAGE

Step 1:   Principal balance × Annual interest ÷ 12 = First month's interest

Step 2:   Monthly mortgage payment − First month's interest = Payment on principal

Step 3:   Beginning principal balance − Principal payment = New principal balance

must be done over again, based on the new principal balance. The new balance must be treated as if it were to be applied to the entire 12 months.

E X A M P L E : A home for sale has a mortgage of $30,000 at 8 percent interest. Your buyer wants to know how much of the $220.13 monthly payment will go for interest and how much for principal during the first three months.

Step 1: $30,000 unpaid balance × .08 rate = $2,400 interest ÷ 12 months
= $200 first month's interest

Step 2: $220.13 monthly payment − $200 interest = $20.13 payment on principal

So the first month's interest was $200, and the principal reduction in month one was $20.13.

But the buyer wanted to know about the first three months. So take credit for the $20.13 paid on the principal by subtracting that amount from the $30,000.

Step 3: $30,000 − $20.13 principal paid first month = 29,979.87 new principal balance

Now repeat the steps above to determine the answers for the second and third months, beginning with:

Step 4: $29,979.87 new principal balance × .08 rate = $2,398.3896 ÷ 12 months
= $199.87 interest

Repeat steps 2 and 3 to determine the unpaid balance remaining after payment of the second month's principal. Begin with this new principal balance at the end of the second month and repeat steps 1, 2, and 3 to find the amount paid for interest and principal during the third month. Thus, the answer to your buyer's question is:

First month: Principal = $20.13; Interest = $200.00
Second month: Principal = $20.26; Interest = $199.87
Third month: Principal = $20.40; Interest = $199.73

If the amount paid for interest from the first month's mortgage payment is given along with the interest rate and loan-to-value (LTV) ratio, the sale price of the property for which payment was made can be found.

E X A M P L E : The interest portion of the first month's mortgage payment is $770, the interest rate is 10.5 percent, and the LTV ratio is 80 percent. Calculate the sale price of the property.

$770 × 12 months = $9,240 interest per annum
$9,240 ÷ 10.5% = $9,240 ÷ .105 = $88,000 mortgage amount
$88,000 ÷ 80% or .80 LTV ratio = $110,000 sale price

PRE-CLOSING STEPS

All real property sales or exchanges eventually conclude with a transfer of title. This occurs at the *title closing,* when the seller delivers title to the buyer in exchange for the purchase price. The date and place of title closing should be specified in the sale contract. There are usually several things to accomplish between the time of signing the sale contract and the title closing. For example some of the pre-closing steps include the following:

1. *Mortgage application.* If the buyers intend to finance the purchase, they will complete a mortgage application. The contract for sale and purchase specifies the number of days within which the buyer must submit a loan application. The real estate contract typically contains a financing contingency clause that provides for cancellation of the sale contract and return of the buyer's escrow deposit if the buyer is unable to secure financing.

2. *Survey.* The buyer should have the property surveyed to determine the exact location and size of the property and to make sure there are no encroachments, such as a neighbor's fence across the property line.

3. *Appraisal.* Because the property is pledged as collateral for the mortgage loan, the lender will order an appraisal to determine whether the property's value is sufficient to ensure recovery of the loan amount should a default occur. In a cash transaction the buyer may want the property appraised to verify the property's value for tax or investment reasons.

4. *Title insurance.* A search is made of the public records for condition of the title and existing liens, judgments, or other encumbrances. The seller is responsible for removing any encumbrances on the title. Typically there is a simultaneous issue of the owner's policy and the lender's policy. (See also Condition of Title, Chapter 9.)

5. *Closing documents.* The closing agent, usually a title company or an attorney, prepares the closing documents.

6. *Property inspections.* It is advisable for the buyer to have a certified property inspector check the condition of the structure and mechanical parts. An inspection for wood destroying organisms (WDO) including termites and wood rot is also recommended and may be required by the lender.

7. *Pre-closing inspection.* Before the closing date, the buyer makes a final **pre-closing inspection** of the property (a *walk-through*) with the sales associate. The purpose of the pre-closing inspection is to verify that repairs have been completed and that the property has been left in good condition.

CLOSING STATEMENTS

475.25(1)(d), F.S.

The Florida real estate license law places the responsibility on the broker for an accurate accounting and delivery of all monies, deposits, drafts, mortgages, conveyances, leases, or other documents entrusted to the broker by the parties to the transaction. The customary method of discharging this responsibility is to have the closing agent prepare and deliver complete and accurate closing statements to the buyer and the seller, plus a summary that reconciles all of the debits (charges) and credits involved.

CLOSING STATEMENT ITEMS

It is important for sales associates to have an understanding of the closing documents. Sales associates should be able to explain and verify the entries on the closing documents. The day prior to the closing, licensees should examine and review the HUD statement with the buyer or seller to correct any errors and explain each entry. Sales associates usually attend the title closing with the buyer and seller in case their knowledge of the transaction is needed to assist with answering any questions or concerns that may arise.

Prorated Expenses

To **prorate** means to divide various charges and credits between buyer and seller. Every sale contract should specify a date and time for prorating items. It is customary when transferring title to have all prorated items determined as of the midnight before the date of closing. This means that (1) the buyer is charged for property taxes on the day of closing; (2) the buyer is charged for interest on an assumed mortgage on the day of closing; and (3) the buyer is credited for any rental income earned on the day of closing. In some areas or by negotiation, it is possible that the day of closing will be charged to the seller. In that case, the seller is charged with an additional day.

Prorating is usually required when rents are paid in advance, property taxes are paid in **arrears** (that is, at the end of the period for which payment is due), and interest on mortgages is paid in arrears (the usual practice). Therefore, all items that are to become a **credit** (reimbursed) or **debit** (charged) to either buyer or seller are *prorated* because the item applies to both the buyer and the seller.

To prorate costs, two methods may be used: 30-day-month method and 365-day method. The 365-day method is preferred and more accurate.

30-day-month method. This method is also called the *statutory month* method. In this method, all months are considered to have 30 days (even February). To use a *statutory year* (360-day year), determine the yearly cost of the item, next divide by 12 to find the cost per month, then divide by 30 to find the cost per day.

> **E X A M P L E :** Closing date is July 23. The annual property taxes are $3,400 and have not yet been paid. How much is the seller to pay the buyer for the days the seller owned the property? (The day of closing is charged to the buyer.)

$$\$3,400 \div 12 \text{ months} = \$283.333 \text{ per month}$$
$$\$283.333 \div 30 \text{ days} = \$9.444 \text{ per day}$$

The seller will credit the buyer for 6 months (January through June) and 22 days in July:

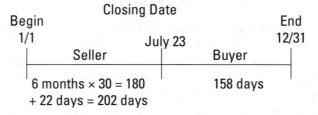

$283.333 per month × 6 months = $1,699.998

22 days in July × $9.444 per day = $207.768

$1,699.998 + $207.768 = $1,907.766 rounded to $1,907.77

(debit seller; credit buyer)

365-day method. This method calculates the proration using the actual number of days in the proration period. To use this method, first divide 365 into the annual cost of the item to find the exact daily rate, then multiply the number of days involved by the daily rate.

EXAMPLE: Using the same information as in the previous example:

$3,400 ÷ 365 days = $9.315 per day

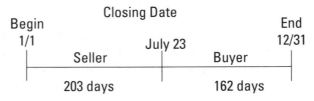

The exact number of days owed by the seller are:

January 31 + February 28 + March 31 + April 30 + May 31 + June 30 + July 22 = 203 days

$9.315 per day × 203 days = $1,890.945, rounded to $1,890.95

(debit seller; credit buyer)

Prepaid rent. Normally, any rental income collected in advance belongs to the new owner as of the date of closing; therefore, the unused portion of advance rent belongs to the buyer. The total rent amount should be divided by the number of days involved in the rental period and allocated on a daily basis.

EXAMPLE: Assume that a property rents for $1,250 per month. The closing date is on the 21st day of a 30-day month. The method of prorating is as follows:

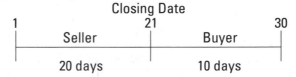

$1,250 ÷ 30 days = $41.6666667 per day

$41.6666667 × 10 days = $416.67 (due buyer)

$1,250 − $416.67 = $833.33 (earned by seller)

On the closing statements, *credit* the buyer with $416.67 and *debit* the seller $416.67. The $833.33 was earned by the seller before closing and is not mentioned on either closing statement.

County and/or city property taxes. (See also chapter 18.) Property taxes are paid in arrears (at the end of the tax year). The seller will have had possession and use of the property for some portion of the year, unless the transfer of title is effective on January 1. To apportion the property taxes fairly, they are prorated on the basis of a 365-day year. The total tax assessment is divided by the number of days in a year to determine the tax cost per day. Then the property tax chargeable to the seller, on departure from the property, is calculated by multiplying the tax cost per day by the number of calendar days before title is conveyed. The resulting amount is entered on the seller's closing statement as a debit. It is also shown on the buyer's closing statement, but as a credit. The buyer's share of property taxes is not reflected on either closing statement because the tax bill is not settled at closing. The buyer pays the entire year's property tax after November 1, which includes the amount paid to the buyer by the seller.

> **E X A M P L E :** The closing date is April 15. The annual property taxes are $2,283.44. (The day of closing is charged to the buyer.) The proration is calculated as follows:

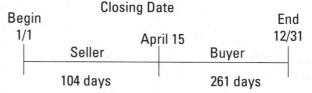

Closing Date

Begin
1/1

April 15

End
12/31

Seller

Buyer

104 days

261 days

> The seller will owe the buyer for three months (January through March) and 14 days in April: January 31 + February 28 + March 31 + April 14 = 104 days

$$\$2,283.44 \div 365 = \$6.256 \text{ per day}$$
$$\$6.256 \times 104 \text{ days} = \$650.624, \text{ rounded to } \$650.62$$
$$(\text{debit seller; credit buyer})$$

If the closing occurs late in the year (November or December) and the seller has already paid the taxes for the year, the buyer will reimburse the seller for the remainder of the year. Thus the buyer will be charged a debit for taxes for the days remaining in the year, but the seller will receive a credit for the same amount.

Mortgage interest on assumed mortgages. Because mortgage payments are normally made each month, one month is usually the period used to calculate interest owed. Interest is paid at the end of the period (in arrears or, in other words, after having the use of the money). It is therefore charged to the seller up to the date of closing. This item is prorated in the same manner as property taxes. Interest is figured from the last date for which interest was paid. The exact number of days in each month is used, and interest is figured on a daily basis.

> Mortgage balance × Annual interest rate ÷ 12 months = Month's interest
> Month's interest ÷ Days in month = Daily rate
> Daily rate × Days interest is owed = Prorated interest

State Transfer Taxes

Just as buying most things in life involves paying state taxes, so real estate transactions involve the payment of state taxes at closing. Florida has three types of state taxes that apply to deeds, notes, and mortgages associated with the transfer of ownership of real property.

State documentary stamp tax on deeds. First, the state requires the payment of a tax on deeds and other conveyances. This state *documentary stamp tax on deeds* is assessed at the rate of $.70 ($.60 in Miami-Dade County) for each $100 of the full purchase price (or any fraction of $100). It makes no difference whether the purchase is all cash, all financed, or some combination of cash and financing because this tax is based on purchase price. This is a one-time tax and is *not* paid annually.

201.02, F.S.

> **E X A M P L E :** If a home sells for $71,200, the documentary stamp tax on the deed will be:

$$\$71,200 \div \$100 = 712 \text{ taxable increments}$$
$$712 \times \$.70 = \$498.40 \text{ documentary stamp tax on deed}$$

If any portion or fraction of $100 remains after dividing the purchase price by $100, a full $.70 tax is charged for the fractional part. For example, if the purchase price in the above example had been $71,250, the state "doc stamp" tax on the deed would be increased by $.70 (to $499.10) because the purchase price was $50 more than an even increment of $100.

The law requires that the seller deliver a recordable deed. Because a deed may not be recorded until the stamp tax has been paid, the seller is obligated to either deliver a deed having paid the stamp tax or negotiate with the buyer to assume the obligation. If the buyer does not agree to pay the stamp tax on the deed, the tax remains the seller's responsibility.

On normal sales or exchanges, the doc stamp tax is shown as a *debit* to the seller on the closing statement. (See Seller's Closing Statement, Figure 14.4 on page 326, for an example.)

State documentary stamp tax on notes. Second, the state requires the payment of a documentary stamp tax on notes for all executed notes and written promises to pay money. The tax rate is $.35 per $100, or fraction thereof, on the face value of the promissory note. This tax is paid on all new and assumed mortgage notes. In an assumption, the borrower pays the tax on the unpaid balance of the note. This tax is due when the note is executed.

> **E X A M P L E :** A home sold for $90,000. The buyer paid $10,000 cash, assumed a recorded mortgage of $55,000, and created a new second mortgage in the amount of $25,000. The documentary stamp tax on notes resulting from this transaction would be:
>
> $55,000 ÷ $100 = 550 taxable increments × $.35 = $192.50 (assumed)
> $25,000 ÷ $100 = 250 taxable increments × $.35 = $87.50 (new note)
> $192.50 + $87.50 = $280 (tax on notes)

The tax on notes is shown as a *debit* to the buyer on the closing statement.

State intangible tax on new mortgages. Third, the state requires the payment of an *intangible tax* before a mortgage is recorded, regardless of when the mortgage was executed (signed). An assumed mortgage recorded previously should not be taxed again, provided the deed or assumption document clearly identifies the county record book and page number where the assumed mortgage was recorded. (Some counties, however, are taxing an already recorded mortgage a second time.) The tax rate for this state intangible tax on new mortgages is two mills ($.002 or two-tenths of one cent) per dollar of debt. Because this is supposed to be a one-time tax, examples throughout this book will not show a second intangible tax on previously recorded mortgages. When a mortgage is recorded, it signifies that the intangible tax has been paid to the clerk of the circuit court or to the county comptroller.

> **E X A M P L E :** Use the figures from the previous example. The intangible tax on the new second mortgage would be:
>
> $25,000 × $.002 = $50 tax on second mortgage

The law expects this tax to be paid by the mortgage owner (lender). However, the mortgagor (buyer-borrower) usually agrees to pay the tax to obtain the loan. Thus, this tax is normally shown as a *debit* to the buyer on the closing statement.

201.08, F.S.

199.133, F.S.

> **T O   R E M E M B E R :   S T A T E   T R A N S F E R   T A X E S**
>
> | S | Stamps on deed | $.70 per $100 |
> |---|---|---|
> | N | Note, stamps on notes | $.35 per $100 |
> | I | Intangible on new mortgages | $.002 per $1 of debt |

E X A M P L E : To illustrate the application of all three of the previous state taxes, suppose a property sold for $79,950. The buyer paid $15,000 cash down and arranged for a $64,950 mortgage loan. The state taxes on this transaction would be:

Deed: $79,950 ÷ $100 = 799.5, rounded up to 800 taxable increments
          800 taxable increments × $.70 = $560 tax on deed

Mortgage: $64,950 × $.002 = $129.90 tax on mortgage

Note: $64,950 ÷ $100 = 649.5, rounded up to 650 taxable increments
          650 taxable increments × $.35 = $227.50 tax on note

Total: $560 + $129.90 + $227.50 = $917.40

Other Charges

In addition to the various mandatory taxes, several other charges are associated with a title closing.

Preparation of documents. The customary method of handling charges for preparation of documents is to require the person who must sign the document to pay the fee for its preparation. Therefore, the seller (grantor) pays for preparation of the deed, and the buyer (mortgagor) pays for preparation of the mortgage and note. The charges that result are shown as a *debit* on the closing statement of the person required to pay. Such fees shown on the seller's statement are not shown on the buyer's statement, and vice versa.

Recording fees. Several of the legal instruments signed at closing should be recorded to give constructive notice of new ownership and debt status. Charges associated with recording these documents are usually paid by the person who wants a particular document recorded. For example, the grantee (buyer) wants the deed recorded and pays for this service, even though the grantor (seller) paid for its preparation by an attorney. The various recording fees are shown on only the appropriate party's closing statement.

Broker's commission. Normally, the person who employed the broker is required to pay the commission. The broker's commission is listed on the employer's closing statement as a charge but, of course, does not appear on the other party's closing statement.

Abstract continuation or title insurance. Legally, the seller of a property is not required to provide an abstract of title, title insurance, or an opinion of title without contractually agreeing to do so. However, title insurances are used to protect the lender and the buyer. Lenders usually will not accept abstracts of title but do demand up-to-date *lender's title insurance*. A buyer's representative should recommend that the buyer's interest be protected by obtaining *owner's title insurance*. Actually, these charges, like many, are negotiable regarding who pays what. (See also chapter 9.)

KEY CONCEPTS REGARDING CLOSING STATEMENTS

- Total purchase price is entered as a credit to the seller and as a debit to the buyer.

- A (new) purchase-money mortgage and assumed mortgage loans are entered as a credit to the buyer and as a debit to the seller (entries are made for both the buyer and the seller because both are involved in the financing).

- New mortgages from nonseller sources (loans from banks) and the binder deposit (earnest money or good faith deposit) are entered as a credit to the buyer (there is no entry on the seller's side).

- Unpaid property taxes appear as a credit to the buyer and as a debit to the seller (prorations have the same dollar amount in each entry).

- When a prorated item is paid in arrears (such as interest on an assumed loan and property taxes for closings between January 1 and October 31), "seller days" are used to calculate the proration.

- When the prorated item is paid in advance (prepaid rent), "buyer days" are used to calculate the proration.

- Expenses are always a debit to the party paying for the expense (single entries).

Liens. The seller is responsible for all existing liens of record. (See also chapter 9.) At the time of closing, the seller must have satisfied all liens, or the buyer and the seller must reach an agreement about disposition of the liens.

Cash Reconciliation Statement

When the closing statements for both the seller and the buyer have been completed, the broker or closing agent is prepared to summarize the entire transaction in a cash reconciliation statement (Figure 14.7, Broker's Closing Statements Cash Reconciliation Statement, on page 329). This clearly and accurately shows the amount of money deposited by the buyer plus the balance due from the buyer at closing. It also shows the expenses chargeable to each party, including the brokerage commission and the amount due the seller at closing. Normally, the person making out the closing statements will have prepared the checks to be disbursed. After the seller and the buyer examine the closing statements, they should be instructed to sign all copies.

Rules of Thumb

The following five general rules of thumb may help the person who is not familiar with the proper preparation of these instruments:

1. On the *seller's closing statement*, the only entries in the *credit* column are the overall purchase price and any prepaid items.

2. On the *buyer's closing statement*, the total purchase price plus all charges and expenses are entered in the *debit* column. The resulting total is the key to the buyer's statement. When all entries in the credit column are totaled, the *difference* between total credits and total debits is the amount the buyer must pay at closing.

3. All entries from the total purchase price down through the prorated items, with the exception of (1) the buyer's deposit, (2) an existing mortgage being paid off, or (3) a new mortgage obtained from a financial institution, are "double entry" items and appear on the closing statements of both parties. *Double entry items* are shown as a credit to one party and as a debit to the other.

4. All *expenses* (attorney's fees, documentary stamps, etc.) are shown on the statement of the appropriate person and are *not* double entry items.

5. All items are subject to negotiation between contracting parties. In the absence of a negotiated agreement, Florida statutes normally regard the parties responsible as follows:

- Items *credited to seller*
    - Total purchase price
    - Other prepaid items
- Items *debited to seller*
    - Mortgages assumed or paid off
    - Mortgages newly created—held by seller (purchase-money mortgage)
    - Prorated taxes, interest, advance rent
    - Security deposits
    - State documentary stamps on the deed
    - Broker's commission
    - Title insurance (owner's policy)
    - Preparation of deed
    - Seller's attorney's fees (if any)
- Items *credited to buyer*
    - Earnest money deposit
    - Mortgages assumed
    - Mortgages newly created
    - Prorated property taxes (city and county)
    - Prorated unpaid interest
    - Prorated advance rent
    - Security deposits
- Items *debited to buyer*
    - Purchase price
    - Title insurance (mortgagee's policy)
    - State intangible tax on the mortgage
    - State documentary stamp tax on the note
    - Recording of the deed
    - Recording of the mortgage
    - Buyer's attorney's fees (if any)
    - Preparation of mortgage and note

A copy of the author's "Work Organizer for Closing Statements" and completed samples of the work organizer, closing statements, and a reconciliation statement appear in Figure 14.2 through Figure 14.7, at the end of this chapter. The author has chosen these formats with the knowledge that many versions exist.

SUMMARY OF IMPORTANT POINTS

- *Profit* is the amount you make over and above cost.

- A *level-payment plan* is a mortgage in which the monthly payments are a fixed amount, but the amount applied to principal increases each month and the amount applied to interest decreases each month.

- Three facts that are needed to calculate a mortgage amortization are (1) principal balance, (2) interest rate, and (3) monthly principal and interest payment.

- A *pre-closing inspection* is a final walk-through with the sales associate to verify that repairs have been completed and that the property is left in good condition.

- To *prorate* means to divide various debits (charges) and credits between buyer and seller. A *proration* is a shared expense between the buyer and seller.

- Property taxes are paid in arrears and are prorated using a 365-day year (actual number of days in the proration period). Unpaid property taxes appear as a credit to the buyer and as a debit to the seller. Prorations have the same dollar amount in each entry. Seller days are used to prorate items paid in arrears.

- Rental income collected in advance belongs to the new owner as of the date of closing. Advance rental income appears as a credit to the buyer and a debit to the seller. Buyer days are used to prorate items paid in advance.

- Documentary stamp tax on deeds is paid on the full purchase price. The rate is $0.70 per $100, or fraction thereof.

- Documentary stamp tax on notes is paid on the amount of debt. This tax is paid on all new and assumed mortgage notes. The rate is $0.35 per $100, or fraction thereof.

- Intangible tax is paid on new debt. The rate is $.002 per $1 of new debt.

SAMPLE CLOSING STATEMENT PROBLEM

Mr. and Mrs. Bravo have decided to buy Lot 14, Block C, Page 641, public records of Foam County, Florida. They have given the sellers, Mr. and Mrs. Sierra, a $7,500 binder deposit, to be held in escrow until the transaction is closed. The contract stipulates that the Bravos will pay a total purchase price of $72,500. They are to assume a recorded VA first mortgage of $59,760, give the Sierras a new $3,640 second mortgage, and pay all taxes related to the financing arrangements.

The closing is scheduled for July 1, 20AA, with the proration time midnight, June 30, 20AA. The sale contract specifies that the property taxes will be prorated on the basis of the previous year's taxes, which were $429 for the city and $684 for the county. The sellers have agreed to pay the broker a 7 percent commission and to pay half of the title insurance costs of $600. Title will be conveyed with a general warranty deed, and the Sierras will pay the taxes on the deed.

Attorneys for the sellers and buyers have agreed to charge $150 for preparation of the deed and $175 for the mortgage instrument and note. Recording fees will be $10 for the mortgage and $6 for the deed. The various applicable items from above are computed and listed on the "Work Organizer for Closing Statements" in Figure 14.3. In Figure 14.4 through Figure 14.6, the Seller's, Buyer's, and Composite Closing Statements are also completed to show their use. The 365-day method of prorating is used throughout.

Note:

Do not try to make the Seller's and Buyer's Closing Statement balance with each other—they are not supposed to balance. The closing statements for both seller and buyer are supposed to balance with the Cash Reconciliation Statement in Figure 14.7.

F I G U R E 14.2 ■ Work Organizer for Closing Statements

DEBIT BUYER	CREDIT BUYER	DEBIT SELLER	CREDIT SELLER
Purchase Price _____	Deposit _____	1st Mortgage _____	Purchase Price _____
	1st Mortgage _____	2nd Mortgage _____	
1st Mortgage _____	2nd Mortgage _____	Doc. Stamps	1st Mortgage _____
2nd Mortgage _____	Prorated:	on Deed _____	
Doc. Stamps	City Taxes _____	Title Ins. _____	2nd Mortgage _____
1st Note _____	County Taxes _____	Intang. Tax	
2nd Note _____	Rent _____	on Mortgage _____	TOTAL
Intang. Tax	Mort. Int. _____	Prorated:	CREDITS _____
on Mortgage _____	Security	City Taxes _____	···
Atty. Fees _____	Deposit _____	County Taxes _____	
Record Deed _____		Rent _____	Total Credits _____
Record Mort. _____	TOTAL	Mort. Int. _____	
Title Ins. _____	CREDITS _____	Atty. Fees _____	less
	···	Commission _____	Total Debits _____
TOTAL BUYER		Miscellaneous _____	
DEBITS _____	Total Debits _____		BALANCE
		TOTAL SELLER	DUE SELLER _____
	less	DEBITS _____	
	Total Credits _____		
	DUE FROM		
	BUYER _____		

CITY TAXES	COUNTY TAXES	PREPAID RENT
Annual taxes ÷ 365 = daily cost	Annual taxes ÷ 365 = daily cost	Amount/period ÷ days in period
Daily cost × no. of days used by seller	Daily cost × no. of days used by seller	Days owned by Buyer _____
(DEBIT SELLER; CREDIT BUYER)	(DEBIT SELLER; CREDIT BUYER)	× amount per day _____
		(DEBIT SELLER; CREDIT BUYER)

1ST MORTGAGE INTEREST	2ND MORTGAGE INTEREST	COMMISSION
Balance due × % = annual interest	Balance due × % = annual interest	Purchase price
Annual interest ÷ 365 = daily interest	Annual interest ÷ 365 = daily interest	_____ × _____ %
Daily interest × no. of days used	Daily interest × no. of days used	

DOC. STAMPS DEED	DOC. STAMPS NOTE	INTANG. TAX MORT.	MISCELLANEOUS
$.70 × $100 on purchase price	$.35 × $100 on note face value	.002 (mills) × $1 mortgage face value	

Note: The debiting/crediting of all items may vary and is negotiable.

F I G U R E 14.3 ■ **Work Organizer for Closing Statements (Completed)**

DEBIT BUYER		CREDIT BUYER		DEBIT SELLER		CREDIT SELLER	
Purchase Price	$72,500.00	Deposit	$ 7,500.00	1st Mortgage	$59,760.00	Purchase Price	$72,500.00
		1st Mortgage	59,760.00	2nd Mortgage	3,640.00		
1st Mortgage	_____	2nd Mortgage	3,640.00	Doc. Stamps		1st Mortgage	_____
2nd Mortgage	_____	Prorated:		on Deed	507.50		
Doc. Stamps		City Taxes	212.74	Title Ins.	300.00	2nd Mortgage	_____
1st Note	209.30	County Taxes	339.19	Intang. Tax			
2nd Note	12.95	Rent	_____	on Mortgage	_____	TOTAL	
Intang. Tax		Mort. Int.	_____	Prorated:		CREDITS	$72,500.00
on Mortgage	7.28	Security		City Taxes	212.74		
Atty. Fees	175.00	Deposit	_____	County Taxes	339.19	Total Credits	$72,500.00
Record Deed	6.00			Rent	_____		
Record Mort.	10.00	TOTAL		Mort. Int.	_____	less	
Title Ins.	300.00	CREDITS	$71,451.93	Atty. Fees	150.00	Total Debits	69,984.43
				Commission	5,075.00		
TOTAL BUYER		Total Debits	$73,220.53	Miscellaneous	_____	BALANCE	
DEBITS	$73,220.53					DUE SELLER	$ 2,515.57
		less		TOTAL SELLER			
		Total Credits	71,451.93	DEBITS	$69,984.43		
		DUE FROM					
		BUYER	$ 1,768.60				

CITY TAXES	COUNTY TAXES	PREPAID RENT
Annual taxes ÷ 365 = daily cost	Annual taxes ÷ 365 = daily cost	Amount / period ÷ days in period
Daily cost × no. of days used by seller	Daily cost × no. of days used by seller	Days owned by Buyer _____
(DEBIT SELLER; CREDIT BUYER)	(DEBIT SELLER; CREDIT BUYER)	× amount per day _____
		(DEBIT SELLER; CREDIT BUYER)
$429 ÷ 365 days =	$684 ÷ 365 days =	
$1.17534 × 181 days =	$1.8797 × 181 days =	
$212.73654	$339.18857	
Round to: $212.74	Round to: $339.19	

1ST MORTGAGE INTEREST	2ND MORTGAGE INTEREST	COMMISSION
Balance due × % = annual interest	Balance due × % = annual interest	Purchase price
Annual interest ÷ 365 = daily interest	Annual interest ÷ 365 = daily interest	$72,500 × 7 %
Daily interest × no. of days used	Daily interest × no. of days used	
		$5,075.00

DOC. STAMPS DEED	DOC. STAMPS NOTE	INTANG. TAX MORT.	MISCELLANEOUS
$.70 × $100 on	$.35 × $100 on	.002 (mills) × $1	
purchase price	note face value	mortgage face value	
$72,500.00 ÷ $100 =	$59,760 ÷ $100 = 597.6	$3,640 × .002 = $7.28	
725 × $.70 = $507.50	598 × $.35 = $209.30		
	$3,640 ÷ $100 = 36.4		
	37 × $.35 = $12.95		

Note: The debiting/crediting of all items may vary and is negotiable.

FIGURE 14.4 ■ **Seller's Closing Statement**

Date of Closing: July 1, 20AA	Debits	Credits
Purchase Price		$72,500.00
First Mortgage—Balance	$59,760.00	
Second Mortgage	3,640.00	
Binder Deposit		
Prorations:		
Rent		
Interest: 1st Mortgage		
2nd Mortgage		
Taxes: City	212.74	
County	339.19	
Expenses:		
Title Insurance	300.00	
Attorney's Fee	150.00	
Documentary Stamps		
Mortgage-Note		
State on Deed	507.50	
Intangible Tax–Mortgage		
Recording:		
Mortgage		
Deed		
Brokerage Commission	5,075.00	
Miscellaneous		
Total Debits and Credits	$69,984.43	$72,500.00
Balance Due Seller	2,515.57	
Grand Total	$72,500.00	$72,500.00

FIGURE 14.5 ■ **Buyer's Closing Statement**

Date of Closing: July 1, 20AA	Debits	Credits
Purchase Price	$72,500.00	
First Mortgage—Balance		$59,760.00
Second Mortgage		3,640.00
Binder Deposit		7,500.00
Prorations:		
Rent		
Interest: 1st Mortgage		
2nd Mortgage		
Taxes: City		212.74
County		339.19
Expenses:		
Title Insurance	300.00	
Attorney's Fee	175.00	
Documentary Stamps		
Mortgage-Note	209.30	
2nd Mortgage-Note	12.95	
Intangible Tax–Mortgage	7.28	
Recording:		
Mortgage	10.00	
Deed	6.00	
Brokerage Commission		
Miscellaneous		
Total Debits and Credits	$73,220.53	$71,451.93
Balance Due Seller		1,768.60
Grand Total	$73,220.53	$73,220.53

FIGURE 14.6 ■ **Composite Closing Statement**

Seller's Statement			Buyer's Statement	
Debit	**Credit**	**Item**	**Debit**	**Credit**
		Purchase Terms		
	72,500.00	Total Purchase Price	72,500.00	
		Binder Deposit		7,500.00
59,760.00		First Mortgage Balance		59,760.00
3,640.00		Second Mortgage		3,640.00
		Prorations & Prepayments		
		Rent		
		Interest: First Mortgage		
		Interest: Second Mortgage		
		Prepaid: First Mortgage		
		Prepaid: Second Mortgage		
212.74		Taxes: City		212.74
339.19		Taxes: County		339.19
		Other:		
		Expenses		
300.00		Title Insurance	300.00	
150.00		Attorney's Fees	175.00	
5,075.00		Brokerage Commission		
		Documentary Stamps		
507.50		State Tax on Deed		
		State Tax on Note (209.30 + 12.95)	222.25	
		State Intangible Tax on Mortgage	7.28	
		Recording		
		Mortgage	10.00	
		Deed	6.00	
		Miscellaneous_____		
		Totals		
69,984.43	72,500.00		73,220.53	71,451.93
To		**Balance Due**	**From**	
2,515.57				1,768.60
		Grand Totals		
72,500.00	72,500.00		73,220.53	73,220.53

FIGURE 14.7 ■ Broker's Closing Statements Cash Reconciliation Statement

	Receipts	Disbursements
Deposit	$7,500.00	$
Check from buyer at closing	1,768.60	
Brokerage commission		5,075.00
Check to seller at closing		2,515.57
Seller's expense (less brokerage commission)		957.50
Buyer's expense		720.53
Totals	$9,268.60	$9,268.60

Note: It is assumed that the broker handles the recording of all instruments and the payment of the title insurance, attorney's fees, stamps, recording fees, etc.

R E V I E W   Q U E S T I O N S

(This quiz is intended not only to help you review this chapter but also to assist with the various computations in other chapters.)

1. Change the percentages to decimals.
   a. 39½%   _____
   b.   2%   _____
   c.   75%   _____
   d. 145%   _____

2. Change the percentages to fractions.
   a. 50%   _____
   b. 20%   _____
   c. 25%   _____
   d. 40%   _____

3. Change the fractions to decimals.
   a. ⅛   _____
   b. ⅗   _____
   c. 1/16   _____
   d. 1/20   _____

4. Divide the numbers below.
   a. 44,032 ÷ 1.72   _____
   b.   493.8 ÷ .60   _____
   c. 18,768 ÷ 25.5   _____
   d.   7,735 ÷ .17   _____

5. A senior sales associate receives 55 percent of all sale commissions earned. His broker has listed a motel for $1,450,000. The listing contract specifies a 6½ percent sale commission for the first $600,000 of selling price, 7 percent for the next $800,000, and 8 percent commission on all of the actual sale price exceeding $1.4 million. What will the sales associate's commission be if he sells the motel for the listed sale price?
   a. $44,550
   b. $54,450
   c. $95,000
   d. $99,000

6. The interest portion of a man's first monthly payment on a 30-year, 12 percent mortgage amounts to $550. If the loan-to-value ratio for the man's house is 80 percent, how much did he pay for the house?
   a. $44,000
   b. $55,000
   c. $68,750
   d. $110,000

7. You bought a house in Citrus, Florida, for $130,000. You gave a deposit of $19,480, assumed a recorded mortgage of $90,520, and signed a new second mortgage and note for $20,000. What are the total state taxes due as a result of this transfer of property?
   a. $1,337.10
   b. $1,336.82
   c. $1,336.75
   d. $1,297.50

8. A broker lists a property, a 7 percent commission is agreed to, and the listing is placed in the MLS. The sale commission is to be split as follows: 45 percent to the listing broker and 55 percent to the selling broker. A sales associate who works for a cooperating broker sells the property for $160,000. The sales associate's agreement with her employer calls for a 60 percent share to her of all commissions she brings to the company. How much is due the sales associate?
   a. $2,016
   b. $2,464
   c. $3,024
   d. $3,696

9. A woman owned ⅜ of a property. She was paid $45,000 as her share of the proceeds from the sale of the property. What was the total selling price of the property?
   a. $120,000
   b. $90,000
   c. $72,000
   d. $61,875

10. To get a mortgage loan of $31,000, a buyer has agreed to pay all state tax costs incurred by creation of the new mortgage. What is the total cost?
    a. $62.00
    b. $108.50
    c. $170.50
    d. $217.00

11. You have a VA mortgage of $48,000 at 9 percent with a 30-year term. The monthly principal and interest payment is $386.21. What portion of the second month's payment will apply to amortization of the mortgage?
    a. $26.21
    b. $26.41
    c. $359.80
    d. $360.00

12. In the mortgage cited in question 11, what would the monthly payments amount to if your property taxes were $840 and your annual insurance $570?
    a. $433.71
    b. $456.21
    c. $474.71
    d. $503.71

13. A woman bought three 200-foot lots on a lake for $500 per front foot each. She then subdivided these lots into six lakefront lots, which she then sold for $62,500 each. What was her percentage of profit on the sales?
   a.   20 percent
   b.   25 percent
   c.   75 percent
   d.   80 percent

14. A warehouse measures 720 feet by 500 feet and rents for $118,000 a month. What is the rent per square foot per month?
   a. $0.25
   b. $0.33
   c. $3.05
   d. $3.96

15. A man incurred a 20 percent loss when he sold a 10-acre parcel (Tract A) for $100,000. He also owns a 25-acre parcel (Tract B) for which he paid $200,000. How much must he sell Tract B for if he wishes not only to recover his loss from Tract A but also to realize a 20 percent profit on his investment in Tract B?
   a. $260,000
   b. $265,000
   c. $270,000
   d. $275,000

16. A couple is purchasing an apartment building. Each of the five apartments rents for $815 per month. The closing is scheduled for September 16, and the rents were collected on September 1. What is the rent proration for this transaction and to whom will the amount be credited? (Day of closing belongs to the buyer.)
   a. $407.50, credit buyer
   b. $1,901.67, credit seller
   c. $2,037.50, credit buyer
   d. $2,173.33, credit seller

17. A 28.5-acre parcel of land in Orange County sells for $4,100 per acre. What is the documentary stamp tax on the deed?
   a. $818.30
   b. $817.95
   c. $642.85
   d. $409.15

18. How is the buyer's binder deposit entered on the closing statement?
   a.   Debit to buyer only
   b.   Credit to buyer only
   c.   Debit to seller and credit to buyer
   d.   Debit to buyer and credit to seller

19. How is the purchase price entered on the closing statement?
    a. Credit to seller only
    b. Credit to buyer only
    c. Credit to seller and debit to buyer
    d. Credit to buyer and debit to seller

20. How are unpaid property taxes entered on the closing statement?
    a. Debit to seller only
    b. Debit to buyer only
    c. Credit to seller and debit to buyer
    d. Credit to buyer and debit to seller

Note to Readers

If you need to learn and practice more than this chapter offers about math as it relates specifically to real estate, obtain the self-study guide written by the author, *Real Estate Math: What You Need to Know*, 6th edition. It covers the basics of arithmetic and provides practice opportunities in all areas. An answer key and step-by-step solutions are included.

15

ESTIMATING REAL PROPERTY VALUE

OVERVIEW

To *appraise* real property means to estimate its value. Appraising is considered to be an art, not a science, because although the appraisal process involves mathematical calculations, appraisers also use their own judgment when appraising real property. There are many reasons for appraising real property. Local communities hire appraisers to estimate the value of property for assessment of property taxes (chapter 18) and to determine the amount of compensation in a condemnation proceeding that involves a taking by eminent domain. However, the most prevalent use of an appraisal is to establish the value of real property that will be used as collateral to finance its purchase.

This chapter will help students learn the basics of appraising required to develop and complete a comparative market analysis. It also will help to improve licensees' communications with professional appraisers.

After completing this chapter, the student should be able to:

- differentiate among the terms *price, cost,* and *value;*
- describe the four characteristics of value;
- differentiate among the three approaches to estimating the value of real property;
- describe the three types of depreciation and recognize examples of each type; and
- apply the steps in the various approaches to estimating value when given an appropriate scenario.

KEY TERMS

assemblage	highest and best use	progression
cost-depreciation approach	income capitalization	reconciliation
curable	approach	regression
depreciation	incurable	replacement cost
economic life	investment value	reproduction cost
effective age	market value	sales comparison approach
effective gross income (EGI)	net operating income (NOI)	situs
federally related transaction	overimprovement	subject property
gross income multiplier (GIM)	plottage	transaction value
gross rent multiplier (GRM)	potential gross income (PGI)	vacancy and collection losses
	principle of substitution	

APPRAISAL REGULATION

475.612, F.S.
475.25, F.S.

Active real estate licensees are allowed to perform a comparative market analysis (CMA) for the purpose of obtaining a listing or a prospective sale. Chapter 475, F.S., prohibits referring to a CMA as an appraisal. Real estate licensees who do conduct actual real estate appraisals are required to comply with the *Uniform Standards of Professional Appraisal Practice (USPAP)* and may charge a fee for performing an appraisal. Florida statute empowers the Commission to discipline brokers and sales associates who violate any of the standards or any other provisions of *USPAP*. (CMAs and broker price opinions are exempted.) The Uniform Standards are developed by the Appraisal Standards Board (ASB) of the Appraisal Foundation.

The Appraiser Qualifications Board (AQB) of the Appraisal Foundation establishes the qualifications for state-certified and licensed appraisers. Qualification criteria include appraiser education and appraisal experience. Appraisal reports involving a federally related transaction must be prepared by a state-certified or licensed appraiser, *unless* the real estate licensee *also* holds such certification or license. A **federally related transaction** is any *real estate-related financial transaction* that a federal financial institutions regulatory agency (FFIRA) has either contracted for, or regulates, and requires the services of an appraiser. There are five federal financial regulatory agencies—the Office of Thrift Supervision (OTS), the Office of the Comptroller of the Currency (OCC), the Board of Governors of the Federal Reserve System (FRB), the Federal Deposit Insurance Corporation (FDIC), and the National Credit Union Administration (NCUA).

A real estate-related financial transaction is any transaction involving the:

1. sale, lease, purchase, investment in or exchange of real property, including interests in property, or the financing thereof; or
2. refinancing of real property or interests in real property; or
3. use of real property or interests in property as security for a loan or investment, including mortgage-backed securities.

Appraisals for real estate-related financial transactions require a state-certified or licensed appraiser unless the transaction has been specifically exempted from the requirement. A state-certified or licensed appraiser is *not* required if the transaction value is $250,000 or less (exceptions to this are discussed below). What is meant by the **transaction value** varies from assignment to assignment depending on the intended use of the appraisal. In most appraisal assignments, the transaction value is the loan amount. However, the transaction value in some situations is the market value. For example, if the assignment involves estimating the value of a foreclosed property, the transaction value is the market value. The specified value threshold of $250,000 is referred to as the *de minimis* requirement.

Real estate licensees are cautioned that just because a transaction is not a federally related transaction, it does not mean that real estate licensees are allowed to provide the appraisal services. FHA and VA transactions and appraisals for loans sold to Fannie Mae and Freddie Mac are not federally related transactions. However, Fannie Mae, Freddie Mac, HUD, and the VA require the use of state-certified or licensed appraisers for all loans with which these entities are involved, regardless of the amount of the loan.

It is a violation of federal law for a financial institution to seek, obtain, or compensate a person who the institution knows is not a state-certified or licensed appraiser for the performance of an appraisal associated with a federally related transaction. Furthermore, it is a violation of federal law for the Federal National Mortgage Association (Fannie Mae) or the Federal Home Loan Mortgage Corporation (Freddie Mac) to knowingly contract for the performance of an appraisal by a person who is not a state-certified or licensed appraiser in connection with a real estate-related financial transaction.

All appraisals for federally related transactions must be in writing and conform to the *Uniform Standards of Professional Appraisal Practice (USPAP)*. Florida law goes further to require that *all appraisals* (regardless of whether the assignment involves a federally related transaction) performed by real estate appraisers *and* real estate licensees conform to *USPAP*. Real estate licensees must be familiar with the standards. Failure to do so may subject the licensee to discipline. Florida real estate licensees who are not state-certified or licensed appraisers and who perform appraisal assignments are cautioned to get a statement in writing from the client that the appraisal is not associated with a federally related transaction and does not require the services of a state-certified or licensed appraiser before accepting the assignment.

WEB LINK

To order a current edition of the standards or to learn more about appraiser qualifications and licensure, visit www.appraisalfoundation.org.

TYPES OF VALUE

There are many types of value that an appraiser may be hired to estimate. The type of value of most importance to real estate licensees is *market value*. (Market value will be discussed separately later in this chapter.) A brief explanation of the different types of value follows:

- *Assessed value* is the value used as a basis for property taxation. (For additional information concerning assessed value, refer to chapter 18.)

- *Insurance value* is an estimate of the amount of money required to replace a structure in the event of some catastrophic event such as fire.

- *Investment value* is the price an investor would pay, given the investor's own financing requirements and income tax situation. This type of value is personal to a particular investor. (For a more detailed discussion of investment value, refer to chapter 17.)

- *Liquidation value* is the value associated with a rapid sale. The amount of dollars a property should bring in a foreclosure sale is an example of liquidation value. (See also chapter 17.)

- *Going-concern value* is the value of an income-producing property or business characterized by a significant operating history. (See also chapter 17.)

- *Salvage value* is the estimated amount for which improvements can be sold at the end of a structure's useful life.

MARKET VALUE

While the word *value* has many different meanings, *market value* is of special interest to the field of real estate. The concept of market value is based on a theory that in any open market there will be a number of buyers and sellers. (See also chapter 19.) If hundreds of transactions are concluded over time, some parties will pay too much and some will pay too little. But the vast majority of value decisions by both buyers and sellers will tend to converge in a fairly small range. That range represents a range of market value, whether the market is dealing in houses, oranges, cattle, or something else.

Many definitions of market value, or *fair market value* as it is sometimes called, can be found. Fannie Mae and Freddie Mac require the following definition of **market value** for the appraisal of all real property securing a mortgage intended for sale to either of those major secondary market agencies:

The most probable price that a property should bring in a competitive and open market under all conditions requisite to a fair sale, the buyer and seller each acting prudently and knowledgeably, and assuming the price is not affected by undue stimulus.

Inherent in this definition are the assumptions that:

- market value applies to a specified date and may change with the passage of time;

- the seller is able to convey a marketable title;

- buyer and seller are typically motivated, and neither buyer nor seller is under any compulsion or pressure to conclude a sale;

- both buyer and seller are well informed and acting in their individual best interest;

- the property is exposed for sale on the open market for a reasonable time;

- the terms of sale are in cash in U.S. dollars or in terms of financial arrangements comparable thereto; and

- the price represents a normal consideration for the property, unaffected by creative financing or sales concessions such as seller contributions or buydowns.

Cost, Price, Value

Cost is the total expenditure required to bring a new improvement into existence plus the cost of the land. A contractor will install site improvements (water, sewer, and so forth); acquire the necessary permits; secure the services of architects, engineers, surveyors, and other professionals; construct the building; landscape the site; market the property; and so forth. The total of these expenditures is referred to as *cost*. A contractor wants the *cost* to be less than the *price* a consumer will pay—and the consumer will pay more than the cost only if the consumer perceives the property's *value* to exceed its cost.

Price refers to the amount of money actually paid in a transaction. Price and value are not necessarily equal. For example, you might purchase a computer for $2,000. Its *price* was $2,000. However, it may actually command less (or more) than $2,000 in exchange if you were to attempt to sell the computer. In real estate, *price* is synonymous with *contract price*.

The *value* of a good or service is determined by its ability to command other goods or services in exchange. *Exchange value* is the monetary value of a good or service to many buyers and sellers at a particular time. Today, we regard exchange value as market value, which is the consensus of the interactions of many buyers and sellers in the marketplace.

TO REMEMBER: COST, PRICE, AND VALUE

Cost	**C**reate	Expenditure to **create** an improvement including, materials, labor, and land
Price	**P**aid	The amount **paid** in a particular transaction; the contract price
Value	**VV**orth	The **worth** of something between many market participants

---

Practice Problem 1

A property owner purchases a lot and builds a house for $270,000. Ten years later, the owner is thinking of selling the property and has the house appraised. The property is appraised at $525,000. Shortly before putting the property on the market, the owner's son graduates from law school and lands a position with a firm in the owner's hometown. The property owner decides to help the young lawyer and his family by selling the house to them for $450,000. What is the cost, price, and value of this home?

(The solution to the Practice Problem is at the end of this chapter on page 359.)

Overimprovement

An owner can pour more money into a property than good judgment would indicate might be recaptured (recovered). For example, if the owner of a $60,000 house in a neighborhood of similar homes adds a $12,000 swimming pool or a $20,000 addition to the house, it is doubtful that the total cost will be recaptured when the property is sold. The two additions are examples of overimprovement. An **overimprovement** occurs when an owner invests more money in a structure than the owner can reasonably expect to recapture.

A $125,000 home in a neighborhood of $50,000 homes is an overimprovement. Buyers who can afford to pay $125,000 for a home usually will prefer a $125,000 neighborhood. So the owner of the overimprovement finds few buyers willing to pay a price approaching the owner's investment. This is another example of the point that cost and value are not the same thing. Value, then, is a concept. Price equals value only when the requirements of a so-called perfect market are approximated. Some "perfect market" requirements are: many buyers and sellers; a homogeneous product; and easy and free entry into the marketplace. Due to the unique nature of each parcel of real estate, this market can only *approach* perfection.

Characteristics of Value

To have value, goods or services must possess the following four traits:

1. Demand
2. Utility
3. Scarcity
4. Transferability

Demand. In economics, demand is more than a desire or need. Demand also implies the available means to obtain what is desired. Herders and farmers who live in the infertile desert lands of the world desire more fertile land, but they do not have the financial means to obtain other, more expensive land. Consequently, their desires alone have no economic impact on the supply of fertile land or on the price of such lands. In contrast, look at Miami Beach, where people desire to live and have the money to acquire the use of part of the available supply. The need or desire combined with the economic means creates effective demand.

Utility. To be valuable, goods or services must be useful and able to fill a need. In real estate, *utility* means the ability to provide useful services and benefits to an owner or tenant.

Scarcity. The availability of goods or services in relation to present or anticipated demand determines *scarcity*. If the supply exceeds demand, there is less scarcity, and the value falls. If demand exceeds supply, more scarcity is created, and value increases. When the number of available apartment units in an area exceeds the demand, apartment units are relatively less scarce, and landlords must reduce rents or lose tenants. When apartments are scarce, landlords can increase rents, and the excess demand will fill any resulting vacancies.

Transferability. The legal ability to convey title and possession of goods creates *transferability*. This is an unusually important factor in real estate. Value cannot exist in cases where rights in land and the use of property cannot be transferred.

TO REMEMBER: CHARACTERISTICS OF VALUE

D Demand
U Utility
S Scarcity
T Transferability

Highest and Best Use

The most profitable use to which a property may be put is the property's **highest and best use**. The use must be:

- legally permissible (zoning);
- physically possible (soil type, the site's shape, size, and slope); and
- financially feasible (income generated considering cost of improvements).

The use that meets these three criteria and that yields the highest return to the land is the highest and best use. An appraiser estimates two types of highest and best use, which are described below.

Highest and best use of the land as though vacant. The appraiser considers what use would yield the highest return to the land taking into account the three elements previously described. If the site has existing improvements, the appraiser considers what type of use should be placed on the site if it were vacant.

Suppose there are three potential buyers for a site. The first buyer estimates the property would yield a net income of $6,000 per year. The second buyer estimates the property would yield $8,000 net income, and the third buyer estimates the property would yield $12,000 per year after expenses. Which buyer will offer the most for the land? Assume a 10 percent rate of return in all three cases. The use that produces $12,000 annually has a value of $120,000 compared to just $60,000 for the use that produces $6,000 annual net income. Therefore, assuming the three criteria (listed above) have been met, the use that yields a net income of $12,000 per year is the site's highest and best use.

Highest and best use of a property as improved. The highest and best use of a property as improved pertains to how a property that already has improvements erected on the site can be best used. The appraiser considers whether (1) the improvements should continue as is, or (2) the improvements should be renovated, or (3) the improvements should be demolished and new improvements erected. In each case, the appraiser must consider the costs associated with each option in relation to the income that will be generated. Therefore, highest and best use is a *residual* concept because it is concerned with value after expenses are deducted. Demolishing an existing structure and building a new apartment building may generate more monthly income compared with remodeling the existing apartment building. But the highest and best use will be the use with the greatest yield after deducting the costs of renovation or the costs of demolition and new construction.

APPROACHES TO ESTIMATING REAL PROPERTY VALUE

There are three approaches to estimating real property value:

1. Sales comparison approach (comparable sales method)

2. Cost-depreciation approach (cost method)

3. Income capitalization approach (income method)

In theory, an appraisal report uses all three approaches to estimate the value of a property. If all the information used to prepare the appraisal were perfectly accurate, and if the real estate appraiser's judgment were perfect, the results from each of the three approaches theoretically would be the same.

However, in this imperfect world, most appraisers must *reconcile* the usually different results from each of the three approaches. In a **reconciliation** any detected errors are corrected and, based on the type of property, a degree of priority (importance) is assigned to each approach used. For example, if the property being appraised is a vacant lot in an established neighborhood, the sales comparison approach is considered the most relevant approach to value. If the property is an income-producing property, the income capitalization approach usually is given the most importance. The cost-depreciation approach usually is most significant for newly constructed homes and for cross-checking the other

1 two approaches. It is also considered to be the most relevant approach when appraising
2 special-purpose properties such as hospitals, schools, or government buildings.

3   The **principle of substitution** is the basis for all three approaches to market value. It
4 means that a prudent buyer or investor will pay no more for a property than the cost of
5 acquiring, through purchase or construction, an equally desirable alternative property.
6 This economic concept thus sets an upper limit of value for a property by establishing the
7 cost of acquiring an equally desirable substitute property on the open market, provided no
8 additional problems are encountered.

9   The remainder of this chapter provides insight into basic appraising functions. Cor-
10 rect application of the information discussed should help licensees produce reasonably
11 accurate opinions of value and comparative market analyses.

Sales Comparison Approach

13 The **sales comparison approach** to value is based on the theory that a knowledgeable
14 purchaser will pay no more for a property than the cost of acquiring an equally accept-
15 able substitute property. The sales comparison approach (also called the *comparable sales
16 approach* or *market approach*) is based on the premise that the value of a property can be
17 estimated accurately by reviewing recent sales of properties (*comparables* or *comps*) similar
18 to the property being appraised (**subject property**) and comparing those properties with
19 the subject property. Because time can affect property values, the sales used for compari-
20 son purposes must meet two qualifications:

21   1. They must have occurred recently in the same market area where the subject
22   property is located.
23   2. The comparable properties selected must be similar to the subject property.

24   Because no two properties are exactly alike, adjustments must be made for any differ-
25 ences between the subject property and each of the comparable sale properties.

26   Adjustments are made for transactional differences (changes in market conditions
27 since date of sale, for example) and property differences (size, location, etc.). All adjust-
28 ments necessary to achieve the maximum degree of similarity must be made to each
29 comparable property, *not* to the subject property. The intent is to adjust the comparable
30 property to make it as similar to the subject property as possible. If a comparable property
31 is *inferior* to the subject property on a given feature, an *upward* adjustment is made to that
32 comparable property (add the value of the difference). If a comparable is *superior* on a
33 given feature, a *downward* adjustment is made to the comparable property (subtract the
34 value of the difference).

TO REMEMBER: CBS VERSUS CIA			
C	Comp	C	Comp
B	Better	I	Inferior
S	Subtract	A	Add

35   The process of comparison in the sales comparison approach is organized into an *adjust-*
36 *ment grid*. The adjustment grid is used to ensure that no adjustment factor important to
37 a value conclusion is overlooked. Figure 15.1 is an abbreviated adjustment grid example.

FIGURE 15.1 ■ **Adjustment Grid: Sales Comparison Approach**

	Comparable 1	Comparable 2	Comparable 3
Address	3752 Shamrock Dr.	3748 Shamrock Dr.	3619 Shamrock Dr.
Date of sale	(6 months ago)	(3 months ago)	(0 months ago)
Sale price	$141,500	$136,000	$140,000
Financing	Conventional	Conventional	Conventional
Conditions of sale	Normal	Normal	Normal
Market conditions	+ $2,830	+ $1,360	Same as subject
Square footage	− $9,600	+ $1,200	Same as subject
Landscaping	Same as subject	Same as subject	− $1,000
Total Adjustments	−$ 6,770	+ $2,560	− $1,000
Adjusted Sale Price	$134,730	$138,560	$139,000

Reconciliation:	Comp 1: = $134,730 × .20	$26,946
	Comp 2: = $138,560 × .30	$41,568
	Comp 3: = $139,000 × .50	$69,500

Indicated Value:		$138,014 or
		$138,000 (rounded)

1 The example illustrates the procedure for adjusting the sale prices of selected comparable
2 properties to arrive at an approximate market value for the subject property.

3 **Adjustment process.** The appraiser prepares the adjustment grid by first entering the
4 street address and sale price for each selected comparable. Adjustments for transactional
5 differences such as conditions of sale, financing terms, and changes in market conditions
6 since the date of sale are made first, followed by adjustments for property characteristics.
7 Those adjustments include the following:

8 ■ *Financing terms.* Appraisers must confirm the financing associated with each sale
9 because the sale price could reflect special financing terms, such as seller financ-
10 ing or seller-paid points. For purposes of the example presented in Figure 15.1,
11 Adjustment Grid, assume the financing associated with each of the sales was
12 conventional financing and that it was typical financing for the market area.

13 ■ *Conditions of sale.* Appraisers must research the conditions of sale to determine
14 if the buyer or seller was under abnormal pressure to buy or sell or if there was a
15 special relationship between the parties to the transaction, such as between fam-
16 ily members or business associates. In the example in Figure 15.1, Adjustment
17 Grid, the appraiser verified the conditions of sale for each of the sales and found
18 them to be normal.

19 ■ *Market conditions.* A property that sold last month or last year may sell for
20 more, or for less, today, even though the property itself has not physically
21 changed. The criterion for making an adjustment for market conditions is
22 whether the price paid for a comparable property, if that property were sold

on today's market, would differ from the price paid during some other period of time. Referring to Figure 15.1, we see that the appraiser adjusted Comparable (Comp) 1 *plus* $2,830. Assume that Comp 1 sold six months ago and the appraiser has estimated a market conditions adjustment of 4 percent annually (or 2 percent for six months). The appraiser is adjusting the sale price of the comparable to estimate what the comp would have sold for under today's market conditions. Similarly, Comp 2 sold three months ago so the appraiser has entered a *plus* $1,360 adjustment (or 1 percent). Comp 3 sold very recently, so a market conditions adjustment was not needed.

- *Square footage.* Assume Comp 1 is 160 square feet larger than the subject property. Because Comp 1 is superior to the subject property with respect to square footage, a downward adjustment is needed. The appraiser has estimated $60 per square foot as an appropriate unit of comparison and has entered an adjustment of *minus* $9,600 (or 160 square feet × $60). Because Comp 2 is 20 square feet smaller than the subject, the appropriate upward adjustment is needed.

- *Landscaping.* Because Comp 3 has nicer landscaping, compared with the subject property, a downward adjustment is made to Comp 3.

Practice Problem 2

An appraiser is estimating the value of a single-family house. The house has three bedrooms, two bathrooms, and a pool. The appraiser has located one comparable that sold for $184,500. The comparable has four bedrooms and two bathrooms but does not have a pool. Based on the market in the neighborhood, the appraiser estimates that a fourth bedroom adds $6,000 of value and a pool adds $11,000. What is the adjusted sale price of the comparable?

(The solution to Practice Problem 2 is at the end of this chapter on page 359.)

Practice Problem 3

The subject property is a vacant lot. It is located at the end of a cul-de-sac. A comparable lot in the same neighborhood recently sold for $27,000, but it is on an interior lot on a through-street (not as desirable a location). However, the comparable lot is larger than the subject. The difference in location is valued at $5,000 and the difference in size is valued at $4,000. What is the adjusted sale price of the comparable?

(The solution to Practice Problem 3 is at the end of this chapter on page 359.)

Reconciliation. Note in Figure 15.1, Adjustment Grid, the method of reconciling the three adjusted sale prices. If the comparables are all equally suitable, the appraiser may simply average the adjusted sale prices. On the other hand, if the appraiser considers one comparable to be a better indicator of the subject property's value than the others, the appraiser may "weigh" that comparable more heavily. This is entirely a matter of judgment. In Figure 15.1, because Comp 3 was considered most similar to the property being appraised, it received a reconciliation weight of 50 percent. This means that 50 percent of whatever the appraised value of the subject property is going to be should be based on the adjusted sale price of Comp 3. Comp 2 was next in similarity and therefore was awarded a reconciliation weight of 30 percent. In each case, the adjusted sale price is multiplied by the reconciliation weight assigned, producing a part of the eventual reconciled value, which will be the estimated market value.

The comparable sales approach is the real estate market "speaking" through past sales. By using only sales already transacted, the market tells us about that particular type of property. Regardless of what one might wish for a sale price, the market indicates what value buyers and sellers have already established for properties similar to the subject property.

The same technique is employed for vacant lots. Select eight to ten recent lot sales, and from those, pick the four to six lots most similar to the subject lot. Differences in size or shape are neutralized by using a common unit of comparison such as front feet or square feet. Using the recent four to six sales selected as market indicators, one can find the price paid per square foot or front foot for each lot. The reconciled average of all comparable sales gives the approximate value per square foot or front foot of the subject lot. To calculate the average cost per square foot of any property, always divide dollars by square feet.

> **EXAMPLE:** What is the estimated market value of a subject lot that is 110' × 120' (13,200 sq. ft.)?

Adjustment Analysis

Comparable Sales:

Sale 1: A lot 100' × 120' located across the street from the subject lot sold recently for $36,800.

Sale 2: A lot 110' × 120' in the same neighborhood as the subject lot sold recently for $37,000.

Sale 3: A lot 100' × 100' in a different but similar-quality neighborhood sold recently for $36,000.

Sale 4: A lot 130' × 150' located in a different but similar neighborhood but near a railroad sold recently for $39,800.

Solution:

Sale 1: $36,800 ÷ 12,000 sq. ft. = $3.067 per sq. ft.
Sale 2: $37,000 ÷ 13,200 sq. ft. = $2.803 per sq. ft.
Sale 3: $36,000 ÷ 10,000 sq. ft. = $3.600 per sq. ft.
Sale 4: $39,800 ÷ 19,500 sq. ft. = $2.041 per sq. ft.

Reconciliation:

Sale 1: $3.067 × .35 = $1.073
Sale 2: $2.803 × .30 = $ .841
Sale 3: $3.600 × .20 = $ .720
Sale 4: $2.041 × .15 = $ .306
$\overline{\hspace{3cm}}$
100% = $2.940 = $2.94 per sq. ft.

Total square footage of subject lot   13,200
Reconciled value per sq. ft.   × $2.94
Estimated market value of subject lot $38,808 (round to $38,800)

Note that in the reconciliation process, Sale 3 was given less weight in the final analysis because it was in a different neighborhood, and Sale 4 was given the least weight because of its proximity to a railroad track and its location in a different neighborhood. If

1 all of the comparables had been considered good representations of the subject property,
2 the appraiser would have given all four comparables equal weight and simply averaged
3 them to arrive at a value per square foot.

Practice Problem 4

An appraiser has assigned the following weights to three adjusted sale prices:

Comparable	Adjusted Sale Price	Weight Assigned
Comp 1	$334,500	35 percent
Comp 2	$338,700	45 percent
Comp 3	$369,200	20 percent

Reconcile the adjusted sale prices using weighted averaging to determine the estimated market value.

(The solution to Practice Problem 4 is at the end of this chapter on page 359.)

---

4 ## Cost-Depreciation Approach

5 The **cost-depreciation approach** to value is based on the theory that a knowledgeable
6 purchaser will pay no more for a property than the cost of acquiring a similar site and
7 constructing an acceptable substitute structure. The maximum value of a property can
8 be measured by determining the cost to acquire an equivalent site and to reproduce a
9 structure as if new, and then subtracting accrued depreciation. There are four steps in the
10 cost-depreciation approach:

11 **Step one.** Estimate the current reproduction (or replacement) cost of the improvements as
12 of the appraisal date. **Reproduction cost** is the amount of money required to build an exact
13 duplicate of the structure. **Replacement cost** is the amount of money required to replace
14 a structure having the same use and functional utility as the subject property, but using
15 modern, available, or updated materials. Consider a historic bungalow home. The cost to
16 duplicate the home in exact detail, including the hand carved trim on the porch, is repro-
17 duction cost. However, if the home were to be reconstructed in the same bungalow style
18 but with modern materials and techniques, this cost is replacement cost.

19 Several methods are available to help in estimating building reproduction costs. Three
20 cost estimating methods are described here, with the most technical and precise method
21 first:

22 1. *Quantity survey method.* This method involves a detailed inventory of all labor,
23 materials, products, and indirect costs, plus the builder's profit, required to repro-
24 duce a building. The number of items is then multiplied by the cost per item. For
25 example, in a single-family dwelling with three baths, multiply the cost of one
26 commode by 3, the cost of one bathtub by 3, etc. If 1,000 linear feet of 2 × 6s are
27 required at a cost of $.50 per foot, the cost would be $500.
28 The man-hours for each type of labor involved are estimated and multiplied
29 by the cost per hour. All costs are totaled, then added to overhead and indirect

FIGURE 15.2 ■   Comparative Square-Foot Method

Estimated reproduction cost new:		
Main dwelling:	1,241 sq. ft. @ $50 per =	$62,050
Utility room:	117 sq. ft. @ $32 per =	3,744
Entrance porch:	75 sq. ft. @ $12 per =	900
Carport:	412 sq. ft. @ $15 per =	+ 6,180
Total estimated reproduction cost new		$72,874
Less accrued depreciation		− 4,802
Total depreciation reproduction cost		$68,072
Add value of land (by comparison)		+16,000
Add value of improvements:		
Landscaping	$2,128	
Driveway: 300 sq. ft. @ $4 per sq. ft. =	+1,200	
Total value of property via cost depreciation		+ 3,328
		$87,400

costs. The builder's profit then is added. The aggregate of all costs is the reproduction cost of a new building.

Cost Depreciation Approach Formula:

Reproduction cost of the building

− Accrued depreciation

= Indicated value of the building

+ Estimated value of the site

= Indicated value of the property

---

2. *Unit-in-place method.* This method is more practical for appraisers and requires
   less technical ability. The cost of materials plus the cost of labor to install them
   is calculated for each component of a structure, such as the driveway, parking
   area, roof, foundation, walls, and floors. For example, the unit-in-place cost for a
   square of roofing (100 square feet) can be obtained. The unit cost is then multiplied by the number of units in the entire roof. Each separate component is
   treated in the same manner. Adding the costs of installed equipment and fixtures
   and builder's profit results in the total reproduction cost of the structure.

3. *Comparative square-foot or cubic-foot method.* This method is sometimes called the
   comparative unit method or the *unit comparison method.* The cost of reproducing
   a recently built property similar in size and function to the subject property is
   often used as a basis for estimating the reproduction cost. To reduce errors in this
   method, square-foot or cubic-foot costs are obtained for a standard (or *benchmark*) house of average size for the locality. Exterior walls are used for measurements. Adjustments are then made for quality, shape, and extra features.

This method is relatively fast and easy. It is probably the predominant cost-ing method used for appraisal purposes. However, its use is limited to relatively small, uncomplicated structures such as single-family homes and small office buildings. Many cost-calculation publications and computer programs are available to assist appraisers determining standard square-foot costs in different geographic regions. (Widely used cost-information publications include *Dodge Building Cost Calculator and Valuation Guide*, published by McGraw-Hill, *Residential Cost Handbook and Residential Cost Explorer CD*, by Marshall and Swift, and *Boeckh Building Valuation Manual*, by the American Appraisal Company.) An abbreviated version of the comparative square-foot method is provided in Figure 15.2, Comparative Square-Foot Method, to illustrate its use.

Step two. Estimate the amount of depreciation from all causes (physical deterioration, functional obsolescence, and external obsolescence) and deduct it from the reproduction (or replacement) cost.

The appraiser begins with an estimate of what it would cost to reproduce the structure as if new today. But the subject property is usually not a brand new structure. The difference between the structure's reproduction (or replacement, if applicable) cost new and the perceived market value of the structure today in its actual condition is referred to as accrued depreciation. **Depreciation** is the loss in value caused by things such as wear and tear, poor design, or the structure's surroundings (proximity). *Accrued* depreciation is the total depreciation that has accumulated over the years.

Depreciation can be curable or incurable. **Curable** depreciation occurs when a building component has been added or repaired and the owners are able to get their money back in added value. For example, assume it costs $1,500 to repair and clean the screens in a screened-in porch. If potential buyers would pay at least $1,500 more for the home because of the condition of the porch, the depreciation was curable. **Incurable** depreciation occurs when a building component has been added or repaired but the owners are unable to get their money back in added value. For example, assume a home has 5-year-old kitchen appliances in excellent working order. The owners purchase all new kitchen appliances for $20,000. If potential buyers are unwilling to pay an extra $20,000 for the home with new appliances, the depreciation was incurable.

Generally, accrued depreciation is associated with a structure's age. As a building grows older, it loses value due to exposure to the sun and rain as well as general usage. However, not all depreciation is associated with age. Depreciation in a structure can be attributed to three major causes:

1. *Physical deterioration.* Physical deterioration includes ordinary wear and tear caused by use, lack of maintenance, exposure to the elements, and physical damage. Brittle roof shingles or a worn out central air-conditioning compressor are examples of physical deterioration.

2. *Functional obsolescence.* Anything that is inferior due to operational inadequacies, poor design, or changing tastes and preferences is functional obsolescence. Examples include a poor traffic pattern, too few bathrooms, or an inadequate amount of insulation. An overimprovement is also considered to be functional obsolescence.

3. *External obsolescence.* Any loss in value due to influences originating outside the boundaries of the property, such as an expressway adjacent to a residential subdivision or deterioration of the neighborhood is external obsolescence. Because

external obsolescence is normally beyond the control of the property owner it is considered to be incurable.

Land is not depreciated in the cost-depreciation approach. Only the buildings or other improvements to land are subject to these three types of depreciation because the *site value* is estimated separately, typically using the sales comparison approach. Any adjustments to the site for size, location, and nonstructural improvements were already made when the appraiser applied the sales comparison approach to estimate the site value. When the cost to reproduce the improvements is determined, depreciation is applied only to that portion of the property.

Lump-sum age-life method. Sometimes appraisers estimate each category of depreciation separately. However, the vast majority of residential appraisals that employ the cost-depreciation approach use the lump-sum age-life method to estimate accrued depreciation. The method is so named because it estimates a single value for accrued depreciation.

The lump-sum method is based on a ratio of a property's effective age to its economic life. **Effective age** is the age indicated by a structure's condition and utility. Chronologically, a home may be five years old. However, if the structure has been well maintained, its effective age may be only two years. There is no precise method for estimating effective age. The appraiser estimates a structure's effective age by observing the structure's current condition. A structure's total **economic life** (or useful life) is the total estimated number of years that the structure is expected to contribute to the property's value.

The appraiser divides the effective age of the structure by the total economic life of the structure. Refer to the formula in the text box below.

Accrued Depreciation Formula:

Effective age ÷ Total economic life × Reproduction cost new = Estimated total accrued depreciation

EXAMPLE: Suppose an appraiser estimates that the effective age of a ten-year-old building is four years. The appraiser estimates the cost to reproduce the structure as if new today is $225,000. If the total economic life is 60 years, what is the amount of accrued depreciation?

(4 years effective age ÷ 60 years economic life) × $225,000 reproduction cost new = $15,000 accrued deprecation

The lump-sum age-life method of calculating depreciation assumes that a structure depreciates at a constant rate. For this reason, it is sometimes referred to as straight-line depreciation (the same amount of depreciation each and every year).

EXAMPLE: To demonstrate this point, let's calculate the accrued depreciation in the previous example by first determining the amount of annual depreciation. Divide the reproduction cost by the economic life. The result is the annual depreciation. Multiply the annual depreciation by the effective age to derive the total accrued depreciation:

$225,000 reproduction cost new ÷ 60 years economic life = $3,750 annual depreciation × 4 years effective age = $15,000 accrued depreciation

> Alternate Accrued Depreciation Formula:
>
> Reproduction cost new
>
> ÷ Total economic life
>
> = Annual depreciation
>
> × Effective age
>
> = Accrued depreciation

The value of the structure today, in its current condition, is estimated by subtracting the accrued depreciation from the reproduction cost new:

$225,000 reproduction cost new – $15,000 accrued depreciation
= $210,000 depreciated structure

Step three. Estimate the value of the site and nonstructural site improvements, assuming the site is vacant and will be put to its highest and best use. The value of land is normally determined by the sales comparison approach, explained earlier.

Step four. To derive the property's estimated value, add the estimated value of the site, including site improvements, to the depreciated structure value. For example, if neighboring comparable properties are selling for $5 per square foot and the lot on which the subject structure stands has an area of 11,000 square feet, the land value is estimated to be $55,000. The estimated property value of the subject property is:

$210,000 depreciated structure + $55,000 site value
= $265,000 estimated value of subject property

(Refer also to the Cost Depreciation formula in the text box on page 347.)

Income Capitalization Approach

The object of the income capitalization approach is to measure a flow of income projected into the future. This method is a complete departure from the sales comparison and cost-depreciation approaches. The **income capitalization approach** develops an estimated market value based on the present worth of future income from the subject property. It is the primary approach for appraising income-producing property and for comparing possible investments.

Let's begin with an explanation of the various types of income.

Potential gross income. The total annual income a property would produce if it were fully rented and no collection losses were incurred is called **potential gross income (PGI)**.

Effective gross income. When vacancy and collection losses are *deducted* from annual PGI and any income from other sources (e.g., laundry, vending machines, parking) is *added*, the result is annual **effective gross income (EGI)**. **Vacancy and collection losses** consist of the expected income loss that will result from occasional turnover of renters and periodic vacancies as well as the likelihood that not all rental income will be collected. Even when a property is 100 percent occupied, the probability of *continuous* total occupancy is unlikely. Therefore, some vacancy and collection losses always should be deducted from PGI.

Net operating income. Net operating income (NOI) is the income remaining after subtracting all relevant operating expenses from EGI. *Operating expenses* are grouped into three separate categories: (1) *fixed expenses* (e.g., property taxes, hazard insurance); (2) *variable expenses* (e.g., utilities, maintenance, management, supplies, janitorial, garbage collection); and (3) *reserve for replacements*. The term *reserve for replacements* refers to a reserve allowance that provides for the periodic replacement of building components such as roof coverings and heating and air-conditioning equipment that wear out at a faster rate than structural components.

Effective Gross Income Formula:

Potential Gross Income (PGI)

– Vacancy and collection losses

+ Other income

= Effective Gross Income (EGI)

Net Operating Income (NOI) Formula:

Effective Gross Income (EGI)

– Operating expenses

= Net Operating Income (NOI)

All costs of financing, income taxes, personal expenses, and business-related expenses (such as payroll and advertising) that do not contribute to actual operation of the property are *business expenses*, not operating expenses. Depreciation is not an operating or a business expense (it does not involve an outlay of cash) and is not used to calculate NOI.

NOI is thus the annual income (before mortgage or income tax payments) that may be expected to occur over the remaining economic life of a property. It is this income (NOI) that is capitalized into *present value*. To use the income capitalization approach, an appraiser must know the annual NOI produced by the property, or an appraiser must be able to forecast the annual NOI based on reasonable estimates.

Licensees may have access to the accounts; may be provided the information required; or, in the case of a vacant lot on which a business building will be constructed, may project a pro forma NOI statement from several existing similar properties (see below).

EXAMPLE: Suppose your client is considering construction of a 10-unit apartment building. You are estimating the value of the vacant property zoned for apartments. Your survey of other apartment projects of similar size and quality in the market area reveals that each of the proposed new apartments could be competitive if rented at $665 per month. The survey also discloses that an annual vacancy and collection loss rate of 10 percent is typical for the area. By using normal costs of operation, a pro forma statement can be developed to indicate the probable annual NOI. (Note: Begin by estimating the potential gross income [$665 rent × 10 units × 12 months = PGI].)

Solution:

Potential annual gross income	$79,800
Vacancy and collection losses (10%)	− 7,980
Effective annual gross income	$71,820
Expenses (per year):	
Taxes	$5,494
Insurance	996
Management	24,600
Repairs and maintenance	4,100
Reserve for replacements	+ 1,800
Total annual operating expenses	$36,990
Effective annual gross income	$71,820
Total annual operating expenses	− 36,990
NOI	$34,830

Once known or estimated, the NOI is usually divided by an *overall capitalization rate* (OAR). The OAR normally is determined by using the sale prices and NOIs of similar properties in the market area. Dividing the NOI of a property by its current value or sale price produces an OAR.

Income (NOI) ÷ Value (Sale price) = Rate (OAR)

The components of this formula are said to be *market-driven*, that is, income figures and recorded sale prices represent the market in action. That is the reason most licensees, appraisers, and others prefer the OAR as a capitalization rate.

EXAMPLE: Sales data, income records, and expense records indicate:

Comparable Garden Apartment Complex	Annual NOI	÷	Sale Price	=	Indicated OAR
A	$ 31,400		$ 325,000		.097
B	$ 48,230		$ 450,000		.107
C	$ 39,600		$ 400,000		.099
D	$ 37,400		$ 395,000		.095
E	$ 44,700		$ 440,000		.102
	$ 201,330		$ 2,010,000		.500 ÷ 5 = .100

$201,330 ÷ $2,010,000 = .100 or 10% OAR

The same procedure could be used to determine the OAR for other types of income-producing properties. Once an appropriate capitalization rate and NOI are determined, the IRV formula is used to estimate the present value of income-producing properties:

For example, using the results of the pro forma statement in the earlier problem and the market area OAR of 10 percent, the estimated value of the property is calculated.

$34,830 (NOI) ÷ .10 rate = $348,300 estimated value

Investors, on the other hand, often prefer to specify a capitalization rate because investors are free to choose the acceptable rate of return they desire. When the type of estimated value is investor-driven, the minimum rate of return acceptable to the investor is frequently used as the capitalization rate. Net annual income is then divided by the specified capitalization rate to obtain the investment value of the property. It is important to mention, however, that this is not *market value*, but rather *investment value*. **Investment**

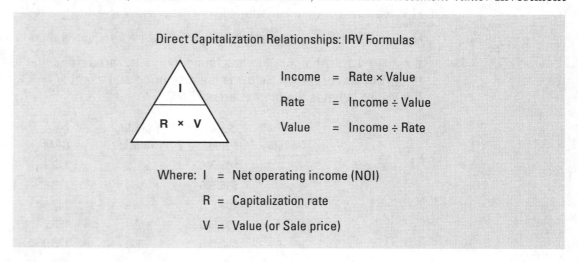

Direct Capitalization Relationships: IRV Formulas

Income = Rate × Value

Rate   = Income ÷ Value

Value   = Income ÷ Rate

Where: I = Net operating income (NOI)

R = Capitalization rate

V = Value (or Sale price)

value is the value of property to a particular investor based on the investor's desired rate of return, risk tolerance, and so forth. Market value is objective and impersonal; investment value is subjective and based on personal criteria.

> **EXAMPLE:** A small income property produces an annual net income of $8,000. Your client wants you to tell her the amount of money that she may invest in the property to provide a return of 10 percent per year from the investment.
>
> $$V = I \div R = \$8,000 \div .10 = \$80,000$$
>
> So the investment value to this investor is $80,000 if a 10 percent rate of return is required from the subject property.

Sound income and expense data are critical in the use of the income capitalization approach. It is also important to realize that a definite relationship exists between present value, net income, and capitalization rate. If, for example, the capitalization rate (R) is increased and the net income (I) remains constant, the present value (V) will be less. Or if the net income (I) goes up and the capitalization rate (R) remains constant, the present value (V) will be greater.

Gross rent multiplier (GRM). A **gross rent multiplier (GRM)** relates sale price to monthly rental income. The GRM is a simple substitute for the income capitalization analysis for one- to four-unit residential rental properties. The GRM applies to rental income only. Although one can use either monthly or annual rent, it is customary to use monthly rent when calculating a GRM. The GRM is found by dividing the sale price by the gross income:

Sale price ÷ Gross monthly rent = Gross rent multiplier (GRM)

> **EXAMPLE:** A single-family property sold for $229,400. This residential investment property earns a monthly rental income of $1,850. What is the property's GRM?
>
> $229,400 Sale price ÷ $1,850 Gross monthly rent = 124 GRM

1   Multipliers must be determined for each local area. A multiplier is market-derived
2   by using comparable properties and averaging the results. To establish a market-derived
3   GRM, an appraiser must locate recent sales and rental data from at least four rental prop-
4   erties that are comparable to the subject property. The sale price of each comparable
5   rental property is divided by the property's gross rent to calculate each property's GRM.
6   The individual GRMs are averaged to estimate a market area GRM. Then the market area
7   GRM is used to estimate the subject property's market value:

8   Rental income × Market area GRM = Estimated market value

9   **EXAMPLE:** An appraiser has found five rental properties that are comparable
10   to the subject property. Below is the sale price and monthly rent for each of the
11   five sales. What is the market area GRM?

	Sale		Monthly		
Sale	Price	÷	Rental	=	GRM
1	$98,000		$575		170.4
2	$96,600		550		175.6
3	$99,900		595		167.9
4	$92,500		550		168.2
5	$98,000		560		175.0
					857.1

20   857.1 (sum of GRMs) ÷ 5 comparable sales = 171.4 market area GRM

21   **EXAMPLE:** The appraiser has estimated the fair market rent for the subject
22   property to be $560 per month. What is the estimated market value of the subject
23   property using the market area GRM of 171.4?

24   $560 Rental income × 171.4 GRM = $95,984 or $96,000 (rounded)

Practice Problem 5

What is the market value of a subject property using a market area GRM of
126.5 and gross monthly rent of $1,500?

(The solution to Practice Problem 5 is at the end of this chapter on
page 359.)

25   **Gross income multiplier (GIM).** The **gross income multiplier (GIM)** is used with small
26   income-producing properties. Notice that the procedure for calculating a GIM is basically
27   the same as for calculating a GRM. However, the GIM refers to all income a property
28   may produce, while the GRM refers to rent only. The GIM typically uses annual income,
29   whereas the GRM typically applies monthly rent.

30   Sale price ÷ Gross annual income = Gross income multiplier (GIM)

31   **EXAMPLE:** A commercial property produces $50,000 of annual gross income.
32   The property recently sold for $400,000. What is the property's GIM?

33   $400,000 Sale price ÷ $50,000 Gross annual income = 8.0 GIM

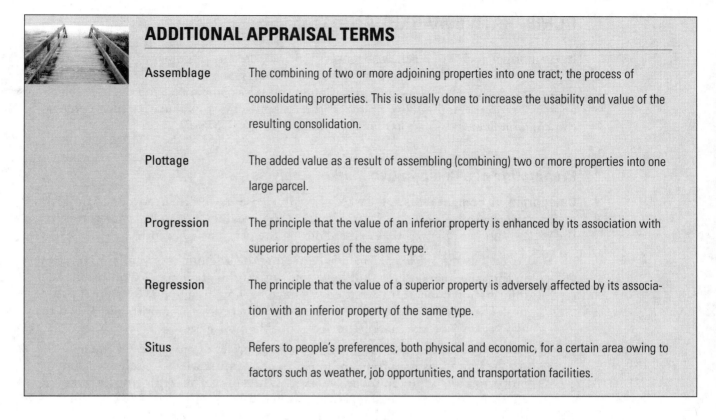

ADDITIONAL APPRAISAL TERMS

Assemblage	The combining of two or more adjoining properties into one tract; the process of consolidating properties. This is usually done to increase the usability and value of the resulting consolidation.
Plottage	The added value as a result of assembling (combining) two or more properties into one large parcel.
Progression	The principle that the value of an inferior property is enhanced by its association with superior properties of the same type.
Regression	The principle that the value of a superior property is adversely affected by its association with an inferior property of the same type.
Situs	Refers to people's preferences, both physical and economic, for a certain area owing to factors such as weather, job opportunities, and transportation facilities.

1 **EXAMPLE :** The appraiser has projected that the subject property can gener-
2 ate a gross annual income of $58,000. What is the estimated market value of the
3 subject property using the market area GIM 8.0?

4           $58,000 Annual gross income × 8.0 GIM = $464,000

Practice Problem 6

What is the market value of a subject property using a market area GIM of 12.5 and gross annual income of $25,500?

(The solution to Practice Problem 6 is at the end of this chapter on page 359.)

Practice Problem 7

What is the GIM of a small income producing property that sells for $425,000 and has a projected gross annual income of $72,000?

(The solution to Practice Problem 7 is at the end of this chapter on page 359.)

COMPARATIVE MARKET ANALYSIS

In the normal course of business, licensees typically prepare a comparative market analysis (CMA) for sellers or buyers as a means to help them make informed decisions on pricing a property. Although CMAs are a variation of the sales comparison approach, they are *not* appraisal reports. Appraisals employ all three approaches to value and must conform to the *Uniform Standards of Professional Appraisal Practice (USPAP)*.

Preparation of a Comparative Market Analysis

Categories of comparables. A CMA typically presents information concerning three major categories of properties: (1) sold within the previous 12 months, (2) currently on the market, and (3) listings that expired during the previous 12 months.

- *Sold within the previous 12 months.* Studying the sale prices of similar properties in the same market area that have sold within the previous 12 months provides information concerning what buyers have been willing to pay for similar properties. The amount of sale activity during the preceding 12-month period and the average days on the market are also valuable information.

- *Currently on the market.* Studying the asking prices of properties in the market area provides important information concerning what the sellers of similar properties are asking in today's market. When properties with equally desirable characteristics are available, buyers normally choose the property with the lowest price. Therefore, the seller should price the property taking into consideration the average asking price of competing properties.

- *Expired during the previous 12 months.* Properties that were listed but failed to sell during the previous 12 months often were priced too high. This information helps to explain to sellers the consequences of overpricing listings.

Common elements of comparison. It is important that all properties used in the CMA be similar to the subject property in size, age, amenities, and location. Adjustments should be made for important differences compared with the subject property, such as swimming pools, condition, style, and so forth. Examples of features that must be considered include location, size, and shape of the lot; landscaping; construction quality; style, design, and age of the structure; square feet; and number of rooms. Adjustments are made to the comps (comparables) using the same procedure as discussed in the sales comparison approach.

Computer-generated CMAs. Software programs are available that will organize the data sales associates gather into attractive presentations. Many MLS service providers offer software for REALTOR® members to download the comparable information directly into a listing presentation package.

S U M M A R Y   O F   I M P O R T A N T   P O I N T S

- Real estate licensees who conduct real estate appraisals are required to comply with *USPAP*. Appraisal reports involving a federally related transaction must be prepared by a state-certified or licensed appraiser.

- *Market value* is the most probable price that a property should bring in a competitive and open market under all conditions requisite to a fair sale, with the buyer and seller each acting prudently and knowledgeably, and assuming the price is not affected by undue stimulus.

■ *Value* is determined by what consumers are willing to pay in the marketplace. *Price* refers to the amount of money actually paid. *Cost* is the total expenditure to create the improvement.

■ An *overimprovement* occurs when an owner invests more money in a structure than the owner can reasonably expect to recapture.

■ To have value, goods and services must possess four traits: (1) demand, (2) utility, (3) scarcity, and (4) transferability.

■ *Highest and best use* is the most profitable use of a property. The use must be legally permissible, physically possible, and financially feasible.

■ The three approaches to estimating value are (1) sales comparison approach, (2) cost-depreciation approach, and (3) income capitalization approach. The principle of substitution is the basis for all three approaches.

■ The *sales comparison approach* compares similar properties to the subject property. The comparable properties' sale prices are adjusted upward or downward to reflect differences between each comparable and the subject property. If a comparable is superior to the subject property on a given feature, a downward adjustment is made to the comp. If a comparable is inferior to the subject property, an upward adjustment is made to the comp. The adjusted sale prices of the comparables are reconciled using a weighted average to estimate the market value of the subject property.

■ The *cost-depreciation approach* estimates the market value of a property based on the cost to buy an equivalent site and to reproduce the structure as if new, less depreciation. *Reproduction cost* is the amount of money required to build an exact duplicate of the structure. *Replacement cost* is the amount of money required to replace a structure having the same use and functional utility as the subject property but using modern, available, or updated materials.

■ The three methods used to estimate reproduction cost are (1) quantity survey method, (2) unit-in-place method, and (3) comparative square-foot method.

■ *Depreciation* is the loss in value. *Accrued depreciation* is the total depreciation that has accumulated over time. Depreciation is curable when a building component has been added or repaired and the owners are able to get their money back in added value. If the owners are not able to recoup the cost of the repaired or added item, it is said to be incurable depreciation. The three major causes of depreciation are (1) physical deterioration, (2) functional obsolescence, and (3) external obsolescence.

■ The lump-sum age-life method of estimating depreciation is based on a ratio of the property's effective age to its economic life. *Effective age* is the age indicated by a structure's condition and utility. *Total economic life* is the total estimated number of years that a structure is expected to contribute to the property's value.

■ The *income capitalization approach* develops an estimated value based on the present worth of future income from the subject property. The approach capitalizes net operating income into value.

■ *Potential gross income* (PGI) is the total annual income a property would produce if it were fully rented and no collection losses were incurred. *Effective gross income* (EGI) is calculated by subtracting vacancy and collection losses from the PGI. *Net operating income* (NOI) is the income remaining after subtracting operating expenses from EGI. The three categories of operating expenses are (1) fixed, (2) variable, and (3) reserve for replacements.

■ The *gross rent multiplier* (GRM) is the ratio between a property's gross monthly rent and its selling price. The *gross income multiplier* (GIM) is the ratio between a property's gross annual income and its selling price.

Practice Problem 1 Solution

(Practice Problem 1 is located on page 339.)

The cost is the amount paid to purchase the lot and build the house: $270,000.

The price is the transaction price paid by the son: $450,000.

The value is the market value based on an appraisal: $525,000.

Practice Problem 2 Solution

(Practice Problem 2 is located on page 344.)

Comparable sale price	$184,500	
Fourth bedroom	−$6,000	CBS (comp better, subtract)
Pool	+$11,000	CIA (comp inferior, add)
Adjusted sale price	$189,500	

Practice Problem 3 Solution

(Practice Problem 3 is located on page 344.)

Comparable sale price	$27,000	
Fourth bedroom	+$5,000	CIA (comp inferior, add)
Pool	−$4,000	CBS (comp better, subtract)
Adjusted sale price	$28,000	

Practice Problem 4 Solution

(Practice Problem 4 is located on page 346.)

Comp 1	$334,500 × .35	= $117,075
Comp 2	$338,700 × .45	= $152,415
Comp 3	$369,200 × .20	= $ 73,840

$117,075 + $152,415 + $73,840 = $343,330

Practice Problem 5 Solution

(Practice Problem 5 is located on page 354.)

$1,500 Monthly rental income × 126.5 GRM = $189,750 Market value

Practice Problem 6 Solution

(Practice Problem 6 is located on page 355.)

$25,500 Gross annual income × 12.5 GIM = $318,750

Practice Problem 7 Solution

(Practice Problem 7 is located on page 355.)

$425,000 Sale price ÷ $72,000 Gross annual income = 5.90 (rounded) GIM

[1]   *Note:* The examples of comparable sales used in this chapter are hypothetical and
[2]   offered for educational purposes only.

R E V I E W   Q U E S T I O N S

1. Valuation of real property is an
   a. estimate of cost.
   b. estimate of value.
   c. exact value.
   d. assessment of cost.

2. The total expenditure required to bring a new improvement into existence is referred to as
   a. cost.
   b. price.
   c. market price.
   d. market value.

3. Which assumption does NOT apply to definition of market value?
   a. Payment is made in cash or its equivalent.
   b. Neither the buyer or the seller is under any compulsion to act quickly.
   c. Market value is the median price a property will bring.
   d. Both buyer and seller are fully informed.

4. The approach to estimating value that is referred to as *the real estate market speaking through past sales* because it uses actual sales transactions is the
   a. transactional comparison method.
   b. economic indicator method.
   c. sales comparison method.
   d. sales transaction method.

5. When more money is invested in a building than can reasonably be expected to be recaptured, it is referred to as
   a. economic lack of utility.
   b. overimprovement.
   c. underimprovement.
   d. depreciation.

6. The most probable price in terms of money that a property should bring in an open market is called the
   a. highest and best use.
   b. sale price.
   c. market value.
   d. exchange value.

7. Loss of value for any reason is called
   a. transferability.
   b. substitution.
   c. depreciation.
   d. economic obsolescence.

8. All below are characteristics required to create value EXCEPT
   a. demand.
   b. supply.
   c. utility.
   d. transferability.

9. The approach to value most likely to be relevant for appraising a community college is the
   a. comparable sales approach.
   b. cost-depreciation approach.
   c. income capitalization approach.
   d. straight-line approach.

10. The subject property has 200 less square feet of living area than a comparable. The market area value of 200 square feet is $20,000. Which adjustment should the appraiser make?
    a. Add $20,000 to the subject
    b. Add $20,000 to the comparable
    c. Subtract $20,000 from the subject
    d. Subtract $20,000 from the comparable

11. The most relevant approach to estimate the value of a vacant lot in a residential neighborhood usually is the
    a. square-foot approach.
    b. cost-depreciation approach.
    c. unit-in-place method.
    d. sales comparison approach.

12. In the comparable sales approach
    a. adjustments are made to the subject properties.
    b. adjustments are made to the comparable properties.
    c. the subject property must have sold recently in the same market area as the comparable property.
    d. the result is considered to be the median value.

13. The basis of all three approaches to market value is the principle of
    a. situs.
    b. substitution.
    c. overimprovement.
    d. economic potential.

14. When applying the cost-depreciation approach which item is NOT subject to depreciation?
    a. A poor traffic pattern in a home
    b. New solid oak wood cabinets and marble tile floors in a neighborhood of $80,000 homes
    c. Older site improvements
    d. Land

15. Which would be considered to be external obsolescence?
    a. Peeling exterior paint
    b. One bathroom in a three-bedroom home
    c. Metal utility shed that is in poor condition located just inside the property line
    d. A residential property's proximity to an industrial area

16. Loss in value due to operational inadequacies, poor design, or changing tastes is referred to as
    a. physical deterioration.
    b. functional obsolescence.
    c. external obsolescence.
    d. underimprovement.

17. A small income-producing property has a projected effective gross income of $48,000. Expenses are estimated at 20 percent of effective gross income. An appraiser has determined that an appropriate capitalization rate, based on property type and competing properties, is 9 percent. The estimated market value of this property (rounded to the nearest dollar) is
    a. $106,667.
    b. $311,111.
    c. $426,667.
    d. $533,333.

18. The economic characteristic that refers to the preference for a certain location owing to various factors such as climate, employment outlook, and so forth, is called
    a. highest and best use.
    b. plottage.
    c. economic preference.
    d. situs.

19. The total estimated time in years that an improvement can be profitably useful is referred to as
    a. effective age.
    b. economic life.
    c. accrued depreciation.
    d. chronological age of the improvement.

20. In the income capitalization approach, if the capitalization rate is increased and the net income is unchanged, the
    a. present value will be less.
    b. future value will be less.
    c. present value will be more.
    d. future value will be more.

21. A home has 1,800 square feet of living area and 200 square feet of garage. The reproduction cost new is $48 per square foot for living area and $28 per square foot for finished garage area. The site measures 75 feet wide by 110 feet deep and is valued at $3 per square foot. The economic life of the home is estimated to be 50 years. The house is 10 years old. The value of the property using the cost-depreciation approach is
    a. $73,600.
    b. $86,400.
    c. $92,000.
    d. $98,350.

22. A limited partnership wishes to purchase an apartment building that has a monthly net income of $4,000 and monthly expenses of $1,000. If the partnership is to get a 12 percent return on its investment, what should it pay for the property?
    a. $25,000
    b. $33,000
    c. $300,000
    d. $400,000

23. An income-producing property has a potential annual gross income of $81,420. Vacancy and collection losses are estimated at 10 percent of potential gross income. Expenses are estimated at $40,000. The estimated value of the property is $250,000. The capitalization rate for this property is
    a. 13.31 percent.
    b. 14.91 percent.
    c. 16.57 percent.
    d. 17.5 percent.

24. A home recently sold for $58,500. The rent on the home is $450 per month. The GRM for the home is
    a. 130.
    b. 108.
    c. 10.83.
    d. 1.08.

25. An appraiser is calculating the reproduction cost new of a home, using the comparative square-foot method. The appraiser measures the exterior dimensions of the home, which are 27 feet by 52 feet, plus a detached garage measuring 22 feet by 24 feet. The appraiser consults an accepted cost manual and estimates the reproduction cost for heated and air-conditioned living area to be $52.50 per square foot and the finished free-standing garage to be $32.50 per square foot. The reproduction cost new of the improvements is
    a. $62,790.
    b. $73,710.
    c. $90,870.
    d. $101,430.

26. Effective gross income is
    a. net operating income divided by an appropriate capitalization rate.
    b. potential gross income minus vacancy and collection losses.
    c. net operating income minus annual mortgage expense.
    d. before-tax cash flow divided by equity invested.

27. You are preparing a CMA for a single-family home that has a two-car garage. You have located a comparable house that sold for $226,000, but it does not have a garage. If a two-car garage is valued at $18,000, which adjustment would you make?
    a. Add $18,000 to the comparable
    b. Subtract $18,000 from the comparable
    c. Add $18,000 to the subject
    d. Subtract $18,000 from the subject

28. A building is valued at $150,000 when NOI is capitalized at a rate of 8 percent. NOI is 40 percent of effective gross income. The effective gross income is
    a. $12,000.
    b. $22,000.
    c. $30,000.
    d. $32,000.

29. A commercial property has a potential gross income of $40,000. Vacancy and collection losses are 5 percent of PGI. Additional operating expenses total $12,920. The property has a first mortgage requiring payments of $1,070.75 per month. Using a capitalization rate of 12 percent, which amount is an accurate estimate of the property's value?
    a. $101,333
    b. $107,667
    c. $209,000
    d. $316,667

30. The annual income earned on a commercial property is $85,000 and the sale price is $722,500. What is the GIM?
    a. 6.5
    b. 7.5
    c. 8.5
    d. 9.5

16

PRODUCT KNOWLEDGE

¹ OVERVIEW

² Real estate professionals should have general product knowledge. Understanding basic
³ construction methods and familiarity with common building materials and techniques are
⁴ invaluable when working with customers.

⁵ After completing this chapter, the student should be able to:

⁶ ■ contrast pier and slab-on-grade foundations;

⁷ ■ distinguish among the various lot types;

⁸ ■ distinguish among the three types of frame construction;

⁹ ■ identify various roof styles;

¹⁰ ■ explain how a basic electrical system works;

¹¹ ■ describe basic residential plumbing and mechanical systems; and

¹² ■ identify the various window types.

¹³ KEY TERMS

corner	flag	key
cul-de-sac	gable	R-value
dormer	hip	single-hung
double-hung	interior	t-intersection

¹⁴ LOT TYPES

¹⁵ A property is characterized by many elements such as the structure's architectural design,
¹⁶ its roof style, and so forth. The shape of the lot is also an important feature of a property.

¹⁷ **Corner** lots are bounded with streets on two sides. Commercial corner lots are gener-
¹⁸ ally worth more than interior lots. Residential corner lots are often desirable because of
¹⁹ their "curb appeal." (See lot 1 in Figure 16.1, Lot Types.)

Interior lots are bounded on each side by another lot. (See lot 2 in Figure 16.1, Lot Types.)

T-intersection lots are interior lots that suffer from their location at the end of a T intersection. They are usually less desirable because of the inconvenience of car headlights shining into the home and a possible danger from speeding "runaway" cars. (See lot 3 in Figure 16.1.)

Cul-de-sac lots occur when a street is open at one end only and it has a circular turnaround at the other end. Lots located on the cul-de-sac are desirable because they usually are more spacious providing ample room for backyard features such as swimming pools. Residential cul-de-sac lots also tend to have less vehicular traffic. (See lot 4 in Figure 16.1.)

Flag lots are characterized by a long access road or driveway back to the main part of the lot. The access road suggests the staff of a flag. Typically flag lots occur as a result of residential development in what once was a large homestead. The long access road usually increases the cost of bringing utilities to the lot. (See lot 5 in Figure 16.1.)

Key lots are generally long skinny lots similar to the shaft of a key that are often bounded by as many as five or six lots. (See lot 6 in Figure 16.1.) *Note:* The term *key lot* is also used to indicate a lot that has added value because of its strategic location.

FIGURE 16.1 ■ **Lot Types**

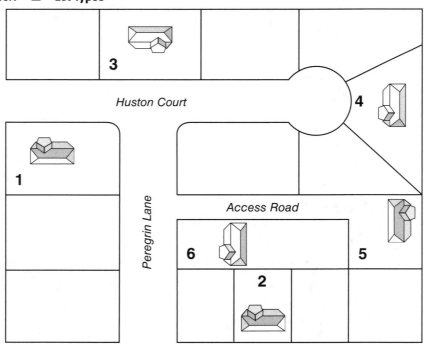

STRUCTURAL ELEMENTS

Footer and Foundation

The footers and foundation provide support for the structure. The footer is usually strengthened with two ⅝-inch rods, called *rebar*, resting on metal *chairs* imbedded in concrete. The footer extends around the perimeter of the building and is the base on which the structure rests. Two basic styles of residential foundations used in Florida are the pier and slab-on-grade foundations.

Pier. A *pier* is a column of masonry. Four or more piers are used to support a structure. Piers lift the structure above ground level to allow a *crawl space* below the structure. This type of foundation has the advantage of allowing easy access to plumbing and electrical connections as well as providing space to run ductwork. Piers can raise the structure even higher if needed in coastal and other flood-prone areas.

Slab-on-grade. *Slab-on-grade* construction involves pouring a concrete slab directly on the ground. The slab is reinforced with steel *mesh*, and the ground is covered with a plastic, waterproof *vapor barrier*. If the footers are poured with the slab, it is a *monolithic slab*. A monolithic slab is both a foundation and a first-floor slab. This type of construction is suitable for nearly flat lots only. If the footers and slab are poured separately, the slab is referred to as *floating*.

Framing

The most common type of residential construction is wood frame. The vertical framing members are called *studs*, which are either 2 × 4 inch or 2 × 6 inch lumber. The top and bottom horizontal members are called *plates*. Anchor bolts and metal straps are used to connect the studs to the top and bottom plates. Pressure-treated wood must be used for the bottom (sole) plate because it comes in contact with the concrete slab. *Pressure-treated lumber* is treated with chemicals to make it resistant to wood rot and termites. A vapor barrier is attached to the exterior face of the studs, and sheathing is then installed. Various types of siding, stucco, or brick or stone veneer are applied to finish the exterior.

There are three methods of wood-frame construction: platform, balloon, and post-and-beam. Platform framing is the most common construction method today. However, balloon framing is common in older homes. Post-and-beam construction is popular in contemporary architecture.

Platform. Each floor is built separately, with the first floor providing a work platform for the structure above. This method of construction is safer for the framers because a flat surface is provided on which to work. The subfloor extends to the outside edges of the structure and provides a platform on which exterior walls are erected. Typically, the wall framing is assembled on the concrete slab and then hoisted into place and anchored. If the house has more than one story, additional layers of floor platforms and walls are stacked on top of the first floor walls. The structure is completed with ceiling and roof framing. (See Figure 16.2, Framing.)

Balloon. Balloon construction is used today for some two-story construction, especially if the structure has a masonry exterior. With balloon frame construction the studs extend continuously to the ceiling of the second floor, providing a smooth unbroken wall surface at each floor level. For example, in two-story construction, the load-bearing wall studs

1 extend in one piece from the foundation to the top plate two stories above. The continu-
2 ous construction reduces uneven settling that can cause cracking of brick, stucco, and
3 stone veneer finishes. Balloon framing is a more expensive type of construction compared
4 with platform construction because of the cost of quality 18-foot to 20-foot studs and
5 higher labor costs. (See Figure 16.2.)

FIGURE 16.2 ■ Framing

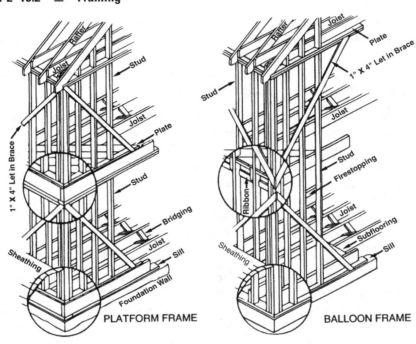

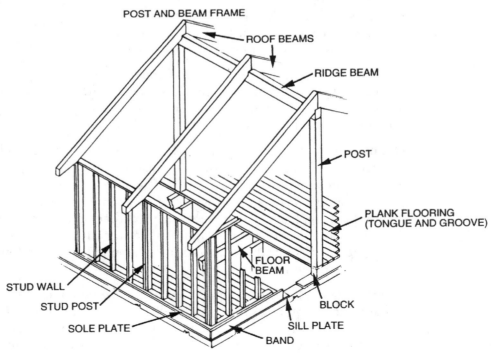

¹ **Post-and-beam.** Sturdy posts support beams that are spaced up to 8 feet apart and covered ² with 2-inch planks that serve to form the floor, ceiling, and roof deck. Because the posts ³ provide some of the ceiling support, rooms can be constructed with larger spans between ⁴ the supporting side walls. This type of framing is popular in contemporary architecture ⁵ where exposed beam ceilings are desired. (See Figure 16.2, Framing.)

Roof Structures

⁷ Most roof structures today use preengineered, factory-built *trusses*. Trusses are lifted into ⁸ place with a crane and then secured to the walls with metal fasteners. Trusses are con-⁹ structed with triangular-shaped internal structural members that transfer the stress load of ¹⁰ the roof away from the center of the span outward to the load-bearing walls.

¹¹ *Roof pitch* (slope) refers to the amount of height (rise) a roof has compared to the hori-¹² zontal measurement (span or run) of the roof. All roofs have some pitch. Even so-called ¹³ flat roofs have a small indiscernible pitch to provide for water runoff. A roof that rises four ¹⁴ inches in height over a one-foot horizontal distance has a pitch of 4/12. Homes are char-¹⁵ acterized by the style and pitch of the roof. Roof styles include gable, hip, saltbox, shed, ¹⁶ flat, gambrel, and mansard. (See Figure 16.3, Roof Designs.)

¹⁷ **Gable.** Gable roofs are cost effective because they use a single truss design. Gable roofs ¹⁸ peak at the center ridge and extend downward on two opposite sides. Gable roofs do not ¹⁹ provide protection from the sun on the two gable ends. Sometimes dormers are incorpo-²⁰ rated into gable and hip (see Figure 16.3) roofs. A **dormer** is a projection that extends out ²¹ of the roof to provide additional light and ventilation.

²² **Hip.** Hip roofs peak at the center ridge but extend downward on four opposite sides. Hip ²³ roofs provide overhang protection on all four sides of the structure and are architecturally ²⁴ pleasing. Trusses for a hip roof are more expensive to manufacture because of the special ²⁵ engineering required.

²⁶ **Saltbox.** Saltbox roofs are characterized by what appears to be a gable roof that then slopes ²⁷ steeply on one side. It gets its name from the old Morton saltbox of the early 1900s.

²⁸ **Shed.** Shed roofs consist of a single steep plane. They are often used in contemporary ²⁹ architecture.

³⁰ **Flat.** Flat roofs are commonly referred to as *built-up* roofs because of the way they are ³¹ constructed in layers of tar and gravel. Flat roofs are used in contemporary residential ³² structures as well as commercial structures.

³³ **Gambrel.** Gambrel roofs are characterized by the American barn style of roof. They pro-³⁴ vide ample headroom in two-story construction.

³⁵ **Mansard.** This style of roof is named after a French architect who is credited with first ³⁶ using the style in Paris, France. Paris had a zoning code that prevented multistory struc-³⁷ tures because structures were being built higher than the fire equipment could reach. The ³⁸ zoning code defined the number of stories of a structure by the number of feet from ground ³⁹ level to where the roofing material began. Mansard cleverly brought the shingles down the ⁴⁰ walls of the top floor, thereby increasing the number of buildable stories without violating ⁴¹ the zoning code. The mansard roof became very common in France and is used in French-⁴² style architecture in the United States. Mansard roofs are very common in the French ⁴³ Quarter district of New Orleans, for example.

FIGURE 16.3 ■ **Roof Designs**

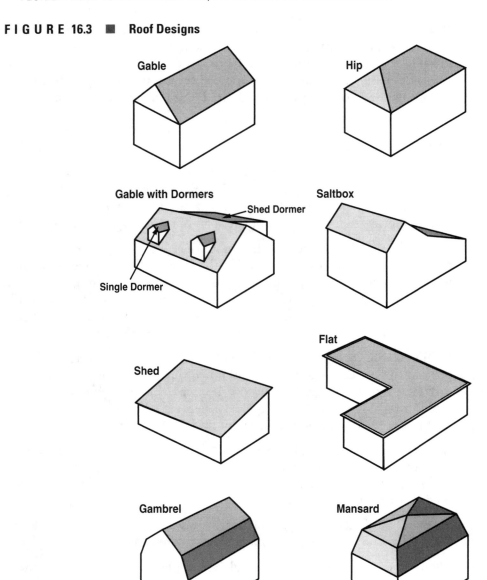

Electrical System

Electrical power is produced by large power plants. From these plants electricity enters large "step-up" transformers that increase voltage to half a million volts or more. Electricity flows easily at high voltages through transmission lines to communities miles away. "Step-down" transformers located at substations reduce the voltage for distribution along street lines. Smaller transformers placed atop utility poles or on concrete pads at ground level further reduce the voltage to 120-volt current for household use.

Years ago, voltage entering houses was rated at 110 and 220 volts. Today it has been increased to 120 and 240 volts. Lines carrying current to the house enter through wires strung overhead and attached to a post called a *weather head* or through an underground

1   conduit. In new construction, even in those subdivisions that are serviced by overhead
2   power lines, the electric service lines from the transformer to the house run underground.
3   In older homes, electric service lines may go from a transformer attached to a power pole
4   to the weather head. The energy is directed through a meter and then to the service panel
5   inside the house.

6   Because electricity travels in a *circuit* (or a closed loop), there must be at least two
7   wires entering the house; one hot wire (power is always present) and one neutral wire (the
8   return path). Older homes with only two wires can deliver only 120-volt current. Most
9   homes built after 1950 have three wires running to the weather head; two lines each car-
10   rying 120 volts of current and a third grounded neutral wire. One hot wire and the neutral
11   wire provide 120 volts for circuits suitable for lights and wall outlets. Both hot wires and
12   the neutral wire provide 240 volts for large appliances such as air conditioners, electric
13   ranges, and electric clothes dryers.

14   The utility company connects the incoming wires to a weatherproof box that holds
15   the meter. The *meter* measures how much electricity the home uses. The wires are then
16   fed to the *service panel*. The two hot wires are connected to the main circuit breaker, and
17   the neutral wire is grounded to a cold water pipe or grounding rod. The electricity is then
18   divided into branch circuits. The *branch circuits* supply power to the different rooms in the
19   house. Each circuit is protected by its own circuit breaker. (See Figure 16.4, Electric Ser-
20   vice Entrance.) *Circuit breakers* are used to protect an electric circuit from damage caused
21   by too much current. A breaker will *trip* (shut off) if the circuit is forced to carry more
22   current than the wire can handle. Inside the breaker is a tripping mechanism that will not
23   allow the breaker to be reset until the wire has cooled. The circuit breaker, once tripped,

F I G U R E   16.4 ■ Electric Service Entrance

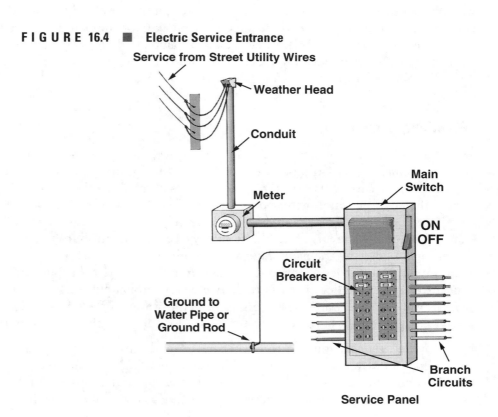

must be reset by hand. In areas of the house where there is a greater danger of electrical shock (in kitchens and bathrooms), *ground-fault-interrupters* (GFIs) are required.

Electricity is distributed in a three-wire system; the hot, neutral, and ground wires. The hot wire carries the current to the switches, the neutral wire carries the current away (completes the loop), and the ground wire routes the excess electricity to the ground. The size of the wire used in a circuit is based on how much current it will carry. According to the American Wire Gauge (AWG) rating system, the smaller the number, the larger the wire. The larger the load, the larger the wire needed. For example, wire supplying power to wall switches may require #12-gauge wire, whereas wire used to supply a clothes dryer may use #8-gauge or #6-gauge wire. Nonmetallic sheathed cable used in residential wiring is identified by the number of wires in the cable. For example, a cable stamped with the words *12/2 with ground* indicates that the cable contains two #12-gauge wires and a ground wire. The individual wires in the cable are color coded. The hot wire is normally black. If the cable has two hot wires, one is black and the other is typically red. The neutral wire is either white or gray. The ground wire can be green, but is usually a noninsulated bare copper wire. The black wire delivers power to the electrical switch and the white is the return path to complete the circuit.

Electric current moving along a wire is measured in units called *amperes*, or *amps*. Amperage describes the amount of electricity or current flowing in a particular circuit. The force that moves the current is measured in *volts*. Voltage represents the "force" in the circuit, which can be compared to water pressure; it is a measure of electricity in terms of pressure. The work performed by the voltage and current is measured in *watts*. Wattage indicates how much energy a device consumes. The electric company charges its customers according to the number of kilowatt-hours (kWh) used. A *kilowatt* is equivalent to 1,000 watts.

You can calculate the wattage or power available in a circuit by first determining the amp rating, which is indicated on the circuit breaker for the particular circuit. Most room circuits have 15-amp or 20-amp service, and 30-amp or 50-amp service is needed for heavy-duty circuits. Voltage times amperes equals watts. In the case of a device designed to operate on 120 volts and a 15-amp circuit, 120 volts × 15 amps = 1,800 watts.

Plumbing System

Residential plumbing systems are composed of two basic systems. The *high-pressure system* delivers *potable* water (suitable for drinking) to the various parts of a home, and the *low-pressure system* carries wastewater away from the home. Potable water typically enters the house through the water meter on the street side of the house. The potable water is delivered under pressure. Forty pounds of pressure per square inch is typical in many localities and is higher in some large cities. The *supply pipe* has a main shutoff valve near the meter. Opening and closing the *main shutoff valve* controls the water supply to the entire home. The supply pipe carries water to the house from the municipal supply and then branches out into pipes of smaller diameter to deliver water throughout the home. A *cold water main* carries water to the water heater and to all cold-water-using fixtures. *Hose bibs* (exterior water faucets) run from the cold water line to locations on the exterior of the house.

A *hot water main* starts at the water heater and runs parallel to the cold water main, providing hot water to all hot-water-using fixtures. The water heater is normally located in the garage area and has a pressure valve at the top of the tank that releases if the pressure inside the tank becomes too great, preventing a potential explosion. The hot and cold

FIGURE 16.5 ■ Plumbing System

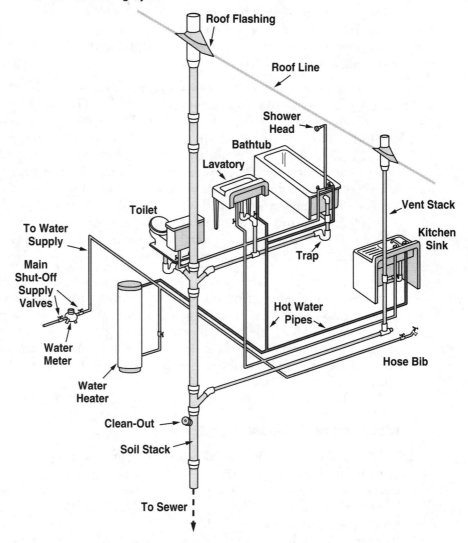

Reproduced with permission of the Council of Residential Specialists.

1 water mains are usually ¾-inch pipe and feed into smaller ½-inch pipes that supply the
2 various fixtures throughout the home. Except for the shutoff valve, these pipes are buried
3 in the ground or hidden in the walls or attic until they arrive at the various fixtures. There,
4 a shutoff valve is normally installed and the pipe diameter is reduced again. Hot water
5 controls on all plumbing fixtures are normally located on the left-hand side.

6   Waste water, under normal atmospheric pressure, is drained off by gravity to main sewer
7 lines. There are two important components of the low-pressure system. *Traps*, which are
8 beneath sinks, tubs, and showers, are typically U-shaped pipes that stay full of water. The
9 water forms a seal in the waste line and prevents odors and combustible gases from entering
10 the home. *Vent stacks* are pipes that protrude through the roof from the waste lines. The
11 vent stacks equalize the air pressure in the drain system and prevent suction generated by
12 flowing water from siphoning the water out of the traps. Drain pipes slant slightly downward
13 so that wastewater flows by the force of gravity. Fixtures empty into slanting branch drains

that connect to a large vertical drain called the *main soil stack*. The *soil stack* is a vertical 3-inch-diameter to 4-inch-diameter pipe that carries waste away from toilets and other fixtures. The soil stack empties into a slanting main drain that carries the waste water to the public sewer system or to the individual septic tank system for the house. (See Figure 16.5, Plumbing System.)

There are two general types of water meter faces. The direct-read meter has numerical readings and looks like an automobile odometer. The other type is a cumulative-reading meter that typically has five or six dials. The dials are numbered clockwise or counterclockwise and look like single-hand clock faces. The six-dial meter is labeled 1, 10, 100, 1,000, 10,000, and 100,000 for the number of cubic feet of water they record per revolution. Each dial turns the opposite direction from the one next to it. Read the dials from left to right, recording the number each pointer has just passed. When the pointer lies between two numbers, record the *lower* number. To read a six-dial meter, begin with the 100,000 dial, noting the smaller of the two numbers nearest the needle. Then read the dial labeled 10,000, and so on. Contact your local utility company for instructions regarding how to read the type of meter in your local area.

You can keep track of water used for a particular purpose (such as filling a swimming pool) by simply subtracting the "before" reading from the "after" reading on the meter, assuming no other water usage is going on at the same time. To help determine if a water stain is caused by a leak in the plumbing (as opposed to a roof leak, for example), turn off all the water outlets in the house and note the position of the one-cubic-foot dial on the meter. After 30 minutes, check the dial. If the dial has moved, it indicates a leak in the plumbing.

Mechanical Systems

Mechanical components include air cooling and heating systems. The most common type of heat distribution system is a *forced air/ducted* system that distributes warm air through ducts to each room of the house. There are two sets of ducts. The *supply air ducts* carry the hot air from the furnace to the distribution registers throughout the house. The return air intake collects the cooled air through *return ducts* to a filter located in the furnace, where it is reheated and recycled throughout the home. Older homes may have a gravity system that distributes heat and returns air throughout the system. Today, ducted systems are equipped with a blower to force the flow of air throughout the home. Heating cycles are rated by a Heating Seasonal Performance Factor (HSPF). The higher the rating, the more energy-efficient the heater.

Air-conditioning systems are rated either in BTUs (British thermal units) or in tons. Twelve thousand BTUs are equivalent to a one-ton capacity. The efficiency of electric air-conditioning systems is measured by a Seasonal Energy Efficiency Ratio (SEER). National minimum standards for central air conditioners require a SEER of 13. The higher the rating, the more energy-efficient the equipment. Increasing the SEER from 10 to 13 means that you are increasing the equipment's efficiency by about 30 percent.

A *heat pump* is equipped with a reversing valve that allows it to collect heat from cold outside air or from well water. This reversing mechanism allows a heat pump to heat the home in the winter and cool it in the summer. Heat pumps are very efficient in Florida, where winter temperatures are mild. In the event of a cold snap, electric heating coils are activated when the outside temperature drops to about 25 degrees.

F I G U R E 16.6 ■ Window Types

Fixed	Awning	Casement	Jalousie
Sliding	Hopper	Center Pivot	Double-hung or Single-hung

WEB LINK

To learn more about energy efficient homes, visit the U.S. Department of Energy's Office of Energy Efficiency and Renewable Energy at **www.eere.energy.gov**.

Insulation and Windows

The measure of the effectiveness of insulation is its resistance to heat flow, or **R-value**. The higher the R-value, the better the energy efficiency. Insulation materials include batt and blanket insulation (typically fiberglass); loose fill (blown cellulose); foam insulation (polyurethane and urea formaldehyde); and rigid board insulation. The U.S. Department of Energy (DOE) has established minimum recommended R-values specific to ZIP code areas.

Many existing homes have *single pane* or *single glazed* glass windows. In an average building, windows cover about 20 percent of the total wall area. As a result, in well-insulated structure, 20 percent to 50 percent of the total energy loss typically occurs through and around the windows. *Thermal pane* or *storm windows* are an energy-efficient alternative to single pane windows.

Thermal pane windows consist of two panes of glass in one frame with an air space in between. Thermal pane windows provide better insulation than regular glass and will help to keep your home warmer in the winter and cooler in the summer. Thermal windows reduce heating and cooling costs. It's the layer of air between the glass that acts as the insulation.

The width of the space between the panes is important because air spaces that are too wide or too narrow generally permit too much heat to be transferred. The best R-values are achieved when the spacing is between about ½ inch and ⅝ inch.

Although air is a good insulator, other gases work even better in preventing heat to move from one pane to the next. Today, most thermal window manufactures use argon gas, which is very stable, and thus has a low reaction rate to changing temperature. However, the windows need to be properly sealed so that the argon can't escape. If the seal becomes

1　defective, the window can cloud up. This is a result of water vapor's building up and con-
2　densing when the weather turns colder. Today, a special moisture-absorbing material is
3　used to catch any water vapor trying to sneak through the window seal.

4　　　Window styles include fixed, awning, casement, jalousie, sliding, hopper, center pivot,
5　and double or single-hung. (See Figure 16.6, Window Types.)

6　**Fixed.** Fixed pane windows are also called *picture* windows. They do not open, which
7　means they do not permit ventilation or easy cleaning. Fixed pane windows have sealed
8　edges to protect against air filtration. Fixed pane windows come in almost any size or shape
9　and with various degrees of glazing. In Florida, double-glazing or triple-glazing should be
10　considered for fixed pane windows, especially if they are large.

11　**Awning.** Awning windows typically are fixed at the top and tilt out with the aid of a crank
12　to provide ventilation but have a limited open space. Because they are easy to clean and
13　provide more security than other types of window, they are common in schools and in
14　multifamily housing.

15　**Casement.** Casement windows consist of one or more sashes hinged at the side like a door,
16　swinging horizontally out or in, usually with the aid of a crank. Older casements swing on
17　hinges while newer ones have pivot mechanisms. Most swing outward, but models that
18　swing inward are available.

19　　　Casements provide excellent ventilation because both halves of the window open.
20　Because they seal tightly when closed, they are considered energy efficient. Another
21　advantage of casements is they are easier to clean than most other windows because both
22　inside and outside surfaces are accessible from indoors. However, for safety reasons, it is
23　best to locate a casement window away from traffic areas such as sidewalks.

24　**Jalousie.** Jalousie (or louver) windows were common in older homes in south Florida
25　because they allowed maximum ventilation. Glass louvers that overlap one another form
26　the panes of a jalousie window. Operated with a crank or turn-screw, the glass louvers tilt
27　to open, permitting airflow. A major disadvantage of jalousie windows is that they are
28　almost impossible to seal. When closed, each glass louver rests against the one below it,
29　rarely if ever making an airtight seal, and the hinges along the sides are almost impossible
30　to seal without covering the entire window. They are not energy efficient and may be a
31　security risk.

32　**Sliding.** Horizontal sliding windows move back and forth on tracks. Usually only one
33　of the sashes moves and the other is fixed. Because only half of the window area can be
34　opened, sliding windows provide less ventilation area than casement windows. An advan-
35　tage is they are inexpensive, especially if the frame is aluminum, and easy to clean if the
36　moveable sash is removed.

37　**Hopper.** A hopper window is hinged at the bottom and opens into the room. A major dis-
38　advantage is that it does open into the room and thus interferes with window coverings.

39　**Center pivot.** This window pivots from a point at the center of the frame. It can be hazard-
40　ous if located in an area where people walk, such as near a sidewalk.

41　**Double-hung.** **Double-hung** windows open by sliding the bottom half of the window up
42　or sliding the top half down. Because only half of the window area can be open at one
43　time, they provide less ventilation than casement style windows. An advantage of double-
44　hung windows is they can be used to create air movement in the home by opening the top
45　portion of the windows on the coolest side of the house. Air will naturally rise out of the
46　higher opening, pulling cooler air in the lower opening.

Older double-hung windows have weight-and-pulley systems to make them easier to open. However, the weight-and-pulley system tends to stick or rattle and it is hard to stop air from leaking around the pulley openings. Newer models have spring-tension devices that work more efficiently.

Single-hung. **Single-hung** windows are probably the most common type of window today. They are similar to the double-hung window, but only the lower sash is movable.

WEB LINK

An informative fact sheet about insulation is available from the U.S. Department of Energy at www.ornl.gov/sci/roofs+walls/insulation/ins_01.html.

To view the U.S. Department of Energy's recommended R-values for existing homes by region, visit www.energysavers.gov/tips/insulation.cfm. Scroll down the page to the map and chart of R-values.

SUMMARY OF IMPORTANT POINTS

- The major lot types are the following: corner, interior, T-intersection, cul-de-sac, flag, and key.

- Two types of residential foundations used in Florida are (1) pier and (2) slab-on-grade. Pier foundations are used in coastal and flood-prone areas. Slab-on-grade foundations may be monolithic slabs or floating slabs.

- Three types of wood-frame construction are (1) platform, (2) balloon, and (3) post-and-beam. Platform is the most common of the three types.

- Roof styles include the following: gable, hip, saltbox, shed, flat, gambrel, and mansard. A dormer is a projection that extends out of the roof to provide additional light and ventilation. The pitch of a roof is its slope. Height (rise) is divided by distance (span or run) to determine the pitch.

- *R-value* refers to the effectiveness of insulation and is measured by its resistance to heat flow. The higher the R-value, the better the energy efficiency.

- Today's homes typically have electrical systems that provide 120-volt circuits plus 240-volt circuits for large household appliances. Circuit breakers are used to protect an electric circuit from damage caused by too much current. Ground-fault-interrupters (GFIs) are required in kitchens and bathrooms to protect a home's occupants from possible electrical shock.

- Amperage describes the amount of electricity or current flowing in a circuit. Wattage indicates how much energy a device consumes.

- Window styles include the following: fixed, awning, casement, jalousie, sliding, hopper, center pivot, and double- or single-hung. Single-hung windows have a lower sash that moves up and down and are most common today.

REVIEW QUESTIONS

1. A type of foundation that is used in low-lying coastal areas is called
   a. slab-on-grade.
   b. floating foundation.
   c. pier foundation.
   d. monolithic slab foundation.

2. A type of frame construction that allows for large spans between supporting side walls is
   a. balloon frame.
   b. post-and-beam construction.
   c. platform construction.
   d. pier frame.

3. If you were to build a commercial structure and because of limited ground space wanted to install the mechanical equipment on the roof, which roof design would be most appropriate?
   a. Flat
   b. Gambrel
   c. Mansard
   d. Saltbox

4. In areas near water in kitchens and bathrooms, building codes require special electrical outlets referred to as
   a. circuit breakers.
   b. grounded outlets.
   c. ground-fault-interrupters.
   d. step-down outlets.

5. You want to replace a ceiling fan and have removed the old fixture. The wiring to the old fixture consists of three wires: a black wire, a white wire, and a green wire. Which wire is the ground wire?
   a. Black
   b. White
   c. Green
   d. There is no ground wire.

6. The pipe that carries water to the water heater is referred to as a
   a. hot water main.
   b. cold water main.
   c. soil stack.
   d. supply pipe.

7. The purpose of a U-shaped trap under a kitchen sink is to
   a. prevent food debris from traveling through the plumbing pipes.
   b. catch a small object such as a wedding ring before it enters the soil stack.
   c. equalize the air pressure in the drain system.
   d. prevent combustible gases from entering the home.

8. An electrical cable stamped with the words *6/2 with ground* is MOST appropriate for wiring to
   a. a ceiling fan.
   b. a table lamp.
   c. an air conditioner.
   d. a home fax machine.

9. You are interested in adding roof insulation to your home to reduce your monthly electrical bill. Which government agency establishes minimum recommended R-values specific to your local area?
   a. Department of Energy
   b. Department of Housing and Urban Development
   c. Fannie Mae
   d. Environmental Protection Agency

10. You are walking through a seller's contemporary-design home. There are windows set high into a loft area, that are not designed to be opened. They function simply to bring light into the loft. What window type does this describe?
    a. Jalousie
    b. Casement
    c. Fixed
    d. Hopper

11. Which type of lot provides an open view down the street but may also suffer from vehicular headlights shining into the windows?
    a. Flag
    b. Key
    c. T-intersection
    d. Interior

12. Which type of lot is bounded by five or six other lots?
    a. Flag
    b. Key
    c. T-intersection
    d. Interior

CHAPTER

17

REAL ESTATE INVESTMENT ANALYSIS AND BUSINESS OPPORTUNITY BROKERAGE

OVERVIEW

Investors consider different factors in their attempt to achieve various investment objectives according to their individual financial status, income tax bracket, motives for investing, and access to credit. Different types of real estate offer various abilities to meet investor objectives. Experience indicates that investors are motivated by one or a combination of objectives: (1) safety of principal, (2) protection against inflation, (3) liquidity, (4) increased income (current and/or future), and (5) tax advantages.

This chapter compares business brokerage with real estate brokerage. It emphasizes the importance of special knowledge when practicing business brokerage. This chapter also defines basic accounting terms, and discusses the methods of appraising businesses.

After completing this chapter, the student should be able to:

- identify the advantages and disadvantages of investing in real estate;
- distinguish among the various types of risk;
- explain the concepts of liquidity and leverage;
- describe the similarities and differences between real estate brokerage and business brokerage;
- describe the types of expertise required in business brokerage;
- distinguish among the methods of appraising businesses; and
- describe the steps in the sale of a business.

KEY TERMS

appreciation	going concern value	liquidity
asset	goodwill	REIT
balance sheet	income statement	risk
cash flow	investment	static risk
dynamic risk	leverage	
equity	liquidation analysis	

NEED FOR REAL ESTATE INVESTMENT ANALYSIS

A knowledge of real estate investment analysis is important to a licensee in Florida because a real estate licensee is allowed to sell investment property. The public regards a real estate broker or sales associate as an expert in all types of properties. While the rewards of negotiating the purchase or sale of investment property are often greater than they are for other types of real estate, so are the liabilities for untrained or unknowledgeable people. Cases have gone to court because real estate licensees either gave bad advice or did not properly analyze an investment before recommending a course of action that could have been avoided by a knowledgeable professional.

Potential investors go to real estate professionals for help and guidance. Licensees must be qualified to provide the needed expertise when they accept the trust and confidence of a client. At the beginning of this book, the point was made that real estate licensees have one major commodity to offer the public—expertise. But part of being a professional also includes knowing when to consult a specialist (e.g., an attorney or an accountant) and when to have one's seller or buyer consult a specialist. The purpose of this chapter, therefore, is familiarization, a first step toward developing expertise in real estate investment matters.

Nature of Real Estate Investment Analysis

An **investment** is the outlay of an investor's money in anticipation of income or profit. Investors use some of their own money called **equity** and borrowed funds. *Real estate investment analysis* is the process of determining the extent to which real estate investments will achieve an investor's objectives.

REAL ESTATE AS AN INVESTMENT

Investors may choose to invest in real estate through a limited partnership. Another alternative is to invest in real estate through a *real estate investment trust* (REIT). A **REIT** offers investors the opportunity to invest in income-producing real estate properties. Individual REITs generally specialize in a particular type of property, such as multifamily communities, retail malls and shopping centers, office properties, and so forth. They provide a means for individuals to pool resources for investment in a professionally managed portfolio of real property and/or mortgages secured by real property. REITs are attractive because they offer diversification and liquidity, they are similar to mutual funds, and they offer the advantages of skilled centralized management and continuity of operation. REITs may be purchased through a stockbroker.

Types of Real Estate Investments

Investors interested in real estate can choose from several general types: residential, commercial, industrial, agricultural, and business opportunities.

Residential. Investments in residential properties include single-family homes, condominiums, apartments, and other multifamily complexes. Most experts agree that investing in an apartment project (or other income-producing property) is economically feasible when the projected future net income over a predetermined period will permit return of the investment (recover invested capital) and allow the investor an appropriate rate of return over the investment period.

In assessing the desirability of an apartment complex, several criteria should be considered, including the following: location, effective gross income, operating expenses, and property taxes. Existing properties should be inspected carefully, and repair and maintenance records should be studied to ensure that the property has been well maintained. A lack of proper maintenance is referred to as *deferred maintenance*.

Commercial. This category includes retail and office properties. Retail properties include downtown commercial properties, shopping centers, and regional malls. A shopping center's economic characteristics depend on the nature of existing leases and on operating expenses. An investor should study all leases carefully to find out how much of the original term remains, whether investors participate in tenant income from sales, and whether the leases provide for appropriate costs to be shifted to tenants. Long-term leases and a tendency on the part of tenants to renew their leases are among the main attractions of investing in office properties.

Industrial. Industrial uses of real estate in urban areas generally involve manufacturing, assembly, and/or distribution. To be suitable for industrial use, a site should be located near transportation facilities such as railroad stations, expressways, and airports because of the need to receive and ship by rail, truck, and air.

Agricultural. Agricultural properties are often purchased by farsighted investors-developers looking for large tracts of land that lie in the path of foreseeable urban growth. However, the holding period to realize such development potential may be many years.

Business opportunities. One of the categories that Chapter 475, F.S., defines as real estate is "any interest in business enterprises or business opportunities." This category includes the sale or lease of a business and goodwill of an existing business, including business assets such as the stock of a corporation.

Advantages of Real Estate as an Investment

Real estate investments have the following advantages:

- *Good rate of return*. Historically, real estate has produced a high rate of return for the owner-investor, compared with other types of investments.

- *Tax advantages*. Although the Tax Reform Act of 1986 eliminated or seriously reduced some of the tax advantages, real estate investments still receive some tax benefits.

- *Hedge against inflation*. The Bureau of Labor Statistics publishes the Consumer Price Index (CPI). The CPI measures the average change in prices over time for a fixed "market basket" of goods and services. Each of the thousands of items in the market basket is assigned a weight, according to its current relative importance to a consumer's budget. Costs of housing, food, clothing, transportation, medical care, entertainment, and other goods and services are obtained to determine price movements. The results then provide a reliable indicator of inflation. Historically, real estate prices have increased (property **appreciation**) at a faster pace than inflation. If a parcel of real property is acquired at market value or less, an owner will normally find that the sale price increases faster than other "market basket" prices. This ability to maintain or increase purchasing power is one reason real estate is regarded as one of the best protections against inflation.

1 ■ *Leverage*. Real estate is typically highly leveraged. An investor can usually borrow
2   70 percent to 75 percent of the appraised value to finance a real estate investment.
3   The goal of leveraging is to increase one's yield (return) on equity (investor's own
4   capital) by using borrowed funds.
5 ■ *Equity buildup*. As a property appreciates in value and the mortgage debt is
6   reduced, the investor's equity grows.

7 ## Disadvantages of Investing in Real Estate

8 Following are some of the disadvantages of investing in real estate:

9 ■ *Illiquidity*. The term **liquidity** refers to the ability to sell an investment very
10   quickly without loss of one's capital. Real estate is *not* considered to be a liquid
11   investment. Therefore, it is said to be illiquid. Recall that two of the critical
12   assumptions associated with the definition of market value (chapter 15) were
13   that (1) neither the buyer nor the seller is under any compulsion to buy or sell
14   and (2) the property is exposed on the market for a reasonable period of time.
15 ■ *Market is local in nature*. The real estate market is very local in nature. An inves-
16   tor usually is interested in a particular property type and geographic area. Other
17   types of investments, such as stocks, are bought and sold in an international
18   marketplace.
19 ■ *Need for expert help*. Many expenses are associated with investing in real estate,
20   including the need for property managers, financial consultants, and legal experts.
21 ■ *Management*. Real estate is a labor-intensive investment. Properties must be
22   cared for, rents collected, and so forth.
23 ■ *Risk*. An investor must weigh the chance of losing invested capital. Tenant turn-
24   over, increasing property taxes, and increased costs associated with operations
25   are a few examples of the types of risk to which a real estate investor is exposed.

26 # ANALYZING INVESTMENT PROPERTIES

27 A number of factors (influences or forces) affect supply and demand, and thus the value, of
28 investment real estate. Each of the various types of investment properties has a particular
29 set of considerations that real estate licensees need to recognize. These value-creating
30 influences affect a property, depending on its relationship to the economy, location, physi-
31 cal characteristics, and legal characteristics.

32 ## Relationship to the Economy

33 One of the external forces affecting a property is the economy or, more appropriately, the
34 economi*es*. Both the local and the national economies must be considered.

35 **Local economy.** Local economic considerations include the existing stock of available units
36 and new development of competing properties. Supply and demand factors are important
37 considerations. An investor would be ill-advised to begin construction of a new apartment
38 complex in a community already experiencing a surplus of new apartment units. The pro-
39 ductivity of the property would be impaired to the extent that the investor could not hope
40 to achieve maximum return on the investment.

National economy. The national debt, employment levels, interest rates, availability of credit, and construction costs are some of the factors that influence the national economy and also the real estate market.

Location

The importance of *location* is undisputed as it applies to real property. No two parcels of real property are exactly alike because location alone creates a difference. Each property is unique and in a fixed location. Investor preferences for location vary. The economic characteristic referred to as *situs* (the preference by people for a certain location) indicates the influences on value created by location. Because real property is fixed in its location, it is affected greatly by its immediate surroundings. A change in land use of surrounding properties, for example, can have a positive or a negative impact on a particular property.

Destination properties. Because the land is immobile, investors must find ways to direct an income stream to the property. Destination properties include *service industries* that support the needs of a local community, such as local repair shops, barbershops, local real estate agencies, and financial institutions.

Origin properties. *Origin properties* are just as immobile and fixed as destination properties, but often they are not as attractive or as well situated on access routes. As a result, they must originate something (a product) to seek out an income stream. Assembly plants, manufacturing facilities, and distribution centers represent origin properties. These properties are regarded as *export activities* in any analysis of a community's economic base.

Physical Characteristics

If one site and building's size, shape, and form were the same as all others, an investor could make investment decisions based on location alone. Seldom, if ever, are two properties found with identical physical characteristics.

Site. In evaluating properties, investors are faced with the same problems as appraisers are. One of the more common ways of neutralizing variables of a site is through the use of *units of comparison*. Usually, both appraisers and investors use square feet, front feet, or acres as units of comparison. These methods of comparing sites are practical because they permit direct comparison of competing sites, regardless of differences in size or shape. For residential properties, the square-foot method is usually used. For commercial properties, either the front-foot or the square-foot unit of comparison may be used. For farms or large tracts of undeveloped land, the acre normally is used.

Other physical characteristics of a site that deserve an investor's consideration are related to topography. A site's surface, subsoil structure, drainage, orientation and view, and exposure to or protection from possible noxious environmental influences are all elements for consideration in a thorough site analysis.

Building. Potential real estate investors will normally have at least one alternative to buying an existing property: They could buy a vacant site and construct a new building. Even when this course of action is not a serious consideration, the cost of this alternative approach tends to set the maximum price they will pay for an existing property. If the existing building has deficiencies, the value of these deficiencies subtracted from the cost of a new building indicates a reasonable market value for the building. Notice the use of the term *market value*, rather than the term *investment value*. Investment value is *not* market value. Investment value is the worth of a building or property to an individual investor based on that investor's individual standards for achieving a goal. It is not established by market activity, although that may be a major influence. The value of investment property should be based on the return and appreciation it will yield, not only on the cost to build. The following are three considerations that influence a building's investment value:

1. *Exterior considerations*. The first impression a building makes on both tenants and customers is its exterior and its environment. The visual image (*curb appeal*) is of great importance: building age and design, landscaping, walkways, and parking areas. Is it well maintained? What is lacking? What needs repairing? Is each repair major or minor? Is each deterioration *curable* (correction adds value) or *incurable* (correction costs more than the value added)?

2. *Interior considerations*. Investors need to make a deliberate and thorough inspection of the premises and make a record as the inspection progresses. All of the following should be noted: the number and condition of each individual office or apartment (the size, layout, number of rooms and baths, and the views from each location); the overall physical quality of the building from the inside; the condition of the plumbing, hardware, carpeting, walls, appliances, and electrical fixtures; and the condition of halls, foyers, entrances, laundry rooms, storage rooms, and recreation facilities.

3. *Building operating expenses*. While the cost of property taxes and insurance are beyond the control of investors, these costs should be verified. All other operating expenses should be examined carefully before investing. Have previous owners allocated annual amounts to a reserve for replacement of short-lived items (e.g., appliances, carpets, drapes)? Do recorded expenditures for repairs and maintenance reflect the approximate condition of the building? Will the investor be required to spend more in the future for maintenance and repairs?

In many instances, the exterior and interior features of a building at first may satisfy a potential investor. Analysis of operating expenses, however, may eliminate the property from further consideration because of unusual expenses attributable to building location, orientation, or design. For example, there may be an abnormally high expenditure for electricity owing to faulty design or an exceptionally high expense for cooling and heating because of glass walls or inadequate insulation.

Legal Characteristics

Investors in real estate are investing in more than land, buildings, and equipment. They are investing in a bundle of legal rights and protected interests. The value of their investment is influenced by the degree to which these rights and ownership interests are present.

Rights. Before investing, investors must determine what type of legal entity will be best to accomplish their investment objectives. A variety of legal ownership forms are available, and each has its own legal and tax consequences. The most commonly used forms of investment ownership are sole proprietorships, tenancies in common, joint tenancies, limited partnerships, corporations, business trusts, and REITs.

Whether a property is expected to show a tax loss or profit frequently determines the type of ownership form to use. The desirability of having the survivorship feature of joint tenancy sometimes determines whether to use tenancy in common. Both a limited partnership and a corporation provide liability protection. While the corporate form is more complex, the ability to raise capital by selling stock might influence investors to use the corporate form. Each of the forms of ownership offers advantages and disadvantages. Investors should seek professional advice in determining the greatest net advantage.

Limitations. Many authorities believe that a type of risk termed *legal risk* is associated with real estate investments: Risk is inherent in acquiring title to real property. Warranty deeds and title insurance serve to minimize such risk but do not entirely eliminate it. Additionally, litigation against real property owners because of alleged noncompliance with ordinances, tenant suits, or liability for accidents occurring on the property is a potential problem that is part of the legal risk.

An important consideration for all investors should be to determine if the use of a site represents its highest and best use. In most situations, the legal use of land is prescribed by zoning ordinances and represents the highest use of a site. It is up to the potential investor to decide which of the alternative types of available improvements and uses might represent the best use, in accordance with the concept of highest and best use. Fortunately, procedures have been developed by appraisers to assist in making such decisions. (See chapter 15.)

ASSESSMENT OF RISKS

Risk is the chance of losing all or part of an investment. Some degree of risk is always associated with an investment. **Static risk** is risk that can be transferred to an insurer such as the risk of vandalism, fire, and so forth. **Dynamic risk** is risk that arises from the continual change in the business environment and therefore dynamic risk cannot be transferred to an insurer.

Risks Associated with General Business Conditions

Business risk. Sometimes referred to as *operating business risk*, this category of risk is associated with the degree of variance between budgeted (projected) income and expenses and actual income and expenses.

Financial risk. Sometimes referred to as *operating financial risk*, this category of risk is associated with the ability of a property to pay operating expenses from funds provided from operations, borrowing, and equity sources.

Purchasing-power risk. This category of risk is related to inflation. In an inflationary period, the ability of a property to produce a good yield may be offset by a corresponding loss of purchasing power due to inflation. After paying all expenses, a loss may result from what first appeared to be a profitable investment. The reason is that if the rents are fixed by the lease, the gross income may not keep pace with inflation, while the operating expenses increase at the inflation rate.

Interest-rate risk. Remember the IRV formula in chapter 15? To find the value of a property using this formula, the net operating income (NOI) is divided by the rate of capitalization (required rate of return). While debt service (financing cost) is not deducted from gross income to arrive at net income, an investor nevertheless has to pay that debt service, which effectively reduces the real yield.

Assume, for the moment, that the only change in a real estate investment is that the interest rate is raised by the lender. The property remains unchanged, the owners remain the same, management does not change. However, with the increase in interest rates, the value of the property as an investment goes down. That is interest-rate risk at work.

Risks That Affect Return

Historically, businesses and individuals have put money in investments that offer the highest return commensurate with the liquidity and safety of the money.

Liquidity risk. Real estate investments are particularly susceptible to liquidity risk (illiquidity). *Liquidity risk* is the possible loss that may be incurred if the investment has to be converted quickly into cash. There is no highly organized market for real estate investments, and their resale usually requires time and considerable expense.

Safety risk. *Safety risk* is the possible loss of invested capital (return of investment) and/or expected earnings (return on investment). Safety risk is composed of market risk (possible loss of invested capital) and risk of default (possible loss of earnings):

- *Market risk* is the type of risk associated with a decrease in the market value of an investment as a result of increased interest rates (the interest-rate risk at work). Often, market risk is magnified by long periods of time. Leaving the money invested exposed to the cyclical gyrations of the money markets over extended periods increases the risk of loss. For example, savings associations can lose money by holding long-term investments in low-yielding mortgages.

- *Risk of default* is the risk that promised earnings will be lost by the investor because of the failure of the investment to earn as expected.

If everything were equal, an investor would prefer a liquid, short-term investment because less risk would be involved. However, the possibility of a higher yield will induce some investors to commit funds to a less-liquid, long-term investment. It is a basic economic premise that risk and the desired rate of return are directly related (e.g., high risk, high return).

LEVERAGE

Leverage is the use of borrowed funds to finance the purchase of an asset. Leverage is the use of other people's money to make more money. Most investors use leverage to increase their purchasing power. For example, an investor purchases a property for $1 million and 10 percent down. The investor has increased purchasing power by using borrowed funds to purchase a property costing ten times the cash investment.

An investor's goal is not only to increase purchasing power but also to earn a higher return on equity. The investor wants an investment property that can produce cash flow in excess of the cost of borrowing the funds. If the benefits from borrowing exceed the costs of borrowing, it is called *positive leverage*. If the borrowed funds cost more than they are producing, it is called *negative leverage*.

To understand the impact of leveraging, consider a property that costs $100,000 and produces net income of $10,000 per year. If purchased for cash, the investor's annual rate of return on the equity invested is 10 percent ($10,000 income ÷ $100,000 equity). Assume instead that this investor leverages the purchase by borrowing $75,000 at 8 percent ($6,000 interest) annually and makes a down payment of $25,000. The $10,000 income earned from the investment in the previous example is reduced by the cost of financing to $4,000. The resulting *return on equity* invested is an attractive 16 percent

($4,000 income taking into account financing cost ÷ $25,000 equity = .16 or 16% rate of return on equity). This is positive leverage at work!

The higher the interest rate and the higher the loan-to-value ratio, the more cash flow from operations required to pay the principal and interest payments. If cash flow is reduced by increasing vacancy rates or an overzealous earnings forecast, the risk is greater because the larger the loan amount, the greater the chances that the investor will either have to invest more out-of-pocket funds or default on the mortgage. This increased risk is the price an investor pays for the higher potential benefits of leverage.

BUSINESS BROKERAGE

Nearly 25 percent of the 14 million businesses in this country change hands each year! Business brokers and business entities engaged in the sale, purchase, or lease of businesses must qualify and hold real estate licenses. Business brokerages may be classified into business enterprise brokerages and business opportunity brokerages.

Business enterprise brokers normally deal in corporate transactions involving the sale and purchase of businesses that provide goods and/or services. Ordinarily, business enterprises are large transactions usually involving the purchase or exchange of corporate stock and the purchase of corporate assets (an **asset** is anything of value).

Business opportunity brokers typically deal in the sale and purchase of smaller businesses, such as sole proprietorships. These businesses have limited amounts of fixed assets (e.g., real property, equipment). Sometimes the real estate owned by the business is the primary component of value. Other times the real estate involved is in the form of a lease. Most business leases are assignable. Whether an existing lease is assigned to the new business owner depends on the terms of the lease.

Business brokers must understand and be able to value a business opportunity, including tangible assets and intangible assets. A *tangible asset* can be touched and has actual substance such as inventory. *Intangible assets* are assets that cannot be touched and that do not have actual substance such as a business opportunity's reputation.

Similarities to Real Estate Brokerage

475.01, F.S.

A real estate relationship is established every time the sale of real property or the assignment of a lease is an integral part of a business brokerage transaction. The transfer of some interest in real property is often involved in business brokerage activities.

Differences from Real Estate Brokerage

Business brokerage differs from real estate brokerage in at least five ways. (See Figure 17.1, Brokerage Comparisons.)

1. Business brokerage usually involves assets other than real estate, such as *personal property* and *goodwill*. **Goodwill** is the intangible asset attributed to a business's reputation and the expectation of continued customer loyalty. The value of goodwill may be approximated by subtracting the value of tangible assets from the value of the business. Other intangible assets that add value include licenses, franchises, copyrights, and patents.

FIGURE 17.1 ■ **Brokerage Comparisons**

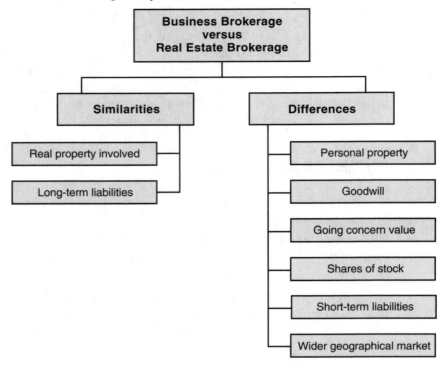

2. The value of an established business may differ from the value of the real estate. This means that the total value, called the *going concern value*, may be different from the real estate value. **Going concern value** is the value of an established business property compared with the value of just the physical assets of a business that is not yet established.

3. Unlike real estate, the value of a business may be allocated among shares of corporate *stock*, which may be either traded publicly or privately held.

4. Business brokerage transactions frequently involve the assumption by the purchaser of short-term liabilities as well as long-term liabilities such as a mortgage. Examples of short-term liabilities include accounts payable and sales taxes collected by the seller but not remitted to the state.

5. As noted in chapter 19, the real estate market is local in nature. On the other hand, the business brokerage market is much wider in geographic scope, perhaps nationwide or even international.

EXPERTISE REQUIRED IN BUSINESS BROKERAGE

Business brokerage brings the broker or sales associate into contact with many problems not normally encountered in real estate brokerage. For example:

- What is the value of a business opportunity that consists solely of an intangible interest in a going concern?

- What is the impact on existing clientele if the business is sold?

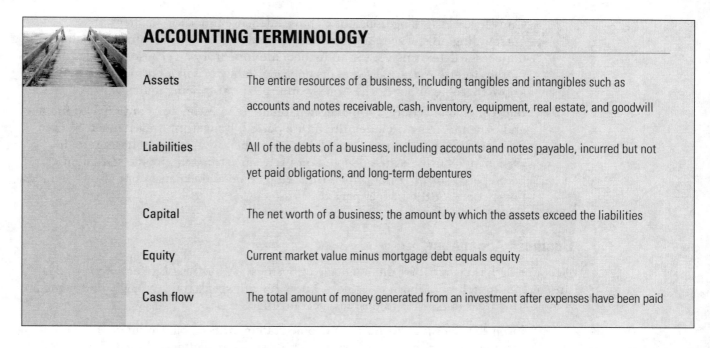

ACCOUNTING TERMINOLOGY

Assets	The entire resources of a business, including tangibles and intangibles such as accounts and notes receivable, cash, inventory, equipment, real estate, and goodwill
Liabilities	All of the debts of a business, including accounts and notes payable, incurred but not yet paid obligations, and long-term debentures
Capital	The net worth of a business; the amount by which the assets exceed the liabilities
Equity	Current market value minus mortgage debt equals equity
Cash flow	The total amount of money generated from an investment after expenses have been paid

- What of a purchaser's concern that the seller might go into competition with the purchaser?
- If the business is to be acquired by another corporation, would the seller be well advised to take stock in the other corporation?

These few questions illustrate that licensees need expertise in areas other than real estate for business brokerage. Some of the more important areas in which business brokers should be knowledgeable are corporate finance, business accounting, valuation of businesses, and the applicable laws that govern business dealings.

Corporate Finance

Business brokers know that efficient financial management is as important to profitability as good production know-how. This fact dictates that business brokers have a working knowledge of the following:

- *The classes and characteristics of corporate stock.* There are two basic types of stock: *preferred* and *common.* Some firms do not issue preferred stock, but all corporations must have common stock because it represents ownership.
- *Securities analysis and valuation.* Just as real estate brokers advise their principals, business brokers must be capable of providing advice and assistance to their principals, especially in areas of securities analysis and valuation. New owners often feel a need to raise additional funds or to refinance the capital structure. Then the question of selecting the proper type of security, or securities, must be decided. Among the factors involved in selecting sources of funds are market conditions, debt or equity funds, tax impact, voting control, stability of profits, and rate of earnings.
- *The management of working capital.* Working capital is defined as the difference between total current assets and total current liabilities. Management of this working capital is of paramount importance to the success of a business. Efficiency is lost if funds kept on hand are in excess of foreseeable needs.

Conversely, it is dangerous not to have adequate funds for payment of outstanding bills, wages, and salaries. Keeping excessive inventory on hand is unnecessarily expensive, yet an inadequate inventory can cause lost sales or production time. Business brokers engaged to buy or sell a business need to be knowledgeable about how a firm's working capital is being managed.

- *Budgeting.* The generic term *budgeting* refers to an estimate of anticipated income and expenditures over a definite future period. Budget information can be used for planning and also to control borrowing, spending, and purchasing. If all aspects of a business are budgeted properly, an estimated income statement can be prepared showing not only estimated income and expenses but also estimated net income for the budget period.

Business Accounting

Accounting has been called the language of business. A business broker who is to deal in the sale and purchase of businesses must know how to speak the language. Following are some of the areas important to business accounting:

- *Income statement analysis.* The **income statement** is a concise summary of all income and expenses of a business for a *stated period of time*. It is designed to show the results of business operations over a specific period and to provide the basic data for analyzing the reasons for a firm's profits or losses. Other names sometimes given to the income statement are *profit and loss statement*, *operating statement*, *statement of income*, and *statement of net earnings*.

- *Balance sheet analysis.* The **balance sheet** shows the company's financial position at a stated *moment in time*, the close of business on the date of the balance sheet. It is customary to prepare an income statement and a balance sheet at the same time. This allows the net income or loss shown on the income statement for the prior period to be reflected on the balance sheet as of that particular moment.

- *Cash flow analysis.* **Cash flow** is the total amount of money generated from an investment after expenses have been paid. Operating expenses include reserves for replacement and payment of mortgage principal and interest. Cash flow disregards depreciation because depreciation does not involve an outlay of cash. A business broker is usually more interested in cash flow and the extent to which cash flow is sheltered from taxes than in whether the business produces a taxable income.

- *Asset depreciation.* Business brokers must be able to separate the depreciable assets of a business into real property and personal property.

- *Taxation.* Anyone interested in buying or selling a business knows the critical role taxes play in the success or failure of that business. Also known is that tax laws are forever changing. Thus, business brokers must be alert to the client's need for expert tax advice. (See also chapter 18.)

VALUATION OF BUSINESSES

In addition to being knowledgeable in the above areas, business brokers who specialize in business valuation may be called on to appraise businesses. Some of the more frequently encountered situations in which businesses need to be appraised include:

- the contemplated sale, purchase, or exchange of businesses;

- allocation of the assets of a business for tax depreciation purposes;

- obtaining of a loan or insurance coverage;

- the exercise of eminent domain by a governmental entity;

- drafting buy-sell agreements;

- in the event of partial or complete destruction or when businesses voluntarily go out of business;

- estate settlements; and

- assigning reasonable values to the business and its assets for businesses with stock option plans.

Methods of appraising businesses. The methods used to estimate a business's value are similar to those used in appraising real property. (See chapter 15.)

- *Comparable sales analysis.* Where records reveal previous sale prices for businesses with a high degree of similarity, the appraiser can use professional judgment to account for existing differences and to arrive at a close approximation of the market value of a business.

- *Reproduction or replacement cost less depreciation analysis.* This method is appropriate for estimating the value of improvements of any type. When reproduction cost is used as a basis, the appraiser calculates the amount required to duplicate exactly the business or building being appraised. When replacement cost is used, the appraiser calculates the cost that would result in a business's (or building's) having the same use and capabilities as the one being appraised, even though the new business/building might differ physically.

- *Income capitalization analysis.* Most income-producing properties derive a large portion of their value from their ability to produce an income stream. This method of appraising attempts to estimate accurately the present value of expected future benefits (earnings and appreciation of assets) by converting the anticipated income stream into a present value through the use of a capitalization rate. The income capitalization approach is the best approach for valuing a business.

- *Liquidation analysis.* The liquidation of a business may become necessary because of failure of a business, the death of a sole proprietor, the dissolution of a partnership, a court order, or any number of other reasons. In a **liquidation analysis**, business brokers and financial experts must consider such factors as the ability of the firm to pay off short-term obligations, the value of the inventory on hand, and the liquidation value of preferred stock.

Key Applicable Laws

In addition to all of the activities mentioned above, a business broker is required to observe the many regulatory provisions, including Chapter 475, F.S., and state and federal securities laws.

STEPS IN THE SALE OF A BUSINESS

The sale of a business generally can be described as a series of steps. In the case of an outright purchase (and sale), the following nine-step sequence normally occurs:

1. List the business for sale.
2. Identify all assets belonging to the business and separate them from all assets that are not part of the business sale (personal).
3. Establish a value for the business, using the various methods of appraisal previously mentioned.
4. Subtract the value of all short-term and long-term liabilities (including the value of preferred stock) from the value of the business.
5. If organized as a corporation, divide the net value of the business by the number of common shares of stock outstanding. The value per share resulting then can be multiplied by the number of shares to be transferred. (*Note*: Most small businesses are sold as an asset sale even if the business is held as a corporation.)
6. Check and recheck to ensure compliance with all pertinent laws.
7. Market (advertise) the business.
8. Secure a buyer and have the buyer sign a confidentiality/non-disclosure agreement before releasing the name, location, and financial information regarding the business.
9. Enter into a contract with both parties.
10. Establish a due diligence period for the buyer to inspect the financials of the business.
11. If real estate is not sold with the business, an assignment of the lease or a new lease from the landlord is prepared; if real estate is included in the sale, title work is ordered.
12. Coordinate with all parties involved to schedule a date for closing the transaction.

SUMMARY OF IMPORTANT POINTS

- Real estate investment trusts (REITs) offer investors the opportunity to invest in a pool of income-producing properties under professional management.
- Investors can choose from several types of real estate investments: residential, commercial, industrial, agricultural, and business opportunities.
- Advantages of real estate investment include the following: good rate of return, tax advantages, hedge against inflation, leverage, and equity buildup.
- Disadvantages of investing in real estate include the following: illiquidity, local market, need for expert help, management requirements, and risk.
- Destination properties include service industries that support the needs of the local community. Origin properties originate a product (export activities) to seek an income stream from outside the local community.
- *Investment value* is the worth of a building or property to an individual investor based on that investor's individual standards for achieving a goal.

- *Risk* is the chance of losing all or part of an investment. *Static risk* is risk that can be transferred to an insurer. Dynamic risk arises from the continual change in the business environment. Dynamic risk cannot be transferred to an insurer.

- Risk associated with general business conditions include the following: business risk, financial risk, purchasing-power risk, and interest-rate risk.

- *Leverage* is the use of borrowed funds to finance the purchase of an asset. Positive leverage occurs when the benefits exceed the cost of borrowing. Negative leverage occurs if the borrowed funds cost more than they are producing.

- An *asset* is anything of value. A tangible asset can be touched and has actual substance. An intangible asset has value but does not have physical substance, such as the goodwill of a business. Goodwill is attributed to a business's reputation and the expectation of continued customer loyalty.

- *Going concern value* is the value of an established business property compared with the value of just the physical assets of a business that is not yet established.

- An *income statement* is a concise summary of all income and expenses of a business for a stated period of time. A balance sheet shows the company's financial position at a stated moment in time.

- *Cash flow* is the total amount of money generated from an investment after expenses have been paid.

- The methods of appraising business are comparable sales analysis, reproduction or replacement cost, income capitalization analysis, and liquidation analysis.

R E V I E W   Q U E S T I O N S

1. Investors who want to invest in office buildings and apartment complexes but want the advantages of liquidity and diversification often consider investing in
   a. a real estate investment trust.
   b. a large property management company.
   c. a mutual fund that invests in the broad stock market.
   d. none of the above.

2. A case in which the interest paid for borrowed funds is less than the overall rate of return to an investor is an example of
   a. loan-to-value ratio.
   b. positive leverage.
   c. negative leverage.
   d. yield.

3. Business risk (operating business risk) is chance of loss associated with the
   a. variance between projected and actual income and expenses.
   b. ability to pay all operating expenses from proceeds generated by the investment.
   c. increase in interest rates during the period of investment.
   d. effect of inflation on purchasing power.

4. Investment value is
   a. market value.
   b. effective gross income capitalized by an appropriate rate of capitalization.
   c. the worth of an investment property offered on the open market with no time constraints.
   d. the worth of an investment property to an individual investor based on the investor's standards.

5. What should an investor consider in evaluating a real estate investment?
   a. Liquidity
   b. Tax considerations
   c. Stability of income
   d. All of the above

6. A phosphate mining facility would be regarded as
   a. a destination property.
   b. an origin property.
   c. a secondary industry.
   d. a commercial property.

7. For investment purposes, the value of an investment property should be based on the
   a. property's return and the appreciation it will yield.
   b. cost to reproduce the property.
   c. prestige and appreciation the investment will afford.
   d. net income of the property capitalized by current market capitalization rates.

8. Intangible assets of a business do NOT include
   a. goodwill.
   b. customer loyalty.
   c. trademarks.
   d. improvements.

9. Which class of stock must all corporations have?
   a. Debenture bonds
   b. Preferred stock
   c. Convertible bonds
   d. Common stock

10. A firm's working capital is customarily defined as the difference between the firm's total
    a. current assets and total current liabilities.
    b. current liabilities and total cash on hand.
    c. short-term liabilities and total cash on hand.
    d. long-term liabilities and total accounts receivable.

11. How does business brokerage differ from real estate brokerage?
    a. There is usually the need for an appraisal.
    b. An interest in real property is involved.
    c. Intangible assets must be considered.
    d. A lease may be involved.

12. The financial report that indicates a firm's financial position at a stated moment in time is the
    a. operating statement.
    b. balance sheet.
    c. working capital statement.
    d. statement of net earnings.

13. The value of an established business property, compared with the value of just the physical assets of a business that is NOT yet established, is referred to as
    a. going concern value.
    b. goodwill.
    c. business enterprise.
    d. tangible assets.

14. Reasons for appraising a business and its assets do NOT include
    a. to obtain financing.
    b. when a governmental unit intends to exercise its power of eminent domain over a business location.
    c. when a business has been destroyed by known or unknown causes.
    d. to ensure compliance with all pertinent state and federal securities laws.

15. A concise summary of all income and expenses of a business for a stated period of time is the
    a. balance sheet.
    b. income statement.
    c. cash flow statement.
    d. asset sheet.

16. All of the resources of a business, including tangibles and intangibles, are referred to as the
    a. net worth.
    b. capital.
    c. gross income.
    d. assets.

17. The cost to duplicate exactly the business or building being appraised is the
    a. replacement cost.
    b. benchmark.
    c. reproduction cost.
    d. liquidation analysis.

18. Investment in an apartment building is regarded as economically feasible if it
    a. shows an appropriate return on the investment within two years.
    b. shows an appropriate return on the investment and recovers the invested capital.
    c. does not show a negative cash flow.
    d. does not show a negative after-tax cash flow.

19. Which expense is NOT considered in a cash flow analysis of a manufacturing plant?
    a. Mortgage loan principal
    b. Depreciation of factory equipment
    c. Reserve for replacement of factory equipment
    d. Expense associated with making the plant energy efficient

20. The market value of an apartment building is $350,000. The investor has leveraged $300,000. What is the investor's equity in the property?
    a. $50,000
    b. $300,000
    c. $350,000
    d. $650,000

18

TAXES AFFECTING REAL ESTATE

1 OVERVIEW

2 City, county, school board, and numerous special tax districts are empowered to impose
3 taxes directly on real property in Florida as part of the powers delegated to them by the
4 state government. The U.S. Constitution prohibits the federal government from taxing
5 real property, passing that right on to the state and local governments. Florida is one of
6 the states, however, that does not tax real estate at the state level.

7 After completing this chapter, the student should be able to:

8 ■ distinguish between immune and exempt or partially exempt properties;

9 ■ calculate the total tax exemptions on a property, given a scenario;

10 ■ describe the various personal exemptions available to qualified owners of home-
11 stead property;

12 ■ compute the property tax on a specific parcel, given the current tax rates,
13 assessed value, and eligible exemptions;

14 ■ list the steps involved in the tax appeal procedure;

15 ■ describe the purpose of Florida's Green Belt Law;

16 ■ calculate the cost of a special assessment, given the conditions and amounts
17 involved; and

18 ■ list tax advantages resulting from home ownership.

19 KEY TERMS

adjusted basis	depreciation	mill
ad valorem	exempt	partially exempt
assessed value	Green Belt Law	special assessments
boot	immune	taxable value
capital gain	just value	tax shelter

F I G U R E 18.1 ■ Property Tax Schedule

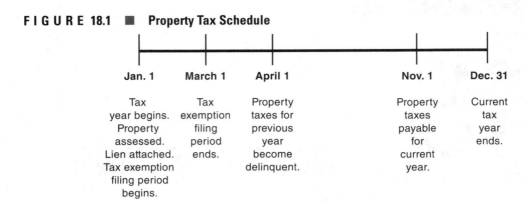

Jan. 1	March 1	April 1	Nov. 1	Dec. 31
Tax year begins. Property assessed. Lien attached. Tax exemption filing period begins.	Tax exemption filing period ends.	Property taxes for previous year become delinquent.	Property taxes payable for current year.	Current tax year ends.

CITY AND COUNTY PROPERTY TAXES

193, F.S.

Property taxes provide the bulk of local government revenues in Florida. They account for a large portion of the revenue needed to provide law enforcement, fire protection, and other services.

The Real Property Taxation Process

197.122, F.S.
193.023(2), F.S.

Real estate taxes (commonly called *property taxes*) are based on the value of real property, hence the term **ad valorem** tax, which means *according to value*. Florida law requires that the county property appraiser assess real property for all levels of government, thus avoiding duplication and possible controversy. All real property assessments must be updated annually.

Property taxes in Florida are levied on a calendar-year basis. Taxes are paid *in arrears* (at the end of the tax year) for the period January 1 through December 31 each year. (See Figure 18.1, Property Tax Schedule.) Property taxes become a lien on all real estate in Florida on January 1 each year. This lien is legally superior to any other lien, regardless of date. Taxes are payable to the county tax collector on or after November 1 each year. Property owners may pay property taxes in four installments or in a single payment. A discount system permits property owners to realize a discount through prompt payment of taxes. All payments made on or after March 1 must be for the full amount of taxes levied. Property taxes for the previous year become delinquent on April 1.

Determining "Just Value"

193.011, F.S.

Property taxes are levied against land and all improvements to the land. The assessed values of the land and improvements are arrived at separately and then combined to reflect a single assessed value. The state supreme court has interpreted Florida statutes as requiring that all real property be assessed at **just value**. Just value is the fair and reasonable value based on objective valuation methods. In arriving at a just valuation, county property appraisers take into consideration property characteristics such as location, size, and condition of the property. The county property appraiser also considers the highest and best use of the property and, if income producing, the income generated from the property. Just value, for ad valorem purposes, may not conform to market value, but it is calculated in relation to a market value base.

Property appraisers apply three approaches to value: the sales comparison, cost-depreciation, and income approaches. (See chapter 15.) If the property is sold during the year, the sale price becomes a factor for consideration in assessing the value of the property, but it is not the controlling factor. Representatives of the property appraiser's office typically go into the community to assess property, collecting data using specific forms and recording procedures. The information obtained from field trips is then processed through a computer, using appropriate valuation formulas to render an objective estimate of assessed value. **Assessed value** is the value of a property established for property tax purposes.

Once an assessment has been placed on a property, the owner must be informed. A Notice of Proposed Property Taxes is mailed to the property owner at the address of record. The notice is also called a TRIM (Truth in Millage) Notice. It is the responsibility of each property owner to see that a current mailing address is on file for all properties owned. Current addresses are needed to ensure that owners receive a notice of change in assessment before the time allowed for protest has expired.

Any property owner is entitled to protest a property assessment, but not every protest will be successful. For example, an owner of a home on a *standard lot* in a large, completely developed subdivision who complains that the lot was assessed too high will have little hope of getting the assessment changed. If the assessed value of the lot were changed, all of the owners of similar lots could protest their assessments.

The same homeowner might have a better chance of obtaining a lowered assessment if the evidence indicates the *house* was assessed at a value greater than justified. The county property appraiser has fairly complete details on the square footage, construction materials, year built, and amount of estimated depreciation since the date of construction, as well as records showing the assessed values of similar structures in the neighborhood.

Protest Procedure

When a Florida property owner feels the assessed value is inaccurate or does not reflect fair market value, the owner can use the following three-step protest procedure:

Step one. The first step is to seek an adjustment by contacting the county property appraiser or a representative of that office. A property owner is allowed 25 days after the TRIM Notice is mailed to protest the assessment to the county property appraiser. If the arguments of the property owner are valid and have a basis in fact, the county property appraiser is authorized to make a change and to lower the assessed value.

194.015, F.S.

Step two. If the property owner's request for an adjustment is rejected, the owner may file an appeal (petition) with the Value Adjustment Board. This board is made up of five members: two county commissioners, one school board member, and two citizen members. If the board agrees with the taxpayer that the assessed value of the property is too high, the board has the authority to change the assessment. If the board decides that the county property appraiser assigned the correct assessment value, the board will reject the taxpayer's request.

Step three. The final step available to a property owner seeking a change in assessed value is litigation in the courts. The taxpayer may pay the taxes under protest and file a suit (a *certiorari proceeding*, meaning a review of the matter by the courts) against the county property appraiser and the county tax collector. The property owner's petition must be filed within the statutory period (Chapter 194, F.S.). The court may not arbitrarily assign an assessment value to a property. It may, however, specify the methods and procedures

F I G U R E 18.2 ■   Protest Procedure: Property Owner Disagrees with Assessed Value

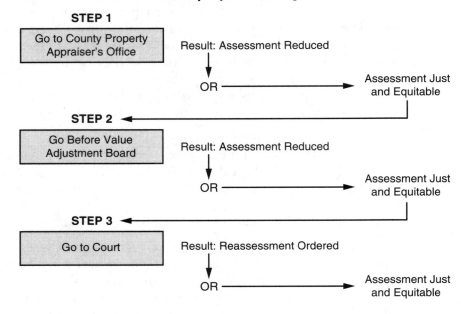

that the county property appraiser should use in reassessing the subject property. If the
court judges the original assessed value to be just and equitable, the property owner has
used all the steps available under the protest process, other than to appeal to a higher
court. Figure 18.2 illustrates this protest procedure in chart form.

Tax Districts: Budgets and Tax Rate Levy

Every fiscal year, each tax district (city, county, school board, or special tax district) prepares an operating budget for the next fiscal year. The operating budget prepared by each
tax district is actually a summary of several departmental budgets. For example, the police
department submits a budget that reflects the estimated cost of operating every phase of
that department's activities during the coming fiscal year. The same process is followed by
public works, health, welfare, finance, fire, and all other departments or agencies. When
consolidated, all of the individual department budgets makeup the total city or county
budget for the next fiscal year.

With the budget in hand, the tax district knows just about what expenses to expect for
the next year. The next issue is obtaining sufficient revenue (income) to pay the expenses.
No elected official is eager to levy higher property taxes than are absolutely necessary
to operate the tax district. So before a general real estate tax is calculated, an attempt
is made to estimate the revenue that can reasonably be expected from all sources other
than real property taxes. Each tax district may have different or unique sources of income,
ranging from outright federal grants to profits resulting from municipally owned utilities.
Fines paid in courts, parking meter income, fees from occupational licenses, and tax funds
returned by the state government are a few of the other sources of income. Estimating the
amount of income from these nonproperty tax sources is made easier by records of preceding years, which indicate a predictable trend.

With a reasonable estimate in hand of the revenue expected from all nonproperty tax sources, the tax district is able to predict the amount of money needed from property taxes. The amount of property taxes paid to a tax district must come from its *tax base*. The tax base is the total assessed value of all taxable property in the tax district. The next component needed to compute a tax rate is the number and type of property tax exemptions granted.

Exemptions from Property Taxes

The owners of certain properties are relieved of the obligation to pay property taxes. Others are partially exempted.

Immune properties are city, county, state, and federal government properties. Examples of immune properties include county courthouses and military facilities. Immune properties also include special properties, such as municipal airports, that have been made immune by statute or ordinance. Immune properties are not assessed and are not subject to taxation.

Exempt properties include property belonging to churches and nonprofit organizations. Exempt properties are subject to taxation, but the owner is released from the obligation.

Partially exempt property is subject to taxation, but the owner is partially relieved of the burden. For example, all owners of homesteaded property are granted a partial tax exemption. For this reason, one cannot always regard the assessed value of a property as the taxable value of that property. The *taxable value* of a property is not known until existing exemptions are subtracted from the *assessed value*. **Taxable value** (nonexempt assessed value) is determined by beginning with assessed value and subtracting appropriate exemptions.

Homestead Tax Exemption

196, F.S.

Florida residents who hold *title* to a home in Florida and use the home as their *permanent residence* may establish their residence as a homestead. Floridians who homestead their residence receive a homestead exemption, which reduces the amount of property taxes owed. A person who holds title to more than one residence in the state of Florida may homestead only one residence.

Applicants must reside in the home and have legal title to the property as of January 1 to be eligible to file for the homestead tax exemption. First-time applicants must file an application with the county property appraiser's office on or before March 1. Some counties allow homeowners to file the initial application throughout the year. However, if the application is filed after the March 1 deadline, the homestead exemption will not take effect until the following year.

The procedure for renewing the homestead exemption varies from county to county. In most counties the property appraiser mails a renewal card on or before February 1 of each year. A county may choose to waive the requirement to renew the exemption each year once the initial application is made and the exemption is granted. However, if an individual no longer qualifies for the homestead exemption and fails to notify the county, the law provides for payment of penalties and interest on unpaid property taxes.

Homeowners are entitled to a $25,000 homestead exemption from the assessed value of the home for city, county, and school board taxes. Homeowners are entitled to an

F I G U R E 18.3 ■ Applicable Homestead Exemption

Increments of Assessed Value	Applicable Homestead Exemption That Applies
First $25,000 of assessed value	Base $25,000 exemption from city, county, and school board taxes
Assessed value of $25,001 up to $50,000	Base $25,000 exemption from city, county, and school board taxes on first $25,000 of assessed value No additional exemption—assessed value of this increment is fully taxed
Assessed value between $50,001 up to $75,000	Base $25,000 exemption from city, county, and school board taxes on first $25,000 of assessed value plus $25,000 additional exemption from city and county taxes only, prorated to the amount of assessed value that exceeds $50,000
Assessed value greater than $75,000	Base $25,000 exemption from city, county, and school board taxes on first $25,000 of assessed value, plus entire $25,000 additional exemption from city and county taxes only

1 additional $25,000 exemption from city and county taxes (but not school board taxes)
2 on the property's assessed value between $50,000 and $75,000. Figure 18.3 displays the
3 applicable homestead exemption depending on the amount of assessed value.

4   Homesteaded properties with an assessed value of $75,000 or more are entitled to the
5 entire $50,000 homestead exemption. Homes with an assessed value of $50,000 or less are
6 entitled to the base $25,000 exemption.

7   The property tax exemption for a homestead is deducted from the assessed value of the
8 property before property taxes are calculated.

Taxable Value Formula:

Assessed value − Homestead exemptions = Taxable value

9   **E X A M P L E :** A homesteaded condominium unit has an assessed value of
10 $49,000. What is the amount of the homestead exemption? What is the taxable
11 value of the property?
12   The assessed value is less than $50,000. Therefore, the homestead exemption
13 is $25,000:

14   $49,000 assessed value − $25,000 homestead exemption = $24,000 taxable value

15   The total exemption that applies to the homesteaded property in the above example
16 is $25,000. The additional $25,000 exemption applies to property with a value greater
17 than $50,000. The additional exemption will apply only if the assessed value of the

property exceeds $50,000, and it will apply to the amount by which the value exceeds $50,000, up to a total additional exemption of $25,000. Homesteaded property valued at more than $50,000 but less than $75,000 receives a prorated exemption.

> **EXAMPLE:** A homesteaded duplex unit has an assessed value of $66,000. What is the amount of the homestead exemption? What is the taxable value of the property?
>
> The base $25,000 homestead exemption applies to the assessed value up to $50,000:
>
> $66,000 assessed value − $50,000 = $16,000 additional exemption
>
> $25,000 base exemption + $16,000 additional exemption
> = $41,000 total homestead exemption

$66,000 assessed value − $41,000 applicable homestead exemption = $25,000 taxable value

Note: The $16,000 additional exemption does not include an exemption for school board taxes. Only the base $25,000 homestead exemption is exempt from school board taxes.

To be entitled to the full $50,000 homestead exemption, a homesteaded property must have an assessed value greater than $75,000.

> **EXAMPLE:** Mr. Pasco owns a homesteaded single-family residence that has an assessed value of $350,000. What is the amount of the homestead exemption for this property? What is the taxable value of the property for calculating school taxes? What is the taxable value of the property for calculating city and county taxes?
>
> This homesteaded property qualifies for the entire $50,000 homestead exemption because its assessed value exceeds $75,000.
>
> $25,000 base homestead exemption + $25,000 additional exemption
> = $50,000 total homestead exemption
>
> The taxable value for calculating school taxes uses only the base $25,000 homestead exemption because only the base $25,000 homestead exemption is exempt from school board taxes.
>
> $350,000 assessed value − $25,000 base homestead exemption
> = $325,000 taxable value for school taxes only
>
> Use the total homestead exemption to calculate the taxable value for city and county taxes:
>
> $350,000 assessed value − $50,000 homestead exemption
> = $300,000 taxable value for city and county taxes

Additional $500 exemptions. The following individuals qualify for an additional $500 exemption from the assessed value of their homesteaded property:

196.202, F.S.

- Widows and widowers (surviving spouse who has not remarried)
- Legally blind persons
- Nonveterans who are totally and permanently disabled

1   A Florida physician, the Division of Blind Services, or the Social Security Adminis-
2   tration must certify the disability.

196.24, F.S.
196.081, F.S.

3   **Disabled veteran exemption.** Veterans who are at least 10 percent disabled by military
4   service-connected misfortune are entitled to an additional $5,000 exemption on their
5   homesteaded property. A veteran who is totally and permanently disabled due to a ser-
6   vice-connected injury is entitled to a total exemption from property taxes on homesteaded
7   property. In some cases, this may carry over after the veteran's death to the widow or
8   widower.

196.075, F.S.

9   **Age 65 and older exemption.** Florida law authorizes counties and municipalities to grant,
10   by ordinance, an additional homestead exemption of up to $50,000 for persons aged 65
11   and older. Household income is restricted to no more than $20,000 (adjusted annually
12   for inflation) to qualify. If a county or a municipality chooses to pass this ordinance, they
13   can grant the person who is 65 and older a tax exemption. Counties and municipalities,
14   however, are *not* required to pass this ordinance.

196.101, F.S.

15   **Special exemption for quadriplegics.** A homestead owned by a quadriplegic is exempt
16   from taxation. Also, low-income individuals with total and permanent disabilities may
17   be eligible for a total tax exemption on their homesteaded property (statutory restrictions
18   apply).

19   **Order of cumulative homestead tax exemptions.** The taxable value of a homesteaded
20   property is calculated by adding up all of the tax exemptions that apply to a particular
21   owner and deducting this amount from the assessed value. Therefore, a widower with an
22   assessed value of more than $75,000 would qualify for a total tax exemption of $50,500.
23   And if the same individual were also legally blind, the legally blind widower would qualify
24   for a total tax exemption of $51,000 on his homesteaded property.

WEB LINK

The Florida Department of Revenue has information concerning Florida property tax exemptions posted on
its Web site at http://dor.myflorida.com/dor/property/taxpayers/exemptions.html.

Download and print the Department of Revenue's official application for filing homestead exemption at
http://dor.myflorida.com/dor/forms/2009/dr501.pdf.

25   Florida's Green Belt Law

193.461, F.S.

26   Florida law authorizes county property appraisers to assess agricultural land by a more
27   favorable method than that used for other properties. If a taxpayer's land is so classified
28   for assessment purposes, the county property appraiser must base the property tax assess-
29   ment solely on the basis of the land's current character and use. The highest and best use
30   of such land (such as commercial development) is not a factor in arriving at just value for
31   agricultural purposes.

32   Florida's **Green Belt Law** was designed to protect farmers from having taxes increased
33   just because the land might be in the path of urban growth and therefore well suited for
34   development. An agricultural land classification results in a lower property assessment.
35   Without such protection, a farmer's taxes could be raised to the point where it no longer
36   would be economically feasible for that farmer to continue the agricultural use. Because of
37   lower taxes on agricultural land, speculators often have been attracted to such properties
38   when they are located in the path of urban growth. In many instances the law, which was
39   intended to protect the farmer, has been used as a tax protection by speculators. To stop
40   this practice, the Florida Green Belt Law was changed to require that all county property

1 appraisers annually classify all lands within the county. Property owners desiring that their
2 land be classified differently must request and rejustify such classification before March 1
3 each year. If the request is denied, these property owners may appeal the denial through the
4 regular protest procedure used by other property owners.

Save Our Home

193.155, F.S.

6 The *Save Our Home* amendment of the Florida Constitution caps how much the assessed
7 value of homesteaded property may increase in a given year. According to Chapter 193,
8 F.S., the just value of homesteaded property may be increased either:

9 ■ 3 percent annually (based on the assessed value for the prior year); or

10 ■ the percentage change of the Consumer Price Index (CPI) for the preceding
11 year, whichever percentage is less.

12 The Save Our Home (SOH) benefit is the difference between the assessed value and
13 the market value of a homesteaded property due to the annual limit on increases in assessed
14 value. The SOH benefit is portable. Homeowners who have had the homestead exemption
15 on their current home in either of the two preceding years can transfer their SOH benefit
16 to a new home. A homesteaded property owner can transfer up to $500,000 of SOH ben-
17 efit to a new homestead. Property owners moving to a more expensive home transfer up to
18 the entire $500,000 benefit. Property owners moving to a less expensive home transfer the
19 same proportion of tax savings realized in the previous homestead.

WEB LINK

The Department of Revenue has prepared a set of examples concerning how to calculate the portability
benefit when downsizing homesteads plus other scenarios at http://dor.myflorida.com/dor/property/
legislation/amendment1/.

689.261, F.S.

20 When homesteaded property is sold, it is assessed at just value as of January 1 of the
21 year following a change in ownership. The assessed value of a homesteaded property may
22 significantly increase after a change in ownership if the previous owners lived in the
23 home for a number of years and the property in the area has experienced strong property
24 appreciation.

25 Licensees should avoid estimating a buyer's property tax liability by referring to a seller's
26 current taxes because the purchaser may be liable for substantially higher property taxes
27 than the previous owner of the home. Prospective purchasers of residential property must be
28 given a disclosure summary regarding property taxes. The disclosure summary informs pur-
29 chasers that they cannot rely on the seller's current property taxes as the amount of property
30 taxes the purchaser may be obligated to pay in the year following purchase of the property.
31 The disclosure further explains that the sale of the property triggers a reassessment of the
32 property's value. (See Property Tax Disclosure Summary on page 253.) Buyers who have
33 questions concerning the amount of property taxes they can expect to pay on the homes
34 they are considering buying should be referred to the county property appraiser's office.

Tax Rates

36 To calculate the dollar amount of property taxes owed, the taxable value of the property is
37 multiplied by the appropriate tax rate. The *tax rate* is expressed in mills. A **mill** is one one-
38 thousandth of a dollar (or one-tenth of a cent). There are 1,000 mills in a dollar. Thus, a tax

rate of .010 is expressed as 10 mills. Florida has legislated a "cap" (ceiling) that limits cities, counties, and school boards to a basic real property tax rate of no more than 10 mills each.

The following simple formula is commonly used for determining the tax rate of cities and counties:

$$\frac{\text{Approved budget} - \text{Nonproperty tax revenue}}{\text{Total assessed value} - \text{Exemptions}} = \text{Tax rate}$$

EXAMPLE: Assume that a county has an approved operating budget for the next fiscal year with expected expenditures of $10,500,000. A review of past and present experience indicates a reasonable expectation of $500,000 in revenue from sources other than property taxes. The county property appraiser reports a total assessed valuation of all taxable properties in the amount of $1,050,000,000 less $50,000,000 in exemptions. Apply the previously cited formula to these figures.

$$\frac{\$10,500,000 - \$500,000}{\$1,050,000,000 - \$50,000,000} = \frac{\$10,000,000}{\$1,000,000,000} = .010, \text{ or } 10 \text{ mills}$$

Thus, the tax rate to be applied to all taxable real property in the county will be 10 mills (.010) per dollar of taxable value.

One mill is properly written in decimals as .001. When the decimal .010 is used, it means one cent, or 10 mills. To convert the tax rate from a decimal form to mills, simply move the decimal point three places to the *right*. Add zeros, if necessary. Always use three digits when expressing tax rates to prevent confusion. For example, .009 = 9 mills and .010 = 10 mills. To convert millage to its decimal form, move the decimal point three places to the *left* of the written or unwritten decimal point. For example, 20 mills = .020 and 25.9 mills = .0259.

Annual Property Taxes Due Formula:

Taxable value × Tax rate = Annual property taxes due

EXAMPLE: Using the tax rate of .010 for a home assessed at $180,000 that has qualified for homestead tax exemption, the calculation of the county property taxes is as follows:

$180,000 assessed value – $50,000 homestead exemption
= $130,000 taxable value × .010 tax rate = $1,300 property taxes due

Note that two separate types of value are involved in determining the actual property tax. The tax rate, in mills, is always applied to the taxable value. Any exemption must be deducted from the assessed value to find the taxable value. Where no exemptions apply, the taxable value and the assessed value are the same. The taxable value is always multiplied by the tax rate to find the amount of tax. The tax rate usually changes each year owing to differences in operating budget costs and revenues.

Not all property owners are subject to the same tax rates. A homeowner living in a city pays city, county, and school board taxes. Perhaps additional taxes will be required as a result of bonds or other obligations approved by the voters. Usually a homeowner living in the county but outside the city limits pays only county and school board taxes. Often, additional taxes are required of county residents who are located in special tax districts.

EXAMPLE: Mr. Pasco's homesteaded single-family residence has an assessed value of $350,000. The millage rate for the school board is 6 mills, city 7.1 mills, and county 8.2 mills. How much is owed for school board taxes? How much is owed for city and county taxes? What is the total property tax bill for this property?

Taxable value for calculating school board taxes applies to the base $25,000 homestead exemption. To multiply by 6 mills, convert to a decimal: 6 mills = .006.

$350,000 assessed value − $25,000 base homestead exemption
= $325,000 taxable value for school taxes only

$325,000 taxable value × .006 = $1,950 school board taxes

Taxable value for calculating city and county taxes applies to the entire $50,000 homestead exemption. (The assessed value of this property exceeds $75,000.)

$350,000 assessed value − $50,000 homestead exemption
= $300,000 taxable value for city and county taxes

7.1 mills city + 8.2 mills county = 15.3 mills = .0153 (decimal form)

$300,000 taxable value × .0153 = $4,590 city and county taxes

Add the property taxes for schools and the property taxes for city and county:

$1,950 school board taxes + $4,590 city and county taxes = $6,540 total taxes due

EXAMPLE: Mr. Pasco is interested in finding the amount of savings in property taxes realized from the tax exemptions. What is the amount of savings to the homeowner resulting from the homestead exemption applied to school board taxes? What is the amount of savings resulting from the homestead exemption applied to city and county taxes? What is the total amount of savings from property taxes realized by this homeowner?

To calculate the savings resulting from the homestead exemption applied to school board taxes, multiply the millage rate for schools (in decimal form) by the base homestead exemption:

$25,000 base homestead exemption × .006 = $150 savings from school board taxes

To calculate the savings resulting from the homestead exemption applied to city and county taxes, multiply the millage rate for city and county by the total applicable homestead exemption:

$50,000 total homestead exemption × .0153 = $765 savings from city and county taxes

Add the property tax savings for the school board to the property tax savings for the city and the county:

$150 + $765 = $915 total savings realized

E X A M P L E : What if Mr. Pasco lived outside the city limits in the same county? How would this affect Mr. Pasco's property taxes? (Remember that Mr. Pasco will still owe the school board taxes of $1,950.)

Calculate the property taxes omitting the city taxes:

$350,000 assessed value – $50,000 homestead exemption
= $300,000 taxable value for county taxes

8.2 mills county = .0082 (decimal form)

$300,000 taxable value × .0082 = $2,460 county taxes

$2,460 county taxes + $1,950 taxes = $4,410 total taxes due

Practice Problem 1

Ms. Sammis owns a home in St. Petersburg, Florida, in Pinellas County that is homesteaded. The city tax rate is 8.7 mills, the county tax rate is 9.2 mills, and the school board tax rate is 6 mills. Ms. Sammis is legally blind. She has quali-fied for homestead exemption. Her home has been assessed at $165,000. What is the taxable value of the property for calculating school taxes? What is the taxable value of the property for calculating city and county taxes? What must Ms. Sammis pay in property taxes? (Hint: Remember to apply an additional $500 exemption because the homeowner is legally blind.)

(The solution to the Practice Problem is at the end of this chapter on page 418.)

Special Assessments

Special assessments are one-time taxes levied on properties to help pay for some public improvement that benefits the property. When city sewers are extended to neighborhoods previously dependent on septic tanks or when unpaved streets are paved, it is assumed that the properties affected receive an increase in value owing to the improvement. Sometimes the municipal authority that levies the special assessment considers affected properties to have benefited in value when the improvement actually may have caused a decrease in value. A quiet residential street that is widened into a four-lane boulevard to relieve con-gested access routes might be an example. The increased traffic, with its resultant noise, pollution, and danger to children, could cause property values to drop instead of increase. In such cases, the property owners can look for relief from the courts.

Laws that allow the levying of special assessments specifically require that all improve-ments *benefit* any property against which a special assessment is levied. Court records are abundant with instances where courts at all levels, up to and including the U.S. Supreme Court, have ruled in favor of property owners when improvements did not enhance the value of affected properties.

Special assessments are *not* ad valorem taxes—they are not levied according to the value of a property. Usually, special assessments are levied on a front-foot basis for items such as sidewalks and street paving. They are often levied on a per hookup basis for utility and sewer improvements.

> **E X A M P L E :** You live on an unpaved street. The city is petitioned to pave the street and agrees to do so. The paving cost is $24 per foot, and the city is to pay 30 percent of the cost. If your lot frontage on the street is 100 feet, what will your special assessment be for street paving? (Don't forget that your street has two sides and the property across the street must bear its fair share.)

$$100 \text{ front feet} \times \$24 \text{ per foot} = \$2,400$$
$$\$2,400 \times .70 \text{ (owner's share of cost is } 100\% - 30\%) = \$1,680$$
$$\$1,680 \div 2 \text{ (one-half of the street paving cost)} = \$840$$

Nonpayment of Real Property Taxes

Property taxes constitute a lien superior to all other liens on real property. Special assessments are next in priority. When a property owner fails to pay property taxes, the taxing authority must take steps to obtain the tax money needed to help pay for the cost of government.

In Florida, unpaid property taxes are considered a debt, just as if the property owner had signed a promissory note for the amount of the taxes. Further, the property is security for the debt and can eventually be sold to satisfy the obligation.

197, F.S.

The city or county government is responsible for the cost of its day-to-day operation and must collect delinquent taxes in some manner. To do this, a property *tax certificate* in the amount of taxes owed is issued for each delinquent property. A list of all delinquent properties is published in a newspaper having general circulation throughout the county. This publication gives all delinquent owners notice that tax certificates on their properties will be sold if the taxes are not paid before the date of sale.

The published list of properties, including the amount of taxes in arrears, specifies a date, time, and place for public auction of tax certificates on each property listed. The county tax collector may conduct electronic online sales of tax certificates. At the auction, any qualified person is entitled to bid for the tax certificate on any property. Instead of bidding in dollars, investors bid interest rates at the auction, starting at 18 percent and going down. The bidder who is willing to accept the lowest interest rate is issued the tax certificate. Once the certificate is sold, the bidder must pay the face amount of the certificate to the county (taxes, interest, and advertising cost). For a certificate to be redeemed by the owner of the property, the tax collector must collect the face amount of the certificate plus all accrued interest. The certificate holder is then paid the face amount of the certificate plus accrued interest.

The holder of the tax certificate can force a public auction of the property by requesting a tax deed after two years but no later than seven years. A tax certificate expires seven years from the date of issue. Anyone can bid at the foreclosure sale and the property will be sold to the highest bidder. If not the successful bidder on the property, the holder of the tax certificate then will be paid the amount invested plus interest. If there are no bidders, the holder of the certificate is issued a tax deed. Once the property is transferred by tax deed, all other liens against the property—including mortgages—are wiped out, with the exception of any government liens.

FEDERAL INCOME TAXES

Current federal tax laws greatly affect the benefits that may be obtained from the purchase, ownership, and disposition of real property. The tax considerations of owning personal or investment property are important, but they are also complex. Let's begin with a discussion of a principal residence.

Principal Residence

Tax laws are designed to encourage homeownership and give preferred treatment to taxpayers who own their residences. The owner-occupied residence may be a house, condominium, mobile home, or houseboat. Regardless, the homeowner has certain tax advantages. If homeowners-taxpayers itemize deductions rather than claiming the standard deduction on their annual federal income tax returns, they may deduct the following:

- *Mortgage interest.* Interest paid on a mortgage loan on a principal and second home is deductible. (Certain limitations apply.)
- *Property taxes.* The annual property taxes paid on principal and second homes are deductible.
- *Interest on a home equity loan.* The interest paid is deductible if the loan does not exceed $100,000.
- *Mortgage origination fees (points).* Points are deductible in the year they are paid, unless they are paid when refinancing a loan—in such cases, the points must be deducted over the life of the loan.

Additional tax advantages of homeownership include the following:

- *First-time homebuyers.* First-time homebuyers may make penalty-free (but not tax-free) withdrawals up to $10,000 from their tax-deferred individual retirement funds (IRAs) for a down payment. (Different IRS rules apply to withdrawals from Roth IRAs.)
- *Exclusion of gain from the sale of a principal residence.* An exclusion of up to $250,000 of gain ($500,000 for married couples filing a joint return) realized on the sale or exchange of a principal residence.

Sale of real property. Federal tax laws classify real property as a *capital asset*. **Capital gain** income is profit from the sale of a principal residence, an investment property, a property used in a trade or business, or an income-producing property, and it must be reported for tax purposes. The taxable gain on real estate is determined by two factors: the amount realized from the sale and the adjusted basis. The gain is the amount realized from the sale less the adjusted basis.

Amount Realized from Sale Formula:

Sale price − Expense of the sale = Amount realized

E X A M P L E : Assume a homeowner sells her home for $165,000 and pays the broker $8,250, and state transfer taxes of $1,155. What is the *amount realized*?

$165,000 sale price – $9,405 = $155,595 amount realized from sale

Adjusted Basis Formula:

Original purchase price + Purchase expenses and capital improvements = Adjusted basis

The **adjusted basis** is the owner's original cost plus buying expenses plus capital improvements (less certain deductions, if applicable).

E X A M P L E : If the homeowner's original cost was $80,000 and there were purchase costs of $800 and capital improvements totaling $5,200, how much is the adjusted basis?

$80,000 price + $800 costs + $5,200 improvements =
$86,000 adjusted basis

Capital Gain (or Loss) from Sale Formula:

Amount realized – Adjusted basis = Capital gain (or loss)

A taxpayer-seller's capital gain (loss) is the amount realized from the sale less the adjusted basis.

E X A M P L E : Using the information above, how much *capital gain* must be reported?

$155,595 amount realized – $86,000 adjusted basis = $69,595 capital gain

While profit from the sale of a principal residence (if not excluded) is included as a capital gain, a loss from such a sale is not allowed as a capital loss and thus may not be deducted.

The IRS allows homeowners to exclude up to $250,000 of gain ($500,000 for married couples filing a joint return) realized on the sale or exchange of a principal residence. Any gain above the exclusion is taxed at the applicable capital gains rate. The exclusion is allowed each time taxpayers sell or exchange a principal residence, as long as the homeowners have occupied the property as their residence for at least two years during the five-year period ending on the date of the sale. The taxpayer is not required to reinvest the sale proceeds in a new residence to claim the exclusion. The exclusion of gain is generally allowed only once every two years. However, homeowners who do not meet the two-year requirement due to a change in health, job transfer, or other allowable reasons may be eligible for a prorated exclusion of gain.

Purchase of real property from foreign sellers. Another federal government regulation that licensees need to be aware of concerns the purchase of real property in the United States from foreign sellers. To prevent foreign sellers from avoiding the payment of taxes due on the sale of real property, the IRS requires that buyers withhold 10 percent of the gross sale price (including cash paid and any debt assumed by the buyer). The buyer must report the purchase and pay the IRS the amount withheld. There are a few exceptions to this rule. All licensees should encourage their buyers and sellers to consult the IRS or a tax specialist regarding the application of this rule.

Tax laws are constantly changing, and they are also very complex. For example, the home equity loan as a source of funds on which the interest is tax deductible may either benefit careful homeowners or result in disaster for homeowners who mishandle their finances. For these and other reasons, it is always wise to retain professional counsel regarding tax situations.

Investment Property

Federal income tax laws encourage real estate investment. Tax benefits include the following: allowable deductions from income, tax deferral and exemptions on resale, installment sale treatment, and like-kind exchanges. Each of the tax benefits is discussed later in the chapter. Buyers and sellers should always seek competent tax advice to ensure the most favorable tax treatment in a real estate transaction. Advance planning is necessary if an investor's after-tax return on investment is to be maximized.

Income classification. For tax purposes, *ordinary income* consists of three types:

1. *Active income* includes wages, tips, commission, and so forth.
2. *Portfolio income* includes income from interest, stock dividends, capital gains, royalties, and annuity income.
3. *Passive income* includes income from activities in which the taxpayer does not participate. Most income from rental or leased real property is classified as passive income.

The significance of these income classifications is that income losses from *passive* activities cannot be used, with few exceptions, to reduce *active* and *portfolio* taxable income. Investors in rental properties should be advised to consult their tax specialist.

Capital gains and capital losses. Real estate, stocks, bonds, and so forth that are owned for investment purposes are capital assets. When you sell a capital asset, the difference between the amount that you sell it for and your basis, which is usually what you paid for it, is a capital gain or a capital loss. You have a capital gain if you sell the asset for more than your basis (for profit). You have a capital loss if you sell the asset for less than your basis. Capital gains are taxed at the applicable capital gains rate.

A capital gain from the sale of real estate investment property can be used to offset a capital loss from the sale of other investment property. Furthermore if an investor's capital loss exceeds capital gains, the investor may deduct up to $3,000 in losses in a given year. Assume, for example, an investor has two investment properties. One earns a capital gain of $10,000 and the other has a capital loss of $15,000. The investor can offset the $10,000 gain with $10,000 of the loss. This leaves a net $5,000 loss of which the investor can deduct $3,000. The investor must carry forward the remaining $2,000 loss to the next year. (Remember, as previously discussed, a loss from the sale of your personal residence is *not* deductible.)

Deductions from gross income. Three types of deductions from gross income are allowed when calculating the taxable income from investment real property:

1. *Operating expenses.* Operating expenses are those cash outlays necessary for running and maintaining the property, and they are deductible in the year paid. Property taxes are considered operating expenses and are deductible. While reserve for replacements is deducted when determining NOI (see chapter 15), it is not a cash expense and is not deductible when computing taxable income. Replacement *expenses* (not capital improvements), however, are deductible in the year paid.

2. *Financing expenses.* Financing expenses include the interest paid as well as the costs of obtaining borrowed money. While mortgage interest is deductible, principal payments are not. Costs associated with obtaining borrowed funds, such as loan origination fees and points, must be amortized over the life of the loan.

3. *Depreciation.* Depreciation is a means of deducting the costs of improvements to land over a specified period of time. The land itself is *not* depreciable. Depreciation (or cost recovery) allows taxpayers to recover the cost of depreciable property by paying less tax than they would otherwise have to pay. Under present tax law the depreciation deduction usually bears little relationship to actual changes in property value. Depreciation is used to stimulate economic expansion by making certain types of real property more attractive to investors. Depreciation is allowed only for business property and income-producing property (which includes investment property). It is not allowed for inventory property or for a personal residence.

As it relates to annual income from a property, depreciation provides favorable tax relief as an allowable deduction that requires no current outlay of cash, as is necessary to deduct other expenses (such as property taxes and mortgage interest). In addition, depreciation is based on the total cost of improvements, including that portion paid for with borrowed funds (the leveraged portion).

Depreciation components. The *depreciable basis* of the property is the amount that may be depreciated. For real property, it is generally the initial cost of the asset plus acquisition costs minus the value of the land. Acquisition costs generally include such items as the buyer's attorney's fees, appraisal fees, survey fees, and title insurance costs. Because land is not depreciable, this basis (total cost) must be allocated between the improvements (buildings, etc.) and the land, based on the respective values of each.

Straight-line method. Depreciation is calculated using the straight-line method. An equal amount of depreciation is taken annually over the useful life of the asset. The Internal Revenue Service (IRS) has currently established useful asset life as 27.5 years for residential rental property and 39 years for nonresidential income-producing property.

Straight-Line Method Depreciation Formula:

Depreciable basis ÷ 27.5 years (or 39 years) = Annual depreciation

EXAMPLE: Assume that in 2010, a residential real estate investment property is purchased for $250,000, with a land value of $50,000. The depreciable basis is $200,000 ($250,000 sale price less the land value). What is the amount of the yearly depreciation deduction?

$200,000 depreciable basis ÷ 27.5 years =
$7,273 annual depreciation deduction

Tax on gain at time of sale. In general, when income property is sold for cash, all gain or loss must be recognized (reported) immediately for income tax purposes. The total realized gain is the difference between the net sale price (selling price less selling expenses) and the depreciated basis of the property. The seller pays tax on the gain from the sale of real estate in the year the gain is collected. Because of the tax consequences of the immediate recognition of gain, the installment sale method or a like-kind exchange may provide beneficial tax results.

Installment sale method. Under the *installment sale method*, the gain is received over a number of years and the seller recognizes the gain for tax purposes over the same period. The installment sale method relieves the seller of paying tax on gain not yet collected. Generally, it calls for the gain to be reported only as payments are actually received, with each payment treated as part profit and part recovery of investment in the property sold. If an installment sale results in a loss, however, the seller may not use the installment sale method to report the loss over a period of years for tax purposes. A qualified loss must be recognized (reported) in the year of sale. Because the IRS requirements regarding the installment sale method are complex, early tax counsel is mandatory.

Like-kind exchange. Real estate investors can defer paying taxes by exchanging real property. The income tax is *deferred, not eliminated.* A *like-kind exchange* enables a taxpayer-investor to realize the benefits of investment and property appreciation immediately while paying taxes later. When the investor sells the property, the capital gain will be taxed.

To qualify as a tax-deferred exchange under Section 1031 of the Internal Revenue Code, real property must be exchanged for other real property (hence the term "like-kind"). However, it may be a different type of real property. For example, a multifamily complex can be exchanged for an office complex. Any additional capital or personal property included with the transaction to even out the value of the exchange is called **boot.** The IRS requires tax on the boot to be paid at the time of the exchange by the party who receives it. Because exchanges are subject to a number of IRS rules that must be strictly adhered to, the transactions must be carefully structured, with early tax counsel mandatory. Personal residences and foreign property do not qualify.

Tax shelter. **Tax shelter** is a term that describes some of the advantages of owning real estate (or other investments). An investment is a tax shelter when it shields income or gain from payment of income taxes. One of the features of a tax-sheltered real estate investment is depreciation. **Depreciation** is a key deduction because it reduces taxable income without involving a cash outlay. Depreciation protects at least a portion of income from tax and also may produce a tax loss, thus possibly creating additional tax sheltering of other income. Under the tax code, sheltering of income is restricted due to income classifications (active, portfolio, or passive).

Sound real estate investments depend primarily on the inherent productivity of a property, not on its tax aspects. A good real estate investment always combines positive cash flow (if income-producing property) with appreciation of property value. If a property declines in value in an amount equal to or greater than the depreciation deduction allowable for tax purposes, that property is *not* a tax shelter.

SUMMARY OF IMPORTANT POINTS

- Property taxes are payable for the current year on or after November 1. Unpaid property taxes become delinquent on April 1 of the following year.

- *Assessed value* is the value of a property established for property tax purposes. Property owners use a three-step procedure to protest the assigned assessed value: (1) contact the county property appraiser, (2) appeal to the Value Adjustment Board, and (3) file a suit in court (certiorari proceeding).

- The Value Adjustment Board is made up of five members: two county commissioners, one school board member, and two citizen members.

- Immune properties consist of city, county, state, and federal government properties. Immune properties are not assessed and are not subject to taxation.

- Exempt properties include property belonging to churches and nonprofit organizations. Exempt properties are subject to taxation, but the owner is released from the obligation.

- Partially exempt property is subject to taxation, but the owner is partially relieved of the burden. Taxable value is determined by beginning with assessed value and subtracting appropriate exemptions.

- Florida residents who hold title to a home in Florida and use the home as their permanent residence may homestead the property. Homeowners are entitled to a $25,000 homestead exemption from the assessed value of the home for city, county, and school board taxes. Homesteaded properties with an assessed value of $75,000 or more are entitled to an additional $25,000 homestead exemption from city and county taxes (but not school board taxes).

- An additional $500 exemption from the assessed value of homesteaded property is available to widows and widowers, legally blind persons, and nonveterans who are totally and permanently disabled. An additional $5,000 exemption is available to veterans who are at least 10 percent disabled by military service–connected misfortune.

- Florida's Green Belt Law shields agricultural property from higher tax assessments.

- The Save Our Home amendment caps how much the assessed value of homesteaded property may increase each year to 3 percent annually or the CPI, whichever is less.

- A *mill* is one one-thousandth of a dollar or one-tenth of a cent. Cities, counties, and school boards are capped at a basic real property tax rate of no more than 10 mills each.

1   ■   *Special assessments* are one-time taxes levied on properties to help pay for a public improvement that benefits the property. A special assessment becomes a lien on the property.

4   ■   Property taxes constitute a lien superior to all other liens on real property. Property taxes become a lien on January 1 of each year.

6   ■   Property owners who itemize deductions may deduct interest, property taxes, and mortgage origination fees on a principal residence and second home, and interest on a home equity loan.

9   ■   Deductions from taxable income on investment property include operating expenses (but not reserve for replacements), financing expense, and depreciation.

12   ■   *Depreciation* is a means of deducting the cost of improvements to land over a specified time. The land itself is not depreciable. Depreciation is calculated using the straight-line method; an equal amount is taken annually over the useful life of the asset. The IRS has established the useful life of 27½ years for residential rental property and 39 years for nonresidential income-producing property.

Practice Problem 1 Solution

(Practice Problem 1 is located on page 410.)

$165,000 assessed value – $25,000 base homestead exemption and $500 blind exemption = $139,500 taxable value for school taxes only

$139,500 × .006 = $837

$165,000 assessed value – $50,000 homestead exemption and $500 blind exemption = $114,500 taxable value for city and county taxes

8.7 mills city + 9.2 mills county = 17.9 mills (.0179 decimal form)

$114,500 × .0179 = $2,049.55

$837 + $2,049.55 = $2,886.55 total taxes due

R E V I E W   Q U E S T I O N S

1. In Florida, real property taxes are levied on a
   a. county fiscal-year basis.
   b. calendar-year basis.
   c. fiscal-year basis.
   d. quarterly basis.

2. Each year in Florida, property taxes for the previous year become delinquent on
   a. January 1.
   b. April 1.
   c. November 1.
   d. December 31.

3. The first step in protesting the assessed value of real property is to
   a. contact the county property appraiser or a representative.
   b. contact the county tax collector or a representative.
   c. contact the Value Adjustment Board.
   d. file suit against the Value Adjustment Board.

4. The Value Adjustment Board is composed of
   a. the city manager, property appraiser, and three other elected officials.
   b. three school board members and two county commissioners.
   c. one school board member, two county commissioners, and two citizen members.
   d. five school board members and two county commissioners.

5. You have been granted homestead tax exemption. Your assessed property value is $65,000. What is your taxable property value for county taxes?
   a. $65,000
   b. $60,000
   c. $40,000
   d. $25,000

6. What would be your city and county property taxes if the property assessment is $38,000, you are a Florida resident receiving homestead tax exemption, and the total tax rate is 28 mills?
   a. $364
   b. $380
   c. $429
   d. $924

7. A 25 percent service-disabled veteran, who is 75 years of age, has been granted a homestead exemption on his $270,000 residence. How much is his total homestead exemption for county taxes?
   a. $25,500
   b. $30,000
   c. $55,000
   d. Totally tax-exempt

8. In arriving at a just value for agricultural property, the highest and BEST use
   a. is not a factor.
   b. of the property must be for agricultural purposes only.
   c. discourages speculative investing in agricultural land.
   d. encourages speculative investing in agricultural land.

9. Which statement is FALSE concerning Florida's Green Belt Law?
   a. The law is intended to protect owners of agricultural property.
   b. Farmers' lands are shielded from excessive taxation.
   c. The law has been strengthened by qualifying agricultural land annually.
   d. The law intended to promote open green spaces along our nation's interstates.

10. If a lot frontage is 100 feet, street paving costs are $40 per running foot, and the city
    will pay 25 percent of paving costs, what will be the assessment to the property owner?
    a. $1,000
    b. $1,500
    c. $3,000
    d. $4,000

11. A widow owns a home in Gainesville, Florida, in Alachua County. The city tax
    rate is 9.3 mills, the county rate is 9.7 mills, and the school board tax rate is 6 mills.
    The woman has homesteaded her principal residence. Her home has been assessed
    at $178,000. The amount of savings in property taxes realized by all allowable tax
    exemptions is
    a. $1,100.00.
    b. $1,112.50.
    c. $1,250.00.
    d. $1,262.50.

12. Current state law allows the buyer of property tax certificates to collect interest up to
    a maximum of
    a. 12 percent.
    b. 18 percent.
    c. the tax rate in each county.
    d. allowable interest voted by the residents of each county.

13. A county or city millage rate is determined by
    a. taking into account the operating budgets of the various government depart-
       ments within the city or county.
    b. majority vote of the registered voters.
    c. the mayor or county commissioners after the period for filing a protest has expired.
    d. the State Legislature.

14. In 2010, a taxpayer had a $20,000 gain from the sale of investment property A, a $19,000 loss from the sale of investment property B, and a $5,000 loss from the sale of his principal residence. All three properties were owned for more than 12 months. The taxpayer's only other income was his $50,000 salary. What is his 2010 total income for tax purposes, using just this information?
    a. $46,000
    b. $47,000
    c. $50,400
    d. $51,000

15. If a married couple who files jointly realizes a profit from the sale of their home that exceeds $500,000, what is the result?
    a. The homeowners will not pay capital gains tax if at least one of them is older than 55.
    b. Up to $125,000 of the excess profit will be taxed as a capital gain.
    c. The excess gain will be taxed at the current applicable capital gains rate.
    d. The excess gain will be taxed at the homeowner's income tax rate.

16. The maximum amount of profit that may be excluded from taxation on the sale of a home for a qualifying couple, filing separately, is
    a. $125,000.
    b. $150,000.
    c. $250,000.
    d. $500,000.

17. Tax advantages of homeownership do NOT include
    a. a tax deduction of property taxes paid.
    b. penalty-free withdrawal from an IRA if used as a down payment on a personal residence for first-time homebuyers.
    c. exclusion of gain from the sale of a principal residence up to $500,000 for married couples filing a joint return.
    d. a tax deduction of homeowners hazard insurance.

18. For tax purposes, when the installment sale method is used
    a. gain is reported as payments are received.
    b. gain or loss is reported as payments are received.
    c. gain must be deferred.
    d. gain or loss must be deferred.

19. Which item is NOT a deductible expense for an income-producing property?
    a. Depreciation
    b. Reserve for replacement
    c. Hazard insurance
    d. Mortgage interest

20. A tax-sheltering real estate investment is one in which
    a. debt service is greater than net operating income.
    b. the secondary purpose is the productivity of the property.
    c. the primary purpose is reduction of personal taxable income.
    d. the amount of depreciation taken for tax purposes is greater than the actual depreciation of the property.

19

THE REAL ESTATE MARKET

OVERVIEW

The word *market* has many meanings, depending on usage. It can mean a place where farmers and tradespeople display their produce and products for buyers. It can mean a place where securities are exchanged, such as the commodities market or the stock market. Regardless of difference in form, the basic principles of market operation hold true for all. A market can function only when sellers and buyers interact. Many markets use intermediaries to facilitate activity between seller and buyer, and the real estate market is one such market.

After completing this chapter, the student should be able to:

- list factors that influence supply and demand for real estate;
- describe the five characteristics unique to the real estate market; and
- distinguish between buyer's and seller's markets.

KEY TERMS

buyer's market	household	supply
demand	seller's market	vacancy rate

THREE KEY QUESTIONS

Every economy in every land in the world has to deal with the following three basic questions:

1. *What will be produced?* Any producer can place a product or service in the marketplace, where it competes with similar products or services offered by other producers. Consumers evaluate the worth, quality, and price of the competing products and services. The products or services sold and the profitability of the producers' efforts tell them which products or services are preferred by consumers. Those products or services that do not generate a profit will no longer be produced. So *the consumer actually decides what will be produced.* Products not

desired by consumers will produce little or no profit and will be replaced by new products for consumers to evaluate.

2. *Who will do the producing?* Imagine you are a producer of canned grapefruit sections. You are competing in the marketplace against four other producers of canned grapefruit sections of similar quality and price. After a thorough analysis of your production methods, you conclude that a change in procedure will permit you to reduce your price slightly below that of your competitors, while retaining the quality and quantity of the product. Gradually thereafter, consumers begin to select your product more and more frequently. You decide to expand your factory and increase the amount of grapefruit sections produced. In time, other producers obviously must either become more efficient, as you have, or face being forced out of business because of a decrease in their sales and profits. The *most efficient* producer of a comparable-quality product will go on doing the producing.

3. *Who will get what is produced?* If more than one person wants the same article, the one willing to spend the most money usually gets the item. Therefore, *those people who have money and are willing to spend it in the marketplace will get what is produced.* We do not worry about whether there will be enough television sets or cars for us to be allowed the privilege of buying one. We know that television sets and cars will be available. Our problem is in selecting between products and services within the limits of our income. So it is with real estate. The marketplace determines sale prices, *not* sellers and *not* real estate agents.

The consumer is the individual who exercises freedom of choice in the marketplace and, therefore, is the real decision maker. Thus, one of the characteristics of the free enterprise system is that individual consumer desires and decisions are the primary determinants in the system. In a controlled economy, the government makes those decisions.

Another characteristic of a relatively free enterprise system is the "automatic" working of the system. No committee from the Department of Commerce or any other agency has to survey the national market to determine which goods and services are selling well and which ones should be removed from the marketplace. Better results are accomplished automatically by the millions of individual consumer choices exercised every minute of every day. Those products that sell well will be replaced with more of the same. Those products that do not sell well will be removed and replaced by other products.

CHARACTERISTICS OF THE REAL ESTATE MARKET

There are five characteristics of the real estate market that set it apart from other markets (see Figure 19.1, Real Estate Market):

1. *Immobility of real estate.* The geographic location of real estate is fixed. The land and the improvements on the land are immovable. Because of the immobility of real estate, the surrounding area largely influences the value of a particular parcel.

2. *The market is slow to respond to change in supply and demand.* Design, land acquisition, site preparation, and construction phases of real estate are time-consuming. For this reason, when the equilibrium between supply and demand is upset, it can be years before the imbalance is corrected.

FIGURE 19.1 ■ Real Estate Market

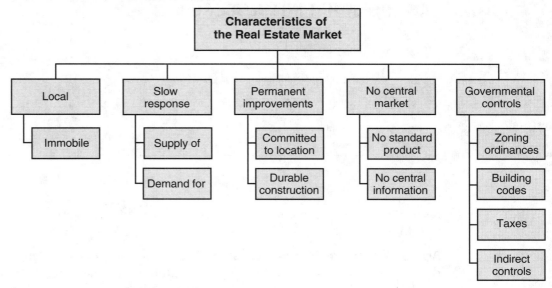

3. *Land is indestructible*. Land is permanent. The physical structures (improvements)
   on the land are durable, however, they deteriorate and become obsolete over
   time.
4. *Real estate is unique*. No two tracts of land are identical. There is no standard
   product. Even two lots side by side have different geographic locations. The
   uniqueness of land is also referred to as *heterogeneity*.
5. *Government controls influence the market through zoning, building codes, taxes, and
   so forth*. Government controls play an important role when compared with other
   markets. Zoning, building codes, and health ordinances that govern septic tank use
   and other health-related matters are examples of *direct* controls. The government
   also uses *indirect* controls such as the monetary policies of the federal government.

SUPPLY AND DEMAND FACTORS

A study of markets and their operations reveals several factors that influence supply and
demand.

Supply

Supply is the amount and type of real estate available for sale or rent at differing price
levels in a given real estate market. The variables that influence supply are listed in the
text box on the following page.

Availability of skilled labor. Numerous skilled laborers, such as carpenters, roofers, and
electricians, are required for construction. The availability and cost of labor depend on such
things as unemployment rates, skill levels required, and the influence of foreign labor. When
an area is growing rapidly, the growth usually is characterized by much construction with

VARIABLES THAT INFLUENCE SUPPLY

- Availability of skilled labor
- Availability of construction loans and financing
- Availability of land
- Availability of materials

1 resulting high employment in the construction industry. These conditions cause competi-
2 tion for labor and its cost increases.

3 **Availability of construction loans and financing.** New construction is directly related to
4 the availability of construction loans and short-term financing. As money becomes more
5 available and less expensive, more speculative homes will be built, increasing the avail-
6 able supply of housing. The same is true for commercial development.

7 **Availability of land.** Although land seems physically plentiful, the supply of the type and
8 location of land most in demand is always scarce. Two factors influence the availability of
9 land: (1) the scarcity of readily usable land and (2) the regulations affecting its use and
10 cost of development.

11 **Availability of materials.** The availability of construction materials influences the supply
12 of new housing. In the late 1970s and early 1980s the construction industry nationwide
13 was severely crippled by a shortage of drywall. Drywall couldn't be found anywhere. New
14 construction was stalled, and construction costs spiraled.

Demand

16 **Demand** is the desire and ability to purchase or rent goods and services. In real estate,
17 demand is the amount and type of real estate desired for purchase or rent in a given market
18 at a given period of time. The variables that influence demand are listed in the text box
19 on the following page.

20 **Price of real estate.** There is an *inverse* relationship between price and the demand for real
21 estate. When prices rise, demand goes down. When prices decrease, demand goes up.

22 **Population numbers and household composition.** Other important variables related to
23 demand are population numbers and household composition. Most of the transactions
24 in the real estate market are residential property transactions. Shelter is a basic need and
25 cannot be long ignored. However, the demand for dwelling space depends on both num-
26 bers of the population and composition of households in every market area. An increase in
27 population creates demand for additional shopping centers, office buildings, and so forth.

28 Mere population size does not provide sufficient information for accurately estimat-
29 ing the demand for dwelling space, nor does a *count* of households. Modern lifestyles,
30 changes in economic conditions, and reduced family size have caused the household to
31 become the basis for most population analysis. A **household**, as defined by the Bureau of
32 the Census, U.S. Department of Commerce, is any person or group of persons occupying a

VARIABLES THAT INFLUENCE DEMAND

- Price of real estate
- Population numbers and household composition
- Income of consumers
- Availability of mortgage credit
- Consumer taste or preferences

separate housing space. Thus, a household may be a single person living in a rented apartment, a husband and wife with four children living in their own home in the suburbs, or two unmarried adults living in a condominium near the city center. Each constitutes a household.

It is only when Bureau of the Census data are analyzed that the benefits of *demand trend forecasting* are realized. Just before the end of the 19th century, 100 dwelling units housed 490 people, due to the average size of households at that time (4.9 persons). The 2010 census revealed that the decreased size of the average household (about 2.58 people per household) required approximately 190 dwelling units to house 490 people. The change in average household size alone had therefore caused an increase of 90 percent in demand. Demographers and others who study population trends state that a further reduction in average household size is anticipated. This again will change the demand for housing, not only in numbers of units but also in size of dwellings.

Demand for new dwellings every year does not mean that each of the 50 states and the District of Columbia will share this growth on a proportional basis. Natural increase in population (that is, the number of births exceeding the number of deaths) and *in-migration*—new residents moving to a location from other places—are two important components of the population factor. Increased longevity of the elderly contributes to the natural increase of population by increasing the number of births over deaths, even if the birth rate remains static. As a result, Florida, along with a few other states, such as California and Arizona, has experienced exceptional population gains. This has been reflected in increased demand for housing.

The most important cause of population increase for Florida as a whole has been *in-migration*. Every reason exists to suppose that this trend will continue.

WEB LINK

The 2010 U.S. Census is available at **www.census.gov**. For valuable information, visit **www.census.gov/cgi-bin/briefroom/BriefRm**. Data concerning construction spending, new home sales, and housing starts are updated monthly.

Income of consumers. Whereas change in price is inversely related to change in demand, income is directly related to demand. As individual income increases, so does demand for dwelling space. Any change in local employment numbers or salary-wage levels causes a change in demand for dwelling space and related loan considerations.

Availability of mortgage credit. The availability and cost of mortgage credit has been called the barometer of the real estate market. Because the typical purchase of residential property involves two or three times the buyer's annual net income, it is easy to understand why a large number of homebuyers use credit to arrange the purchase. If a potential homebuyer can afford the monthly mortgage payments (principal and interest), plus property taxes and hazard insurance, the total cost of the house is of secondary importance.

The amortized (principal) portion of a monthly payment can be increased or decreased by (1) the amount of the down payment made on the property and (2) the term of the loan. Both of these have a direct bearing on demand for housing.

When a *tight money market* develops and interest rates rise, a corresponding drop is reflected in housing demand because the amount of money needed to make monthly mortgage payments increases. For example, a $90,000 mortgage loan at 7 percent interest for a period of 30 years requires a monthly payment of $598.77, not including taxes and insurance. The same amount of money for the same period of time but at 9 percent interest requires a monthly payment of $724.16, an additional $125.39 per month. An increase in mortgage interest rates of even 1 percent causes a definite drop in demand for housing.

Consumer tastes or preferences. Another factor related to demand concerns changing consumer tastes or preferences. Different architectural designs are sometimes introduced into the residential market and may enjoy brief periods of popularity. Generally speaking, however, enduring changes in consumer tastes occur slowly, over extended time periods. In recent years, the "green movement" has consumers preferring energy efficient homes. Whatever style and type of house the buying public prefers at a given time is the type of dwelling that will be built more often, until a new demand creates a new preference.

Changes in demand for condominiums or second homes for vacation purposes also reflect changes in consumer preferences. For years, *empty nesters* (those parents whose children are grown and have moved away) continued to live in the same house where they had reared their children, although it was then entirely too large for their needs as a couple. The numerous chores of the homeowner related to maintenance, repairs, and grounds upkeep were often a joy but sometimes too physically demanding. The advent of condominiums and other forms of smaller, maintenance-free housing units offered a solution to these empty nesters and other small families.

Interpreting Market Conditions

Whenever the supply and demand equilibrium of a market is upset by excess supply, a **buyer's market** develops. The number of excess units in that particular market allows a potential buyer to shop among anxious owner-sellers to obtain better prices and terms. When this condition exists, more intelligent builders may stop building because the excess supply results in a lack of profit. On the other hand, whenever the supply and demand equilibrium is upset by excess demand, a **seller's market** develops. This allows sellers to demand higher prices from buyers, who are forced to compete for available space. More building again takes place until market equilibrium occurs.

What the average real estate sales associate and broker would like is some sort of dependable reference guide to help interpret market conditions. Fortunately, several indicators help to clarify what the market is doing. Market indicators include:

- price levels,

- vacancy rates, and
- sales volume.

Price levels. The changes in price levels of home sales and the number of building permits issued for a given period of time are indicators of new housing supply and demand for certain price ranges.

Vacancy rates. A **vacancy rate** is the percentage of rental units that are not occupied. Vacancy rates are one indicator of the need and demand for housing in a certain market area. An increase in vacancy rates in rental housing indicates a surplus of housing space. A 5 percent vacancy rate (95 percent occupancy rate) is usually considered indicative of a healthy housing market. As the occupancy rate increases, rental rates tend to increase, and apartment dwellers who have been waiting to buy homes of their own are given impetus to start looking for houses for sale and to move out of apartments. This causes increased apartment vacancies and eventually a drop in rents as well as a halt in construction of new apartments.

One of the first indications of a revived real estate market has always been an increase in rental occupancies that cannot be attributed to reduced rents or giveaway programs. High occupancy rates lead to increased rents. Increased rents lead to new construction and a revived real estate market.

Calculating occupancy and vacancy rates. To calculate the occupancy rate, divide the number of occupied units by the total number of units in the building.

> **E X A M P L E :** Assume that 200 apartments are rented in a 250-unit apartment building. What is the building's occupancy rate?
>
> 200 rented units ÷ 250 total units = .80 or 80 percent occupancy rate

To calculate the vacancy rate, divide the number of vacant units by the total number of units in the building.

> **E X A M P L E :** What is the building's vacancy rate if 225 units are rented in a 300-unit apartment building?
>
> 300 total units − 225 rented units = 75 vacant units
> 75 vacant units ÷ 300 total units = .25 or 25 percent vacancy rate

Sales volume. There are many ways to collect information on the number and prices of homes sold during the recent past. One can go to the public records, either in person or via the Internet, and extract the number of houses sold. Then, from the state documentary stamp tax on deeds, the approximate sale price of each can be calculated. Tax laws require that the price of each real estate sale be reported. This requirement reduces the problem of collecting housing data.

Most towns and cities have newspaper publication of sales during the previous week or previous month. From these published accounts one can extract information on how many sales occurred, the approximate sale prices, where the properties sold were located, and sometimes, the types of houses involved. Licensees in towns and cities that have multiple listing services find the job a great deal easier.

No market indicator is of any value unless one learns how to use it. A database system arranged by subdivision, by streets, or alphabetically can be of great value in building a current sales data file. A large-scale map of a town or those areas of a city where interest is high can become a valuable tool to pinpoint areas of greatest activity and to forecast direction of growth. When a sale is reported in a publication, a color-coded pin can be placed on the map to indicate price range and location of property. A glance at such a map shows where most sales are occurring and the general price ranges. Direction and rate of growth also can be estimated from a sales data map.

SUMMARY OF IMPORTANT POINTS

- The five characteristics of the real estate market are (1) immobility of real estate; (2) a market that is slow to respond to change in supply and demand; (3) land that is indestructible; (4) the uniqueness of real estate; and (5) government controls that influence the market through zoning, building codes, taxes, and so forth.

- *Supply* is the amount and type of real estate available for sale or rent at differing price levels in a given real estate market. Variables that influence supply are availability of labor, availability of construction loans and financing, availability of land, and availability of materials.

- *Demand* is the desire and ability to purchase or rent goods and services. Variables that influence demand are price of real estate, population numbers and household composition, income of consumers, availability of mortgage credit, and consumer taste or preferences.

- A buyer's market occurs when the supply and demand equilibrium is upset by excess supply (supply exceeds demand).

- A seller's market occurs when the supply and demand equilibrium is upset with excess demand (demand exceeds supply).

- A vacancy rate is the percentage of rental units that are not occupied.

R E V I E W   Q U E S T I O N S

1. Any economy in any nation must find answers for three questions: what will be produced, who will do the producing, and
   a. when will production cease?
   b. what will production cost?
   c. who will get what is produced?
   d. which producers will produce what?

2. The company who will do the producing is the
   a. biggest producer of a given product.
   b. company that budgets the most for product promotion.
   c. company that uses only part-time help to avoid expensive employee benefits.
   d. most efficient producer of a comparable-quality product.

3. The ultimate decision makers in the marketplace are
   a. salespersons.
   b. producers.
   c. manufacturers.
   d. consumers.

4. Which characteristic does NOT describe the real estate market?
   a. Land is indestructible.
   b. The market is quick to respond to changes in supply and demand.
   c. Real estate is heterogeneous.
   d. Real estate is immobile.

5. Which statement is FALSE regarding the relationship between price and demand?
   a. An increase in price causes a decrease in demand.
   b. A decrease in price causes an increase in demand.
   c. There is an inverse relationship between price and demand.
   d. An increase in price causes an increase in demand.

6. Government controls influence the real estate market both directly and indirectly. An example of an indirect control is
   a. zoning ordinances.
   b. building moratoriums.
   c. monetary policy.
   d. building codes.

7. Which statement is NOT associated with the economic concept of demand?
   a. Demand is the desire and ability to purchase or lease goods and services.
   b. Changes in price cause an inverse change in demand.
   c. Consumer preferences influence demand.
   d. The availability of building materials influences demand.

8. Variables that influence demand include
    a. consumer tastes and preferences.
    b. population size and household composition.
    c. consumer income.
    d. all of the above.

9. Which statement does NOT describe the real estate market?
    a. Real estate has become standardized thanks to technology.
    b. Real estate is fixed in its location.
    c. Land is permanent.
    d. Federal monetary policy has an indirect influence on the real estate market.

10. When the equilibrium of the real estate market is upset by an excess supply
    a. builder activity increases in response to the need.
    b. a seller's market exists.
    c. a buyer's market exists.
    d. demand decreases.

11. One person or a group of persons occupying a separate housing space is technically defined as a
    a. unit.
    b. household.
    c. family.
    d. multiple ownership unit.

12. The most important cause of population increase in Florida has been the
    a. increase in consumer income.
    b. number of births exceeding deaths.
    c. in-migration of new residents.
    d. expansion of mortgage credit.

13. The barometer of the real estate market is considered to be the
    a. change in consumer income.
    b. cost and availability of credit.
    c. number of housing starts.
    d. change in consumer tastes.

14. The typical homebuyer today is concerned primarily with the
    a. style of the house being current.
    b. total cost of the house.
    c. amount of the monthly mortgage payment.
    d. occupancy and vacancy ratios.

15. Factors affecting the supply side of the real estate market are related to
    a. availability of land.
    b. availability of skilled labor.
    c. availability of material.
    d. all of the above.

CHAPTER

20

PLANNING AND ZONING

OVERVIEW

In a residential community located in a fashionable area, homes are meticulously land-scaped with rose bushes and beautiful fountains. It is a neighborhood of executives and their families. Across the street from one of the fashionable homes is a small candy factory, and farther down the street is a soft-drink bottling company. This is just one example of what happens when community planning and land-use control are absent.

After completing this chapter, the student should be able to:

- distinguish among the six types of land-use planning background studies;
- distinguish among zoning ordinances, building codes, and health ordinances;
- explain the purpose of a variance, a special exception, and a nonconforming use;
- calculate the number of lots available for development, given the total number of acres contained in a parcel, the percentage of land reserved for streets and other facilities, and the minimum number of square feet per lot; and
- describe the characteristics of a planned unit development.

KEY TERMS

base industries	environmental impact	service industries
buffer zone	statement (EIS)	special exceptions
building codes	health ordinances	special flood hazard area
certificate of occupancy	nonconforming use	(SFHA)
concurrency	planned unit development	variance
economic base studies	(PUD)	zero lot line
		zoning ordinances

HISTORY OF PLANNING AND ZONING

Planning and land-use control have been practiced in this country to varying degrees since the first European settlers arrived. During the colonial period, the British colonies enacted ordinances restricting slaughterhouses and gunpowder mills to the outskirts of the community. Later in the 1800s, cities established fire districts and building height restrictions.

Industrialization brought a decreased interest in planning and land use regulations. The philosophy of *laissez-faire* (French for "let alone") prevailed among business and political leaders. Laissez-faire, a philosophy of noninterference by the government in private business affairs, advocated letting the owners of land and business fix the rules of competition. Planning and growth management were largely ignored. Property owners used their land to produce the greatest private gain without regard to the impact on the community. As industrialization expanded, people left the farms for city jobs. Unorganized growth resulted.

In 1916 the first serious efforts were made to create and enforce zoning ordinances. The garment industry in New York City was about to expand into the exclusive Fifth Avenue district. A zoning ordinance was enacted to protect Fifth Avenue property values by prohibiting all but specified property uses in that district. Other cities began to adopt zoning ordinances to create or protect local property values. Many property owners objected to the introduction of zoning laws. Most of the objections were raised because of zoning ordinances that prohibited owners from using their land to generate profit or income without compensating them for the rights lost. In 1926 the U.S. Supreme Court ruled that legally enacted zoning laws were constitutional. This ruling gave powers of enforcement to municipalities that had enacted zoning laws for the purpose of regulating future growth. These controls gave rise to city planning and growth management all across the nation.

Planning Goals

As part of the *growth management* process, *city planning* attempts to regulate city growth as required to achieve four basic goals:

1. To plan future land uses that allow the highest and best use of the maximum number of properties
2. To reduce the possibility that a particular type of land use may cause loss of value to neighboring properties
3. To reduce present and future growth costs that must be borne by taxpayers
4. To create an optimal social and economic environment as a result of community growth

Florida's growth management laws require that all local governments discourage urban sprawl and inadequate infrastructure in their comprehensive plans. *Urban sprawl* is the unplanned expansion of a municipality over a large geographic area. Typical urban sprawl patterns of leapfrog development, ribbon or strip development, and low-density residential uses over large land areas increase the cost of public *infrastructure* services (for example, bridges, sewers, utilities, and roads). Growth management planning by a city or county increases the likelihood of goal accomplishment.

LOCAL PLANNING AGENCY

Hartford, Connecticut, organized the first official land-use planning agency in the United States, in 1907. Today there are planning agencies at all levels of government. Planning commissions in Florida are primarily at the city and county level. The **concurrency**

1 provision in Florida's Growth Management Act of 1985 mandates that the infrastructure,
2 such as roads and water and waste treatment facilities needed to support additional pop-
3 ulation, be in place before new development is allowed. Many communities have expe-
4 rienced complete curtailment of new construction because of a building moratorium until
5 a new sewage treatment plant, for example, was completed.

163.03, F.S.

6 Cities and counties compete with each other to attract new residents and industries. To
7 plan efficiently beyond local community boundaries, a *comprehensive plan* (or master plan)
8 is thought necessary. The process of developing such plans often uncovers unexpected
9 obstacles. Chapter 163, F.S., charged the Department of Community Affairs (DCA) with
10 the regulation and standardization of regional, county, and city comprehensive plans and
11 required that all levels of government within the state develop comprehensive plans to
12 guide and control future growth.

Composition

14 Planning commissions are most effective when composed of members who represent all
15 walks of life. Members most often are not trained professional planners. The overriding
16 goal is to have representatives from a cross section of interests. A planning commission
17 composed entirely of developers, for example, could not possibly speak for all the people.
18 The homes, desires, and goals of all residents should be considered.

19 Members of the planning commission are usually appointed (not elected) and serve
20 in a voluntary, unpaid capacity. The primary legislative body of the city or county is the
21 appointing authority, normally a city council or a county commission. Planning commis-
22 sions vary in size, and the terms for which planning commissioners are appointed may
23 vary from the terms of their colleagues. This ensures a staggered rate of replacement and is
24 designed to prevent any one appointing authority from selecting an entire planning com-
25 mission. Planning commissioners are usually appointed for terms longer than the term of
26 the appointing authority to reduce the commissioners' obligation to any single political
27 body. This minimizes political influence within the planning body.

28 The planning commission or board serves as an advisory body to the elected city or
29 county government. As important as the planning function may be to the future welfare
30 of a community, the commission is not the final authority in matters related to planning.
31 The commission is responsible for planning, just as the police department is responsible
32 for law enforcement, but the elected government must make the final decisions based on
33 recommendations from subordinate agencies.

Authority

35 Three areas of responsibility for which city planning commissions are commonly dele-
36 gated final authority are: (1) subdivision plat approval, (2) site plan approval, and (3) sign
37 control.

38 **Subdivision plat approval.** A developer planning to create a subdivision must submit a
39 *subdivision plat* to the planning commission for approval. (See also chapter 1.) A developer
40 is not issued a building permit until final approval is granted by the planning commission.
41 When approval is received, the developer may proceed to record the plat in the public
42 records and receive a building permit.

Site plan approval. The *site plan* serves the same function that a subdivision plat serves for a subdivision. It is a detailed plan of how the project is to be developed, how traffic and parking will be dealt with, and what impact on neighboring properties may be expected. This is an area in which the expertise of the planning commission's support staff can be of great assistance. Reviewing and checking site plan proposals requires painstaking attention to detail and a well-rounded background of information. This ensures compliance with all physical, economic, and environmental requirements.

Sign control. More and more cities are exercising control over signs. The primary aims of sign control are to minimize distraction to motorists and to eliminate actual safety hazards created by signs at blind corners, lighted signs that glare into the eyes of drivers at night, and the like. Any aesthetic improvement resulting from sign control is a welcomed by-product.

Support Staff

While appointed members of the commission may be experts in their own fields, they often are not urban planning experts. The planning commission's function is to make policy recommendations regarding the type of city it feels that citizens want in the future. It sets goals and provides residents with a number of feasible alternative plans for achieving those goals. The job of collecting, sorting, analyzing, and reporting is handled by the staff of the planning commission.

The planning commission support staff is composed of full-time city or county employees. Staff members are normally college-trained or university-trained planners. They have learned how to evaluate the economic base of a city. They know the most productive sources of information regarding population, proper land uses, and support requirements for future growth. The planning support staff collects and refines the raw data to produce the basic studies needed to develop a flexible, comprehensive plan for future growth.

THE PLANNING PROCESS

Basic Background Studies

Before the goals, objectives, and policies can be finalized, the planning commission and its support staff must have a good idea of what has happened in the past, what the present situation is, and what projections indicate for the future. Six types of background studies (see Figure 20.1, Comprehensive Plan) are used by planners:

1. Population background studies
2. Area economic base studies
3. Existing land-use studies
4. Physiographic studies
5. Recreation and community facilities studies
6. Thoroughfare studies

Population background studies. The population and its geographic distribution are the basic determinants of comprehensive planning. Population studies are the most basic and important of all planning studies. These studies identify the following: the composition of the population; the number of households and their approximate incomes; and the numbers and locations of different ethnic groups, occupations of residents, and educational

F I G U R E 20.1 ■ Comprehensive Plan

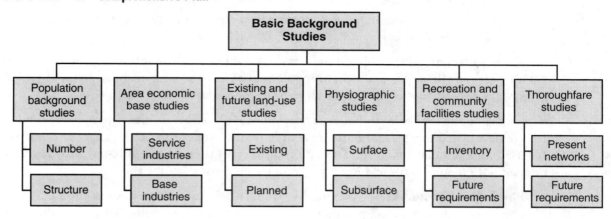

1   levels. With this demographic information, predictions can be made for the future. In
2   Florida, predictions normally are limited to periods of five years to ten years into the future.
3   In states where growth is slow, the planning predictions may be projected for 15 years to
4   20 years into the future.

5   Population studies give planners an indication of the number of new households
6   expected to move into an area. This information is of great assistance in estimating the
7   cost of social services for a larger, and in some cases older, population. Planners can alert
8   cities and counties to the number of additional police officers, firefighters, teachers, medi-
9   cal facilities, and the like that will be required to handle the new residents.

10 **Economic base studies.** **Economic base studies** analyze the effect of base-industry employ-
11 ment in the area. **Base industries** are those industries that attract outside money to the
12 area, such as film making, fertilizer plants, and the citrus industry. **Service industries** are
13 those such as grocery stores, barber shops, and retail stores, whose customers are primarily
14 local residents. These industries keep money already in the area circulating but attract
15 little outside money to the area.

16   These studies also will reveal whether an area is principally tourist-oriented, indus-
17 trial, commercial, educational, or agricultural in character. Perhaps the area can boast of
18 several economic activities. The more diversified the economic base, the more stable the
19 area economy tends to be. This contributes to growth and stable property values.

20 **Existing land-use studies.** To plan for future land use, the planning commission takes
21 an inventory of all public and private land uses. The commission does a complete survey
22 of land uses, with detailed maps plotting each separate land parcel. Individual lots and
23 tracts can be identified on land-use maps with colors or codes to indicate the present use
24 of the land. Once completed, existing land-use patterns dictate, to a great degree, the
25 location of future land uses. Generally, professional planners use five basic land-use cat-
26 egories: (1) residential, (2) commercial, (3) industrial, (4) agricultural, and (5) special
27 use. Basic land-use classifications are divided further into subcategories. For example, a
28 county might use:

29   ■   *residential:* single-family, one-family to four-family, multifamily;

30   ■   *commercial:* neighborhood shopping, community business, professional offices,
31   shopping center, central business district;

- *industrial:* component assembly, light manufacturing, heavy industry, warehousing; and
- *special use:* public schools, churches, recreational areas (community parks and national parks).

Unfortunately, there is no uniform standard of land-use classification that applies to all parts of the state. Each planning commission or zoning authority may establish any system desired to prevent encroachment of incompatible uses.

Once the land-use studies are complete and all of the current uses of individual parcels are accounted for, it is a relatively simple matter to determine the number of acres being used for each classification. This information can then be coordinated with results of the population studies to develop a preliminary land-use plan for the future.

Physiographic studies. Physiographic studies help avoid unexpected problems with soil conditions: drainage, soil percolation, and load-bearing capacity. They describe the physical structure of the land. All of the various soil types are cataloged and then plotted on a map. Each soil type is coded to indicate recommended usage. For example, some soil types require floating foundations or special pilings. Areas where these types of soil conditions are found are not suitable for high-rise buildings. Some soils do not drain well, necessitating special storm drainage systems. Physiographic studies with accompanying maps are a factor in determining the highest and best use of specific tracts of land.

Recreation and community facilities studies. These studies, which should be coordinated with the population studies, plan for public and private recreation areas. Parks, playgrounds, beaches, and municipal facilities are identified and plotted on a map. A relationship then can be established to indicate the population number and type to be served.

When the existing community facilities are located and plotted, plans can be made for the location of appropriate similar facilities in those areas marked for future growth. Projections can be made for the number and location of additional parks, playgrounds, and community recreational facilities needed to serve the planned residential areas.

Thoroughfare studies. Thoroughfare studies are designed to identify existing and projected traffic circulation systems. They are closely related to population and economic studies. Federal and state laws require that cities of 50,000 people or more do urban area thoroughfare studies to reflect present and future transportation networks. Because cities of that size have an effective market area much larger than that contained within the city limits, these studies must include the surrounding urban areas, which are considered part of the metropolitan market area.

Thoroughfare studies are normally a joint venture involving city, county, and state transportation departments and regional planning commissions. Such studies must anticipate requirements for ingress and egress and traffic flow to future residential and commercial areas that may be still in the planning stage. They also must anticipate increased amounts of roadway and pedestrian traffic generated by new residents. In addition, they must consider the transportation requirements of neighboring cities and counties. Because most counties share transportation problems with their neighbors, they share the need for joint planning efforts.

Goals Formulation

When the background studies are completed, the planning support staff will have provided the planning commission with the information needed to enter the next phase of city planning: formulating goals. Before the data from the background studies are converted into a single comprehensive plan for growth management, the planning commission attempts to find out what type of city the residents want. Some cities mail each resident a questionnaire, some use inserts in local newspapers, some hold public hearings, and some have members of the planning commission make presentations to social and civic clubs. The main purpose of this phase of city planning is to identify broad planning objectives that the community residents want to achieve.

Time and time again, experience has demonstrated that the desires of the population must be considered if a comprehensive plan is to be effective. This is one of the reasons a planning commission should include representatives from occupations not related to real estate or development.

ZONING LAWS AND CODE ENFORCEMENT

Zoning ordinances are enacted to ensure that property owners adhere to the planned types of land uses and to protect the integrity of the comprehensive plan. No other land-use controls affect all properties in a community to a greater degree than zoning ordinances. Used in conjunction with building codes, they are effective in protecting property values.

Zoning ordinances are local laws that implement the comprehensive plan. Local government exercises *police power* by regulating and controlling the use of land and structures within designated land-use districts or zones. Each zone is assigned a specific land-use classification. Unless an exception is granted, only the assigned land use is allowed in a particular zone to protect against uses that might reduce the value of neighboring properties. Zoning ordinances regulate the following:

- Permissible uses for each parcel of land
- Lot size
- Type of structures
- Building heights
- Setback requirements (the space between lot lines and building lines)
- Density (the ratio of land area to structure area also known as *floor area ratio*—determined by dividing the total floor area of a building by the total land area of the site)

Building codes protect the public health and safety from inferior construction practices. Building codes set minimum standards for materials and quality of workmanship, sanitary equipment, electrical wiring, fire prevention, and so forth. Florida has a statewide building code called the *Florida Building Code*. Additionally, cities and counties may enforce more (but not less) stringent building code requirements.

WEB LINK

To learn more about the Florida building code, visit **www.floridabuilding.org/c/default.aspx**.

553.72(2), F.S.

Local government enforces building codes. The process begins by issuing a *building permit* after review of the architectural and engineering drawings. Municipal inspectors visit each job site and conduct building inspections at various phases of the construction. The inspections must pass before the next phase of construction can proceed. A final **certificate of occupancy** is issued once construction is completed and the municipal building inspector agrees that the structure conforms to code.

Health ordinances control maintenance and sanitation of public spaces. The local health department inspects and enforces sanitary standards in a community's food and drinking establishments.

Residential

Residential zoning regulates *density*, meaning the number of units (homes) per acre. Several subcategories establish different minimum sizes for lots.

> **EXAMPLE:** Imagine that residential zone R-1A requires that all lots in that subcategory contain at least 9,000 square feet of land. This automatically restricts the number of lots a developer can create from each acre in a subdivision. Every acre of land contains 43,560 square feet. A given developer is going to develop 100 acres. In the process of turning raw land into a subdivision, between 20 percent and 25 percent of the land is commonly used for streets and open space. Wider streets and open green space add quality but reduce the amount of land available for lots. Using 25 percent loss for streets, the developer can determine the number of lots per acre (density) permitted by the R-1A zoning.

$$43{,}560 \text{ square feet per acre} \times .75 \text{ land available for lots}$$
$$= 32{,}670 \text{ square feet available per acre}$$

$$32{,}670 \div 9{,}000 \text{ minimum square feet per lot}$$
$$= 3.63 \text{ lots per acre (density)}$$

$$3.63 \times 100 \text{ acres} = 363 \text{ total subdivision lots}$$

In the same county, residential zoning subcategory R-1AA may require one-acre lots, and R-1B may require only a minimum of 8,000 square feet per lot. Zoning authorities may create as many zoning subcategories as needed. They also fix the criteria for each subcategory.

Commercial

The purpose of *commercial zoning* is to regulate *intensity* of use. Intensity is determined by the type and amount of pedestrian and vehicular traffic generated by a commercial enterprise. Businesses that generate a great deal of traffic, such as service stations, are normally less desirable next to quiet residential areas. In contrast, a physician's office or an attorney's office does not create the same degree of threat to residential values. Zoning ordinances normally recognize these conditions by creating a *buffer zone* between residential and commercial zones. A **buffer zone** is a strip of land separating one land use from another. Frequently, the buffer zone will allow multifamily zoning (for example, apartments) next to single-family residential areas, then a professional business zone, then higher intensity zones.

Industrial

Industrial zoning also is intended to *regulate* intensity of use. In addition, industrial zoning subcategories are used to control the amount and location of industrial offshoots resulting from different kinds of industrial activity. A wide industrial-base city may have many subcategories of industrial zoning, whereas a city oriented toward agriculture, tourism, or education may have only one or two industrial subcategories. One innovation in industrial zoning has been industrial subdivisions, or *industrial parks*. (See also chapter 1.)

Agricultural

The *agricultural zoning* classification is an all-inclusive category; it is not divided into subcategories. If the existing use of the property is for some type of agriculture, no zoning controls will attempt to regulate the type of agriculture permitted. If the use fails to qualify for an agricultural classification, the property then can be rezoned into another zoning category.

Special Use

Although the county property appraiser may be interested in knowing exactly what level of government owns what property, most zoning authorities consider all property owned by all levels of government as a type of special-use property. Public zoning is a subcategory of special-use zoning, which includes, for example, city parks, county courthouses, and federal post office buildings. This zoning category is exempt from local zoning regulation.

APPEALS AND EXCEPTIONS

Zoning Board of Adjustment

Owners of real estate may appeal enforcement of zoning restrictions in cases where strict compliance would cause undue hardship or reduce property values. To handle appeals and requests for relief, most zoning authorities have established a semijudicial body called the *Zoning Board of Adjustment,* or simply *Board of Adjustment.* The primary function of the Zoning Board of Adjustment is to provide property owners some degree of relief from otherwise rigid zoning codes. The board must take all possible precautions to render objective, unbiased decisions because its quasi-judicial powers give it some of the characteristics of a court. Once the Zoning Board of Adjustment renders a decision, most zoning laws will allow a property owner only one additional avenue of appeal, litigation in the courts.

Variances. A **variance** allows a property owner to *vary* from strict compliance with all or part of a zoning code because to comply would force an undue hardship on the property owner. Two conditions must be met before a property owner may be granted a variance from existing zoning requirements:

1. The property owner must show that a *hardship* exists or will be created by strict compliance with zoning requirements and that the owner did nothing to cause the hardship. This will prevent a property owner or developer from taking some action designed for private benefit with the expectation that the Zoning Board of Adjustment will accept or approve the situation the property owner or developer created.

2. The Zoning Board of Adjustment must use the same established criteria to judge the validity of all requests for a variance. This ensures fair and impartial treatment for each property owner requesting a variance.

Many people have trouble with the word *hardship*. It has nothing to do with economic or personal hardships. It involves land *use*, and the hardship must relate to the use of the property. For example, suppose you bought a nice lot on a river where zoning restrictions require "setback" distances of 25 feet from the front of the lot and 30 feet from the river or rear of the lot. Imagine you are about to start construction of a new house designed to fit precisely the above setback requirements when a survey reveals that erosion by the river over time has carried away 10 feet from the river side of your lot. The maximum setback distance possible is now only 20 feet. Because zoning restrictions require 30 feet, you will be in violation if you go ahead with construction. Violation of zoning laws can cause removal of the offending structure. To prevent potential trouble, you request a variance. The hardship exists, and you did nothing to cause the hardship. You would have met the hardship requirement for a variance (the first condition in the preceding list).

Special exceptions. The Zoning Board of Adjustment is authorized to issue **special exceptions** for controlling the location of particular land uses. A dentist's office might be granted a special exception in an area located near a large mobile home community. Another example is an adult day-care facility in a residential area composed primarily of retirees. A special exception grants a specific use of a particular parcel. Special exceptions are a departure from the zoning ordinance, generally permitted in cases where it is determined that the surrounding area would be better served by allowing the special exception. Most communities require public hearings before a special exception is granted so that property owners of surrounding parcels have an opportunity to provide input in the decision process.

Legally nonconforming uses. If a property's use was lawfully established but no longer conforms to the use regulations of the zone in which it is located because of the enactment of a new zoning ordinance, the use is allowed to continue as a **nonconforming use**. For example, a small neighborhood gas station might have located in an area that was later zoned residential. The small gas station within the new residential zone is *grandfathered* as a nonconforming use.

The U.S. Constitution prohibits depriving a person of property without due process or fair compensation. Local governments may not employ eminent domain powers to correct nonconforming uses unless the property is taken for a public use. The methods used to correct a nonconforming use vary around the state. Most zoning authorities allow a time period long enough for nonconforming property owners to recapture their investment in the property. After the expiration of this designated period, the property owner must convert the use of the property to that use for which the area is zoned. If, during the designated period, the structure on the property is damaged or more than 50 percent destroyed, the property must be converted to a use that conforms with area zoning. Other communities allow a legal nonconforming use to continue until ownership changes. Nonconforming-use properties usually are not permitted to be increased in size or to undergo structural changes. Most zoning authorities restrict repairs and maintenance of such properties to those needed for sanitation and safety purposes. These procedures are designed to result in all properties eventually becoming conforming-use properties. (See Figure 20.2, Government Land-Use Controls.)

F I G U R E 20.2 ■   Government Land-Use Controls

Method	Function
Building code	Controls construction and materials
Zoning ordinance	Controls use
Health ordinance	Controls maintenance and sanitation
Variance	Permission to build or use to relieve a hardship *not* caused by owner
Special exception	Permission to build or use in apparent conflict with existing zoning ordinance
Nonconforming use	Permission to continue to use in spite of enacted zoning ordinance

Developments of Regional Impact

As the state grows, planning assumes an ever-increasing importance and responsibility. Regional planning groups are becoming more instrumental in controlling growth. In fact, no planned development of sufficient size to affect surrounding areas can be approved without regional planning approval. Developments of Regional Impact (DRIs) have become the subject of a separate statute in Florida to ensure better control of the environment, today and in the future.

The term *development of regional impact* means any development that, because of its character, size, or location, will have a substantial effect on the health, safety, or welfare of citizens of more than one county in the state. Statewide guidelines and standards, along with numerical "thresholds" (limits), are used to determine whether particular developments must undergo DRI review. The review process evaluates everything from air quality to roads and schools. DRIs include projects such as shopping centers and malls, industrial plants and parks, sports facilities, and residential developments.

Regional planning commissions (or councils) are organized in much the same manner as county or city planning groups. The commission members are appointed, and a trained professional support staff assists with administrative and technical matters. Like their local counterparts, regional planning commissions are advisory in nature. This means that the appointing authority (city or county for the area in which a project is located) makes the decision to implement, reject, or modify recommendations submitted by the regional planning group.

Planned Unit Development

A **planned unit development (PUD)** is a type of special land use allowed under most local zoning ordinances. The developer clusters residential units on smaller lots to create maximum open spaces. The open spaces are typically developed into parks and recreation areas. The dwelling lots and structures are individually owned. A nonprofit community association is organized to provide for maintenance of the common areas. The special characteristics of PUDs are summarized below.

Clustered homes. Clustering homes together on smaller lots allows for large open green spaces. Clustering results in the same overall density as in a conventional development; however, the clustered improvements result in more open common areas.

Mixed land use. A variety of types of housing may include single-family detached homes in addition to, for example, townhouses and garden apartments. Some PUDs incorporate shopping, restaurants, and entertainment facilities into the development to create a sense of community. For this reason, PUDs are also referred to as multiple-use zoning.

Planned open spaces. The open space resulting from clustering dwelling units is often developed into recreational areas that are maintained by a community association.

Zero lot line is a term used to describe the positioning of a structure on a lot so that one side rests directly on the lot's boundary line (no side setback requirement). Zero lot line homes are sometimes marketed as garden homes or patio homes. Such homes may feature large patios for entertaining or neighbor-friendly front porches.

Environmental Impact Statement

When a large project is proposed, an environmental impact study is conducted to analyze the long-term impact the project will have on the quality of the surrounding environment. The study must estimate the impact on waste-disposal systems, air quality, traffic, local employment, and so forth. An **environmental impact statement (EIS)** summarizes into a single document the long-term effect the proposed project will have on the surrounding environment. The EIS provides local government agencies and the public with important information regarding the environmental impact that can be expected from proposed development.

Federal Flood Insurance Program

Congress created the National Flood Insurance Program (NFIP) to help provide property owners with coverage against losses due to flooding. The NFIP offers flood insurance to homeowners, renters, and business owners if their community participates in the NFIP. Participating communities agree to adopt and enforce ordinances that meet or exceed FEMA requirements to reduce the risk of flooding. The Federal Emergency Management Agency (FEMA) administers the flood program. FEMA prepares flood maps for every city and county in the United States.

Flood insurance can be purchased for any property located in a community participating in the NFIP. Homes and buildings located in the 100-year flood plan, referred to as **special flood hazard areas (SFHA)**, financed with mortgage loans from federally regulated or insured lenders are required to have flood insurance (flood map zones A and V). SFHA have a 1 percent or greater chance of flooding in any given year, which is equivalent to a 26 percent chance of flooding during a 30-year mortgage.

S U M M A R Y   O F   I M P O R T A N T   P O I N T S

- ■ City planning commissions are delegated final authority for subdivision plat approval, site plan approval, and sign control.
- ■ Basic background studies include population background studies, economic base studies, existing land-use studies, physiographic studies, recreation and community facilities studies, and thoroughfare studies.

- ■ Economic base studies analyze the effect of base-industry employment in the area. Base industries are those industries that attract outside money to the area. Service industries are those establishments whose customers are primarily local residents.

- ■ Zoning ordinances authorize the segmentation (dividing) of a community into districts or zones in keeping with the character of the land and structures and their suitability for particular uses to protect against uses that might reduce the value of neighboring properties.

- ■ Building codes protect the public health and safety from inferior construction practices. The Florida Building Code is a statewide building code.

- ■ Residential zoning regulates density, meaning the number of homes per acre. Commercial zoning regulates intensity of use, such as vehicular traffic generated by a commercial enterprise.

- ■ A *buffer zone* is a strip of land separating one land use from another.

- ■ The Zoning Board of Adjustment handles appeals and requests from property owners for zoning changes.

- ■ Variances allow property owners to vary from strict compliance with all or part of a zoning code because to comply would force an undue hardship on the property owner.

- ■ *Special exception* is permission to build or to use property in apparent conflict with existing zoning ordinances.

- ■ *Nonconforming use* is continuing land use that is not in compliance with a newly enacted zoning ordinance.

- ■ A *planned unit development* (PUD) is a self-contained development planned under special zoning ordinances that allow maximum use of open space by reducing lot sizes and street sizes.

- ■ *Zero lot line* is a term used to describe the positioning of a structure on a lot so that one side rests directly on the lot's boundary line (no setback requirement).

- ■ Environmental impact statements summarize the effect that proposed development will have on the surroundings.

R E V I E W   Q U E S T I O N S

1. One of the major reasons for the lack of emphasis on city planning in the 1800s was the
   a. focus on identifying and locating rural tracts for farming using a new method of describing real property.
   b. philosophy of laissez-faire.
   c. reduction in university course offerings in real estate and urban development.
   d. exodus from the farms to the cities for jobs.

2. The subsection in Florida's Growth Management Act that requires that parks, roads, sewers, and drinking water be available before new development is allowed is referred to as the
   a. utilities provision.
   b. infrastructure provision.
   c. concurrency provision.
   d. level of service provision.

3. A planning commission is normally composed of
   a. trained professional planners.
   b. elected officials.
   c. appointed unpaid members.
   d. members of the primary legislative city or county body.

4. The best composition of a planning commission is generally thought to be one with representation from
   a. each licensed professional occupation.
   b. senior adult homeowners because of their experience.
   c. real estate and mortgage lending firms.
   d. a cross section of interests.

5. In municipalities with planning commissions, the final authority in planning matters is the
   a. planning commission chairperson.
   b. professional staff director.
   c. elected city government officials.
   d. planning commission support staff supervisor.

6. The primary function of a planning commission is to
   a. make policy recommendations to the elected government body.
   b. make policy recommendations to the trained professional staff.
   c. advise the next higher planning board (county, regional, etc.) of its recommendations and actions.
   d. collect, refine, and produce the basic studies needed to develop a comprehensive plan for future growth.

7. A strip of land that separates one land use from another is referred to as
   a. an easement.
   b. an egress.
   c. a buffer zone.
   d. a median.

8. The MOST basic of all the background planning studies is the
   a. economic base study.
   b. land-use study.
   c. community facilities study.
   d. population study.

9. A land-use study
   a. shows where future land uses should be.
   b. involves plotting each parcel on a land-use map.
   c. requires an inventory of public and private land uses.
   d. involves all of the above.

10. Population background studies include an estimate of
    a. the number of new households expected to move into the area.
    b. the best housing markets of the future.
    c. the future cost of social services.
    d. all of the above.

11. Base industries contribute to stability and growth; service industries are the businesses that
    a. do not attract much outside money to the area.
    b. attract outside money to the area.
    c. manufacture and export products.
    d. create and export service assistance.

12. Physiographic studies reveal the
    a. physical location of shopping centers and subdivisions.
    b. transportation network structure.
    c. surface and subsurface structure of land.
    d. density and intensity structure of population.

13. Thoroughfare studies are normally a
    a. city project.
    b. county project.
    c. state project.
    d. cooperative project.

14. To be granted a variance, a property owner must provide evidence that
    a. the same treatment has been afforded other owners.
    b. a hardship related to land use exists.
    c. the variance, if granted, will be for the owner's use only.
    d. the land use existed before passage of zoning laws.

15. Residential zoning is designed to regulate
    a. intensity.
    b. frequency.
    c. density.
    d. all of the above.

16. Commercial zoning is designed to regulate
    a. intensity.
    b. frequency.
    c. density.
    d. all of the above.

17. A small general store that existed before a change to residential zoning would be an example of a
    a. special exception.
    b. variance.
    c. PUD.
    d. nonconforming use.

18. The legal right to enact zoning laws is derived from
    a. police powers.
    b. public policy.
    c. property taxation.
    d. all of the above.

19. Zoning ordinances regulate
    a. the firewall rating of a wall located between the kitchen and dining areas of a restaurant.
    b. the setback requirements of a building from the property lines.
    c. the electrical rating of the wiring in a residential home.
    d. all of the above.

20. A parcel of land contains 75 acres. A developer has reserved 25 percent of the land for streets and green space. Applicable zoning regulations require a minimum of 9,500 square feet per residential lot. The number of permissible lots is
    a. 86.
    b. 232.
    c. 257.
    d. 260.

APPENDIX A: PRACTICE END-OF-COURSE EXAM

This practice exam consists of 100 multiple-choice questions. A student who achieves a score of at least 80 percent without using any reference material should be in a strong position relative to subsequent examinations. It is recommended that at least two hours or more of uninterrupted time be budgeted to take this exam.

1. A licensed real estate broker has been hired by a lender to appraise a home for a buyer who has made application for an FHA loan. Which statement is TRUE regarding this situation?
   a. The broker's license entitles him to appraise this property.
   b. The broker may not charge for this assignment.
   c. The broker is required to be a state-certified appraiser to perform this appraisal assignment.
   d. The broker may not accept this appraisal assignment because to do so would be a conflict of interest.

2. Leasehold estates do NOT include
   a. a tenancy at will.
   b. a holdover tenancy.
   c. an estate for years.
   d. a remainder estate.

3. The Florida Real Estate Commission must notify which agency when it takes disciplinary action against any of the agency's licensees?
   a. Division of Time Shares
   b. Division of Professions
   c. Division of Regulation
   d. Division of Florida Condominiums, Timeshares, and Mobile Homes

4. Failure to comply with the statute of frauds will result in
   a. a charge of fraud.
   b. an illegal contract.
   c. an unenforceable contract.
   d. a revocation of licensure.

5. Which statute prohibits discrimination in hotels, restaurants, and other places of public accommodation if such discrimination is based on national origin?
   a. Civil Rights Act of 1866
   b. Civil Rights Act of 1964
   c. Fair Housing Act of 1968 (as amended)
   d. Florida Fair Housing Act

6. A broker received a $5,000 deposit from a buyer on Tuesday at 1:00 PM. The seller will not be available until Monday. The broker's normal banking day is Monday. The broker is required to deposit the $5,000 before the end of
   a. the next business day.
   b. business on Wednesday.
   c. business on Thursday.
   d. business on Friday.

7. Which expense is subtracted to derive NOI?
   a. Vacancy and collection losses
   b. Mortgage payments
   c. Income taxes
   d. Depreciation

8. An investor wanted to build a motel. A broker showed him three choice sites zoned hotel-motel. The investor promised to decide on a site in three weeks, so the broker took a two-week vacation. When the broker returned, the investor bought one of these sites. The broker sold the site, not knowing that the zoning on that site had been changed to industrial. Which is correct?
   a. The broker is guilty of culpable negligence.
   b. The broker is not guilty of wrongdoing.
   c. The property owner is guilty of fraud.
   d. The broker is guilty of fraud.

9. The mortgage clause that requires the lender to waive the right to a deficiency judgment against the borrower, relieving the borrower of personal liability to repay the loan, is referred to as
   a. a right to reinstate clause.
   b. an indemnity clause.
   c. an exculpatory clause.
   d. a hold-harmless clause.

10. The broker is a single agent of the seller. The principal has disclosed to the broker that the roof leaks, although there is no visible evidence of a water problem. The broker has satisfied her legal obligation to both the principal and all prospective buyers if she discloses
    a. that the roof leaks.
    b. that the roof appears to be in good condition.
    c. nothing about the condition of the roof unless specifically asked about the roof's condition.
    d. that she is bound by confidentiality to her principal.

11. The seller instructs the listing broker not to show his home to members of a protected class. The broker informs the seller that this would be a violation of the Fair Housing Laws, but the seller is insistent. Which choice is the broker's BEST course of action under these circumstances?
    a. Report the incident to the Fair Housing Administration.
    b. Report the seller to the DBPR.
    c. Withdraw from the listing agreement.
    d. Follow the seller's instructions because to do otherwise would violate the broker's fiduciary duties to the seller.

12. A broker has a listing priced at $120,000. An uninformed buyer offers her $125,000. The broker buys the property for $120,000, then sells it for $125,000. Which statement is FALSE?
    a. The $5,000 profit is called an "overage."
    b. The $5,000 profit is called a "secret profit."
    c. The broker has violated her duties to the seller.
    d. This is legal as long as the broker withdraws from the listing first.

13. A woman has homesteaded her residence. Her home has an assessed value of $279,000. She is a nonveteran who is totally and permanently disabled due to a serious car accident. She is also legally blind. What is her cumulative tax exemption on her homesteaded residence?
    a. $26,000
    b. $50,500
    c. $51,000
    d. $55,000

14. The duties of a real estate licensee, owed to a buyer or seller who engages the real estate licensee as a single agent, include all EXCEPT
    a. dealing honestly and fairly.
    b. limited confidentiality, unless waived in writing by a party.
    c. presenting all offers and counteroffers in a timely manner, unless previously directed otherwise in writing.
    d. loyalty.

15. Federal savings associations that are members of the Federal Home Loan Bank System are regulated by the
    a. Federal Home Loan Mortgage Corporation.
    b. Office of Thrift Supervision.
    c. Federal Reserve System.
    d. Resolution Trust Corporation.

16. A sales associate who is employed by an owner-developer who owns properties in the name of various entities may be issued
    a. multiple licenses.
    b. a group license.
    c. a commercial license.
    d. a branch office license.

17. A tenant signed a lease for ten years requiring a monthly base rent of $1,900, plus 2 percent of all monthly gross sales volume over $95,000. The tenant also must pay all property taxes, insurance, and other costs normally considered property owner's costs. This is a
    a. gross lease.
    b. fixed lease.
    c. variable sale lease.
    d. net lease.

18. A real estate license may be revoked or canceled without prejudice for which action?
    a. Culpable negligence
    b. Failure to account and deliver escrow funds
    c. Issuance of a license by mistake by the Commission
    d. Conversion

19. A broker's license was involuntary inactive for two years and one month. To operate again as an active licensee, the broker must complete
    a. 60 hours of the broker's postlicensing education course, 28 hours of continuing education, and pass the broker's licensing exam.
    b. 42 hours of continuing education and pass the continuing education course exam.
    c. FREC Course I and pass the sales associate's licensing exam.
    d. FREC Course II and pass the broker's licensing exam.

20. A man successfully negotiated (and was paid for) the sale of a Federal Communications Commission license for a television station. He is not a licensed real estate broker or sales associate. The man
    a. has violated SEC regulations.
    b. has not violated F.S. 475.
    c. has acted as an unlicensed real estate broker.
    d. must secure a communications license from the DBPR.

21. Which statement concerning characteristics of the real estate market is FALSE?
    a. Real estate is immobile.
    b. The market is slow to respond to changes in supply and demand.
    c. The real estate market is organized and controlled centrally.
    d. Land is indestructible.

22. A comparable property has one more bedroom ($8,000) and is on a slightly larger lot ($2,000) than the subject property. The comparative market analysis requires a net adjustment of
    a. minus $8,000 to the comparable property.
    b. plus $2,000 to the subject property.
    c. plus $10,000 to the subject property.
    d. minus $10,000 to the comparable property.

23. Which entity may NOT be registered as a real estate brokerage?
    a. Corporation for profit
    b. Corporation sole
    c. Partnership
    d. Sole proprietorship

24. The formula to calculate the overall capitalization rate is
    a. NOI ÷ Value (or price).
    b. NOI × Value (or price).
    c. Debt service × Value (or price).
    d. NOI ÷ Owner's equity.

25. Which is NOT a requirement under RESPA?
    a. Use of the HUD-1 form by the closing agent
    b. A copy of the HUD information booklet to the mortgage applicant within three business days
    c. Give mortgage applicant a list of competing lenders so that the consumer can comparison shop for the best rate
    d. Give mortgage applicant an estimate of settlement costs within three business days

26. A transaction broker does NOT have which duty?
    a. Duty of using skill, care, and diligence in the transaction
    b. Duty of accounting for all funds
    c. Duty to disclose all known facts that materially affect the value of residential real property and are not readily observable to the buyer
    d. Full fiduciary duties to both the buyer and the seller

27. A license becomes ineffective when it is
    a. revoked.
    b. suspended.
    c. canceled.
    d. expired for more than two years.

28. A real estate brokerage company is a transaction broker for a buyer. The buyer wants to purchase a new home so the sales associate takes him to three model centers listed by three competing real estate companies. The sales associate must give a written no brokerage relationship notice to
    a. the buyer.
    b. the model home employees at each model center.
    c. no one.
    d. the owner-developer of each new homes subdivision.

29. Title to real property is technically conveyed when the deed is
    a. recorded in the public records.
    b. voluntarily delivered and voluntarily accepted.
    c. signed and witnessed.
    d. acknowledged.

30. Which variable does NOT influence demand?
    a. Availability of mortgage credit
    b. Availability of construction loans
    c. Income of consumers
    d. Consumer tastes and preferences

31. A real estate licensee is obligated to communicate to the seller
    a. all offers, unless specifically instructed by the seller to accept on the seller's behalf.
    b. only all written offers.
    c. all oral and written offers, regardless of how worthy they may be in the licensee's opinion.
    d. all offers up until such time as there is a contract pending.

32. A single agent broker received an offer on a listed property at the seller's price and terms. Before informing the seller, the broker received a higher offer. She submitted only the first offer, and the seller, her principal, accepted it. The broker
    a. has violated her fiduciary duty to her principal.
    b. is guilty of conversion.
    c. has fulfilled her duty to the seller because the offer was for the seller's full price and terms.
    d. is not required to submit the second offer.

33. A man earned a $7,500 commission by selling a coin-operated laundry business, which has six more years before the expiration of its present lease. The man
    a. must be registered with the Florida Retail Commission as a business broker.
    b. must be registered with the Florida Real Estate Commission as a business broker.
    c. must be registered with the Florida Real Estate Commission as a real estate licensee.
    d. need not be registered with any state agency in the given situation.

34. Three claimants have come before the Commission requesting relief from the Real Estate Recovery Fund. All three claimants were involved in the same real estate transaction. Payment for their claims, in the aggregate, is limited to
    a. $150,000.
    b. $75,000.
    c. $50,000.
    d. $25,000.

35. The rate of interest that the Federal Reserve Bank charges member banks for borrowing from the Federal Reserve Bank is referred to as
    a. discount points.
    b. the discount rate.
    c. the prime rate.
    d. the reserve requirement.

36. Local government exercises its greatest effect on the real estate business by
    a. creating tax shelters for those developing low-income housing.
    b. using zoning, taxation, and the planning process.
    c. providing financing where justified.
    d. supervising contractors and their on-the-job performance.

37. Which information must be disclosed to all prospective buyers?
    a. The seller's brother was murdered in the residence.
    b. A previous occupant was infected with HIV.
    c. The home is situated in a flood-prone area.
    d. The neighborhood residents are Hispanic.

38. Which statement does NOT describe a planned unit development?
    a. A variety of types of housing may be used.
    b. Dwelling units are typically clustered, with planned green space areas between clusters.
    c. Industrial parks are a welcomed offshoot of the PUD concept.
    d. The open space areas are maintained by a community association.

39. Insulation is rated by its ability to resist
    a. cold temperatures.
    b. heat flow.
    c. cold wind.
    d. severe temperatures.

40. A licensee makes a statement that is material to the transaction as if it were a fact when the licensee does not know if the statement is true or false, and the buyer relies on the statement. As a result of the statement made by the licensee, the buyer suffers damages. This situation constitutes
    a. culpable negligence.
    b. fraud.
    c. breach of trust.
    d. deceptive services.

41. The DBPR may issue which penalty for an initial offense of a minor violation by a licensee?
    a. Notice of noncompliance
    b. Subpoena to appear
    c. Notice of assignment
    d. Final order

42. A man owns a farm in fee simple. He deeds the farm to a friend until the friend dies, at which time a woman will acquire a fee simple title to the farm. The woman's interest in the farm is a
    a. life estate.
    b. fee simple estate.
    c. reversion estate.
    d. remainder estate.

43. Business brokers appraise businesses using appraisal methods similar to real estate appraisal EXCEPT for the additional technique of
    a. stock, bond, and debenture analysis.
    b. asset appreciation analysis.
    c. working capital analysis.
    d. liquidation analysis.

44. What authority originates from the U.S. Constitution and relates to protection of health and welfare of citizens at local levels?
    a. Escheat
    b. Situs
    c. Police power
    d. Community protection power

45. Which element is NOT essential in a valid real estate sale contract?
    a. A legal objective or purpose
    b. Competent parties
    c. An earnest money deposit
    d. The vendor's signature

46. A provision in all mortgages that allows the delinquent mortgagor to avoid foreclosure by paying all of the back mortgage payments, late penalties, and costs of collection up until the time of foreclosure sale is the
    a. equity of redemption.
    b. due-on-sale clause.
    c. acceleration clause.
    d. defeasance clause.

47. The statute of limitations is the authority that outlines the
    a. requirement that real estate sale contracts be in writing.
    b. essential elements of a contract.
    c. remedies available in case of breach.
    d. period of time during which a contract may be enforced.

48. The statute of frauds applies to
    a. all legal contracts and other documents.
    b. the transfer of personal property.
    c. instruments of conveyance of real property.
    d. acts of fraud by licensees.

49. The documentary stamp tax on deeds is based on the
    a. "new" money involved in the transaction.
    b. amount of the mortgage loan.
    c. amount of the new mortgage.
    d. entire sale price of the property.

50. Which statement concerning tenancy by the entireties is FALSE?
    a. It is a form of concurrent ownership.
    b. The estate includes right of survivorship.
    c. The property must be owned by a wife and her husband.
    d. The deed must specifically state intent to create such a tenancy.

51. The financial term applied to the use of borrowed funds to finance the purchase of an office building is
    a. leverage.
    b. liquidity.
    c. intermediation.
    d. disintermediation.

52. A mortgage in which changes in the interest rate may cause changes in the monthly payment amount is called
    a. a partially amortized mortgage.
    b. an adjustable-rate mortgage.
    c. a graduated-payment mortgage.
    d. an escalator mortgage.

53. Depreciation (cost recovery)
    a. may be taken on a principal residence.
    b. includes the cost of land in the amount to be depreciated.
    c. is an allowable deduction that requires no current outlay of cash.
    d. does not include the mortgaged portion of an apartment building in the amount to be depreciated.

54. Constructive notice is
    a. information learned by reading, seeing, or hearing.
    b. information advertised in the newspaper.
    c. provided by recording in the public records.
    d. notarizing a conveyance.

55. In a deed, the warranty of quiet enjoyment pertains to
    a. peace and tranquility on and around the property.
    b. peaceful possession undisturbed by others' claims of title.
    c. guaranteed satisfaction with the property.
    d. property that is completely vacated.

56. The law that requires that the annual percentage rate be disclosed to consumers is the
    a. Real Estate Settlement Procedures Act.
    b. Equal Credit Opportunity Act.
    c. Truth in Lending Act/Regulation Z.
    d. Florida "Little FTC Act."

57. Homeowners who have a homestead exemption on their current home in either of the two preceding years can transfer up to what amount of their Save Our Home benefit to a new home?
    a. $50,000
    b. $100,000
    c. $225,000
    d. $500,000

58. The government survey method of legal description
    a. is the most accurate method.
    b. was used in the 13 original colonies.
    c. has as a basis a principal meridian and a base line.
    d. features a critical reference called the *point of beginning*.

59. A buyer who obtains a mortgage loan that covers the purchase of a condominium plus furniture, appliances, and other personal property such as towels and kitchen utensils has a
    a. blanket mortgage.
    b. chattel mortgage.
    c. wraparound mortgage.
    d. package mortgage.

60. A type of roof style that slopes from the ridge to four opposite sides and allows continuous eave venting around the entire house perimeter is the
   a. gable.
   b. hip.
   c. mansard.
   d. saltbox.

61. Which estate includes the right of survivorship?
   a. Joint tenancy
   b. Fee simple estate
   c. Tenancy in common
   d. Tenancy for years

62. A title theory state is one in which a mortgage
   a. transfers title to the lender or escrow agent until the loan is paid.
   b. creates only an encumbrance on title to a property.
   c. creates a tenancy in common until the loan is paid.
   d. creates a joint tenancy for the lender until the loan is paid.

63. Which term refers to a situation where during the early years of a loan the principal balance increases?
   a. Graduated payments
   b. Positive leverage
   c. Negative amortization
   d. Reverse annuity

64. Which statement is TRUE regarding the monthly payments on a 30-year, fully amortized loan?
   a. Initially, interest is the smallest portion of the payment.
   b. Initially, principal and interest are approximately equal.
   c. Initially, interest is the larger portion of the payment.
   d. Level monthly payment means the same amount of principal is paid each month.

65. When the Fed wants to ease a tight money supply, it may
   a. increase the discount rate.
   b. issue new Treasury securities.
   c. raise the reserve requirement.
   d. buy Treasury securities.

66. How much personal money may a broker place in a property management escrow account?
   a. None
   b. $200
   c. $1,000
   d. $5,000

67. An example of an ad valorem tax is
   a. a special assessment.
   b. a property tax.
   c. an income tax.
   d. a zoning tax.

68. Which individual is NOT exempt from real estate licensure under F.S. 475?
    a. An individual who sells cemetery lots for compensation
    b. A salaried county employee who appraises railroad property for tax purposes
    c. A business broker who negotiates leases of business property only
    d. A court-appointed personal representative liquidating the real property of an estate

69. If a developer wants to develop a new subdivision, she must submit
    a. a subdivision plat map to the planning commission.
    b. a site plan to the Zoning Board of Adjustment.
    c. an existing land-use study to the planning commission.
    d. a thoroughfare study to the Department of Transportation.

70. You have been hired to appraise the local public library building. The approach that is likely to be the MOST relevant is the
    a. comparable sales approach.
    b. cost-depreciation approach.
    c. public land and property approach.
    d. income capitalization approach.

71. In the cost-depreciation approach, estimating accrued depreciation involves estimating
    a. the amount of allowable cost recovery.
    b. the value of allowable expenses.
    c. the loss in value of the improvements.
    d. effective gross income.

72. The purchase price of a business minus the value of the tangible assets of that business equals the intangible assets of the business. This is referred to as
    a. personal property.
    b. real property.
    c. common stock.
    d. goodwill.

73. A sales associate received a $5,000 earnest money deposit from a buyer. She immediately delivered the deposit to her broker. The broker deposited the check on the third business day into his general operating account.
    a. This is the proper procedure for the handling of earnest money deposits.
    b. This is an example of commingling of escrow funds.
    c. The broker is guilty of dishonest dealing by trick, scheme, or devise.
    d. This is the proper procedure, provided the broker uses a title company that has trust powers.

74. Sales associate Terry Stoufer may have which information entered on her license, if applicable?
    a. Terry's Real Estate Services
    b. Terry Stoufer, LLC
    c. Terry Stoufer Enterprises, LLC
    d. Best Homes, Inc.

75. If all legislated requirements have previously been met, an active broker in Florida may hold an active license in
    a. Florida only.
    b. Florida and any other state whose licensing laws have not been violated; however, a licensee may hold only one active license at any one time.
    c. Florida and any other state or foreign country whose licensing laws have not been violated.
    d. any other state or foreign country whose licensing laws have not been violated, provided the Florida license was placed on inactive status.

76. Which statement is FALSE regarding a corporation for profit that is doing business as a real estate broker?
    a. The broker must file the articles of incorporation with the Florida Department of State.
    b. There must be at least one officer who is an active real estate broker.
    c. The corporation must be registered with the FREC.
    d. All stockholders must be registered with the FREC as inactive brokers.

77. A broker who changes the business address must notify the Commission of the address change within how many days?
    a. 60
    b. 30
    c. 10
    d. 5

78. In relation to Section 1 of a township, Section 12 is due
    a. north.
    b. east.
    c. west.
    d. south.

79. A man is a 72-year-old retired college professor. The local lender to whom the man applied for a 30-year mortgage denied the man's loan application, even though he has sufficient income from his pension plan and an excellent credit history.
    a. This is a violation of the Fair Housing Laws.
    b. The lender's actions are legal because it is unlikely that the man will survive the term of the loan.
    c. This is an example of redlining.
    d. The lender's actions are a violation of the Equal Credit Opportunity Act.

80. Essential elements of a deed do NOT include
    a. voluntary delivery and acceptance.
    b. good or valuable consideration.
    c. signature of two witnesses.
    d. signature of a competent grantee.

81. A person must hold an active real estate license if, for express or for implied compensation, the person
    a. advertises a list of available rental properties.
    b. manages an apartment building complex on-site and for salary only.
    c. rents mobile home lots in a mobile home park.
    d. manages condominium rentals as a salaried manager for single-unit owners.

82. Individuals who solicit mortgage loans, accept applications for mortgage loans, and negotiate the terms of new mortgage loans on behalf of a borrower are referred to as
    a. mortgage bankers.
    b. mortgage finders.
    c. mortgage loan originators.
    d. mortgage agents.

83. The Florida Real Estate Commission is empowered by law to
    a. levy fines up to, but not exceeding, $500.
    b. impose prison sentences up to 60 days.
    c. assess damages resulting from breach of contract suits.
    d. reprimand, fine, or otherwise discipline licensees.

84. If a seller refuses to pay a broker her sales commission after the residential property is sold, the broker may
    a. file a vendor's lien on the owner's property.
    b. file a suit in the courts for her commission.
    c. refuse to permit the closing to occur.
    d. keep the binder deposit as just compensation.

85. If you have located a township numbered T2S, R4E, the township due south of that township is
    a. T2N, R1E.
    b. T2S, R5E.
    c. T3S, R4E.
    d. T2S, R3E.

86. In Florida real property is assessed on January 1 of each year, and property taxes become a lien on the property on
    a. January 1, the same year.
    b. April 1, the next year.
    c. November 1, the same year.
    d. December 31, the same year.

87. Brokers should not accept the task of appraising a parcel
    a. unless they also hold an appraisal license or certification.
    b. unless the appraisal assignment is contingent on securing the listing on the property.
    c. if they have previously sold the property.
    d. if their fees are contingent on the appraised value.

88. Which information is confidential?
    a.   Minutes of the meetings of the FREC
    b.   Final disciplinary action taken against a licensee
    c.   An examinee's grade on the state licensing examination
    d.   The name and address of the principal broker for a particular brokerage entity

89. A prospective tenant purchased a rental list from a broker and then rented a duplex
    that the list said included all utilities. The tenant discovered that only water was
    included in the rent and notified the broker within the legislated time limit. The
    tenant is entitled to
    a.   nothing unless the request for a refund is made in writing.
    b.   75 percent of the rental list fee.
    c.   100 percent of the fee paid.
    d.   no refund because the tenant agreed to rent the property.

90. A real estate company represents a motel owner who wishes to list one of his motels
    for sale. The owner has told the listing agent that he does not want to sell the motel
    to any racial minorities.
    a.   Because this is not a sale of a residential dwelling under the Fair Housing Act,
         the listing agent may honor the owner's instructions.
    b.   The listing agent may not refuse to show or sell the motel to a minority buyer;
         however, the owner may refuse to sell to certain individuals if he sells the prop-
         erty "for sale by owner."
    c.   It would be a violation of the Fair Housing Act to abide by the owner's wishes.
    d.   To refuse to sell or lease any real property based on one's race is a violation of
         the federal Civil Rights Act of 1866.

91. A property closes on April 8 with the day of closing charged to the seller. The
    annual property taxes are $1,486.00. Which entry will appear on the closing state-
    ment for the property taxes?
    a.   Debit to seller and credit to buyer in the amount of $394.91
    b.   Credit to seller and debit to buyer in the amount of $394.91
    c.   Debit to seller and credit to buyer in the amount of $398.98
    d.   Credit to seller and debit to buyer in the amount of $398.98

92. The following taxes were paid at the closing of a new home: $1,540 state documen-
    tary stamp tax on the deed, $693 state documentary stamp tax on the note, and $396
    state intangible tax on the mortgage. What was the purchase price of the home?
    a. $198,000
    b. $220,000
    c. $346,500
    d. $440,000

93. What would be the total required taxes for the loans on a $47,500 tract that sold
    with $10,000 cash down, a new second mortgage of $15,500, and an assumed mort-
    gage of $22,000 that was previously recorded?
    a. $332.50
    b. $206.25
    c. $162.25
    d. $131.25

94. You have a level-payment, amortized mortgage of $42,000 at 12½ percent for 30 years. The monthly payment is $448.25. What amount of interest will be paid from the second monthly payment?
    a. $432.83
    b. $432.94
    c. $437.39
    d. $437.50

95. Your seller owns a home appraised at $52,500. She still owes $32,760 on the first mortgage and $4,200 on a second mortgage. Your sales commission will be $3,640. What is your seller's equity in the home?
    a. $11,900
    b. $13,589
    c. $15,540
    d. $19,740

96. The city has decided to pave the streets of a recently incorporated community. Property owners are to be assessed 70 percent of the cost of paving, which is found to be $25 per foot. The 70 percent assessment tax is to be apportioned between owners on both sides of the streets. What will the special assessment be for a property with 80 feet of frontage?
    a. $350
    b. $700
    c. $1,400
    d. $2,000

97. A property has been assessed at $40,000. The city tax rate is 10 mills, the county tax rate is 9 mills, and the school board levy is 8 mills. The owner has qualified for and received homestead tax exemption. How much will the owner save from his county taxes as a result of the homestead tax exemption?
    a. $135
    b. $225
    c. $405
    d. $675

98. A developer purchased three oceanfront lots, each measuring 75 by 110 feet, for $20 per square foot. The developer later sold the lots for $200,000 each. What was the developer's percentage of profit on the sale of the three lots? (Round to nearest percent.)
    a. 18 percent
    b. 2 percent
    c. 21 percent
    d. 25 percent

99. A sales associate accepts employment with a broker at 45 percent of sales commissions earned as a result of his sales efforts. The broker lists a property for $48,000, with a 7 percent sales commission agreed to by the owner. The sales associate sells the property at the listed sale price. What is the broker's share of the commission?
    a. $1,512
    b. $1,848
    c. $1,884
    d. $3,360

100. A licensed real estate broker has a buyer who is interested in investing in income-producing property. The broker finds a property producing net income of $1,750 per month. The buyer informs the broker that she will buy the property if she can get it for a price that will return her 14 percent per year on her investment. If the desired 14 percent rate of return is regarded as a 14 percent capitalization rate, what will the buyer be willing to pay for the property?
    a. $12,500
    b. $21,000
    c. $125,000
    d. $150,000

APPENDIX B: LIST OF ACRONYMS

A BAR SALE	Real estate services (chapter 2)
CBS vs. CIA	Appraisal adjustments (chapter 15)
CEDDING	Elements of a deed (chapter 9)
COLIC	Elements of a valid real estate contract (chapter 11)
CPI	Consumer Price Index (chapter 15)
DELL	Private restrictions (chapter 9)
DUPE	Bundle of rights (chapter 8)
DUST	Characteristics of value (chapter 15)
FHA	Federal Housing Administration (chapter 11)
HOT CAN	Conditions for alienation by adverse possession (chapter 9)
IRMA	Test for fixtures (chapter 8)
IRV	Income capitalization formula (chapter 15)
MALE	Conflicting demands settlement procedure (chapter 5)
PET	Government restrictions (chapter 9)
PITT	Four unities of a joint tenancy (chapter 8)
SNI	State transfer taxes (chapter 14)
WILD CARD	Ways an offer is terminated (chapter 11)

assignor: person who transfers a legal right to another (e.g., mortgagee selling mortgages and notes; a buyer transferring rights to another person in a sale contract)

assignee: person to whom a legal right is transferred (e.g., Fannie Mae buying mortgages and notes in the second mortgage market)

grantor: party giving the deed that conveys title (e.g., seller in a sale contract)

grantee: party receiving the deed and acquiring title (e.g., buyer in a sale contract)

lessor: landlord who gives lease

lessee: tenant who receives lease

lienor: person who has a claim on another's property

lienee: person whose property is subject to a claim or charge by another

mortgagor: borrower who gives note and mortgage to obtain a loan

mortgagee: lender who receives note and mortgage

offeror: buyer making an offer to purchase

offeree: seller receiving an offer to purchase, who accepts, counters, or rejects the offer

optionor: owner who gives an option to a buyer

optionee: buyer who receives an option contract

vendor: seller in a sale contract

vendee: buyer in a sale contract

Rental Rate Formulas (Chapter 9)

- Percentage Lease

Annual gross sales – Gross sales level specified in lease = Sales subject to rent
Sales subject to rent × Percentage in lease = Additional rent
Base rent from lease + Additional rent = Total annual rent

- Index Lease

New index – Original index = Change in index ÷ Original index = Percentage of change
Original rent × Percentage of change = Increase in rent
Increase in rent + Original rent = New rent

Financial Ratio Formulas (Chapter 12)

- Housing expense ratio (HER)

Monthly housing expenses ÷ Monthly gross income = Housing expense ratio (HER)

- Total obligation ratio (TOR)

Total monthly obligations ÷ Monthly gross income = Total obligations ratio (TOR)

- Loan-to-Value (LTV) ratio

Loan amount ÷ Sale price (or value) = Loan-to-value ratio (LTV)

Profit or Loss Formula (Chapter 14)

- Profit (or loss)

Sale price – Cost = Profit (– Loss)

- Percent of profit (or loss)

Profit (– Loss) ÷ Cost = Percent of profit (or loss)

Amortizing a Mortgage (Chapter 14)

Loan amount x Interest rate = Annual interest ÷ 12 months = Interest payment for first month
Monthly mortgage payment – Interest for first month = Principal payment for first month
Beginning loan amount – Principal payment for first month = New loan amount
For second month, repeat formula using new loan amount

Proration Formulas (Chapter 14)

- Prepaid Rent

Rent paid for the closing month ÷ Number of days in closing month = Daily rental rate

Daily rental rate × Number of days buyer owns property in closing month = Proration amount

Credit Buyer proration amount and Debit Seller proration amount

- Unpaid Property Taxes

Property taxes for year ÷ 365 days = Daily tax rate

Daily tax rate × Number of days seller owns property in year = Proration amount

Credit Buyer proration amount and Debit Seller proration amount

- Prepaid Property Taxes

Property taxes for year ÷ 365 days = Daily tax rate

Daily tax rate × Number of days buyer owns property in year = Proration amount

Credit Seller proration amount and Debit Buyer proration amount

- Interest on Assumed Mortgage

Loan balance × Interest rate = Annual interest ÷ 12 months = Interest for closing month

Interest for closing month ÷ Number of days in closing month = Daily interest rate

Daily interest rate × Number of days seller owns property in closing month = Proration amount

Credit Buyer proration amount and Debit Seller proration amount

State Transfer Taxes (Chapter 14)

- Documentary Stamp Taxes on Deeds

Purchase Price ÷ $100 = Number of stamps (rounded up to a whole number)

Number of stamps × $.70 = Cost of doc stamps on deeds

- Documentary Stamps Taxes on Notes

Each new or assumed loan amount ÷ $100 = Number of stamps (rounded up to a whole number)

Number of stamps × $.35 = Cost of doc stamps on notes

- Intangible Tax on New Mortgages

New loan amount × $.002 = Cost of intangible tax

Estimating Value Formulas (Chapter 15)

- Accrued Depreciation

Effective age ÷ Economic life × Reproduction cost new = Accrued depreciation

Or

Reproduction cost new ÷ Economic life × Effective age = Accrued depreciation

■ Calculating Net Operating Income (NOI)

Potential gross income (PGI) – Vacancy and collection loss + Other (non-rental) income = Effective gross income (EGI)

Effective gross income (EGI) – Operating expenses = Net operating income (NOI)

■ IRV Formulas

NOI ÷ Capitalization rate = Value
NOI ÷ Value (or sales price) = Capitalization rate
Capitalization rate × Value = NOI

■ Gross Rent Multiplier (GRM)

Sale price ÷ Monthly rent = Gross rent multiplier (GRM)
Subject's monthly rent × Market GRM = Value

■ Gross Income Multiplier (GIM)

Sale price ÷ Annual gross income = Gross income multiplier (GIM)
Subject's annual gross income × Market GIM = Value

Property Tax Formulas (Chapter 18)

■ Calculating Annual Property Taxes Due

Assessed value – Exemptions = Taxable value
Taxable value × Tax rate = Property taxes due

■ Calculating Property Tax Savings

Total exemptions × Tax rate = Property tax savings

Street Paving Special Assessment (Chapter 18)

Front feet of lot facing the street × Paving cost per foot = Total cost to pave
100% – Percentage of cost government will pay = Percentage for property owners
Total cost to pave × Percentage for property owners = Cost to property owners
Cost to property owners ÷ 2 = Assessment for individual property

IRS Depreciation Deduction (Chapter 18)

Total cost to acquire property × Percentage for building = Depreciable basis
Depreciable basis ÷ Useful life (27.5 or 39 years) = Annual IRS depreciation deduction

Calculating Buildable Lots (Chapter 20)

Number of acres in development × 43,560 sq ft per acre = Square footage of development
100% – Percentage for streets, sidewalks, and green space = Percentage that can be developed
Square footage of development × Percentage that can be developed = Buildable sq ft
Buildable sq ft ÷ Minimum lot size = Number of buildable lots

APPENDIX E: CROSS-REFERENCE TO FEDERAL AND FLORIDA LAW

To assist with exam preparation, the following tables cross reference each of Florida statutes, administrative rules, and federal regulation with the chapter and section title of this textbook. The legal references are listed in the margin of the corresponding chapter and section title.

FIGURE E.1 ■ **Florida Statutes**

Statute	Chapter	Section
475.001, F.S.	2	Historical Perspective of Florida Real Estate Law
475.001, F.S.	3	Florida Real Estate Commission
475.01, F.S.	2	General Licensing Provisions
475.01, F.S.	2	Real Estate Services
475.01, F.S.	3	Real Estate Regulation
475.01, F.S.	4	Brokerage Relationships in Florida
475.01, F.S.	5	Advertising
475.01, F.S.	5	Types of Business Entities that May Register
475.01, F.S.	8	Definition of Real Property
475.01, F.S.	17	Business Brokerage
475.011, F.S.	2	Individuals Who Are Exempt from a Real Estate License
475.011, F.S.	5	Business Arrangements and Entities that May Not Register as Brokers
475.011, F.S.	8	Cooperatives, Condominiums, and Time-Sharing
475.011, F.S.	9	Deeds
475.02, F.S.	3	Florida Real Estate Commission
475.021, F.S.	3	Florida Real Estate Commission
475.021, F.S.	3	Department of Business and Professional Regulation
475.021, F.S.	6	Procedures for Investigations and Hearings
475.03, F.S.	3	Florida Real Estate Commission
475.04, F.S.	3	Florida Real Estate Commission
475.04, F.S.	3	Real Estate Regulation
475.045, F.S.	3	Real Estate Regulation
475.05, F.S.	3	Florida Real Estate Commission

F I G U R E   E.1 ■ **Florida Statutes (Cont.)**

Statute	Chapter	Section
475.10, F.S.	3	Florida Real Estate Commission
475.125, F.S.	3	Florida Real Estate Commission
475.15, F.S.	5	Types of Business Entities that May Register
475.161, F.S.	5	Types of Business Entities that May Register
475.161, F.S.	5	Trade Names
475.17, F.S.	2	Sales Associate Qualification for Licensure
475.17, F.S.	2	Regulations Pertaining to Prelicense Courses
475.17, F.S.	2	Post-Licensing Education
475.17, F.S.	6	Violations and Penalties
475.175, F.S.	2	Broker Requirements
475.175, F.S.	2	General Licensing Provisions
475.175, F.S.	2	Regulations Pertaining to Prelicense Courses
475.181, F.S.	3	Florida Real Estate Commission
475.181, F.S.	6	Violations and Penalties
475.182, F.S.	3	Real Estate Regulation
475.183, F.S.	3	Real Estate Regulation
475.215, F.S.	2	Registration and Licensure
475.215, F.S.	3	Real Estate Regulation
475.22, F.S.	5	Brokerage Offices
475.23, F.S.	3	Real Estate Regulation
475.23, F.S.	5	Change of Employer
475.24, F.S.	5	Brokerage Offices
475.25, F.S.	1	Real Estate Brokerage
475.25, F.S.	3	Florida Real Estate Commission
475.25, F.S.	5	Advertising
475.25, F.S.	5	Escrow or Trust Accounts
475.25, F.S.	5	Broker's Commission
475.25, F.S.	5	Change of Employer
475.25, F.S.	6	Complaint Process - Seven Steps
475.25, F.S.	6	Violations and Penalties
475.25, F.S.	6	Types of Penalties

FIGURE E.1 ■ Florida Statutes (Cont.)

Statute	Chapter	Section
475.25, F.S.	9	Acquiring Legal Title
475.25, F.S.	11	Contracts Important to Real Estate
475.25, F.S.	14	Closing Statements
475.25, F.S.	15	Appraisal Regulation
475.255, F.S.	4	Brokerage Relationships in Florida
475.272, F.S.	4	Brokerage Relationships in Florida
475.2755, F.S.	4	Brokerage Relationships in Florida
475.278, F.S.	1	Real Estate Brokerage
475.278, F.S.	4	Brokerage Relationships in Florida
475.31, F.S.	3	Real Estate Regulation
475.31, F.S.	6	Complaint Process - Seven Steps
475.31, F.S.	6	Violations and Penalties
475.37, F.S.	6	Complaint Process - Seven Steps
475.42, F.S.	5	Brokerage Offices
475.42, F.S.	5	Brokerage Commission
475.42, F.S.	5	Trade Names
475.42, F.S.	6	Violations and Penalties
475.42, F.S.	6	Types of Penalties
475.43, F.S.	11	Contracts Important to Real Estate
475.451, F.S.	3	Florida Real Estate Commission
475.451, F.S.	3	Real Estate Regulation
475.4511, F.S.	3	Real Estate Regulation
475.453, F.S.	5	Rental Information and Lists
475.453, F.S.	6	Types of Penalties
475.455, F.S.	6	Violations and Penalties
475.482, F.S.	6	Real Estate Recovery Fund
475.483, F.S.	6	Real Estate Recovery Fund
475.484, F.S.	6	Real Estate Recovery Fund
475.5015, F.S.	4	Brokerage Relationships in Florida
475.5015, F.S.	5	Escrow or Trust Accounts
475.5017, F.S.	5	Escrow or Trust Accounts

FIGURE E.1 ■ **Florida Statutes (Cont.)**

Statute	Chapter	Section
475.5018, F.S.	11	Contract Negotiation
475.611, F.S.	1	Real Estate Brokerage
475.612, F.S.	1	Real Estate Brokerage
475.621, F.S.	15	Appraisal Regulation
475, Part III, F.S.	5	Broker's Commission
475, Part IV, F.S.	5	Broker's Commission
455.02, F.S.	3	Real Estate Regulation
455.10, F.S.	2	General Licensing Provisions
455.201, F.S.	2	Historical Perspective of Florida Real Estate Law
455.201, F.S.	3	Florida Real Estate Commission
455.203, F.S.	3	Real Estate Regulation
455.203, F.S.	6	Procedures for Investigations and Hearings
455.207, F.S.	3	Florida Real Estate Commission
455.207, F.S.	6	Complaint Process - Seven Steps
455.209, F.S.	3	Florida Real Estate Commission
455.213, F.S.	2	License Application
455.217, F.S.	2	Sales Associate Qualifications for Licensure
455.217, F.S.	3	Real Estate Regulation
455.2171, F.S.	3	Real Estate Regulation
455.2175, F.S.	3	Real Estate Regulation
455.219, F.S.	3	Florida Real Estate Commission
455.223, F.S.	3	Department of Business and Professional Regulation
455.2235, F.S.	5	Escrow or Trust Accounts
455.224, F.S.	3	Department of Business and Professional Regulation
455.224, F.S.	6	Types of Penalties
455.225, F.S.	3	Department of Business and Professional Regulation
455.225, F.S.	6	Procedures for Investigations and Hearings
455.225, F.S.	6	Complaint Process - Seven Steps
455.225, F.S.	6	Types of Penalties
455.227, F.S.	6	Violations and Penalties
455.227, F.S.	6	Types of Penalties

FIGURE E.1 ■ Florida Statutes (Cont.)

Statute	Chapter	Section
455.2273, F.S.	6	Complaint Process - Seven Steps
455.2273, F.S.	6	FREC Disciplinary Guidelines
455.2277, F.S.	6	Types of Penalties
455.228, F.S.	6	Types of Penalties
455.27, F.S.	3	Real Estate Regulation
455.275, F.S.	6	Complaint Process - Seven Steps
61J2-1.014, F.A.C.	3	Real Estate Regulation
61J2-1.015, F.A.C.	3	Real Estate Regulation
61J2-2.027, F.A.C.	2	Sales Associate Qualifications for Licensure
61J2-2.029, F.A.C.	2	Sales Associate Qualifications for Licensure
61J2-2.030, F.A.C.	2	Sales Associate Qualifications for Licensure
61J2-2.032, F.A.C.	6	Complaint Process - Seven Steps
61J2-3.008, F.A.C.	2	Sales Associate Qualifications for Licensure
61J2-3.008, F.A.C.	2	Regulations Pertaining to Prelicense Courses
61J2-3.008, F.A.C.	2	Post-Licensing Education
61J2-3.008, F.A.C.	2	Broker Requirements
61J2-3.008, F.A.C.	3	Real Estate Regulation
61J2-3.009, F.A.C.	2	Continuing Education
61J2-3.010, F.A.C.	3	Real Estate Regulation
61J2-3.012, F.A.C.	2	Sales Associate Qualifications for Licensure
61J2-3.020, F.A.C.	2	Post-Licensing Education
61J2-3.020, F.A.C.	2	Broker Requirements
61J2-3.020, F.A.C.	3	Real Estate Regulation
61J2-4.009, F.A.C.	5	Types of Business Entities That May Register
61J2-5.012, F.A.C.	5	Types of Business Entities That May Register
61J2-5.013, F.A.C.	5	Types of Business Entities That May Register
61J2-5.014, F.A.C.	5	Types of Business Entities That May Register
61J2-5.015, F.A.C.	5	Types of Business Entities That May Register
61J2-5.016, F.A.C.	5	Types of Business Entities That May Register
61J2-5.017, F.A.C.	5	Types of Business Entities That May Register
61J2-5.018, F.A.C.	5	Types of Business Entities That May Register

FIGURE E.1 ■ **Florida Statutes (Cont.)**

Statute	Chapter	Section
61J2-5.019, F.A.C.	5	Types of Business Entities That May Register
61J2-5.020, F.A.C.	5	Types of Business Entities That May Register
61J2-6.006, F.A.C.	3	Real Estate Regulation
61J2-9.007, F.A.C.	5	Trade Names
61J2-10.022, F.A.C.	5	Brokerage Offices
61J2-10.023, F.A.C.	5	Brokerage Offices
61J2-10.025, F.A.C.	5	Brokerage Offices
61J2-10.027, F.A.C.	5	Membership in Organizations
61J2-10.028, F.A.C.	5	Broker's Commission
61J2-10.030, F.A.C.	5	Rental Information and Lists
61J2-10.032, F.A.C.	5	Escrow or Trust Accounts
61J2-10.034, F.A.C.	5	Trade Names
61J2-10.038, F.A.C.	3	Real Estate Regulation
61J2-14.008, F.A.C.	5	Escrow or Trust Accounts
61J2-14.009, F.A.C.	5	Escrow or Trust Accounts
61J2-14.012, F.A.C.	5	Escrow or Trust Accounts
61J2-14.014, F.A.C.	5	Escrow or Trust Accounts
61J2-17.009, F.A.C.	3	Real Estate Regulation
61J2-17.013, F.A.C.	3	Real Estate Regulation
61J2-17.015, F.A.C.	3	Real Estate Regulation
61J2-20.009, F.A.C.	6	Complaint Process - Seven Steps
61J2-20.040, F.A.C.	3	Florida Real Estate Commission
61J2-20.048, F.A.C.	3	Department of Business and Professional Regulation
61J2-20.049, F.A.C.	3	Florida Real Estate Commission
61J2-23.001, F.A.C.	8	Cooperatives, Condominiums, and Time-Sharing
61J2-23.002, F.A.C.	8	Cooperatives, Condominiums, and Time-Sharing
61J2-24.001, F.A.C.	5	Broker's Commission
61J2-24.001, F.A.C.	6	Complaint Process - Seven Steps
61J2-24.001, F.A.C.	6	Types of Penalties
61J2-24.001, F.A.C.	6	FREC Disciplinary Guidelines
61J2-24.001, F.A.C.	9	Acquiring Legal Title

FIGURE E.1 ■ **Florida Statutes (Cont.)**

Statute	Chapter	Section
61J2-24.002, F.A.C.	3	Real Estate Regulation
61J2-24.002, F.A.C.	5	Escrow or Trust Accounts
61J2-24.002, F.A.C.	5	Membership in Organizations
61J2-24.002, F.A.C.	5	Types of Business Entities That May Register
61J2-24.002, F.A.C.	6	Violations and Penalties
61J2-24.002, F.A.C.	6	Types of Penalties
61J2-24.002, F.A.C.	6	FREC Disciplinary Guidelines
61J2-24.002, F.A.C.	11	Contracts Important to Real Estate
61J2-24.003, F.A.C.	6	Types of Penalties
61J2-24.003, F.A.C.	6	FREC Disciplinary Guidelines
61J2-24.005, F.A.C.	3	Real Estate Regulation
61J2-24.005, F.A.C.	6	Violations and Penalties
61J2-25, F.A.C.	3	Real Estate Education and Research Foundation
61J2-26.001, F.A.C.	2	General Licensing Provisions
20.03, F.S.	2	Historical Perspective of Florida Real Estate Law
20.052, F.S.	3	Florida Real Estate Commission
20.165, F.S.	3	Florida Real Estate Commission
20.165, F.S.	3	Department of Business and Professional Regulation
61.075, F.S.	8	Special Ownership Interests
83.04, F.S.	8	Estates and Tenancies
83.49, F.S.	7	Florida Residential Landlord and Tenant Act
83.51, F.S.	7	Florida Residential Landlord and Tenant Act
83.52, F.S.	7	Florida Residential Landlord and Tenant Act
83.53, F.S.	7	Florida Residential Landlord and Tenant Act
83.56, F.S.	7	Florida Residential Landlord and Tenant Act
83.57, F.S.	8	Estates and Tenancies
83.59, F.S.	7	Florida Residential Landlord and Tenant Act
83.60, F.S.	7	Florida Residential Landlord and Tenant Act
83.62, F.S.	7	Florida Residential Landlord and Tenant Act
95.18, F.S.	9	Acquiring Legal Title
120.52, F.S.	6	Complaint Process - Seven Steps

FIGURE E.1 ■ Florida Statutes (Cont.)

Statute	Chapter	Section
120.569, F.S.	2	Sales Associate Qualifications for Licensure
120.569, F.S.	6	Complaint Process - Seven Steps
120.57, F.S.	2	Sales Associate Qualifications for Licensure
120.57, F.S.	6	Complaint Process - Seven Steps
120.575, F.S.	6	Complaint Process - Seven Steps
120.60, F.S.	6	Complaint Process - Seven Steps
120.62, F.S.	6	Procedures for Investigations and Hearings
120.68, F.S.	6	Complaint Process - Seven Steps
163.3180, F.S.	7	State Housing and Growth Management Laws
173.03, F.S.	18	City and County Property Taxes
193, F.S.	18	City and County Property Taxes
193.011, F.S.	18	City and County Property Taxes
193.023, F.S.	18	City and County Property Taxes
193.155, F.S.	18	City and County Property Taxes
193.461, F.S.	18	City and County Property Taxes
196, F.S.	18	City and County Property Taxes
196.075, F.S.	18	City and County Property Taxes
196.081, F.S.	18	City and County Property Taxes
196.101, F.S.	18	City and County Property Taxes
196.202, F.S.	18	City and County Property Taxes
197, F.S.	18	City and County Property Taxes
199.133, F.S.	14	Closing Statement Items
201.02, F.S.	14	Closing Statement Items
201.08, F.S.	14	Closing Statement Items
404.056, F.S.	11	Contracts Important to Real Estate
494.001, F.S.	13	Primary Mortgage Market
501.6, F.S.	5	Advertising
501, Part II, F.S.	7	State Laws Requiring Real Estate Disclosures
542, F.S.	5	Broker's Commission
553.72, F.S.	20	Zoning Laws and Code Enforcement
553.996, F.S.	11	Contracts Important to Real Estate

FIGURE E.1 ■ **Florida Statutes (Cont.)**

Statute	Chapter	Section
607, F.S.	5	Types of Business Entities That May Register
608, F.S.	5	Types of Business Entities That May Register
608.406, F.S.	5	Trade Names
609, F.S.	5	Business Arrangements and Entities That May Not Register as Brokers
617, F.S.	5	Types of Business Entities That May Register
619, F.S.	5	Business Arrangements and Entities That May Not Register as Brokers
620, F.S.	5	Types of Business Entities That May Register
621.12, F.S.	5	Trade Names
673.1041, F.S.	12	Loan Instruments
689, F.S.	9	Deeds
689.25, F.S.	4	Brokerage Relationships in Florida
689.261, F.S.	11	Contracts Important to Real Estate
689.261, F.S.	18	City and County Property Taxes
695.03, F.S.	9	Acquiring Legal Title
697.02, F.S.	12	Legal Theories of Mortgages
701.01, F.S.	12	Loan Instruments
701.04, F.S.	12	Loan Instruments
712.02, F.S.	9	Acquiring Legal Title
718, F.S.	3	Department of Business and Professional Regulation
718, F.S.	8	Cooperatives, Condominiums, and Time-Sharing
718.503, F.S.	8	Cooperatives, Condominiums, and Time-Sharing
718.504, F.S.	8	Cooperatives, Condominiums, and Time-Sharing
719, F.S.	3	Department of Business and Professional Regulation
719, F.S.	8	Cooperatives, Condominiums, and Time-Sharing
719.503, F.S.	8	Cooperatives, Condominiums, and Time-Sharing
720, F.S.	3	Department of Business and Professional Regulation
720.401, F.S.	11	Contracts Important to Real Estate
721, F.S.	3	Department of Business and Professional Regulation
721, F.S.	8	Cooperatives, Condominiums, and Time-Sharing
721.20, F.S.	5	Escrow or Trust Accounts
721.20, F.S.	8	Cooperatives, Condominiums, and Time-Sharing

FIGURE E.1 ■ Florida Statutes (Cont.)

Statute	Chapter	Section
725.01, F.S.	11	Statute of Frauds
726.102, F.S.	9	Ownership Limitations and Restrictions
732.01, F.S.	9	Acquiring Legal Title
732.2065, F.S.	8	Special Ownership Interests
732.501, F.S.	9	Acquiring Legal Title
733.107, F.S.	9	Acquiring Legal Title
733.301, F.S.	9	Deeds
760.21, F.S.	7	State Housing and Growth Management Laws
760.50, F.S.	4	Brokerage Relationships in Florida
775.081, F.S.	6	Types of Penalties
865.09, F.S.	5	Trade Names

FIGURE E.2 ■ Federal Regulations

Federal Regulation	Chapter	Section
Real Estate Settlement Procedures Act (RESPA): Title 12, Chapter 27, Sections 2601-2617, U.S. Code	5	Broker's Commission
Real Estate Settlement Procedures Act (RESPA): Title 12, Chapter 27, Sections 2601-2617, U.S. Code	7	Federal Laws Regarding Mortgage Lending
Truth in Lending Act: Title 15, Chapter 41, Subchapter I, Part A, Section 1601-1615, U.S. Code	7	Federal Laws Regarding Mortgage Lending
Equal Credit Opportunity Act: Title 15, Chapter 41, Subchapter IV, Sections 1691-1691f, U.S. Code	7	Federal Laws Regarding Mortgage Lending
Interstate Land Sales Full Disclosure Act: Title 15, Chapter 42, Sections 1701-1720, U.S. Code	7	Federal Laws Regarding Mortgage Lending
Coastal Zone Management Act: Title 16, Chapter 33, Sections 1451-1465, U.S. Code	7	Federal Laws Regarding Mortgage Lending
Civil Rights Act of 1866: Title 42, Chapter 21, Sections 1981-1996b, U.S. Code	7	Federal Fair Housing Law
Civil Rights Act of 1964: Title 42, Chapter 21, Sections 1997-2000h, U.S. Code	7	Federal Fair Housing Law
Fair Housing Act: Chapter 42, Sections 3601-3631, U.S. Code	7	Federal Fair Housing Law
Residential Lead-Based Paint Hazard Reduction Act: Title 42, Chapter 63A, Sections 4851-4856, U.S. Code	11	Contracts Important to Real Estate
American Disabilities Act: Title 42, Chapter 126, Sections 12101-12213, U.S. Code	7	Federal Fair Housing Law

GLOSSARY

abandonment A surrender of rights; point when a broker makes no effort to service or sell listed property; failure to perform.

absentee owner A property holder who does not reside on the property and who usually relies on a property manager to supervise the investment.

abstract of title Condensed history of title to real property consisting of a summary of the links in the "chain of title" extracted from documents bearing on the title status.

acceleration clause Stipulation in a mortgage that the entire unpaid balance of the debt may become due and payable if a default of expressed conditions should occur.

acceptance Voluntary receipt of an item offered by another.

accretion Gradual addition of land caused by natural forces, such as wind, tide, flood, or watercourse deposits.

acknowledgment Formal declaration before an authorized official, by the person who executed the instrument, that it is a free act.

acre 43,560 square feet.

actual notice Information a person has actually learned by reading, seeing, or hearing.

address of record A licensee's last known mailing address or e-mail address.

adjudication A judicial or court decision.

adjustable-rate mortgage (ARM) A financing technique in which the lender can raise or lower the interest rate according to a set index.

adjusted basis The owner's original cost plus buying expenses plus capital improvements.

administrative complaint An outline of allegations of facts and charges against the licensee.

administrative law judge An attorney employed by the Division of Administrative Hearings, Department of Administration, to hear complaints and issue recommended orders.

ad valorem tax According to the value; in proportion to worth.

advance fee A commission or partial compensation received by a broker prior to completing the real estate service.

adversary Opponent; a person or group that opposes another.

adverse interest A purpose in opposition to the interest of another party (as, for example, with a buyer and a seller).

adverse possession A method of obtaining title to real property by occupying it in an open and hostile manner contrary to the interests of the owner.

affidavit A sworn statement written down before a notary or public official.

affiliated business relationship An arrangement in which (a) a person who is in a position to refer business incident to or a part of a real estate settlement service involving a federally related mortgage loan, or an associate of such person, has either an affiliate relationship with or a direct or beneficial ownership interest of more than 1 percent in a provider of settlement services; and (b) either of such persons directly or indirectly refers such business to that provider or affirmatively influences the selection of that provider.

after-tax cash flow (*See* cash flow.)

agency Express or implied authorization for one person to act for another.

agent A representative; one who is authorized to act on behalf of another.

agreement for deed (*See* contract for deed.)

agricultural Defined in Chapter 475, F.S., to mean property zoned as such, consisting of more than ten acres.

air rights The freedom to use the open space above a property.

alienation The act of transferring ownership, title, or an interest or estate in real property.

allodial system A theory of land ownership that individuals may own land free of the rights of an overlord.

alluvion (alluvium) The increase of land by the gradual and imperceptible action of natural forces (e.g., deposits of sand and mud on a riverbank).

amortized mortgage A loan characterized by payment of a debt by regular installment payments.

anniversary date Recurring each year; the date an insurance policy must be renewed to continue in effect.

annual debt service The amount of money required each year for the payment of all mortgage interest and principal.

annual percentage rate (APR) Total yearly cost of credit.

appeal A request to some authority for a decision or judgment.

applicant A person who applies for something; a candidate.

appraisal The process of developing and communicating an opinion of a property's value as of a certain date.

appraisal plant Copies of current statistics and publications kept by appraisers in their library or record room.

appraised value Estimated worth of a property determined by someone qualified in valuation.

appraiser, real estate One who is a registered, licensed, or certified by the DBPR and provides an estimate of value.

appreciation An increase in value.

arbitration The act of having a third party render a binding decision in a dispute between two parties.

arrears The state of being behind in the discharge of an obligation; paid at the end of the period for which due (the opposite of in advance).

assemblage The combining of two or more adjoining properties into one tract.

assessed value Worth established for each unit of real property for tax purposes by a county property appraiser.

assessment The imposition of a tax or charge according to a preset rate; the allocation of the proportionate individual share of a common expense in a condo or co-op building.

asset Anything of value.

assignee Person to whom a right or interest is transferred.

assignment Written instrument that serves to transfer the rights or interests of one person to another.

assignment of mortgage A legal instrument that states that the mortgagee assigns (transfers) the mortgage and promissory note to the purchaser.

assignor Person who gives his or her legal rights or interests to another person.

associate Person working for a broker.

association An organization of persons having a common interest.

assumption The buyer of real property that is already mortgaged assumes liability for the mortgage payments of the original loan that remains on the property.

at arm's length Conducting negotiations on one's own behalf without being subject to the other party's control or influence.

attachment A legal writ obtained to prevent removal of property that is expected to be used to satisfy a judgment.

attorney-in-fact One who is authorized to perform certain acts for another under a power of attorney.

attorney, power of Designation of another person to act for a principal who may not be present.

automated underwriting A service that enables lenders to obtain a credit risk classification using applications software in the loan underwriting process.

balance sheet A financial report that shows the company's financial position at a stated moment in time.

balloon payment A single, large payment made at maturity of a partially amortized mortgage to pay off the debt in full.

bargain and sale deed A type of deed in which title is transferred and a limited number of warranties are made respecting title to or use of the property.

base industries Businesses that attract outside money into the area; primary.

base lines Imaginary lines running east and west and crossing a principal meridian at a definite point; used by surveyors for reference in locating and describing land under the government survey system.

before-tax cash flow (BTCF; cash throwoff; gross spendable income) The resulting amount when annual debt service is subtracted from net operating income.

biennium (biennial) A period of two years.

bilateral contract An agreement wherein both parties are legally obligated to each other to perform.

binder A memorandum given subject to the writing of a formal contract for sale, usually acknowledging receipt of a portion of the down payment for purchase of real property.

biweekly mortgage A mortgage loan amortized the same way as other loans with monthly payments, except that the borrower makes a payment every two weeks.

blanket mortgage One debt instrument covering two or more parcels.

blind advertisement An advertisement that provides only a telephone number, a post office box, and/or an address without the licensed name of the brokerage firm.

blockbusting The illegal practice of inducing homeowners to sell their property by making misrepresentations regarding the entry or prospective entry of minority persons in order to cause a turnover of properties in the neighborhood; discriminatory acts against sellers.

bona fide Without deceit or fraud; genuine; in good faith.

boot Money or other property that is not like-kind, which is given to make up any difference in value or equity between exchanged properties.

borrower (debtor) The mortgagor; one who gives a mortgage as security for a debt.

branch office A business location other than the real estate broker's principal place of business.

breach Failure to do or perform what has been promised.

broker An individual or business entity licensed by the DBPR to perform services of real estate for others for compensation.

broker associate An individual who is qualified to be issued a broker's license but who operates as a sales associate in the employ of another.

broker's price opinion (BPO) A written opinion of the value of real property. Florida real estate licensees are allowed to prepare and charge for BPOs provided the BPO is not referred to as an appraisal. Price opinions are often requested by relocation companies and lenders involved in short sales of distressed properties.

buffer zone A strip of land separating one land use from another.

building codes Government ordinances regulating construction practices and materials.

business brokerage The sale, purchase, or lease of businesses that provide goods and/or services.

business broker Real estate licensees who engage in the sale, purchase, or lease of businesses.

business opportunity brokerage The real estate activity dealing in the sale, purchase, or lease of businesses.

business trust (syndicate) A group of people who associate with each other for the purpose of purchasing shares or units at a specified amount per unit, with the money raised to be used to purchase the real property, often for subdividing and resale.

buydown A financing technique in which points are paid to the lender by the seller or builder that lowers (buys down) the effective interest rate paid by the buyer/borrower, thus reducing the amount of the monthly payment for a set period of time.

buyer brokerage agreement An employment contract with a purchaser.

buyer's market The supply of available properties exceeds the demand.

bylaws Rules that govern the administration of the condominium.

canceled A license ceases to exist, effective as of the date approved by the Commission, and does not involve disciplinary action.

capital The collective wealth (money and property) of a person or business; the investment in a property. (*See also* equity.)

capital asset Certain property held by a taxpayer, not including inventory for sale to customers.

capital-deficit area A region where the total amount of local savings is not sufficient to finance economic development already under way in that area.

capital gain The profit from the sale of an asset, including real property.

capitalization rate The relationship between the net income from a real estate investment and the present value.

cash flow (after-tax cash flow) The resulting amount when annual debt service, tax liability, and capital improvement costs are subtracted from net operating income.

caveat emptor Latin for "let the buyer beware."

cease and desist order An action by a government agency to require a person or business to stop an illegal or unfair practice.

cease to be in force (cease to be in effect) A licensee cannot perform real estate services because certain events occur, such as when a broker changes business address.

censure An official act of strong disapproval.

certificate of occupancy An occupancy permit issued by the local government after construction is completed and the final inspection is approved.

certificate of title opinion (opinion of title) A document signed by a title examiner (attorney or title company agent) stating the judgment that, based on an examination of the public records, the seller has good title to the property being conveyed to the buyer (not to be confused with title insurance).

certified appraiser (*See* state-certified appraiser.)

certiorari, writ of An order to bring from a lower court to an appellate court an action or record of proceedings in a case.

chain of title A successive listing of all previous holders of title (owners) back to an acceptable starting point.

chattel Any item of personal property. (*See also* personal property.)

check A square measuring 24 miles on each side and representing the largest unit of measure in the government survey system.

circuit breakers Devices that will shut off the flow of electricity if more electrical current is flowing through the wire than the wire can handle.

citations Statements of alleged violations and the penalties to be imposed.

Civil Rights Act of 1866 A federal act that prohibits any type of discrimination based on race in any real estate transaction (sale or rental) without exception.

clause A distinct provision in a written document.

closing Final settlement between the buyer and seller; the date on which title passes from the seller to the buyer.

cloud on title Any defect, valid claim, or encumbrance that serves to impair the title or curtail an owner's rights.

collateral Real or personal property pledged as security on a debt.

collusion Two or more parties jointly attempting to defraud a third party.

color of title A condition in which ownership of real property appears to be good but is not good because of a defect.

commercial A classification of real estate that includes income-producing properties such as office buildings, gasoline stations, restaurants, shopping centers, hotels and motels, and parking lots. Commercial property usually must be zoned for business purposes.

commingle To mix together money or a deposit with personal funds; combine; intermingle.

commission Compensation paid to a broker or sales associate for successfully concluding a real estate transaction.

Commission Short for the Florida Real Estate Commission (FREC).

common elements The parts of a multiple-ownership property not included in the units; those parts in which each unit owner holds an undivided interest.

common law A system of law based on accepted customs and traditions.

community property Real property acquired during a marriage. (Florida is not a community property state.)

comparable property (comparable; comp) A recently sold property similar to one being evaluated.

comparative market analysis (CMA) An informal estimate of market value performed by a real estate licensee for the seller to assist in arriving at an appropriate listing price, or if working with the buyer, an informal estimate of market value to assist the buyer in arriving at an appropriate offering price.

compensation Anything of value or a valuable consideration, directly or indirectly paid, promised, or expected to be paid or received.

competent A party to a contract who possesses the legal capacity to enter into a binding contract.

complainant A person who makes an allegation or a charge against another (the respondent). (*See also* plaintiff.)

complaint Formal allegation or charge.

comprehensive plan (master plan) A statement of policies for the future physical development of an area (e.g., city, county, region).

concealment The act of keeping from sight or keeping secret.

concurrency A provision in Florida's Growth Management Act that mandates that the infrastructure, such as roads and water and waste treatment facilities needed to support additional population, be in place before new development is allowed.

concurrent ownership Ownership by two or more persons at the same time, such as joint tenants, tenants by the entirety, or tenants in common.

condemnation The taking of private real property for a public purpose under the right of eminent domain for a fair price.

condominium A multiunit project consisting of individual ownership of a dwelling unit and undivided ownership of common areas.

conflicting demands When different parties each make claims that are inconsistent with one another.

conforming loan A standardized conventional loan written on uniform documents that meets the purchase requirements of Fannie Mae and Freddie Mac.

consideration Inducement offered to conclude a contract.

construction lien A claim based on the principle of "unjust enrichment"; favors parties who have performed labor or delivered materials or supplies for the repair or building of an improvement to real property.

constructive notice The recording of a document or an instrument in the public records designed to give adequate notice to all.

consumer member A member of the Florida Real Estate Commission who does not hold a real estate license.

Consumer Price Index (CPI) A measurement of average price changes of goods and services using a base period.

contract An agreement between two or more competent parties to do, or not do, some legal act for a legal consideration.

contract for deed A financing technique wherein the seller agrees to deliver the deed at some future date and the buyer takes possession while paying the agreed amount (also called land contract, an installment sale contract, and an agreement for deed).

conventional mortgage A real estate loan granted that is neither FHA-insured nor VA-guaranteed.

conversion Unauthorized use or retention of money or property that rightfully belongs to another person.

convertible mortgage A financing instrument allowing a change from an adjustable-rate to a fixed-rate mortgage.

conveyance Written instrument that serves to transfer an interest in real property from one party to another.

cooperative A multiunit project consisting of individual dwelling units owned by the corporation in which the individual apartment tenants own stock rather than owning their respective units.

co-ownership (concurrent or multiple ownership) Title to real property held by two or more persons at the same time.

corner lot A lot bounded with streets on two sides (intersecting).

corporation An artificial or fictitious person formed to conduct specified types of business activities.

corporation not for profit An artificial or fictitious person organized for business purposes and similar to a corporation for profit.

corporation sole An artificial or fictitious person formed by an ecclesiastical body.

cost The amount to produce or acquire something.

cost-depreciation approach A method for estimating the market value of a property based on the cost to buy the site and to construct a new building on the site, less depreciation.

counselors Professionals who analyze existing or potential real estate problems and recommend a course of action.

counteroffer A rejection of the original offer by proposing a new offer, thereby terminating the original offer.

covenant A warranty, guarantee, or promise formally given in a legal document.

credit As a verb, to make an entry on the right or credit side of an account; as a noun, payment or value received.

creditor A lender; person or business entity to whom a debt is owed.

cul-de-sac lot A lot located where a street is open at one end only and the street has a circular turnaround at the other end.

culpable negligence Inadequate attention to duties and obligations by one who knows, or should know, what is required of him or her.

curable When the correction of a defect results in as much added value as the cost to correct the defect.

curbstone operation Conducting business without maintaining an office.

current mailing address Where a licensee receives letters and so forth through the U.S. Postal Service.

customer One with whom the broker or sales associate hopes to be successful in accomplishing the purpose of employment. Per Section 475.01, F.S., a member of the public who is or may be a buyer or seller of real property and may or may not be represented by a real estate licensee in an authorized brokerage relationship.

damages Losses incurred as a result of a breach of contract or some other cause. (*See also* liquidated damages and unliquidated damages.)

debit As a verb, to make an entry on the left or charge side of an account; as a noun, a charge or expense.

decedent A deceased person, usually one who has recently died.

declaration The legal document that the developer of a condominium must file and record in order to create a condominium under state law.

declaration of trust A formal instrument filed by a business trust with the Department of State as a prerequisite for creating the trust.

declaratory judgment A course of action declaring rights claimed under a contract or statute intended to prevent loss or to guide performance by the party or parties affected.

dedication An offer of land for some public use, by an owner, together with acceptance by or on behalf of the public.

deed A type of conveyance; a written instrument to transfer title to real property from one party to another.

deed in lieu of foreclosure A friendly foreclosure (nonjudicial procedure) in which the mortgagor gives title to the mortgagee.

deed restrictions Provision placed in deeds to control future uses of the property.

default Failure to comply with the terms of an agreement or to meet an obligation when due.

defeasance clause A provision in a mortgage that specifies the terms and conditions to be met in order to avoid default and thereby defeat the mortgage.

defect (*See* cloud on title.)

defendant The person or party being sued or charged.

deficiency decree Judgment brought when a mortgage is foreclosed and the sale proceeds fail to cover the costs of the sale, taxes, and the unpaid mortgage balance.

demand The quantity of goods or services wanted by consumers.

demand deposits Checking accounts; payable on demand by holder.

denial A refusal or rejection.

density The number of homes or lots per acre.

deposit Earnest money or some other valuable consideration given as evidence of good faith to accompany an offer to purchase or rent. (*See also* binder and earnest money.)

Deposit Insurance Fund (DIF) A fund that insures banks and savings associations.

deposition Written testimony of a witness under oath.

depreciation A loss in value for any reason; a deduction for tax purposes.

descent The passage of title to real property upon the death of the owner to the legal descendants.

designated sales associates Two real estate licensees designated to represent the buyer and the seller as single agents in a nonresidential transaction. The buyer and seller must have assets of $1 million or more and sign disclosures stating their assets meet the required threshold.

development of regional impact (DRI) A large project affecting more than one county.

devise A gift of real property by a will.

devisee One who receives real property under a will.

devisor One who gives real property through a will.

discount points A method for increasing a lender's yield. (*See also* point, mortgage discount.)

discount rate The amount of interest the Federal Reserve charges to lend money to its eligible banks.

disintermediation A disengagement process when depositors withdraw money from savings for direct investment in stocks, money market funds, and other securities.

Division of Administrative Hearings (DOAH) The governmental entity that hears all formal hearings resulting from an administrative complaint against a licensee.

doc stamps An abbreviated term for documentary stamp tax.

document Any written paper that provides information or evidence.

documentary stamp tax on deeds, state Tax required on all deeds or other documents used as conveyances. The charge is based on the total purchase price.

documentary stamp tax on notes, state Tax required on all promissory notes. The cost is based on the face value of the note.

dormer A projection built out from the slope of a roof, used to house windows on the upper floor and to provide additional light and ventilation.

double-hung A window consisting of two sashes that move up and down in a pair of channels and are held open by tension springs.

down payment A portion of a purchase price paid prior to closing the transaction. Earnest money may be part of or the entire down payment.

draw (installment) Disbursement made by a lender to a builder.

dual agency Representing both principals in a transaction (not a legal agency relationship in Florida).

dual agent A broker who represents both the buyer and the seller of a transaction in a fiduciary capacity.

due-on-sale clause A provision in a conventional mortgage that entitles the lender to require the entire loan balance to be paid in full if the property is sold.

dynamic risk The risk that arises from the continual change in the business environment and therefore dynamic risk cannot be transferred to an insurer.

earnest money deposit A type of money that a broker may handle for others in the ordinary course of business; also referred to as good-faith deposit or binder deposit.

easement A right, privilege, or interest in real property that one individual has in lands belonging to another; a legal right to trespass; right-of-way authorizing access to or over land.

easement appurtenant An easement that runs with the land and benefits an adjacent parcel of land.

easement by necessity An easement created by a court of law in cases where justice and necessity dictate it, such as when property is landlocked.

easement by prescription A right acquired by an adverse user to use the land of other, created through a court of law after longtime uninterrupted use.

easement in gross A type of easement that benefits an individual or business entity and is not related to a specific adjacent parcel, for example, utility easements.

economic base studies An analysis of employment in the primary industries of a region.

economic life The period of time a property may be expected to be profitable or productive; useful life.

effect a sale A provision in a listing contract requiring the broker to obtain a signed contract from a ready, willing, and able buyer on the terms specified.

effective age The age indicated by a structure's condition and utility.

effective gross income (EGI) The resulting amount when vacancy and collection losses are subtracted from potential gross income. (*See also* vacancy and collection losses.)

elective share An estate defined as consisting of 30 percent of the decedent's personal property and Florida real property, except homestead-exempt property and claims.

eminent domain The constitutional right given to a unit of government to take private property involuntarily if taken for public use and a fair price is paid to the owner.

employer The individual who hires the services of another.

empty nester Older parents whose housing needs change after their children have moved away.

encroachment Unauthorized use of another person's property.

encumbrance Any lien, claim, or liability affecting the title or attaching to real property.

encumbrance clause A provision in a deed to real property that warrants that no liens, claims, or liabilities exist on the property being conveyed, except as specified.

enforceable contract A legally binding contract that the law will recognize.

entitlement That portion of a VA-guaranteed loan that protects the lender if the borrower defaults.

environmental impact statement (EIS) A document that summarizes the effect proposed development will have on the surroundings.

equitable title The beneficial interest in real estate that implies that an individual will receive legal title at a future date.

equity The market value of a property less any debt against it; in a business entity, assets minus liabilities equals capital (owner's equity); a system of legal rules administered by a court of chancery.

equity of redemption The right of a mortgagor, before a foreclosure sale, to reclaim forfeited property by paying the entire indebtedness.

erosion Gradual loss of land due to water or other natural causes.

escalator clause A provision in a mortgage permitting the lender to increase the interest rate that is usually tied to an event or a contingency.

escheat Reversion of property to the state when an owner dies without leaving a will or any known heirs.

escrow account An account in a bank, title company, credit union, savings association, or trust company used solely for safekeeping customer funds and not for deposit of personal funds; impound account or trust account.

escrow disbursement order (EDO) A course of action for determining the disposition of a contested deposit.

estate Tenancy; the interest one holds in real property; the total of one's property and possessions.

estate by the entireties A tenancy created by husband and wife jointly owning real property with instant and complete right of survivorship.

estate for life (*See* life estates.)

estate for years A tenancy measured from a starting date to a termination date (may be for a few days or longer than any natural life; e.g., a leasehold is an estate for years).

estate in fee (*See* fee simple estate.)

estate in reversion An estate that comes back to the original grantor.

estate in severalty Ownership of property vested in one person alone, also known as sole ownership.

estate in sole Real property owned by a corporation sole.

estate of freehold (*See* freehold estate.)

estate of remainder An estate that can become effective only after another estate has terminated.

estoppel A principle of law that prohibits (stops) people from defending themselves against their own acts or lack of action.

estoppel certificate A written statement that bars the signer from making a claim inconsistent with the instrument (commonly used with a mortgage assumption).

ethics The moral obligations and duties that a member of a profession or craft owes to the public, to a client, or to other members of the profession or craft.

evidence Any proof that may legally be admitted in settlement of an issue.

exclusion The right of an owner to control entry onto the property.

exclusive-agency listing Employment contract given to one real estate broker as the sole agent for the sale of an owner's property.

exclusive-right-of-sale listing An employment contract given to one real estate broker as the sole agent for the sale of an owner's property, with the commission going to that broker regardless of who actually sells the property during the employment contract period.

exculpatory clause A provision in a mortgage or note in which the lender waives the right to a deficiency judgment against the borrower and the borrower is relieved of personal liability to repay the loan.

executed contract An agreement in which the terms have been fully performed by all parties; a signed document.

executive power, FREC Duties related to the education of licensees, the regulating of professional practices, and the publishing of materials.

executory contract An agreement containing some act or condition that remains to be completed.

exempt property Property that has been decreed to be excluded from taxation or claim by others.

express contract An agreement wherein the terms are specifically stated by the parties, either orally, in writing, or by a combination of the two.

facsimile ("fax") An exact copy.

factor market A resource pool representing the four major elements (factors) of production that are bought and sold.

failure to account for and deliver The act of failing to pay money to a person entitled to receive it.

Fair Housing Act An act contained in Title VIII of the Civil Rights Act of 1968 that created protected classes of people and prohibits discrimination when selling or renting residential property when based on race, color, religion, sex, national origin, familial status, or handicap status.

familial status A protected class as defined in the Fair Housing Act consisting of one or more individuals under age 18 living with a parent or legal guardian and pregnant women.

Fannie Mae A private institution in the secondary mortgage market that buys and sells mortgages.

farm area A selected and limited geographical district to which a sales associate devotes special attention and study; to farm an area or neighborhood.

Federal Deposit Insurance Corporation (FDIC) A federal agency that insures deposits of member banks and savings associations.

Federal Housing Administration (FHA) Insures mortgage loans made by FHA-approved lenders on homes that meet FHA standards in order to make mortgages more desirable investments for lenders.

Federal Housing Finance Board (FHFB) Supervises regional Federal Home Loan Banks and oversees their mortgage lending.

Federal Reserve System (the Fed) A central banking authority that influences the cost, availability, and supply of money.

Federal Trade Commission (FTC) A federal agency that investigates and eliminates unfair and deceptive trade practices.

federally related transaction Any sale transaction that ultimately involves a federal agency in either the primary or secondary mortgage market. Under FIRREA, state-certified or state-licensed appraisers must be used for certain loans in federally related transactions.

fee simple estate The most comprehensive and complete interest one can hold in real property; freehold estate. Also known as fee or fee simple absolute.

fictitious name (*See* trade name.)

fiduciary A person in a position of trust and confidence with respect to another person.

fiduciary relationship An alliance of trust and confidence that creates a moral and legal obligation when extended by one person and accepted by another.

final order A decision rendered by the FREC.

find a purchaser A provision in a listing contract requiring a broker to produce a ready, willing, and able buyer or offer on the terms specified.

fixture An object that was once considered to be personal property but has become real property because of attachment to, or use in, improvements to real property.

flag lot A lot characterized by a long access road or driveway leading back to the main part of the lot.

Florida resident For application and licensing purposes, a person who has resided in Florida continuously for four calendar months or more within the preceding year.

follow-up What a sales associate does after a sale to maintain customer contact and goodwill.

foreclosure A court process to transfer title to real property used as security for debt as a means of paying the debt by involuntary sale of the property.

formal complaint An outline of the charges against a licensee that must be answered within the statutory time limit.

formal contract Any agreement that contains all the essentials of a contract, including that it is in writing and under seal; a contract dependent on a particular form.

formal hearing (*See* hearing.)

fraud The intent to misrepresent a material fact or to deceive to gain an unfair advantage or to harm another person.

Freddie Mac Formerly called the Federal Home Loan Mortgage Corporation (FHLMC). A secondary mortgage market institution that buys and sells conventional, FHA, and VA loans.

free and clear Title to real property that is absolute and unencumbered.

freehold estate A tenancy in real property with no set termination date that can be measured by the lifetime of an individual or can be inherited by heirs.

further assurance A provision in a deed containing a covenant or warranty to perform any further acts the grantee (buyer) might require to perfect title to the property.

gable A roof design that peaks at the center ridge and extends downward on two opposite sides.

general agent A representative authorized by the principal to perform only acts related to a business or to employment of a particular nature.

general lien A claim that may affect all of the properties of a debtor.

general partnership An association of two or more persons for the purpose of jointly conducting a business, each being responsible for all the debts incurred in the conducting of that business.

general warranty deed An instrument of conveyance containing the strongest and most comprehensive promises of further assurance possible for a grantor (seller) to convey to a grantee (buyer).

going concern value The worth of a business, including real estate, goodwill, and earning capacity.

good consideration A promise that cannot be measured in terms of money, such as love and affection.

good faith A party's honest intent to transact business, free from any intent to defraud the other party; each party's faithfulness to one's duty or obligations set forth by contract.

good-faith estimate A preliminary accounting of expected closing costs. The Real Estate Settlement Procedures Act requires lenders to give loan applicants a good-faith estimate that lists the charges the buyer is likely to pay at closing.

goodwill An intangible asset (value) of a business.

government lot Fractional piece of land less than a quarter section resulting from geographical features (e.g., lakes, streams) interfering with land surveying.

Government National Mortgage Association (GNMA) ("Ginnie Mae") A federal agency that is part of the Department of Housing and Urban Development (HUD). Ginnie Mae plays an important role in achieving the HUD's goal of providing low-cost mortgage credit to traditionally underserved sectors of the housing market.

government survey system A type of land description, developed by the federal government for subdividing lands using surveying lines.

grantee Party who receives a deed or grant; buyer.

granting clause The provision in a deed that specifies the names of the parties involved, the words of conveyance, and a description of the property.

grantor Party who signs and gives a deed; seller.

Green Belt Law, Florida Legislation that authorizes county property appraisers to assess land used for agricultural purposes according to its current value as agricultural land.

gross income multiplier (GIM) A rule of thumb for estimating the market value of commercial and industrial properties; the ratio to convert annual income into market value.

gross lease An agreement for the tenant to pay a fixed (base) rent and the landlord pays all of the expenses associated with the property.

gross rent multiplier (GRM) A rule of thumb for estimating the market value of income-producing residential property; the ratio to convert rental income into market value.

ground lease An agreement for the tenant to lease the land only and erect a building on the land.

group license A right granted a sales associate or broker associate to work various properties owned by affiliated entities under one owner developer.

habendum A provision in a deed to real property that stipulates the estate or interest the grantee is to receive and the type of title conveyed.

Handbook Published by the Florida Real Estate Commission for study and guidance of students, applicants, licensees, and members of the general public on Florida Statute 475 and other laws, acts, rules, and regulations. (Available on the DRE's Web site.)

handicap status A protected class as defined in the Fair Housing Act and the Americans with Disabilities Act consisting of a physical or mental impairment that substantially limits one or more major life activities.

hazard insurance Coverage by contract whereby one party undertakes to guarantee another party against loss resulting from physical damage to real property.

health ordinances Local codes that regulate maintenance and sanitation of public spaces.

hearing A session in which testimony and arguments are presented, especially before an official.

highest and best use A principle of value that focuses on the most profitable legal use to which a property can be put.

hip Pitched roof with sloping sides and ends.

home equity loan A mortgage secured by a personal residence. It provides a line of credit available for draws when needed by the homeowner. It is sometimes used as a home improvement loan.

homestead Term used to describe three separate but related situations: (1) a tax exemption, (2) a tract of land limited in size, and (3) a statutory condition designed to protect the interests of a spouse and lineal descendants.

household One individual, or a group of individuals, living in one dwelling unit.

hypothecation To pledge real or personal property as security for a debt or obligation without giving up possession of the property.

immediately The time period during which a broker must deposit escrow funds; no later than the end of the third business day after the broker's sales associate or an employee has received the funds.

immune Real property that is owned by a unit of government and is not subject to taxation.

implied Expressed indirectly (e.g., an implied contract).

implied contract An agreement wherein the terms are not stated but are inferred from the conduct of the parties.

implied listing An employment contract that arises from the conduct of the broker and seller and may be enforceable even though not clearly spelled out in words.

improvement Addition that increases the value of real property (not repairs).

income Amount earned or gained, not return of capital.

income capitalization approach A method for estimating the market value of a property based on the present and future income the property can be expected to generate.

income statement A summary of all income and expenses of a business for a stated period of time.

incurable When the cost to correct a defect is greater than the value added by the cure.

index The variable component that is added to the margin to calculate the interest rate in an adjustable rate mortgage.

industrial Properties that include (1) sites in industrial parks or subdivisions, (2) redeveloped industrial parcels in central areas, and (3) industrial acreage.

ineffective Status of a license when it is inactive or has been suspended.

informal hearing A respondent who does not dispute allegations of material fact in the administrative complaint may request an informal hearing before the FREC for final action on the complaint.

injunction A writ or order by a court forbidding a party from doing something.

in-migration Movement into a community or region by new residents.

instrument Any legal or formal writing, such as a will, option, lease, contract, or deed.

insurance (See hazard insurance.)

insurance clause A provision in a mortgage that requires the mortgagor to obtain and keep current a hazard insurance policy.

intangible asset Something of value lacking physical substance; existing only in connection with something else (e.g., the goodwill of a business).

intangible tax on mortgages, state Tax required prior to a mortgage being recorded. The cost is based on the face value of the mortgage.

intensity The concentration of activity (pedestrian and vehicular traffic) used as a means of designating land for commercial zones.

interest The price paid for the use of borrowed money; estate.

interest rate The percentage charged for the use of borrowed money.

interior lot A lot that is bounded on either side by another lot (lots in the middle of the block—not on the corner).

intermediation The process whereby financial middlemen consolidate many small savings accounts belonging to individual depositors and invest those funds in large, diversified projects.

intermingle (See commingle.)

interpleader A course of action when two contesting parties cannot reach an arbitrated agreement; a legal proceeding whereby the broker, having no financial interest in the disputed funds, deposits with the court the disputed escrow deposit so that the court can determine who is the rightful claimant.

interval ownership Fee simple possession, for the limited time purchased (one or more weeks), of a time-share unit, complete with deed, title, and equity.

intestate Without a will.

investment The outlay of money in anticipation of income or profit; the sum risked or the property purchased.

investment contract A type of security using the sale of real property as the investment.

investment value The worth of a property to a particular investor based on the investor's desired rate of return, risk tolerance, etc.

involuntary inactive The license status that results when a license is not renewed at the end of the license period.

involuntary liens Claims imposed against real property without the consent of the owner (e.g., taxes, special assessments).

joint tenancy An estate or interest owned by more than one person, each having equal rights to possession and enjoyment; the interest a deceased tenant conveys to surviving tenants by specific wording in the deed establishing the joint tenancy.

joint venture (joint adventure) Two or more parties in an arrangement confined to only one or a limited number of business deals.

judgment Decree of a court that not only declares that one party owes another party a debt but also fixes the debt amount.

judicial review The power of a court to reexamine statutes or administrative acts and to determine their validity; a rehearing or appeal to a higher court.

just value The fair market value.

key lot A long skinny lot similar to the shaft of a key that is often bounded by as many as five or six lots (the term also refers to a lot that has added value because of its strategic location).

kickback Payment of money from someone other than the buyer or seller associated with real estate business.

laissez-faire Allow to act; noninterference by government in trade, industry, and individual action generally.

land The surface of the earth and everything attached to it by nature.

land contract (See contract for deed.)

land description (legal description) A definite and positive written identification of a specific parcel of land and its location without additional oral testimony.

lay member One not belonging to or connected with a particular profession.

lease An estate for years; an agreement that does not convey ownership but does convey possession and use for a period of time and for compensation.

leasehold estate A tenancy in real property held under a lease arrangement for a definite number of years; nonfreehold.

legal description A series of boundary lines on the earth's surface.

legally sufficient A complaint that contains facts indicating that a violation has occurred of a Florida statute, a DBPR rule, or a FREC rule.

lender's policy Title insurance issued for the unpaid mortgage amount to protect the lender against title defects.

lessee A tenant or leaseholder; party given a lease.

lessor The landlord or owner; party granting a lease.

level-payment plan A method for amortizing a mortgage whereby the borrower pays the same amount each month.

leverage The use of borrowed funds to finance the purchase of an asset; the use of another's money to make more money.

liabilities Debts; financial obligations; drawbacks.

license A privilege granted by the state to operate as a real estate broker, broker associate, or sales associate; a type of time-share interest.

licensee An individual who has qualified for, and been registered as, a real estate broker, broker associate, or sales associate.

licensure Certification as a licensee; the granting by the state of a license to practice real estate.

lien A claim on property for payment of some obligation or debt.

lienee One whose property is subject to a claim or charge by another.

lienor One who has a claim or charge on the property of another.

lien theory Legal concept that regards a mortgage as a just claim on specific property pledged as security for a mortgage debt.

life estates Tenancies whose durations are limited to the life of some person; freehold.

limited liability company (LLC) An alternative, hybrid business entity with the combined characteristics and benefits of both limited partnerships and S corporations.

limited liability partnership A business entity that features protection from personal liability but with fewer legal restrictions compared with other business entities.

limited partnership A business entity consisting of one or more general partners and one or more limited partners.

lineal Descended in a direct family line; relating to or derived from ancestors.

liquidated damages The amount of valuable consideration specified in an agreement as a penalty for default. (*See also* damages.)

liquidation The process of determining liabilities and apportioning the assets in order to discharge the indebtedness of a business to be sold.

liquidation analysis An appraiser's methodology and estimate of the value of a business that is being liquidated. An assessment of such factors as the ability of the firm to pay off short-term obligations, the value of the inventory on hand, and the liquidation value of preferred stock.

liquidity The ability to convert noncash assets into cash quickly; refers to a firm's cash position and its ability to meet obligations.

lis pendens A pending legal action.

listing Oral or written employment agreement between a broker (or a sales associate employed by a broker) and the property owner; authorization to sell, rent, or exchange.

litigation A lawsuit; the act of carrying on a lawsuit; a case before a court of law.

littoral rights Legal rights related to land abutting an ocean, sea, or lake, usually extending to the high-water mark.

loan correspondent Generally, a mortgage banker or company that provides services for lending institutions.

loan-to-value (LTV) ratio Relationship between amount borrowed and appraised value (or sale price) of a property.

lot and block A type of legal description of land.

maintenance clause A provision in a mortgage agreement that requires mortgagors (borrowers) to maintain mortgaged property in good condition.

majority A person having attained 18 years of age, or having married, or by court order; no longer a minor; a number greater than half the total.

malfeasance The committing of an unlawful act, especially by a public official.

mandamus, writ of An order of a superior court directing a lower court or body to do some specified act.

mandate Directive from a higher authority to a lower body.

margin The fixed component that is added to the index to calculate the interest rate in an adjustable rate mortgage.

marital assets Real and personal property acquired during marriage.

marketable title (merchantable title) Rights to real property that are so clear that a buyer may have peaceful and quiet enjoyment of the property free of litigation.

market value The most probable price a property will bring from a fully informed buyer, willing but not compelled to buy, and the lowest price a fully informed seller will accept if not compelled to sell.

master in chancery An appointed assistant to a court.

material fact A piece of information that affects the value of real property and is relevant to a person making a decision about that property.

mechanic's lien (*See* construction lien.)

mediation The act of having a third party attempt to reconcile a dispute between two parties.

meeting of the minds The point when two people, thinking of the same thing, reach an agreement through an offer and acceptance.

meridian Any of the imaginary lines of longitude on the earth's surface; in land description, the vertical lines running in a north-south direction parallel to the principal (prime) meridian and separating the various ranges.

metes-and-bounds description A method of legal description that identifies a property by specifying the shape and boundary dimensions of the parcel. A metes-and-bounds description starts at the point of beginning and follows the boundaries of the land by compass direction and linear measurements and returns to the point of beginning.

middleman An intermediary who merely brings two parties together.

mill A unit of money used to specify a property tax rate ($1 for each $1,000 of taxable value).

millage A tax rate, expressed as the number of mills to be applied.

ministerial duties The duties of the Division of Real Estate that involve record keeping.

misdemeanor Any crime punishable by fine or imprisonment other than in a penitentiary.

misfeasance A lawful act done in a negligent or unlawful manner.

misrepresentation A false or misleading statement of a material fact; concealment of a material fact.

monetary policy The actions undertaken by the Fed to influence the availability and cost of money and credit.

monument Man-made or natural object used to establish boundaries of land.

moral turpitude An act of corruption, vileness, or moral depravity; a disgraceful action or deed.

mortgage A written agreement that pledges property as security for payment of a debt.

mortgage broker company (mortgage lender) A business entity that originates, sells, and then services mortgage loans. Mortgage broker companies are not depository institutions. They originate loans and then package the loans together and sell the entire package.

mortgage lender A company that makes loans with the expectation of reselling them to institutional lenders. (*See also* mortgage broker company.)

mortgage loan originator One who finds a lender for a potential borrower, and vice versa.

mortgagee A lender who holds a mortgage on specific property as security for the money loaned to the borrower.

mortgage insurance premium (MIP) Fee paid by FHA borrowers to obtain a loan (up-front and annual).

mortgagor A borrower who gives a mortgage on the borrower's property in order to obtain a loan from a lender.

multiple licenses Licenses held by a broker in two or more real estate brokerage firms.

multiple listing service (MLS) An arrangement among members of a real estate board or exchange that allows each member broker to share listings with other members so that greater exposure is obtained and a greater chance of sale will result.

mutual assent The making and acceptance of an offer.

mutual recognition agreement A transactional agreement between Florida and another state that provides for the two states to recognize each other's real estate license education.

negative amortization A financing arrangement whereby monthly mortgage payments are less than required to pay both interest and principal. The unpaid amount is added to the loan balance.

net income Profit from property or business after expenses have been deducted; effective gross income less operating expenses.

net lease An agreement for the tenant to pay fixed rent plus property costs such as taxes, insurance, and utilities.

net listing An agreement or contract to sell or rent a property for a specified minimum net amount for the owner.

net operating income (NOI) The resulting amount when all operating expenses are subtracted from effective gross income.

no brokerage relationship The broker doesn't represent either the buyer or the seller.

nolo contendere A pleading of no contest by a defendant; a plea in a criminal action not admitting guilt but subjecting the defendant to punishment as if it were a guilty plea.

nonconforming use Continuing land use that is not in compliance with zoning ordinances.

nonconventional mortgage A mortgage loan that is insured or guaranteed by the federal government (FHA or VA).

nonfreehold estate (leasehold interest) An estate in real property in which ownership is for a determinable time period, as in a lease.

note Legal evidence of a debt that must accompany a mortgage in Florida; a legally executed pledge to pay a stipulated sum of money. (*See also* promissory note.)

notice (*See* actual notice and constructive notice.)

notice of noncompliance Issued by the DBPR in the case of a minor rule violation that does not endanger the public health, safety, and welfare.

novation The substitution of a new party and/or new terms to an existing obligation.

obligee A lender or mortgagee.

obligor A borrower or mortgagor.

obsolescence A cause of loss in value. (*See also* depreciation.)

occupancy rate The percentage of rental units that are occupied.

offer An intentional proposal or promise made by one party to act or perform, provided the other party acts or performs in the manner requested.

offeree One who receives an offer, usually the seller.

offeror One who makes an offer, usually the buyer.

Office of Thrift Supervision (OTS) A branch of the U.S. Treasury Department that replaced the Federal Home Loan Bank Board as regulator of the thrift industry.

open-end clause A provision in a mortgage allowing the borrower to increase the loan amount as long as the total debt does not exceed the original mortgage loan amount, with the lender often reserving the right to adjust the interest rate to current market rates; a mortgage for future advances.

open listing An employment contract given to any number of brokers who work simultaneously to sell the owner's property.

open market operations Purchase and sale of U.S. Treasury and federal agency securities.

opinion of title A formal statement by an attorney regarding the status of a title after examination of the chain of title.

opinion of value An estimate of a property's worth given by a licensee for the purpose of a prospective sale.

option contract A right or privilege to purchase or lease real property at a specified price during a designated period based on a sufficient consideration.

optionee The party who takes an option and pays a consideration.

optionor The party who gives an option and receives a consideration.

origination fee, loan A charge by a lender for taking a mortgage in exchange for a loan.

ostensible partnership One or more parties cause a third party to be deceived into believing that a business relationship exists when no such arrangement exists.

overage (secret profit; secret commission) Retaining more than the agreed amount of sales commission, without the express knowledge and consent of the parties involved; a form of fraud.

overall capitalization rate (OAR) The relationship between annual net operating income and the value or sale price of a property.

overimprovement An addition or change to property not in line with its highest and best use, or a betterment that exceeds that justified by local conditions.

owner-developer An unlicensed entity that sells, exchanges, or leases its own property.

owner's policy Title insurance issued for the total purchase price of the property to protect the new owner against unexpected risks.

package mortgage A loan covering both real and personal property.

parol contract An agreement that is not in writing.

partially exempt Property subject to taxation, but the owner is partially relieved of the burden.

partial release clause Stipulates the conditions under which the mortgagee will grant freeing building lots from a mortgage lien upon payment of a certain amount of money.

partnership Two or more competent individuals each of whom agrees to share in the profits and losses of the business.

pass-through securities Certificates pledging a group (pool) of existing government-backed mortgages used for the purpose of channeling funds into housing markets.

patent The instrument that conveys real property from the state or federal government to an individual.

penalty clause A provision in a mortgage that requires the borrower to pay a penalty in money if the mortgage payments are made in advance of the normal due date or if the mortgage is paid in full ahead of schedule.

percentage lease An agreement for the tenant to pay rent based on the gross sales received by doing business on the leased property.

per diem By the day; per day; an allowance for daily expenses.

performance Point when a party or parties to a contract fulfill the promises or obligations in the contract.

personal property Tangible and movable property (transferred by bill of sale); property not classified as real property. Also known as personalty or chattel.

personal representative Administrator of a deceased person's estate.

personalty (*See* personal property.)

petition for review A request to a court of appeal (appellate court) asking it to examine the record of the proceedings in a specific case. (*See also* judicial review.)

pier A type of building foundation that uses columns of masonry to support the structure.

pitch The slope of a roof.

plaintiff The person or party bringing suit or charges; the complaining party; complainant.

planned unit development (PUD) A residential project with mixed land uses and high residential density.

planning Devising ways and means for achieving desired goals.

planning commission (board) An official agency, usually made up of appointed lay citizens, that directs and controls the use, design, and development of land in a city, county, or region.

plat (plat map) (*See* subdivision plat map.)

plottage The added value as a result of combining two or more properties into one large parcel.

point, mortgage discount A charge of 1 percent of the mortgage value; assessment by a lender to increase the interest yield to compete with the interest yield from other types of investments. (*See also* Discount points.)

point of beginning (POB) The starting (and ending) place in a land survey using the metes-and-bounds method of property description.

point of contact information Any means by which to contact the brokerage firm or individual licensee including mailing address(es), physical street address(es), e-mail address(es), telephone number(s), or facsimile telephone number(s).

police power The authority of government to protect the property, life, health, and welfare of its citizens.

policy manual The notebook of written rules and regulations that set desired standards and procedures in an office.

potential gross income (PGI) The total annual income a property would produce with 100 percent occupancy and no collection or vacancy losses.

power of attorney (*See* attorney, power of.)

premises section (*See* granting clause.)

prepayment clause A provision in a mortgage that allows the mortgagor to pay the mortgage debt ahead of schedule without penalty.

prepayment penalty The amount set by the creditor that the debtor is charged for retiring the debt early.

prescription, easement by A method of acquiring an interest in real property through long and continued use.

present value The worth of all future benefits of an investment in terms of today's dollars.

price The amount paid for something.

prima facie evidence Requiring no further proof; acceptable on the face of.

primary lender Financial institution that makes mortgage loans directly to borrowers (e.g., savings association, bank).

primary market A source for the purchase of a mortgage loan by a borrower.

principal The party employing the services of a real estate broker; amount of money borrowed in a mortgage loan, excluding interest and other charges.

principal meridians Imaginary lines running north and south and crossing a base line at a definite point; used by surveyors for reference in locating and describing land under the government survey system.

private mortgage insurance (PMI) Needed to insure all of the mortgage representing more than 80 percent of appraised value or purchase price.

probable cause Reasonable grounds or justification for prosecuting.

probation An administrative penalty imposed by the FREC that allows the licensee to continue to practice real estate under the guidance of the FREC.

procuring cause The person whose efforts are the cause of an executed sale contract, regardless of who actually writes the contract.

professional association (PA) A business corporation consisting of one or more individuals engaged in a primary business that provides a professional service (e.g., lawyer, doctor).

professional member A member of the FREC who holds either an active broker license or an active sales associate license.

profit The amount one makes over and above one's cost.

pro forma statement An estimate of the economic results of a proposed project; a projected income statement.

progression The principle that states that the value of an inferior property is enhanced by its association with superior properties of the same type.

promissory note A written promise to pay a specific amount. (*See also* note.)

promulgate The formal act of announcing a statute or an administrative rule. To publish and officially announce a new or amended rule or statute. The FREC may promulgate rules and regulations.

property A bundle of legal rights.

property insurance (*See* hazard insurance.)

property management The leasing, managing, marketing, and overall maintenance of property for others.

property manager A person who manages properties for various owners. A property manager's primary duties are to secure and keep tenants, to provide financial records and accounts, and to provide upkeep and maintenance of the properties.

property report A disclosure document required under the federal Interstate Land Sales Full Disclosure Act.

proprietary lease A written agreement between the owner-corporation and the tenant-stockholder in a cooperative apartment.

prorate To divide or assess proportionate shares of charges and credits between the buyer and the seller according to their individual period of ownership.

prospectus A document prepared by a developer of 20 or more new condominium units that summarizes some of the major points contained in the condominium documents.

public accommodations Private entities that own, lease, lease to, or operate facilities such as restaurants, retail stores, hotels, movie theaters, private schools, convention centers, doctors' offices, homeless shelters, transportation depots, zoos, funeral homes, day care centers, and recreation facilities, including sports stadiums and fitness clubs.

puffing Comments or opinions not made as representations of fact and thus not grounds for misrepresentation.

purchase-money mortgage (PMM) Any new mortgage taken as part of the purchase price of real property by the seller.

quadrant Quarter; any of the four quarters into which something is divided.

qualification The process of reviewing prior to approval (of a buyer's housing needs and financial abilities, of a borrower's mortgage loan application, or of an application for licensure). (*See also* underwriting.)

quasi As if; of a similar nature; seemingly.

quasi-legislative Powers delegated to the FREC to enact rules and regulations, decide questions of practice, and validate records (imprint with FREC's seal).

quasi-judicial Powers delegated to the FREC to discipline real estate licensees for violations of real estate license law and FREC administrative rules.

quasi partnership (*See* ostensible partnership.)

quiet enjoyment A provision in a deed guaranteeing that the buyer may enjoy possession of the property in peace and without disturbance by reason of other claims on the title by the seller or anyone else.

quiet title A suit or action in a court to remove a defect, cloud, or claim against the title to real property.

quitclaim deed A type of deed that will effectively convey any present interest, claim, or title to real property that the seller (grantor) may own.

quorum The minimum number of persons who may lawfully transact the business of a meeting (51 percent or four of the members of the Florida Real Estate Commission).

R-value Resistance to heat flow. The measure of the energy-effectiveness of insulation.

range In the government survey system of land description, a vertical strip of land six miles wide located between two consecutive submeridians or range lines.

range lines (submeridians) The surveyed north-south lines running every six miles east and west of the principal meridian.

ratio The relationship in quantity, size, or amount between two things; proportion.

ready, willing, and able "Ready" indicates the buyer is in a position and of a mind to complete the transaction; "willing" implies that the buyer desires to do so at the price and terms agreed; "able" refers to the buyer's financial ability to produce the required money when necessary.

real estate Land, including the air above and the earth below, plus any permanent improvements affecting the utility of the land; real property; property that is not personal property.

real estate brokerage A part of the real estate business that is concerned with bringing together buyers and sellers and owners and renters and completing a real estate transaction.

real estate business A commercial activity in which the sale, purchase, leasing, rental, exchange, or management of real property is conducted by qualified and licensed parties acting either for themselves or for others for compensation.

real estate profession A profession requiring knowledge of real estate values, experience in dealing with the public, plus exceptional personal integrity and character as qualifications to act as advisors and agents for members of the public.

real estate services Real estate activities involving compensation for performing the activities for another.

real property Any interest or estate in land, including leaseholds, subleaseholds, business opportunities and enterprises, and mineral rights; real estate.

REALTOR® A real estate broker who is a member of a local board of REALTORS® and is affiliated with the state association (Florida Association of REALTORS®) and the National Association of REALTORS® (not synonymous with "real estate agent").

realty A synonym for real estate and real property.

reasonable time A variable period of time, which may be affected by market conditions, desires of the owner, supply and demand, fluctuations of values, or an official decision.

receiver An independent party appointed by a court to impartially preserve and manage property that is involved in litigation, pending final disposition of the matter before the court.

receivership clause A provision in a mortgage, related to income-producing property, that is designed to require that income derived shall be used to make mortgage payments in the event the mortgagor (borrower) defaults.

reciprocity The practice of mutual exchanges of privileges. Some states have reciprocal arrangements for recognizing and granting licenses to licensed real estate professionals from other states.

recommended order A determination by an administrative law judge that includes findings and conclusions as well as other information required by law or agency rule to be in a final order.

reconciliation The process of weighting the estimates of value derived from the sales comparison, cost, and income approaches to arrive at a final estimate of market value.

record To place any document or instrument affecting title or an interest in real property in the public records of the county in which the property is located.

recovery fund (Real Estate Recovery Fund) A state-regulated account to cover claims of aggrieved parties who have suffered monetary losses from licensee's actions.

recovery period The assigned time over which property is depreciated for tax purposes.

rectangular method (*See* government survey system.)

redemption To repurchase, to buy back, to recover property used as security for a mortgage by paying the debt. (*See also* Equity of redemption.)

redlining Discriminatory financing by a lending institution.

registration Authorization by the state to place an applicant on the register (record) of officially recognized individuals and businesses.

regression The principle that states that the value of a superior property is adversely affected by its association with an inferior property of the same type.

REIT A method of pooling investment money using the trust form of ownership.

release clause A provision in a blanket mortgage covering more than one unit of real property that provides for the mortgagor to obtain freedom from the mortgage for each unit when a designated amount has been paid to the mortgagee for each unit.

reliction Gradual receding of water and resulting permanent increase in land once covered.

remainderman The party designated to receive an estate at the end of a life estate.

renunciation To abandon an acquired right without transferring that right to another.

replacement cost The expenditure of constructing a building with current materials and techniques that has the same functional utility as the structure being appraised.

replacement reserves (reserve for replacements) A portion of the annual income set aside for covering the cost of major components (e.g., air-conditioning) that wear out faster than the building itself.

reprimand An official act of oral and/or written criticism with a formal warning included.

reproduction cost Amount required to duplicate the property exactly.

rescind To annul, cancel, repeal, or terminate.

reserve for replacements (*See* replacement reserves.)

reserve requirements The amount of funds that an institution must hold in reserve against deposit liabilities.

resident of Florida (*See* Florida resident.)

residential sale The sale of improved residential property of four or fewer units, the sale of unimproved residential property intended for use as four or fewer units, or the sale of agricultural property of ten or fewer acres.

respondent A person who answers to an informal complaint proceeding prior to being adjudged innocent or being named as a defendant.

restriction Any device or action that controls or limits the use of real property.

restrictive covenants Conditions placed by developers that affect how the land can be used in an entire subdivision.

reversion That portion of the net proceeds from the sale of property that represents the return of the investor's capital.

revocation To cancel, rescind, annul, or make void; the permanent cancellation of a person's license.

right of survivorship A situation by which the remaining joint tenant succeeds to all right, title, and interest of the deceased joint tenant without the need for probate proceedings.

right-to-use A leasehold interest in a time-share unit based on the limited time (one or more weeks) specified in the agreement.

riparian rights Private ownership rights extending to the normal high-water mark along a river or stream and including access rights to water, boating, bathing, and dockage in accordance with state and federal statutes.

risk The chance of losing all or a part of an investment; the uncertainty of financial loss.

Rural Housing Services Administration An agency of the Department of Agriculture that offers assistance to rural residents and communities.

SAFE Act Secure and Fair Enforcement of Mortgage Licensing Act (SAFE Act) sets a minimum standard for licensing and registering mortgage loan originators. (MLOs were previously licensed as mortgage brokers.)

sale and leaseback A financing arrangement in which an investor buys property owned and used by a business accompanied by a simultaneous leasing back of the property to the business by the buyer-investor.

sale contract (deposit receipt contract; purchase agreement; contract for sale and purchase) An agreement whereby one party agrees to sell and the other party agrees to buy according to the terms set forth.

sales associate A licensed individual who, for compensation, is employed by a broker or owner-developer.

sales comparison approach A method for estimating the market value of a property by comparing similar properties to the subject property.

satisfaction of mortgage A certificate issued by the lender when the debt obligation is paid in full.

seal A mark, emblem, or impression on a document used to authenticate the document or a signature.

secondary lender Agency or financial institution that buys mortgage loans previously made by primary lenders.

secondary market A source for the purchase and sale of existing mortgages.

second mortgage (secondary financing) A loan that is junior or subordinate to a first mortgage, normally taken out when the borrower needs more money.

secret profit or commission (*See* overage.)

section One of the primary units of measurement in the government survey system of land description. A section is one mile square and contains 640 acres.

security Evidence of a debt or of ownership.

seisin (seizin) A covenant in a deed that warrants that the grantor (seller) holds the property by virtue of a fee simple title and has a complete right to dispose of same. Also known as seizin clause.

seller's market The demand for available properties exceeds the supply.

separate property Real property owned by a husband or wife prior to the marriage with the spouse having no present rights in such property; property owned individually.

service industries Businesses that attract local money (e.g., grocery stores, retail shops).

servicing disclosure statement A disclosure statement given to borrowers that discloses whether the lender intends to service the loan or transfer it to another lender or servicing company.

setback Restrictions established by zoning or deed on the space required between lot lines and building lines.

severalty Sole ownership of real property ("severed" from all others).

severance The act of removing something attached to the land (e.g., fruit, timber, fence).

single agent Per Section 475.01, F.S., a broker who represents, as a fiduciary, either the buyer or seller but not both in the same transaction.

single-hung A window characterized by a movable lower sash.

site plan A document that indicates the improvement details for a project of greater-than-average size.

situs Relationships and influences created by location of a property that affect value (e.g., accessibility, personal preference).

slab-on-grade Concrete foundation poured directly on the ground.

sole proprietorship Dealing as an individual in business.

special agent One authorized by a principal to perform a particular act or transaction, without contemplation of continuity of service as with a general agent.

special assessments Taxes levied against properties to pay for all, or part of, improvements that will benefit the properties being assessed.

special exception An individual ruling in which a property owner is granted the right to a use otherwise contrary to law.

special flood hazard area (SFHA) An area located in the 100-year flood plan.

special information booklet A booklet containing consumer information regarding closing costs the borrower may incur at closing. The Real Estate Settlement Procedures Act requires lenders to give the booklet to loan applicants.

specific liens Claims that affect only the property designated in the lien instruments or agreements.

specific performance A remedy for an injured party obtained through a court of equity, which requires specific accomplishment of the contract terms by a defendant.

state-certified appraiser A person verified by the DBPR as qualified to issue state-certified real property appraisals.

static risk Risk that can be transferred to an insurer such as the risk of vandalism, fire, and so forth.

statute An established rule or law passed by a legislative body.

statute of frauds An act that requires that certain real estate instruments and contracts affecting title to real property be in writing in order to be enforceable.

statute of limitations An act that prescribes specific time restrictions for enforcement of rights by action of law.

statutory month method A proration method in which each month is considered to have 30 days.

stay Delay temporarily; stop for a limited time.

steering Discriminatory acts against buyers.

stipulation An agreement as to the penalty reached between the attorneys for the DRE and the licensee or licensee's attorney.

stock The ownership element in a corporation usually divided into shares and represented by transferable certificates (may be divided into two or more classes of differing rights and stated values).

subagent A person authorized to assist and represent the agent and whose duties are delegated by the original agent.

subbaselines (*See* township lines.)

subdivide To segment large, acquired tracts of real property in order to create small tracts for the purpose of resale.

subdivision plat map A plan of a tract of land subdivided into lots and showing required or planned amenities.

subject property The real property under discussion or appraisal.

subject to the mortgage A buyer makes regular periodic payments on the mortgage but does not assume responsibility for the mortgage.

sublease A lessee leasing a property to a third party for a period of time less than the original lease (also referred to as subletting).

submeridians (*See* range lines.)

subordination Made subject to or subservient to; assignment to a lesser role or position.

subordination clause A provision in a mortgage in which the lender voluntarily permits a prior or subsequent mortgage to take priority over the lender's otherwise superior mortgage; the act of yielding priority.

subpoena A writ or order commanding the person named to appear and testify in a legal proceeding.

subrogation (*See* subordination.)

substitution, principle of An economic law of value: No prudent buyer will pay more for a property than the cost of an equally desirable replacement property.

suit An act of suing; an action in a court of law for the recovery of a right or claim.

summary suspension Emergency or immediate action against a license to protect the public.

supersedeas, writ of A stay of enforcement; temporary stop in a legal proceeding; restraining order.

supply The quantity of goods or services offered for sale to consumers.

survey The procedure used to measure and describe a specific tract of real property for the purpose of determining exact boundaries and the area contained therein.

survivorship, right of A legal concept whereby the surviving owners of a joint interest in real property are entitled to the interest formerly owned by one or more deceased owners.

suspension To cause to cease operating for a period of time; the temporary withholding of a person's license rendering it ineffective; a period of enforced inactivity.

syndicate (*See* business trust.)

tangible asset Anything of substance; personal and real property (e.g., cash, building, equipment, land).

tax Compulsory payment paid by a citizen to a unit of government.

taxable income Gross income minus tax deductions; net operating income plus reserve for replacements minus financing costs and allowable depreciation.

taxable value The assessed value less allowable exemptions resulting in an amount to which the tax rate is applied to determine property taxes due.

tax certificate A document sold by a local tax authority granting the certificate buyer the right to receive delinquent taxes plus interest when paid by the legal property owner.

tax clause A provision in a mortgage that requires the borrower to pay all legitimate property taxes.

tax deed A type of deed used to convey title after real property is sold at auction by public authority for nonpayment of taxes.

tax district An authority, such as a city, county, school board, or special levy area (e.g., water district), with the power to assess property owners annually in order to meet its expenditures for the public good.

tax lien A claim against real property arising out of nonpayment of the property taxes.

tax rate The percentage of value that is used to determine the amount of tax to be levied against each individual unit of property; ad valorem (according to the value).

tax shelter An investment that shields items of income or gain from payment of income taxes; a term used to describe some tax advantages of owning real property (or other investments), including postponement or even elimination of certain taxes.

telephone solicitation The initiation of a telephone call for the purpose of encouraging the purchase of, or investment in, property, goods, or services.

tenancy The estate or rights of a tenant. (*See also* estate.)

tenancy at sufferance An estate lawfully acquired for a temporary period of time but retained after a period of lawful possession has expired; nonfreehold estate.

tenancy at will An estate that may be terminated by either party at any time upon proper notice; nonfreehold estate.

tenancy by the entireties An estate created by husband and wife jointly owning real property with instant and complete right of survivorship.

tenancy in common A form of ownership by two or more persons each having an equal or unequal interest and passing the interest to heirs, not to surviving tenants.

tenant A person or party with rights of occupancy or possession of real property.

term mortgage A nonamortizing loan that normally calls for repayment of the principal in full at the end of the loan term.

testate Having left a will.

testator (testatrix) A person who makes a will.

third party Generally, a member of the public; not the principal or agent in a transaction.

tier An east-west row of townships (as used in the government survey method of land description).

time is of the essence A phrase in a contract making failure to perform by a specified date a breach or violation of the agreement.

time-share An individual interest in a real property unit together with a right of exclusive use for a specified number of days or weeks per year.

T-intersection lot An interior lot that suffers from its location at the end of a T-intersection (a street ends in front of the lot).

title Evidence of ownership of real property, such as a deed.

title insurance A policy of insurance that protects the holder from any loss resulting from defects in the title.

title plant Copies of recorded documents from the public records kept by title insurance companies; record room.

title search An examination of all of the public records to determine whether any defects exist in the chain of title.

title theory Legal concept that vests title to mortgaged property in the mortgagee (lender) or a third party.

topography Surface features (natural and manufactured) of land (e.g., lakes, mountains, roads).

township A square tract of land measuring six miles on each side and including 36 sections (formed by the crossing of range and township lines).

township lines (subbaselines) The east-west survey lines located every six miles north and south of the primary base line.

trade fixture An article that is attached by a commercial tenant as a necessary part of the tenant's business and is personal property.

trade name Any adopted or fictitious name used to designate a business concern.

transaction broker A broker who provides limited representation to a buyer, a seller, or both in a real estate transaction, but does not represent either in a fiduciary capacity or as a single agent.

triggering terms The Truth in Lending Act requires creditors to disclose certain information if certain credit terms, called triggering terms, are included in the advertisement. Triggering terms include the amount or percentage of down payment, number of payments, period (term) of repayment, amount of any payment, and the amount of any finance charges.

trust A right of property, either real or personal, held by one party for the benefit of another.

trust account (*See* escrow account.)

trustee (escrow agent) A person or party, either appointed or required by law to administer or manage another's property.

trust funds Cash, checks, money orders, and items that can be converted into cash, such as deeds and personal property, that a person (broker) holds in trust for another person.

underwriting (loan qualification; risk analysis) The analysis of the extent of risk assumed by a lender in connection with a proposed mortgage loan.

undivided interest An interest in the entire property, rather than ownership of a particular part of the property.

unenforceable A contract that was valid when made but either cannot be proved or will not be upheld by a court.

Uniform Standards of Professional Appraisal Practice (USPAP) The set of standards that must be followed when performing appraisal services.

unilateral contract An agreement in which only one party promises to perform without receiving a reciprocal promise to perform from the other party.

unincorporated association A group of people associated together for some common, noncommercial purpose.

unities (four unities) Individual prerequisites required to constitute a single joint tenancy.

universal agent A representative authorized by the principal to perform all acts that the principal can personally perform and that may be lawfully delegated to another.

unliquidated damages The amount of valuable consideration awarded by a court to an injured party as a result of default. (*See also* damages.)

usury Charging a rate of interest greater than the legal one; unlawful interest.

vacancy and collection losses A deduction from potential gross income for (1) current or expected future space not rented due to tenant turnover and (2) loss from uncollected rent due from delinquent tenants.

vacancy rate The percentage of rental units that are not occupied.

vacate To set aside, cancel, or annul; to leave empty.

valid Sufficient to be legally binding; enforceable.

valid contract An agreement binding on both parties and legally enforceable against all parties to the agreement.

valuable consideration The money or a promise of something that can be measured in terms of money.

value The worth of something.

variable lease An agreement for the tenant to pay specified rent increases based on a predetermined index (CPI) at set future dates.

variance An exception to zoning regulations or ordinances granted to relieve a hardship.

vendee The buyer or purchaser of real property under an agreement of sale.

vendor The seller of real property in an agreement of sale.

vendor's lien A claim against property giving the seller the right to hold the property as security for any unpaid purchase money.

Veterans Affairs, Department of (VA) Guarantees mortgage loans to encourage private lending agencies to give liberal mortgages to veterans and their spouses.

void Invalid; without force; no longer effective.

voidable A contract that because of the manner or method in which it was brought about, one of the parties is allowed to avoid contractual duties.

voluntary inactive The license status that results when a licensee has met all of the requirements for licensure, yet the licensee chooses not to engage in the real estate business, and has requested that the license be placed in this status.

voluntary liens Claims imposed against real property with the consent of the owner.

warrant A guarantee or covenant, as in a warranty deed.

warranty deed (*See* general warranty deed.)

warranty forever A provision in a deed guaranteeing that the seller will for all time defend the title and possession for the buyer.

waste An improper use or abuse of property by one who holds less than the fee simple ownership of it.

will A written document legally executed by which an individual disposes of an estate, effective after death.

withhold adjudication When the court determines that a defendant is not likely to again engage in a criminal act and that the ends of justice and the welfare of society do not require the defendant suffer the penalty imposed by law, the court may withhold adjudication of guilt, stay (stop) the imposition of the sentence, and place the defendant on probation.

witness A person who gives testimony; one who observes and attests to the signing or executing of a document.

wraparound mortgage A financing technique in which the payment of the existing mortgage is continued (by the seller) and a new, higher interest rate mortgage, which is larger than the existing mortgage, is paid by the buyer-borrower.

writ A court order directing a party to do a specific act, usually to appear in, or report to, a court of law.

writ of certiorari (*See* certiorari, writ of.)

writ of mandamus (*See* mandamus, writ of.)

writ of supersedeas (*See* supersedeas, writ of.)

yield The rate of return; the return on an investment or the amount of profit stated as a percentage of the amount invested; the ratio of the annual net income from a property to the cost or market value of the property.

zero lot line The positioning of a structure on a lot so that one side rests directly on the lot's boundary line (there is no side setback requirement).

zoning ordinances Classification of real property for various purposes; the government power to control and supervise the use of privately owned real property (actually, the exercise of police powers).

INDEX

Notes

Notes

Notes